Kathy Rooney ©2001

THE CHIEF

Art Rooney and his Pittsburgh Steelers

By Jim O'Brien

"You had a special bond with my father. Being an Irish kid, and from Hazelwood, which was a lot like the North Side, made you a real Pittsburgh guy to him. It gave you a decided advantage with my father. I know he liked you."
— Note to Jim O'Brien from Art Rooney, Jr.

Books By Jim O'Brien

COMPLETE HANDBOOK OF PRO BASKETBALL 1970-1971

COMPLETE HANDBOOK OF PRO BASKETBALL 1971-1972

ABA ALL-STARS

PITTSBURGH: THE STORY OF THE CITY OF CHAMPIONS

HAIL TO PITT: A SPORTS HISTORY OF
THE UNIVERSITY OF PITTSBURGH

DOING IT RIGHT

WHATEVER IT TAKES

MAZ AND THE '60 BUCS

REMEMBER ROBERTO

PENGUIN PROFILES

DARE TO DREAM

KEEP THE FAITH

WE HAD 'EM ALL THE WAY

HOMETOWN HEROES

GLORY YEARS

THE CHIEF

To order copies of these titles directly from the publisher, send $28.95 for hardcover edition. Please send $3.50 to cover shipping and handling costs per book. Pennsylvania residents add 6% sales tax to price of book only. Allegheny County residents add an additional 1% sales tax for a total of 7% sales tax. Copies will be signed by author at your request. Discounts available for large orders. Contact publisher regarding availability and prices of all books in Pittsburgh Proud series, or to request an order form. Some books are sold out and no longer available. You can still order the following: Doing It Right, MAZ And The '60 Bucs, Remember Roberto, Keep The Faith, We Had 'Em All The Way, Hometown Heroes, Glory Years and The Chief. They cost $26.95 apiece, plus sales tax and shipping charges. E-mail address: jpobrien@stargate.net.

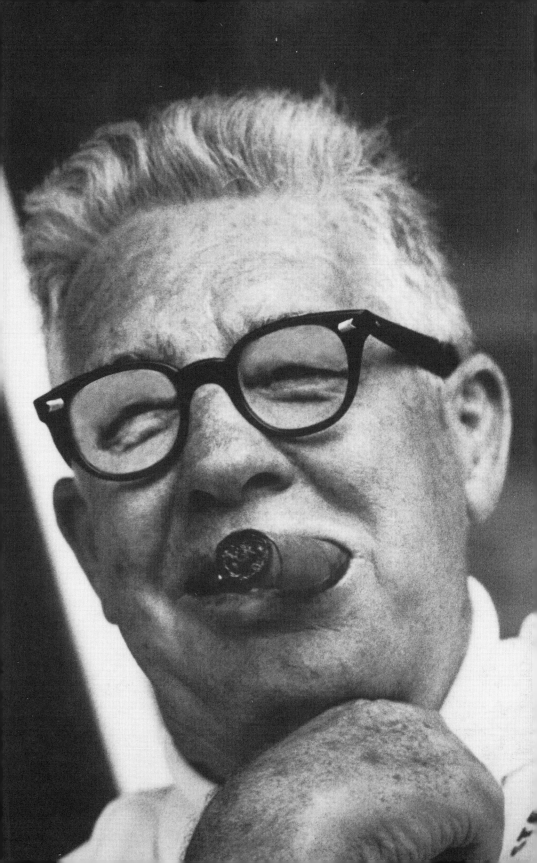

Art Rooney strikes relaxed pose in his office in March of 1983.

This book is dedicated to the memory of Arthur J. Rooney and my mother-in-law, Barbara A. Churchman

Cover drawing by Marty Wolfson

Profile photos by Jim O'Brien

All autograph signatures are reproductions and are used with permission

Copyright © 2001 by Jim O'Brien

All rights reserved

James P. O'Brien — Publishing
P.O. Box 12580
Pittsburgh PA 15241
Phone: (412) 221-3580
E-mail: jpobrien@stargate.net

First printing: August, 2001

Manufactured in the United States of America

Printed by Geyer Printing Company, Inc.
3700 Bigelow Boulevard
Pittsburgh PA 15213

Typography by Cold-Comp
810 Penn Avenue
Pittsburgh PA 15222

ISBN 1-886348-06-5

Contents

Acknowledgments

Tampa is Art Rooney's kind of town. It's on the West Coast of Florida, the weather is balmy in the winter, it's easy to find a good cigar, and there's gaming activity all around the area. Tampa is famous for its cigars. It's also a town that has a high regard for pirates — that's with a lower case p — and holds annual festivals and parades where the locals dress up like pirates and the folks who founded Florida as they did during Super Bowl XXXV in late January, 2001.

I traveled to Tampa during Super Bowl Week so I could talk to some of Art Rooney's old friends among the National Football League elite. Wellington Mara of the New York Football Giants and Art Modell, the owner of the Baltimore Ravens and before that the Cleveland Browns, were the principals of the opposing teams in the league's showcase contest. Then, too, there were oldtimers like Tex Schramm, who knew Rooney when Schramm was running the Los Angeles Rams and the Dallas Cowboys.

Mara, Modell and Schramm shared stories of their relationship with Rooney, one of the grand old men of the NFL, as did so many of the most esteemed and respected sportswriters and broadcasters in the nation who were there to cover the contest. Spending time with the greats of the sports media has always been one of the highlights of attending the Super Bowl festivities.

Pat Hanlon, vice-president for media relations with the New York Giants, and a former assistant of mine in the sports information office at the University of Pittsburgh, continued to provide valuable assistance, as did other NFL officials with their support at Super Bowl XXXV.

I went back to Florida for another five-day stay in May, this time visiting Palm Beach and West Palm Beach, where the Rooneys have wintered and resided for many years. I am indebted to Art Rooney's five sons, Dan, Art, Jr., Tim, John and Pat for their time and cooperation. Art, Jr. and Pat's son, Joe, were particularly helpful. So was Art's secretary, Dee Harrod, and his sister-in-law, Sandy Sully Rooney. I am grateful to all the NFL folks who were willing to be interviewed and shared stories of their relationship and regard for Art Rooney.

I came upon more information in Florida than I had anticipated to complete the picture of a man for whom I had always had the highest respect and admiration and, yes, love. He was an original.

Everyone needs help to get anything worthwhile accomplished. I have been privileged to have a great support team in my efforts to write and publish my "Pittsburgh Proud" sports book series. It would not be possible to do this without the broad-based support I have enjoyed the past 20 years.

Special thanks are offered to Robert G. Navarro and Bob Czerniewski of Stevens Painton Corporation and Tom Snyder of Continental Design & Management Group for their loyal support.

Special thanks to patrons who contributed to the building of the new football stadium on the North Side: Jack Mascaro of Mascaro

Construction Co., Fred Sargent of Sargent Electric Co. and Miles Bryan of Bryan Mechanical Inc. Bryan was a fullback in the same backfield as Dan Rooney (quarterback) and Richie McCabe (halfback) on the 1950 North Catholic High School football team.

Other loyal patrons include John Rigas and Anthony W. Accamando, Jr. of Adelphia Cable Communications; Louis Astorino and Dennis Astorino of LD Astorino Associates, Ltd.; Pat McDonnell and Allison Hoffman of Atria's Restaurant & Tavern; Ronald B. Livingston, Sr. of Babb, Inc.; Bill Baierl of Baierl Automotive Group; Rich Barcelona of Bailey Engineers, Inc.; Andrew F. Komer of Bowne of Pittsburgh; the National Baseball Hall of Fame and Museum, the Frick Art & Historical Center, Howard "Hoddy" Hanna of Hanna Real Estate Services.

Don Carlucci of Carlucci Construction Co.; Kenneth F. Codeluppi of Wall-Firma. Inc.; Tom Sweeney of Compucom, Inc.; James T. Davis of Davis & Davis Law Offices, Armand Dellovade of A.C. Dellovade, Inc.; Don DeBlasio of DeBlasio's Restaurant; Jim and Suzy Broadhurst of Eat'n Park Restaurants; Everett Burns of E-Z Overhead Door & Window Co.

John E. McGinley, Jr. of Grogan, Graffan, McGinley & Luccino, P.C.; John R. McGinley of Wilson-McGinley Co.; Steve Fedell of Ikon Office Solutions; Joe Faccenda of Giant Eagle, Inc.; Lou Grippo of The Original Oyster House; Frank Gustine, Jr. of The Gustine Company; Ed Lewis of Oxford Development Co.; William R. Johnson and Jeffrey Berger of Heinz, U.S.A.; Mike Hagan of Iron & Glass Bank; William V. Campbell of Intuit; Larry Werner of Kechum Public Relations; Joseph A. Massaro, Jr. of The Massaro Company.

F. James McCarl, Robert Santillo and Danny Rains of McCarl's, Inc.; David B. Jancisin of Merrill Lynch; Jack B. Piatt of Millcraft Industries, Inc.; Thomas W. Golonski, John C. Williams, Jr. and Angela Longo of National City Bank of Pennsylvania; Jack Perkins of Mr. P's in Greensburg; Dan R. Lackner of Paper Products Company, Inc.; A. Robert Scott of *Point*; Joe Browne, Sr. of National Football League; Joseph Piccirilli of Pittsburgh Brewing Company.

Lloyd Gibson and John Schultz of NorthSide Bank; Pat and John Rooney of Palm Beach Kennel Club; Patrick J. Santelli of Pfizer Labs; Thomas H. O'Brien, James E. Rohr and Sy Holzer of PNC Bank Corp.; Tim Rooney of Yonkers Raceway; Joseph Costanzo, Jr. of The Primadonna Restaurant; Sam Sciullo of *Inside Panther Sports*; Pennsylvania Sports Hall of Fame.

Jim Roddey and Michael J. Fetchko of SportsWave, Inc. (International Sports Marketing); Daniel A. Goetz of Stylette, Inc.; Charles H. Becker, Jr. of Marsh USA Inc.; Dick Swanson of Swanson Group Ltd.; Robert J. Taylor of Taylor & Hladio Law Offices; Barbara, Ted and Jim Frantz of Tedco Construction Corp.; W. Harrison Vail of Three Rivers Bank.

John Paul of University of Pittsburgh Medical Center; John Lucey and Alex J. Pociask of USFilter; Thomas J. Usher of USX Corporation; Clark Nicklas of Vista Resources, Inc.; Charles and Stephen Previs of Waddell & Reed Financial Services; John Seretti Chevrolet Inc.;

Ray Conaway of Zimmer Kunz; John Williamson of J.C. Williamson Company; Tom Volovich of Interstate Baking Co.; Gordon Oliver of Steeltech, Inc.; Bill Shields of McCann Shields Paint Company.

Friends who have been boosters include Aldo Bartolotta, Andy Beamon, Jon C. Botula, Judge John G. Brosky, John Bruno, Tim Conn, Beano Cook, Bob Friend of Babb, Inc., Ralph Cindrich of Cindrich & Company in Carnegie, Bill Dudley, Joe Gordon, Dave R. Hart, Darrell Hess of DJ Hess Advertising, Harvey Hess, Mrs. Elsie Hillman, Zeb Jansante, Tommy Kehoe, Robert F. McClurg, Ken Malli, George Morris of Norton Co., Andy Ondrey, Dr. Edward Sweeney, Richard Mills, George Schoeppner, Ruth and Lester E. Zittrain.

Friends who have offered special encouragement and prayer and those who have opened up doors for our endeavors include Bill Priatko, Rudy Celigoi, Ron Temple, Bob Shearer, Jim Kriek, Dennis Meteny, Foge Fazio, Stan Goldmann, Ed Lutz, Pete Mervosh, David E. Epperson, Thomas J. Bigley, Mike Ference, Mario Tiberi, Bob Wissman, Kenneth E. Ball, Bob Lovett and Art Stroyd of Reed Smith Shaw & McClay, Bob Harper and Art Rooney II of Klett Lieber Rooney & Schorling, Patrick T. Lanigan of Lanigan's Funeral Home, Tom O'Malley, Jr., Sally O'Leary of the Pirates' Black & Gold Alumni Newsletter, Chuck Klausing, Nellie Briles of Pittsburgh Pirates, John Longo of WCNS Radio in Latrobe, Rob Pratte of KDKA Radio and Jack Bogut of WJAS Radio. My heartfelt thanks to Mavis Trasp, my "Christmas angel" and her daughter, Sherry Kisic, and their friends at Century III Mall for all their kindness.

Special thanks for his cooperation and efforts to Donald "Doc" Giffin of Arnold Palmer Enterprises.

I do all my work with Pittsburgh firms. All of my books have been produced at Geyer Printing. Bruce McGough, Tom Samuels, Charlie Stage and Keith Maiden are great to work with each year. Denise Maiden, Cathy Pawlowski and Becky Fatalsky of Cold-Comp Typographers did their usual outstanding job. Cathy came through under difficult circumstances. The cover drawing of Art Rooney was done by an old friend and co-worker on some earlier books in this series, Marty Wolfson. A drawing on the dust jacket by Merv Corning was commissioned by Art Rooney, Jr. The cover design was done by Guiseppi Francioni and Christopher Longo of Prisma, Inc.

The Almanac newspaper in the South Hills, for which I have been writing a man-about-town column for the past decade, has promoted my book signing appearances through the years, as has *The Valley Mirror* in Homestead-Munhall. I have always appreciated the efforts of Pittsburgh photographers David Arrigo, Michael F. Fabus, Jack A. Wolf, Teddy Thompson and George Gojkovich. Tony DeNunzio also provided a photograph.

My support team begins with my wife of 34 years, Kathleen Churchman O'Brien, and our daughters, Dr. Sarah O'Brien-Zirwas and Rebecca O'Brien and her dog Bailey. They make it all worthwhile.

All history is partial history, and all truth is the writer's truth, we're told. This is not intended to be a definitive history of the Rooneys

9

or the Steelers, but rather a collection of reflections and anecdotes. I am proud of this collection of stories about Arthur J. Rooney. He always liked the fact that my full name was James Patrick Joseph O'Brien. The Rooneys got a lot of use out of a few names and all three of my names can be found many times on the Rooney family roster. No matter how well dressed I might be on a particular day, Art Rooney brought me down to earth by saying with a smile, "Lookit this dude from Hazelwood."

— *Jim O'Brien*

Author Jim O'Brien and Steelers owner Art Rooney shortly after Steelers won their fourth Super Bowl in 1980 before 103,985 at Rose Bowl in Pasadena, California.

Introduction
Rooney reunion

"It's a reminder of family roots."

The Rooney family, some 150 strong, gathered for a reunion the weekend of July 13-15, 2001 at Idlewild Park, an amusement park in Ligonier, Pennsylvania, about 60 miles east of Pittsburgh. They came from across the country for this reunion, held ten years after the first such assembly.

A golf tournament was scheduled for Friday, a picnic and two touch football games — one for adults and one for the kids — were planned for Saturday, with a Mass and brunch set for Sunday morning at nearby St. Vincent's College in Latrobe, site of the Steelers' summer training camp. The brunch was being provided courtesy of Dan Rooney, the oldest son of Steelers' founder Arthur J. Rooney and the president of the Pittsburgh team.

There is much about the Rooneys that reminds one of the Kennedy clan and the kind of things they would do when they would gather at the family's summer getaway in Hyannisport, Massachusetts. The Rooneys relish the comparison as they have long admired the Kennedys and have even enjoyed some social events in their company. Tim Rooney, the third oldest of Art Rooney's sons, boasts of a collection of nearly all the books written about the Kennedys.

Sandy Rooney, the wife of Pat Rooney — one of the twin sons of Art and Kathleen Rooney — did a lot of research on the Rooney family tree, and provided such information to all members of the family in a 12-page publication prior to the reunion. It was an impressive publication.

There were over 200 descendants from the marriage of Daniel M. Rooney and Margaret Murray on January 9, 1899. Daniel and Margaret were married at St. Patrick's Church in Alpsville, Pennsylvania by Reverend P.J. O'Neil. Daniel's brother, John, and sister, Mary Ellen, were the couple's attendants.

Dan, an Irishman from Wales, operated Rooney's Saloon at 528 West Robinson Street on the North Side of Pittsburgh. Margaret was a homemaker. They lived upstairs of the bar, and later the couple moved to 2514 Perrysville Avenue. They had nine children.

Arthur Joseph was the first born, on January 27, 1901. Then came Daniel Michael, James Patrick, John Paul, Vincent Timothy, Katherine, Margaret Katherine, Mary Ellen (Marie) and Thomas Joseph. One child, Katherine, died at the age of two. Tommy, the youngest, was killed in World War II. He was known as Private Tommy Rooney. He was stationed in Guam in the South Pacific. He went to Duquesne Prep School and Bullis Prep School in Washington, and was a quarterback in high school. He joined the Marine Corps when he came out of high school.

Pat Rooney, the other twin son of Art Rooney, was scheduled to offer some reflections about Private Tommy Rooney. Art, Jr. was scheduled to say a few words about his father and mother, Kathleen Rooney, both deceased. John Rooney would talk about James Patrick Rooney. Patricia Rooney Moriarty would talk about her parents, Joanna and John Rooney. Timmy Rooney, a former NFL talent scout, would speak about his parents, Anne and Vincent Rooney. They still talk about the heartfelt reflections delivered by Dan at the last reunion.

"It's a reminder of family roots," explained Art Jr.

Margaret Katherine Rooney Laughlin and Marie Rooney McGinley, the sisters and only surviving members of Art Rooney's siblings, planned to be in attendance at the reunion. Margaret's son, Jimmy Laughlin, and Marie's son, Jack, would talk about their parents. The idea was to make sure all the grandchildren and great-grandchildren knew their roots as Rooneys. "It was a fast ten years," it was noted in Sandy Rooney's newsletter. "Many changes have taken place, a lot more members, a few funerals, many weddings, and a couple of divorces." There were about 50 newcomers since the last reunion.

There was much on the menu that sounded appetizing: barbecue ribs, charcoal chicken, hot dogs, hamburgers, potato salad, coleslaw, fresh melon, corn on the cob, dinner rolls, frozen deserts, pecan pie, brownies and unlimited soft drinks. The kids would enjoy the usual Idlewild Park fare of swimming, music, six waterslides and the Story Book Forest. I am hoping the younger Rooneys will learn much about their family by reading this book. They are, for sure, a fascinating family that has left its mark on Pittsburgh and other places where people enjoy sports and a sporting proposition. It's a good bet that Art Rooney's spirit as well as his relatives were all present, somewhere behind those trees, in Story Book Forest.

I thought I knew Art Rooney, but I learned so much more about him while working on this book, and now I admire and love him more than ever. Here's hoping you will feel the same way.

The Rooneys held a family reunion in the summer of 1991 at Idlewild Park in Ligonier, Pennsylvania.

Art Rooney

He showed the way

*"He's at least five-to-one over
anybody else we know."*
— Jimmy "The Greek" Snyder

One of the joys of being a sportswriter was to stroll the sideline on a sunny afternoon during a practice session of the Pittsburgh Steelers and talk to club owner Art Rooney. It's my fondest memory of days spent at Three Rivers Stadium. The second best memory was sitting in his office, listening to his stories.

I had a chance to do that on many occasions during a four-year period from 1979 to 1982, when I was reporting on the activities of the Steelers for *The Pittsburgh Press*, and for a too brief period a few years later while working on books about the Steelers. You learned a little about football and a lot about life on those sideline strolls and office chats. Mr. Rooney usually wore a white shirt and a tie to work during the week. He might show up without the tie on Saturday. He favored black or dark blue suits and sport coats. There were often traces of cigar ashes on them. I found myself flicking off the ashes when I'd be close to him, as if I were his valet. He'd smile at my concern about his appearance. He would wear button-down sweaters over his shirt and tie often in the winter. The sweaters were always snug on his frame. Mr. Rooney always had a rumpled look about him. He was comfortable in his casualness. It made you comfortable, too.

He had thick lips. Sometimes they appeared downright blue. Sometimes they had a tobacco stain or a bit of tobacco on them. His eyes were often squeezed tight because he was laughing or smiling about something. He was such a joy. Most fans wanted the new football stadium named in his honor, but they will have to settle for Art Rooney Avenue and other testimonials. The stadium is named Heinz Field. That's a strong Pittsburgh name, too.

"I'm always available," he'd say when you asked if he had time to talk. "I appreciate being interviewed. I remember when we lived for the days we'd get our games mentioned in the papers, when papers were all that kept pro football going, but they didn't interview people much."

A little background on Art Rooney might be helpful here.

Arthur Joseph Rooney was born in Coultersville, Pa., just northeast of McKeesport, on January 27, 1901, and the world was better for it. This year of 2001 is the 100th anniversary of his birth. He was the oldest of Daniel and Margaret Rooney's nine children. He grew up in Old Allegheny, now known as the North Side of Pittsburgh, living at first in rooms over his father's saloon and then a home on Western Avenue. He later lived in another home in the same neighborhood, near Three Rivers Stadium, and remained there until his death.

13

He died on August 25, 1988, following a stroke at the age of 87. His funeral was a civic event, and drew thousands to St. Peter's Church. Some had suggested he was such an important Pittsburgh personality that services should be held at St. Paul's Cathedral in Oakland, the bishop's church, which was larger and could better accommodate the anticipated crowds. "If you do," said someone who knew him well, "he might not show up." I remember sitting behind former Pirate slugging star Frank Thomas at St. Peter's. Thomas told me a story about how Art Rooney had attended the funeral for Frank's daughter, who had died in a tragic accident years earlier. "The snow was deep in the streets, and there was a long line on the sidewalk outside the funeral home," said Thomas. "Mr. Rooney took his place at the end of the line, and was out in the cold for quite a while I was told. He wouldn't think of going to the head of the line."

I also recall seeing Pete Rozelle sitting behind Al Davis directly across the aisle from where I was sitting. They both had been seated on the aisle. They were constantly feuding at the time. The NFL Commissioner wasn't happy with the way Davis was conducting his affairs as owner of the Raiders, always challenging his NFL colleagues. They had to shake hands when the priest instructed everyone to offer a peace greeting to those around them. I thought that Art Rooney was up there somewhere pulling strings. He liked Rozelle and Davis.

Rooney attended St. Peter's Catholic Grade School and Duquesne University Prep School. He attended Indiana (Pa.) Normal, later known as Indiana University of Pennsylvania, as well as Georgetown University and Duquesne University. He had a brother, Jim, who lettered in football for three years at Pitt (1926,1928, 1929).

Art Rooney was an exceptional all-around athlete and competitor. Knute Rockne tried to persuade him to enter Notre Dame to play football. The Chicago Cubs and Boston Red Sox expressed interest in his baseball talents. He held middleweight and welterweight titles from the AAU Boxing Championships and was named to the U.S. Olympic boxing team in 1920 for the Games in Antwerp, Belgium. He did not compete in the Olympic Games because he was studying in the seminary at the time. He played minor league baseball from 1920-25, including a stint with his brother Dan (Father Silas) Rooney with the Wheeling (West Virginia) Stogies of the Middle Atlantic League (he batted .369 and Dan hit at a .359 clip), before his career was cut short by an arm injury. Rooney continued playing semi-pro football on the Pittsburgh area sandlots.

"What's the difference between being a winner and being a loser?" Rooney once observed. "And I'm in a position to know. This is what I tell them. A loser dodges through the alleys. A winner walks up the main street.

"I've had enough people ask, 'How did you stand all the bad years?' I hated to lose, and we did a lot of losing, but it was always fun. The sports business is just a great life."

MARGARET and DANIEL ROONEY
Art Rooney's parents

"It was a different time."

He was married on June 11, 1931 to Kathleen McNulty, and the couple had five sons — Daniel, Art Jr., Tim, John and Pat. If you have spent one day in your life in the company of Art Rooney you should know enough about public relations to last a lifetime.

He was simply the best person I've met. "He's at least five-to-one over anybody else we know," observed Jimmy "The Greek" Snyder, who came to Pittsburgh to pay his respects at the funerals of, first, Kathleen Rooney, and then for the funeral of the Steelers' owner. Snyder and his wife took my wife and I to dinner at Tambellini's on Route 51 and spoke in detail of his affection for Art Rooney. Snyder had come out of Steubenville to make his mark as an oddsmaker in Las Vegas and then a national sports analyst and handicapper. He said Rooney was one of the all-time greats as a handicapper.

Art Rooney was always reluctant to discuss his historic cleanup at the races in the '30s, but the legend of the story found its way into various reports through the years. He went to New York with a $300 bankroll in his pocket. He ran that up to $21,000. Bent on taking his winnings home, he and a Pittsburgh boxer, Buck Crouse, dropped into a friend's restaurant. Within a few hours, however, Rooney and Crouse and their friend were on their way to Saratoga Springs.

There, Art is said to have bet $2,000 at odds of 8 to 1 on one Quel Jeu. It won. Four more times he collected on nip-and-tuck finishes, making his big killing on a $10,000 wager. When the day was over, Rooney had between $250,000 and $300,000. But that was a few years after he invested in an NFL franchise. He could well afford the $2,500 the National Football League franchise cost him in 1933 before he'd won any bets of that kind. When he did have his two-day bonanza at the track, though, he did ship a portion of his winnings to his brother, Father Silas Rooney, who was struggling against great odds as a missionary in China at the time. There are stories told that Father Rooney had to use his fists on occasion to maintain his turf in China. Father Rooney was a big man, about 6-2, whereas The Chief stood about 5-8 or 5-9 at best.

After hearing various accounts of that two-day winning spree at race tracks, Roy Blount Jr., the author of *About Three Bricks Shy Of A Load*, wrote, "You can talk about Man o' War and (Eddie) Arcaro all you want. The Chief for my money is the biggest figure in horse racing history." Art Rooney loved the action. He controlled the jukebox and slot machine business at bars and restaurants and after-hours clubs throughout Allegheny County as a young man. He was familiar with gamblers and sporting types across the country. He attended racetracks, sports events of all kinds, even cockfights where he could find such underground activity. He bet on everything except, he always insisted, pro football games.

Art Rooney could drink and rumble with the best of them in his early days. As a senior he became a teetotaler and a saint. His boys wouldn't have a drink in his presence. Their playmates knew not to swear in the backyard of the Rooney home. "My dad didn't drink at all the last 30 years of his life," said Art Jr.

He kept the company of notable figures like New York saloon-keeper Toots Shor and Pittsburgh boxing god Billy Conn, as well as old neighborhood buddies and priests. It's intriguing to think about the varied company he kept in his lifetime.

His gambling activity and early entrepreneurial efforts in shady areas are alluded to in Blount's book about the Pittsburgh Steelers, regarded by many as the best book ever written about the Black & Gold. "He raised hell in the old days," wrote Blount.

Like his friend "Jimmy the Greek," Rooney cleaned up his act and became a beloved national figure. That's to be admired. Most of us did things as young men and women that we wouldn't do now. The lucky ones grow up and get smarter.

When I was ten to 14 years old, I took great pride in my ability to go out and solicit money to pay for our football and basketball uniforms. I would take what they called a booster card around town and talk to the merchants and shop-keepers about making a donation to the team. In turn, their name would appear in one of the boxes on the booster card. The booster card would be displayed in the windows of all the participating boosters. It was good advertising. Anytime you saw a box that read "Compliments of a friend," it was a good bet that the booster was a local bookie or numbers writer. I knew all the bookies and numbers writers in Hazelwood. They were all interested in sports. Hey, they bet on the games and they took bets on all the sports action. They were some of the best guys in town. They liked me and I liked them. One of them, an Italian fellow who was reputed to be the major numbers guy in the community, once asked my dad, Dan O'Brien, if he wanted to join him as a numbers runner — someone who would pick up the bets around town. My father rejected the offer. "I'm Irish," he said, "and I'll get caught."

"The Irish sports section."

Art Rooney kept a diary of sorts, with a succinct sum-up of each Steelers game. After his team's first appearance in the NFL in 1933, for instance, a game with the New York Giants, he jotted down just three sentences: "The Giants won. Our team looks terrible. The fans didn't get their money's worth."

It wasn't easy to make money in pro football back then, as an owner or as a player. "In those times," recalled Rooney, "everybody in the league traveled by bus or Pullman. Once, going to Boston, we took the cheapest bus, and the players had to get out and push the thing up the steeper hills. Another time, coming home from Boston, the bus broke down 30 miles from home and we all had to hike the rest of the way to Pittsburgh. Then we started taking jets here and there and a trip to the West Coast was no big deal.

"There were no game films or terminology like red dog, zig out, flare and things like that back then. One of the biggest changes, I guess, would be the payroll. The total team payroll in the early days would be scarcely over $25,000. We used to do our scouting by mail, and by reading sports magazines."

I was always amused by how Mr. Rooney carried a big wad of dollar bills in his back pocket. It was wrapped tight with a rubber band, or gum band as Pittsburghers prefer to call such things.

"I didn't know you could go to the bank and borrow money," he said. "I thought you had to have it in your pocket."

He knew the best of times and the worst of times.

"Before we had Three Rivers Stadium," he said, "we used to practice so often in mud and snow at old South Park, where players had to dress in the cellar of a house. There were about three or four showers that worked and the toilets didn't have seats on them. Imagine that, with the luxuries we have today. But, you know something, they sort of liked it. It was a different time."

Rooney had a brief fling with politics. He was a candidate for Register of Wills, and a typical campaign speech went like this: "I don't know where the office is, but if I'm elected I'll see to it that you get a fair shake because I'll get good people to run the office." He was not elected. An honest politician may have been too much for the voters to accept.

He would have been proud that his grandson, Jim Rooney, named after one of his brothers, ran for a state senatorial position in the North Hills in March of 2001, and would have consoled him after he lost an expensive campaign. He could understand what that was all about. Dan Rooney, the president of the Steelers, was behind his son all the way, lending his personal presence as well as his bankroll to Jim's campaign. The winner, Jane Orie, a Republican, said the voters couldn't afford a Rooney because of the high cost of imploding Three Rivers Stadium and building a new stadium when voters had overwhelmingly opposed the idea.

In 1987, at age 86, Art Rooney seemed to be still going strong. He traveled that year to take in horse racing's Triple Crown — at the Kentucky Derby, the Preakness and Belmont — and the only thing he enjoyed more than a day at the races was a day at the Super Bowl with his Steelers in the battle. In July of that same year, he took his annual sojourn to Canada, something he had done for 50 years. He visited religious shrines there, and did some fishing there once upon a time. His boys suggested there might have been some gaming activity across the border that attracted their father as well.

In August of that same year, he presented John Henry Johnson, one of his old workhorse fullbacks, for induction at the Pro Football Hall of Fame in Canton, Ohio. One of his other stars, Joe Greene, was introduced for induction by head coach Chuck Noll at the same

Art Rooney loafing with some North Side kids on a Sunday afternoon in early November, 1980, at the corner of North Lincoln Avenue and Allegheny Avenue near his home.

Jim O'Brien

Rooney's 11-room Victorian manse on North Side as it appears today following recent renovations.

ceremonies. It was a glorious day for Art Rooney and the Pittsburgh Steelers. Then again, all days were glorious for this great man.

I was privileged to know him. He was the grandfather I never had, as both of mine died before I was a year old. It was always comforting and fun to be in his company. Everyone who knew him thought they enjoyed a unique relationship with him. He had that capacity for making you feel special. Horse racing never appealed to me and I was the only member of my immediate family who didn't gamble but I sure felt a lot in common with Mr. Rooney.

"From the time I was a kid," he said, "I was the manager of teams, running things, selling tickets. Kids don't have the opportunity to organize that I had then."

I did have that opportunity growing up on Sunnyside Street in Hazelwood. My boyhood friends tell me now that they never worried about what they were going to do on a summer's day because I always had the games lined up for that day. "You scheduled our summers," one of them said.

Asked how he got along so well with his employees, Rooney once remarked, "I loafed with 'em. Never expected 'em to do anything I wouldn't do. If there were any fights, I was right there."

The only individuals I met on the sports beat in Pittsburgh who came close to approaching Art Rooney were Frank Gustine, the former Pirates infielder who owned a restaurant near Forbes Field in Oakland, and Doc Carlson, a Hall of Fame basketball coach at Pitt who was the director of student health services during my student days, and maybe Baldy Regan, the unofficial mayor of the North Side. Former Pirates manager Chuck Tanner is in that class. "Gus was a close second," offered Tom "Maniac" McDonough, a retired insurance salesman who moonlighted as a bartender at Gustine's in his heyday.

It was also McDonough who referred to the obituary section of the newspaper as "the Irish sports section" when I was having lunch with him, Frank Gustine Jr., a commercial real estage mogul, and Mike Hagan, president of Iron & Glass Bank, at the City Café on the city's South Side in the summer of 2000. I had never heard that wonderful phrase before. Art Rooney was famous for attending more funerals than any other public figure in Pittsburgh during his lifetime. He and his staffers — Joe Carr, Mary Regan and Ed Kiely in particular — used to circle names in the obituary section of the newspaper each morning the way they might circle names on the racing form in the sports section. When Art Rooney attended the annual owners' meetings in all those stylish resort spots such as Maui, Hawaii, Palm Springs and Phoenix, nobody had a better time than he did. Nobody had more fun. If they had been on the North Side of Pittsburgh he'd have enjoyed their company just as much.

The first time I ever stood on a sideline and talked with Art Rooney was during my senior year at the University of Pittsburgh, back in the fall of 1963. It was at the Fairgrounds in South Park, just outside of Pittsburgh, where the Steelers trained in a spartan setting.

John Henry Johnson was one of them. The Steelers had a good team that year and nearly made the playoffs for the first time.

I was 20-years-old and the co-publisher, along with Beano Cook, of a 5,000-circulation newspaper called *Pittsburgh Weekly Sports*. Rooney was treating me as if I were a lead columnist for *The New York Times*. He told me that Jimmy Cannon, a syndicated columnist out of New York, was his favorite sportswriter. He talked of other sports writers he'd known and enjoyed through the years.

Cannon once wrote of his profession as a sportswriter: "I like my life because it's pleasant. I function in glad places."

Art Rooney was definitely Jimmy Cannon's kind of guy. I got to know Jimmy Cannon when I worked in New York and lapped up his stories and wisdom. He told stories about meeting Ernest Hemingway in Paris during the War, and of spending time with the great Joe DiMaggio, his favorite ballplayer. About a week after I had spoken to Rooney at South Park, I received a hand-written letter from him apologizing if he'd come of as "something of a know-it-all."

Rooney was concerned, mind you, about how he came off to a cub reporter. He didn't want to leave the wrong impression. He never did.

"We shouldn't brag."
— Art Rooney

In the years that followed, I was blessed to receive similar notes, and postcards from all over the world, especially Ireland, with warm, often humorous, messages from The Chief. I kept most of them. The only other people in sports who did the same thing for me were Angelo Dundee, the wonderful boxing trainer from Miami who looked after Muhammad Ali among many boxing champions, and Marquis Haynes, the marvelous dribbling wizard of the Harlem Globetrotters who lived in Tulsa. Dundee and Haynes are both Hall of Fame honorees in their respective sports.

Art Rooney also paid for a small ad in each issue of *Pittsburgh Weekly Sports*, but he just wanted an item about the next game, the date and kick-off time. He didn't want it to look like an ad. He didn't want every other newspaper in town coming after him for an ad. He just wanted to help us out.

Art Rooney was always thinking about his friends. He cared. One of his closest pals, Rich Easton, drove a truck for *The Pittsburgh Press*. Mr. Rooney was often accompanied by priests. Ed Kiely, the Steelers' publicist for many years, was a constant companion in the last decade of Rooney's life. Wherever Rooney went each day, Kiely was always at his side to make sure everything was OK. "Kiely thinks he's a Rooney," Art Jr. once observed.

Rooney always asked those who approached him, "How's your family?" or "How's your mother?" And, unlike most people, he was eager to hear the answer.

"The day after we beat Minnesota (16-6 in Super Bowl IX) down in New Orleans, I called our office and our switchboard lady answered, 'World champion Pittsburgh Steelers!' I'm not much of a memo-writer, but I sent out a memo on that," said Art Rooney. "I told them not to do that anymore. We don't have to tell people we are champions. We shouldn't brag."

Back in 1980, when the NFL started to hold a two-day draft, I made a call from a desk just outside Rooney's office to my mother, Mary O'Brien, to inquire about how she was doing. She had a muscle snap behind one of her knees the day before, and was in pain. Rooney came out of his office and saw me standing alongside the desk of his secretary, Mary Regan, who'd given me permission to use her phone He asked about my mother's health when I got off the phone.

I told him how she was doing, about her difficulties.

On the second day of the draft, I called my mother again from the same phone. "I had the nicest thing happen to me today," my mother said. "I got a Mass card from Mr. Rooney, and he had a lovely note attached to it. He had some Masses said in my name."

About three years later, just after Rooney had been released from Mercy Hospital where he had a pacemaker implanted, I mentioned to him that my mother was a patient in the same hospital. The next day when I visited her at the hospital, she pulled a letter out of a table next to her bed. It was, of course from Art Rooney. It was hand-written, with an uplifting message of encouragement. Oh, how I wish I had kept that letter. He said all the sort of things you'd like someone to say about you to your mother. For a year or so after that, he always asked me about my mother whenever he'd see me.

He came to the funeral home when my father and my brother died, and he made sure some other Steelers' officials paid their respects as well. He moved around the room at the funeral homes, quietly, exchanging remarks with everyone. It was like having a cardinal coming to console us in our grief. He had that kind of calmness about him, a presence that pacified everybody else in the room.

I always hated to go to funerals and avoided them like the plague. I hated to look at dead people. From Art Rooney, I learned that you're there to pay your proper respects, to comfort the family and friends of the deceased, that you're there for the living. He said you didn't have to look at the deceased if you didn't want to. You were there for the living, not the dead. He was the best man at more funerals in Pittsburgh than anybody else in town. When I went to three funerals on a Friday in February — a personal high — I blamed Art Rooney for my itinerary. He also led the National Football League in visiting hospitals, sending get-well cards and, of course, collecting Mass cards and funeral cards. He used the latter for bookmarks. The books he left behind in what is now a library named in his honor all have Mass cards and funeral cards in their pages. Art Rooney Jr. does the same thing with his books.

1969 Pittsburgh Steelers

Postcards from Art Rooney

Dear Jim, Thanks for paper. We don't know what to do with our first @hoice, what ever we do I hope we guess right. Good wishes Art

Jim O'Brien
Miami News
Miami Fla.

For the record, the Steelers selected Terry Bradshaw with their No. 1 draft choice in 1970.

Concelebrated Mass in the Basilica, Knock Shrine, Co. Mayo, Ireland.

Photo: P. O'Toole, John Hinde Studios.

2/1977

Dear Jimmy,
Hope you and
yours are OK.
The O'Briens over
here asked if you
O'Briens from Pittsburgh
were the McCoys. I
told them yes. At

PAR AVION
AERPHOST
O.E. 78.

EIRE
26
24 VI
82

Jimmy O'Brien
c/o Pittsburgh Steelers
300 Stadium Circle
Pittsburgh Pa
15212 U.S.A

KNOCK SHRINE, CO. MAYO. On 21st August, 1879, Our Lady, St. Joseph and St. John with the Altar the Lamb and the Cross appeared at the Church Gable in a blaze of heavenly light. A Diocesan Commission accepted the evidence as "trustworthy and satisfactory". Many privileges have been granted by the Holy See and Knock is recognised as one of the great Marian Shrines. Over a million pilgrims and invalids come to the Shrine annually from all over the world, including His Holiness Pope John Paul II who visited the Shrine in 1979.

IRELAND

Published by Our Lady's Shrine, Knock and Printed by John Hinde Ltd, Cabinteely, Dublin 18.

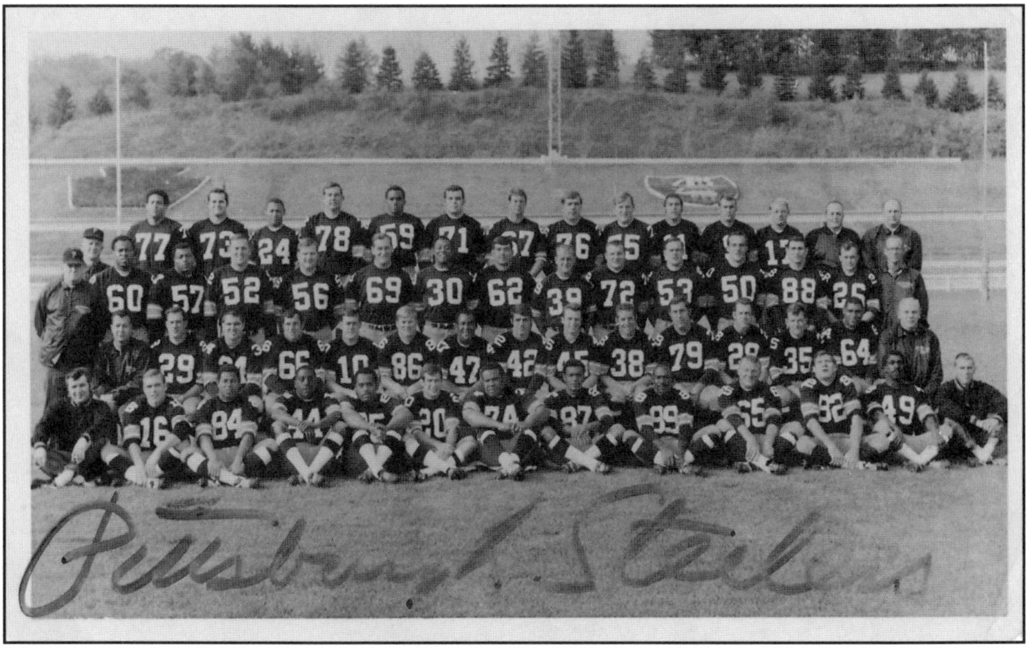

Pittsburgh Steelers

Dear Jim: - Hope all goes OK. We are well. Our team plans to be improved. Noll has done a fine job. We need about 4 good men to be a good team. The Stadium will be ready for us and baseball. Base Ball may not open their season at the new Stadium. Jim we send you our news releases. Many Reporters tell me everyone in the AFL gets them - So did Joe Gordon tell me - Hope Miami has a good year - Good luck
Art
PITTSBURGH
SEP 20 '69
P.A.
U.S. POSTAGE
.05
PB METER
863045
Jim O'Brien
Miami News
Sports
Miami Fla

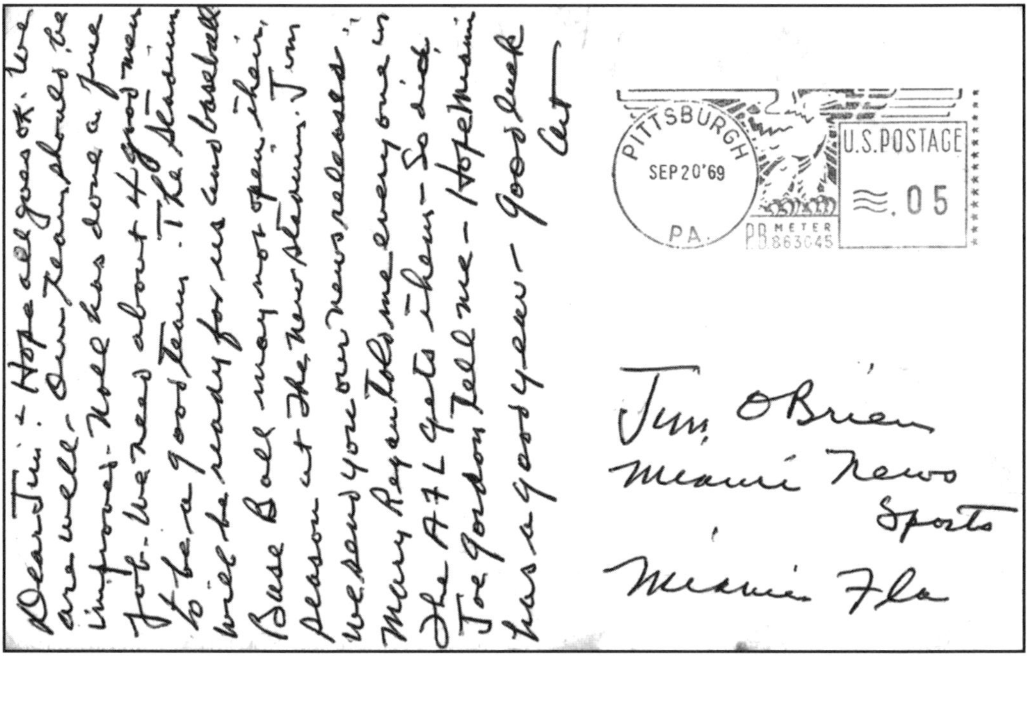

Dear Jimmy - Hope
you and yours are
as this guy your Uncle
Have had a fine trip
seeing old friends
and visiting the
tracks - Good luck
Art

Farmer with hay cart near Athlone,
Co. Westmeath.

Real Ireland
THE PEOPLE & LANDSCAPE
4a Hagan's Court, Lad Lane, Dublin 2, Ireland. Tel: 766N8. (Photo: Liam Blake)

EIRE
2

EIRE
2

22 EIRE

Jim O'Brine
Pittsburgh Press
Bloof Allie's
Pittsburgh Pa
USA

"He wanted us to be fair in our dealings with people."
— Joe Gordon
Steelers' public relations director

When the Steelers had their 50 Seasons Celebration in 1982, a photographer friend of mine took some pictures of some of the young Steelers with some of the greats of the game who'd come back for a reunion. I sent copies of the photos a week later to about 30 people, and asked them to drop a "thank you" note to the photographer for his kindness. I didn't ask Art Rooney to do that. I didn't have to. He was the only one, my photographer friend later told me, who sent him a "thank you" note.

I sent a special publication to about 200 people in Pittsburgh to acknowledge their support of a particular project, and the only one who responded with a "thank you" note was Dan Rooney, the president of the Steelers.

That brings something else to mind. None of the Rooneys are big on show. There have never been any biographical sketches about any of them in the Steelers' press guides. Their names and titles are simply listed. Some information about them has crept into the copy relating to the team's history in more recent editions of the annual publication. During Rooney's lifetime, though, any reference to him was simply Arthur J. Rooney, Chairman of the Board. That was it. Other owners have three- and four-page biographical sketches, complete with photos of them with famous personalities, or their favorite horse.

It was the same way at the Pro Football Hall of Fame. Each team has a display there and some of them seem to be shrines to the club owners.

Art Rooney's bust was in the Pro Football Hall of Fame ever since he was inducted in 1964 for his contributions to the league and the growth of the pro game. That was good enough. The Steelers' display was always devoted to the team's outstanding players.

The Steelers remain a testimonial to Art Rooney. The Steelers were the fifth-oldest franchise in the NFL. They were founded on July 8, 1933 by Rooney. They were originally named the Pittsburgh Pirates because he loved the Pirates.

They were a member of the 10-team NFL, playing in the Eastern Division. The other four NFL teams who were in existence at the time who are still in the league are the Chicago (Arizona) Cardinals, Green Bay Packers, Chicago Bears and New York Giants.

I will never forget two remarks Rooney made at the Steelers' 50 Seasons Celebration dinner at the David L. Lawrence Convention Center, named after his old friend, the former mayor of Pittsburgh and governor of Pennsylvania. Rooney said, "I never had a player on my team I didn't like." And, "I never had a player on my team I didn't think was a star." He also paid personal tribute that night to his wife — "I may never get a chance to do this again," he explained from the podium — and it wasn't long after the dinner that his wife, Kathleen, the mother of his five sons, died.

Other owners through the years have worked so hard to have the same sort of reputation, and league-wide regard, as Rooney, but they have failed to place or show. They tried too hard, that's why. With Art Rooney, it all came so naturally. There was no pretense, no guile. He was simply a nice man, a nice guy.

Joe Gordon, who served as the Steelers' public relations man since 1969, said, "Mr. Rooney doesn't always say things in so many words, but he always gave me the impression that he wanted us to be fair in our dealings with people, to try and be helpful, and to treat people the way you wanted to be treated. That's all."

Rooney always enjoyed the company of sportswriters, though toward the end he said he missed the days when there was a more easy-going exchange between the owners and the sportswriters, and the team officials and players and the sportswriters.

"The romance has gone out of the business," he would say.

Another time, he said, "If I were not a sports owner I'd want to be a sportswriter. And if I were a sportswriter I would always go to the losing locker room first because that's where the action is going to be. That's where people are going to be upset and saying things."

And unlike so many owners, Rooney seldom went into the locker room when the media was present, or when the TV cameras were capturing the scene. He preferred to go in when it was less crowded. "The locker room belongs to the players," he said. "It's like their second home."

I recall a scene at Three Rivers Stadium around 1980 that points up his manner in that regard. The Miami Dolphins were in the visitors' locker room just prior to a game with the Steelers. Miami coach Don Shula spotted Art Rooney coming down the hallway, and asked him to come in and say hello to Dan Marino, the Dolphins' quarterback who hailed from Pittsburgh and played his college ball at the University of Pittsburgh.

Art Rooney begged off, briefly. "I don't go into our own locker room before the game," said Rooney. Shula persisted, and brought Marino to the area just outside the visitors' locker room doors. Art Rooney congratulated Marino on the fine season he was having, told him how much he enjoyed watching him play at Pitt, and how he wished the Steelers had selected him in the draft. Finally, Rooney offered Marino a few words of advice, "Beware of newfound friends and acquaintances," said Rooney.

Another time, during a players' strike in 1987, he came upon John Bruno, a young ballplayer filling in for three games, as Bruno was coming out of the showers, wearing a towel around his waist. Rooney greeted him by saying, "John Bruno, the punter from Penn State. How are you?" Bruno couldn't believe he knew who he was. "That's when I felt like I was really a Steeler," said Bruno.

Prime figures at retirement luncheon after 1987 season are, left to right, Coach Chuck Noll, receiver John Stallworth, Art Rooney, strong safety Donnie Shell, and team president Dan Rooney.

Pirates owner John Galbreath pays tribute to Pittsburgh Steelers and their owner Art Rooney at April 7, 1979 ceremonies at Three Rivers Stadium.

> *"You can tell a Pittsburgher by the warmth of their handshake."*
> — Art Rooney, Sr.

The Immaculate Reception
The Chief missed it

"What happened?"
— Art Rooney

The two greatest moments in Pittsburgh sports history were Bill Mazeroski's home run that won the 1960 World Series for the Pirates, and "The Immaculate Reception" by Franco Harris that gave the Steelers their first playoff victory in the team's 40-year history. The irony of both momentous events is that they were not seen by someone who would have appreciated them the most.

Pirates' broadcaster Bob Prince didn't see Maz hit the ball over the left field wall at Forbes Field to defeat the mighty New York Yankees in the seventh game of the World Series. Maz connected on a 1-0 slider from Ralph Terry to spark a city-wide celebration unlike any ever seen in Pittsburgh. The ball soared over Yogi Berra's head in left field at 3:36 p.m. on October 13, a day that has become almost a religious holiday in Pittsburgh.

It took a long time, but Mazeroski, who may be the best fielding second baseman in history, was inducted into the Baseball Hall of Fame on August 5, 2001. The day before, Lynn Swann of the Steelers, was inducted into the Pro Football Hall of Fame. That, too, took a long time to happen. It was quite a doubleheader for Pittsburgh sports fans and brought back memories of the best of times.

Prince was on his way to the locker room to do post-game interviews and had no idea how the game ended. By coincidence, the first man he spoke to was Mazeroski. Prince asked him, "Billy, how does it feel to be a member of a world championship team?" Then he dismissed the man of the hour. Steelers owner Art Rooney did not see Harris score the game-winning touchdown in the closing seconds for a 13-7 victory over the Oakland Raiders in an AFC playoff contest on December 23, 1972 at Three Rivers Stadium. It has been judged the greatest single play in the history of the National Football League. It was the first playoff victory in Steelers' history.

Raiders quarterback Ken Stabler had scrambled 30 yards for a touchdown, followed by a conversion kick by George Blanda, to give the Oakland team a 7-6 lead with 83 seconds remaining to play. That's when Rooney left his box to beat the crowd to the clubhouse. He wanted to console his Steelers after a tough defeat.

"It's typical that he was worrying about how we were feeling," said former Steelers' safety Mike Wagner.

Rooney and his cronies took the elevator down to the lobby, just outside of the clubhouses. They didn't see Terry Bradshaw throw a desperation pass on a fourth-and-10 play from his own 40. Jack Tatum, a tough Raiders' defensive back, and Frenchy Fuqua, a Steelers' running back, both reached the ball at the same time.

It's felt that Tatum hit the ball off Fuqua's shoulders and that it deflected into the air. Harris was hustling downfield to block for Fuqua when he found the ball floating toward him. He reached down and grabbed it and raced for the end zone from the Oakland 42.

As Rooney came off the elevator he was greeted by none other than Bob Prince. "Congratulations, Chief!" cried Prince, as only he could.

"What happened?" asked Art Rooney.

"What a helluva way to win a football game!" shouted Prince.

"What happened?" asked Art Rooney once again.

Imagine trying to explain to the Steelers' owner what had just occurred. We're still not sure what happened.

With Franco Harris at 50 Seasons Celebration in 1982.

31

The Patriarch
Stories of the good ol' days

"I'd rather be lucky than good."

It was always a pleasure to visit with Art Rooney in his office at Three Rivers Stadium. He would sit behind his desk, comfortable in his well-padded chair, and simply tell stories. This was in mid-January of 1980, before the Steelers were to play in Super Bowl XIV in Pasadena, California. He had a chance to be the first owner ever to win four Super Bowls. Only George Halas had been in the league longer than Art Rooney, but no one had waited as long to win his first NFL title than Mr. Rooney. "You know how we're just sitting here talking," he said. "Chuck Noll never comes in here and just sits and talks. It's always business. But he talks to Dan a lot. That's the way it should be, I guess. He's Dan's man." Here's what Art Rooney had to say that day:

My mother's people were all coal miners and my father's people were all steel workers. They all worked in the mills. Our neighborhood on the North Side was made up of Irish, most of them from Galway, Ireland, with a mixture of Polish, Italian and black. We lived on the second floor of my father's saloon — Dan Rooney's Saloon. So my dad's name was Dan and my mother's name was Margaret. My dad owned that saloon for years and years.

It was a rough neighborhood, in a way, but in those days kids were on the playground from the time the sun came up to the time it went down. We played baseball and football and we boxed.

In the earlier days, before they raised the streets and built the reservoirs, it wasn't unusual at all that we would go to school out of our second-story window in a skiff. The river came up six or seven times a year. Since they raised the streets and built the reservoirs, we haven't had many floods here, except the year before last when all those rugs and that wood paneling were ruined here.

My brothers Jim and Dan were into all the sports as well. Jim played football at Pitt in the late '20s. I had a try-out with the Red Sox and won some amateur boxing titles. I boxed those guys who came around in the carnivals. They'd give you $3 a round if you could last with the guy. Sometimes the problem was carrying them for three rounds. They couldn't fight. If they could fight, they wouldn't be in the carnival. Every time I hit a town, I'd always ask if there was a carnival around.

I not only participated in sports, but I started to organize and promote sports, too. I guess I liked it better than anybody else. I founded my first football team, a semi-pro club, in 1916. In a way, I guess that was the start of the Steelers. It grew from that. My first team was called the Hope Harvey team.

Hope was the name of the fire engine house that furnished all our dressing rooms and that. And Harvey was a doctor who never charged us anything to take care of the players. They played right here at Exposition Park and sometimes we had 12,000 people in the stands. Later on, we called the team the J.P. Rooneys.

I never joined the National Football League, which was led by George Halas, back then because the league played its games on Sundays, and Pennsylvania's blue laws prohibited any competitive athletics on the Sabbath. But portions of the blue laws were repealed in 1933, and that opened the door for us to get into what was thought then to be a big-time football league.

Even so, I was still more interested in horse racing. I have made tremendous bets on horse racing. That's the only game I ever bet on. Never football. I've enjoyed betting on horses and winning. If I'm losers, I don't enjoy it at all. If I'm winners, I really enjoy it and I make a good player, as good a player as there is. If I lose, I back off.

I had a big day at Empire City in 1936, so see I didn't get the money to buy an NFL franchise from my big day at the track. That came later. Then I went to Saratoga and had an even bigger day. At Empire City I had the car (winners in all races). Then I went to Saratoga and I had a lot of winners. One day I had five different races that I bet on and won. Sometimes I bet as much as I could get on a horse. I did OK that day. I don't want to say how much I won (estimated at between $250,000 and $300,000), but I did all right.

When we first started, we called our NFL team the Pittsburgh Pirates, but it got mixed up with the baseball team so much that we decided to change the name. Then we had a contest. And we figured Steelers was the proper name because Pittsburgh was the steel center of the world. Joe Carr, our ticket manager, really liked "Steelers" as a nickname. Our first coach was Jap Douds, and we had Joe Bach, and the legendary Johnny Blood — he was something — and Walt Kiesling. We had Jim Leonard; he was an asparagus farmer. We had Jock Sutherland — he was a great coach and he'd have won us a championship but he died too soon — and we had John Michelosen and Buddy Parker and Bill Austin. And, finally, we got Chuck Noll. He was the big difference.

In your lifetime, you make mistakes. I had Joe Bach twice, and he was a good coach. Letting Joe Bach get away was the one big mistake I made. Had I kept him, we would have won championship after championship at Pittsburgh. He was out and out college, a Joe College. He loved the college spirit and the rah-rah. In those days, despite what anyone else tells you, this league was just a couple of jumps ahead of semi-pro ball. We traveled by coach and trains and they didn't have the rah-rah spirit. I didn't have confidence in this pro football and he and I and his wife and my wife were very close friends.

So I actually helped Bach get the head job at Niagara University. When Bach left, we got Johnny Blood, who played and coached (1937 through 1939) for a few years. Johnny was way ahead of his time. He was way ahead of these here college free-spirits. That guy had free spirit before anybody else had it. He used to drive up here on a motorcycle. He'd travel cross-country on a motorcycle. He'd get on a boat between seasons and work around the world. He was a ghost. He used to come out of nowhere. He could show up here tomorrow and I wouldn't be surprised. You know where the Taft Hotel is in New York? On Seventh Avenue? I think it was the Taft. Anyway, Johnny Blood always wore sneakers. And one day Curly Lambeau, the coach of the Green Bay Packers, locked Johnny in his room on the top floor of the Taft. John was playing for Green Bay then and they were in New York to play the Giants. The hotel was made of small blocks. John climbed out of his seventh-floor window by putting his toes between the blocks and crawled down into Walt Kiesling's room, and out his door. What a man! Yeah, Kiesling was playing for the Packers then, too.

I remember another time Blood got cut so bad in the calf of his leg — he was our player-coach — that blood was running down his leg into his shoe, and every time he'd take a step the blood would shoot up until the players couldn't stand it anymore. They kept hollering, "Get rid of him! Get him out of here!"

But you never knew when Blood was going to put on a performance. He could have been a great coach. He had imagination, but he didn't believe in fundamentals. So Blood gave way to Walt Kiesling as our coach. The one thing Kiesling didn't have was the knack for getting along with the ballplayers.

"We put two bad teams together and made them twice as bad."

Then, we joined up with the Chicago Cardinals to form one team. Kiesling and their coach, Phil Handler, were in charge. Handler was from Chicago. We put two bad teams together in 1944 and made them twice as bad. That team, called the Pitt-Cards, went 0 and 10. Handler was a horse player. Both he and Kiesling were handicappers. They were at the racetrack all the time. Kiesling carried the *Racing Form* more than the playbook. And Handler! Both of them. They did more handicapping with the *Racing Form* than with the X's and O's. They were knowledgeable enough about football, but they were horseplayers first and X's and O's guys second.

Then we had Jim Leonard. He could have been a good coach. He had an asparagus farm in New Jersey, and coaching was kinda secondary. Jock Sutherland followed Leonard in '46 and '47. He was great. Sutherland was one of those hard-boiled coaches who practiced and practiced. When he was the coach, we sold out Forbes Field every time. He took us to the playoffs against the Eagles in '47. Unfortunately, he got a brain tumor and died (April 11, 1948).

So Michelosen, who'd played for Sutherland at Pitt, took over (in 1948). We were still using the single-wing. We were the last team in the NFL to employ the single-wing offense. Then it gets complicated. I brought back Joe Bach for two years, but he was not the same rah-rah coach I had known earlier. He had diabetes and died after coaching

Dr. John B. Sutherland (right) posed with co-owners of the Steelers, Bert Bell (left), and Art Rooney, after signing to coach the Pittsburgh professional football team on December 26, 1945. Next to Dr. Sutherland is Johnny Michelosen, his assistant, who would succeed him at the helm of the Steelers.

Steelers coach Buddy Parker and newly-named NFL Commissioner Pete Rozelle meet with Art Rooney before luncheon at Roosevelt Hotel on March 1, 1960.

> *"If you ask a Pittsburgher where some place is, he'll stop and tell you, and if he has nothing to do, he'll take you there."*
> — Art Rooney, Sr.

two years (1952 and 1953). Kiesling came back for three years, until 1956, but he was sick, too. He was not well at all. In fact, he came back from Green Bay because he was sick. It was one of those things. I just took care of him.

Then I hired one of the best coaches available in the business, Buddy Parker, who'd been great with the Detroit Lions. But he had a bad temper and a drinking problem, and he did some irrational things that hurt us. Parker traded our draft choices all the time. Some years we didn't have a draft choice until the eighth or ninth round. But he had been successful at doing that in Detroit and thought he could do it here. That was where I thought he made his major mistake. In fact, that led to one of the things that made Parker resign. We told him that we didn't want him making any more trades giving away our draft choices and that was one of the things that irked him. We told him we wanted to build on draft choices. But he was a tremendous guy, truthful and honest. In 1965, Parker quit after a loss and this time we decided to accept his resignation. He'd done it before when he was upset. We replaced him with one of his assistants, Mike Nixon.

Then we brought in Bill Austin. That was Danny's first hire. Austin came highly recommended by Vince Lombardi. Austin was an assistant coach on all those great teams at Green Bay. Lombardi was very close to my family. One of the problems with Austin was that he wanted to be like Vince, but he couldn't be. It would have been better if he had been Bill Austin in his personality. He'd yell at a ballplayer because Lombardi did things like that. But Austin couldn't do it like Lombardi. The players didn't believe he was for real.

"He gave us class."

That's when we took a chance on Chuck Noll. He'd been with Don Shula on some great teams at Baltimore. It was a good move. He gave us class.

He lost 13 of 14 games his first year, when we played at Pitt Stadium for the last season. When Noll didn't lose the team the first year, I told both of my boys, Dan and Artie, that this guy's got it. I told them that he was going to make it, if we could get him the material. And Dan and Artie did just that.

You never heard a squawk from the ballplayers. They never beefed. They went out and practiced as if they had won the game. The biggest problem with a lot of coaches is that they know everything but they can't put it all together. They can't get the most out of their players.

Things improved after that and we started making some good money. There were other reasons we made a profit. We got $3 million for joining the American Football League. They paid off at $600,000 a year over five years. I remember when we made that decision. That's the first time we had real money to work with.

At first, I wasn't happy about leaving the National Football League. We couldn't arrive at any decision on how to do it. And the wind-up was, we were all going into a hat — the whole league — and we were going to draw out of a hat what division you were in and what team you played. You would think that I, being a horseplayer, would be the last person to be afraid of taking such a chance, but I couldn't take it. I had to be in the same division as Cleveland. We sold out the Cleveland game every year. And out there, too.

I went to Art Modell (the Cleveland Browns' owner) and told him we can't afford to go into the hat. So we agreed to go together, along with Baltimore, and pick up the $3 million, too. I could have made moves to Baltimore, New Orleans and Atlanta, but I'm a Pittsburgher and I like the town. Great people live here. Friendly people. The only problem is that a lot of the people I know are dying off. I probably go to more wakes than anybody in Pittsburgh.

I have few regrets. I could have done it better, I'm sure. I really didn't spend the time on this like I should have, like Halas or Lambeau. It was my fault. There isn't any doubt about that. I was at the racetrack. I was doing what I could do. But we had some bad breaks, too. Bach could have done it. Sutherland could have done it. Parker almost pulled it off. Bach never would have gone if I told him I wanted him to stay. I wasn't high on the pro game. I didn't know it was going to come to where it came. I'll be honest about that. I always thought it was going to be better, but not like this. But I have no regrets. I kept my team. So many guys went by the boards in my time. They lost their teams. I'm still here.

Rooney reassures Mayor David L. Lawrence in meeting at City Hall in November of 1956 that Steelers are staying in Pittsburgh after four other cities made overtures to Steelers' owner to move his team.

Stadium Stories
The Chief recalls early days

"I won't bother you."

Art Rooney remembered how the river would rise when it rained in the spring and summer and, eventually, run over the docks where the Allegheny met the Monongahela to form the Ohio River. The Rooneys resided on what is now known as the North Side of Pittsburgh, but was then known as Old Allegheny, a city unto itself.

"All the kids in the neighborhoods had skiffs," Rooney recalled. "We were always around the river. We swam there and we fished there. If you spit in the Allegheny River there'd be a flood. It happened every year. We'd crawl out the second story of our home, untie our skiffs, and ride around the streets."

Rooney remembers how one of his buddies came by a canoe once, and they were riding in the center of Exposition Park, the ballfield where Honus Wagner and Pie Traynor once played as Pirates.

"I wasn't too keen on the canoe," said Rooney. "It kept tilting so much. After we had paddled round the park for awhile, we got careless and someone tipped the canoe. I had boots on and they filled up with water and I just made it to the left field bleachers to save myself."

Rooney pointed to the spot where he crawled into the stands. It was more than 60 years after the fact. Rooney, white-haired at 72, was sitting in the press box at the brand-new Three Rivers Stadium back in the summer of 1970, built on the same site as Exposition Park.

Rooney was talking to me during a Pirates game at Three Rivers Stadium. He seldom missed a game, walking to the stadium from his home just five minutes away. We'll miss Three Rivers Stadium because it said something about our city, it told the world that we had three rivers in the heart of the city.

The new stadium solved a lot of problems for the Pirates and the Steelers, but it also brought some new ones, as Rooney related. He said his mailbox was flooded with complaints from fans who weren't satisfied with their seats in the new stadium.

"Everybody's squawking and beefing about it," said Rooney. "It pains me to hear all these complaints. I was coming out of church on Sunday and I ran into a guy I went to school with. He was complaining, too. He said, 'Art, I've been going to see your team play ever since you've had a team. I had a seat on the 50 all these years, and now I'm on the 30.' His name is John Callahan and he's the last guy in the world I want mad at me."

He made an interesting point that ought to bring a smile to all those Pitt fans who complained about the leveling of Pitt Stadium and the move to the North Side by their beloved Panthers. Rooney said there were twice as many seats between the 40-yard lines at the college stadium. That had bleacher-type seating and the new stadium had theatre-type seating, and he said that made a big difference.

"These seats here are 23$\frac{1}{2}$ inches wide and they have arm rests," said Rooney, pointing out a positive aspect of the new stadium. "At Pitt Stadium, if a fat guy was sitting on one row, somebody else was half-way in the aisle. These are much more comfortable than hard wood benches, too. Outside of those seats, though, that's a wonderful place to watch a football game. That's a football stadium. This one's built more for baseball, too.

"There's a fancy club here, too," he said, pointing to the windows of the Allegheny Club. "That took up a lot of our good seats. I tried to get them to put it out there (he pointed to deepest centerfield), but the baseball club is bigger than I am and they have something to say, too. I can squawk and complain, too, but it didn't do me any good."

People who complained about that private club in a stadium built mostly with public money called it "the Three Rivers Country Club." Now when's the last time you heard that? If the truth be known, the new stadium caters to the well-heeled customers even more.

Big companies that had two to four season tickets at Pitt Stadium had 200 or more at Three Rivers Stadium, and they were among the best to be had. Long-time season ticket holders were being pushed aside. One would never know that the Steelers had one of the lowest season ticket sales totals for many years in the National Football League.

"Joe Magarac is getting the shaft in the new stadium," said one insider. "It's the shot-and-beer guy who's getting the worst of it. Art doesn't even know what is being done in that respect. He has no control over that anymore."

Joe Magarac is a mythical character, something like Paul Bunyan, who is symbolic of the fire-eating steel worker in western Pennsylvania. Rooney's club, originally known as the Pirates, was named after these very men. Back then, they represented the heart, if not the money, of the city.

They stuck by the Steelers when it wasn't so fashionable to be seen in the stadium. They peeked from behind pillars at Forbes Field for more years than they'd like to count at a club that had gone the longest in the league without winning a championship of any kind.

Still, many of those people suspected that sportswriters were on the team payroll because they continued to refer to Rooney as a wonderful, wonderful man. This was true, however. Though the man was a millionaire, he had never forgotten where he came from, and he was more like the man in the street than he was a man in the stadium club or the Duquesne Club.

Rooney remembered the same thing happened when he moved from Forbes Field to Pitt Stadium. He had about 8,000 season ticket holders at the time and they all had great seats in right-center field that were among the best of any ballpark in the country. There weren't many other seats, however, at Forbes Field that afforded a favorable view of the action, and the capacity was only 40,000 at best.

It rained nearly every game at Pitt Stadium which was an open bowl, as opposed to the seats at Forbes Field that were under a roof.

The cries were so loud that Rooney returned his team to Forbes Field for a few more seasons before he went back to Pitt Stadium.

"If our team wins they'll all be satisfied," said Rooney. "And if you keep on losing the seats get worse each game."

Rooney's logic still holds true now that the Pirates are playing in PNC Park and the Steelers have their own football-only stadium on the North Side, Heinz Field, that they are sharing with Pitt.

Rooney revealed to me that he hadn't even been able to see the Steelers very clearly out on the field for the previous four years. The Steelers' most jaundiced fans would say he was lucky but, in seriousness, Rooney thought he was going blind.

In 1969, however, a doctor fixed him up with a pair of contact lenses, plus eyeglasses that he also had to wear, and he said he could see clearly once more.

He also had a new office in the new stadium. It was about four times as big as the one he shared with the team's business manager at the downtown Roosevelt Hotel. He was comfortable there in an office that was nearly wall-to-wall desk and cigar smoke.

Rooney was contented, and liked the coziness and unkemptness of the place. His desk was right up against that of Fran Fogarty, who always seemed to be banging away at an adding machine, and making notations in a yellow ledger. It was Fogarty who read newspapers to Rooney, and it was a great blow to Rooney when Fogarty died at the outset of the 1969 season. Now Art was asking other staff members if they wanted to share his office with him. "I won't bother you," he assured all he approached with the offer. "Trust me."

The third Lombardi Trophy emblematic of Super Bowl XIII triumph is hoisted by Mayor Richard Caliguiri, at right, along with, left to right, Steelers president Dan Rooney, Coach Chuck Noll and Art Rooney, in early 1979.

Dan Marino
Saw Rooney at Steelers' practice sessions

"He touched you."

Miami Dolphins

Dan Marino remains a hometown hero in Pittsburgh where he starred at Central Catholic High School and as an All-American quarterback at Pitt, not far from his home in South Oakland. Marino set many NFL career passing records during his 17 seasons with the Miami Dolphins before retiring after the 1999 season. When Marino was a senior at Pitt, Steelers' owner Art Rooney remarked, "We've got to find a way to keep that kid in Pittsburgh." But the Steelers passed on Marino with the 21st pick on the first round of the 1983 college draft and selected Gabe Rivera, a defensive lineman from Texas Tech. Rivera was left crippled by an auto accident during his rookie season. Marino is No. 1 in several all-time major categories, including passes attempted (8,358), completed (4,967), yards passing (61,361) and touchdown passes (420). He joined the "Inside the NFL" team on HBO for the 2000 season and was an immediate hit, teaming up with Lenny Dawson, Nick Buoniconti, Chris Collins and Jerry Glanville on the popular weekly cable show. Marino remembered Art Rooney from his schooldays:

Growing up in the city of Pittsburgh, I knew about the history and tradition of the Steelers. And it all started with Mr. Rooney. Being a kid who loved the game of football, I respected the fact that he was the man most responsible for the Steelers being in Pittsburgh. He bought the team. It was his baby.

I worked one summer, back in 1980, for Massaro Construction Company when they were doing a job at Three Rivers Stadium. Joe Massaro's people were building new suites on the luxury box level. I would see Mr. Rooney walking around the field, and see him talking to the ground crew. A lot of the guys on the ground crew were from Oakland. They had started working on the ground crew when the Steelers and Pirates were playing in Oakland. So I knew a lot of them from our neighborhood. I remember how open and friendly he was, and how well he treated those guys on the ground crew. I heard he used to take two of them on the airplane for every Steelers' road game, and that he would have a drawing and take some of them to the Super Bowl when the Steelers were in it. They named Mr. Rooney an honorary member of the ground crew.

Dan Marino

13

If you grew up in Pittsburgh, as I did, Mr. Rooney was as big a name as there was in sports. Later on, when I established myself in football there, I started to see him at sports banquets in Pittsburgh. I'd talk to him a little bit. He'd always congratulate me about something. I admired him, so it meant a lot to me.

He was the tradition; he built the Steelers. And he was always telling stories, and he was always talking to somebody. He treated people like they were important. He touched you. He'd ask me about what was going on at Pitt, and about my family. If I were with my father, he'd make a fuss over him, too.

My boyhood hero was Terry Bradshaw. I grew up as a big Steelers fan, and I wanted to be a quarterback in the NFL. That was my dream. Bradshaw was the best back then. So he was my man. I got to meet him when I was at Pitt, and that was a big thrill.

Pitt had everyone back from our team last season (2000) when they were playing at Three Rivers Stadium. That was nice. And when I came in for the Mario Lemieux Celebrity Golf Invitational they presented me with a No. 13 Steelers jersey with my name on the back of it. I treasure that jersey. Sure, you wonder what it might have been like to play for the Steelers, but it couldn't have worked out better than it did for the Dolphins.

I was back recently and I got to see the new practice facilities for Pitt and the Steelers on the South Side. From where I was standing, I could see the hillside and the lights over what was Frazier Field when I was growing up and playing there for St. Regis Grade School, which was just across Parkview Avenue from my house. My grandmother lived near Frazier Field, which overlooked the J&L Steel Company down on Second Avenue back in those days. It made me smile to know that you could see my boyhood field (now named the Danny Marino Field) from where the Steelers and Pitt are practicing these days.

I'll never forget those days. Willie Stargell of the Pirates lived near my grandmother, and he used to play catch with me and my friends in the street there. Bruno Sammartino, the champion wrestler, lived in the same neighborhood. We weren't far from Forbes Field and Schenley Park. We knew everybody in the neighborhood, and they all seemed to be big sports fans.

People are always asking my dad if he wished I had been drafted by the Steelers instead of the Dolphins. He tells them, 'Yeah, I missed going on all those vacations to the North Side.' No, the Marinos are all in Miami now, and we're quite happy with that scene. We're treated well there and feel at home there. But Pittsburgh will always be my hometown.

> *"He always said he wasn't a saint, that he touched all the bases in life."*
> — Dan Rooney

Dan Marino is seated between Bishop Leonard and Art Rooney on upper level, directly behind Mayor Sophie Masloff at CYA dinner where he was honored.

During his senior season at Pitt in 1982, Dan Marino meets with his idol, Terry Bradshaw of Steelers and former pro football player turned broadcaster Ahmad Rashad at Pitt Stadium.

Hard Times
The summer of 1933

What it was like at the start

A young fan who follows the Pittsburgh Steelers today would have a difficult time imagining what it must have been like when the team started out in the summer of 1933.

Today the Steelers dominate the sports coverage in the city's media. Hardly a day goes by that there isn't a story about the Steelers in the sports pages of the area newspapers. During the season, there are special pullout sections, full-page posters of star players, and statistics and notes to satisfy the most ardent of fans. The Steelers are the subjects of conversation on sports talk shows on radio and TV on a year-round basis. People never seem to tire of talking about the Steelers, even though it's been over 20 years since they last won a Super Bowl.

Back in 1933 the Steelers were known as the Pittsburgh Pirates, for one thing. They were renamed the Steelers in 1940. In the beginning, they were often limited to a single paragraph in the daily newspapers, and the copy for the item was set in agate, the smallest type size, the size usually reserved for statistics and boxscores. There would be an item about some player signings, and the announcement would be attributed to Art Rooney, the owner and founder of the franchise. The item would take up an inch of space or less in a single column.

> The Pittsburgh Pirates professional football team secured their biggest name to date with the signing of Angel Brovelli, a fullback from St. Mary's of Oakland, Calif., according to team owner Art Rooney. Brovelli will report to training camp on Sept. 2-3. The Pirates hope he'll be in a class with Benny Friedman and Red Grange.

There was no television in those days, of course, and there were no sports talk shows on the radio.

There would be some sports highlights to be seen at the movie theaters during the news segment. The news was usually about two weeks old, but it was nearly as popular as the cartoons that went with the main fare.

There would be half-page spreads, with four or five players pictured, about the college football teams in the area, including Pitt, Duquesne and Carnegie Tech, which all fielded top-flight teams that went to bowl games, as well as Washington & Jefferson, Geneva and Westminster.

Major league baseball ruled the day and the Pirates were the biggest professional team in town. Boxing, horseracing, golf and tennis — women's as well as men's for the latter two — were given extensive coverage. Sandlot teams often were given more attention than the city's pro football team. Local amateur baseball teams had boxscores of their games in the papers.

Rooney, who had been operating semi-pro teams for years in his native North Side, purchased the National Football League franchise for $2,500. Money was as tough to come by as newspaper space for the Steelers in that era.

Men were selling apples on street corners for 5 cents in 1933. You could also buy a loaf of bread for 5 cents. The country's banking system collapsed that same year. The stock market had crashed in 1929 and the country was still deep in The Depression. Half the nation's workers had lost their jobs. That was true in the Pittsburgh mills as well. The other half of the workers were on part-time duty. The workers at the Thompson Works of U.S. Steel in Braddock, for instance, were working two or three days a week at best, but happy they were working at all. Poverty was a way of life for over 40 million people. This was the era of the "Okies" — migrant farmers going West seeking work — as portrayed in the book and movie in John Steinbeck's "The Grapes of Wrath."

Herbert Hoover, the 21st President of the U.S.A., stumbled out of bed at 6 o'clock on the chill, grey morning of March 4, 1933 to be told that on his last day as president the banking system in the U.S. had collapsed. Soon after, "Hoovervilles" sprung up throughout America. These were squalid villages in vacant lots where the homeless sheltered themselves in sheds made of packing boxes and scrap metal while they foraged through garbage cans for food.

Those who were working weren't making much money. The average yearly salaries for some fields went like this: bus driver $ 1,373; college teacher $ 3,111; priest $ 831.00; public school teacher $ 1,227; steelworker $ 422.87; attorney $ 4,218.

Anyone who wants to gain some appreciation for this period in our nation's history, and some background on the Steelers and Pittsburgh sports scene could go to the Carnegie Library in Oakland and scan the microfilm of the city's daily newspapers from the summer of 1933. There were three dailies serving the city back then, the *Pittsburgh Post-Gazette*, *The Pittsburgh Press* and the Pittsburgh *Sun-Telegraph*. Only the *Post-Gazette* has survived and the *Tribune-Review*, once just a Greensburg newspaper, has expanded its coverage to Pittsburgh as well.

"You're supposed to pretend to be nice to people. That's how you become a nice person."
— Rebecca, the barkeep in "Cheers," explaining to the regulars why they should visit someone in the hospital they don't particularly like.

Some haven't used their revolvers for years.

Prohibition banning the sale of alcoholic beverages was lifted on December 5, 1933 when the 21st amendment was adopted and 40 Prohibition agents in Pittsburgh lost their jobs. That same year, Pennsylvania ended its Blue Laws which prohibited charging admission for spectator sports on Sunday. That really opened the doors for a pro football venture. Fridays belonged to high school sports, Saturday to the colleges, so Sunday was all that remained of the weekend for the pros to play.

There was much going on in 1933.

The ban on "Ulysses," a controversial book by the Irish writer James Joyce was lifted by a federal judge.

It was a time of "Hooverville," NRA, CCC, WPA, PWA, FDR and his public works programs and John L. Lewis looking after the coal miners' union.

It's the year that Franklin Delano Roosevelt said, "The only thing to fear is fear itself."

Franklin J. McQuaide, the superintendent of police in Pittsburgh, wanted to get the rust out of guns carried by police officers. "I am tired of seeing policemen with revolvers only as ornaments," said McQuaide. "Some haven't used their revolvers for years. A lot of service pistols are so corroded I doubt they would discharge if someone pulled the trigger."

Our Marines were in Haiti. There was a World's Fair in Chicago featuring controversial fan dancer Sally Rand. Two daring French fliers, Paul Codos and Maurice Rossi, flew out of Floyd Bennett Field on Long Island on a straight line to Rayack, Syria, setting some sort of flight record.

John S. Herron was running for re-election as mayor of Pittsburgh. The late mayor, Charles H. Kline, left an estate of $7,000 to his widow and his secretary. Roy A. Hunt was the president of Alcoa. Chancellor John G. Bowman was in charge at Pitt.

There was a civil war in Havana and there was a call for President Gerardo Machado to resign. Troops were called out by Machado to stop the uprising. Later in the summer, the Cuban military force overthrew Machado and forced him to step down. President Franklin D. Roosevelt sent warships to Cuba to keep things under control.

Meanwhile Adolph Hitler and Joseph Goebbels were making public appearances to promote their "Aryan supremacy theories" in Germany.

You could buy a Frigidaire for $99 at Gimbel's at Sixth Avenue at Smithfield Street, or dress shirts for $1.69 to $2.98 at Rosenbaum's on Sixth Street between Liberty Avenue and Penn Avenue. A tweed woman's suit cost $16.75 at Joseph Horne Co. You could also get gifts at Frank & Seder Department Store or Kappel's.

46

At the Graham Packard Motor Co. of Pittsburgh on Baum Boulevard an eight-cylinder automobile cost $845 and a six-cylinder automobile cost $745. A top of the line Packard cost $2,150.

Gillette razor blades were 49 cents for a pack of 10 blades. Eggs were 19 cents a dozen, soap was 48 cents for 10 "giant" bars. A two-pound bag of coffee grounds was 49 cents. Two dozen oranges were 35 cents. Pears were five for 10 cents. Cantaloupes were three for 25 cents.

Other prices were 25 cents for a tube of toothpaste; $20 for a typewriter, 22 cents a pound for bacon; 22 cents a pound for chicken; 5 cents a pound for sugar; 2 cents a pound for potatoes, 29 cents a pound for sirloin steak; 55 cents for a silk necktie; $2.69 for a raincoat; $1.79 for leather shoes; $2 for an electric iron.

Pittsburgesque was a popular man-about-town column in the *Post-Gazette* written by Charles F. Danver. Cy Hungerford was the paper's political cartoonist.

Mae West was starring in "She Done Him Wrong," a movie at the Davis Theater in Sheridan Square. Constance Bennett was starring in "Bed of Roses"; at the Enright Theater in East Liberty. Marie Dressler and Walter Berry were in "Tugboat Annie" at the Loew's Penn in downtown Pittsburgh. Also downtown were "Whoopee," starring Eddie Cantor, at the Fulton.

On the national scene, the Marx Brothers were in "Duck Soup," Laurel & Hardy were in "Song of the Desert," Ginger Rogers was in Busby Berkeley's extravagant musical production "Gold Diggers of 1933," Katharine Hepburn and Joan Bennett were in "Little Women." Playwright Eugene O'Neill's newest show was "Ah, Wilderness."

It was the time of "Little Orphan Annie" and "Leapin' Lizards."

It was six years before the public debut of television at the World's Fair in New York.

George Bernard Shaw, the Irish writer, said, "There are three things which I shall never forget about America — the Rocky Mountains, the Statue of Liberty and Amos 'n Andy."

Cab Calloway was directing his band at the Duquesne Gardens, a show that was being aired on WWSW. Ho-de-ho!

Pittsburgh-born Dick Powell was appearing with dancer Ruby Keeler in "42nd Street," a musical on Broadway.

Newly-published books included "God's Little Acre" by Erskine Caldwell and "Miss Lonelyhearts" by Nathanial West.

Popular songs were "Lazybones" by Hoagy Carmichael, "Let's Fall In Love" and "It's Only A Paper Moon" by Harold Arlen, and "Sophisticated Lady" by Duke Ellington. It was the heyday of Cole Porter, Irving Berlin and Moss Hart.

Southern Cal, the 1932 national college football champion, beat Pitt, 35-0, in the Rose Bowl on January 1, 1933. Primo Carnera of Italy KOd Jack Sharkey at Long Island City Bowl to win the world heavyweight boxing title. In the first All-Star Game, the American League defeated the National League, 4-2.

Postmaster General James A. Farley, a friend of Art Rooney, was delivering an address on WJAS Radio. Nationally-syndicated sports columnist Grantland Rice was doing a sports report that was carried by KDKA Radio. Fiorello LaGuardia was elected mayor of New York City.

There were picnic listings in the local newspapers for Kennywood Park, West View Park, North Park and South Park, among others. On August 8, the Monongahela Businessmen's Assn. was at Kennywood Park; the Jewish Big Brothers Club was at Willows Grove at North Park, and the First Presbyterian Church of Crafton was at the Stone Manse at South Park.

A riot broke out and police had to be called to restore order at the Lithuanian Club picnic at Adams Grove in Castle Shannon. Patrolman John Higgins was arrested for hitting patrons of a movie theater over the head with a mace as they left a midnight show. According to witnesses, Patrolman Higgins had been drinking.

Some of most popular offerings on the radio were Amos & Andy, of course, Kate Smith, George Burns and Gracie Allen, Ozzie and Harriet, Fibber McGee and Molly, Jack Benny, Fred Allen, Charlie McCarthy with Edgar Bergen, W.C. Fields and Dick Tracy.

It was a time of super heroes like Jack Armstrong — The All-American Boy, Tarzan, Flash Gordon, Tom Mix and Buck Rogers.

The "Most Wanted" list included the likes of John Dillinger, George "Machine Gun" Kelly, "Pretty Boy" Floyd, Ma Barker and Her Boys, Bonnie & Clyde and chasing after them was FBI director J. Edgar Hoover.

Some of the top movie stars were Shirley Temple, Jean Harlow, Clark Gable, Gary Cooper, Marlene Dietrich, Errol Flynn, Bette Davis, Will Rogers, Fred Astaire, George Raft, Paul Muni, Mickey Rooney, Jimmy Cagney and Edward G. Robinson.

Teddy Yarosz, a 161-pound fighter from Monaca, won every round in a 10-round main event before 6,000 fans at Dreamland Park in Newark, New Jersey, defeating Al Rossi of Silver Lake, New Jersey. Yarosz was one of eight children of Polish immigrants who originally settled on the North Side, but moved to Monaca to be closer to the mill where Teddy's father worked. The father died in 1927, leaving his widow with eight children to raise.

The Pirates were running second to the New York Giants in the eight-team National League standings. They finished the season in that same position, with an 87-67 record under second-year manager George Gibson. He would be fired after 51 games the following summer and replaced by Pie Traynor. The Pirates fell to fifth place that season. The Pirates played an exhibition game against the Wheeling Stogies, the team that Art Rooney and his brother, Dan, had once played for.

The Pirates opening day lineup in 1933 was centerfielder Lloyd Waner, centerfielder Fred Lindstrom, rightfielder Paul Waner, third baseman Pie Traynor, first baseman Gus Suhr, shortstop Arky Vaughan, second baseman Anthony Piet, catcher Earl Grace and pitcher Bill Swift.

The New York Giants defeated the Washington Senators, 4 games to 1 in the World Series.

Elmer Layden was the head football coach at Duquesne University, and Joe Bach was one of his assistants. Bach would later coach the Steelers on several occasions. Buff Donelli was the coach of the freshman football team at Duquesne. Howard Harpster was the football coach at Carnegie Tech. That team was covered by Jack Sell, who would cover the Steelers for nearly 40 years.

Sell did a series of stories throughout the summer on the off-season activity of local college football players. Among those profiled was Bob Timmons, who had prepped at Allegheny High School on the North Side before attending Pitt. Timmons was working as a lifeguard on the Allegheny River with the river patrol officers. Timmons would later become an assistant football coach and then the head basketball coach at Pitt.

Helen Wills Moody was the reigning woman tennis player and Ellsworth Vines was one of the men's champions. Dr. John O'Loughlin was the Pittsburgh men's tennis singles champion. His brother, Dr. David O'Loughlin was another top local player. They were quite the doubles team.

Helen Jacobs was playing in the U.S.Open at the West Side Tennis Club at Forest Hills, making her debut in shorts, the scantiest attire ever worn by a woman competitor at the exclusive Long Island club. Alice Marble planned to do the same.

"They're really a tremendous advantage," said Miss Jacobs. "Nothing but prudishness has prevented our wearing them for years. I knew they improve my game and all the other girls say the same. I know I've lost many points through the racket catching in my skirt."

Newsweek and *Esquire* began publishing in New York.

The Chicago Bears defeated the New York Giants, 23-21, in the first championship playoff in National Football League history. Bronko Nagurski was the game's star performer.

There was boxing at Hickey Park. Charles Baxter of the North Side lost a TKO in the fourth round to Harry Dublinsky of Chicago. On the same card, Jimmy Thomas, "a Pittsburgh colored boy," fought to a 10-round draw with Charles Burns of Johnstown. In the opener, Fritzie Zivic, 134½ pounds, of Lawrenceville won an easy six-round victory over Joey Greb of Wilkes-Barre. Jackie Wilson was another Pittsburgh fighter of note back then. It wasn't until 1934 that Billy Conn became a pro fighter.

Havey J. Boyle was the sports editor of the *Post-Gazette*.

There were polo matches played at South Park.

Four of the nation's outstanding swimmers, Johanna Gorman, Lenore Kight, Anna Mae Gorman and Louise Clark, all from the Carnegie Library swimming team in Homestead, were honored at the pool at Kennywood Park.

Heavyweight champion Primo Carnera started a national tour of boxing exhibitions in Erie, Pennsylvania.

There were boxscores in the papers for both the Homestead Grays and the Pittsburgh Crawfords, two of the best teams in the Negro Leagues.

There were standings and boxscores for minor league and local sandlot baseball teams. The Crawfords were playing the House of David and the New York Black Yankees.

Julius "Moose" Solters, who had gotten his start on the Hazelwood sandlots, was batting .370 for Baltimore in the International League.

Joe Sartory and Ed Sarangue were going to do the Pirates professional football games on WWSW. The Pirates were holding their first football training camp at Newell's Grove in Champion, Pennsylvania. Jap Douds was the first head coach. The backfield coach was Jimmy Rooney, one of Art's brothers who had played at Pitt. Their season opener with the New York Giants was scheduled for September 20 at Forbes Field.

There were cigarette ads in the papers for Chesterfields, Lucky Strike and Camels.

"The Duquesne," a passenger train on the Pennsylvania Railroad was derailed in Bloomfield enroute from Pittsburgh to Philadelphia.

There were radio listings in the newspaper each day the way they now carry TV listings. The top local radio stations were WWSW, KDKA, WJAS, WCAE and KQV.

A young wife, Mrs. Hazel McCarthy Mazza, stole a purse so she would get sent to the Workhouse — a corrections facility in Blawnox for minor offenders — so she could be with her husband. She turned herself in at a police station on the North Side, shouting to the officers, "Arrest me."

Her husband was serving three years for robbing a North Side laundry.

A jealous wife, Mrs. Fred Miller of Stanley Street in Greenfield, shot and killed her husband because of "the other woman" in his life.

"Bookmakers are always sad looking."
— Damon Runyan

Al Abrams had a story in his column about the Yankees' Lou Gehrig breaking the major league baseball "iron man" record of 1,307 games set by Everett "Deacon" Scott, a former Yankee and American League all-star player, in a game against the Red Sox. Gehrig started his streak 26 days after Scott's streak came to an end.

The Yankees later played an exhibition game against the Pirates at Forbes Field. The Pirates played an exhibition game the day after that in Scranton, the hometown of pitcher Bill Swift, against ballplayers in that northeastern Pennsylvania community. The Pirates were on their way to Brooklyn to play the Dodgers in a regularly scheduled game. The Pirates were also referred to as the Corsairs.

There was a heart-wrenching story about the death of a young fan who was killed while traveling to Pittsburgh to see Babe Ruth and

50

Lou Gehrig. James Jack, 16, of Oil City, was "bumming his way" to Forbes Field when he fell off a freight car. The train ran over his leg and crushed it. He died from shock when his injured leg was amputated at Franklin Hospital. During his hospital stay, Jack was told that a baseball autographed by Ruth was being sent to him. Jack and William McMonigal, 18, were eager to see Ruth play and they hopped a Pennsylvania Railroad freight car that was Pittsburgh-bound. Jack was jolted from a gondola a short distance between Oil City and Franklin.

When Ruth heard what happened he tried to hit a home run over the fence at Forbes Field. He hoped to retrieve the ball, sign it, and send it to Jack. He didn't succeed in that regard, however. Jack died before a signed ball arrived at the hospital.

The Pirates beat the Yankees, 10-2, in the first game the two teams played since the Yankees swept the Pirates in four games in the 1927 World Series. There were 10,500 fans at Forbes Field — not much of a crowd — for the exhibition contest, many of them sitting in right field to be close to Babe Ruth.

Ruth singled over second base with two out in the third inning, but was forced out by Lou Gehrig. Gus Suhr hit a three-run homer to pace the Pirates.

Syndicated New York columnist Damon Runyan wrote about Man O' War, one of the greatest racehorses in history. The dateline on all of Runyan's columns during the summer of 1933 was Saratoga Springs, where he attended the racing program each day. By coincidence, it was at Saratoga Springs that Art Rooney had the second day of his legendary two-day winning spree. Sounded like nice duty for Damon Runyan. He later became a Broadway notes columnist. The musical, "Guys and Dolls," was based on characters popularized in Runyan's stories.

Runyan often referred to a New York bookmaker named Tim Mara, who was the owner of the New York Giants, being in attendance at Saratoga Springs. Runyan wrote this line: "Bookmakers are always sad looking." Runyan also referred to George Preston Marshall, the owner of the Washington Redskins, being a frequent visitor to the racetrack.

Fred Waring and his Pennsylvanians appeared in Pittsburgh for a concert, which was carried on WWSW. There was a commercial for Iron City Beer: "A cold leg of chicken and a bottle of ice-cold thirst-quenching Iron City — could anything taste better?"

Teddy Yarosz fought Vince Dundee at Forbes Field for a Pennsylvania boxing title on August 21. Dundee won a unanimous verdict before a crowd of 16,000. Among the fighters on the undercard were Joe Bazzone of McKeesport, Eddie Zivic of Lawrenceville, Johnny Riska of the South Hills and Al Becker of Sheraden.

Presbyterian Hospital was added to the Oakland hospital center.

It was some "last meal."

Edward A. Sabel, 47, from West North Avenue on the North Side was slain for reporting bootleg ring activity to Prohibition agents. He told the agents the location of some bootleg stills. Soon after his death the ban on booze was lifted. Five men, all from the North Side, were arrested in connection with his death.

In golf, Gene Sarazen won the PGA title.

There was a sandlot gridiron league formed by the Pittsburgh Sports Shop, which also outfitted the Pirates football team. It included the Rox Rangers, Tarentum Firemen, Scott Morgans, Etna Sycamores and Oakland Community Club. This was the top division of nine divisions in the league.

Two stars for the Pittsburgh Pirates, Honus Wagner and Pie Traynor, owned a sporting goods store in downtown Pittsburgh and they also supported sandlot leagues, outfitting the teams in their respective leagues. One sandlot league lineup included Turtle Creek Universal, Creighton, Natrona Bennetts, Brackenridge Independents, St. Rosalia's, Millvale Amici, J.J. Doyles of Hazelwood, and Soho Oakleafs.

Frank Joy was hacked to death and his body was covered with slate in a coalmine near Pitcairn. Two suspects were arrested in a Trafford home. Joy had boasted of his knowledge of bootleg gangs, but was not connected to rackets himself. He was buried from St. Michael's Church in Pitcairn. He had been warned not to talk about the rum business. Tony Morrocco of Trafford was found guilty of the murder of Frank Joy.

Three men were executed on the same day in the electric chair at Ossining, New York on August 17. One of them, George Swann, 21, was allowed to order anything he wanted for his last meal. He took this invitation seriously.

His last meal consisted of two fried chickens, lobster salad, shrimp salad, celery, tomatoes, smoked herring, lettuce, stringbeans, shortcake, a pound of candy, three packs of cigarettes, cigars, apples and a couple of cups of coffee. While his head was being shaved, Swann said, "It's all over and I guess I won't have much chance to suffer from indigestion."

With so many people out of work, it seemed like a strange year to establish the 40-hour workweek, with a maximum of 48 hours and a six-day workweek. A minimum wage was also established. One thousand striking miners at the Pittsburgh Coal Company's Montour Mine No. 10 at Library went back to work.

Jean Osberg, 13, of Glen Willard near Coraopolis, would give blood as part of an experiment to find a serum to prevent polio. She had been crippled by infantile paralysis. It would be more than 20 years later that Dr. Jonas Salk would develop the anti-polio vaccine while doing research at the University of Pittsburgh.

Art Rooney talked the manager of world heavyweight boxing champion Primo Carnera into fighting an exhibition at North Side Stadium for the benefit of St. Peter's Athletic Association. Carnera had won the title from Jack Sharkey and was fighting on the North Side without a payday. He normally commanded $1,000 per exhibition, but didn't get paid for this one.

His manager Bill Duffy had promised Art Rooney — "a local sports figure," according to the newspaper report — to bring him to Pittsburgh free of charge, if he won the title. Tickets sold for $1.10 and $2.20 for the fight. A crowd of 3,000 watched the exhibition. Joe Zivic refereed all the bouts. Some of the fighters were referred to as "colored boy" and "colored fighter" in a story by John S. Herron.

Carnera was honored at a luncheon by local Italians. Carnera was pictured with Art Rooney and Milt Jaffe at Kramer's Restaurant. There was a story by Havey Boyle in the *Post-Gazette* that indicated that Rooney owned a piece of Carnera, but Rooney denied the report.

He said he and Duffy were friends and had promised to help each other if they could. He said there were no strings attached.

Ricordo della visita di Primo Carnera
Campione del mondo Massimi
Pittsburgh, Pa   Agosto 25 1933-XI   Verzella Studio
Pgh, Pa

From Jim O'Brien collection

Heavyweight boxing champion Primo Carnera is the tall fellow front and center at this luncheon gathering hosted by the Italian community of Pittsburgh on August 25, 1933. The fellow with folded arms two figures to the right of Carnera is Art Rooney, the first-year owner of the NFL's Pittsburgh Pirates. It was Rooney who arranged for Carnera to fight an exhibition to raise money for the athletic programs at St. Peter's Grade School.

Snapshot:

Johnny Blood
One of the pro pioneers

"It's like your wedding day."

Johnny Blood was a legend in his time, a zany football player and coach in the pioneer days of the National Football League. He played for the Steelers in 1934 and again as a player-coach from 1937 through 1939. He came back to Pittsburgh for the 50 Seasons Celebration in late September, 1982. He was born Johnny McNally but Johnny Blood fit his lifestyle better and the name stuck. He was inducted in 1963 into the Pro Football Hall of Fame

"Some people have the gift for football; this is what they can do," said Blood. "And they would do it whether you pay them or not. It's more organized now, but the basic motivation is the same. They are in it for the money, women and glory — and the chance to hit each other. And all that can be classified as fun. The fun of the game.

"The sports business is just a great life. It depends on what you want out of life. And I've come to believe there is one major purpose for human beings on this planet. That's to maximize your emotional income. That's why people play football after all. You get out on the field and the adrenalin starts flowing. The moment has come and your glands start pumping and you just feel more alive than you do most of the time.

"It's like your wedding day, or at least the first time you were married. You certainly felt different that day. You were doing more living per second than any ordinary day. It feels good."

55

Rudy Celigoi

Mike Ditka
Respected Mr. Rooney and Mr. Halas

"I loved the old man."

Mike Ditka was born in Carnegie and grew up in Aliquippa. He was an All-American end at Pitt in 1960 and was a first round draft choice in 1961 of the Chicago Bears. He was an All-Pro end there, and later starred with the Philadelphia Eagles and Dallas Cowboys. He's the only Pitt man to win the Super Bowl as both a player and a coach. He was with the Cowboys when they defeated Miami in Super Bowl VI. In 1986, Ditka coached the Chicago Bears to victory against the New England Patriots in Super Bowl XX. He later coached the New Orleans Saints, and has done several network TV stints as an NFL analyst and color man. He and Joe Schmidt are both honored in the Pro Football Hall of Fame. He received a "Lifetime Achievement" award at the Dapper Dan Sports Dinner in Pittsburgh in February, 2001, and was honored as a distinguished alumnus a few months earlier at the University of Pittsburgh. He was in Tampa, Florida in January, 2001 for Super Bowl XXXV when we last talked. We also spoke at length on November 13, 2000. Ditka offered these thoughts:

You gotta go back to what Mr. Rooney meant to Pittsburgh and the Steelers. He was one of the characters that formed and shaped the National Football League, and set the standard for sports in Pittsburgh. He was a winner before his team was a winner. I loved him.

He and the Steelers fought through hard times. George Halas was like that with the Bears. They did it for the love of the game. They had a vision that football would be a great thing.

I loved the old man. Every time I'd see him, he'd hand me a cigar. He knew I liked them. He and Halas lived in the same place most of their lives. They never moved up, so to speak, when they started making big money. They stayed put, through thick and thin. They weren't swayed by success. Halas lived in a condominium in Chicago. He never moved.

Mr. Rooney and I would stand around and talk and smoke cigars. There were not too many places you could smoke a cigar any more, so it was special.

Mr. Rooney, the legacy. Who he was. He was people; he was good people. He was a guy who cared. He was for the people who worked for him. He talked to them. He was genuine. They weren't just a cog in the machine. He talked to the equipment guy or ground crew guys the same as he would the president of U.S. Steel. He considered the Pittsburgh Steelers his family.

His son, Danny, is a man of character and he learned a lot from his dad.

"I like to roll the dice."

I remember seeing Mr. Rooney at the league meetings every year. He was always a presence. When I got into coaching, I was always struck by the posture he maintained. He was never a guy who made a lot of noise. What he did he did. He let Dan run the team. I have to respect someone like Mr. Rooney. I go back to the game itself. It was here before we came along. He left his mark on the game and he certainly left his mark on the Steelers. He left his mark on the city.

I liked the fact that he'd been a gambler all his life. He liked the ponies, he liked the action. He liked to compete on every field, as I did. I like to roll the dice. If that keeps me out of heaven, that's OK.

I heard some stories about the big money he won at the track when I was in Pittsburgh. That always made him more appealing to me.

I remember playing in a game when I was with the Bears and we beat the Steelers at Forbes Field (on Nov. 24, 1963). I had a good day. That was the Sunday right after President Kennedy had been assassinated. Pete Rozelle got some heat for not calling off those games. I had that catch and run where I went back and forth across the field. It looked like it was in slow motion. They still show that play on TV from time to time. I think the first guy who hit me was Clendon Thomas.

I was asked if I could go deep on that play. I was dead tired. I had caught about nine passes already. I said, "I can run down and make a hook. I'll get a first down out of it." I caught the ball and broke a few tackles. I couldn't run. It was like being in wet cement. But I guess it was quite a play.

(Author's note: I had a great view of Ditka's great zig-zag run against the Steelers. I watched that game from a photographer's perch on the right-centerfield roof of Forbes Field and had a bird's-eye view. A game between Pitt and Penn State at Pitt Stadium the day before was canceled because of the death of JFK two days earlier. The delay may have cost the Panthers, with a 9-1 record, a post-season bowl game invitation. Imagine not going to a bowl game with a 9-1 record.)

Playing against the Steelers was always special for me. I grew up with guys like Chandnois, Tarasovic, Rogel and Stautner. I was a big Eagles' fan, too, for some reason. I loved Steve Van Buren. I was also a big Pirates' fan and a baseball fan. My favorite ballplayer was Stan Musial, a Polish guy from Donora. I was a Hunkie and he was a Hunkie, so I liked him. No one was insulted being called a Hunkie back in those days.

When I went to Pitt, I played basketball against some of those Steelers. Guys like Red Mack and Bobby Layne were just good people, and fun to be around. When I first played football against the Steelers, I think Ernie Stautner tried to kill me. He had a hard box, I swear, on his forearm, and he whacked you with it. Pound for pound, he was as tough a player as there was in the game. I loved guys like that; that's the way I played the game. John Henry Johnson was another tough guy on those Steelers' teams. He was a running back, but he'd played linebacker, too, and he loved to hit you with a stiff arm.

I have to smile when I think of those guys. I am almost as old as all of them. I love to go back to Pitt, and I liked having an opportunity to speak to the students. Pittsburgh is still important to me. Pitt will always be important to me. And people like Art Rooney are still important to me. I used to get a Christmas card from him all the time, and a few notes when I did something special. I'd get postcards from around the country from time to time.

I think the intimacy he enjoyed with so many people makes everyone miss him. He was pretty special. He cared. He wasn't trying to impress you. He just did it.

John Alexandrowicz

Ditka was known as "Iron Mike" during his All-American days at the University of Pittsburgh where he was a defensive terror and clutch receiver as a senior in 1960.

Inducted into the Pro Football Hall of Fame in Canton, Ohio ceremonies in Class of 1988 were Fred Biletnikoff of Erie and the Oakland Raiders, Mike Ditka of Aliquippa and the Chicago Bears, Philadelphia Eagles and Dallas Cowboys, Jack Ham of Johnstown and the Pittsburgh Steelers and Alan Page of Canton and the Minnesota Vikings.

Mike Ditka had one of the greatest catch-and-run performances in pro football history in November 24, 1963 game against the Steelers — and another former Pitt star Dick Haley (No. 27) — at Forbes Field. NFL Commissioner Pete Rozelle drew criticism for allowing games to be played that weekend in wake of assassination of President John F. Kennedy.

Coultersville

A small community called Coultersville was the birthplace of Arthur J. Rooney. It was a coal-mining community at the eastern tip of Allegheny County, sandwiched between White Oak, just outside of McKeesport, and North Huntingdon in Westmoreland County. It was called Coultersville. Nowadays they call it Coulters or Coulter.

By any name, the 450 or so people who live there still claim Art Rooney as "one of our very own," according to accounts in a book called "Golden Memories of Coulter, Alpsville and Osceola," authored by JoAnn and Ray Shepherd and Sue and Orville Drescher. Those three communities that make up South Versailles Township are located on a horseshoe curve along the Youghiogheny River. A railroad runs along that shoreline. The road that runs next to those tracks is known as Railroad Street.

Coultersville was named for the Coulter family of Westmoreland County. Eli and Priscilla Coulter, who settled the 262-acre tract around 1788-1790, were of Scotch-Irish descent. It was once written in Ripley's "Believe It Or Not" that there was only one road in and one road out of Coultersville.

Art Rooney was born in a hotel and tavern owned by his parents, Dan and Margaret Rooney, on January 27, 1901. In those days, most babies were born at home with the help of a midwife. The Rooneys were running that hotel, located in an alley between Third and Fourth Streets, when the first three of their nine children were born. One girl, Katherine, died in infancy. The family had earlier operated the Colonial Hotel in Monaca.

The eight surviving children were Art, Daniel, James, John, Vincent, Margaret Katherine, Marie and Thomas. John and Thomas served with honors in World War II. Thomas was killed in action in the Phillipines. James was a talented punter at Pitt whose political career was cut short by a serious auto accident.

There were boom times when coal, often called "black gold," was mined in that area. The miners toiled six days out of seven to make $5 for a week's work. They still tell stories about how the Youghiogheny would freeze over, with ice 6" deep, and you could walk across the river to Greenock and Duncan.

According to community history, Dan Rooney was born in Wales and came to the country as an infant. Margaret Murray was born in Alpsville. Her father, Robert Murray, came from Ireland and was a coal miner. Her mother, Maria Somers, was of English descent and was born in this country.

The Rooneys were married on Jan. 9, 1900 at St. Patrick's Roman Catholic Church in Alpsville. They operated a hotel in

Street sign in Coultersville, Pennsylvania was dedicated in 1967.

Coultersville until 1909, when Dan opened a saloon on the North Side, just across the Allegheny River from Pittsburgh on the site of Exposition Park.

In later years, Art would bring his parents and sister Margaret back to Coultersville to visit relatives and friends. They were related to families in Coultersville named Murray, Dreer, Skillen, Deemer, Barry, Summers and Greenway.

People in Coultersville cite how Art, Dan and Jim played baseball for a semi-pro team on the North Side, and played against black teams like the Homestead Grays and Kansas City Monarchs.

Coultersville also claimed Joe "Moon" Harris, who had a career batting average of .317 for ten years in the Major Leagues. Harris played nearly a 1,000 games in the big leagues as a first baseman and outfielder with the likes of the Yankees, Indians, Red Sox, Senators and Pirates. He played in two World Series, one with the Pirates in 1927 in his next-to-last season. The Pirates were swept in four games by the Yankees featuring Babe Ruth, Lou Gehrig and the "Murderers Row" lineup.

Folks in Coultersville long believed that Harris belonged in the Hall of Fame, just like Art Rooney.

Art Rooney attended community ceremonies in 1967 when a street — ROONEY STREET — was dedicated in his family's honor. The sign is still there.

50 Seasons Celebration
Man of the hour

"He's always done things to brighten other people's days."
— Pete Rozelle
NFL Commissioner

The food was fine, which is rare at $100-a-plate dinners. The highlight film and all the trimmings were equally top-shelf. Pete Rozelle, Howard Cosell, Count Basie and all the football greats, past and present, were supposed to be the show-stoppers at the Steelers' 50 Seasons Celebration dinner-dance at the David L. Lawrence Convention Center.

But ageless Arthur J. Rooney Sr. stole the show.

It was appropriate.

The Steelers owner seldom missed a sports dinner or luncheon — he was in his usual seat the following day at the Curbstone Coaches gathering at the Allegheny Club at Three Rivers Stadium — but he never sought the limelight or asked to say anything. He liked to listen.

He liked seeing all the people. He was always surprised when they recognized him. Unlike so many other National Football League owners, he didn't think he was a big deal. He never thought he had all the answers.

At the dinner to honor his team and its history, Rooney had the best lines. They were classics, and worth repeating. They are elsewhere in this book, I know, but they are that good.

"I never had a ballplayer play for me that I didn't think was a star," remarked Rooney.

"I never had a ballplayer play for me I didn't like," he added.

Before he paid tribute to his ballplayers, Rooney pointed to his wife, Kathleen, seated at a front-row table among the 2,500 in attendance, and said, with a slip of the tongue, "She has been a very devoted husband."

He had been married to Kathleen for 52 years, two years longer than he had been married to the Steelers.

"When this thing started," said Mr. Rooney, "I had no idea it would be this big a deal. My wife, to this day, keeps asking me questions about it, and I don't know what was going on. She said, 'I've been married to you for 52 years and you never know anything.' I just thought we'd have a 50th year and we'd invite in some old ballplayers. I like this — it's a big deal — and I'm happy to see everybody."

He didn't figure that Count Basie would be there. He figured that Harold "Mr. Trombone" Betters, the pride of Connellsville, would be providing the music as usual, or Walt Harper. It pleased him that Myron Cope and Jack Fleming got to offer some tributes even if Cosell was put in a starring role.

Chuck Noll with Howard Cosell

With legendary player/coach Johnny Blood

With wife Kathleen at 50 Seasons Celebration

Photos by Robert Pavuchak

"Art Rooney was a tremendous people person."
— "Bullet Bill" Dudley

Speaking of his long-time association with sports, Rooney said, "I enjoyed every minute of it. Sports has been my life. I'm glad we brought back all our ballplayers. I enjoyed seeing them, and talking to them."

Rozelle referred to Rooney's "wonderful quiet dignity. Between the Rooneys and their players exists a strong mutual trust. Unfortunately, it's not that way throughout all of the National Football League."

Rozelle presented Rooney with a special award from the league. "You have to love him," remarked Rozelle. "He's so honest and down-to-earth. He has a heart of gold, and that was the Steelers' problem once upon a time.

"He'd go back and forth with coaches, taking care of old friends, and that sort of thing. He has a feeling for the tradition of this league, and that's so important in these times. He's always done things to brighten other people's days."

Dan Rooney, the president of the Steelers, said, "I think this is just tremendous. We have players here from every year, and we're celebrating each and every one of them, not just the Super Bowl years. We wanted to make it fun, and we wanted the fans to be a part of it. That's why I didn't want it to be a black tie affair. The fans are a big part of this."

Franco Harris added to that when he told the crowd, "We want to thank you. You've been a big part of this."

It was a night when Howard Cosell said all the right things about the Steelers — something the fans didn't feel he did when he was providing color commentary on Monday Night Football Games. Cosell came across as downright lovable, telling it like it was, or at least the way Cosell saw it.

Among Cosell's many complimentary remarks about the Steelers, he said, "The Rooneys are the finest people, the people I most respect in American sports ownership. I've always felt that way. And there's no reason to change. They are people of integrity and character.

"The way they put the Steelers together, to hire a man like Chuck Noll, to emphasize the team concept. It's more than coincidence that a man like Joe Greene played for the Pittsburgh Steelers. The Steelers have a great sense of community.

"It's more than a coincidence that Willie Stargell and Joe Greene were contemporaries in the same city. I have a whole transcendental feeling for the Steelers and the Rooneys and Pittsburgh. Speaking for ABC Sports and the Monday Night Football Series, I can't think of a team more responsible for our success than the Pittsburgh Steelers. We have to be grateful for that."

Talking about Pittsburgh in a personal interview over the telephone prior to the dinner, he said, "It's still the City of Champions. It has nothing to do with victories. It has a winning character. Whether they win or lose in athletic events doesn't matter. They rise above it."

Cosell was surprised when told that he was often credited for coining the phrase "City of Champions," a banner the city carried with great pride.

"I never really knew that I was being held responsible for that," he said. "I talked about Pittsburgh during the 1979 World Series between the Baltimore Orioles and the Pirates. I did a commentary on 'The Tale of Two Cities.' Tommy LaSorda was in the broadcast booth with me that night, and he couldn't get over how I used a sports situation to draw a broader picture of American life.

"I pointed to Pittsburgh and Baltimore as natural models for urban renewal in this country, and what can be accomplished by cities with effective mayoral leadership. I'm glad to hear that Pittsburghers take pride in that. They should."

The mayor of Pittsburgh, Richard S. Caliguiri, was an old friend of mine. He had looked after his father's bowling establishment on Second Avenue in my hometown of Hazelwood when I was 14 and working as the sports editor of *The Hazelwood Envoy*. I'd get bowling scores off Caliguiri. He had always been kind to me, and continued to do the same when he became the mayor of Pittsburgh.

"This is a remarkable evening," said Mayor Caliguiri, one of those seated at the dais. "I realize the importance of majors sports teams in our community. It builds pride. It is easy to get emotional about Art Rooney."

Joe Greene, the honorary chairman of the event, and a unanimous choice on the All-Time team after 13 outstanding seasons with the Steelers, said "It was a lot of work, and Joe Gordon deserves a lot of credit for pulling this off. It was an idea when he first asked me to serve as chairman. Now it's a reality. The banquet was a sell-out affair. There were so many people involved in it.

"I get goose pimples being here and seeing all these people. And I felt that way going into the first Super Bowl."

Joe "The Screamer" Tucker, the "Voice of the Steelers" for 32 seasons (1936-68), said, "I'm just thrilled to see it all. Especially because they have so much of the past. The past led to the present. And the present leads to the future. People can get a look at another era of pro football, and see what the single-wing and power football was all about."

Armand Niccolai, a tackle and place-kicker (1934-1942) from Duquesne University who resided in Monessen, was looking trim and dapper. "It brings back a lot of memories," said Niccolai, one of Art Rooney's all-time favorites and a frequent visitor to his office at Three Rivers Stadium. "I have to think of those fellows I played with. A lot of them have passed away. I realize how lucky I've been to see how Art brought this team from nothing to what it is today."

Writing this chapter brings back a lot of memories of that special night in Pittsburgh. Realizing how many of the luminaries have died since then is a sobering reminder of the passage of time. Among those now deceased are Art and Kathleen Rooney, Pete Rozelle, Howard Cosell, Mayor Caliguiri, Count Basie, Joe Tucker, Jack Fleming and Armand Niccolai, Ray Mansfield and Steve Furness, Rollie Dotsch and Jack Hart, Johnny Blood and Joe Gilliam.

Three Hall of Famers in Steelers' history were, left to right, Terry Bradshaw, Johnny Blood and Lynn Swann, as seen at 1982 Steelers 50 Seasons Celebration at David L. Lawrence Convention Center.

Terry Bradshaw

Among the all-time Steelers greats who gathered for 50 Seasons Celebration were, left to right, John Henry Johnson, Chuck Noll, Lynn Chandnois and "Bullet Bill" Dudley.

Paul Martha, the Steelers' No. 1 draft pick in 1964, and Pitt assistant coach Ernie Hefferle, are greeted by Art Rooney at Curbstone Coaches luncheon at Roosevelt Hotel.

Rooney and John Michelosen stick with single-wing offense at start of 1950 season.

Paul Martha

At his office in December of 1961.

Boyish-looking Rooney in 1938, his fifth year as owner of the Pittsburgh pro team, then called the Pirates.

In the '70s . . .

Joe Gordon
Grad school at Rooney U.

"We don't do things for show."

Joe Gordon was associated with the Steelers for 29 years, from 1969 to 1998. He was the team's publicity director until 1987, and he had five different titles relating to business management and marketing over the last six years before he retired. Whatever his title, he was Dan Rooney's right-hand man and loyal lieutenant for most of those latter years. He remained on the Steelers' payroll — as Noll did — and Rooney still discussed certain club issues with him from time to time, but Gordon was seldom seen at the Steelers' offices on the South Side. He said he was happily retired.

During the Steelers' glorious run of the '70s, Gordon was generally regarded as one of the finest publicists or public relations men in the National Football League. "He's the very best," pronounced Paul Zimmerman, a former co-worker of mine at *The New York Post* who is acclaimed as the pro football expert at *Sports Illustrated*. "No one gets it done like Joe Gordon gets it done. No one."

Gordon went at his job like few others. He was always on the telephone, it seemed, his dark, protuberant eyes ablaze, but he would be speaking to someone in his office at the same time. It might be a sportswriter, or an advertising executive, or a secretary, or an ad dealer — or all of them at the same time — and Joe was typing a to-the-point reply to a letter he received that very day from someone seeking an appearance by a Steeler at a school sports award banquet in DuBois. He prided himself on still using an old-fashioned manual typewriter. He did things right away. Today, not tomorrow. Or next week. He attacked his assignments. It was the best way. Gordon was a sports information man who realized that he was in the service industry. And he serviced everybody, as quickly as possible. If he was out when you called, he returned the call within the hour. He could be tart at times, but you learned to live with that.

Gordon was good at what he did and he knew what he was doing. He learned a lot about public relations, though, and treating people the right way from his father, Manny Gordon, who owned a bar in Homestead, and from Art Rooney, whose father once owned a bar on the North Side and who owned the Pittsburgh Steelers. You couldn't be around Rooney and not learn something about public relations. Gordon cultivated a loyal following from the smallest dailies in the tri-state area, inviting them to travel with the team at the Steelers' expense during their heyday.

Gordon was fiercely loyal to the Rooneys, resented those who were not, and believed in giving an honest day's work for an honest dollar. He was well-paid, invested wisely, and had profited from the

Steelers' success in the '70s — when they won four Super Bowls, lest we forget — but he could have done better in another business. Or with another ballclub looking for a sharp front-office executive. One of the other Pittsburgh pro teams — the Pirates or Penguins — or one of the local universities would have been wise to throw money at him to get him on their side. Like his bosses, Gordon took great pride in being a Pittsburgher ("I'd like to see us get back that 'City of Champions' tag again," he said).

Gordon grew up in Squirrel Hill. "I lived and died with the Pirates and the Steelers," he said.

Upon graduating from Taylor Allderdice High School, he went to Pitt and played baseball there in the mid-50s for Bobby Lewis. "I wanted to be a big league baseball player," recalled the former infielder. While at Pitt, he worked as a go-for in Beano Cook's sports information office. That's how Gordon got started. "I found out I wasn't good enough to be a major league baseball player," he said.

In his early 20s, Gordon was the publicist for the Pittsburgh Rens of Archie "Tex" Litman and the American Basketball League, Abe Saperstein's brainchild. Later, he was its general manager at age 27, the youngest general manager in the pro sports world at the time.

When the ABL folded, Gordon went to work selling space for the Yellow Pages — "one of the best work experiences I ever had" — before hooking on as the publicist for the Pittsburgh Hornets of the American Hockey League. He was there when the Hornets won the AHL's Calder Cup Trophy as champions in 1967, the team's last season. The next season, he was working for the Pittsburgh Penguins of the National Hockey League.

From there, he was hired by the Steelers in 1969 — the same year they hired Chuck Noll to coach the team. That was fortuitous. Everybody knows what happened after that. A guy could learn a lot from covering the Steelers on a daily basis for four years, from 1979 to 1983, as I did. It's the same span one requires for a college education. You had great teachers because of gentlemen like Gordon, his predecessor Ed Kiely, Noll and the Rooneys.

When Jack Sell covered the Steelers during the first 40 years of their existence for the *Pittsburgh Post-Gazette*, he often referred to them as "Rooney U." In this regard, it was appropriate. Anyone interested in a public relations education could get it from the front-office types at the Steelers' complex at Three Rivers Stadium.

Gordon never screened phone calls, for instance. If you asked for Joe Gordon, you got Joe Gordon. You didn't get music while you were on hold, as you might have when you called the Civic Arena (now Mellon Arena) at the same time in history. No secretary asked for your name, or the nature of your call, as happened when you called certain other offices. Nobody ever answered by saying, "Thank you for calling the Super Bowl champion Pittsburgh Steelers. May I help you?"

You got Gordon; that's what you got. You may have had to share him, but you got Gordon. And Gordon gave you all he had. Almost,

69

anyhow. "Being a sports fan helps in my job," he would say. "It tends to make you more enthusiastic."

He could have been called Flash Gordon.

"We're not concerned about being America's Team (like the Dallas Cowboys)," he liked to say. "We want to be Pittsburgh's team.

"We don't do things for show; we don't do things just to look good. We'll worry about the Pittsburgh Steelers and not everyone else. I say live and let live. The key is to be able to communicate; then you can have success. You have to communicate on every level."

That's something else Gordon practiced as well as he preached. When he was a publicist for the Penguins in the mid-60s, I was publishing a newspaper along with Beano Cook on a shoestring budget called *Pittsburgh Weekly Sports*. It sold for 20 cents a copy and had a high of about 5,000 weekly sales. Yet Gordon always treated us like we were from *The New York Times*.

Gordon gave us credentials, and major league treatment. When my father died early in 1969, Gordon called and asked if there was anything he could do. He meant it. I told him we'd be busy burying my father on the day when the paper usually went to press.

So Gordon went to the printers that day, proofread and okayed all 12 pages, and put the paper to bed, as they say. I never forgot that, certainly not 11 years later when I came back to town — after a year in Miami and nine in New York — to cover the Steelers for *The Pittsburgh Press*.

That's why the words ring true when Gordon, talking about the challenge of being the main press liaison at four Super Bowls, said, "You must do the same thing for 2,000 people as you would for one. You also have to devote time and attention to the little guy as well."

"They could never quite get over the hump."

"My first awareness of the Steelers came after World War II," said Gordon. "That was as a kid, listening to Joe Tucker broadcasting the games. Those were the days (in the mid-40s) of Johnny 'Zero' Clement and Buist Warren. They had other running backs like Bill Dudley — he was the star — and Joe Glamp.

"I really got involved in the early '50s. That's when they had Jim Finks, Ernie Stautner, Lynn Chandnois, Ray Mathews, Fran Rogel, Elbie Nickel and Bill McPeak. That's when they had Jack Butler. Butler was definitely the best Steeler not in the Hall of Fame. If he played with winning teams he would have been a first ballot selection to the Pro Football Hall of Fame. He was a phenomenal football player.

"They were playing at Forbes Field in those days. My younger brother Mark —— he was a year, a month and a week younger than I was — and I would wait outside Forbes Field before the game to get

From Tucker Family collection

Press Club sports night in March 1971 attracted Chuck Noll, club manager Adolph Donadeo, Art Rooney and Joe Tucker.

With Willie Stargell, honoree at CYA dinner on October 21, 1976.

Pittsburgh Post-Gazette Archives

In minor league baseball days

Chuck Klausing

Don Stetzer/Pittsburgh Post-Gazette Archives

With Chuck Klausing, CMU football coach, in January, 1979 meeting in press box during a Steelers' playoff game at Three Rivers Stadium.

tickets. About ten or fifteen minutes before the kick-off, Tim Rooney, one of Art's five sons, would come out with a fistful of tickets and give them to the kids. We'd be out there on Sennott Street near the corner of Bouquet Street. That was my first association with Tim Rooney.

"They had good teams in those days, but they could never quite get over the hump. We were there (in 1952) when the Steelers beat the New York Giants, 63-7. Finks and Mathews had big days. We were there (in 1954) when the Steelers beat the Cleveland Browns, 55-27. Lynn Chandnois returned the opening kickoff for a touchdown.

"I remember one day (in 1954) we went to see Pitt play Penn State at Pitt Stadium (the Panthers lost 13-0) in the afternoon in November. A kid could get into a Pitt game then for a quarter. Then we went down to Forbes Field and waited around for three hours to go to see the Steelers play the San Francisco 49ers in a Saturday night game at Forbes Field. The 49ers didn't come here very often in those days (The Steelers lost that game, 31-3.) Even though our teams lost, it was quite a day.

"Finks was my favorite player in those days. He was also at one time a professional baseball player — he played minor league baseball — and that's probably why he appealed to me so much. My first love was baseball. I liked Sid Gordon when he was an infielder for the Pirates in the mid-50s. Finks also came to the Steelers before they switched from the single-wing offense to the T-formation. He started off as a tailback.

"Stautner was also a favorite. He was their greatest player during that period. He was an All-Pro and he played in the Pro Bowl just about every year (nine times over a 14-year span). He was tough. He played injured. He never missed a game. He probably epitomized the image of the Steelers in that era. Other teams might know they could beat the Steelers but they also knew they would feel it two weeks later. The Steelers were such a physical team. They beat you up even if they didn't beat you on the scoreboard.

"Then Bobby Layne came in and the Steelers got better. They had better teams and they almost won it in 1963. But you could always get tickets. And we did. People have no idea of how subordinate the NFL was in the total sports picture in those days. Baseball and college football were so dominant in those days. Pitt got better coverage, and so did Duquesne and Carnegie Tech, even when they dropped down and played a Class B schedule. They would still get more coverage than the Steelers.

"My dad owned a saloon in Homestead in the 1950s. That's something else I think Art Rooney liked about me. When they first started televising pro football games, there were three teams on all the time in Pittsburgh. That was the Steelers, the Colts and the Cardinals. It was on the Dumont Network. We didn't even have a TV at home then. My dad would go down to his bar on Sunday afternoon to clean up and we'd go with him. My brother and I would go to watch the games on TV at the bar. It was called the Hi-Lite, and it was on 8th Avenue near

McClure. Now there's a parking lot there. We read about the Steelers in the sports pages then, too.

"We always had a greater interest in pro football than the average sports fan around here. Just like us going to our dad's bar on Sundays so we could watch the games."

"The Chief would sit down and talk to my dad."

Asked to assess Art Rooney, Gordon said: "The most important thing was loyalty. It was not your ability or your work ethic. The highest priority was loyalty. He was loyal to everybody he ever dealt with. Dan's the same way. The Rooneys believed in a loyalty to Pittsburgh, a loyalty to church, a loyalty to their family, and a loyalty to the NFL.

"The thing I cherish the most was Art Rooney's relationship with my father. They had a box lounge at Three Rivers and Art instructed Mary Regan to give me two tickets for every home baseball game. They were for my dad. If The Chief was in town, he'd always attend every Pirates' game. He might not stay the entire game, but he always made an appearance and said hello to everyone. If my dad was there, The Chief would sit down and talk to my dad. And whenever he'd see me, he'd always ask me, 'How's your dad? How's he doin'?' He'd ask my dad when he was coming down to the stadium to have lunch with him. He was really sincere. He had an unbelievably genuine interest in people.

"During our football games, he sat in a small box above the press box, not in the big luxury box that belonged to his family. He was happy to have others sitting there. Show was never important to him. He just wanted to watch the game with a few good friends. There was always a priest or two with him.

"Hundreds of times I'd see him walking through our lobby and he'd see someone sitting there. He'd go over and say, 'Hello there, my name's Rooney. What's your name? Where you from?' The guy might say he was from McKeesport. The Chief would say, 'Oh, McKeesport. I played ball there when I was young. I always loved McKeesport. Nice people there. Do you know so-and-so?' And it would go on like that. The visitors couldn't believe they were meeting Mr. Rooney, the owner of the Pittsburgh Steelers. But Art was as excited about the meeting as whoever was in the lobby.

"The news media guys loved him. They saw him for what he was. He had a genuine interest in them. He'd say to them, 'Are Gordon and Kiely taking care of you?' Or he'd pop his head in my office and say, 'Joe, Ed Pope's out here! Everything OK?'

"Never, never, in all my years with the Steelers, and I think this is the most important thing...there was never ever a mandate to be nice to people or to accommodate the media in any special way. You just followed the example they set. Dan's not as gregarious as his father, but he's always been big on accommodating the media. It was this simple. They believed in the Golden Rule. You were to do unto others as you would want others to do to you. With Art, it came naturally.

"He was gifted with remarkable people skills. There was nothing phony about him. He was a big hockey fan, too, for instance. He was a Hornets fan when we didn't have a whole lot of fans. He'd come to about 15 or 20 games a year. He'd stop in the pressroom and say hello to everyone. That's how I first met him. I remember the first Christmas after I met him he sent me a Christmas card with a hand-written note on it. It was written on a personal level, like we'd been friends for years. He made some comments about the Steelers and why they had a bad year.

"He had the ability to make people think at that time they were the most important person in the world.

"I remember my first year (1969) with the club, we played an exhibition game in Green Bay. All the teams then stayed in the Northland Hotel. It was ancient, but it was the only big hotel in town. We came in on Saturday afternoon. We were together at a table and he spotted four nuns at a nearby table. When the waiter came over, The Chief said, 'Make sure I get their check.' He did that all the time. I saw him do that with nuns or clergy many times when we were at the Roosevelt Hotel. If the clergy knew what time Art Rooney would be going to lunch there they could have eaten for free every day.

"I remember something else about that game in Green Bay my first year. Dick Shiner was our starting quarterback that night. The Steelers were driving for the go-ahead touchdown. The ball squirted through Shiner's hands on one snap and it rolled about 20 yards. Shiner fell on the ball. But it killed the Steelers' hopes. The Chief was sitting in the front row of the press box. He had a cigar and he took it out of his mouth and threw it up against the glass. It fell down on the table in front of him. I always thought of that incident when people said he didn't care if we won or lost. That was an exhibition game, and he was upset like that."

"He knew who was phony."

"When we were at the Roosevelt Hotel, I had a desk in a small room behind the ticket office. Nearby was the desk of our receptionist, Mary Regan. Art Rooney shared the office next door with Fran Fogarty, who was our business manager. Dan Rooney and the coaches were in offices upstairs in the hotel. Fran Fogarty died in August of 1969. It was the night of his daughter's wedding. The Steelers were playing the St. Louis Cardinals in Norfolk, Virginia that night. It was our first exhibition game of the year. Fran was watching our game on TV. He had a heart attack and died.

"I remember this street guy comes in one day to see The Chief. Meanwhile The Chief has the mayor, Joe Barr, in his office. The Chief knows the guy is out there. So he asks Mayor Barr if he can go outside for a few minutes, and he excuses himself. This guy comes in and he had to be a regular because Mary Regan recognized him and knew The Chief would see him. The guy complains to The Chief about having to wait to see him. The Chief says, 'I'm sorry, Joe. The mayor was here.' And he slips him a $20 bill.

"There's another incident that comes to my mind. We were going to Memphis late in the exhibition season in 1972. We're playing the New Orleans Saints in Memphis. One day, The Chief says to me, 'When are you going to Memphis? I said, 'I think on Tuesday.' He says, 'How about if I go along with you?' I said, 'That would be great.' He says, 'We have to stop at a few places on the way to Memphis, and I'd like to leave on Monday.' I said, 'That's fine with me. You're on.'

"So we go to Philadelphia on Monday. The Eagles had an exhibition game there that night. We stayed for the first half, and then we took off for New York. I think Jack Butler went with us. When we came out of the Lincoln Tunnels in New York, The Chief started telling me where to turn right and left to get to our hotel. This is at 12 o'clock at night. He knew New York the way I know Pittsburgh.

"When we got to the hotel, the doorman and the bellboys all addressed him by name. 'Hello, Mr. Rooney, welcome to New York.' Stuff like that. Everyone seemed to know him.

"He went to Mass the next morning at St. Patrick's Cathedral in Manhattan. He tells Butler, who is also Catholic, 'I'll see you in the lobby at a quarter to eight.' He knew I was Jewish, so he turns to me, 'Be ready to leave at 10 o'clock.' That's when we went out to Belmont Racetrack. He gave me directions from the hotel to the track, taking some shortcuts here and there. He was uncanny. It was the same story at the track as it was at the hotel. Everyone knew him. The guy in the parking lot, the valet, the people who worked at the track, they all knew him. I thought I was traveling with the President. We spent the day at the track. I think a hundred different people came up to say hello.

"Then we went to the airport and flew to Memphis that night. When the media found out The Chief was in Memphis they all wanted to interview him. It was the easiest week I had advancing a game. I'd set up appointments for people to come and interview him. The Rooneys were interested in a dog track in Arkansas at that time. Memphis is right on the border between Tennessee and Arkansas. So one night we go to the dog track to check it out. He'd give me money to bet on the dogs. I forget how he did that night. It didn't really matter. It was such a memorable trip.

"When I think of how Ed Kiely accompanied him to so many places for nearly 20 years. Kiely was his constant escort. He got to go to so many special places and met so many special people with Art. What an assignment. I wish I could have gone with him to a lot of those places. It had to be unreal sometimes. Art Rooney got a lot out of life. He always wanted to be where the action was. That's why he liked baseball more than football, because there were more games. You could have a game every day. You could go to the ballpark every day. You could be with people every day. He could size up people fast with phenomenal accuracy. He knew who was legitimate and he knew who was phony. Art Rooney was, by far, the most fascinating and perceptive person I've ever known."

Jim O'Brien

Steelers' highly-respected publicist Joe Gordon is flanked by oil portrait of Art Rooney and Steelers president Dan Rooney in The Chief's former office at Three Rivers Stadium in summer of 1999.

> *"His life was gentle, and the elements so mixed in him that Nature might stand up and say to all the world, 'This was a man!'"*
> — William Shakespeare

The Chief's Favorites

Here's a listing of Art Rooney's personal favorites from his years at the Steelers helm, as provided upon our request by his son, Art Rooney Jr.:

Top Ten All-Time

1. Joe Greene
2. Elbie Nickel
3. Jack Butler
4. Terry Bradshaw
5. Armand Niccolai
6. Franco Harris
7. Jack Lambert
8. John Baker
9. Rocky Bleier
10. Bill Dudley

Steelers of the 1930s
Johnny Blood
Armand Niccolai
Byron White

Steelers of the 1940s
Chuck Cherundolo
Bill Dudley

Steelers of the 1950s
Dick Alban
Pat Brady
Jack Butler
Jim Finks
George Hays
Val Jansante
Johnny Lattner
Richie McCabe
Bill McPeak
Elbie Nickel
Lowell Perry
Fran Rogel
Ernie Stautner
Bill Walsh

Steelers of the 1960s
John Baker
John Brown
Dick Haley
Dick Hoak
John Henry Johnson
Bobby Layne
Paul Martha
Lou Michaels

Steelers of the 1970s
Rocky Bleier
Mel Blount
Terry Bradshaw
Sam Davis
Joe Greene
Jack Ham
Franco Harris
Jon Kolb
Jack Lambert
Ray Mansfield
Andy Russell
Donnie Shell
Lynn Swann
Mike Wagner
Mike Webster

Steelers of the 1980s
Tunch Ilkin

"Bullet Bill" Dudley

A classy guy

"I've always surrounded myself with good people."
— Art Rooney

The Steelers had one more No. 1 pick than expected report to Three Rivers Stadium on a memorable Thursday afternoon, May 24, 1979.

Baylor's Greg Hawthorne, who they hoped would be the second coming of Franco Harris, was scheduled to come in the night before, along with other prospects who had just been selected by the Steelers in the college draft that week. But "Bullet Bill" Dudley was a surprise visitor.

The Steelers' No. 1 selection in 1942 was back to see his old boss, and dear friend, team owner Art Rooney. I have visited with Dudley several times in Charlottesville, Virginia and Pittsburgh in the years since, but this was the first time I was ever in his esteemed company. It was a memorable meeting because his name still had a hint of magic about it, one of those football names from your youth.

"If I had to pick my favorite Steeler of all time," Rooney once remarked. "It would be Bill Dudley. He didn't know the meaning of the word quit."

Dudley was already retired from playing by the mid-50s when I first tuned in to the Steelers. He also served as an assistant coach one year — 1956 — on Walt Kiesling's staff. I was born in the summer of 1942, when he reported for his rookie season with the Steelers, so I never saw him play. I just heard about him, the way you heard about "Red" Grange and Charlie "Choo-Choo" Justice. Dudley was a contemporary of Ralph Kiner, when he was winning major league home run titles with the Pirates. They are the same age. They performed at Forbes Field during the same era.

"I just feel Mr. Rooney's one of the finest fellas I've ever known," declared Dudley, still a formidable figure, even at age 56, and wearing a dark blue pinstripe three-piece suit that May day in 1979, "and when I'm in town I always stop to say hello."

Dudley was doing quite well in those days as an insurance underwriter, working for the same company, the Equitable Life Assurance Company, the previous 29 years. He was based in Lynchburg, Virginia — the same state where he was one of the biggest college football heroes ever to grace any campus. I visited the University of Virginia campus many times during the four years (1992-1996) my daughter Sarah was a student there, and I often came across framed paintings and photographs of Dudley in different buildings. He was still a Big Man on Campus. I even came across him once,

78

by accident, when he was tail-gating before a Virginia football game. He referred to his alma mater simply as "the University." He remained a revered figure in his home state. Rooney's eyes brightened at the sight of one of his all-time favorite Steelers.

Suddenly, Rooney's Wall of Fame came to life. His office, back then, was covered with photos from the past — some actually sepia-toned — of his favorite people in pro sports. He was much closer to his players in the old days, and that was evident by the preponderance of photos from that era. There were photos of Jim Finks, Elbie Nickel, Bobby Layne, John Henry Johnson, Armand Niccolai, Johnny Blood, Johnny Lattner, Paul Cameron, "Big Daddy" Lipscomb, Ernie Stautner, Byron "Whizzer" White and, of course, "Bullet Bill."

Then, too, there were photos of some of Rooney's fellow NFL owners in the early days of the league, such as Bert Bell, Dan Reeves, Bill Bidwill and George Halas, political pals such as David L. Lawrence and Joe Barr, local boxing greats such as Billy Conn and Fritzie Zivic, as well as Joe Louis and Jack Dempsey. It was like being in a museum, with the best of all possible guides.

"I've always surrounded myself with good people," boasted Rooney. "My boys go in for modern art, and say we have to dress up this place, but I prefer to have people around me. I can't relate to that other stuff. I had even more pictures in my old office."

He liked it even more when one of the people who is pictured on the walls stopped in his office for a visit. It could have been Conn or Dudley, Hall of Famers both, but just old friends, as far as The Chief was concerned.

Tim Conn, the godson of Art Rooney, tells a story about how Mr. Rooney originally owned the Steelers with an entrepreneur/promoter named Milt Jaffe. "Jaffe was upset with Mr. Rooney for paying Whizzer White $16,000 a year (1938), when that was unheard of. They were paying most of the guys a few hundred dollars a game, some less. So Rooney bought out Jaffe's share in the team for about $2,000. Imagine what that share would be worth today."

Dudley was also one of the Rooney's better-paid performers.

"We were close friends all the years he was here," Rooney recalled, nodding in the direction of Dudley, "and we continued our friendship all through the years since then. He's always been a classy guy.

"I believe Bill Dudley was as good as any football player who has ever played in the National Football League. He wasn't fast, even though his nickname made you think he was. But nobody caught him. He couldn't pass, but he completed passes. He was one of the top kickers in the game. He was the best all-around ballplayer I've ever seen."

Dudley was once a member of the Virginia legislature, and only "Whizzer" White, a Supreme Court justice, rose higher in the political world. Dudley was a trustee for many years at the University of Virginia. Rooney pointed out a photo on the wall of his office showing "Bullet Bill" and himself with a group of youngsters outside Rooney's North Side home.

Dudley recalled another photo out of the past. "When I first came here," he said, "Mr. Rooney and I went out to dinner and to a couple of other places, and we ended up at an orphanage. I've still got a photo of us with those kids. I treasure it.

"He has a way of establishing relationships with everyone who's ever played for him. Frankly, I'm lucky that I'm one of the guys that's remembered. His entire family is cut out of the same cloth. His boys have all followed in his footsteps."

Dudley performed for the Steelers in 1942, then spent two seasons in the Army Air Corps during World War II, then returned for three more years with the Steelers. Walt Kiesling had been his coach as a rookie, but when he returned the team was run by Jock Sutherland, a strict disciplinarian who had first gained fame as an All-American player and Hall of Fame football coach with the Pitt Panthers. Dudley left the Steelers for the Lions and later the Redskins. He was elected to the Pro Football Hall of Fame in 1966. So how did the Steelers ever let him get away?

He forced a trade because he couldn't stand Sutherland, "the dour Scot," as he was often called. "It was like losing one of my own sons," said Rooney at the time.

"People ask me which team was my favorite," said Dudley, "and I have to say Pittsburgh. I have to root for Pittsburgh. It's where I played first, and where I made my reputation.

"People remember me better here. When I come in — and this doesn't happen in other places — somebody will pick me out of the crowd. I can be standing in front of a hotel here, and someone will holler out to me 'Hey, Bill, what the hell are you doing in town?' This is Pittsburgh, and I've always felt at home here.

"I always get a good reception here. It's my home away from home. When I first came here, being a Southerner, I was a stranger. And, so to speak, they took me in."

He noted the changes that had taken place since he had played for the Steelers at Forbes Field. "It was a different era in those days," he said. Pointing out the guy with the telegraph pole of a cigar extending from chapped lips, Dudley allowed, "but he hasn't changed. And our relationship has grown."

Just then, a yellow taxicab pulled in front of the Steelers' complex. "Is there a Mr. Dudley here?" hollered the cabbie. "Bullet Bill" was off and running, and I wondered whether the cabbie had any idea who he had for a fare. Or, had Greg Hawthorne ever heard of him?

I spent some quality time with Bill and his wife, Libba, at a dinner hosted by his friend and former Steelers teammate Jerry Nuzum at the P.A.A. in Oakland a year or so later, and again when he came to town for the Steelers' 50 Seasons Celebration in 1982. Also in attendance at the P.A.A. dinner were Fran Rogel, Lynn Chandnois and Joe Gasparella. I was the only sportswriter there, along with my wife, Kathie. I felt privileged to be there. Then there was the time I had breakfast with him and his wife, Libba, at the Farmington Country Club on the outskirts of Charlottesville.

Photos from Pittsburgh Steelers Archives

"Bullet" Bill Dudley was a Hall of Fame football performer for the Pittsburgh Steelers, Detroit Lions and Washington Redskins. He remains one of the most respected figures in the history of the University of Virginia.

Jim O'Brien

Libba and Bill Dudley are frequent visitors to the University of Virginia in Charlottesville.

He had just turned 70. I asked him again about his relationship with Art Rooney.

"Why or how that developed one never knows," he responded. "I don't know if I was one of his favorites or not. I always looked at him as a friend. In the nine years I played in the National Football League, what I cherish most are the people I got to meet. I regret not having played all my years with Pittsburgh.

"But I got to meet Mr. Rooney, and Mr. Bell, and Mr. Marshall, and Mr. Mara, and Mr. Halas. They were great owners; they were great people. I got to know them all on a first-name basis, but I refer to them by Mr. out of habit. I was brought up that way to respect my elders.

"My relationship with Mr. Rooney helped me to get to know all those people. We used to get postcards from him all the time, especially when he went to Canada. Art was a tremendous people person.

"I thought Mr. Rooney was a man of his word. Where I growed up, my word was always my bond. That's the way Mr. Rooney was. One time he was supposed to have sent a wire to bookies at racetracks around the country, and he could place a bet for several thousand dollars, and it was honored. They knew he was good for the money. I don't know if that's true or not, but that's what I understood."

"Bullet Bill" Dudley and "The Chief" Art Rooney can be found in the midst of children at St. Paul's Orphanage in Crafton in December, 1945 visit. Dudley has a copy of this picture in his office in Lynchburg, Virginia.

"I always wanted to win."

Excerpt from "About Three Bricks Shy Of A Load" by Roy Blount, Jr.

Copyright 1974.

Roy Blount, Jr., at right, enjoys a "toddy" with Myron Cope.

The Chief looks like a cross between Charles Coburn and Jiggs. He is chunky, big in the middle, not tall. He has shaggy eyebrows and thick white hair, combed back. Since he was not wearing one of his out-of-whack soft felt hats, the hair was stirring a bit in the breeze. He is a man who, once he has become acquainted with you, looks almost comically glad to see you again. For that matter, I have seen him look at a brand-new acquaintance, of no particular prominence, with the expression of a little boy who has just been handed a puppy. The Chief is hard on his sons but I never heard him say one critical word about anybody else. Chuck Noll and Dan Rooney — especially Noll — run the Steelers, but the Chief is perhaps the most fondly regarded figure in all of pro football. The people in Pittsburgh who denounce him do so because he got rich, coming up from nothing, without ever giving the city a winner. Asked once how he felt about having the image of a good loser, the Chief bristled. "I *hate* losing!" he snapped. "I *hate* it! I *always* wanted to win." But he probably ran the Steelers too permissively to win. It was in those enterprises where he was least soft-hearted — such as in raising five sons, who now control the Steelers, Yonkers Raceway in New York, two other horse-racing operations and one dog track — that he had the most concrete results. Some of the things he permitted to go on before the Noll Revolution were more engaging, though, than victory. When he gets to reminiscing it seems that the things he enjoyed the most, at least in retrospect, were the things that went wrong. Comic spirits appreciate incorrigibility. "In 1941, I went up to our summer camp in Hershey," the Chief has said, "and the team had new uniforms on. They looked terrible and when a sportswriter asked me what I thought I told him so. I said, 'The only thing different is the uniforms. It's the same old Steelers.' The papers have never let me forget that."

Irish Blessing

*May the road rise
to meet you
May the wind be
always at your back
May the sun shine
warm upon your face
May the rains fall soft
upon your fields
And until we meet again
May God hold you
In the palm of His hand.*

In Memory of
Arthur J. Rooney
January 27, 1901
August 25, 1988

REMEMBER, MAN,
  AS YOU PASS BY,
THAT AS YOU ARE
  SO ONCE WAS I,
THAT AS I AM
  SO WILL YOU BE,
REMEMBER, MAN,
  ETERNITY.

Read on a tombstone in Ireland

Ed Kiely
The Chief's escort

"He had a touch."

Ed Kiely started out with the Steelers in 1950, handling the team's public relations, and stayed until 1989, retiring a year after Art Rooney died. In the last six or seven years, Kiely was a constant companion of the Steelers' owner, accompanying him on most of his travels. Kiely, at 83, worked out daily to stay in shape, and remained an ardent reader of many newspapers and magazines. His late wife, Pat Kiely, was a popular TV news anchorwoman in Pittsburgh for years. Their children, Kathy, Timmy and Kevin, were all in the media business, with newspapers in Kathy's case, and television with the boys. I had a luncheon interview with Kiely and former Pittsburgh Press *sports editor Pat Livingston on April 6, 2001 at Poli's Restaurant in Squirrel Hill. Kiely's comments follow:*

I was with Art quite a bit. You were on the road and I was like a traveling secretary. He wouldn't like the room we had so we would move. I would take care of stuff like that, just trying to make it easier for him. No matter where we went people would be falling over one another to greet and meet him. A lot of big people made a fuss over him. He knew everybody.

In the latter years, we were more friends than anything else. He was still the boss, but we had grown really close. I felt like part of his family; I had gotten so close to everybody. His kids said I ended up being a part of the family. It became a friendship more than just a job. He got to think I knew everything he knew. "You know what I'm talking about!" he'd rail from time to time. But I wasn't always on the same page.

One time we were having dinner in Luchow's, a famous German restaurant — one of the best — in New York. He got into a conversation with Hume Cronyn and Jessica Tandy. They were married and one of the great husband-and-wife teams on Broadway. They were in movies, too. Art was related somehow to Anne Jackson, an actress who was married to the actor Eli Wallach, so they talked about that.

Art had once decked a guy in that same restaurant. The guy apparently had been loud and abusive, out of control, giving everybody a bad time. He said something smart to the Chief. Art cold-cocked the guy with one punch. He said that was the last fight he ever was in.

After his wife died, I really spent a lot of time with him. I accompanied him most of the time when he went somewhere. I just made sure everything was the way it ought to be. We went to a lot of things. Sometimes he balked at things. Some of that stuff became a pain.

Everyone could learn a lot about charity and humility from Art Rooney. There were really no bad guys, as far as he was concerned. Everyone got a fresh start with Art Rooney. He got along well with Al Davis, for instance, because he understood Davis. He told Davis he had to get in line, and that he couldn't be fighting the other owners all the time. But Art is gone and Davis is still challenging the league at every turn. Art liked Charles O. Finley, another controversial sports figure. He thought he had a lot of good ideas. He had some imaginative ideas. Those guys would listen to Art because of his reputation. They'd pay attention to what he had to say.

We went to Chicago for the last College All-Star Game. There was thunder and lightning, and a terrible storm and they had to call it off, sometime in the third quarter, I think. We got a call from Mayor Daley's office the next day. I got a message that Mayor Daley wanted to give Art Rooney a key to the city. So we went to his office the next morning to get the key to the city. They had a media office and we went by it to a room nearby. Mayor Daley and Art were talking about politics. Mayor Daley told him he would present the key to him in front of all those newspaper guys. After awhile, Art said to Mayor Daley, "Listen, Mayor, those newspaper guys are probably waiting for you." And the Mayor smiled and said, "Let the bastards wait."

I know that didn't sit well with Art. I don't know anyone who had more respect for the press than he did. He treated the littlest guy from the littlest newspaper like the guy was from *The New York Times* or *The Washington Post*.

And Art made friends with a lot of good guys in the business. I know he and Dick Schaap hit it off. Dick couldn't get over how he was. I told Dick to go down to his office and just go in, but he wasn't comfortable with that, so I took him to see Art. After that, they got to be good friends. After that, Dick felt comfortable calling on Art on his own.

Another thing that comes to mind is when Art Carney came to town. They were doing a made-for-TV movie based on Rocky Bleier's book, "Fighting Back." Carney was going to play the part of Art Rooney. One day, Carney asks me, "What fingers does he use to hold his cigar?" I told him I would be damned if I knew, but that we could go visit with Art and he could see for himself. I was impressed that he wanted to know details like that so he could properly depict him in a movie.

Carney is a frightfully shy guy; it's hard to believe the guy was so funny on TV in those Jackie Gleason shows. After he visited with Art for quite a while, he was about to leave when he asked me, "Do you think you could get him to sign some photos of himself for me?" I told him he could ask Art, but he didn't want to do that. Art signed some photos for him, and then he asked Art Carney, "Say, Art, do you have any pictures with you? You ought to be autographing photos for me."

"To me, life's been good since the day I was born. Smoking cigars can make a day great."
— Ray Mansfield

Art Rooney was portrayed by actor Art Carney in 1980 made-for-TV movie about Rocky Bleier's heroic comeback called "Fighting Back."

"The father was very firm."

Art Rooney was more a politician than any politician you'd ever meet. Once he met you he wouldn't forget you. I met Jim Farley, the old Postmaster General, through him. They both did the same things. They were natural politicians. They had a way with people. Art made people feel important. He was a people person.

You had to be a real goofball to mess up with him. That's the way the politicians operated. They treated everyone like they were special. If you were just an everyday bloke and you got a hand-written post-card from Art Rooney it made you feel special.

They had important friends. Tim, for instance, was close to Teddy Kennedy. Several of the Kennedys came to the Super Bowl when we were in it. Ethel was there. Timmy could have been something in politics, too. He had that flare. He was a product of his father, a born politician. The father was very firm with those boys. He made sure all five of them went to school and that they stayed out of trouble. Art told them never to act like they were rich. They never drank around their dad. He drank alcohol in his early years, but not the last 30 years of his life.

When his eyes went bad, I used to read articles in the newspaper to him, or call certain stories to his attention. I knew what would be of interest to him. I'd cut out editorials from the *Wall Street Journal* for him, for instance, and out-of-town newspapers. He had wide interests. When he died, I received a note from (NFL Commissioner) Pete Rozelle in which he wrote, "I hope you'll take as good care of Dan as you did his father."

When Dan took over running the team, his father took a backseat to him. Art might come into the room in the middle of an owners' meeting, and they'd see him moving across the back of the room, looking for a place to sit, and they clapped their hands to acknowledge his presence. He was as respected as anybody. He did more public relations for the league than any public relations guy. He had a feel for people and things that are hard to replace.

When I would ride with him on an airplane, people would come up to me when I'd be walking down the aisle to go to the bathroom, and they'd say, "Can I get an autograph?' And I'd tell them just to go up and see him. When they did I'd see him talking to them. He'd be wonderful with them. He had a touch.

I remember going to funeral homes with him. We'd go to see one person and there might be a funeral home full of bodies. He'd go see them all. People would be so surprised to see him and taken aback by him walking in. He might be introduced to the widow, and he'd say, "There are going to be tough times for you. You'll have to be strong. Can you do that?" He'd comfort them and lecture them at the same time. I remember when he did this sort of thing when they were always running that United Way commercial featuring him. That made him even more recognizable. We'd come out of the funeral home and he'd say to me, "How did they know me?" That always cracked me up.

His evolution must have been something to see. When he was a young man, he was a tough guy, quite the ballplayer, a boxer, quite the competitor. Then he became an influential politician. He was a ward leader on the North Side. Jimmy Coyne was the boss and Art was one of his lieutenants. There were no Roosevelt programs for the poor then. Guys like Coyne and Rooney got food for everybody who needed it in the neighborhood for Thanksgiving and Christmas. He was always loyal to Jimmy Coyne. So he remained a Republican. No one could get him to become a Democrat, not even his good friend David Lawrence.

He was a religious guy, but he hated it when they wrote about it. He didn't want people to make a big deal about it.

"He saw a lot of fun in life."

Everybody was his friend. You could go with him to the racetrack, and everybody would fuss over him. He'd drive up in his car, and the valet parking people would all come over to greet him. He knew every one of them by name. It was the same with the people who worked in the dining room. He'd say, "Mary, how are you? How are the kids?" He knew the kids' names. It was that way with everyone in the dining room. How could he do that? That's an art.

He loved baseball and the baseball people loved him. I remember some baseball managers, guys like Joe Torre and Whitey Herzog, would come in to see him when their teams were in town. He'd sit in their dugouts during workouts on the day of the game. He really enjoyed that. He and Torre would talk about cigars and they'd smoke them together. He liked loafing with those guys. He was really close to baseball.

If you screwed up, he'd let you know. He might have been the nicest guy, but he'd get on you from time to time.

At the same time, he had a tremendous sense of humor. He saw a lot of fun in life. As serious as life was, he found the fun in it.

If you're in a town with competition, like we had, you had to work the local media to get your share of attention. When I got started with the Steelers, the Pirates were the biggest thing in town. Baseball was the biggest sport in the country.

People don't know what our business used to be like. When I was working as the Steelers' public relations guy, I used to drive down to Monongahela or Uniontown, places like that, and spend the day with the sportswriters there. I used to drive everywhere. You went into the city of the opposing team before road games, and you'd take photos and handouts and set up telephone interviews. There were seven daily newspapers in New York at one period and you had to visit all of them.

Television made football a big deal and a big business. Art knew that, but he was never comfortable with it. He always worried about what would happen if TV pulled out of football, and left us with a TV-driven economy. I remember him saying to Terry Bradshaw, "Big boy, when they turn that red light off on TV someday, could you play for $10,000 a year?" And Bradshaw would say, "What else could I do?"

He liked Bradshaw and he liked Lambert and Mel Blount. He liked guys he thought would have fit in and played tough like the guys he knew in the old days. When he came into the locker room everyone felt they were special to him. He'd say, "How are ya? Howya doing? Where ya from?" And they loved him. When guys got traded, they hated to leave him. He'd continue to write to them wherever they went. He was unreal like that. To him, they were always Steelers.

Ed Kiely, left to right, chats with long-time friends in the Steelers' family, Dr. Bernard Kobosky, an executive at both Duquesne University and the University of Pittsburgh in his educational career, Blesto scouting director Jack Butler and club vice-president Jack R. McGinley.

"When I got traded to San Francisco, Mr. Rooney sent a letter to my mom saying how proud he was to have had me on the team. I was only a backup there for a short time (1977-78), but that letter was a thrill for my parents. He did that kind of stuff all the time."
— Tony Dungy, head coach
Tampa Bay Buccaneers

Talking Boxing with Billy Conn
Rooney was a champion, too

"I could hit...I was a champion."
— Art Rooney

"**T**hink about it," boasted Billy Conn, "the best guys in the world are former boxers. You've got Bob Hope, Frank Sinatra and Art Rooney.

"Hope fought under the name of Packy East when he was a kid in Cleveland. He had about 13 pro fights and won all but one of them. Sinatra boxed a little bit out of Hoboken, New Jersey. Sinatra's the highest-class guy in the world. He raised over a million dollars for Joe Louis. No one can put a patch on him...except Art Rooney.

"He's the quarterback on the first-team of the all-nice guy team. There are a lot of bad guys and fools in this world, but a few good guys. A guy like Art Rooney takes up the slack. He's an unassuming real nice guy, the way he treats you, he's just another guy."

Billy Conn, of course, was a former boxer himself. He was the light-heavyweight champion of the world for parts of 1939 and 1940, vacating the title to box in the heavyweight ranks. Twice Conn fought Joe Louis for the title, and twice came up short, though he was ahead on the scoring cards when Louis knocked him out in the 13th round in their first meeting.

Their meetings provided Louis with two of his three biggest purses as a prizefighter until, that is, Sinatra tossed a fund-raising testimonial to him in the late '70s. Conn was talking about Hope, Sinatra, Louis and Rooney in the summer of 1981, when Conn was 64 and Rooney was 80. They were dear friends.

Rooney's life-long love affair with horse racing was more celebrated and chronicled than his romance with boxing, but he was always a big fan of the fight game. He was once both a national and international amateur boxing champion and qualified for the U.S. Olympic team in the 1920 Games at Antwerp, Belgium.

During his early days as owner of the Steelers, Rooney also promoted pro boxing matches in Pittsburgh with Barney McGinley, a minority owner of the Steelers and the father of Jack McGinley, who still owns a piece of the pro football franchise.

Conn and Rooney were reminiscing about boxing's grand old days during lunch at the Allegheny Club at Three Rivers Stadium where diners had an expansive view of the playing field where the Steelers and Pirates played their home games. I was fortunate to be sharing their table.

Conn had offered his highly complimentary remarks about Rooney while the latter was visiting some other friends at a nearby table, pumping hands as usual and inquiring about the health of everybody's wife and family. Rooney rejoined Conn and this writer to continue talking about their boxing ties.

Asked about his boxing skills, Rooney replied without a hint of boasting in his voice, "I could hit. I was a champion."

He began boxing when he was 16, and fought in the national amateur tournaments a few times, and fought in an international tournament in Toronto. He won the lightweight title there. "I beat Arnold Thornberg for an AAU title here at the P.A.A. (Pittsburgh Athletic Association) in an outdoor match around 1917," recalled Rooney. "There was great inner-city competition for amateurs in those days, between teams from the Boston and New York athletic clubs. You could keep real busy."

Rooney turned down a chance to box in the 1920 Olympic Games because he did not want to interrupt his studies at a Catholic school. Friends say Rooney was interested in becoming a priest, not a boxer, at the time.

"I beat Sammy Mossberg to go to the Olympics," Rooney recalled, "and then I didn't go. He won the gold medal at the Olympics and when he came back I beat him again. I boxed for about two or three years; I boxed professional twice. I forgot the first guy I fought, but the second was Sammy Mandell, who later became a champion. We fought in a preliminary in Chicago to a main event in which Tommy O'Brien fought Pinky Mitchell.

"That's the only time I almost seriously became a fighter. I was supposed to go to Australia and fight Mandell, and stay there and do some fighting. Tommy O'Brien was a champion in Australia at the time. Tommy O'Brien's wife talked me out of going to Australia, and did me the biggest favor of my life."

To which Conn interjected, "That's for sure!"

As Rooney and Conn chatted about their boxing experiences, they tossed around some of the great names of the fight game as casually as other diners at the Allegheny Club were exchanging salt and pepper shakers.

Sammy Mandell and Tommy O'Brien were openers. Others that came into their conversation — and I had to write these names down quickly and check them out later in the *Ring* magazine record book — included Joe Louis, Rocky Marciano and Muhammad Ali. Rooney referred to him as Muhammad Ali and Conn kept calling him Cassius Clay, which gives you additional insight into Rooney and Conn.

Others mentioned were Melio Bettina, Tony Galento, Teddy Yarosz, Harry Greb, Sammy Angott, Frank Klaus, Fritzie Zivic, Tommy Farr, Mickey Walker, Benny Leonard, Jimmy McLarnin, Jersey Joe Walcott, Ezzard Charles, Tommy Loughran, Gene Tunney, Jack Dempsey, Tony Canzoneri, Freddie Miller, Solly Krieger, Oscar Rankins, Charlie Burley, Jackie Wilson, Billy Soose, Joe Frazier, Billy Petrolle and Henry Armstrong.

They spoke of a period when Pittsburgh could have been called "The City of Champions," because the area could boast of having five champions out of the eight weight categories in the pro game. Between July 13, 1939 and November 18, 1941, Conn, Angott, Zivic, Soose and Wilson held world boxing titles, but not all at the same time. Angott was from Washington, Pa. and Soose was from Farrell.

Conn and Rooney agreed that Greb, who grew up in Garfield, was the greatest fighter in the history of the game. "I never saw him, but I heard plenty about him," said Conn. "He was always in great shape, and he'd fight anybody. Sometimes he'd fight a few times in the same week. He was always willing and ready to go. He must've been something."

Rooney responded with a Greb story on his own. "I saw the first Greb-Tunney fight," recalled Rooney. "Greb beat him twice, though he got robbed once. They fought five times (and, for the record, Tunney won twice, lost once, and there were two no-decisions).

Greb died October 22, 1926, following an operation on his eye. "He's buried here in Calvary Cemetery, near my mother," said Conn. (When he died, Conn was also buried in Calvary Cemetery.)

Greb, who was elected to the Boxing Hall of Fame, was the middleweight champion of the world and the American light-heavyweight champion. He was managed by Red Mason, who once tried to get Rooney to turn pro, and George Engel, who was Rooney's best man when he was married. There is a vintage photo of Greb displayed on the wall behind the bar at Tessaro's Restaurant on Liberty Avenue in Bloomfield, not far from Greb's old neighborhood. It's a prized possession of owner Kelly Harrington.

To give further proof of his ties to boxing people, Rooney served as godfather for Timmy Conn, one of Billy's sons, and for Charlie Jones, who managed Sammy Angott, when Jones converted to Catholicism.

Rooney once promoted a fight in Pittsburgh between Angott and another local hero, Fritzie Zivic, who often visited him in his Steelers' office.

"I hate to live in the past," said Rooney, "but that's all the guys coming to my office want to talk about every day. I like Sugar Ray Leonard and Roberto Duran, but most of the young guys never saw the kind of fighters I saw."

Rooney recalled a classic fight held in 1936 in Pittsburgh, one of three meetings between Solly Krieger and Oscar Rankins. "It was at Duquesne Gardens," interjected Conn. "It was one of the world's greatest fights. I was there. I fought both of them later."

Rooney was fond of telling a story about the first Conn-Louis fight to his players, as he did later that day with Sam Davis and Gerry Mullins. "Billy, in later years, asked Joe Louis why he didn't let him win that fight," related Rooney. "Billy said it would have been good for both of them if he'd taken the title away from Louis. He told Joe they could have fought for the title again in a return match in six months, for really big money, and Louis could have reclaimed his title at that time. Joe told him, 'Billy, I gave you the title for 13 rounds, and you didn't know what to do with it. What would you have done with it for six months?' "

Later, Rooney said he brought Conn into the Steelers' clubhouse a year earlier and none of the players recognized his name. "But I asked the black guys if they'd heard about Joe Louis, and they all sure knew him!"

It was a two-way street, however. This writer was present when Jack Lambert, the Steelers' All-Pro linebacker and the UPI's Defensive Player of the Year in the AFC, was confronted by Conn and Rooney in the hallway at Three Rivers Stadium one afternoon.

Rooney said, "Jack, you know my friend, Billy Conn," and Lambert nodded. Then Rooney turned to Conn, and said, "You know Jack here, don't you, Billy?" And Conn nodded and said, quite seriously, "Sure, Jack Ham, right?" The sour look on Lambert's face should've tipped off Conn to his mistake.

"I have an excuse," Conn conceded later on. "I took too many punches to the head. But what's the big deal?"

To which Mary Regan, Rooney's long-time secretary and Gal Friday, offered, "Billy, how'd you like somebody to mistake you for Fritzie Zivic?"

Louis and Conn did fight again, and for big money. In fact, it was a record gate at the time. A crowd of 45,266 showed up at Yankee Stadium, and the gate was $1,925,505. Louis got $625,916.44 and Conn received $325,958.22. Conn was KO'd at 2:19 of the eighth round the second time around.

Even so, Conn remained popular in New York, more so than in Pittsburgh, at least to hear Conn. "Here, I'm a bum!" bellowed Conn. He told a story to make that point.

"Budd Schulberg, who's a wonderful guy, wanted me to be in a movie based on his book, 'On The Waterfront,' but I told him I made one stink-bomb movie about myself — 'The Pittsburgh Kid' — and I didn't want to make another.

"So I went to see the movie when it was playing in Pittsburgh. Marlon Brando is this fighter who raises pigeons, and he's sitting in a taxi talking to his older brother, who was played by Rod Steiger. Steiger tells him, 'If you behaved yourself, you'd have been another Billy Conn.' And this guy tells his girlfriend in front of me in the theater, 'Isn't he a big enough bum as it is now?' Even I had to laugh at that one."

Conn couldn't stop with one story. "Do you know who the toughest, guttiest guy is of all time in the fight game?"

Even Rooney didn't respond to that one.

"It was Battling Siki," Conn came back. "He had to be the gamest guy to ever come along. He was black and he defended his title against Mike McTigue on St. Patrick's Day in Dublin, Ireland. He had as much chance as a snowball in hell of winning that fight."

Sure enough, a check of *The Ring Encyclopedia and Record Book* revealed that Battling Siki, born Louis Phal in French West Africa, lost his title in a 20-round fight to McTigue on March 17, 1923 in Dublin.

Then Conn talked about Cuddy D'Marco, who came from the western Pennsylvania community of Charleroi. "They called him 'The Sheik,' and he was the handsomest, best-dressed guy," recalled Conn. "He once beat 161 guys in a row. Hell, you can't beat 161 girls in a row!"

Rooney chortled over Conn's tales, and told a few of his own. "There used to be a romance aspect to boxing," said Rooney. "You had some great managers, and they were real characters in their own right. There was Billy Gibson, Red Mason, George Engel — I could listen to him all day — Mike Jacobs, Jimmy Johnson and Johnny Ray."

Rooney recalled the time Conn came home on a three-day pass from the Army to attend his son's christening. Art was there as the godfather for Timmy Conn. Billy's father-in-law, a storied gentleman named "Greenfield Jimmy" Smith, was still smarting over his daughter's decision to marry Conn.

"I could tell there was going to be trouble," recalled Rooney, "just by the look in their eyes. They both had a short fuse. Before you knew it, they were tossing punches at one another in the kitchen. Billy broke his right hand hitting his father-in-law. But the father-in-law got in some good licks, too. You should have seen the wall in the kitchen. It looked like somebody had tossed a bucket of red paint on it."

Conn kept laughing as Rooney told the twice-told tale. "When I was 23," recalled Conn, "a guy wanted to lay an 8-to-5 bet I'd never be 27. Art said, 'I agree.'"

That was good for another laugh. "The Pittsburgh Kid" and "The Chief" were having a good time.

From Jim O'Brien collection

Rooney and good friend and former light-heavyweight boxing champion Billy Conn, the original "Pittsburgh Kid," check out photo of Conn's famous title fight with the great Joe Louis that was displayed on the wall of Rooney's office at Three Rivers Stadium.

A Christmas Carol
Special relationship with players

"When you win, you have all the answers."

'Twas two nights before Christmas, 1979, and all through the then 130-year-old Victorian house of Art and Kathleen Rooney, not a creature was stirring. Until Art asked, "What's that?" Singing could be heard, coming from outside. "Why don't you go see?" Kathleen suggested to her husband.

Mr. Rooney, the owner of the Steelers, went to the door and, much to his surprise, he found three of his players — Terry Bradshaw, Lynn Swann and Gerry Mullins — standing on the doorstep, with their wives, singing Christmas carols.

Art and his wife were delighted, naturally.

Later, the Steelers carolers left the North Side house where the Rooneys had lived nearly half a century, and moved on to Mt. Lebanon where they sang carols at the homes of Dan and Art Rooney, Jr. Then they went to nearby Upper St. Clair for more carols at the home of Chuck Noll. Ask yourself how many pro sports owners and head coaches have been serenaded lately by players and you can see why the Pittsburgh Steelers are something special. The Rooneys are special, that's for sure. They were elite citizens in "the City of Champions." Mayor Richard Caliguiri had given them more keys to the city than they could possibly need.

During the Camelot years of the '70s, the Rooneys were Pittsburgh's answer to the Kennedys. They were Irish, rich, politically connected, powerful and everywhere. Then, too, the specifics of their early years and entrepreneurial efforts were somewhat murky. Art was the patriarch of the pro franchise in Pittsburgh, and the main reason the Steelers stayed through many slim seasons. "I'm a Pittsburgh guy, that's why," he often said.

He owned the club for 40 years before it ever played for a title.

His oldest son, Dan, who was 47 when the Steelers won their fourth Super Bowl, served as club president during these heady times, and ran the business end of the operation during the '70s when it was the most successful and most universally admired franchise in the National Football League.

Art, Jr., the second son in the chain of command, was in charge of the scouting and player personnel department, and contributed to the success of the Steelers in the draft during that period. "Chuck Noll has taught our scouts so that they know exactly what he's after," said Art, Jr.

"When you win," said the father, one of the most famous sports figures in the country and certainly one of its most popular and endearing leaders, "you have all the answers. We weren't always so smart or so popular in Pittsburgh. When you're losing, people don't think you're smart enough to come in out of the rain. When you win, you get smart in a hurry."

The elder Rooney was responsible for public relations during the team's terrific run in the '70s. He greeted everybody who entered the Steelers' inner sanctum. He offered them a firm handshake, a first-class cigar and the comfort of his company. The boys looked after the business.

"We have to pay full attention to it, and we do," said Dan Rooney, one of the most respected executives in the NFL. "My dad's different, too. He's a legend. He comes up to people now, and he's a somebody. It wasn't always like that. He wasn't always like he is now. He wasn't that visible 20 years ago."

Like the ghosts in "The Christmas Carol."

Art Rooney and his wife, Kathleen, are in the forefront of this family reunion photo from a Thanksgiving gathering at their North Side home in 1964. Their five sons and ten of their grandchildren are pictured here. Front row, left to right, are John and his wife JoAnn, holding Sean; Mr. and Mrs. Rooney, with Duffy; Peggy and Art II. Center row: Peggy, Rita, Bridget, Kathleen and Patsy. Rear row: Kathleen and Art Jr., holding Art III, Dan's wife, Pat, holding Danny; Pat and his wife, Sandy; June and her husband,Tim; and Dan Rooney

"What is a family after all, except memories?"
— From "We Were The Mulvaneys"
by Joyce Carol Oates

Day in the Sun
NFL flips over Mr. Rooney

"My dad's really enjoying himself."
— Dan Rooney

There are special sequences that stand out in my personal experience with Art Rooney that provide insights into his character. Sometimes it's simple things, every-day behavior, not big stuff. It was the essence of Art Rooney, though, because he was consistent. He was always a source of goodness, a reason to smile. The stories are still illuminating.

This was in mid-January, 1980 as the Steelers were preparing to play the Los Angeles Rams in Super Bowl XIV. The National Football League had announced that Mr. Rooney — I can't refer to him any other way — was going to flip the coin at midfield to determine the kickoff. The Steelers, as the American Football Conference champions, were going to be the home team in the game to be played at the Rose Bowl in Pasadena. It's their turn. Rooney was hoping the Steelers would win the coin flip and that he could match their call.

The Steelers' owner always enjoyed the game of chance, so this was right up his alley. It was NFL Commissioner Pete Rozelle's way of recognizing Art Rooney's contributions to the league. He wanted to put his favorite owner in the spotlight he usually shunned but merited. Mr. Rooney was having a wonderful time during this period. He was busier than usual, at his office in the Steelers' complex at Three Rivers Stadium. He continued to lead the league in hospital visitations and wake appearances, and now he was obliging out-of-town reporters who wanted to interview him for stories relating to the Steelers' successful run of the '70s.

These were the best of times and the worst of times for Mr. Rooney. His Steelers were going to the Super Bowl, but his brother, Father Dan "Silas" Rooney, 76, a Franciscan priest, was gravely ill and the family's horse racing interests in the East, which several of his sons were looking after, were experiencing difficult days.

Mr. Rooney would be celebrating his 79th birthday on January 27, the Sunday after the Super Bowl, but he was still going strong.

Twice in the previous two weeks, he had gone to St. Petersburg, Florida to visit his brother, Father Silas. He was quite concerned about him. "He's led a full life," remarked Mr. Rooney, "but he's fading badly."

His brother was to be transferred to St. Bonaventure University where he could get better care and where he was once the athletic director and the magnet that drew the Steelers to establish their training camp there some years back on the Olean, New York campus. That was in the days when Eddie Donovan was the basketball coach there. Donovan would later gain fame as a coach and administrator in the NBA and is honored in the Basketball Hall of Fame in Springfield,

Massachusetts. I remember when I covered the Knicks that Donovan, the team's general manger, often asked me about Mr. Rooney. So did the Knicks' trainer, Danny Whelan, an Irishman who performed similar chores for the Pirates' World Series winners in 1960.

The Roooneys had recently unloaded their William Penn Meet holdings at Liberty Bell Race Track in Philadelphia. Their Yonkers Raceway was getting some stiff competition from the newer Meadowlands track in New Jersey.

Being in the Super Bowl again was good for whatever ailed the Rooney clan.

After the previous Sunday's 27-13 victory over the Houston Oilers in the AFC title game at Three Rivers Stadium, Mr. Rooney had received congratulatory calls that same night from George Halas, the owner of the Chicago Bears, and Art Modell, the owner of the Cleveland Browns. Mr. Rooney had recently attended the funeral of Halas' son, "Muggsy," in Chicago.

"My dad's really enjoying himself," offered Dan Rooney. "I hope we have as many Super Bowl tickets as he's promised his friends.

"He called me at home Thursday night — I was in bed — and told me he had to get some tickets for the mailman. I told him he could do whatever he wanted to do with his tickets, but that he shouldn't be worrying about the mailman. After he hung up, he left his house and went to the post office nearby to leave tickets for the mailman."

It was a trip that some stout-hearted men in Pittsburgh might not make at that hour of night without a police canine corps escort. Or unless Jack Lambert was along for the walk. Somebody up there must have liked Mr. Rooney, because he made the trip without any problems.

Behind his desk, there was a portrait of Pope John Paul II, pictures of former mayors David L. Lawrence and Joe Barr, a brand-new studio portrait of Terry Bradshaw and wife Jo Jo Starbuck — personally autographed by both — and Mass and funeral cards were stacked neatly on his desk. Near the box of cigars he offered to all visitors.

The week before, Mr. Rooney went to Mercy Hospital to see Armand Niccolai, who played tackle and kicked for Duquesne and the Steelers (1934-42) and remained one of Mr. Rooney's all-time favorites. "He's been wearing a pacemaker and he just had a heart attack," said Mr. Rooney, waving some smoke from his face.

Two weeks earlier, on the Friday following New Year's Day, he had visited Mike Wagner, the Steelers' free safety, at Divine Providence Hospital. Wagner had undergone surgery two days earlier for a hip injury.

"While I was there," related Mr. Rooney, "Rocky Bleier and Jack Ham and their wives all came into the room, dressed up in surgical gowns and masks and carrying operating tools. They were pushing a patient cart that was draped with a white sheet. They pulled off the sheet and they had all kinds of good food under there."

As Mr. Rooney was leaving his office, he bumped into Mel Blount, who walked by wearing a cowboy hat.

"You look like a Cowboy," chortled Mr. Rooney.

"No, Mr. Rooney, I'm a Steeler, all the way," replied Blount, the big defensive back. "I want to congratulate you on this season."

"You guys get the congratulations," Mr. Rooney responded. "Even if you don't win the Super Bowl you'll still be big in this town."

"No, Mr. Rooney," Blount came back. "This will be a wasted year if we don't win that last game. But don't worry. We'll win it for you."

From Art Rooney Jr.

The Chief sits with his brother, Dan, a Franciscan priest known as Father Silas, in the stands at Three Rivers Stadium in 1972.

Pittsburgh Post-Gazette Archives

Art Rooney at his desk at Three Rivers Stadium in January, 1976 shortly after Steelers had defeated Dallas Cowboys, 21-17, in Super Bowl X in Miami, Florida.

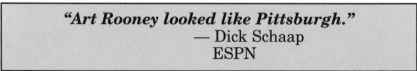

"Art Rooney looked like Pittsburgh."
— Dick Schaap
ESPN

"Just Shoving And Pushing."

From an interview with Steelers' owner Art Rooney:

"The kind of football I played in the 1920s, I suppose you'd call it semi-pro, but our teams were as good as the teams in professional football. We were as good as the teams in the National Football League, which was just getting started. I was no more than twenty-two when I started up a team called Hope-Harvey. I owned it and coached it and in the important games played halfback. The team was called Hope-Harvey because Hope was the name of the fire-engine house in The Ward and Harvey was the doctor in The Ward. For home games we dressed and got our showers in the engine house, and Harvey took care of anybody who got hurt. So nothing cost us a cent. And a lot of guys in that semi-pro ball got up to a hundred dollars a game — a lot of them got more money than fellows in the National Football League.

JIM THORPE

"I remember we played the Canton Bulldogs and Jim Thorpe in Pittsburgh once. I tried a field goal but it was blocked. Thorpe picked it up and ran for a touchdown, and as I recall, they beat us, 6-0. Oh, I played against Thorpe a number of times. He was certainly very fast, but Thorpe was pretty much at end of his rope then. Anyhow, the game in those days was just shoving and pushing, compared to what it is now. Not long ago I went to a gathering of some old-timers, just wonderful people. I really enjoy myself loafing with those old fellows that I played ball with and against, but at this gathering they showed a film of one of the football games we played. They thought it was great. They thought it was tough football. But watching it, you know, I thought, 'It's strictly shoving and pushing.'"

Thanksgiving at Mercy Hospital
Dan Rooney counts his blessings

"Accidents happen to people every day."

Steelers president Dan Rooney lay in a bed in Mercy Hospital on Thanksgiving, 1980, and was thankful he was still alive. On his way to work from Mt. Lebanon to Three Rivers Stadium the day before, he lost control of his station wagon when it hit an icy patch on Banksville Road, about two miles from the Fort Pitt Tunnels, and struck a utility pole. Four other autos were involved in a chain-reaction collision. Nobody else had to be hospitalized.

Rooney suffered facial lacerations and a broken right hip. He was already afflicted with rheumatoid arthritis — which pained him on his bad days and stiffened his gait — so there was concern about how that might complicate matters

He underwent surgery for 3½ hours and a steel pin was inserted in his hip bone. He looked far worse than anyone on the Steelers' injured-reserve list.

While members of his family were counting the lacerations on his forehead, he was counting his blessings.

"Accidents happen to people every day," he said when someone suggested his mishap was the latest in a string of Steelers' misfortunes. He regarded that as a bit melodramatic. That's just the way many well-wishers saw his setback.

Some started their conversation, whether at bedside or by phone, by saying, "With everything else that's gone wrong, and now this…"

Dan didn't go along with that kind of thinking. He didn't see any relationship between what happened to him and what had been happening to his football team that season.

Dan didn't become a fat cat during the Steelers' sensational run in the '70s, and he had kept everything in perspective. He remained on an even keel, while others about him took a ride on the proverbial roller coaster.

The previous Monday, only a few days before his accident, I visited Dan at his office at Three Rivers Stadium. It was the day after a resounding setback at Buffalo. Dan was at his desk in the Steelers' office complex. He was cheerful, as he seemed to be back then more often than not, and volunteered conversation about mutual friends.

One of his brothers was married to a woman I knew as a student at St. Stephen's Grade School in Hazelwood and the Rooneys — from The Chief on down — were always eager to talk about hometown ties. So while many Steelers fans were wondering what was wrong with their team — they were 7-5 en route to a 9-7 record after winning their fourth Super Bowl the year before — Dan wanted to know if a knew a Lynch family from Hazelwood.

One of the brood, Pat Lynch, I learned, was the attorney representing the National Football League in the court case surrounding the attempt by Al Davis to move the Oakland Raiders to Los Angeles.

I asked Dan how he was dealing with all the adversity after so many successful seasons over the last eight years. He smiled his you-should-know-better smile. After all, Dan was 48, the same age as the Steelers, and his dad didn't promise him a garden of roses when he turned the team over to him at the outset of the '70s.

More than most people, Dan realized how much hard work went into the Steelers' success, and he knew it would be difficult to stay on top. He had put together an organization, beginning with Chuck Noll, that he believed would build upon that excellence.

Dan Rooney didn't expect that Super Bowls would become part of his family's table setting.

"I think," he said the day after the debacle in Buffalo, "that it's too early to say anything or do anything."

It was my contention that so much had gone wrong with the Steelers this particular season that it simply wasn't their year. Everything that could go wrong had gone wrong. Dan didn't look for excuses, so he wouldn't buy this argument. The show goes on, as he saw it, and you still do your very best. But it ran through my mind when I learned about Dan's accident.

An on-the-scene witness to his auto accident said that Dan Rooney's head was bloodied to the point that he didn't recognize him. "The window was shattered and there was a bubble in it where Dan's head had struck it," he related. "There were bloody towels all over the place. It was bad." Art Rooney, Jr., who headed the team's scouting department at the time, stayed overnight with his brother at his hospital bedside. Their mom and dad made several visits to the family's hospital suite. Dan's wife and their nine children were frequent visitors. It's not the way Dan would have chosen to spend Thanksgiving, but such holidays were always special to the Rooneys.

Dan could see their faces, he was alert, and he smiled and talked with them. To him, it was still a special day.

> *"Art Rooney led his beloved Pittsburgh Steelers for more than half a century in the NFL, but he was a man who belonged to the entire sports world. It is questionable whether any sports figure was any more universally loved and respected. His calm, selfless counsel made him a valuable contributor within the NFL. But he will be remembered by all he touched for his innate warmth, gentleness, compassion and charity."*
> — Pete Rozelle
> NFL Commissioner

Al Davis
Not such a bad guy

"He's a good football man."

During his 19-day stay at Mercy Hospital, where he was recovering from some nasty injuries suffered in an auto accident the day before Thanksgiving, in late November, 1980, Steelers president Dan Rooney received all sorts of get-well offerings.

Each day, men from local florists shops, would come into his hospital room and deposit flowers, plants and baskets of fruit.

"They'd come and go without a word," recalled Rooney. "Until one day, this guy comes in carrying a basket, and he says to me, 'Mr. Rooney, you better check this one out. It's from Al Davis.'"

There was no bomb in the basket, which might surprise some Steelers fans, but not Dan Rooney. Not then. He laughed and immediately penned a letter to the owner of the Oakland Raiders, whose reputation preceded him where he or his gifts go. "You'd have loved it," Rooney wrote to Davis, telling him of the comment from the florist deliveryman. One could picture Davis chuckling over Rooney's correspondence a few days later. He, indeed, would have loved it.

Al Davis had a well-earned reputation few would covet. He never minded being labeled a "devious genius," but there are some other names ascribed to him that he could do without.

The Raiders, under the direction of Davis, were having a great year, certainly a better year than Dan Rooney and his Steelers. A year away from their fourth Super Bowl championship effort in six years, the Steelers had slipped to what would be a 9-7 record and failed to qualify for the playoffs. The Raiders meanwhile were going to be playing the Philadelphia Eagles in Super Bowl XV in New Orleans.

For an entire year, Davis had been feuding with the National Football League — especially commissioner Pete Rozelle — to move his franchise to the Los Angeles Coliseum, which the Rams had vacated for new quarters in Anaheim.

Neal Colzie, a former defensive back for the Raiders who was now employed by the Miami Dolphins, called Davis "a back-stabber."

Colzie continued, "Anybody who treats people the way Al Davis does is going to get his."

Ken Stabler, who didn't speak to Davis during the 1979 season and was traded to the Houston Oilers soon after, said of their spat, "I'd like to bury the hatchet — right between Al Davis' shoulder blades."

Dave Casper, whom Davis dealt to the Oilers early in the 1980 season, said "You don't really know what Al really, really means when he talks."

Richie McCabe, who worked as a coach for the Raiders and had grown up with the Steelers, first as a waterboy and later as a defensive back, had no use for Davis. "He's the worst human being I've ever been around," he told friends in Pittsburgh. "You can't trust him."

Chuck Noll has never had any use for Al Davis. He believes Al Davis has a problem and that problem is Al Davis. They were both coaches on the staff of Sid Gillman with the Chargers in the early '60s.

For a change of pace, put this in your pipe: I like Al Davis. I always did. I first met him when he came into Beano Cook's office in the Pitt Field House to pick up his press box credential as a scout for the Los Angeles Chargers in 1960. I met him again in 1969, when I was covering the Miami Dolphins in the last year of the AFL. Davis was a sportswriter's dream. He always remembered your name, he liked to talk about all sports — just like Art Rooney — and he was available for interviews. He was cooperative.

He understands sportswriters. He's a soul brother, in some ways. He knew more about professional football than just about any owner still active in running his organization then except Paul Brown, and he was doing a better job with the Raiders than Brown was doing at the time with the Bengals.

Davis didn't go out of his way to seek publicity, though his critics would claim otherwise. He's just comfortable talking to people, that's all, especially sportswriters. Some other owners of those times — Bud Adams in Houston and Robert Irsay in Baltimore — would have loved to have Davis' notoriety, but none of them could come close. Those guys couldn't get picked out of a police lineup in their hometown.

Davis doesn't just know his football, but also his basketball, baseball and most other major sports. George Steinbrenner of the New York Yankees, I know from personal experience, is like that, too, and not a bad guy to be around, as long as you're not working for him. Davis religiously reads the sports pages. So how can he be a bad guy?

He was always quick to introduce his wife, Carol, and I liked that. It showed she was important to him. He called her "Caroli." When she was deathly ill in the early '80s, he recalled how Art Rooney kept in constant touch, sent her flowers often, sent her encouraging words, went to visit her. Davis said he would never forget Rooney's concern and personal kindness toward him and his wife. Carol accompanied her husband when he attended Art Rooney's funeral.

During the playoffs at the end of the 1980 season, I spotted Al Davis making his way through the stands to the press box high up in the rafters at Cleveland Stadium where Al's Raiders were about to play the Browns. His golden hair combed high on his head, with the old Fabian Forte flair, and wearing a full-length black fur coat, Oakland Al was instantly recognized by many of the fans as he made the steep climb to the press box.

The fans called out to him, "Hey, Al, why don't you move your club to Cleveland? Come here, Al, we'll treat you right!"

Or, "Hey, Al, what brings you here?"

And some booed him.

Davis didn't duck his head into the high collar of his coat. He smiled back, shouted good-naturedly to some and had a good time. He enjoyed the give-and-take with the fans. They were his kind of people.

There were few owners who would have been recognized under those circumstances, maybe Cleveland's Art Modell, Paul Brown, Art Rooney and George Halas. But none of them were able to climb those steep steps anymore.

Dan Rooney conceded that Davis was, indeed, a celebrity.

"He's a good football man, no denying him that," related Dan Rooney. "I just don't like it when he attempts to take his team out of Oakland the way he has. I can enjoy Al otherwise."

The relationship of Dan Rooney and Al Davis deteriorated by the spring of 2001 when they got into nasty name-calling over differences. Rooney called Davis "a lying creep" in May and Davis referred to Rooney and Carmen Policy of the Cleveland Browns as "two punks who cheated flagrantly on the salary cap." It's unlikely Rooney still regards Davis as "a good football man."

Al Davis and Dan Rooney discuss football issues during "better days" back in the late '70s the day before their teams met at Three Rivers Stadium.

> "It may be that the people we think to be mad are the really sane ones, and it's we ourselves who are mad."
> — Frank O'Connor

Among the many NFL officials who attended Art Rooney's funeral Mass on Saturday, August 27, at St. Peter's on the North Side were, left to right, Al Davis of the Oakland Raiders, Carl Petersen and Leonard Tose of the Philadelphia Eagles, and Carol Davis, Al's wife. In background are George Whitmer, left, of Stadium Authority, and TV analyst and oddsmaker Jimmy "The Greek" Snyder.

Art Rooney often came to the defense of Al Davis at league meetings. "He's a good football man, if he'd keep his mind on football," the Steelers' owner told me once at an NFL owners' meeting at Palm Springs, California. "I get a kick out of him, and I argue with him. But we like each other. I communicate with him, and talk to him. I'm one of the few guys in the league who does. He likes to think he's the devil, but he's not." Davis later disclosed the special nature of some of the communications he had received from Rooney. The previous October (1979), Al's wife, Carol, suffered a stroke and nearly died.

"Art Rooney sent me letters like you wouldn't believe," Davis said. "He kept my spirits up, and gave me strength and confidence that things would turn out okay. I love that man. He's one of a kind. We get along because he's not afraid of me. The rest of the establishment — don't ask me why — is afraid of me for some reason."

Carol Davis confirmed the goodness of the Steelers' owner. "He's one of the last of a vanishing breed," she said. "When you find somebody as special as him, you better treasure him. He's such a good man. He said he remembered me in his prayers."

St. Patrick's Day in Maui
Art Rooney leads parade to church

"Where's your green?"

C an you imagine what it was like to spend St. Patrick's Day in Hawaii with Art Rooney? It's one of my favorite memories from covering the Steelers and an NFL owners' meeting in Maui in mid-March, 1981. And I was getting paid to do this by *The Pittsburgh Press*.

When the Steelers owner first appeared on the morning of March 17 in the atrium lobby of the Hyatt Regency the black cloth covers were still draped over the gilded bird cages throughout the tropical garden, and the talking birds inside them were silent.

It was 6:30 a.m. when Wellington T. Mara, and his wife, Ann, met Rooney as scheduled to drive to a Catholic church near the Kaanapali Beach Resort where the annual NFL owners were holding their annual meeting. I had arranged to go along for the ride with them.

Rooney and Mara were long-time friends. Their relationship had been strengthened by the recent marriage of one of Mara's sons, Chris, to one of Rooney's granddaughters. Kathleen Rooney was the daughter of Tim Mara, who ran Yonkers Raceway. Father Robert J. Reardon of Pittsburgh performed the service.

Both Mara and Rooney were wearing green slacks. Rooney also wore a plaid sport coat that had a trace of green in it, and a blue club tie covered with green shamrocks. Rooney jokingly reprimanded me for wearing a light blue tie on this big day for the Irish. I told him I had grown up on a street where everyone else was of Italian heritage, so it was wise to keep a low profile on St. Patrick's Day.

Mara and Rooney were followed closely in a caravan to the church by Jim Murray, the general manager of the Philadelphia Eagles. That's not Jim Murray, the marvelous sports columnist for *The Los Angeles Times*. This Jim Murray owned one percent of the reigning National Football Conference champions. The Eagles earlier in the year had lost out to the Oakland Raiders for the Super Bowl title.

Murray was accompanied by his wife, Diane, and four of their five children.

Murray was always dressed for St. Patrick's Day. He favored Philadelphia's team colors of Kelly green, silver and white, and his family was similarly attired on this special occasion. New England Patriots owner Billy Sullivan was also in step, wearing the brightest green slacks. I owned a pair of bright green slacks like that for years, but I couldn't bring myself to wear them, not even on St. Patrick's Day.

In short, the NFL had its own St. Patrick's Day parade in the Hawaiian Islands.

The Maria Lanakila Church in Lahaina was a modest white-walled edifice, with fans whirling languidly overhead. It was beautiful in its simplicity. The first Catholic mission on Maui was established on the site in 1846. This was truly an island paradise in the Pacific.

There is a native saying that goes like this: "*Maui no ka oi.*" It means "Maui excels" or "Maui is the best," and nobody from the NFL would dispute that.

On this Monday in Maui, as Rooney and the Maras and Murrays were coming out of the church, they came upon a Hawaiian schoolboy wearing a Steelers' T-shirt. Rooney greeted him and patted him on the shoulder. Murray told the young man that the white-haired gentleman who was talking to him was the owner of the Pittsburgh Steelers.

"The kids eyes just lit up," said Murray.

As this party was departing the church after Mass, they came upon Ray Malavasi, the coach of the Los Angeles Rams, and his wife, Mary. The Rams' leader, whose real name was Raymondo Guiseppi Giovanni Baptiste Malavasi, called Jim Murray out of the crowd and kidded him.

"You Irish only go to church one day a year," mocked Malavasi.

Murray didn't miss a beat. He held up his balding head and beamed. "Accounts, accounts," Murray said to Malavasi. "Hey, we wear it on our sleeve today. We don't have to be on defense today. We get to carry the ball one day a year."

Murray's sons, Jimmy Joe, 10, and Brian, 9, raced by on that note, their first names emblazoned on the back of their green sweatsuits. His daughters, Karin, 21, and Amy, 12, ambled by in floor-length green outfits. The youngest Murray, 2-year-old John Paul — named after you know-who — was back home in Philadelphia with relatives.

"Ah, it's a great day for the Irish," intoned the proud father.

As Rooney was about to cross a road to get to Mara's rented automobile, he saw two smiling young girls serving as crossing guards. "Happy St. Patrick's Day to you," he said. "Where's your green? Why aren't you wearing green today?"

As he seated himself beside Ann Mara in the backseat, Rooney spotted another youngster crossing the road in the direction of the church. The boy had a backpack that was gold with a black Steelers' insignia on it.

"Hey, look at that!" directed Rooney. "Another Steeler fan! All the way out here!"

He was 5,000 miles from his North Side home and nearby Three Rivers Stadium, but the distance had been closed considerably by the native Hawaiian kids.

Rooney and our party returned in Mara's rented automobile to the hotel that served as headquarters for the weeklong meeting, where Rooney would be constantly approached by reporters for interviews. They would want to know whether the Steelers were expecting Terry Bradshaw to be back the next season, what was developing at Three Rivers Stadium where the Steelers had expressed concern about deteriorating conditions — that was back in 1981, mind you — and other league matters.

"The stadium has been good to us," said Art Rooney. "We'd still be a second-class operation without it. That's the way it was when we were practicing at South Park, dressing in the basement of a building at the Fairgrounds, and playing our games at Forbes Field and Pitt Stadium.

"But the Pirates and the Steelers are well-established teams, so you get taken for granted. We've got to get something done."

Rooney headed a six-man Steelers' delegation. His son, Dan, the team president, was there. He had recently shed his crutches from injuries suffered in a mid-November automobile accident on an icy stretch of road on the way to work. Dan was hoping to do some swimming in the hotel pool as part of his rehabilitation regimen. Chuck Noll, the team's coach, and Art Rooney Jr., the team's scouting director, and team publicists Joe Gordon and Ed Kiely came along, too.

Dan addressed the team's concerns about conditions at Three Rivers Stadium. "We've got 29 years left on a 40-year lease and we're concerned," he said. "We don't think the Pirates are holding up their end of the bargain. We don't see repairs being made. Nothing's happening. We're not improving the park for the future. We don't have the sort of scoreboards and other stuff in our stadium that you're seeing at other teams' stadiums.

"My brother Pat prefers to watch a game on TV because of the instant replays and close-ups, so we've got to compete and hold our own live audience with modern technology."

The Rooneys weren't about to abandon the city in favor of someplace where the local citizenry would do anything to accommodate their desires. "Of course not," declared Dan Rooney, "but sometimes when I see what other teams are doing to increase their revenues, I think we're just like rubes just in from out in the country." It was a feeling Dan didn't like much, understandably.

So going to Mass had been a pleasant respite for Rooney.

Rooney, Mara, Sullivan and Murray were not in Hawaii to get a tan. Mara, whose light blue eyes are hidden by a perpetual squint, once told me as we strolled the sideline at a Giants' practice at Pace University in Pleasantville, New York. "The Irish are not meant to be out in the sun. We were born to be in caves, peat bogs and other dark places." Or churches. Or saloons.

In any case, it was a St. Patrick's Day I wouldn't soon forget.

A year earlier, the NFL owners had their annual meeting at a posh California desert resort near Palm Springs — known as "the waiting room to heaven" — and I spotted The Chief dressed like one of the local residents.

He was wearing a bright blue sport jacket and silver-gray slacks, quite a contrast to his usual conservative attire at Three Rivers Stadium. He was walking with his wife, Kathleen, through the downtown shopping area. Palm Springs was a nice place to visit, Rooney reluctantly admitted, but all things considered, he said he'd rather be in "The Ward" — his old neighborhood on the North Side of Pittsburgh. Kathleen questioned his sanity. "But," Rooney conceded, without missing a beat, "this is a nice change of pace."

Pittsburgh Post-Gazette Archives

Kathleen and Art Rooney arrive at Marriott Hotel in Pasadena, California in January, 1980 for Super Bowl XIV game between Steelers and Los Angeles Rams.

Kathleen Rooney
A special woman

"She runs our house."
— **Art Rooney**

The Steelers were down, 9-0, at halftime, and assistant coach Woody Widenhofer was hollering at an official for what he felt was a bad call, and suddenly the game just didn't seem important at all. "The Chief's wife died," somebody said, and there was a hollow feeling in my stomach.

Kathleen Rooney, 78, the wife of Steelers' owner Art Rooney for 51 years, died at Allegheny General Hospital not far from her home on Pittsburgh's North Side, following a heart attack on Sunday, November 28, 1982.

Just a few days earlier, on Thanksgiving Day, Rooney had been talking about his wife's condition as he watched the Steelers practice at Three Rivers Stadium. She had just returned after a 12-day stay at Divine Providence Hospital following an accident at home in which she had fallen down stairs and broken her leg.

"I told her she's in for the winter." Rooney had related. "She didn't believe me when I first told her that. She thought she was going to be up and about in a short time. She's taking it pretty well."

Rooney's remarks were running through my head as I heard that his oldest sons, Dan and Art, Jr., had left the press box at the Kingdome in Seattle after they heard the shocking news.

Their dad had been talking Thanksgiving Day about the spills he had taken in recent years. He told me how he had to be careful when going up and down steps these days, holding on to banisters, seeking help from strangers when the sun was bright and he couldn't see the steps well. He recounted the different spills, and how the doctor had told him he was lucky he didn't lose his vision altogether on one occasion. "It was a bad fall," he said.

I remembered him talking about the outcome of a political election earlier in the month — making more sense of it than any of the TV analysts — and how he drifted into a conversation about his wife, and how she often dictated what he watched on TV.

"She runs our house," he said with a smile and a wave of his cigar. "It's a laugh a minute in our house with her."

She was the one who bought their home on the North Side, in fact, back in the mid-40s, for $5,000.

She once asked him, "Are you expecting to die soon?" He wanted to know what prompted that question. "Because you haven't bought a new suit in five years," she replied.

I remembered him telling me a story once where she asked him a question, "I read in the papers where you're a multi-millionaire," she told him, "so why don't you throw me a crumb once in a while?"

She was a lady, regal-looking, who liked fine clothes and good jewelry, and was concerned about her appearance. She liked to have her hair done on a regular schedule. She never took sports too seriously, and was usually the source for a smile whenever I'd see her or speak to her. She didn't talk a great deal to outsiders, choosing her words carefully, for the most part. She had a good sense of humor, like her husband.

"She was the wittiest woman I ever knew," said her husband. "She knew more Irish sayings than anyone. She said the Rooneys didn't know they were sick until they were in the coffin. Then one of them says, 'Hey, he must've been sick.'"

I remembered how someone was talking to her at the National Football League owners' meeting at Palm Springs, California three years earlier and, learning that she was from Pittsburgh's North Side, asked her, "Do you know the Heinz family?"

"Oh, yes," she replied, "we use their ketchup and mustard all the time."

Another time, she and Art went to dinner at a fine French restaurant late one night in Maui, where the NFL owners' meeting was held the following year. They didn't get back to their hotel until 11 o'clock. Yet they were up at 5:30 a.m. to catch an airplane to Phoenix to see some friends. From there, they were to travel to Las Vegas the next day. "She liked being on the move," explained her husband. Oh, how Art Rooney loved this woman who bore him five sons. He loved to tell stories about her. Before the Steelers held their 50 Seasons Celebration Dinner the month before, he related how she asked him for details about the dinner, but he came up blank because he wasn't involved in the planning. "I've been married to you for 51 years," she told him, "and you never know anything."

During the dinner, he paid tribute to her and had a slip of the tongue, saying she "has been a very devoted husband." Reflecting on that after her death, he said, "I introduced her when I got up to speak, and I never did that before. She stood for quite a while. I told her later, 'I didn't think you were ever going to sit down.' I just thought maybe I might not get a chance to introduce her like that again."

When it was mentioned that there had been a tremendous turnout for her funeral Mass, he said, "It was nice that so many people came to pay their respects." He always thought it was more important to go to a funeral when someone close to a friend died than it was to go to the funeral of the friend.

When they were married, he took her to New York where they spent considerable time at Belmont Racetrack, and they traveled cross-country and ended up watching the Rose Bowl in Pasadena. "She kept asking me questions about the game and I told her never to ask me any questions about football again. She never did."

When somebody asked Mrs. Rooney about her honeymoon when she returned to Pittsburgh, she said, "Oh, we had a lovely time. I think I saw every racetrack and stadium in North America."

Her husband was known to everybody in the sports world and beyond, yet she managed to remain well in the background, as his wife and the mother of his children.

Thanksgiving was always a big day at the Rooney home on the North Side. Sometimes Kathleen could count as many as 50 members of the family for dinner. But she wasn't up to it this time. "She's not happy unless the house is full," said her husband. "The more the merrier."

From Art Rooney Jr. collection

Family portrait in 1945 shows proud parents, Art and Kathleen Rooney, with their five sons, left to right, Art Jr., John, Pat, Tim and Dan.

"If I had to be somebody else, I'd like to be Art Rooney. I've learned so many lessons from him. His religiousness, his sense of fair play, his decency. I think his greatest quality is his fairness with everyone. He's such a beloved figure to people in all walks of life. I've been with him in Pittsburgh when people just walked up to him like he was their dearest friend."
— Ed McCaskey
Chairman of the Board
Chicago Bears

Art Rooney and his son, Dan, enter St. Peter's Church on North Side for funeral Mass for Kathleen Rooney on December 1, 1982. Behind them are Jim Boston, who negotiated contracts for the club, and Dan's oldest son, Art II.

Bishop Leonard
He grew up on The Hill

Saying goodbye to a good friend

This is an excerpt from the book, "Blessed Are The Poor In Spirit, For Theirs Is The Kingdom of Heaven." It's the story of the Most Reverend Vincent Martin Leonard, the first Pittsburgh-born priest to become Bishop of Pittsburgh. This was written by Father John B. McDowell.

A sermon I recall is one Bishop Leonard gave at the funeral of Art Rooney, one of the outstanding Catholics of the diocese, and outstanding citizen of the city and long time friend of the Bishop. Art was a good, solid citizen and a daily communicant. He attended St. Peter's Church, North Side most of his life and resided in the same humble home in that same area for as long as one can remember. He was an exemplary husband and father, and he gave his family every opportunity to follow his spiritual lead in life.

His national fame came from the famous Steelers. Today the family is well settled in life, living exemplary Catholic lives, and they are outstanding citizens in the Pittsburgh community.

Art Rooney was a close friend of both Father Campbell and Bishop Leonard. They frequently went out to dinner together and occasionally accompanied Art on his visits around the horse track and dog track circuit. Art was an expert on horses, not riding but judging (handicapping), and owned a few tracks, one in New York, West Palm Beach, Philadelphia and Vermont. Father Campbell, so he said, accompanied Art on these trips and, so it goes, to "bless the good ones and to give the last Sacraments to the poor ones."

Art died when he was 87 years old, on August 25, 1988. His funeral Mass was offered in St. Peter's Church, his home parish, two days later, August 27. It is interesting to note that the family always has an anniversary Mass for their dad on August 25 and treat those invited (and there are many) to lunch. Art is still a legend and much loved by Pittsburghers and many others to this day. He was truly a great man, yet quite simple, humble and kind. He was exceptionally good to people. It would take pages to record even in part, his extraordinary charitable work.

By the way, his brother Dan was very close to Art. They grew up together and participated in every sport for years. His brother was especially a good baseball player as was Art and both played in the twenties for the Wheeling Stogies. In 1925 Dan was ordained a priest, taken into the Franciscan Order, and given the name Silas.

Bishop Leonard was a few years younger than Art, but they were fast friends. The Bishop spent his time at the theater while Art and Father Campbell went to the horse track. Art's wife preferred the theater to the track, so Kathleen, it is said, went to the theater with the Bishop while Father Jim and Art gave last rites or blessings to the local quadrupeds.

At the funeral Mass, a crowd from around the country overflowed the church. Afterwards, he was buried in North Side Catholic Cemetery. Bishop Leonard presided at the Mass and gave the sermon. The Bishop spoke about Art's younger days and how Art and Dan played every sport every place they could. Finally, he told the interested crowd (largely from the sports world) how Art organized the Steelers, the famous, local professional football team. He also told stories of Art's kindness and charity to local people and institutions. The main part of the sermon about Art Rooney concerned his great devotion to the Sacred Heart of Jesus.

If one glances at a picture or statue of the Sacred Heart, the exposed heart tells the whole story. The heart is a symbol of love, and in this case, the symbol of God's love through Jesus for all people.

Using well-known quotes from the Bible, Bishop Leonard went on to tell how this love (which God, His Spirit, and His Son Jesus lavish on men and women), makes the world go around. He spoke in a special way of Art Rooney having this love from God and dispensing it through his life and actions toward others. He lived a life of great charity — great love — for God and also for his neighbors, helping them in every possible way by his gifts of time, possessions, funds and prayers. It was a moving sermon that touched the thousands of friends, Catholics and non-Catholics, present for the final salute to Art Rooney. It wasn't an easy crowd, but when the Bishop spoke there wasn't a sound in the Church.

Perhaps the sermon in front of the sports world in miniature (players, coaches and owners from around the country) tells us very much about the Bishop's touching friendship for his friend, Art, as well as his preaching style. He could speak their language.

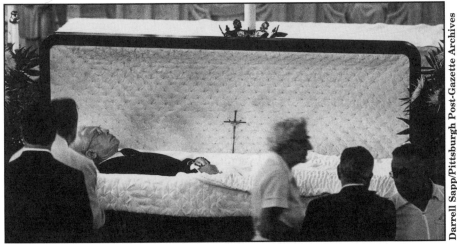

Mourners pass the casket of Steelers' owner Art Rooney in sanctuary of St. Peter's Church on North Side on August 26, 1988.

Dave Anderson
An admirer from New York

"The players were like Art Rooney."

Dave Anderson is a Pulitzer Prize-winning sports columnist for The New York Times. *He has written several popular sports books with John Madden. He was in Tampa, Florida for Super Bowl XXXV in January, 2001. We talked several times at the Media Center at the Tampa Convention Center. He remains one of the class acts in the business. His reflections follow:*

I was around Art Rooney a lot through the years, and it was like talking to your grandfather. You knew that he suffered through all those years, mostly out of loyalty to friends in the coaching business. He took care of his guys.

I met him a couple of times at Yankee Stadium. He'd just blend in with the furniture. He could get comfortable in a hurry. He enjoyed being with sportswriters.

The pro football guys today are different. They're not football guys; most of these guys today are corporate guys. I just spent some time with Wellington Mara of the Giants, and his heart is in football, too. That's why I'm happy he's here.

He was eight years old when he first got involved with the Giants. He'll talk to you forever. He has a team picture of every one of his teams that won a championship hanging in his office. There are 19 of those. There are four rows — with five pictures in three of them, and one with four.

When George Steinbrenner does some charitable act he always makes sure the word gets out through his p.r. people. I remember Art Rooney saying, "If people know about it then it's not charity."

He was a wonderful man; there was no show about him.

I heard a story about how Terry Bradshaw was talking to Art Rooney at lunch one day, and moping about his first marriage ending in divorce. Rooney told him, "Terry, you're a country boy. Why don't you find a girl who knows how to milk a cow?"

I always loved to go to Pittsburgh. People would ask me why. And I'd say, "There's great people in Pittsburgh and Art Rooney is the best of them all." I loved to go to Pittsburgh because the players were like Art Rooney.

To me, the Steelers were great. They were never a spoiled team. They were a team that had continued success, but it didn't change them. Chuck Noll was a great coach, but he was useless for us writers. We'd crowd around him after a game, but I never bothered asking him any questions. You didn't get anything. I'd go to Joe Greene. He'd give you a column. Art Rooney was always a good column.

118

I remember Art Rooney's funeral. It was the only out-of-town funeral outside the family that I've ever gone to since I've been a sportswriter. He was a special person; that's why I went. There were a lot of priests and Irish guys there. It was a great scene, like something out of a movie.

Pat and Dan Rooney lead family members from St. Peter's Church on North Side following funeral Mass in honor of Art Rooney on August 27, 1988.

John Kaplan/Pittsburgh Post-Gazette Archives

Jim O'Brien

Tom Jackson
Remembers Rooney's ghost

"He's the man."

Former Denver Broncos linebacker Tom Jackson has been an NFL analyst on TV for years. He remembers paying a visit to Art Rooney's office at Three Rivers Stadium prior to a contest there. Art Rooney had died five years earlier, but his office was preserved as a library.

He was a great man, from all that I've heard. He had the ultimate, and I mean ultimate, respect of every player who passed through Pittsburgh, and those who heard about him on other teams throughout the league. The one thing I heard about him over and over was how well he treated his players. There were all kinds of memorabilia in his office, but most of all there were pictures of former players and NFL associates. There were helmets and pictures. The Rooneys were one of the pioneer families in league history. I remember if you looked at the glass pane that fronted the office in a certain way you could see his image. It was a reflection of an oil portrait of Mr. Rooney that was on a nearby wall. You had to stand in a certain spot to see it. It was like a ghost. We used that on our pre-game show. He was one of those guys that every player who played for him said, "If there's ever a guy you want to play for he's the man."

Donald J. Stetzer/Pittsburgh Press photo in PG Archives

Art Rooney shows Dwight White his gallery of Steelers' greats when White announced his retirement on January 28, 1981 after ten seasons as a defensive end for Pittsburgh's NFL entry.

Johnny "Blood" McNally makes his old boss laugh.

Robert J. Pavuchak

"*I think there's something about the Irish experience — that we had to have a sense of humor or die. That's what kept us going — a sense of absurdity, rather than humor. And it did help because sometimes you'd get desperate. And I developed this habit of saying to myself, 'Oh, well,' I might be in the midst of some misery, and I'd say to myself, 'Well, someday you'll think it's funny.' And the other part of my head will say, 'No you won't, you'll never think this is funny. This is the most miserable experience you've ever had.' But later on you look back and you say, 'That was funny, that was absurd.'*"
— Frank McCourt,
Pulitzer Prize-winning author
Angela's Ashes and *'Tis*
At Bethel Park High School, Oct. 5, 1999

Dan Rooney
At Super Bowl XXX

"We're here for the game."

Steelers president Dan Rooney appeared at a press conference in late January, 1996 in Tempe, Arizona prior to the Steelers' game with the Dallas Cowboys in Super Bowl XXX. I was invited by the Steelers to fly to Phoenix on one of their charter airplanes to attend the event and it was great to be there, even though the Steelers came up short in a game they could easily have won. Here are Dan Rooney's remarks:

It's been written that I'm part of the old guard. I consider myself part of the people that think the tradition of the National Football League is very important. I think that includes everyone. There are great new owners in the league. They contribute someone like (Denver's) Pat Bowlen. He goes all-out and participates on committees. He does a fine job. A guy like (Carolina's) Jerry Richardson who just comes in for an expansion team. He's doing quite a bit. Then, of course, you have people like (New York Giants') Wellington Mara who really follows the past and knows the history of the league. I think that our position is that the National Football League really is something that is important.

It's great for us to be back in the Super Bowl regardless of anything else. I have to say that I'm really very, very thrilled about being here. There have been a lot of things written, even the slogan "one for the thumb," which is a problem. This team is its own team. That is a thrill for me to see these young people come of age. It's really their Super Bowl. They're the ones that are doing it. As Neil O'Donnell said, he's looking for one for the ring finger.

We're lucky to have a coach like Bill Cowher. If you will remember back then (when he was hired), everybody talked to us about how young he was. "Do you think he's ready for it? Sure, he's a good coach, but do you think he's ready for it?" I have to say that every time I would talk to Bill, you thought of his age. His enthusiasm, his ability to command a situation and be a leader of people, just came through. I felt here is a guy who can do this job. That leadership and that enthusiasm has come through. He's really shown great leadership for our team.

I think there are differences between the Dallas Cowboys and the Pittsburgh Steelers. I think our approach is a lot different off the field. On the field I think we're similar in that we want the best players. We feel the approach is to get players to come up through your ranks, not go after the big free agent types. Go after people that you are going to bring in and they are going to help you and that everybody is a part of the organization. And I think Dallas does that. Off the field, I think we're totally different. I think their approach is the big sell, the big America's Team, and things like that. The football end of it, which is the important thing, and I think that's important to remember. We're here for the game. We're not here for Nike. We're not here for Pepsi. We're not here for Coke. We're here for the game. I think we're very similar in that regard.

I hated to see Art Modell move his team from Cleveland to Baltimore. I personally think that teams have to stay where they are under most circumstances. I think there are circumstances that could prevail that a team would, should move. They are considerably less than what is happening now. Cleveland is a great football town. It's one of the traditional places like Pittsburgh. Pro football started in Pittsburgh, we say. But it really has developed itself in the nature that we know in the Ohio, western Pennsylvania area. I really hate to see Cleveland without a team. I think the Steeler organization's personality was set by my father. It goes back to the beginning. The thing always meant so much to him. We're trying. I don't think any of us can do it near as well as he did. It is people that mean something. The people in our organization are meaningful. Every player is important. Every coach is important. Our staff, our fans, you have to consider that. I think that if there is a uniqueness, it's people that are meaningful to us. To get very emotional, I'd say it's love. It's the love that exists among us for everybody. I think that's what counts and I think it came from him and I think we're trying to carry it on. We want to do it right.

The Super Bowl has changed since we were last in it. It has gotten a lot bigger. There's more hype. To be quite honest with you, it is more (Cowboys' owner) Jerry Jones. It's more selling. It's more NFL Properties buying into with Jerry on some of these things. I really believe the game is the important thing. That should be our principle purpose here, to play a great football game and do everything we can to make that the best it can be. Everything else should be secondary. It's where we are. It's the biggest sporting event in the world.

Mike Fabus/Pittsburgh Steelers

Steelers President Dan Rooney, left, has been grooming his son, Art II, to succeed him as the club's top executive.

Elbie Nickel
A bricklayer from Ohio

"Art was like a father to me."

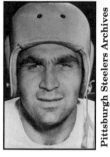

I can still see him standing in the door of his home in Chillicothe, Ohio, and that was two years ago as I am writing this. The face and smile were still familiar. I had last seen him in person 17 years earlier at the Steelers' 50 Seasons Celebration in Pittsburgh, back in 1982. He was one of four players from the 1950s still regarded as one of the team's greatest players.

His name was Elbie Nickel and it still had a magic ring to it. His eyebrows were as dark and bushy as ever, like caterpillars — the sports cartoonists loved those eyebrows — but his dark hair was streaked with more gray and silver now.

He had been a teammate of Jack Butler, Ernie Stautner and Pat Brady, the other all-timers from that period. I had first seen that face on a bubble gum card, one of the last of the black and white cards in my collection, and later on full color cards. I was seven or eight years old and living in a row house in Hazelwood, about four or five miles from Forbes Field where the Steelers played in those days, when I first began collecting such cards.

Elbie Nickel went from wearing a leather helmet to a plastic helmet in that evolution of bubble gum cards. He was an outstanding end for the Steelers for 11 seasons, from 1947 to 1957, back when receivers were simply called ends. He was a Steeler in the days of leather helmets, no facemasks and no TV.

He was a 15th round draft choice out of the University of Cincinnati in 1947, when there were 30 rounds in the college draft and it was all done in one day. Nickel showed me some written information during my visit that showed that the Steelers initially selected Bobby Layne of Texas on the first round of the same 1947 draft, but dealt him to the Chicago Bears before the draft was completed. I never knew that. So add Layne to the list of great quarterbacks who got away from the Steelers, even if they did get him back late in his playing career and he put in some productive years with the Black & Gold. The Steelers were still playing a single-wing offense in 1947; that's why they let Layne go. He said he didn't want to play for the Steelers.

Going into the 2001 season, Nickel still ranked in the top five among all-time Steelers receivers with 329 receptions to his credit, only seven less than Lynn Swann and 23 more than Franco Harris. That gives you some idea of how good this guy was. He played in the Pro Bowl three times.

He topped the Steelers in passes caught in 1952 with 55 and 1953 with 62 when the regular season consisted of 12 games. There were 14 games in a season from 1961 till 1977 and 16 games in a season since 1978. All-time leader John Stallworth had 537 catches in 14 seasons, most of them 16-game seasons. When Nickel retired after the 1957 season, he held the Steelers' team records for reception yards (5,133), touchdowns on receptions in a season (nine) and touchdown passes caught in a career (37), and he's still in the top five in the latter category. So Nickel's name remains in the Steelers' record books.

"I've been in this same house since 1949."

I had seen the road signs for Chillicothe for five years (1995-1999) when my younger daughter Rebecca O'Brien was a student at Ohio University in Athens. I called Elbie Nickel and arranged for a visit to coincide with one of my visits to see Rebecca. I drove to his home in Chillicothe, about 45 miles south of Columbus on February 21, 1999, out where the farm fields are so flat. I had breakfast nearby at Katie's Kountry Kooking, and drove by the Lucky Star Motel. I passed a wild boar hunting ranch, fields with bales of hay here and there, junkyards and roadside churches in Ross County.

I had mixed emotions as I toured his one-story home on McKell Street ("That was also the name of the high school I went to in Kentucky," said Nickel). It bothered me that he lived there alone. His kids were long gone and his wife of 43 years, Roberta, had died nearly eleven years earlier. His son, Joe, 51 at the time of my visit, had five children of his own, and his daughter, Susan, 48, had three children. Joe lived in Cincinnati, and Susan lived in Hudson, near Cleveland. They visited on occasion, their father told me. "I've been in this same house since 1949," he said. "My dad built this house for me and I'm comfortable here. My dad, his name was Richard, was in the construction business. He had been a carpenter. My brother, Eugene, was a carpenter, too, so they made me a bricklayer."

He was proud to have a union card as a bricklayer. In an article by Gay Talese of the *New York Times*, who went on to become a famous book author, Nickel said, "I'll stick to brick-laying. When a brick-layer returns home at night, he doesn't bring any bricks with him." In the summers of his college days, Nickel delivered 25-pound blocks of ice to homes, carrying them on his shoulders in the same way as legendary running back Harold "Red" Grange once did when he gained the nickname of "The Wheaton Ice-Man."

> *"Memory is a funny thing. Recollections slip in and out and around in time, leaving plenty of room to weave, backtrack and drift and glide. In my life I found that memories of the spirit linger and sweeten long after memories of the brain have faded."*
> — Willie Morris
> "My Dog Skip"

"He's the type of fellow coaches dream about."

In 1988, Nickel had suffered two great losses in consecutive months. In August of that year, his dear friend and former boss, Arthur J. Rooney, Sr., passed away, and in September Nickel's wife, Roberta, died as well.

Nickel was one of Rooney's all-time favorite football players. I came across a framed article in Nickel's gameroom in which Rooney was quoted as saying of Nickel: "Elbie is the best all-around end in the league. He's a 60-minute man, a great offensive and defensive player. He's the type of fellow coaches dream about. I wouldn't trade him for any end in football."

A friend of mine, Bill Priatko, who played one season (1957) with Nickel with the Steelers, said, "He was a real professional. It was his final season with the Steelers and he was an established player. He went about his work quietly, but he was a determined competitor. He wanted to win. He was a likable guy."

As I walked through his home, Nickel apologized for its appearance. "I don't keep it up as well as my wife did," he said with a shrug. I thought it looked pin-neat and had been impressed with its polished appearance.

I work at home alone these days and I don't like it. Rebecca and her sister, Sarah, have been gone the past two or three years, and my wife, Kathie, works as a social worker in the oncology department at Allegheny General Hospital during the day. Writing is supposed to be a lonely profession, but I liked it better when my family filled the home.

"Yeah, I get lonely now and then," admitted Nickel, "but I'm OK. You wake up at night when you have a bad dream and you wish someone were here. I've been doing pretty well. It's something you have to live with. My wife and the kids had a lot of great times here together. Sometimes something will happen that reminds me of those days."

Another thing that struck me when I was in the Nickel home was finding a photograph on the wall of his game room in which I was pictured at a Curbstone Coaches Luncheon in the fall of 1982. The late Bob Prince and I were co-emcees of a monthly sports luncheon series co-sponsored by The Pittsburgh Brewing Company and *The Pittsburgh Press*. When I returned home to Pittsburgh in 1979, I got the folks who produced Iron City beer to bring back the luncheon series that I enjoyed so much during my student days at the University of Pittsburgh in the early '60s. Back then it was held on a weekly basis at the Roosevelt Hotel, where the Steelers' offices were located. I couldn't believe there had been no such luncheons during the '70s when Pittsburgh had the best decade of sports successes in the city's history. So we revived it and the luncheon series is still going strong.

Dan McCann, who was in charge of sales at Iron City and moonlighted as the football coach at Duquesne University, coordinated the luncheon and had gotten handsome plaques to present to players from the '50s who were honored on the Steelers' all-time team.

Curbstone Coaches pay tribute to the senior members of Steelers' 50th Anniversary All-Time team, as sportswriter/emcee Jim O'Brien and Pittsburgh Brewing Company executive Dan McCann are bookends for Jack Butler, Art Rooney, Elbie Nickel and Pat Brady. Ernie Stautner was unable to attend this 1982 season affair.

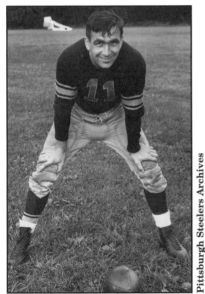

ELBIE NICKEL

Elbie Nickel relaxes in his family room at his home in Chillicothe, Ohio on February 21, 1999. The walls were covered with photos and plaques from his playing days at University of Cincinnati and with the Steelers (1947-1957).

So I was in a photo, from left to right, with Jack Butler, Art Rooney, Elbie Nickel, Pat Brady and McCann. And it was on the wall in Nickel's game room that was a veritable Hall of Fame for a former Steelers' star. It felt strange to know I was on Nickel's wall, in the home of a boyhood hero, all the way out in Chillicothe, Ohio.

"You never knew when Art was winning or losing."

Seeing Art Rooney in the photo prompted Nickel to talk about their special relationship. "Art was like a father to me," he said. "He was a super person. He took me to the Kentucky Derby for thirty years. I think I started going with him in 1948 or 1949. They used to drive a lot and they'd come through Chillicothe and pick me up on their way to Louisville. That's a couple of hundred miles from here. Joe Tucker, Ed Kiely, Jack Sell and sometimes Bob Drum would be with Art. He loved the sports announcers and the sportswriters. And they loved him.

"You never knew when Art was winning or losing. He could win a bundle or lose a bundle and he'd be the same mild guy. You'd never hear him root for a horse when it's running, the way most people do. He seemed to like everybody. I didn't know of a player who disliked him. Because of him, I still like to go to the racetrack, like Beulah Park in Columbus or River Downs in Cincinnati, but I don't get there like I used to. I learned that from Art Rooney. He made a horseplayer out of me. He even named one of his racehorses after me. Here, I have a photo of me with the horse and Mr. Rooney. It was a mare and it won some races out here in Ohio and in West Virginia. It won and paid $32 at Beulah Park. It paid $92 when it won at Waterford Racetrack in this picture. It broke its maiden there," said Nickel.

Elbie Nickel showed me the photos from his high school, college and pro days. He had some video tapes — in black and white — with game film from his playing days with the Steelers which he shared with me, as well as game programs from that period. It was a trip down memory lane. It was a handsomely paneled room, a warm room, and Nickel enjoyed reminiscing.

He gave me two copies of his bubble gum card from the Topps Football Archives, reprints of the Ultimate 1957 series. I was 15 that year and had just become the sports editor of the local weekly, the *Hazelwood Envoy*, so I recognized it right away. Those cards were my main connection with the Steelers or sports at large in those days. It listed him as a 6-foot-1-inch, 205-pound receiver. Because we didn't get to see sports stars like fans do today — with the 24-hour-a-day all-sports cable outlets and radio stations — there was something almost mystical about them.

Nickel had retired at age 60 from a long-time involvement with the J.H. Butt Construction Company. "I always had a job," noted Nickel.

"It makes you appreciate football more, and I had something to fall back on. I knew I couldn't play football the rest of my life. My first job was working for my father who had a business of his own, and eventually teamed up with Mr. Butt. I worked with him during the off-season and enjoyed it. Being a football player wasn't too important then. We didn't get much publicity. But it helped me to get started in life."

His starting salary with the Steelers was $5,000 a season, and he recalled that Rooney gave him a $500 bonus at the end of the first campaign. "They must've made a little money that year," said Nickel.

There were enough reminders of those days surrounding us that it didn't require much prompting to get Nickel to talk about his fondest memories. He said being named to the Steelers' All-Time Team, considering the club's successful run in the '70s, was the highlight of his sports career.

"I can remember the time (in 1954) we beat the Cleveland Browns, 55-27, at Forbes Field in a Saturday night game," he said, showing me the game ball he'd been given afterward. "And another game (1952) in which we beat the New York Giants, 63-7, at Forbes Field.

"The Giants' coach, Steve Owen, had a book come out a few weeks before about this special 'umbrella' defense he had concocted. Our game was not a good endorsement for the wisdom of his book."

The Steelers could roll up scores like that, yet they finished 5-7 in 1952 and 1954. They had only two winning seasons in Nickel's 11 years.

In his rookie season of 1947, the Steelers, under Jock Sutherland, went 8-4 but lost an Eastern Division playoff to the Philadelphia Eagles. That was as close as the Steelers ever came to winning a conference crown until 1972. Sutherland died after that 1947 season, and Nickel played the next four years under one of Sutherland's disciples from his days at Pitt, John Michelosen.

"We were the last team in the NFL to play the single-wing, and I was the blocking end," noted Nickel. "So I was what was later called a tight end. I didn't have the speed these guys have today. The first three years I was there, I also had to play defense."

In the single-wing, the quarterback is a blocking back. Michelosen had played that position at Pitt. The quarterback in the single-wing scheme lines up directly behind a guard or tackle on one side or the other. The side on which he lines up is called the strong side, and is usually the end to which a sweep is run. There are lots of blockers out front in such a sweep. The tailback takes a direct snap from the center and stands back the way quarterbacks do now in the so-called "shotgun" formation. I told Nickel that Art Rooney used to tell me that he thought Sutherland was a great coach, and that the Steelers would have been successful earlier if Sutherland had lived longer.

"That single-wing was getting pretty old," said Nickel. "We couldn't draft anybody who played it because the colleges were all playing the T-formation. It was about over the hill. His defense was pretty standard stuff. He'd have been behind in that, too."

"Sutherland was the most demanding coach."

Elbie Nickel played for five different coaches in his stay with the Steelers. Michelosen succeeded Sutherland. Then came Joe Bach, Walt Kiesling and Buddy Parker. "We didn't get the coaching like you do today," said Nickel. "Buddy Parker had some pretty good ideas. I was over the hill myself by the time Parker came. I was with him only one year. He was a good modern day coach. He was a little rowdy once in a while, but he was all business when it came to football.

"Sutherland was the most demanding. He was a good coach, but hard to play for because he demanded so much out of you. He believed in hard work. We had two workouts a day. One went three hours in the morning, and then we went four hours in the afternoon. The afternoon session was in pads. There was lots of contact. With Michelosen, it was more of the same.

"I was pretty lucky. I sprained my ankle once, and I was kicked in the back once, but that was about it. And I don't have any old football injuries plaguing me today. I'm grateful for that.

"I enjoyed my stay there. It was a good town. We didn't win too much. One year (1952) we scored 300 points (to 273 for the opposition) and we won only five of 12 games. We were always a little short someplace. We had Jim Finks, Lynn Chandnois, Fran Rogel and Ray Mathews; we had as good a backfield as anybody. Val Jansante was a fine end. But we were thin on the line, and Jack Butler was our only good defensive back. My best friend, Bill McPeak, was a good defensive end. He was my roommate for eight years. He's passed away, too.

"Finks was a smart quarterback. He didn't have much to work with. We had a couple of 190 and 195 pound guards. He took a beating. Finks, McPeak, Stautner, (Dale) Dodril and Butler were great players, but got very little credit for what they did for the Steelers. We had some good players, but we didn't have much depth."

Butler says Nickel was a great receiver. At 30, Nickel caught 62 passes to rank second to Pete Pihos of the Eagles who caught 63. Pihos is in the Pro Football Hall of Fame. Harlon Hill of the Chicago Bears, Hugh "Bones" Taylor of the Washington Redkins and Elroy "Crazy Legs" Hirsch of the Los Angeles Rams were other outstanding receivers in those days. "Some of the catches Taylor made," noted Nickel, "should have counted for two."

Nickel has always been in good company. Since I visited his home, I have been to the Athletic Hall of Fame at the University of Cincinnati, and there was a plaque acknowledging Nickel's UC career, and he was honored there with Oscar Robertson, Jack Twyman, Miller Huggins, Sid Gillman and Danny Rains of Hopewell.

As far as the money went, Nickel said, "I made as much as $10,000 the last few years. Hey, you couldn't make that much money working a regular job in a year. We were rich in other ways. Art Rooney was one of the finest men you'll ever meet, and there wasn't a better boss to be had."

Among those in attendance at Steelers' training camp at St. Bonaventure University in mid-'40s were, left to right, Ernie Stautner, Elbie Nickel, business manager Fran Fogarty and Jack Butler. All three players were Pro Bowl performers and would be on Steelers' 50th anniversary team.

Elbie Nickel is flanked by two of his Steelers teammates, John "Bull" Schweder, left, a guard from University of Pennsylvania, and Bill McPeak, an end from New Castle and the University of Pittsburgh, in mid-'50s.

CHUCK CHERUNDOLO

Nickel's teammates George Tarasovic and Fran Rogel at team's training camp at St. Bonaventure University in Olean, New York

"He was one of the boys."

He was happy for Rooney when the Steelers started winning big in the '70s, and had a six-year tear when they won the Super Bowl four times. "I took a lot of pride in that, being an old Steeler," said Nickel. "I got a lot of publicity around here during that period because I had played for Art Rooney and the Steelers.

"Art Rooney was such a good old guy. He was one of the boys. He'd go out and have a drink with us in his heyday. I've never seen the man get mad. He would come out and walk around the practice field. He never bothered the coaches. He'd tell us if he had a horse running that had a chance to win. I remembered those days fondly, and still have a warm feeling for Rooney and his Steelers. He was such a kind man. We'd go down to Louisville for the Derby and there'd be bums in the streets. We'd walk by them and Art would stop and talk to them. They'd tell him a bad luck story and he'd give them money.

"He never talked about his ballplayers, but some of them touched him up pretty good, too. Some of those guys would be broke in the summer and he'd lend money to them. He sent postcards to me from everywhere in the world. He'd ask about my wife and kids.

"He was a very religious man. No matter where we'd stay he'd get up, and he'd get Kiely up, and they'd go to Mass at 6 a.m. on the road.

"I remember Johnny Unitas, but that's gotten to be an old story. We had Finks, and he was going to be the starting quarterback. We had Marchibroda and we had Vic Eaton. Eaton could punt the ball and play defensive back if need be. All Unitas could do was throw the ball. He was kinda slow, as I remember. They never gave him a chance to show what he could do. We took him in the ninth round, and I don't remember him getting into an exhibition game. As far as practice goes, I don't remember him too well.

"We had another player who could have been great. That was Lowell Perry, who was a receiver from Michigan. He came to us in 1956. He hurt his leg running a reverse play against the Giants. Roosevelt Grier and Emlen Tunnel hit him at the same time. That was the end of his career. He could have been a terrific ballplayer.

"So, of course, I've always rooted for the Steelers. When they were winning all those Super Bowls it was great. People made a fuss about me. They knew that I had played with the Steelers. This is a Browns' town, but they got behind the Steelers in the Super Bowl because I'd been on the ballteam.

"I liked Bradshaw as a quarterback, and Swann and Stallworth as receivers. Defensively, I liked Lambert and Blount. I used to go down to Cincinnati when the Steelers played there. I still root for them. I used to go to Wilmington and see the Bengals at their training camp. That was about 60 miles from here. I knew Paul Brown real well, and I'd talk to him when I was there. Now, he's gone, too."

Brown coached Nickel in the Pro Bowl. "He was a terrific blocker," Brown once said of Nickel. "He really did a job for us in the

Pro Bowl." In his last game as a Steeler at Forbes Field, Nickel nabbed TD passes of 23 and 47 yards. "I don't know why he's quitting," said McPeak. "Who's better?"

Finks called him "the most under-rated end in pro football."

Chuck Cherundolo, a former star at Penn State and with the Steelers, said, "I've watched a lot of football players in my day, but what a guy this Nickel is. He's 100 per cent all the way — a great fellow on and off the field. He's a player's player."

I saw a photo of Nickel in a college baseball uniform. He also played basketball. "The Cincinnati Reds wanted to sign me and send me to Columbia, South Carolina," he recalled. "That was their Class D team. I was 21 at the time. The Reds wanted to pay me $90 a month. I was married and that wouldn't do very much, so I stuck with football. I didn't sign with the Reds. Besides, I knew I couldn't hit big league curves."

I also learned that Nickel's pro career was delayed by a 33-month stint in the military service between his junior and senior years at the University of Cincinnati. He landed on the Normandy beaches with the infantry (engineering division) and collected a chest-full of medals and battle ribbons, according to articles I read about him. There were stories saying Nickel was awarded the Purple Heart, but Nickel pointed out that this was not true.

"I wasn't in the D-Day invasion," Nickel wanted me to be sure to know. "We came in seven or eight days later when it was all cleaned up. I'm proud that I served my country, but I wasn't any kind of hero."

Colorado's Byron "Whizzer" White, the Steelers' No. 1 draft choice in 1937, was the most decorated player in the history of college football. He won the Theodore Roosevelt Award, the NCAA's top award, and the Gold Medal, the top award of the National Football Foundation and Hall of Fame. He was Phi Beta Kappa as a junior, first in his class at Colorado, a Rhodes Scholar and was No. 1 in his class at Yale Law School. He won two Bronze Stars in Pacific combat, and in 1962 at the age of 45 he became the youngest man to be appointed to the U.S. Supreme Court. On the field, he was a consensus All-America, second in the Heisman voting, won four NCAA statistical titles in 1937 (his all-purpose yards per game record stood intact until Oklahoma State's Barry Sanders came along in 1988) and twice was National Football League rushing champion.
— From NCAA Football's Finest

Jerry Izenberg
Always liked Pittsburgh

"It was only right that decency wins once in a while."

Jerry Izenberg is a sports columnist for The Newark Star-Ledger, *a member of the selection committee for the Pro Football Hall of Fame, one of the eight writers who has attended every Super Bowl game, and a proud alumnus of* Pittsburgh Weekly Sports.

This guy, to me, was real. This was a guy who loved the competition. That's why he was in it. He was close to Tim Mara, I know, and Tim passed a lot on to his son, Wellington, and they've been great friends, too. He gave Wellington the knowledge to be one of Art's think-alike friends.

Every time there was a matter to be voted on by the NFL owners, I will bet you that if the issue was what's good for the league and not necessarily the Steelers, Art would vote for it. That's not true of most owners today.

There's a great story involving Rocky Bleier that I've been told over and over. It's still a good story. It tells you a lot about Art Rooney and the regard the players had for him. Mr. Rooney wasn't well and he was in the hospital. Bleier and four or five other Steelers went to the hospital and sang Christmas carols. Try that with Jerry Jones of the Cowboys or David Snyder of the Redskins. That wouldn't happen with them.

Art Rooney was the soul and guts of the Pittsburgh franchise and he changed little over the years. It was difficult to explain him because we were used to a very different type of owner around most pro football teams. This is a man who, for example, when Joe Greene did not make the Pro Bowl one year and thereby lost a $5,000 bonus clause in his contract, simply sent him the money anyway with a short note saying, "In our view, you fulfilled the requirements."

To the end, he was still the same guy. His social friends were Pittsburgh people, real Pittsburgh people. He was still enmeshed in a frenetic love affair with the town and his relationship with his players was clearly the most personal in the NFL. He often invited players to his home for dinner.

He had set routines and he didn't deviate from them, no matter how special the game. He went to Mass in the morning. If the Steelers were playing at home, an old friend (Richie Easton) usually drove him to Three Rivers Stadium. Rooney visited the locker room, stopped by the press box briefly, talked to visitors who were friends rather than reporters, then would retreat to his own private box to watch the proceedings. His pals and priests usually filled his box. It was not so much the residue of habit as it was a labor of pure enjoyment. I rooted for the Rooneys. It was only right that decency wins once in a while and that old loyalties are not square and that Art Rooney, at long last, had a wonderful team.

I told his son, Danny, the other day about my regard for his dad and the people in Pittsburgh. There was something appealing to me about the Steelers owner and the team's fans. They were my father. When the Steelers were on top it was a great experience to be around that pro football team in their town. The Pittsburgh fans were the greatest in the country. You had Franco's Italian Army and Gerella's Gorillas, Myron Cope and the Terrible Towel. You had the whole milieu and it became a great story. Then I lost interest because the whole town became sore winners. As the fans changed, so did the Steelers.

When the Steelers were going strong, though, I loved going up there. Part of it was influenced by two friends of mine. You and Beano Cook introduced me to Pittsburgh. You introduced me to people like Joey Diven, a friend of Billy Conn's who was called "The World's Greatest Streetfighter," and a guy who sold newspapers in Oakland named "Yutzy" Pascarelli, I think. Diven was a Notre Dame fan and Yutzy was a Pitt man and they'd meet at midfield following a Pitt-Notre Dame game at Pitt Stadium and shake hands. I love stuff like that. I kept being drawn to Pittsburgh. You introduced me to an insurance salesman named "Maniac" McDonough, who took pride in crashing the gate for every sports event in the city. The Clemente story was so poignant. After I went to Puerto Rico to do a documentary on Clemente, I was struck by the love the people had for him. He was so much more than a sports figure. He was a man of his people, of his country. He was popular in Pittsburgh, too. I remember a little girl in a grammar school doing a drawing of him, with the line that "Pittsburgh will always love him" written under the drawing. I knew that a lot of racists in Pittsburgh hated him. But if you die and you die doing something good that reinstates you in the pantheon of Pittsburgh. I knew Dick Groat in his pre-baseball days, when he was a great basketball player at Duke.

Clemente and Groat were big guys in Pittsburgh, but they were never looked at in the same way as Art Rooney. He was Pittsburgh. Pittsburgh was Newark with steel mills. I could relate to Pittsburgh. Everybody who grew up in an honest blue-collar neighborhood could understand Pittsburgh. It provided a mosaic of the people there, a common polyglot.

During the great drought, when the Steelers were a mediocre team, I was drawn to Pittsburgh because the fans I met in Pittsburgh, as I said, were my father. He worked seven days a week for seven years in one stretch. He had certain values and we knew what they were. My dad was a fourth grade dropout so he didn't follow any college teams. He was a fan of the Giants. They were our team. The Maras and Rooneys were patriots of the league. They have always represented the best that the NFL had to offer.

Ernie Stautner
Defensive lineman (1950-1963)
Elected to Hall of Fame (1969)

"The one thing I wanted most in my entire career was to be a winner. I wanted to play on a championship team. If the Steelers had come to me and said I was traded to a contender, I would have been out of town so fast they would have never seen my tracks. I never went to a coach and asked to be traded, though. That's one thing I never would have done. I respected Art Rooney too much to do anything like that. Art was probably the finest, kindest man I'd ever met. I feel privileged I was able to play for him all those years. I would have felt I was slapping Art in the face to request a trade out of Pittsburgh. So I kept my mouth shut."

Pro Football Hall of Fame

Ernie Stautner played in Pro Bowl in nine of his 14 seasons as a defensive tackle.

Arnold Palmer
A friend of the Steelers

"He's proud of it."
— Doc Giffin

Arnold Palmer was golf's greatest ambassador for years, but somebody who always remembered his roots. He liked staying close to home in Latrobe and he has been a life-long fan of the Steelers and the Pirates. He was an admirer of Art Rooney and hosted the Steelers and other area athletes at fund-raising golf events frequently at his Latrobe Country Club.

At his club, Palmer proudly displayed a unique glass plaque — the Arthur J. Rooney Award — that he was presented by the Steelers' owner himself at a Catholic Youth Association (CYA) dinner at the William Penn Hotel in 1977. "It has a light in it and it's one of the more unique trophies or awards in Arnie's collection," pointed out Doc Giffin, Palmer's long-time assistant. "He's proud of it."

Asked why it was displayed in such a prominent manner when he won so many internationally-renowned awards and plaques, Palmer said, "I was very pleased to receive that Art Rooney Award one year. Art Rooney was a very philanthropic person. He was very supportive of many charitable causes and, of course, was recognized for that with the establishment of the Arthur J. Rooney Award by the CYA of Pittsburgh. He received many accolades from his many friends in Pittsburgh for the work he did for charity and for the City of Pittsburgh through his Pittsburgh Steelers."

I covered a Press Old Newsboys Celebrity Golf Tournament at the Latrobe Country Club in early June, 1979 where they raised over $50,000 for the benefit of Children's Hospital.

Ex-Steeler Andy Russell, the No. 1 Press Old Newsboy, and Palmer hosted the scramble golf competition, and Palmer conducted a golf clinic for all in attendance. Russell has continued to conduct an annual celebrity golf tournament on his own, and has teamed up with Palmer on other occasions. It's a winning parlay.

"Watching Palmer hitting the ball so cleanly during the clinic," remarked Russell later on, "is an exercise in ego-reduction."

Among the celebrity participants were Steelers coach Chuck Noll and several of his players, past and present, such as Ray Mansfield, Jack Ham, John Banaszak, Mike Webster, Rocky Bleier and Cliff Stoudt, former Pirates Steve Blass and Dave Giusti, Penguins Pete Mahovolich and Gregg Sheppard, Pitt football coach Jackie Sherrill.

Sportscasters Bob Prince, Nellie King and Sam Nover competed, along with Ken Anderson and Chris Bahr of the Cincinnati Bengals, former Miami Dolphins Nick Buoniconti and Paul Warfield, former Denver Bronco Floyd Little, Jim Hart of the Cardinals and the most intriguing participant of all, 7-2 Artis Gilmore of the NBA's Chicago Bulls. Jim Dugan of Xerox Corporation coordinated the activity. So many of these celebrities have since been inducted into one Hall of Fame or another.

Mansfield emceed the dinner that followed and roasted just about everybody in attendance. Mansfield couldn't help himself. "The Ol' Ranger" was a great kidder.

Talking about Webster, his former teammate and successor at the center position with the Steelers, Mansfield cracked, "Webster missed a putt today and knocked down a tree doing it.

"These greens are something here," Mansfield followed up. "We had to put a rope around the waist of one of our guys to make sure he wouldn't fall off while he was putting."

Mansfield even made fun of Noll. "That's when it's great to be retired," he said, turning toward his buddy Russell. "If I talked about Coach Noll like this three years ago when I was playing for him, he'd have me out snapping the ball for field goals until dark."

Turning to Banaszak, he told the gathering, "You know those three golf balls Arnie gives you as a gift when you arrive? John ate them. He thought they were marshmallows."

Mansfield's spoofs spurred Russell to recall the pre-Super Bowl days of the Steelers. "Our offense was so bad in those days," said Russell, "that when our defense came off the field, we'd tell the guys coming on, 'Try to hold them now.' Mansfield was our center, but one game — and this is a fact — he led our team in individual tackles with six. And he missed five."

Noll noted how he saw Palmer practicing chip shots in the morning, getting himself ready for the U.S. Open that was coming up the following week at the Inverness Country Club in Toledo. Noll would later tell his Steelers that story to make a teaching point with them. "Most players want to practice doing what they do best," said Noll, "but you should work at your weaknesses."

It was great just to be around a performer of the stature of Palmer. When Palmer talked about golfing greats, he talked about Bobby Jones, Byron Nelson, Ben Hogan, Sam Snead and Jack Nicklaus. He let others put Arnold Palmer in that elite category.

"There are more good players on the tour now than we've ever had," Palmer observed back then. "Some of them can be great on occasion, but they're not great golfers." Tiger Woods was a mere kitten at the time.

I heard some stories at the Latrobe Country Club that made me appreciate Palmer even more. He had a lot in common with Art Rooney when it came to having the common touch and a way with people. Palmer was proud of his achievements, but he never forgot his humble beginnings, how lucky he was to have had the parents he had, and he remained grateful to his fans.

You've heard stories about nice guys who would give you the shirt off their back. Well, that's Arnold Palmer.

Bill Boyle, a security officer during *The Press* Old Newsboys golf outing, related, "I was here one day when a guy in the clubhouse was admiring Arnie's jersey, and Arnie just pulled the jersey over his head and said, 'Here, if you like it so much, take it.'"

That man, it was later learned, was Carl DePasqua, the former Waynesburg and Pitt football coach who lived in Latrobe.

Major Homer Redd, who oversaw nearly 1,000 state policemen in Westmoreland County, and had been responsible for crowd control at a number of golf tournaments in the area, was a big fan of Palmer

"I don't think a great deal of too many athletes anymore," remarked Redd, "because they give you the attitude these days that they're up here, and you're down there. I have only two pictures of athletes in my office, and one of them is of Arnold Palmer and the other one is of Bill Mazeroski."

Mazeroski, who owned his own golf course in Rayland, Ohio near his boyhood home, was living in Greensburg. "He's a good guy and he likes cops," said Redd. "I even deputized him once to make sure we'd keep law and order at a restaurant party out here. Another ballplayer I really liked was Bill Virdon; he was a real down-to-earth guy, too."

I met a security guy during the summer of 2000 and he made similar observations about Palmer's pleasant nature and why he was so fond of him. It's nice to know that some things don't change. That's why Palmer has been such an enduring figure on the international and local sports scenes.

CYA Archives

Art Rooney presents CYA Man of the Year Award to Arnold Palmer at testimonial dinner in 1977. It remains one of Palmer's favorite mementos in his spectacular professional golfing career.

Hal Bock
A history buff

*"You felt like you were with
such an historical figure."*

*Hal Bock had been with the Associated Press in New York for 38 years,
and had covered all major sports in that time, including the National
Football League. He lives in East Williston, New York.*

What a great man! He was a big leprechaun. Jolly. Just having
a good time. He was enjoying life. For all the hard years he
went through with that franchise, I thought it was remarkable how well he handled the team's success. I thought he kept such
an upbeat attitude through the toughest of times. We were glad to see
him win. I'm a great student of history, and when you met him you felt
you were with such an historical figure. He went through a lot of down
and dirty times. He was a guy who just was a delight to be around.
I loved his stories. I love people who have had experiences and are
willing to share them with me. I'd see him at the Super Bowl or at
league meetings and he'd sit around and tell stories. He'd just visit
with us. He was like one of the guys. He'd sit in the lounge as long as
we'd stay and listen. He'd talk about Johnny Blood and people like
that. I majored in history in college. This was an opportunity to talk
to somebody who'd been there before you where there. He may be the
best owner of them all.

Harry Coughanour/Pittsburgh Post-Gazette Archives

**Art Rooney watches a televised NFL playoff contest on December 23, 1972 after
he missed seeing "Immaculate Reception" by Franco Harris in final minute of his
team's 13-7 victory over Oakland Raiders at Three Rivers Stadium.**

Dave Roderick
Growing up on the North Side

"It means a lot to me."

David M. Roderick had roots similar to his long-time friend Arthur J. Rooney, Sr. They both grew up on the North Side and played football on local sandlots and boxed in the local lyceums and gyms. Roderick graduated from the University of Pittsburgh with a b.s. degree in economics and finance and rose up the business ranks to become the chairman and chief executive officer of USX Corporation. In recent years, Roderick has served as chairman of the board of the Earle J. Jorgensen Co. with offices on the 62nd floor of the USX Tower. He can see PNC Park, the new football stadium, Heinz Field, and his old neighborhood from his office. In 1988, he was honored with the Horatio Alger Award as a distinguished American with a rags-to-riches success story. He received the Distinguished Pennsylvanian Award in 1992. Best of all, he is a member of the North Side Hall of Fame, which raises money each year for Art Rooney's favorite church school, The Cardinal Wright Regional School on West Commons, adjacent to St. Peter's Catholic Church. Roderick was wearing a gray business suit with a red paisley tie and stiff-collared white shirt when we spoke at his office in late November of 1998.

They have been closing certain schools on the North Side so we have been working with Bishop Wuerl to raise money to help them out. We just honored Dan Rooney and Tom Foerster in the North Side Hall of Fame. Nobody has done more for that area than those two, except maybe Dan's father. I was one of the first inductees in that group, so it means something special to me. Mayor Tom Murphy and John Marous, the former CEO at Westinghouse, are active in that group as well. Rooney and Foerster got it all started. We had a dinner and agreed to help fund it. Just completed the third year. Raised about $150,000 a year for three years. I think Rooney is going to do it for two more years.

I was born on May 3, 1924. I went to Horace Mann School until third grade and then we moved and I went to John Morrow Grade School on Davis Avenue. I grew up on the Ohio River side of the 27th Ward, down toward the McKees Rocks Bridge. I went to Oliver High School, and graduated from there in 1942. My dad was a postal worker. During the Depression, he had a steady income. He decided to buy a house. Up till then we were renting.

I think the new ballpark and football stadium on the North Side are going to be great. All those buildings over there will be torn down and we're going to have state-of-the-art sports facilities and a bigger and better convention center on this side of the river. There were some other sites considered, but it ended up on the North Side. It will work.

I think the area will really come alive. I was driving through the Strip District recently late at night. Two blocks from the Doubletree Hotel we could hardly move. I asked, "What the devil is going on? Has there been an accident?" I was told, "No, this is the way it is on Friday night in The Strip." That's become the hub of nightlife for the young people in Pittsburgh. It wasn't planned that way. It just kind of happened. I hope it will be that way on the North Side, too. It has the same kind of potential.

The North Side means a lot to me. My grandfather, David Roderick, was a policeman. I was named after him. He served on city council in Allegheny, when it was a separate city from Pittsburgh.

We were all boxing fans, following Fritzie Zivic and then Billy Conn. Boxing became popular here during the Depression. People participated in sports that didn't cost much money. We played football and baseball on the sandlots and boxing at local clubs. It filled in a lot of time and kept us out of trouble. We could go to the gym in the dead of winter. There was a gang of fellows I loafed around with near the St. Francis School. All my buddies went there. They had a recreation area there, right in my backyard. We boxed there a couple of nights a week. That was from 1938 to 1940. We were boxing from the time we were 12 years old. We started boxing in Lawrenceville and in The Hill.

There were little boxing clubs. There were eight or ten different clubs on the North Side. No one ever got hurt. We wore pretty heavy gloves. It kept you in good condition. It was a good way to spend a winter's night. Our old friend Art Rooney was a product of that. He kept busy with baseball, football and boxing, too. Nobody spent much money on anything in those days. I'd get boxing gloves for Christmas and they had been somebody else's boxing gloves.

Father Burke was the priest who worked with the boys at St. Francis. When the school was closed we'd go into the basement of my house and box there. It was a basement, believe me, not a game room. In those days you went anywhere you could. My parents permitted me to bring kids in the house. As long as we were behaving ourselves. At least they knew where we were. There was a furnace and a coal bin and pillars, and we'd take turns boxing one another. Then we'd sit around and discuss sports. We'd be staying out of the cold. It was a different era. Only a third of the families had cars. You weren't out chasing around. We were about two-and-a-half miles from Downtown. You either walked down or you hopped on the back of a trolley. And I mean on the back. You'd go over to California Avenue and wait for them to stop. Then two of you would jump on.

I didn't grow up with any kid who had an allowance. You did things to make money. Your parents let you keep whatever you could earn. You'd shovel coal or you'd shovel snow. You'd run errands. You'd do anything to make money.

> *"The greatest strength of Pittsburgh is our history, and our sense of ourselves as a community. We remember our heroes."*
> — Mayor Tom Murphy

Your dad might give you a dime to go to a movie, but no one had an allowance. I read Tom Brokaw's book "The Greatest Generation," and he got a good feel for that.

"Everybody in the neighborhood was sort of your mother and father."

My friends went to school a mile away. About two-thirds of the families on my street were Irish Catholic. We were Protestant. We went to a Presbyterian church. My dad was Welsh and Mother was Irish. All of my buddies were learning Latin to be altar boys, so I learned it, too. They'd be practicing, and I paid attention to what they were doing. I think I knew enough that I could have gotten up there and been an altar boy. I married a Catholic girl and my kids were altar boys.

During the summer months you could play in the streets. Your parents were sitting on the porch, watching you. You did a lot of mischievous things, but you didn't do anything to hurt anybody. Everybody in the neighborhood was sort of your mother and father. You couldn't get away with anything. Just catch and play ball.

If I got in a fight, by the time I got home my mother knew about it. By the time your father got home he knew about it, too. If you were dating a girl, everyone in the neighborhood knew about it. I was a Protestant, but I never got to date anybody but Catholic girls and their parents were okay with that most of the time. Some might not have been thrilled about it. That's all I met. I was engaged to a Catholic girl. Her name was Kitty Staley. We got engaged when I was home on leave from the Marine Corps. We called off our engagement when I was overseas for two and a half years. I ended up marrying a Catholic girl, an Irish-Catholic. Her name was Elizabeth Costello. The Irish pronounce that Coslow. She was from Penn Hills. She died three years ago (in 1995).

When I came out of the service in 1945 I went to Robert Morris College. I graduated from there in four years, but Robert Morris wasn't an accredited college back then and I wanted a real college degree. So I started at Pitt in 1949. I graduated from Pitt in 1955. I went there three nights a week and on Saturday morning while I was working during the day.

I had been a big Pitt fan when I was in high school. Pitt was in its heyday in college football in the late '30s. They had guys like Bobby Larue and Marshall Goldberg. My favorite Pittsburgh Pirate then was Arky Vaughan. As I said, I was a big fan of Fritzie Zivic and Billy Conn. All those sports figures were great.

When I was playing baseball and softball I'd always ask for No. 21. That was Arky Vaughan's number before it was worn by Roberto

Clemente. He was stocky and combative. He batted .385 one year (1935) to lead the league. They traded him away. It had to be for the money. Benswanger must have needed the money. Arky Vaughan was from California. He went fishing with a friend one off-season and they both drowned. They never found his body.

People had it different in those days, as Brokaw pointed out in his book. They didn't expect anything. They saw their parents struggle and help friends at the same time. They didn't expect their parents to provide them with a lot of things. When you got out of high school, you went to the military service to contain Hitler and Hirihito and Tojo. You were disciplined and kept humble in the military service. You knew your place.

You came back and you started your life at 21 or 22. There was a marvelous opportunity provided by the G.I. Bill to go to college and get a degree. There were still low expectations. You expected to work for everything you got.

There was no welfare. People wanted to work. There was a certain dignity in earning your own way. Unemployment is less than five percent today. Anybody who wants a job can get one. Most people on welfare are there because they want to be.

In my high school class, under normal conditions, only five per cent would have gone to college. About 80 per cent of the guys in my class ended up in the military service. Probably 40 to 50 per cent from that group went to college under the G.I. Bill. That generation never expected to go to college.

I went to Robert Morris College at night for four years and then six more years at Pitt. That was not painful for me. I was accustomed to work. People would ask me how I could do that. To me, it wasn't all that bad. I wanted it all. I wanted to get married. I wanted to go to school. I wanted to get a good job.

Everything is relative. I grew up in a very good environment. A lot of great men grew up here and immigrated here and turned out to be great men. You had Carnegie, Frick, Westinghouse, Pitcairn, Mellon, Hillman and Phipps.

Those are all Pittsburgh names. We've had our share of history-makers. They've contributed to our industry, our community and civic endeavors. This is a city where the business community can get together and make things happen. There's a lot of pride. There's a tradition here for getting things done. We can get some things done that are not done in bigger cities. This community has always had a great partnership between political leaders and industrial leaders and educational leaders. We can make a difference. There's a cohesiveness of leaders here.

There is a cooperative spirit in our city. You had a person like Art Rooney who took a great deal of pride in being a Pittsburgher, and fostered that idea. We want it to be a great city. Anything we can do to perpetuate the legacy. Whether it's ballparks, Pitt, the Steelers, UPMC, the Pirates or the Pittsburgh Symphony Orchestra. I'd like to help to continue to have this city be a great place to spend your life.

US Steel president David Roderick presents Steelers' MVP award for 1975 season to Mel Blount as Myron Cope and Joe Gordon look on from left.

Roderick is front and center with Steelers' MVP award for 1976 season won by Jack Lambert. With him, left to right, are linebackers coach Woody Widenhofer, and All-Pro linebacker trio of Lambert, Andy Russell and Jack Ham.

North Side scene
Gus serves ice balls for everybody

"We always felt safe."
— Stella Kalaris

A young boy is murdered and his body mutilated. A homeless man in the neighborhood is accused of the hideous crime. Both the boy and the man traveled on the same streets on the city's North Side. They were familiar figures to many. Scott C. Drake, 11 years old, was on those streets too often for someone his age. Joseph Cornelius, 47 years old, had no home at all, and found refuge where he could in back alleys, hostels for the homeless, and under trees in West Park.

Photographs of Scott Drake and Joseph Cornelius appeared in the local newspapers often in the weeks after Drake's death on September 24, 2000. The images stay with us. There is a haunting quality about those faces. They make us all feel vulnerable.

Anybody who has children or grandchildren, or cares about kids, was hurt deeply by what happened. If it could happen there then it could happen in your neighborhood, too.

It hit home with Gus Kalaris, the wonderful Greek gentleman who dispenses ice-balls, popcorn, peanuts and neighborhood news from a mobile bright orange cart in the middle of West Park. His stand sits by the tennis courts, which are always brightly-lit at night.

His stand is sort of an oasis in the park. It's a beautiful park, one of the city's best-kept secrets, but it's thought to be dangerous by some. Employees at the nearby Allegheny General Hospital are warned about walking through there alone.

"People tell me that everybody feels safe when Gus was down here," said Stella Kalaris, his sweet wife. Gus and Stella had been married for 46 years. They grew up in the same neighborhood on the North Side and have known each other since they were kids.

"When Gus was sick last year, and wasn't here for a long stretch, people told me it wasn't the same down here," said Stella. "They didn't feel safe at night."

The Kalaris family has been offering these sidewalk treats at the same stand since 1934. Gus and Stella and their stand are a Pittsburgh institution. His parents started the business. Gus and Stella are the warmest people you will ever meet. We have become friends this past decade. They proudly tell you they get invited to parties at Dan and Pat Rooney's home just three blocks away.

This front-page news story was a different matter, for sure, and a long way from festive Christmas gatherings with good friends.

"We served them both shortly before this happened," Gus said of the accused murderer and the victim. Scott Drake's genitalia had been cut away with a piece of broken glass, and Joseph Cornelius had confessed to the crime. He even confessed to Mayor Tom Murphy.

"Our daughter Chrissie, or Christina, saw the picture of Cornelius in the newspaper and recognized him," said Stella. "She said, 'There's the guy who came to our stand last week. He was wearing a red jacket, and he bought a cherry ice ball. Oh, my.'"

Christina Sfanos, 46, often takes a turn at the family stand in West Park. She and her parents all recognized the face of Scott Drake as well. "He was a street urchin," said Gus. "He was out at all hours, from what I hear. His dad's in jail. He had to be released to go to the funeral."

Stella said that Scott Drake was riding a bike. He was with his cousin, a girl his age who also had a bike. "They dropped their bikes on the sidewalk next to our stand," recalled Stella. "I told them they had to put their bikes over there by the tree, so no one would trip over them on the sidewalk. They were kind of frisky, and I told them they'd have to behave if they wanted us to serve them. They wanted popcorn, but they had only 40 cents instead of the dollar they needed. I told them I'd give them the popcorn if they promised to be good. And I told them if they acted up, or were bad after they got the popcorn, that I wouldn't serve them in the future.

"They were real nice after that. They were well behaved. They came back again, and they were real polite. His grandmother came here, too. That man, he was well known in the neighborhood. He slept on the picnic table across the street from the Allegheny Sandwich Shop. That was one of his places. He slept in three or four different places. It's so upsetting. You think that could be your child. For someone to do that is just unspeakable. This is a beautiful park. You should have been here when we were kids. Gus and I went to a Greek school near here, after we were done with our regular school. We'd be there at the Greek school from 4:30 till 7 o'clock at night. We'd walk through here on the way home. We always felt safe."

Jim O'Brien

Stella and Gus Kalaris are popular with the kids who come to their West Park stand on North Side where they sell ice balls, popcorn and peanuts.

Furman Bisher
A southern gentleman

"Art Rooney was a good citizen."

Furman Bisher, at age 82, was still writing a sports column for the Atlanta Journal-Constitution, *where he had been a sportswriter since 1950. His first hire on the staff in Atlanta was Edwin Pope, later the sports editor of* The Miami Herald. *Bisher grew up in Denton, North Carolina. He was in his 23rd year as a member of the selection board for the Pro Football Hall of Fame. He favored John Stallworth over Lynn Swann in the initial voting for the 2001 class, but went along with the majority in the final vote.*

I was on Art Rooney's Christmas card list and I always felt good about that. It always brought a smile to my face to open his card. I used to see him at the Kentucky Derby and places like that. The first time I saw him I was scared to death. He was such a revered character, and I was afraid to approach him. But you didn't have to worry about that; he approached you. He always made you feel comfortable and at ease. I learned a lot about him, in the beginning, from Red Smith. Smith told me the story about how Rooney broke the bank when he went to the track at Saratoga. That story stayed with me.

Pittsburgh writers like Chet Smith, who was at *The Press* for so many years, and Lenny Pasquarelli, who came from Pittsburgh to Atlanta, knew him well. Lenny used to tell me stories about him, too. Lenny absolutely loves the guy.

The Steelers used to stop by to play an exhibition game in Atlanta in days gone by, and that's how I first met him. He'd make a point to get to know you. He made you feel more comfortable than any other owner. He always had that cigar in his hand or in his mouth. He seemed to welcome you. He seemed to sense your discomfort.

I've known his son, Dan, for a long time, too, and Dan has always been easy to deal with. I appreciate that.

I have very little contact with athletes in this day and age, so I spend more time talking with the owners and administrators. More and more, I rely on my relationships with old-timers. I heard Paul Harvey say on the radio that 20 percent of all the players in the NFL have a criminal record. So I'm not thrilled with most of them these days.

Guys like Art Rooney appealed to me. He was a good citizen. Pittsburgh should have been proud to have an Art Rooney living there, even if he didn't own the Pittsburgh Steelers. He suffered through some of the worst periods. One year it got so bad they had to split the year with the Eagles. It was a different world then. The owners were compatriots, and relied on one another. He leaned on one another. They counted on one another. Nowadays, I don't even know some of these owners. Back in the days of Art Rooney, these guys were in this thing together. It was a fraternity. Wellington Mara and Art Modell, who owned the teams in this year's Super Bowl, would appreciate what I am talking about.

Wellington Mara is a fellow who kept the league together when they decided to go into revenue sharing. He had the best market in the league in New York. He wanted what was best for the league. Rooney came from one of the smaller markets, but he was always for what was good for the league, or so I've heard anyhow.

I think I helped Wellington Mara get into the Hall of Fame. I got up at one of the voting meetings and I said simply, 'What kind of Hall of Fame is this that Al Davis can get into it and Wellington Mara can't?' That's all I said. He got in that year. I think they ought to put Art Modell in, too. Speaking of Al Davis, I think it's a disgrace that he got in. He's a guy who tried to destroy the league, and he's still at it.

I didn't vote for Ralph Wilson of Buffalo. Show me what he did. Art Rooney did something. Wellington Mara did something. I guess I'm getting a little callous.

"The Prez" goes for a ride, as Art Rooney is honored at the Circus Saints and Sinners banquet at the Pittsburgh Hilton in November 1964. In forefront holding up Rooney's legs are two Steelers legends, John "Blood" McNally and "Bullet Bill" Dudley. Others, left to right, are Chicago Bears owner George Halas, Pitt head coach and former Steelers coach John Michelosen, NFL Commissioner Pete Rozelle, Steelers coach Buddy Parker and Art's brother, Father Silas Rooney. "They're trying to make a Saint out of Arthur," said his mother, Margaret Rooney, "but he's not ready for that yet."

149

Steve Furness
Another '70s Steeler dies

"You hate to see this start...
it's going to go on."
— Ralph Berlin

It looked like the locker room of the Pittsburgh Steelers in the '70s when they ruled the pro football world. Except for the flowers. Steve Furness, a defensive lineman on all four of the Steelers' Super Bowl championship teams, had died.

There were many familiar faces on this Friday afternoon, February 11, 2000 at L. Beinhauer & Son Funeral Home on Rt. 19 in McMurray, where Allegheny County gives way to Washington County.

Many of them had been in the same mortuary just over three years earlier when Ray Mansfield was the first player from the glory days of the Steelers to die. Mansfield was 55. Furness was 49. Both lived in the South Hills since they first arrived in Pittsburgh, fresh out of college. Both died of heart attacks. Mansfield had died while hiking through the Grand Canyon, Furness died while sitting at a kitchen table at his home in Bethel Park.

Mansfield had been the heart and soul of the Steelers' first two title teams. Furness was one of only 22 Steelers to claim four Super Bowl champion rings.

"The warrior is gone," said John Banaszak, who along with Furness backed up the famed Steel Curtain defensive line of L.C. Greenwood, Joe Greene, Ernie Holmes and Dwight White. "Four more Super Bowl rings are in heaven."

Banaszak, a big success in his first season as head football coach at Washington & Jefferson in 1999, came to the funeral home with his wife, Mary, and his boss, John Luckhardt, W&J's athletic director at the time. It was easy to recognize that Banaszak was shaken by the loss of a friend. Banaszak's dark brown eyes were moist and he wiped the back of his hand at the corners of his eyes from time to time, before a tear could form.

Many teammates spoke of the tremendous work ethic and competitive fire of Furness. He had a fire in his belly. They also swapped stories about his fun-loving ways and his passion for pulling practical jokes. He had a winning, mischievous smile. I remember how happy he was when Bill Cowher hired him on his coaching staff, one of the first to sign on in 1992.

"I was telling L.C. when we were standing by the casket," added Banaszak, "I expected that at any minute Steve would wink at us, and sit up and say 'gotcha.' It's like something he'd do."

Jim O'Brien

Good times were enjoyed by former Steelers teammates Gerry "Moon" Mullins, Dwight White and Steve Furness at 1999 awards dinner at Doubletree Hotel.

Courtesy of Debby Furness

The Furness family gathers at their Upper St. Clair home in 1993 during Steve's last season as an assistant to Bill Cowher on Steelers' staff. From left to right are Zaban, Debby, Zack and Steve.

Banaszak shook his crew-cut head, however, knowing better. Furness was gone. A friend was gone. Only the memories remained. There were photos and posters showing Steve Furness in his Steelers uniform on display near the casket. There were all those flowers with familiar names from the Steelers Super Bowl lineups wherever one looked. They were all reminders of the special time in the city's sports history. Those were the days, my friend, we thought they'd never end. The funeral home provided quite a contrast from those scenes at Three Rivers Stadium during those glorious seasons of the '70s. This was a more sober side of sports, of life.

Those who had seen him recently spoke about how Furness appeared to be in great shape and great spirits. They felt he had bounced back, at last, from the keen disappointment he felt when he was fired as the Steelers defensive line coach following the 1993 season. He was also bitter when the Steelers traded him to Tampa Bay right before the 1981 season. I was covering the Steelers that summer for *The Pittsburgh Press*, and remember how furious Furness was about being told he was dispensable.

Conversely, I remember how much Furness enjoyed watching his sons, Zachary and Zaban, play football for Upper St. Clair High School. I last saw him sitting in the stands at Mt. Lebanon for a late season sizzler with USC in November of 1999. I had seen him many times through the years in the stands at Upper St. Clair's football stadium, even before his boys were on the team.

Sports broadcasters Myron Cope and Lanny Frattare also paid their respects at the funeral home that Friday afternoon. Cope called attention to a beautiful black and gold ribbon floral arrangement from the Steel Curtain that had the jersey number (64) of Furness in the midst of those of Greene (75), Greenwood (68), Holmes (63) and White (78). The number of Furness was on a black ribbon and the other four were on gold ribbons. Some real thought had gone into this.

Edmund Nelson, who followed those guys as a defensive lineman, was also in attendance.

Banaszak, Luckhardt and Greenwood were in a group at the funeral home that, eventually, would include Steelers owner and president Dan Rooney, who had just been voted into the Pro Football Hall of Fame, and his wife, Pat, and business coordinator Dan Ferens. Moon Mullins, an offensive guard on all four Super Bowl teams, was there with his wife, Joan.

I remembered seeing the Rooneys visit the same funeral home when there was a viewing for Ray Mansfield.

Dan Rooney remarked that Joe Greene had called him that morning and asked him to offer his condolences to everyone.

"It's hard to lose a good kid like Steve," offered Pat Rooney. Then, looking toward Banaszak, she added almost apologetically, "I still call you kids."

Banaszak came back, "And we still like you to see us that way."

Yes, it was far better to be seen as young rather than as old.

Banaszak's wife, Mary, had mentioned earlier though that she was struck a year earlier at a reunion of those Steelers of the '70s at how she didn't recognize some of the players. They had gone gray or bald, and looked different.

"This should make people realize that we're human," said Greenwood.

"You feel vulnerable," said Mullins. "Who's next?"

Ralph Berlin of Bethel Park, who was the head trainer of all those great Steelers teams, was there with his wife, Dee. At age 64, Berlin appeared slim after undergoing open-heart surgery in November and felt fine. "You hate to see this start," observed Berlin. "First Mansfield and now Furness…it's going to go on."

Berlin had babied these guys, looking after all their aches and pains, taping their ankles and whatever. He kept them intact at times. But even Berlin was stumped for any remedies now. He felt a sense of gratitude that he'd gotten better. He was begging his doctor to let him smoke a half cigar once a week, and doing whatever he was told to improve his health. His heart was heavy though he told old war stories, some of them light-hearted ones.

Indeed, we felt similar losses the next day when we heard of the deaths of cartoonist Charles Schulz who brought us "Peanuts," and Hall of Fame football coach Tom Landry of the Dallas Cowboys. His teams were great rivals of the Steelers in the '70s. Landry died of leukemia at age 75.

They were all reminders that it was longer than we would like to think that the Steelers were such a joy for us and we were citizens of the City of Champions.

"We're people, just like they are."
— L. C. Greenwood

It was always good to see L.C. Greenwood. He had such a noble look about him. He had a warm smile, a glint in his eyes, and a bass-voiced laugh, almost a chortle, that was contagious. He was still the tallest and most stately looking of the Steelers at 6-6, but his hair had gone gray. He was now a real graybeard. He had received strong consideration for the Pro Football Hall of Fame in recent years, but his vote totals had diminished and his chances seemed to be slipping.

Rooney had gotten in on his second go-round. Lynn Swann and John Stallworth were still knocking at the door, and still had legitimate chances of being inducted at ceremonies in Canton someday. Greenwood was a long shot, at best. Someday he might get another look-see from the veterans committee that considered old-timers.

Greenwood had grown up in Canton, Mississippi, the son of a hard-working man who had about three jobs, working in a mill, farm-

153

ing his own land, and serving as a lay preacher. So Greenwood had a strong religious upbringing.

He could go to his Canton any time he wished. "My dad taught me that our life was not measured by the number of years you're going to be here," said Greenwood when I sat down next to him in an adjoining room at the funeral home.

"It's unfortunate that we've lost Steve, but it seems that he accomplished quite a bit in his 49 years. You see him like this (and Greenwood looked into the room where Furness was on view) and you remember how we were together all those years. It's sad. It's not as unfortunate as it is sad. When you think of how he and Ray Mansfield died the real surprising thing is that these guys were not sick. They were here one day, gone the next.

"I was talking to people about Steve, and they were saying he was running every day, five miles a day, and was in great shape. There's no way to explain this. At least they both went without suffering. That's something. I've read some things from the National Football League Alumni office, and there are studies that suggest we don't have a long life expectancy.

"It hits home and, yes, it does raise some questions. Who's next? When is my time? Because of our success on the football field, and maybe because of how big and strong we appeared to be, people thought we were different. Now they can see that we're human, too. We're people, just like they are.

"Remember Willie Fry (a defensive end from Notre Dame who was a disappointing 2nd round choice in 1982)? Remember what a physical specimen he was? So muscular. Well, he died, too. So you never know.

"I've got my own comfort level in that regard. My dad died and he used to say we were put here to die. We were all born to die. As they say down home, in the symbolic sense, you better get your act together."

"He really worked and became a guy you could count on."
— Dan Rooney

Furness was a backup to the "Steel Curtain" most of his career, but he was a standout when he replaced an injured Joe Greene during Super Bowls X and XIII against the Dallas Cowboys.

"Steve was a guy who, when he came here, was really not a polished player," said Steelers president Dan Rooney. "He really worked and became a guy you could count on."

Steve Furness was a tough cookie. He came out of Rhode Island University, not exactly a football mill, to stick with the Steelers. He was drafted as a defensive end in the fifth round in 1972. He had earned a bachelor's degree at URI and that's where he met his wife, Debby. They would have two sons, Zachary and Zaban, who both played football at Upper St. Clair High School.

The Furness family lived in Washington, at first, then McMurray and Upper St. Clair. Debby blamed the breakup of their marriage on Steve's keen disappointment when he was fired as defensive line coach of the Steelers after two seasons — 1992 and 1993. He was fired soon after the Steelers suffered their second consecutive first-round playoff loss, this time to the Kansas City Chiefs. "He was so unhappy about everything after that," said Debby. "It didn't seem fair."

In the aftermath, he and Debby had separated and were divorced. Debby was a member of the support staff at Chartiers Valley Middle School. Her good friend, Betsy Steiner, the principal of the school, was at the funeral home with other school officials to offer their respects. Steiner had lost her husband, Dwayne, less than a year earlier and could appreciate Debby's state of mind. Steiner was aware that her husband's health was in decline, however, and knew he was dying. She was at his side through his long illness.

Debby could only wonder what might have been. We often saw each other at our local post office and would talk to one another. I liked Debby Furness. Family was important to her. Steve Furness resided in Bethel Park when he died. He was sitting at the kitchen table when he died. There was no warning. Peggy Bombich identified herself as his fiance when we were introduced at the funeral home.

It was similar to the scene at the funeral for Ray Mansfield with an ex-wife and a fiance both receiving condolences from family and friends. It was awkward. Debby moved back home to Rhode Island in the summer of 2001.

"He overcame an awful lot in his life," said Banaszak. "I feel bad that his family situation didn't work out the way you'd like. It was one of many disappointments."

Banaszak and Luckhardt had seen Furness only the week before his death when Furness paid a visit to Washington & Jefferson College. Furness had been successful in selling W&J on purchasing an artificial football surface from Field Turf, a company he represented as a salesman. W&J was in the midst of a major renovation program of its football facilities.

"He seemed to be in great spirits," said Banaszak, "and he seemed to be excited about what he was doing. He finally seemed to have found something he enjoyed doing. It was so good to see him happy again with his new job. He was going after it; he had that same drive again.

"This makes life seem real fragile," he continued, accepting a hand offered him by his wife, Mary. They squeezed hands. I had inter-

155

viewed John and Mary many times and knew they were much in love. Theirs was a marriage to be envied.

"It's just a shock, a shock," Banaszak said. "Steve and I were pretty close. We'd ride in to the stadium together. I got to know him. I spent a lot of time with Steve. We shared a lot of good times. I played next to him.

"When I made the Steelers as a free agent in 1975 there were just the two of us backing up the Steel Curtain. I learned an awful lot from him: how to handle our job as role players.

"In '77, when Ernie left, and he was the heir apparent to the right tackle job. Steve worked so hard in the off-season and at training camp. Then we go to Buffalo and he gets stepped on and hurts ligaments in the pre-game warm-up and missed six weeks. He didn't give up or get down, though, and he came back strong as soon as he could.

"He lifted weights with those offensive linemen — Mike Webster, Steve Courson, Ted Petersen, Jim Clack and Jon Kolb — at the Red Bull Inn in Washington, and became one of the Men of Steel. Well, it looks like our armor has been cracked. We're not invincible."

Several of those players, including Furness, admitted to using steroids in their bodybuilding efforts. Furness had told us in an interview for one of our books on the Steelers that he quit using steroids early on, after seeing some of their side effects. Even so, people wondered aloud if steroid usage had contributed to the death of Furness. Then, too, there had been a history of heart disease in his family, much like Mansfield's family.

Banaszak and Luckhardt both had serious health scares in recent years. Luckhardt gave way to Banaszak as head coach a year earlier because of health concerns. A few years earlier, during what he thought was routine surgery to clean up an old knee injury, Banaszak got a staph infection and his leg and, indeed, his life were at risk for a scary period.

"I've struggled with this," said Banaszak. "It's difficult for me to put this in the right context. If you looked at all the guys I played with and you'd get asked to pick guys you thought were going to live a long time, Steve would be one of them. It hurt badly when I lost my father, but Steve is really the first good friend I have lost. My first friend in high school committed suicide, but that was a long time ago, and it was different. I look at what happened to Steve and I say, 'This can't happen to us.'"

Steelers and people associated with the ballclub who came to the memorial service at the funeral home the following day included Chuck Noll, with his wife, Marianne. It was Noll, of course, who was the head coach of all those championship teams in the '70s. Former Steelers publicist Joe Gordon and his wife, Babe, came by to pay their respects.

Those same couples had sat directly behind me at a memorial service for Mansfield at Westminster Presbyterian Church, and they were shaken by the loss. The more one is around people like Noll and Gordon you gain a sense of what decent, caring individuals they are, even though they were sometimes gruff when someone rubbed them the wrong way during the Steelers' successful run in the '70s and '80s.

Former assistant coaches Paul Uram and Marvin Lewis were there, along with several former Steelers and their spouses, including Andy Russell, Mike Wagner, Tunch Ilkin, Steve Courson, Lynn Swann, Larry Brown, Billy Davis, John Banaszak and John Luckhardt. Dana Harris, the wife of Franco Harris, was there as well.

"Back in May, I stood next to Steve Furness at the funeral of Steve Courson's wife, Jackie," recalled Ilkin. "This time I was standing next to Steve Courson at the funeral of Steve Furness."

Several Steelers had mentioned to me that the last time they had seen so many of their teammates was at the funeral for Courson's wife. She had accompanied her husband to the weekend reunion of the Steelers of the '70s that was held at the David L. Lawrence Convention Center in the summer of 1999. Terry Bradshaw came back for that promotion on one of his rare returns since he quarterbacked the Steelers to greatness.

Courson was the former Steelers lineman who blamed the ballclub and the National Football League for looking the other way when ballplayers were using steroids and other performance-enhancing drugs. Courson had serious health problems at one point. It was thought his heart was so damaged — he said from steroid use — for him to survive without a heart transplant. Through medical care and a stringent diet and training regimen, however, Courson kept his problem in check. Jackie nursed him through a lot of difficult days and seemed to be good for him.

"Jackie seemed to be enjoying seeing everyone from the team that weekend," said one of the former Steelers. "Then the next day she committed suicide. She shot herself. She suffered from depression. One of the problems that people with that condition have is that they can be on a great high like when everyone was together that weekend. Then when it's over they take an emotional nosedive. She looked happy on Friday, Saturday and Sunday. Then on Monday she kills herself."

Such events are difficult to explain or understand. The Steelers of the '70s seemed so super. As the years pass and problems arise, marriages coming apart at the seams, players and their families having emotional and financial difficulties, and then death, they seem all too human. It was better seeing them in the locker room. They were more protected when they wore pads and helmets. The locker room was secure from the outside world. Visitors needed proper credentials to get into the world of fun and games.

> *"If you don't go to the funeral home*
> *to pay respect to your friends,*
> *they won't visit you when you pass away."*
> — Yogi Berra

Elsie Hillman
A special date

"Imagine me and Jack being friends."

A Christmas Carol, Act I: A special card came in the mail at the outset of 2001. It was from Elsie Hillman and it had a message at the bottom of the card hand-written in red ink. Elsie said she was recovering nicely from a short hospital stay the previous month. She also offered some kind comments about some newspaper columns of mine she had recently read. It made my day.

The message in red ink reminded me of a Christmas card I had received the same week the previous year. It also reminded me of a "date" I had with Elsie Hillman in December of 1998. I'm not a kiss-and-tell guy, but I have to share this story with you.

The Hillmans, for the record, don't do much writing in red ink.

For the few who may not recognize the name, Elsie Hillman happens to be the wealthiest woman in western Pennsylvania. She is also the most politically powerful woman in western Pennsylvania. For a long time, she was the chairperson of the Republican Party in these parts. She has always been a big sports fan, and was a close friend, for instance, of the great boxer, Billy Conn, the original "Pittsburgh Kid," and his wife, Mary Louise Conn.

Elsie's husband is Henry Hillman. He is always referred to in society or "Seen" columns as "an industrialist." I don't know what that means, but let's just say the position pays well. Henry Hillman is one of the richest men in America.

They are an odd couple, but a great team. Henry is reserved. Elsie is not. Elsie is a great lady, but so down-to-earth. She likes to dance. She's a lot of fun. Both are generous with their time and money. They can afford to be. But everyone who can afford to be doesn't do that.

Art Rooney, the late owner of the Steelers, used to say rich people didn't like to spend money. "That's how they got rich," he'd say. Art Rooney would have regarded Elsie Hillman with another of his favorite expressions. He'd say "she's a real Pittsburgh guy."

Elsie has friends in high places. She has been buying ten copies of my newest book annually and having me inscribe appropriate messages on them.

In January of 2000, I received a card with a Houston, Tex. address on the outer flap. I didn't recognize the address. The card read: "Dear Jim, Elsie Hillman sent me 'Hometown Heroes.' I'll read it. Thanks for the good wishes Elsie passed along and for inscribing my copy. Happy 2000!" It was hand-written in red ink, but I couldn't make out the name.

I flipped it over and there was a beautiful portrait photo of the family of former President George Bush. Barbara was behind him. Our future president was to his immediate left. It was dated Dec. 25, 1999. I couldn't get over President Bush taking the time to write me a "thank you" card on Christmas Day. There's a lesson in there for all of us. I had known of Elsie Hillman since I was a kid because my mother, Mary (who turned 94 on Christmas Eve, 2000 by the way), was one of five Republicans in our community in Hazelwood, and she worked the polls every election. Elsie stopped by on occasion to see my mother's boss, a local Republican leader. I didn't get to know Elsie well, though, until we teamed up at a funeral in Greenfield, of all places. Elsie was alone at the funeral of Jack Rafferty, a street ruffian of sorts who was a Republican activist. He also booked numbers as a sideline, illegal in some parts of town. "Imagine me and Jack being friends," she whispered in my ear. I liked his three brothers; that's why I was there.

Elsie latched onto my right arm in the funeral procession at St. Rosalia's Catholic Church. We made a nice couple. I knew the match had the tongues wagging of all my old buddies and rivals from Greenfield. Elsie called me a few weeks later on the telephone. She said she had to speak at a United Way dinner at the Doubletree Hotel the next week, and she needed some background information on Dan Rooney, the owner of the Steelers, who was being honored at the fete. She asked me to fax her something ASAP.

A few days later, she called me again and thanked me for my help. "Remember that dinner I told you about," she began. "Well, Henry has a conflict in his schedule and he can't make it. You'll be my date."

She said a dark suit would be fine. I was to meet her in the lobby at the Doubletree Hotel at 6:15 p.m.

A Christmas Carol: Act II.

I wasn't sure how to behave when I was on a "date" with Mrs. Elsie Hillman. Her husband, Henry, had a schedule conflict and could not accompany his wife when she attended a United Way dinner at the Doubletree Hotel, so she called upon me to go with her.

This was in December of 1998. I had provided Elsie with some biographical information on Dan Rooney, the president of the Pittsburgh Steelers, who was being honored at the dinner saluting the National Football League's efforts on behalf of United Way. You've seen those NFL ads on TV, showing players participating in United Way-funded community activities.

Elsie called me a few days before the dinner and said, rather succinctly, "You'll be my date." She didn't ask me if I would be available, or if I would like to be her escort. It was more of a summons. I liked her style. I should have spoken like that, more authoritatively, when

I called girls for dates back at Taylor Allderdice High School. Then I wouldn't have sounded like I was begging.

Elsie's confidence comes from her status in Pittsburgh social circles. She is also the most pleasant, affable, approachable, good-humored and down-to-earth woman you would want to meet. It's easy to be in Elsie's company. She's a sweet woman.

As soon as I said I would be happy to go with her and hung up the phone, I thought about Kathie. She happens to be my wife. She had met Elsie outside her home in Shadyside when we delivered some books there once, and Kathie was impressed with how personable and gracious Elsie had been with her.

I called Kathie on the telephone to make sure it was OK with her. "Elsie Hillman called me," I began, "and she wants me to go with her to a big dinner. Do you mind if I go with her?"

"Heck, no," Kathie came back. "I hope she adopts you."

I could always count on Kathie for her support.

Elsie met me in the lobby of the Doubletree. She was fashionably late. I was sweating that she was going to stand me up. As she approached, I was wondering how to welcome her. She gave me a little peck on the cheek. She knew what to do.

She showed me a black handbag and opened it slightly to reveal a copy of one of my books, "Keep The Faith," with Steelers' star running back Jerome Bettis on the cover. "I wanted to show this to my friends," she said with a smile.

I followed Elsie wherever she went. I walked one or two steps behind her. I remembered that Prince Phillip did that when he walked with Queen Elizabeth. "You make me feel queenly," Elsie has since written to me.

People were bowing and genuflecting, or so it seemed, as Elsie made her way through the hallways. They were all happy to see her. She introduced me to everyone as "my writer friend." Then she'd give them a peek at the Bettis book in her little black bag.

I felt like a young artist, Raphael perhaps, walking with his patron.We sat at a table that had to be the "power" table in the room of 800 or so guests at the Doubletree. Dan Rooney and his wife, Pat, were at the head of the table. His oldest son, Art II, and his wife, Gretta, were across from me. David Roderick, a Rooney friend and the former president and CEO of U.S. Steel and USX, was there with his friend, Becky Fisher, along with Helge Wehmeier, president and CEO of Bayer Corp. I was seated next to Paul Tagliabue, the NFL commissioner. Joe Browne, the commissioner's right-hand man, made quite a gesture on his own. He swapped seats with me so I could sit next to Tagliabue. Browne sat next to Elsie Hillman.

I imagined Dan Rooney whispering into his wife Pat's ear, "What's O'Brien doing here?" I was asking myself the same question.

When it was Elsie's turn to speak from the platform above us, reciting Rooney's achievements, she started by showing the audience my book. You can't buy that kind of endorsement, especially from Elsie Hillman.

It was an eventful evening. I told Elsie afterward that if Henry ever had another conflict that she could call on me at some future date. She hasn't summoned me since, I must confess. I might have blown it when I drank an IC Light from the bottle. I hope not. She dropped me a card from the Caribbean Islands, written in red ink, after she heard about my concern in this regard. She assured me that another date was on the horizon. She said my Kathie could come next time.

Jim O'Brien

Elsie Hillman, at right, joins her dear friend Mary Louise Conn at ceremonies to name stretch of Craig Street in Oakland (that once ran past Duquesne Gardens) in honor of Billy Conn, the original "Pittsburgh Kid" on June 18, 1998.

> *"I'm not emotional at football games, but if I go to a wake and people break down I break down right with 'em. I can't help myself."*
> — Art Rooney, Sr.

161

Dan Rooney's Top 10 Games
Lists his favorite Steelers' triumphs

*"The first Super Bowl
is a tremendous thing."*

Super Bowl XIII in Miami ranks high on Dan Rooney's list of the Steelers' 10 greatest games of the '70s, which he compiled at my personal request.

The Steelers defeated the Dallas Cowboys, 35-31, to become the first team to win three Super Bowls.

Even so, in the Steelers' president's ratings, Super Bowl XIII ranks only second or third — he's not sure which — among the Steelers' greatest games of the period in which the Steelers were hailed as the NFL's "Team of the Decade."

He rates the Steelers' first Super Bowl success, a 16-6 victory over the Minnesota Vikings in New Orleans in Super Bowl IX, as No. 1.

"You never replace the feeling of that first Super Bowl victory," he said. "The first Super Bowl is a tremendous thing. It's just a great feeling — to be there and to win it."

Rooney's runner-up choice for his "greatest game" either is winning that third Super Bowl title in Miami, which brought immortality to the team by ranking it with the Green Bay Packers of the late 1960s, or the "Immaculate Reception" playoff game on December 23, 1972 in Three Rivers Stadium. Franco Harris' controversial scoring reception with 22 seconds left beat the Oakland Raiders in the AFC playoffs — the Steelers' first-ever playoff victory in team history.

Dan Rooney remembered the play. "I knew right away it was a good play, but I didn't know how it would be ruled."

Rooney refused to list his team's ten greatest games of the '70s in any particular order. It was difficult enough, he insisted, to limit it to ten.

"The game we played after the 'Immaculate Reception' sticks out in my mind, for instance," Dan said. "Even though we lost it. Miami defeated us, 21-17, for the AFC title. But it was a great game in that the people of Pittsburgh gave us a standing ovation when we came off the field."

Still, that game isn't on Rooney's list.

A game in the drive to qualify for the playoffs for the first time in 1972 remains vivid in Rooney's mind.

That was the Steelers' 23-10 victory over Minnesota in Pittsburgh. "What we said was very similar to what Kansas City and Miami said after beating us in our first two games this season," Rooney said. "They talked about what it meant to beat the Pittsburgh Steelers. That's the way we felt when we beat Minnesota that season."

The Steelers went on to win their next three games — over Cleveland, Houston and San Diego — and finished with an 11-3 record.

Rooney regards that last game as an important one, too. "We were playing late that day, and we knew we had to win in order to win our first division championship," he said. The Steelers steamrollered the Chargers, 24-2.

On December 29, 1974, the Steelers defeated the Raiders, 24-13, in Oakland to win their first AFC championship and gain their first Super Bowl.

"What was so unique about that game was that it showed the character of Chuck Noll and the team," Rooney said. "Right before the end of the first half, Bradshaw threw a touchdown pass to John Stallworth, who was a rookie. The officials ruled that Stallworth was out of bounds when he made the catch. The instant replay proved otherwise.

"But we didn't cry or go into hysteria. Not the way (Oakland's managing partner) Al Davis did after 'The Immaculate Reception' two years before." The Steelers went on to defeat the Vikings, 16-6, for their first Super Bowl title.

One of the games Rooney had to scratch to get down to 10 games was a 42-6 victory over the Browns in Cleveland in October, 1975. "There were fights in that game, but it showed how the Browns, who had dominated us for so many years, were frustrated by the turn-around in our fortunes," related Rooney.

"We had won the Super Bowl the year before, and we were really showing Cleveland that we were the team. We finished that season by defeating Dallas (21-17) for our second straight Super Bowl (X) championship."

The Steelers didn't win the Super Bowl the following year, yet Dan shared his father's sentiment that the 1976 Steelers may have been the best football team in history.

The Steelers lost four of their first five games. Terry Bradshaw was hurt in the fifth game at Cleveland. Mike Kruczek, a rookie, replaced him at quarterback.

The Steelers won ten consecutive games as the defense yielded just 42 points, ran up an incredible string of 22 scoreless quarters, didn't allow a touchdown in eight of their last nine regular season games, and shut out five of their last eight opponents.

Rooney chose a 7-3 victory over the Bengals on a snowy day in Cincinnati. "That may have been the best defense ever played in the National Football League," said Rooney.

With some relish, Rooney recalled a 34-5 victory over the Houston Oilers in the AFC Championship at Three Rivers Stadium on Jan. 7, 1979.

"It came up cold and rainy," Rooney said. "There were two inches of water on the field the whole game. And we just completely dominated Houston." From there, the Steelers went on to win Super Bowl XIII.

163

"This made us the first team to win three Super Bowls, which made it a big, big thing," Dan said. "Others had won two. This put us at the top."

The next game Rooney mentioned was in the Super Bowl the following year, a 31-19 win over the Los Angeles Rams at the Rose Bowl in Pasadena. I covered that game for *The Pittsburgh Press*.

Rooney didn't want to stop with ten games. He said, "There were just so many."

Pittsburgh Steelers Archives

Franco Harris breaks away from Raiders pursuing him after his "Immaculate Reception" that won the AFC playoff game for Steelers on December 23, 1972 at Three Rivers Stadium.

"He was one of the greatest guys in sports. We had some giant battles with the Steelers, but Art Rooney was always above that. Win or lose, he would treat you the same. There's a saying, 'Shut up until you win, then talk like hell.' He was never like that."
— John Madden
Former Raiders Coach
Fox Sports

John L. Sullivan
Stadium usher

"He liked my name."

"If I live till January (2001), I'll be 80. I was raised in Greenfield, and I played for the Greenfield Preps in the late '30s and early '40s, and they were one of the best sandlot football teams in the city. I was named for the great heavyweight boxing champion. That's one of the reasons Art Rooney liked me; he liked my name. And he knew I was Irish and a city guy. I remember he used to come to a lot of baseball games. He liked to sit in Section 21, near the end of the dugout, here at Three Rivers Stadium. The first thing he did was give me a dollar tip. He shook my hand with his right hand, and he had a short rosary wrapped around his left hand. He said, 'Here's a rosary for you.' And he slipped the rosary off his hand into my open hand. There was a dollar and a rosary in the palm of my hand. He sure was a nice guy."

Art Rooney was honored in "Hail to the Chief" celebration by Western Pennsylvania chapter of the Arthritis Foundation at a dinner at Carnegie Hall. His son, Dan, accompanied him to the dinner.

Andy Starnes/Pittsburgh Press photo in PG Archives

Dale Robertson
Remembers a favor

*"I couldn't ask Art Rooney
to do that for me."*

Dale Robertson covered the National Football League for 25 years, as a beat man for about five years and mostly as a columnist. He was with the Houston Post for 18 years and then with the Houston Chronicle for 11 years. Robertson's personal reflections follow:

The Steelers and Houston Oilers had such a great rivalry in the '70s and they had some great games in the playoffs. I loved coming around the Steelers. There was a rivalry, but it never got nasty. They respected each other. I liked the Steelers better than any other team I ever dealt with.

I was in Pittsburgh to do some advance stories on the Steelers who were going to be playing the Oilers there on Sunday. I was with the *Houston Post* at the time. This was in early September, 1980 and the Houston Astros just happened to be in Pittsburgh to play the Pirates. The Astros were in the heat of the playoff race. I wrote a story in the Steelers' offices that day, and then went upstairs for the baseball game that night. That's when I realized I had left the power cord for my computer in the Steelers' offices. I was desperate because I couldn't send my story to Houston without it. I was dead without that power cord.

I told the Pirates' public relations guys about my dilemma and they said they had no connection with the Steelers — they were in separate offices — and they couldn't help me get into the Steelers' offices. They said the Steelers' offices were closed for the day. They said they would try to help me if they could. They told me Art Rooney, the Steelers' owner, usually showed up at the Pirates' games, and maybe he could help me.

And, later on, they pointed out Art Rooney to me in a nearby box. I didn't feel comfortable asking him to help me out. I couldn't ask Art Rooney to do that for me. I had told the Pirates p.r. people where the power cord could be found. I didn't know what to do.

I'm scoring the baseball game and the next thing I know Mr. Rooney himself is standing next to me, tapping me on the shoulder. He's standing there and he's holding the power cord. He said, "Young man, is that what you want? Here, I heard you left this in our office. Is this what you need?" And he smiled. I was so grateful. I couldn't believe he did that for me. I don't know if he sent someone else down to get it or what. I didn't care.

He stood there for a few minutes and talked to me. You felt like you were talking to God. Like he was so much a part of history. After that, I had a chance to talk to him on a few occasions. He never talked down to you. I don't know how it trickled down to the team — the front-office people and the players — but it did. There were as many stars on that Pittsburgh team as any in the history of the league. Yet they were always the easiest team to deal with. You never failed to get a call back from a Pittsburgh Steelers player.

In early January of 1980, I got into a scuffle with Dan Pastorini, the quarterback of the Houston Oilers. We were both on the ground and he had to be pulled off me. I went to Pittsburgh the next day. The Steelers players were razzing me about what happened. Terry Bradshaw came over and shook my hand. He said, "Hey, I consider Dan a friend of mine. I don't know what happened, but none of that matters. That was completely inexcusable on his part. He was out of line. That embarrasses me." He shook my hand and walked away. Then I went over to talk to L.C. Greenwood. He said, "Chances are I'll get a little bit of revenge for you when we play the Oilers this week." That meant a lot to me to have those guys give me the benefit of the doubt like that, and kid around with me after that incident in Houston.

Bum Phillips, the coach of the Oilers, was well liked by the Steeler fans. It was a fantastic rivalry. They went at each other with all they had on the field, but they didn't carry it off the field.

After nearly 30 years in the business, and covering the NFL for 25 years, I have no fonder memories than of that great rivalry with the Steelers. You felt like you were covering something special. The highlight was Mr. Rooney recovering my power cord for me and saving the day for a Houston sportswriter.

When he died, that story was the lead in my column.

"The Chief" checks out Steelers' clubhouse prior to first practice when regular players returned following strike in mid-November of 1982 season.

Myron Cope
Still standing for Steelers

*"Chief was terrific. He always had a
soft spot for newspaper guys."*

*Myron Cope is a Pittsburgh institution. He made his mark as a writer
of national distinction as a young man. His fame grew during his reign
as a sports talk show host for a quarter of a century at WTAE Radio,
and as an analyst and color man for Steelers broadcasts on WTAE and
now on WDVE for a total of 32 years. It was Cope who created "The
Terrible Towel," a symbol of Steeler mania. Cope celebrated his 72nd
birthday on January 23, 2001. "Anyone who reaches the 70 mark can't
feel cheated," said Cope. "Being the Steelers' color man was totally
unexpected, but it's been a lot of fun." Cope swapped some stories about
his Steelers experience on March 16, 2001 over a salmon salad lunch
at Atria's Restaurant & Tavern in Mt. Lebanon, the community where
he had been living the last two years. He said he had just started to
write his autobiography. He had bought a computer, and gotten some
lessons from his next-door neighbors, but quickly became frustrated by
his awkward efforts. So he discarded the computer and managed to
find a manual typewriter. "Everyone tells me I'm crazy; they say it's so
much easier to write with a computer," growled Cope. "Writing isn't
supposed to be easy. I can't knock out an honest sentence on that computer. Red Smith said he sweated drops of blood when he wrote, and
that's the way it's supposed to be. I'm re-learning how to write again."*

I was a big sports fan growing up in Squirrel Hill. I became aware
of the Steelers from the time I was able to read a sports page or
listen to the radio. Even when they had losing teams, I was still a
fan. When I was in my teens, back in the mid-'40s, I worked as a
vendor at Forbes Field. During the summer I would go out to Forbes
Field early in the morning to get work as a vendor. Myron O'Brisky
was in charge of concessions. You were never sure you were going to
get picked to work. You reported to the ballpark at eight in the
morning. They had what I would call a dungeon for vendors in the
bowels of Forbes Field. You had to stoop through a short door on
Bouquet Street to get in there. You'd sit around on wooden benches,
and there was a wooden picnic table in the room. You'd sit around for
hours, hoping to get work. They had a shape-up like they did on the
docks in those days. O'Brisky's lieutenants would keep a close eye on
you to make sure you were working and not just there to watch the
baseball game. If they caught you sitting around watching the game
they'd weed you out and send you home. You wouldn't get to work any
more.

> *"I like my life because it's pleasant.
> I function in glad places."*
> — Jimmy Cannon, sports columnist

Myron Cope checks out a cartoon of Steelers' lineman of '70s by the late Bill Winstein of *The Pittsburgh Press* during a visit to Atria's Restaurant & Tavern near his condominium home in Mt. Lebanon.

Photos by Jim O'Brien

Cope compares notes with two long-time colleagues on Steelers' press row, left to right, Norm Vargo, sports editor of the *Daily News* in McKeesport, and Dave Ailes, former sports editor of *Greensburg Tribune-Review,* following press conference at Three Rivers Stadium. "Art Rooney always had a soft spot for sportswriters," commented Cope, who followed the team since his grade school days.

The ushers had a union and they were guaranteed work and they'd laugh at us because we weren't organized. We weren't union. They'd have a shape-up and maybe you'd get work, maybe you wouldn't. I used to always get hot dogs. You had to carry a big metal oven around, with a big strap around your neck and shoulders supporting this big metal oven. It was a load and it was hot in places. You know how big I am now...well, I was even smaller then.

During the baseball season, I went out there to make spending money. We weren't rich, and times were tough. You'd get paid each time you sold a load, but you didn't get money. You got tokens each time you came back to get another load of hot dogs, or a bucket of Cokes, or more peanuts or popcorn. Whatever you were selling that day. You never knew what you'd be doing; you just wanted to work and make some spending money. When you sold out, you'd come back to the dungeon. They had a cashier in a booth and she'd give you your tokens. You'd go back out with another load. After the game, you had to spend a few hours cleaning up Forbes Field. You weren't paid anything extra to do that, either. It was part of your workday.

They used to sell these seat cushions. You had to go around the ballpark and pick those up. You had to pick up all the Coke bottles. Yeah, bottles. Can you imagine them letting you have bottles in the ballpark these days? It was no fun. Sometimes there'd be a doubleheader and it would be raining after the last game. The seats were all wet. You had to store them in great bins. It was a mess when they were wet. You couldn't cash in your tokens for cash until you had cleaned up the park. You might get out at ten o'clock at night, having come there at eight in the morning. You had to get in line with your tokens. Sometimes a kid would drop his tokens while he was in line. Suddenly, there were shoes covering all the tokens. A kid might work all day and go home empty-handed. If you didn't have your tokens you didn't get paid.

On Sundays in the fall and winter, I would go out there for the Steelers' games. When I worked baseball games, I worked to make money. When I went to the Steelers' games, I wanted to watch the games. I loved the Steelers so much. I reported for work on Sunday morning early. There was a gate in the dungeon that was closed to keep you from sneaking out into the ballpark. I'd watch O'Brisky's lieutenants coming and going and I noticed that they closed the gate, but they left it unlocked. As soon as they were out of sight, I opened the gate and raced through the stands until I got to the highest point in right field. I'd go into the men's room. I'd hide in a toilet booth. I'd study my rosters from that day's newspaper.

When the gates would open for the fans to come in, I'd race to this spot where they allowed standing room in the upper deck. It was on the 50-yard line. I'd be the first one there. That area would fill up fast, so once the gates were open I had to get there in a hurry. Sometimes it looked like there were more people there than there were in the seats. To get into a Steelers' game, all you had to do was slip fifty cents to the ticket taker and they'd let you in. You didn't have a ticket for a seat so you had to stand. That's how I saw my Steelers' games. I'd get out of that dungeon before they'd give out the blue uniforms that the vendors had to wear when they were working. I never missed a Steelers' game. I'd do the same thing every game, wait for those guys to open the gate in that dungeon, and then I'd race through the stands. O'Brisky's lieutenants never got wise to my game.

I graduated from high school (Taylor Allderdice) in 1947. So I was working at the ballpark during World War II. Times were tough. So I was happy to be there. Jim Finks was one of my favorites; I liked all those guys. I've been a lifelong fan of the Steelers.

This has been a rough year for anyone who cares about the Steelers. Closing down Three Rivers Stadium was a mixed bag for anybody who cares about the Steelers. I had some great times there, some great memories. We lost some Steelers. Steve Furness died, and then Dan Turk and Jack Fleming, my former partner on the radio broadcasts all those years, died. That was a real blow. He'd been to the final game. Then Joe Gilliam. I've been going to too many funerals. I have a strong sense of my mortality. I won't feel short-changed. My dear wife, Mildred, didn't get to hit 70. She died at 63. I only hope I write my book. I want to get the book done. It's about my life. It's not about athletes. It's about my experiences. I'm working hard at it as much as I can. I'm not a fast writer.

I've always gotten along great with the Rooneys. They never interfered. They never once told me what to say, or what I shouldn't say. They're special people. I knew this before I became their broadcaster. Well, I'm not their broadcaster, but they had to approve of my hiring by the radio station.

Hey, I was just along for the ride and my timing couldn't have been better. Take the "Immaculate Reception," for instance. One of my callers (Michael Ord) came up with that name, by the way. I had left the press box with a few minutes remaining in the 1972 playoff game with the Oakland Raiders and I was in the end zone and I saw that play perfectly. I was standing in the corner of the end zone as the media guys do to get to the locker room faster for the post-game interviews. Franco caught that ball off his shoetops and ran straight at me. I'm hollering, "Come on, Franco. Come on, Franco."

I came up with those black and gold towels and they became the "Terrible Towels." Stuff like that made it all great fun. The fans really got into that. Yeah, it's been a great ride. But I was a Steelers' fan before it was my job to be there.

I used to hang out in the Steelers' offices when I was a sportswriter at the *Post-Gazette*. They weren't my beat. I didn't start there until 1951. They were in the Union Trust Building on Grant Street. Before that they were in the Fort Pitt Hotel. Later on, they relocated to the Roosevelt Hotel. So I hung out in their offices when they were at the Union Trust Building and then the Roosevelt Hotel. I used to go to the draft. I was there because I loved it. I would stop there for a few hours before I'd report to work around 4 o'clock.

Chief was terrific. He always befriended young newspaper guys. He'd stop in the pressroom and he'd see a new face, and he'd go over and introduce himself. He'd say, "Hi, I'm Art Rooney. What's your name? You're new around here, aren't you?" The new kid would be overwhelmed that the owner was talking to him. And then Art would ask all kinds of questions about where the kid came from, who his folks were, what nationality he was, what church he went to. He always had a soft spot for newspaper guys.

I remember him asking me to have lunch with him at the Roosevelt Hotel. The Chicago Cubs were in town, and he was taking all the Chicago writers to lunch. He asked me to join him. He was around the team when it traveled by train, and he always had a lot of fun talking to the newspaper guys. They were together more than they are today. There was more freedom of movement. No one was held suspect. He was just a nice guy. I don't think he ever plotted doing any of these things as a p.r. gesture. The Chief went to more funerals than anyone in town. He had Mary Regan go through the obituaries every day and tell him who he should see.

He developed friendships. He liked newspaper guys. He was just doing what came natural. He was just being a terrific guy. When he died, there were so many stories on the air about acts of charity that he had never talked about. He helped so many total strangers. A lot of these stories never surfaced until he died. Then people started calling in and telling one story after another about something The Chief had done on their behalf. You had to like the Chief.

One day, after he had died, I was walking through the Steelers' offices. I was coming from the kitchen and down the hallway. I was going to go through the lobby and outside to smoke a cigarette. This was after they banned cigarette smoking in the stadium and the Steelers' offices. You can't smoke anywhere anymore. Those damn health Nazis. I had a cigarette in my hand as I was walking down the hall. Tom Donahoe, the head of the football operation at the time, came walking toward me. He said, "No smoking, Myron." I was in front of the library, which used to be Art Rooney's office. I pointed through the window at an oil portrait of Art Rooney with a cigar in hand, and I said, "Why don't you go in and tell 'The Chief' to put out that cigar?"

One time when I was a kid reporter at the *Post-Gazette*, we had to take our vacation in the winter when we weren't as busy. Everything evolved around baseball back then. Baseball ruled the town. I decided to go to Florida. I rented an efficiency apartment in a residential section of Miami. I happened to mention my plans when I was loafing around the Steelers' offices one day. The Chief started asking me questions about it. "Do you have the address where you're going to be staying?" he asked. "Do you have a phone number for it?" I said, "Yes," and I gave him the information. He said, "I'll call you. I'll be down there at the same time. I'll take you out to the track." Sure enough, he called me when I was there, and we made a date to go to the track. Somebody was driving him around town and he came by and picked me up. He took me to Hialeah Racetrack.

You know what a great horseplayer he was. I'm betting $2 a race. I didn't know what 'The Chief' is betting, but he's having a bad day. He's just tearing up tickets after every race.

Finally, before the eighth race, he says, "What horse you betting?"

And I said, "I was just out to the paddock and I took a liking to a gray horse. He just looks nice."

"You like the gray horse?" he says.

"Yeah," I say, "I like the way he looks."

The horse was a real long shot, like 20-to-1, I think, something like that. So he gets down on the gray horse. The gray horse won and he picked up his winnings, and he said, "We can go home now." We didn't stay for the last race.

Now I was an inside man, a desk guy at the *Post-Gazette* back then. I was nothing. Who'd expect the owner of the pro football team in town to come by and pick me up and take me out for a day at the races? He was just amazing that way. I'll never forget his generosity.

Jim O'Brien

Myron Cope, left, and his Steelers' broadcast partner, Bill Hillgrove, far right, flank three of the finest homegrown offensive line coaches in the National Football League, Russ Grimm of Pitt and Mt. Pleasant, Joe Bugel of Munhall and Dan Radakovich of Duquesne.

Dante's
Steelers hangout in the '60s

"It was the best ever."

T here will never be another restaurant and bar like Dante's. Some of the biggest stars of the Steelers and some of the top sports writers and sportscasters used to dine and drink there, and that just doesn't happen anymore. It never will again.

Dante's, owned and operated by Dante Sartorio and his older brother, Bruno, was located on Brownsville Road, just across from the Baldwin-Whitehall Shopping Center. It drew customers from all over the city, especially from The Steel Valley and South Hills. It was in business for 23 years, from 1959 to 1992, and it had quite a spirited run.

Bobby Layne, who quarterbacked the Steelers from 1958 to 1962, helped establish it as the top gin joint in the area. Layne and his buddy (and bodyguard) Ernie Stautner had their own table in the dining room. The Steelers played their home games at Forbes Field back then and practiced at the South Park Fairgrounds. Layne and Stautner are now enshrined in the Pro Football Hall of Fame.

Layne was driving from Dante's the night he collided with a streetcar. Lane told the police it was the streetcar driver's fault. "He swerved on my side of the road and hit me," said Layne. Noting that the streetcar was still on its tracks, the cop said, "I don't think so, Bobby."

I was there one night with my dad and my older brother, Dan, who introduced me to Dante's. I had cautioned my dad to take it easy, that it was going to be a long night. My dad usually drank in bars in Homestead and Hazelwood where everyone drank boilermakers.

He started off at Dante's by ordering an Iron City and an Imperial. That's a boilermaker. It was downhill from there. Dan came to me later in the evening and said, "Ernie Stautner's picking on dad. We're not going to put up with that."

I told him we were going to put up with that, and I grabbed Dan and my dad and hustled them out of Dante's as quickly as possible. None of us was taller than 5-9.

I frequented Dante's at the age of 19 and 20, when I was not legally permitted in the place. I was a writing student at Pitt at the time, the sports editor of *The Pitt News*, and I wanted to be around the writers more so than the Steelers. Layne could be tough on writers.

Tom "The Bomb" Tracy was usually there, too, along with Gary Ballman, Lou Cordileone and Lou Michaels. In later years, Bill Nelsen and Jim Bradshaw would show up regularly. They'd chip away at Myron Cope, then a writer for *Sports Illustrated*, and some of his friends in the media, like Pat Livingston, Bob Drum, Dave Kelly, Tom

Finn, Ed Conway and Tom Hritz. There were some Damon Runyan characters among the regulars, like a not-so-funny fellow named Funny Sam.

There were two long-time waitresses who were great with the crowd, too, Helen Kramer from Bon Air and Hilda Phillips from Dormont.

"It was the best ever," claimed Cope when he was asked to recall Dante's. "It was the 'Cheers' of Pittsburgh. There were so many regulars, and it was the football hangout. Dante was a very congenial guy, a swell guy. He was one of my best friends. He could get along with athletes and he knew how to look after them and how to talk around them."

Cope explained that when he and Dante would be discussing the latest antics of Layne, the blond bomber quarterback of the Steelers, they would refer to Layne as "Whitey."

"That was in case some yahoo was at the bar for the first time," said Cope. "We didn't want them spreading stories about Bobby to their buddies. We protected him that way. Dante knew it was smart to do that."

Cope, then 71 and still doing the Steelers games on the radio, and I were having this conversation because we both learned that weekend in late June, 2000, that Dante Sartorio had died, at age 84, of cancer at his retirement residence in Cape Cod. His brother, Bruno, had died a year or so earlier.

"They had both worked at the Pittsburgher Hotel," recalled Livingston, then 79, the former sports editor of *The Pittsburgh Press*, "and they brought a lot of customers with them from downtown when they opened their place. Dante was a helluva guy and he got along with everybody. He made a good drink and they had good food. It was a fun place to be."

Everybody behaved, for the most part, and you felt safe there, something that couldn't be said for all the nightclubs on Rt. 51 in those days. For me, it was similar to what I enjoyed at Frankie Gustine's Restaurant and Bar on the Pitt campus, near Forbes Field. There were interesting people there from the world of sports, and you could learn something from them.

It was part of my education at the University of Pittsburgh. Dante Sartorio and Frankie Gustine were great guys and they made sure you knew everyone.

The late Bob Drum could give you a rough time, but he taught you some things — things you should do and things you shouldn't do — and you benefited both ways. I was fortunate to know these guys. And now I'm one of the older writers sharing stories.

"Never pass a bar that has your name on it."
— Rule of travel in Ireland

George Blanda *H·O·F·81*

He came from good stock

"You do what you need to do."

George Blanda was bluffing and his brothers knew it. So they chuckled collectively when he raised them one more time as they played the last hand of a poker game at the kitchen table of their boyhood home in Youngwood, Pennsylvania.

There were five of them. Clockwise from George, age 73, they were Tom, 60; Mike, 78; John, 66; and Paul, 68. This was Paul's place now. He and his wife had spruced it up after his mother died and taken over the family manse. Paul was the host for this family reunion. The women, including George's wife, Betty, were next door in the living room, just sharing family news. There was Paul's wife, Marjorie; John's wife, Emily; and Margaret Yakubisin, one of the Blanda girls, who lived nearby.

When the last game began, Paul pitched a quarter into the center of the table and said, "Let's ante up 25 cents this time for the last game." But George had the last word. "No, let's put 35 cents in," he said as he did so. It was Paul's place, but it was still George's game. "If we're going to play this one game," said George, "I've got to get even."

George Blanda has always been like that. It's his game. He's in charge. His brothers were used to it by now, and they simply smiled and followed his lead. He was the eighth-born of 12 children, but he somehow became the boss. Paul just winked at me when George increased the stake.

George gained quite a reputation as a card player — poker and gin — during his 26 years of playing pro football. No sooner had his team boarded an airplane going to or from a football game somewhere in America and George had a blanket spread out on the empty seat next to him. Let the game begin.

Someone mentioned that the Blandas were all born at home, with the help of a midwife. "There were no doctors involved," said Mike. "There was a Mrs. Rady, who lived two blocks down the street. She was a Polish lady. She delivered all of us. We were all Hunkies. "

Noting the size of his family, George offered, "I never slept alone until I got married." That broke up the room. Paul mentioned that he had just played golf that morning with former Pirates' star Bill Mazeroski and former Steelers' star Ray Mathews. "We get out and play golf a lot," he said. "They're good friends."

This was around 7:30 p.m. on Thursday, August 3, 2000. George Blanda had come home via Canton, Ohio where he had attended induction ceremonies five days earlier at the Pro Football Hall of Fame. Steelers president Dan Rooney and former 49ers and Chiefs

Poker game gets competitive when Blanda brothers get together at their boyhood home in Youngwood. They are, left to right, host Paul Blanda, brothers George, Tom, Mike and John.

Blandas always have American flag flying from their front porch on George Blanda Drive. They are, left to right, Paul, Mike, George, Tom and John.

quarterback Joe Montana from Monongahela were among those honored in the Class of 2000.

Montana was the most recent quarterback from western Pennsylvania to gain such honors. The area had a reputation for turning out top-notch quarterbacks. Blanda had been one of them. Joe Namath of Beaver Falls and Johnny Unitas and Danny Marino, both of Pittsburgh, were among the all-time top players at the position. Marino was regarded as a sure-fire first ballot inductee in the Hall of Fame when he became eligible. There were over 30 first-rate quarterbacks in college and pro programs who had come from western Pennsylvania. Blanda had been one of 110 members of the Hall of Fame to be in Canton for a special celebration called for by NFL Commissioner Paul Tagliabue. He'd traveled there from his home in suburban Chicago.

I had caught George at a post-induction party at the Hall of Fame in the company of his former boss on the Oakland Raiders, Al Davis, himself a Hall of Fame inductee. They were conversing in the same area as Tony Dorsett of Hopewell, Mike Ditka of Aliquippa, and two former Steelers greats, John Henry Johnson and Joe Greene. It was Greene who had presented Dan Rooney for induction.

I told George I had spoken to Paul about visiting the Blanda brothers in Youngwood the following week, and asked George if we could get together for an interview. He said that was fine. He knew I was interested in athletes from western Pennsylvania.

Blanda mentioned that Ditka was a No. 1 draft choice of the Houston Oilers when he was with them, but Ditka decided to sign with the NFL Bears. "Mike was a great player," said Blanda. "He could have helped us." He said he saw Ditka at charity golf outings in the Chicago area.

"What man doesn't take a drink?"
— Mrs. Mary Blanda

I recognized the Blanda home as I approached it on what is now called George Blanda Drive. It's in Youngwood, a community of 3,000 citizens near Greensburg in Westmoreland County, about 50 miles east of Pittsburgh. Youngwood is 13 miles southwest of the Steelers' summer training camp at St. Vincent College in Latrobe.

It's a well-kept two-story home with white aluminum siding. It's a shrine to family pride. If everybody looked after their homes and yards the way the Blandas always have this would be a better country. There is an American flag on display on the front porch. The yard is well groomed. There's a chain-link fence surrounding it that wasn't there when I first visited that home on July 30, 1981. That was two days before George was inducted into the Pro Football Hall of Fame. The home was on South Third Street back then. It's also busy Rt. 119. His mother, Mary Blanda, 84 at the time, was mowing the lawn when I arrived. She was doing so with an old push mower. She shook my hand in greeting, and did so with the firmest grip ever offered by any 84-year-old woman. When I met Mary Blanda it helped explain how her son had stayed and played so long in pro football. Soon after, she offered me a shot of whiskey to officially welcome me to her home. She wouldn't take no for an answer. "It's a tradition with men who come here," she said sternly and with a strong Slavic accent. "What man doesn't take a drink?"

I went there that time on assignment from *The Pittsburgh Press*, with Al Herrmann, a first-rate photographer, and Pat Hanlon, an impressive summer intern and Pitt student. In January, 2001, Hanlon was at Super Bowl XXXV in Tampa, Florida as the vice president for communications of the New York Giants. He still remembers meeting the Blanda family way back when.

"He had the will to win."
— Al Davis

George Blanda is best known for his durability, grit, gamesmanship, place-kicking accuracy and orneriness. George Blanda played pro football longer than any other player — 26 years, from 1949 until just before the start of the 1976 season. His goal was to play until he was 50, but he closed his career just one month short of his 49th birthday.

"And I set that goal when I was 47," boasted Blanda.

He played for the Chicago Bears, the Houston Oilers and the Oakland Raiders. As a quarterback, he threw more than 4,000 passes. As a place-kicker, he remained the NFL's leading scorer in pro football history until former Steeler Gary Anderson surpassed him during the 2000 season. Blanda's 840-game tenure was the longest ever. "When I first went to the Bears they had Sid Luckman, Johnny Lujack and Bobby Layne," recalled Blanda. "I played linebacker as a regular with the Bears almost the whole season. I covered little Buddy Young one-on-one."

Blanda's scoring record totaled 2,002 points — almost 400 points more than his nearest rival when he entered the Hall of Fame — with nine touchdowns, 943 conversions and 335 field goals. As a passer, the 6-2, 215-pound Blanda completed 1,911 passes for 26,920 yards and 236 touchdowns. In 1961, when he directed the Oilers to a second straight AFL championship, he threw a record-tying 36 touchdown passes. At Houston, one of his teammates was John Henry Johnson.

"Whenever I'd see Mr. Rooney at Three Rivers Stadium or at the Allegheny Club we'd always trade cigars."
— Ken Malli

Although Blanda held 21 NFL, AFL or AFC championship game marks and had 21 listings in the regular-season record book when he retired, all of his work might have gone relatively unnoticed had it not been for an unreal five-game string of heroics in 1970. It gained him national media attention and admiration.

It began, fittingly enough against the Steelers, his favorite football team as a kid, when he single-handedly produced four victories and a tie for the Raiders when defeat seemed imminent in every outing. Blanda came off the bench each time, at age 43, and rallied the Raiders.

"George never got the recognition he should have," opined Paul. "What he did that year he had done all his life."

George Blanda became the sports hero for the geriatric set that 1970 season. He had Johnny Carson talking about him on his late-night show. George made every senior feel a little better the way he showed those snot-nosed kids how to compete. He was the only player whose pro career spanned four decades.

"I was a math instructor at West Point in 1970," recalled Tom Blanda. "Everybody there wanted to talk to me about George. It never bothered me. I was so proud of him. I admired what he accomplished, that he never gave up. He proved that if you worked hard you could achieve anything. He never got anything given to him. "

Blanda was labeled "the greatest clutch player in the history of professional football" by Davis, the Raiders' owner, at his induction ceremonies. "He had the will to win," declared Davis. "George Blanda was a fierce competitor who had a God-given killer instinct to make it happen when the game was on the line."

It was no different when Blanda was playing cards with his brothers back home in Youngwood. Or when he was recounting the details of that five-game string of comebacks. I had done my homework for this interview, perhaps to a fault. The night before I went to the Blanda home I re-read a book I had in my library called *Blanda*, by the late Wells Twombly.

I had the temerity to correct Blanda about the details of one game. His face reddened, his chin got firmer and he glared at me. "Hey, this is my story!" he scolded me. "Let me tell it. I know what the hell happened!" He grumbled something under his breath, and I was worried that I had blown the interview. He smiled and resumed his story. I never interrupted him again.

I should have remembered from Twombly's book that Blanda never suffered sports writers too well. He could be brusque and treat them with disdain if they annoyed him somehow.

"I seldom talked to sports writers," George once said. "I knew who I could trust. I was usually the first guy dressed and out of the locker room."

I had invited a pal of mine, Bill Priatko, who lived in nearby North Huntingdon, to meet me at the Blanda home. Priatko played pro ball briefly, with short stints with the Cleveland Browns, Green

Bay Packers and Pittsburgh Steelers. He liked and admired men of the Blanda breed. He had played with Paul Blanda at Pitt in the early '50s. Both were linebackers in the same corps as All-American and later All-Pro and Hall of Famer Joe Schmidt.

Priatko managed to get on the wrong side of Blanda that evening, too, with something he said about George's legendary coach at Kentucky, Paul "Bear" Bryant. Blanda doesn't budge once he's expressed a view on any subject, especially sports and politics. George did take me for a tour of his hometown, however, pointing out old haunts, and he took me to the local train station and railroad museum. He said hello to some young people standing in front of a tattoo parlor in midtown. They had some interesting body markings.

As he was sitting on a bench at the train station, he told me a story about how he and his brothers used to pick up pieces of coal that fell from railroad cars that passed on the rails just a few feet from his backyard. If the coal didn't fall on its own, the Blanda boys might poke a stick at the top of the pile. "Hey, we never had much money," said George, "and we needed it to keep the fire going in our home. You did whatever you needed to do."

It was a philosophy that served Blanda well as a football and basketball player at Youngwood High School, at the University of Kentucky and in a roller coaster pro football career. He pointed out the Sell Building nearby. "My sister owned that building," he recalled. "I painted the rooms on all three floors and I got paid $20. Money was hard to come by in those days. Things were a little tight."

Blanda was always a big fan of Art Rooney and the Pittsburgh Steelers. "He had five sons, just like my dad, so I could relate to the Rooneys," said Blanda. "But we had a few girls in our family, too. The Rooneys always seemed like the real McCoys to me. I liked their style."

When he was inducted into the Hall of Fame, Blanda was 53 years old. He chose to boost others. He extolled the American family, especially his own, the American flag, and the American Football League. He praised the Pittsburgh Steelers as well as the Oakland Raiders, Joe Namath and Al Davis.

His mother sat next to him, wearing a white crocheted shawl over her broad shoulders, and he would pat her on the back or on her knee as he made his points.

Blanda spoke about the influence of his mom and dad, Mike Blanda, who had died in 1959. Both had immigrated to this country from Czechoslovakia as teenagers. They provided the proper start.

"I had good guidance and love," he said. "And I had coaches like Bear Bryant. They taught me the virtues of hard work and determination and discipline, and that's what I needed to last so long."

> *"Money is better than poverty.*
> *If only for financial reasons."*
> — Woody Allen

"God sent me a good baby."
— Mary Blanda

There were still traces of an Old World accent in Mary Blanda's voice. She had come to this country as a 15-year-old girl from Prague in 1912, a year after Mike Blanda, whom she would soon marry, had come over from the same Slovak village.

They had 12 children. One of them, Edward, died at six months. "But God sent me a good baby nine months later," recalled Mrs. Blanda with a big smile and much animation. "He gave me George Frederick."

In the hallway of her home, Mrs. Blanda showed off several pictures of her other sons, who were all good at sports. The biggest photograph was of Tom Blanda, who quarterbacked the Army football team, class of 1961. He went on to become an officer in the Army. Tom was the youngest of the Blanda brood.

He played against Pitt when Army last had good football teams, when All-American backs Bob Anderson and Pete Dawkins played behind him.

"You'll notice there are no pictures of the daughters," said Irene, who was one of them. She and Helen and Mary were all present at the time.

The Blandas had lived there nearly 60 years. There was a shrine to the Blessed Virgin Mary in the front yard, a pair of pink flamingos flanking a birdbath in the backyard, and a ceramic deer family grazing in the next yard. Norman Rockwell might have painted the scene.

Directly across the street was the home of one of the Blanda women, Mrs. Margaret Yakubisin, who was looking after two grandchildren. Her home was also neat, with a swing and potted flowers on the front porch. There seemed to be a lot of American flags and potted flowers on the porches along the main streets of Youngwood. It's that kind of town. Actress Shirley Jones, who starred in "The Music Man," grew up just down the road in Smithton. Shirley's dad owned the Stoney Brewing Co. Inside the home of George Blanda's sister, I saw a player piano, dried-up palm from Palm Sunday lying across the top of a plaque picturing the Sacred Heart, and doilies atop furniture, old-fashioned and honest as can be. In a bookcase, beside a Catholic Bible, are two books about George Blanda, the favorite son and beloved brother.

"This is a once-in-a-lifetime thing for us," said Margaret. "It's great. We're a very close-knit family. We never fight or argue, for as many of us as there are."

Their father, Mike, was a coal-miner most of his life. After working the mines near Uniontown, he worked in Youngwood at the Robertshaw Thermostat Company, and later as a custodian at Hempfield Area High School.

The Blanda family of Youngwood poses with an enlarged photo of son and brother, George Blanda, two days before he was inducted into Pro Football Hall of Fame in ceremonies at Canton, Ohio on August 1, 1981. From left to right are Helen, Joe, Mary, Paul, Mrs. Mary Blanda, Mike, Tom, Margaret and Irene.

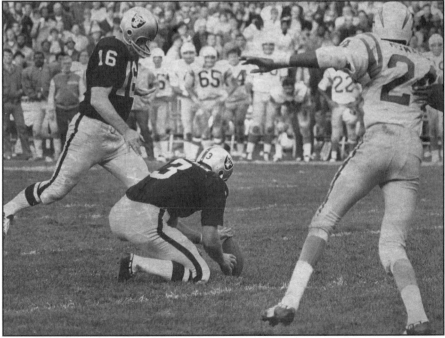

For the fifth time in as many games, George Blanda was the hero as he kicks a game-winning 16-yard field goal with seven seconds left to play as the Raiders defeated the San Diego Chargers, 20-17, on November 21, 1970.

A neighbor, Steve Ersick, 66, who was retired from Robertshaw, remembered Mike as well. "I remember one game at the high school, George was going ten and 15 yards a crack, like a bull, but finally the beating took its toll, and he limped off the field," said Ersick. "Mike was standing behind the bench, and he hollored to George. 'Get the hell back in there.' And George went back."

Margaret Yakubisin told a similar story of how Mike once gave the same advice to Tom, who wanted to quit the U.S. Military Academy and come home. "You have an opportunity there to get a great education," Mike reminded his son. "You stay right there."

He stayed in the Army for 24 years and retired in San Antonio as a full-bird colonel.

Ersick remembered more about the young George Blanda. "He was just an outstanding athlete. A town like this, so small, and tried to compete against bigger schools like Latrobe and Greensburg, which is where I went. George and the other Blandas just stood out like beacons. In basketball, it'd be one star against five.

"Where George really showed himself was in track. He finished first in the shot put, javelin and discus in the county meet. His brother Paul, who later played for Pitt alongside Joe Schmidt, did the same thing a few years later. The Blandas were all good boys."

George remembered his dad well. "If we got out of line, he made us pay for it," said George. "He closed the door at 9 o'clock and we were expected to be home by then."

"The strap was waiting for you if you came home after the curfew," said Paul. "And you were not allowed to cry."

"I always rooted for Joe Namath."

What's so amazing about George Blanda is that he not only helped beat the Steelers in that great streak in 1970, but he scored enough points to help the Bears beat them back in 1949 when he kicked a field goal in the late going. It points up the eras he spanned when you consider that "Bulldog" Turner was centering the ball, and George McAfee was holding it for Blanda. Both have been in the Hall of Fame for quite awhile.

"I remember getting a game ball in 1958 after an exhibition game against the Steelers," he said. "We won a close one when I came off the bench and led the team on an 80-yard drive for the game-winning touchdown. But I've always been a big Steeler fan, and I still am, except when they're playing Oakland.

"My family feels that way, too. They're still basically Steeler and Pirate and University of Pittsburgh fans. But they still have a soft spot in their hearts for the Raiders.

"People asked me why I had Al Davis present me to the Hall of Fame. People really don't need to know. Without him, though, I wouldn't be here. He gave me nine years. He gave me a chance when everybody else frowned on a guy over 35.

"He's a sharp man, a football genius, I'd say. I've had a long rapport with him. I always admired him. We've had our differences, but we dealt with them. He did an awful lot for the American Football League.

"I always rooted for Joe Namath. He was the highlight of the AFL. He gave it credibility with the public. None of us who played needed it, but we did as far as the fans were concerned.

"And what Joe did in Super Bowl III was just the icing on the cake. He not only guaranteed the victory over the Baltimore Colts, but he came through and made good on it when he beat the Colts, 16-7.

"And Pittsburgh can be thankful for the AFL. They got Chuck Noll, and he was basically AFL-oriented in his philosophy. It was great for Pittsburgh, Baltimore and Cleveland.

"We're proud of the AFL. For ten years, I had to live with the stigma that I was a semi-pro football player, even in my hometown. I was just playing somewhere in a minor league, they thought. That's what made the 1970 season so sweet.

"It's a great thrill for all the old AFLers. Jim Otto and I played in all 10 years of the AFL, and were among the few to do so. Then we showed the establishment that we belonged with the best. That's what makes the Hall of Fame award doubly great.

"There were a lot of great players in Oakland and Pittsburgh in that period, and many of them are in the Hall of Fame now. The Steelers were our rivals, but I respect what they did. It was unbelievable to win four Super Bowls. They had to go through three playoff wins to get it. It's unbelievable that they could do that.

"One of my favorites on that football team was Mel Blount. I saw Mel when he was inducted into the Pro Football Hall of Fame, and I got to meet him. I thought he was the best defensive back who ever played. I thought the Steelers were great in the '70s. They knocked us out of the Super Bowl two years. They were a great team. They were better than us the two years they beat us. You gotta give them credit."

Jim O'Brien

George Blanda was a big admirer of the Steelers of the '70s, especially Joe Greene. They got together at the "Greatest Pro Football Reunion" at Hall of Fame in Canton, Ohio in late July, 2000.

Pro quarterbacks who came out of Western Pennsylvania

Team	Name	Hometown	High School	College	RD	Year	Also
Detroit	Charlie Batch	West Mifflin	Steel Valley	Eastern Michigan	2	1998	
Oakland	George Blanda	Youngwood	Youngwood	Kentucky	12	1948	Chicago Houston Baltimore
New Orleans	Marc Bulger	Pittsburgh	Central Catholic	West Virginia	6	2000	
Kansas City	Tom Clements	McKees Rocks	Canevin	Notre Dame	FA	1980	Oakland
Buffalo	Dan Darragh	Pittsburgh	South Catholic	William & Mary	13	1968	
Edmonton (CFL)	Bernie Faloney	E. Carnegie	Scott (Clark)	Maryland	1	1954	San Francisco
Washington	Gus Frerotte	Ford City	Ford City	Tulsa	7	1994	Detroit
Tampa Bay	Chuck Fusina	McKees Rocks	Montour	Penn State	5	1979	
Green Bay	Arnold Galiffa	Donora	Donora	Army	7	1949	New York San Francisco
Pittsburgh	Joe Gasparella	Vandergrift	Vandergrift	Notre Dame	4	1948	Chicago Cardinals
Pittsburgh	Terry Hanratty	Butler	Butler	Notre Dame	2	1969	Tampa
NY Giants	Jeff Hostettler	Davidsville	Conemaugh Twp.	West Virginia	3	1984	Oakland
Denver	John Hufnagel	McKees Rocks	Montour	Penn State	14	1973	
Denver	Ken Karcher	Glenshaw	Shaler	Tulane	4	1991	
Buffalo	Jim Kelly	East Brady	East Brady	Miami	1	1983	Houston (USFL)

Team	Name	Hometown	High School	College	RD	Year	Also
Chicago Bears	John Lujack	Connellsville	Connellsville	Notre Dame	1	1948	
Washington	Richie Lucas	Glassport	Glassport	Penn State	1	1961	
Miami	Danny Marino	Pittsburgh	Central Catholic	Pitt	1	1983	
Washington	Fred Mazurek	Uniontown	Redstone	Pitt	FA	1965	
Tampa Bay	Scott Milanovich	Butler	Butler	Maryland	FA	1998	Cleveland
San Francisco	Joe Montana	New Eagle	Ringgold	Notre Dame	3	1979	Kansas City
NY Jets	Joe Namath	Beaver Falls	Beaver Falls	Alabama	1	1965	LA Rams
Green Bay	Babe Parilli	Rochester	Rochester	Kentucky	1	1952	New England
Montreal (CFL)	Sandy Stephens	Uniontown	Uniontown	Minnesota		1961	
Miami	John Stofa	Johnstown	Bishop McCourt	Buffalo	FA	1966	Cincinnati
Pittsburgh	Rick Strom	Pittsburgh	Fox Chapel	Georgia Tech	FA	1969	
Washington	Harry Theofiledes	Homestead	Homestead	Waynesburg	FA	1966	
Chicago	Willie Thrower	New Kensington	New Kensington	Michigan State	FA	1953	Winnipeg (CFL)
Baltimore	Bill Troup	Bethel Park	Bethel Park	South Carolina	FA	1974	Green Bay
Baltimore	John Unitas	Pittsburgh	St. Justin	Louisville	9	1959	San Diego
San Diego	Matt Vlasic	Monaca	Center	Iowa	4	1987	Kansas City
New England	Scott Zolak	Monongahela	Ringgold	Maryland	4	1991	Miami, New York Jets
Hamilton (CFL)	Joe Zuger	Homestead	Homestead	Arizona State	FA	1962	

Compiled by Dave Miller, Acme, Pa.

Chuck Tanner
An optimist from New Castle

"There's only one."

Chuck Tanner was the manager of the Pittsburgh Pirates for nine years (1977-1985), and directed the team to a World Series victory in 1979. He grew up in New Castle and made his home there during a long career as a baseball player and manager. In recent years, he was a scout for the Milwaukee Brewers. Tanner broke into the big leagues as an outfielder for the Milwaukee Braves in 1955. He hit a homerun in his first at-bat on April 12, becoming the third pinch-hitter in history to smash a home run on the first pitch he saw. I spoke to him about Art Rooney at a Pirates' game during their last summer at Three Rivers Stadium. Here are Tanner's thoughts on a special friend:

A rt Rooney was always in my office when we were playing at home. I'd give him signed baseballs, and he was always giving me some footballs. I signed my name to my World Series jacket and gave it to him. Every home stand at Three Rivers, he'd come down and see me every day. He'd stay for ten or 15 minutes and I really cherish the memories of those times now. Back then it was almost a part of the daily routine, and I was always happy to see him. But now I realize how special that time with him was, and how lucky I was to know him. He wrote me a letter now and then. He'd tell my great stories. He brought his brother, Father Silas, with him a few times. He told me about his big day at the race track. He made a real killing. He said when he came back home from New York he threw the money on his bed in front of his wife. She said, "What did you do — rob a bank?" He laughed at his own story.

There was nobody like Art Rooney. There's only one. Guys like him come along only once in a hundred years and he was the one. Everybody should have had the honor to talk to him. Once, I told him I bought a mare. He said, "You got a free season with one of my horses." He said, "You have a season" — they called it a season — "whenever you want to." I never took him up on his offer.

Chuck Tanner, at right, joins Kent Tekulve, Chuck Noll and Dan Rooney at special promotion at Three Rivers Stadium.

Pittsburgh Pirates Archives

Pat Livingston
The Steelers' first scout

*"You know a good football
player when you see one."*
— Jock Sutherland

*Pat Livingston, at age 80 in October 2000, was retired from The
Pittsburgh Press where he had worked for 33 years (1949-1982). He
had served as the sports editor and columnist and, before that, as a
long-time reporter on the Steelers' beat. In 1979, he received the Dick
McCann Award and was installed in the sportswriters' wing of the Pro
Football Hall of Fame. We met for lunch at Da Lallo's Restaurant in
Bethel Park, where he lived in an apartment complex about two miles
away. He reflected on his days with Art Rooney and the Steelers:*

I saw the Steelers' first game at Forbes Field. It cost about a quarter to get in, as I recall. Jap Douds was the coach. I was a sophomore at Central Catholic High School for the 1933-34 school year
just a few blocks away. We lived in a home in The Hill, near Schenley
High School. We lived near a reservoir and park at the highest point
in Allegheny County. My father, John Livingston, was a streetcar
motorman.

I was the sports editor of the school newspaper — *The Viking* —
at Central Catholic. I used to go to the Duquesne Gardens, which was
just around the corner from Central Catholic, where they had pro
hockey, some great boxing and college basketball and even college
boxing. The Hornets and Duquesne University played there.

I was also the sports editor of the paper when I went to St.
Francis of Loretto College. It was called *The Lorettan*. I was an
English major. I just loved sports. Art Rooney came up to check out
the campus for a possible football camp in 1938. Art Rooney asked me
to see him. I was also the assistant public relations man and secretary
for Jim Leonard, who was the football coach at St. Francis. He would
be the Steelers' coach in 1945.

Art asked his friend Buck Krause, a fighter and boxer, to
accompany him on the trip to St. Francis. I was in a conversation with
Jim Leonard. Leonard was talking about a boxing show they were
having at the school that night. There were a lot of amateur boxers up
there. A guy named Ralph Martz from Bloomfield was promoting it.
Leonard asked Art Rooney to stay around for the show. They had Art
Rooney come up in the ring to pick a winner out of a hat for a $1,000
prize. My mother won the prize. I had the ticket. I took those guys out
to a Burley's Bar in Loretto to celebrate. When I gave my mother the
money, it was short the $40 I had spent on everyone. She wanted to
know where the $40 was. There was an IRS man there and he wanted

189

a cut of it. But I told him the prize belonged to the five Livingston boys, $200 apiece. He said he wouldn't have to report it then. My brother Tom also went to St. Francis of Loretto. He was a good friend of the Rooneys socially.

Art became a good friend. He had five sons and my mother had five sons and he thought that was great. He was just like me. He was like one of my friends from Pittsburgh. Art Rooney never hired me. Bert Bell hired me the first time and then Jock Sutherland hired me. Bert Bell was running the team when I first went to work for them. I just went in to Art's office one day and asked him for a job in public relations. They needed one. He said, "It's too bad you weren't in earlier. I just hired one." He called me a few days later and sent me up to Hershey to talk with Bert Bell. The Steelers were training there. I took the train to Hershey. I called him from the lobby of the hotel, which was the Hershey Inn. He tells me to come up to his room. He's in bed. He's got this big, fat belly. But he got up and talked to me. He hired me to help out.

In 1940, Art sold the Steelers to a guy named Alexis Thompson. He was an heir to a cosmetics fortune. He was a real playboy from New York. He wanted a team closer to New York. He went to Bert Bell with that idea. He said, "I'll be glad to take the Eagles to Pittsburgh if Rooney is all for it." Bell was looking for a partner and Rooney was having second thoughts about getting out of the NFL. So Bell got Rooney to go in with him. They switched franchises and, to this day, Pittsburgh plays under the Philadelphia Eagles franchise, and the Eagles under the Steelers franchise. The Steelers used to have the document hanging in the office. We also swapped some players. We got Chuck Cherundolo from the Eagles. He was the first real hero for the Steelers. When he retired, he stayed around town and sold wines here.

Art Rooney is one of my all-time favorites. He was probably the most sincere person who ever lived. He never avoided answering a question. He genuinely liked people. I went every place with him. He was usually with Jack Sell, who covered the team for the *Post-Gazette* and had grown up with him on the North Side; with Joe Tucker, who broadcast the ballgames on the radio, and Ed Kiely, who was the Steeelers' publicist at the time.

We'd travel together to Chicago and New York. When we played in Los Angeles we'd always go to Las Vegas. We'd go to some of the great restaurants. That was the big thing. He liked the sportswriters everywhere, not just in Pittsburgh.

Art usually did the driving. Before long, he'd have all of us saying the rosary while we were riding along, all except Tucker, that is, who was Jewish. I got Art upset one time with something I said about us saying the rosary. He was passing cars in tunnels as we were heading to New York City. When we came out of one of the tunnels, I said, "Now I know why you have us saying the rosary. The way you drive we better say our prayers." He didn't like that.

Another time we drove to Chicago for the College All-Star Game. I was driving a brand new Pontiac. After that game, we got in my car and took off for Buffalo. This was before Buffalo had its own pro football team. I think we were playing an exhibition game there against the New York Giants. He made me quit driving. He said I drove too slow. He said we'd never get there in time for the kickoff, and he took over the driving. You didn't argue with Art Rooney.

He liked to go to the racetracks. Several of the owners were into horse racing in those days. They were sportsmen. Tim Mara of the Giants, for instance, had been a bookmaker when bookmaking at the track was legal. Bookmakers were put out of business when they introduced parimutuel machines. That's when Art Rooney got out of it. He didn't like gambling machines. When he made that big killing at the track, I think he placed some of his bets with Tim Mara. He never said how much money he made those two days because he didn't want to have to pay tax on it. He was smart enough to know that.

When I was working at the Fort Pitt Hotel, which was located where the Doubletree Hotel is today, Joe Carr, who lived on the North Side, was the ticket manager. Fran Fogarty was the business manager. The football team was strictly a sideline to Art Rooney. He never really got interested in the Steelers until he hired Sutherland. Sutherland got him interested. Sutherland was the second guy to hire me. Rooney asked me, "If you want your job back, you better get to know him." I didn't think I had a chance. He was a great friend of Frank Scott, who had worked for him at Pitt. I thought Scott might get the p.r. job, but he wanted to be the equipment manager. Then halfway through the season Sutherland told me he needed a scout more than a publicist. He didn't want to go for another season with the players he had. I told him I didn't know anything about scouting, and he said, "You know a good football player when you see one." Sutherland was well-connected with the colleges. We had two good drafts in a row and then Sutherland went nuts and he made me quit. I just couldn't stand him anymore. He forgot everything. He'd tell you to do something and the next day he'd forget it. I sent Ray Ary, a big blocking back from Oklahoma, a contract. And he sends it back signed. Not long after Ary gets caught for drunk driving. And Sutherland is screaming, "Who the hell signed that guy? You did! From now on, don't sign anyone without my approval." He kicked Ary off the team right then and there. He never played for the Steelers.

Sutherland had a nephew in England become a doctor. He wanted to bring him here. He needed to send him all kinds of forms to fill out so he could apply to come here. Sutherland asked me if I'd take the package to the post office. He gave me $2. So I came back upstairs after I did that and went to my office. Johnny Michelosen was sitting on my desk. Mike Nixon, Frank Souchak and Mugsy Skladany were sitting there, too. I asked Michelson to give me an envelope from my desk. I wrote Dr. Sutherland on the envelope and put his change in the envelope. Those coaches asked me what I was doing, and

I explained the transaction to them. "I got to put this on his desk," I said, "or he'll be accusing me of stealing his money." They laughed about my concerns. Sure enough, just then the phone rings and Michelosen picks it up. It's Sutherland telling Michelosen to get the change I owed him. It was a dollar and 30 cents or something like that.

Sutherland had a brand new Cadillac. He only had two months on it when he died. In his will, he left it to his 90-plus-years mother. She was in Scotland. The streets in their neighborhood weren't even big enough to handle that car, but it was shipped over to Scotland. A few months before he died, I told everybody "Something's wrong with him." He wouldn't go to a doctor. One of his players was a doctor. He told Sutherland to get a big straw hat. Told him he needed to protect himself from the sun. He'd be sitting at his desk, rubbing his head. He had a brain tumor, and no one knew it.

He was a good coach, first at Brooklyn and then in Pittsburgh. In 1947, we lost to Philadelphia in the playoffs, 21-0. They had Bosh Pritchard and Steve Van Buren; that was "Greasy" Neale's team. That was the only playoff game they ever played in before Chuck Noll came along.

I was very lucky. I met some of the most interesting people through Art Rooney. Like Jim Farley. He was the Postmaster General and head of the Democratic Party. I was waiting for the players to get registered at a hotel in Syracuse. I see this guy going up to Art Rooney in the lobby. He grabbed Art Rooney and hugged him. Later on, I said, "Hey, Art, tell me something. Of all those friends you have, so many guys are in the Democratic Party. How come you're a Republican?" He told me he owed so much to James J. Coyne, who was his political mentor. Art was a big Republican leader on the North Side. He was a big power in politics in his time. Roosevelt came along and they all turned Democrats. Art never did, out of loyalty to Coyne.

One day Art Rooney called me, and he called me every name in the book. He really got hot. I asked him what was wrong. He said he was at the Dapper Dan banquet and he bumped into Les Biederman, who was the sports editor at the time. He told Biederman he had to go ask Pitt to let him out of his agreement to play at Pitt Stadium. They couldn't do any good at Pitt Stadium. Biederman told the editor about it and the editor gave me hell for not writing the story. So I wrote the story. Art was mad about it. I told him, "What are you blaming me for? You shouldn't have told Biederman. Why would you tell him something like that if I was holding back the same story?" He called me back five minutes later and he apologized.

Art's primary interest was in the Chicago Board of Trade. He was a big investor in the commodities market. That's where he made most of his money. He once told me that he if he knew what his sons knew he never would have lost his interest in the Steelers.

Art Rooney didn't work at being a good guy, either. He was born that way. A good man. It wasn't until he won the Super Bowls that he became so respected. Before that, no one took him seriously.

After Art decided to put his mind to football, when he had Sutherland, he was good at it. He made some good coaching choices. Michelosen was a good coach. Buddy Parker was a good coach. Michelosen knew football, but he didn't know the business of football.

The day before Christmas, after my wife died, Jimmy Boston drove up to my house and he unloaded the biggest bag of Christmas gifts. Art Rooney sent him with the stuff. Lots of nice clothes. The greatest Christmas my kids ever had. Art did that for three or four years. That's the way he was. He never expected any favors in return.

Michael Chikiris/Pittsburgh Press photo from PG Archives

Pat Livingston always enjoyed the company of "The Chief" when he was covering the Steelers for *The Pittsburgh Press*. The fellow peeking over Rooney's shoulder is KDKA newsman Bill Burns.

Pittsburgh Post-Gazette Archives

Rooney is flanked by Steelers coach Bill Austin, at left, and Vince Lombardi, then the head coach of the Green Bay Packers, in the late '60s.

Bill Fralic

Bill Fralic [signature]

Remembers Uncle Chuck's funeral

"It meant a lot to me."

Bill Fralic was an All-American tackle at Penn Hills High School in 1980 and the University of Pittsburgh in 1984, a Pro Bowl lineman for the Atlanta Falcons (1985-1993) and finished his NFL career with the Detroit Lions (1993). He was inducted into the College Football Foundation Hall of Fame in 2000. He attended the University of Pittsburgh Varsity Letter Club golf outing at Montour Heights Country Club in April 6, 2001. He explained why he was such a big fan of the Steelers and Art Rooney:

When I first started playing football as a kid with Joe Natoli and the Morningside Bulldogs I began hearing stories about my uncle, Chuck Mehelich. He had played football at Duquesne University and with the Pittsburgh Steelers (1946-1951). He was a defensive end for the Steelers, and he must have been something. He was from Verona, same as me. Pat Livingston, the former sports editor of *The Pittsburgh Press*, once told me that my uncle was an unreal physical specimen. Livingston said, "He may have had the most muscular well-chiseled body until Jimmy Brown came along. He was as tough as nails. He and Ernie Stautner set the standard for being tough with the Steelers."

The one story I was told over and over again was how my uncle tackled Leon Hart on the opening kickoff of the first exhibition game one season (1950) and knocked him out of the game. They carried Hart off the field on a stretcher. Hart apparently had been quoted in the newspaper as saying he didn't think the pros were that much tougher than the college football players.

My Uncle Chuck hollered to Hart, "Does the league seem tougher to you now, Rook?" Now Leon Hart was a legendary football player. He came out of Turtle Creek High School and was a big guy for his day, about 6-3 and 265 pounds, and he played both ways in college and in the pros. My Uncle Chuck was 6-2, 210.

Hart was the only player to win three national championships in college (1946, 1947 and 1949), at Notre Dame, and three more championships in the National Football League, with the Detroit Lions (1952, 1953 and 1957). He was a three-time All-American and he was the last lineman to win the Heisman Trophy (1949).

But my uncle must have really nailed him. Hart missed a few games from that collision.

When my uncle died (1984), I was a senior at Pitt. By attending the funeral, I missed being in Houston as one of the five finalists for the Lombardi Award that went to the best college lineman in the country. My dad thinks that hurt my chances of winning the award.

My uncle's funeral was in Philadelphia and the city had just been hit by an ice storm. I remember that Art Rooney came to the funeral. I was impressed by that. It couldn't have been easy to get there. Mr. Rooney came over and spoke to me.

He told me my uncle was one of the toughest football players he'd ever seen. He said, "He was harder than those statues on the North Side." Coming from Mr. Rooney, it meant a lot to me.

Mr. Rooney knew my mom, Dorothy, who worked for over 30 years as a waitress at the Oakmont Country Club, and my dad, who's also Bill Fralic. There is a large color photograph in my parents' home in Monroeville that shows my mother standing between Art Rooney and Dan Rooney. There's a hand-written message on the picture from Mr. Rooney. It was written to my mother. (It reads: "Good wishes to you and your family. Your son Bill is a superstar. However, I never saw a tougher pro football player than your brother Charlie.") And it was signed by Art Rooney and by Dan Rooney.

Jim O'Brien

Joe Natoli, an official with Italian-American Sports Hall of Fame and former coach of the Morningside Bulldogs, congratulates "Legend" award winners at 2000 banquet at Pittsburgh Hilton, Chuck Noll, at left, and his former Bulldog star, Bill Fralic.

> *"In the end, there are still going to be figures who are larger than life."*
> — Bruce Springsteen

John Baker
The Sheriff of Wake County

"A lot of us called him Daddy Rooney."

Sitting behind his dark mahogany desk, John Baker is a compelling figure. His head and his hands sieze your eyes. They are large. John Baker is a big man. Since 1978, John Baker has been the Sheriff of Wake County, the second largest county after Mecklenburg County in North Carolina. He was 65 years old at the time of my visit, August 24, 2000, and wondering whether he wanted to run again in the next election. He remained respected and popular in his hometown of Raleigh after 22 years on the job.

At an Applebee's Neighborhood Grill in Raleigh, where we had lunch later on, there was a corner table that had a wall behind it covered with Baker football memorabilia. I had asked him to take me some place like that. There was a brass plate in the center of the display that read:

JOHN BAKER
HOMETOWN HERO

At a relatively new school in town, Southeast Raleigh High School, there's a John A. Baker, Jr. Stadium. So he has definitely left his mark there.

One of Baker's top aides, Major Ralph Stephenson, joined us for lunch at Applebee's. "Not many people can eat lunch at their own shrine," said Major Stephenson. John Baker believes he has distinguished himself in some other ways as well.

Baker believes he is the only Steelers player who ever had Art Rooney sleep overnight in his home. That tells you something about John Baker and even more about Art Rooney. More about that later.

Baker's expansive and impressive first-floor offices are in downtown Raleigh. I have relatives who live in suburban Raleigh, Harvey and Diane Churchman, my brother-in-law and sister-in-law, respectively. My wife, Kathleen, and I love to go to Raleigh. It's a great area, a great city. John H. Baker, Jr. is my latest in-law in Raleigh, in a different respect.

He's the No. 1 local lawman, always a good man to know. I have his office phone number and his home phone number.

Sheriff John Baker and one of his top aides, Major Ralph Stephenson, enjoy lunch in John's "Hometown Hero" corner at Applebee's Neighborhood Grill in Raleigh in late August, 2000.

Photos by Jim O'Brien

"Everyone has a story. I'm the link. They all have stories. We just have to find them"
— Gay Talese

There are statues in a nearby park by the state capital building that show three U.S. Presidents from the Carolinas. Andrew Johnson came out of Wake County. James Knox Polk was from Mecklenburg County and Andrew Jackson was from Union County in what is now South Carolina.

John H. Baker, Jr. was born on June 10, 1935 to the late Louise Shepherd Baker and the late John Haywood Baker, Sr., a career veteran of the Raleigh Police Department. His father was the first black police officer in town and remained at the job for 43 years. He was 74 when he died and he was still on the police force. Baker had one sibling, a sister Dolores Baker Wilder.

So John Baker was born to be a lawman. He stood six feet six inches tall and weighed in at 265 or 270 pounds. He has been called "Big John" by his friends and admirers, and by those who fear his baleful glare. He has been called "Big Bad John" by those who've gotten on the wrong side of the law, or who went up against him in his football-playing days.

He is on the telephone, talking with a colleague about a problem at the jail. He winks behind gold wire eyeglasses that sit halfway down his nose, just to remind you that he hasn't forgotten you are there. He smiles and seems less formidable.

"I am the only bad one here," Baker tells somebody on the telephone, having a little fun with his own image, when I was sitting in his office in the summer of 2000. "If you're going to raise hell in my jail, there's no bigger hell-raiser than me around here. So I'm saying 'let's get on with it.' Sometimes these people make mistakes in judgment. They better behave here. We're here to keep the peace."

On the wall behind his desk, a "peacemaker" .45 pistol, a legendary weapon from the Wild West days, was on display. It had been given to Baker as a gift from his senior staff. When he walks out from behind his desk, you notice he is wearing high black cowboy boots. They reach to the top of his calves. He was living up to one of his early campaign slogans: John Baker, The Kind of Sheriff They Make Movies About.

"A sheriff serves a four-year term," said Baker. "I have two years to go on my fifth term. I haven't decided what I'm going to do. I'll start looking at my situation here a year or so down the road."

He was also wearing a white dress shirt with a button-down collar, a black tie with light blue and gold diamond pattern that was much too thin for such a wide body. He wore well-pressed black slacks. His black suit jacket was hanging in his closet. John Baker was all business. John Baker was a professional football player for 12 years. He was employed by four National Football League teams: the Los Angeles Rams, the Philadelphia Eagles, the Pittsburgh Steelers and the Detroit Lions.

There's a famous photograph still on display in the Pro Football Hall of Fame in Canton, Ohio that shows New York Giants quarterback Y.A. Tittle on his knees in the end zone at Pitt Stadium, his helmet off and blood trickling from his bald head down his brow. It's a photograph that won awards for Morris Berman, who was living in retirement in Sun City, Arizona. It's in a book of the best football photos in NFL history.

It's a photo that was not used in the next day's newspaper, interestingly enough, because there were empty seats just above the end zone showing in the background, and that wouldn't look good. The sports editor who made that decision defended his decision years later. Al Abrams said there was no action in the photo.

Tittle had been bloodied by none other than John Baker, defensive end for the Steelers. Nobody blocked Baker and he just blew in on Tittle and dealt a mighty blow to Tittle's ribs as he was releasing a pass. The ball jerked out of Tittle's right hand and was picked off by Chuck Hinton, another defensive lineman for the Steelers, who lumbered 15 yards with the interception for a touchdown. This was on September 20, 1964 and the Steelers upset the Giants, 27-24. The Steelers beat them the year before at Forbes Field, 31-0, also in the second game of the regular season schedule.

I had Baker go to the drawing board in his office, and use a Magic Marker to draw up the play on which he tackled Tittle. He told me that he had Tittle come to town once to boost his candidacy for sheriff during a re-election campaign.

Baker was traded by the Eagles to the Steelers before the start of the 1962 season and stayed for six seasons. He was a tough defensive end. He lined up on the same front four as Chuck Hinton, a former teammate at North Carolina Central College in Durham. Baker and Hinton, both from Raleigh, and Ben McGee, from Jackson State in Mississippi, were the nucleus for tough defensive lines in Pittsburgh in those days. Baker told me that Hinton had died earlier that year, and that McGee was back in Jackson, Walter Payton's old stomping grounds.

I was a junior and senior at Pitt in John Baker's first two seasons in Pittsburgh. The Steelers played their home games at Forbes Field in those days, and moved to Pitt Stadium for the 1964 season. Beano Cook, the sports information director at Pitt then, started a newspaper called *Pittsburgh Weekly Sports* with me during my senior year. I was the editor and Beano looked after the business end of the paper. Ed Kiely, the publicity director of the Steelers, was kind enough to provide us with press box credentials. So I covered John Baker and those Steelers for our lively and controversial tabloid.

Buddy Parker was the coach of the Steelers in those days. He had brought Bobby Layne with him from the Lions a few years earlier, but had talked Layne into retiring prior to the 1963 season. The Steelers' lineup included John Henry Johnson and Ernie Stautner, two of the toughest performers in pro football history. Layne, Johnson and Stautner are all enshrined in the Pro Football Hall of Fame.

"John Henry was here in Raleigh not too long ago," said Baker. "We had a chance to talk."

It's a shame the Steelers didn't have Layne that 1963 season because they might have made the playoffs for the second time in the team's history. Instead they had to wait until 1972, Chuck Noll's third season with the Steelers, to get there. The Steelers came up short of the playoffs when they lost a season-ending game to the Giants in New York, 33-17, and finished with a 7-4-3 record. They had beaten the Giants, 31-0, in the second game of the season, played at Pitt Stadium.

The year before, the Steelers had finished the season in a short-lived post-season bowl game in Miami that matched the runner-up teams in each division. The Steelers had lost that game to the Lions, 17-10. The game was a box-office flop and was soon cancelled.

Baker looks back fondly on those six seasons with the Steelers. He loved and respected Art Rooney, the owner of the Steelers, and was a frequent visitor to his office. In his first season with the Steelers, Baker lived in the Roosevelt Hotel in downtown Pittsburgh. The Steelers offices were located in the lobby of the Roosevelt. So it was easy for Baker to spend time with the boss.

Art Rooney, Jr., the second oldest son of the Steelers owner, stays in touch with Baker, and often sends him postcards and pictures portraying his father. Art, Jr. provided me with a list of his father's all-time favorite Steelers, and John Baker was in the Top Ten.

"I was unhappy in LA from Day One."
— John Baker

John Baker provided background on his football career. "I went to Washington High School here in Raleigh," said Baker. "They built a new high school, Ligon High School, and I moved into that school for my junior year. My class was the first class (1954) to graduate from Ligon High School."

He then starred for the Eagles at North Carolina Central College from 1954 to 1957. The school is now called North Carolina Central University but still competes in the Carolina Intercollegiate Athletic Association. He graduated with a degree in physical education in 1958.

One of his teammates, Julius L. Chambers, was the chancellor at North Carolina Central and I paid a visit to see him on the Durham campus. He was in his office in a corner of the Hoey Administration Building on Fayetteville Street. He was short and stout and didn't look like a former athlete, but he was a valued reserve quarterback for the Eagles in his younger years. He looked more like a former attorney, which he was.

"John Baker was a person determined to achieve," recalled Chancellor Chambers. "He really worked very hard to prepare to compete in all ways. He was much better than the rest of us and went on to great things. I helped him and he helped me. He was a great person who really believed in helping people. He's proof of what a person can accomplish, no matter where you come from, if one puts himself or herself in a position to be the best. John made it happen."

Baker was named All-CIAA and to *The Pittsburgh Courier* newspaper All-American team. That was an All-American team comprised of players from predominantly black colleges. It was a team picked by Bill Nunn, Jr., the sports editor of the *Courier* who would become a personnel scout on the Steelers' staff, working for Art Rooney, Jr. during the period when the team drafted and put together four Super Bowl championship teams in the '70s.

Baker has spent most of his career in government service, starting during the off-season when he was playing in the NFL as a recreation supervisor for the North Carolina Department of Corrections. He was elected sheriff of Wake County in 1978, and remained that county's chief law enforcement officer.

"I went to the College All-Star Game in Chicago," recalled Baker. "That was the year the All-Stars played the Detroit Lions. Bobby Layne was their quarterback.

"I was drafted by the Rams in the 5th round in 1958," continued Baker. "I was unhappy in LA from Day One. My wife and I drove there. It was 2,616 miles from my front door in Raleigh, North Carolina. We traveled the southern route. It was one of the worst experiences of our life, the racist and segregated situations we confronted along the way. We ran into a lot of discrimination that I've tried desperately to forget. I told my wife when we got to Los Angeles that we would never drive that southern route again.

"That's another reason I wanted to play on the East Coast, where I'd be closer to family and friends. But I stayed four seasons with the Rams. Sid Gillman was the coach. We had some great players. We had Bob Waterfield and Billy Wade as quarterbacks. We had Tom Fears, Les Richter and Jon Arnett.

"Every year I went in to LA I asked the Rams people to trade me. In my fourth year, they finally traded me to the Philadelphia Eagles. Shortly thereafter, I was traded again, this time to the Steelers. That was for the 1963 season. "I went to Forbes Field and joined them at practice. I had one year with 'Big Daddy' Lipscomb and I learned quite a bit from him. I had many opportunities to chat with him. That man could play. He told me to hit everybody who came your way. He said you had to sort them out until you get the back with the ball.

"He had played for the Colts before he came to the Steelers, and he continued to live in Baltimore. He was always going back to Baltimore. It was sad what happened to him. His untimely death was a real shock to the team. He died from an overdose of drugs, but nobody on the team believed that because he hated getting shots. He hated needles. Some foul play was suspected.

"When I first went to Pittsburgh, somebody picked me up at the airport and took me downtown to the Roosevelt Hotel. That's where I stayed. Art Rooney and Fran Fogarty, who handled the financial end of the business, shared an office at the Roosevelt. There wasn't much room to get around in that office. Their desks filled it up pretty much. I remember I used to go to a restaurant across the street, and there was a hot dog shop behind it.

"I'd drive out from there to practice at Forbes Field and then South Park. We practiced on a field at the Fairgrounds at South Park. That was rather different from the Rams' situation. Pittsburgh's practice facilities were fairly primitive compared to the Rams' facilities. The Rams' training camp was at the University of California at Redlands. I start to sweat just thinking about that place. It was probably the hottest place in the universe to train."

"I grew up with it."

There are lots of pictures in his downtown Raleigh office. There are framed photos of his son, John H. Baker III, and his daughter, Mrs. Jonnita Elizabeth Baker-Williams. Her first name is a combination of John and Juanita, her parents' first names. There are photos of his grandchildren, both boys. There's John H. Baker IV, whom he said would be two-years-old in October, and Tyler Baker Williams, whom he said would be six-years-old in September.

"When I came in here, the department was at its lowest ebb," said Baker. "My philosophy then was that if I couldn't bring it up I didn't want to be here. Now we have the best law enforcement department in the state. I'm very proud of that. At the time I was elected, there was none more proud of what I'd accomplished than Art Rooney back in Pittsburgh.

"Our county has a population of about 600,000. We have 856 square miles of territory. We're pushing Mecklinburg for No. 1 status.

"I knew early in my life that I wanted to get into law enforcement. I knew how proud my dad was of what he was doing. I grew up with it. I'd come home in the off-season and I worked in the correction system. I handled the physical education program in the prisons and jails.

"My dad was called Big John. He was 6-2, and over 300 pounds. He was more out front than I am; he had a bigger stomach. He was a very respected man in this community. When I was running for political office here, people would say, 'I don't know you, other than that you played pro football. So you're a jock. If you're anywhere near your daddy, you're a good man and I'd probably vote for you.'

"I wanted to come home again. There was a time when I was young when I didn't intend to stay here. But I liked the weather and the people here in North Carolina. I liked the opportunities in North

Carolina. Some people didn't think opportunities for an African-American were good in North Carolina. I made up my own mind and I haven't looked back. I wanted to raise my family here and I haven't regretted it.

"I had good mentors. I worked for awhile for U.S. Senator Robert Morgan. He told me about the importance of returning calls, no matter how critical the caller might be. 'You better respond to everyone within three days,' he said. 'You better have some kind of response.'

"My mom and my dad believed strongly that discipline starts at home. That's the way I am. First of all, you have to have love and discipline in the home. You have to tell your kids, 'We love you.' I made a speech last Saturday. I told them discipline doesn't start in the schools; it starts at home. You can't get around that. Too many parents today turn their kids over to the teachers and expect them to do everything."

Some of Art Rooney must have rubbed off on John Baker because he certainly learned some political skills from his former boss in Pittsburgh.

"My wife and I go to a different African-American church in our county every Sunday," said Sheriff Baker. "Juanita is a Baptist and I am a Methodist. I have worshipped in a different church with her every Sunday. I don't take the church for granted politically, either. I let the pastor know I'm here to worship, but if you would allow me a few minutes I have a message to deliver as well. I want to talk to them about crime.

"The black churches in Wake County have been very important in my re-elections. I let them know that my concern is for the people and citizens of this county, no matter your color. There are close to 150 African-American churches in Wake County. My No. 1 reason for going to church is to worship, but it doesn't hurt to get the word across, either. They help me do my job better, too. They look out for us in their community."

He points to his parents for getting him off to a great start. "My Mom and Dad demanded that you get an education," he said. "They felt that no one could take that away from you. They taught us how to stay out of trouble. I came from a family of educators. I had a lot of aunts — my dad's sisters — who were teachers. My sister became an elementary school teacher in Raleigh. My dad was a coach, too, and helped me with my sports.

"I always wanted to play for the Washington Redskins. That's the team we picked up here. The Redskins weren't interested in black players then, though. George Preston Marshall was the owner of the team, and they were sort of the NFL team of the South. He made it known he didn't want any black players. Bobby Mitchell was the first black player they ever drafted."

He said some of the people he knew from his days with the Detroit Lions, his last team, such as his coach, Joe Schmidt, and teammates like Lem Barney and Mel Farr helped him get ready for life after football.

When Baker ran for office in Raleigh, Barney, a Hall of Fame defensive back, came down to back him in public appearances. He even talked Y.A. Tittle into coming there and boosting his candidacy. Tittle was also a Hall of Famer. Baker even used the photo of the bloodied Tittle in his campaign flyers to show that no criminal would want to mess with him.

"I remember we went to New York the year after I had hit and bloodied Y.A. Tittle at Pitt Stadium," recalled Baker. "I was hoping and praying that we'd win the toss so we'd receive the opening kick. I wanted our offensive unit to be introduced. But it ended up that our defensive team was introduced. Everybody at Yankee Stadium stood up and booed when I was introduced.

"But Y.A. and I have become friends. He knew that I was just doing my job. I had no other choice than to cream him when I could. I had a clean shot at him and I took it. They were trying a screen-play and he was waiting for his receivers to release their blocks. Y.A. threw the ball just as I hit him. They took him off the field. He was out for the rest of the season. We had a mutual friend in the insurance business that contacted him on my behalf to come down here for my campaign. I'm a Democrat and he's a Republican and he still stumped for me. He said, 'John Baker sacked me and now he's trying to sack crime.' Y.A. Tittle is a remarkable guy.

"I never stood over Y.A. Tittle and taunted him after I hit him. No one in my day would do something like that. It just wasn't done. I don't think all that celebrating stuff is necessary. Just do your job and get the hell back to the huddle. Why stand over someone and beat your chest? I had some great teammates in Pittsburgh. Chuck Hinton was from Raleigh and had gone to the same high school and college I went to. Ben McGee was the other defensive end. He came from a black school (Jackson State), too, and he could play. Dick Hoak was a fierce competitor and one who took his job and practice very seriously. John Henry Johnson was an outgoing guy, a funny guy, never a dull moment. He was very much like Hoak as far as being a fierce competitor. John Henry reminded me of Jim Taylor. He would always try to find somebody to hit. He'd run until he could find someone to run over. He was like that in training camp.

"Bobby Layne was their quarterback just before I arrived. He stayed on as assistant in 1963. I heard a lot of stories about Bobby Layne. He was a legend in more ways than one. He'd stay out all night before a game, and then try to grab two or three hours of sleep in the morning. He had to go to bed right before the game and get a good rest. That's all he needed. The more he partied the better he played, or so his friends insisted. He was just an outstanding football player. He had his ways. No one else could do that. We understood that. There were no problems with the other players over that.

"His buddy, Ernie Stautner, was one of the finest persons I ever came in contact with. I can see him now. He had six or seven rolls of

John Bakers draws up play on which he had a clear shot at New York Giants quarterback Y.A. Tittle and left him bleeding from forehead in famous photo that can be found in the Pro Football Hall of Fame in Canton, Ohio. Morris Berman of *Pittsburgh Post-Gazette* took the award-winning photograph.

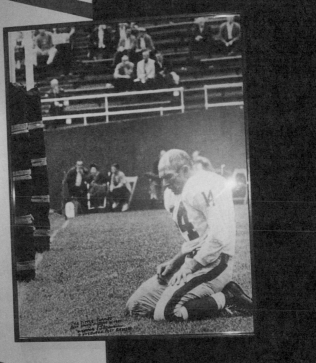

ON DISPLAY ARE WINNING PHOTOGRAPHS FROM THE PRO FOOTBALL HALL OF FAME'S ANNUAL PHOTO CONTEST

OPEN ONLY TO PROFESSIONAL PHOTOGRAPHERS WHO COVER N.F.L. GAMES

Sponsored by CANON...
Official Camera of the
Pro Football Hall of Fame

Photos by Jim O'Brien

tape on his arms. His arms would be like shells. They were weapons. He knew the game from all aspects, and he was as tough as anybody in the NFL. I played with him for one year and then he became an assistant coach and taught me a lot. He went on to become an outstanding coach with the Dallas Cowboys. I was surrounded by a lot of people who are now in the Hall of Fame.

"Pittsburgh was always known for having fierce defensive teams. We had Big Daddy on our defensive line for two seasons. I was the left defensive end and I had good people up there with me."

"He was a player's owner."

"Mr. Rooney was one of the most outstanding individuals that you're going to come in contact with. I had a tremendous amount of respect for him. I went one on one with him a few times at the Roosevelt Hotel. I went into his office. He was always receptive to his players visiting him and chatting with him. Jim, I can see him now, coming out to practice at South Park. I can see that stogie. He was a player's owner. All of us had so much respect for him.

"I believe I'm the only ex-player who has the distinction of saying an owner stayed in my house. During the off-season, I'd come back and work in the corrections system. One of my responsibilities was in the women's system. During a visit to such a prison in Raleigh, I was sitting there speaking to the superintendent, Mrs. Elizabeth McCubbin, and she was telling me that they wanted to build a chapel for the women, but they lacked the funds to do so.

"I was wondering what I could do to help them build this chapel. I went back to Pittsburgh, and I felt I could solicit some friends for the funds. I went to see Mr. Rooney to tell him what I had in mind. I said, 'Boss, these women want to build this chapel, and they're having problems raising the money. I'd appreciate it if you'd give me a contribution. He looked at me and said, 'John, how much do you want?' And I said, 'Mr. Rooney, whatever amount you'd give would be appreciated.' He turned to Fran Fogarty, his business manager. Mr. Rooney had that cigar in his mouth. He said, 'Fran, John has a project in North Carolina. Write him a check for $5,000.' I damn near wet myself when he said that. He came up to me at practice a few months later, and said, 'John, let's go down to Raleigh.' We had Mondays off. 'Get Fran to make airplane reservations for us.' Fogarty was frowning. He was tough to get money out of. He was a real tight guy. We went down Monday morning and came back Tuesday morning in time for me to report to practice at 10 o'clock. We flew United Airlines. My wife picked us up at the airport. He went on a tour of the prison. He got to see the chapel he helped build. He had an opportunity to talk to prison officials. He was a big hit with everybody there.

"Then we went to my house. Juanita cooked one of those big Southern dinners for him. We had grits and country ham, red gravy, hot biscuits, all that good stuff. He seemed to enjoy the meal. And he slept at our home that night. How many owners in the NFL do you think ever stayed at the home of one of their players? He was that kind of man. He always had time for his players. John Henry enjoyed an open-door policy with him, and I think he took pretty good care of John Henry, above and beyond the call of duty.

"He was just an unusual man. He was a very compassionate person, very understanding. He didn't let his wealth deter him from being a compassionate person. He had me to his home, too. They had torn houses down all around him, but his home was still standing. He boasted, 'They didn't tear my house down.' I met his wife, Kathleen. He talked about her quite a bit.

"I remember when I was elected the sheriff here, I received a congratulatory card from him and the Pittsburgh Steelers family. Had I asked him, he'd have come down here and helped me get elected. I can see him now. That stogie. And he drove a black Buick. He never had a chauffeur, but he usually had one of his buddies behind the wheel. A lot of us called him 'Daddy Rooney.' He was like a daddy to a lot of us. You felt at ease talking with him. You could sit down and talk to him.

"He was a fair man. He was just a fine man. That's why I had so much respect for him. He didn't look at the color of my skin. He looked at me as one of the players of the Pittsburgh Steelers. I know I was there to do a job. Professional football is a business. You're there to do a job. Somebody else is going to take your place. I was doing something I enjoyed, and I had a love for the game.

"Last year, I got a call from Artie, his son. He sent me some cards. He's a lot like his dad. I have a strange relationship with the Steelers. Dan is in charge, I know. How did Dan get so powerful? Their dad was different from all of them. They don't make them like Mr. Rooney now. He was dedicated to his players, and all of us had the highest respect and admiration for Mr. Rooney. We still do."

> *"People say to me that he sounded too good to be true. But he was the genuine thing. He wasn't a saint on earth or anything like that. He was just a good, wonderful man."*
> — Mary Regan, Art Rooney's secretary (1952-1988)

Dick Groat
A hometown hero

"Art Rooney was always so kind to me."

Dick Groat began his major league baseball career with the Pittsburgh Pirates in 1952, and was the National League's most valuable player in 1960 when the Bucs won the World Series. He was traded to the St. Louis Cardinals in 1962, and later played with the Philadelphia Phillies and San Francisco Giants. He grew up in Swissvale and graduated from Duke University where he was Player of the Year in basketball in the 1951-52 season. For 22 years, he served as analyst on Pitt basketball broadcasts with sports announcer Bill Hillgrove. He remained one of the city's most popular sports figures. At age 70, Groat was overseeing the activity at his Champion Lakes Golf Course near Ligonier when we spoke. His reflections follow:

I worked with the Pirates in a public relations capacity in the off-season and I'd see the Steelers practicing at Forbes Field. Joe Bach and Walt Kiesling were the coaches when I was first with the Pirates. I was a close friend of Lou Tepe, a center who was at Duke when I was there. We were fraternity brothers at Sigma Chi. He's the first player I can remember being a red-shirt. He played on the same high school basketball team as Sherman White at Englewood, N.J. White was one of the guys who got into trouble with the basketball fixing scandal in the '50s when he was at LIU, playing for the legendary Clair Bee.

Tepe came to the Steelers as their center and linebacker right after Chuck Cherundolo in the early '50s. I worked with Lynn Chandnois at Jessop Steel out in Washington, Pa. We were both on the sales staff. Ray Mathews has always been a good friend. We've played a lot of golf together through the years. I've known him for a hundred years. I'll never forget when Buddy Parker was coaching the team. He was a real character.

Art Rooney was always so kind to me. He liked the fact that I was from Swissvale, and that I was a local guy playing for the Pirates. The Steelers were struggling when I was with the Pirates, but you'd never know it when you were around Mr. Rooney. He sent me a hand-written congratulatory letter after I won the MVP Award and we won the World Series in 1960.

One time I tried to call him when the Steelers were playing the Miami Dolphins in the AFC championship in 1984. They were going to Miami for the game. I called the Steelers offices and asked for Art Rooney, Sr. I was told that Mr. Rooney was there, but that he was not taking any phone calls. I told them that I didn't want any tickets. I just wanted to wish him a happy birthday. His birthday was coming up later in the month. I also wanted to wish him good luck. "I don't want anything," I said. "Just see if he'll take a phone call from Dick Groat." Next thing I know he's on the telephone. "Dick, how are you? Do you need tickets?" I said, "No, I just want to wish you a happy birthday and good luck in the playoff." I used to receive a note from Mr. Rooney from time to time, always hand-written. He was just the nicest man. He was so good for this city.

My daughter Carol Ann was in a serious automobile accident and we thought we were going to lose her. He came to West Penn Hospital to visit her when she was there. He was just the most compassionate man. He also sent me a note about her. He was praying for her. He was just a very special man. And you never met anyone quite like him.

I used to play in exhibition basketball games against the Steelers until Joe L. Brown stopped me from playing basketball. I banged up a knee in Erie, and Dr. Joe Finegold tapped it, and Joe Brown was mad about that. When I was traded to the Cardinals I got a call from Baldy Regan, who ran the Steelers basketball team, and he asked me to play with them during the 1963-64 season. I played with Dick Hoak, Paul Martha and John Henry Johnson. I played with Red Mack, George Tarasovic and John Reger. Those guys protected me. I had 51 points one night in Ligonier. I broke my nose once playing for them.

We played Beaver Falls in the new field house at Geneva. We got down to about 20 seconds. I drove and I took a jump shot and missed it. I got the rebound and put it in to tie the game. I had 63 points in that game. They said there was no such thing as overtime in football, so they went to the showers. They said they didn't get paid for overtime so they wouldn't play overtime. Yeah, I had some great times with the Steelers, and I was always a fan of theirs. Still am. And I'll always have a special place in my heart for Mr. Rooney.

Jim O'Brien

Former Pirates shortstop and 1960 National League MVP Dick Groat, right, has always been a big admirer of Steelers' coach Chuck Noll, who was named a "Legend" at Italian-American Sports Hall of Fame dinner at downtown Hilton in spring of 2000.

Frank Bolden
Still a Pittsburgh Courier

"Rooney was a patron saint."

Frank Bolden, at 88, still loved to tell stories. He was befriended by Art Rooney when he was a college student at the University of Pittsburgh. He grew up in Washington, Pa. and worked for 27 years on the Pittsburgh Courier, *once one of the most powerful black weekly newspapers in the country when it had a circulation of 400,000 in its heyday in 1947. Bolden was the entertainment editor of the* Courier *for 14 of those years, and rose up the ranks to become the city editor. He was one of the first two accredited black war correspondents during World War II. He worked in the Pitt Alumni office during my student days of the early '60s when I first met him. He was always an interesting storyteller. He'd seen a lot in his life. He'd been married to his wife, Nancy, for 40 years. His asthma was causing him problems, but his mind was nearly as sharp as ever. He continued as a consultant to the Baseball Hall of Fame and to the Smithsonian Institute. There is always someone who steals the show, unexpectedly, whenever I do one of my books, and Bolden may be that individual in this offering:*

In a day where there is so much of a clash between the races, Art Rooney was a special man. Here was an Irish Catholic from the North Side who made friends and helped families wherever they might be from. He came up to the Hill District frequently, and he was a friend to all. He helped a lot of families, and he did it without fanfare. I don't think you have those kinds of friendships now.

Art Rooney was the patron saint of Pittsburgh sports, as far as our people were concerned. Not just the Steelers, but all sports. He helped start the Pittsburgh Crawfords baseball team, and a lot of people don't know that. I heard he helped the Homestead Grays, too. He was a natural. He knew where the bodies were, and he had the kind of political connections and clout to get things accomplished, but he used his influence to help families in need. It didn't matter whether they were white or colored, he came through for them. He was also sharp enough not to let his charisma slip around his neck and strangle him. Art Rooney was the jukebox king of Pittsburgh and Allegheny County. Every bar and restaurant got their jukeboxes from Rooney. You couldn't get a jukebox in your bar in Allegheny County unless it came through Art Rooney. He may have had slot machines in many of those places, too. He was into a lot of enterprises. He was a protégé of Pennsylvania Senator James Coyne, and Coyne made sure that no one bothered Art Rooney. Art was the ward leader on the North Side. He controlled a lot of government jobs.

NEGRO NATIONAL LEAGUE
PRESENTS

HOMESTEAD GRAYS

FRONT. ROW - Left To Right: DUKES, JACKSON, CARLISLE, WELMAKER, GULA, HARRIS, ALLEN, BENJAMIN.
BACK ROW - LEONARD, WHITE, PEREZ, G. WALKER, PARKER, J. WILLIAMS, GIBSON, BROWN, E. WALKER.

LEADERS of the 1937 PENNANT RACE

PITTS. vs. CRAWFORDS

AT BUTLER, PA.

ON

Jim O'Brien

He was a close friend of Gus Greenlea, who made his money as a numbers writer in the Hill District. I never liked the term "numbers writers," so I always referred to them in my stories as "digitarians." Greenlea was a powerful Repubican leader, too. Negroes had been Republicans for many years because of the respect they had for President Abraham Lincoln, who was credited with freeing the slaves.

Then Robert L. Vann, who was the publisher of the *Pittsburgh Courier*, wrote a front-page editorial — his editorials were always on the front page — in which he urged the black people of America to turn Lincoln's picture to the wall in their homes because the Republican Party was no longer doing anything to benefit Negroes or colored people. And Vann had been a staunch Republican. Vann succeeded in turning Negroes against the Republicans and they've never come back to the fold. Pittsburgh was a strong Democratic stronghold after that, but Rooney remained a Republican. He gained influence from Senator Coyne. David Lawrence, the mayor of Pittsburgh, was a Democrat. He was one of Art Rooneys' best friends, but he couldn't get Rooney to become a Democrat. Art Rooney wasn't a man to move to the other side of the fence. He became a rich man, but he never moved out of his home on the North Side. I admired that.

He'd come up and have lunch at the Crawford Grill and talk to Gus Greenlea. The Crawford One attracted all kinds of people. There were prostitutes and pimps always hanging around. I didn't like to call them that, though, so I referred to them in my stories as "members of the nocturnal sisterhood and their personal shepherds." I hung out there, too. It was an action place. That's where I first met Art Rooney. Art and Gus were friends. I was working my way through college, and I was in the window of the restaurant, flipping hamburgers. Art Rooney took a liking to me. My fraternity at Pitt had house dances on Friday nights, and Art Rooney lent me a jukebox on a regular basis. It was delivered to our fraternity house on Friday afternoon. He took the governor off it so we could play the songs for free. Usually, it was a nickel a song, and he got his cut of the take. I remember we had to have it back by two o'clock on Saturday.

He was the jukebox king and he was kind to a Negro kid at Pitt. I know all this to be true. There aren't any witnesses still around, but I give you my honest word on all of this. We liked to dance and party, and a jukebox was worth its weight in gold. I don't think Rooney ever got into numbers writing because Coyne already had his designated people in that business. Politicians had their fingers in a lot of pies back then, and they protected their interests. They allowed horse rooms to flourish in the city, too.

There were many policemen on the North Side who retired to Florida. They didn't want them around here so they'd have to answer any questions about what they did.

> "*Where else could you walk in off the street — without an appointment — and visit with the owner of a pro football team? He knew my family from the North Side.*"
> — Bill Berry

The North Side had the biggest whorehouse in the city back then. Nettie Gorman had about 30 young ladies, or "members of the nocturnal sisterhood," in her place. It was for the top men in town. You had a lot of important people and political figures, even judges, going in there. The average guy was turned away. "Horizontal refreshment," as I called it in my column, was limited to the upper crust.

Once a week a few of the white girls there would come up to the Hill District and the best colored girls would go over to the North Side. They were very strict about when that could be done. It was like a swap. They had to be back in their respective houses by 9 p.m. on Sunday.

Wylie Avenue and Crawford Avenue were my beat on weekends, so I was there a lot. The whites used to come up from the city to the Hill District, but the colored men and women weren't permitted to go to the clubs downtown. Those places were still segregated.

Some of the top musicians who played downtown, at the Stanley Theater or Loew's Penn, would come up after their stage shows and play at the Crawford Grill, or at the Musician's Club, which was two doors down the street.

Those big bands included the likes of Benny Goodman, Cab Calloway, Ted Weams, Tommy Dorsey and Jimmy Dorsey. It was a classy crowd that came to see these guys play. You could come up the Crawford Grill and hear Dizzy Gillespie and his group.

We could go to the city and watch a baseball game between the Homestead Grays and the Brookline Eagles. We had to leave right after the game. We couldn't sit in those same seats any other time. When whites and Negroes gathered for entertainment back then there were no problems, no fights that I can recall.

That's how Walt Harper became famous. He attracted the college crowd, and the college kids, of course, were mostly white. They came up to the Hill District to hear him perform. Those clubs had rules. You couldn't come in after five o'clock without a jacket and tie. There was no profanity. You couldn't loiter in the rest rooms, or loaf in the doorways. No one bothered those white kids; they were good for the commerce in our community.

Art Rooney is responsible for the formation of the Pittsburgh Crawfords, one of the most famous baseball teams in the Negro Leagues, right up there with the Homestead Grays. Art Rooney helped Gus Greenlea put that team together. Gus didn't know a first baseman from a shortstop. Rooney taught him how to manage that team, how to put it together. To my knowledge, though, Rooney did not own a piece of the team. He just helped Gus get it going. Gus built a ballpark for the Crawfords in the Hill, and I'm sure Rooney urged him to do that.

Satchel Paige pitched for the Pittsburgh Crawfords. He never pitched for the Homestead Grays. Gus owned Satchel Paige. Art talked Gus into organizing his own team. Gus stole the best ballplayers from the Homestead Grays. He got them by paying them more money. That was it. He gave Satchel Paige a chance to pitch to Josh Gibson.

He signed Oscar Charleston, Ted Page, "Cool Papa" Bell, Josh Gibson, Buck Leonard and Judy Johnson, some of the greatest players in the Negro Leagues. You heard how "Cool Papa" Bell was so fast that he turned out the light switch on the wall and was back in bed before the light went out? The one I liked best was that Bell was so fast that he once hit a single down the right field line and got hit with the ball as he was rounding first and heading for second. I used to stay at the Grill until 2 a.m., and later, to hear stories like that. I loved that stuff.

Later, Batista, the dictator in Cuba, came over and paid these players even more money to bring them to Cuba to play ball. But when the revolution broke out, they came back home. They had been treated like kings in Cuba.

"The Steelers had the first crack at the best black ballplayers."

Bill Nunn, Sr. was the news editor and later the managing editor of the *Pittsburgh Courier*, and he'd hang out at the Crawford Grill, too. He and Art became close friends. They concocted an East-West All-Star Game for the Negro colleges at the Crawford Grill.

To show you how we paid Art Rooney back for all he did, we held an All-American banquet for the ballplayers from the Negro colleges. Our newspaper brought them to Pittsburgh rather than Baltimore or Richmond or Atlanta. We had guys in here like Joe Greene, L.C. Greenwood, Ernie Holmes, John Stallworth. The Steelers people got to meet them and talk to them here before the draft. The Steelers had the first crack at the best black ballplayers.

They signed free agents like Donnie Shell and Sam Davis because of their connections with the black colleges. Many of the other clubs didn't even know where those black colleges were located, except for maybe Grambling.

When the *Courier* went broke who got a job with the Steelers? That's when they hired Bill Nunn on their scouting staff. They just put him back on their staff again after he had retired. He's still a consultant. He helps them when their black ballplayers have problems or need somebody to talk to. That was the payback by the Rooneys for what the Nunns had done for them. Bill Nunn, Jr. winters in Florida. I heard the Rooneys helped him get his place. Rooney had been good to his father, too, Bill Nunn, Sr. And Art Rooney didn't need Bill Nunn, Sr. He never forgot.

Art Rooney helped a lot of people. I know he took care of John Henry Johnson for years. John Henry went through money fast and he didn't have two dimes to rub together a few times, but Rooney always came to the rescue. I know he bailed John Henry out of trouble a few times.

When Lowell Perry got hurt here (as a rookie early in the 1956 season), Rooney got Sammy Weiss, the judge, to use his influence to get Perry into Law School at Duquesne University, which was Weiss' alma mater. Perry worked as an assistant coach with the Steelers while he was going to school. He later transferred to Michigan to finish his degree. Art Rooney took care of all the bills for school and for his family. After Perry passed away this year, I called his family to offer my condolences. They still refer to Art Rooney as "Mr. Rooney" in their conversation. Even after Perry got a good job with General Motors, Rooney would call him and ask him if he needed anything.

When he was helping Gus Greenlea, Art Rooney decried the fact that the major leagues didn't have Negroes on their teams. He knew it was wrong and he said so. Art had a black on his first ballclub, when the Steelers were called the Pittsburgh Pirates, back in 1933. His name was Ray Kemp. He came from Cecil, out near me in Washington County, and he had played ball at Duquesne University.

Art Rooney was more than a sportsman. He was a humanitarian. He took care of families. He didn't care about the color of their skin or their religious preference. It took a tough man to tell David L. Lawrence, "I don't want to join your party."

I was nothing but a little raggedy student at Pitt, a nobody, and he cared about me and did some special things for me. He befriended those in need. There are just a lot of things people don't know about Art Rooney. There were two main "numbers guys" in the Hill, and that was Greenlea and William "Woogie" Harris, who was the brother of the famous photographer Teenie Harris, who worked at the *Courier* all those years. Art Rooney looked after them. The police never bothered Greenlea or Harris, and they controlled the numbers business in this community.

This was during the Depression when cornbread was considered a dessert. Art Rooney would come up from the North Side to the Crawford Grill and he mingled with us.

"He never asked for a line in the newspaper."

Art Rooney was clearly No. 1 of all the men I admired growing up in Pittsburgh. Rabbi Solomon B. Freehof of Rodef Shalom Congregation on Fifth Avenue in Oakland, and Senator John Heinz were next in my personal rankings. And I'm a Democrat. I voted for John Heinz in every election. You had quality Republicans then, not the riffraff you have now.

215

Art Rooney was revered in the black community. I was a little disappointed that his son Dan didn't make sure that there were more black people working on the new ballpark. Dan could have told them he wanted 30 blacks working on the project; he didn't have to hire the whole race.

The sons are not the same as the father. Art Rooney would not have allowed them to build a new ballpark without more Negro workers. We were lucky in that regard back then. Harry Keck of the *Sun-Telegraph* and Al Abrams of the *Post-Gazette* both wrote fairly about Negroes. When "Cum" Posey, who owned the Homestead Grays, died you wouldn't have found two better tributes to him than those guys wrote in their columns.

I thought the writers were fair to Roberto Clemente, and I don't believe they were trying to make fun of him in any way when they quoted him. They were writing sports like that when people weren't writing that way about Negroes in the rest of the newspaper. You couldn't get a story about some of the good things that were going on in the Negro community. We did better in the sports pages than the rest of the paper.

They'd rather write about the cop getting killed in Aliquippa because that's easy to do. They'd rather zero in on those kind of stories instead of the ones about achievement in the Negro community.

I know what Art Rooney did for people in general, not just in sports. He was humble. He never moved from the North Side. He never asked for a line in the newspaper when I was in the business. That's my idea of a real important person.

He was a real role model. He never tooted his own horn. It went farther as a result. He was unselfish. When you can get the respect of your colleagues in the National Football League like he did you must be something special. I never heard anyone castigate Art Rooney. He's a good role model for anyone who wants to aspire to the heights.

He had the attitude to move to the altitude. He's my idea of a real hero.

In my race, we learn early to make stepping stones out of stumbling blocks. He never left from whence he came. His home should be a historical landmark. We had Andrew Carnegie and Richard Mellon and George Westinghouse; now that's money. Rooney was cut from a different cloth. He didn't have to let me have a jukebox. We might have taken it and sold it. He lent it to a minority. He didn't know me. But he trusted me just the same. I'll never forget him. We haven't had an Art Rooney in any sport since his time. The best way I can sum up my description of Art Rooney is that he made each day brighter as he touched it with kindness.

> *"Our Irish blunders are never blunders of the heart."*
> — Maria Edgeworth

Bob Roesler
Saints come marching in

"He made lobby-sitting a rare treat."

Bob Roesler is sports coordinator for the New Orleans Metropolitan Convention and Visitors Bureau, and was in Tampa during Super Bowl XXXV to help promote Super Bowl XXXVI that was set for the New Orleans Superdome in 2002. He was the executive sports editor of the New Orleans Times-Picayune *and was associated with that newspaper for nearly 47 years.*

Art Rooney Sr. often said New Orleans was his kind of town. He liked to recall the night he strolled Bourbon Street after his Steelers beat the Minnesota Vikings, 16-6, in Super Bowl IX. He ran into so many Steelers fans that he thought he was back in Pittsburgh.

The world was a winner every day of Art Rooney's long life. When he died following a stroke, at age 87, he was especially missed at the NFL meetings, where he made lobby-sitting a rare treat.

As it turned out, his Steelers were in New Orleans for an exhibition game on the last weekend of August, 1988, when Art Rooney was buried in Pittsburgh. A sign was hanging from the Superdome loge level that read: "Football will miss you, Mr. Rooney. God bless you." It was signed: "A loyal Saints fan."

Rooney's connections with New Orleans were strong. He was one of the town's strongest supporters in the 1960s, when it was seeking an NFL franchise.

He was influential in mustering support when the city sought to play host to Super Bowl games.

Actually, his connections in New Orleans go back quite a ways. He brought his Steelers to New Orleans to play a regular season game with the Cleveland Rams in 1938. It was not a success.

"In those days," Rooney related, "pro teams didn't stick to formal schedules. We'd call off games, postpone games and transfer games from one city to another. When the weather was bad in Pittsburgh, I decided to transfer our home game with Cleveland to a warmer city. New Orleans was the logical choice."

But New Orleans was not ready for pro football, and ticket sales were horrible. A friend brought Rooney to Mayor Robert S. Maestri, hoping to get help from City Hall. Rooney decided to bring Steelers star Whizzer White with him.

"I thought I'd score a touchdown," Rooney said. "If he didn't know who Art Rooney was, he certainly would have heard of our great star. After all, he'd been an All-American at Colorado and he was one of the highest paid players (at $16,000 a year) in the NFL."

Rooney was wrong. When Rooney introduced his ace, he said Maestri asked, "Who's Whizzer White?" And, of course, he had no idea he was in the company of the ballplayer who would someday serve on the nation's Supreme Court as Justice Byron White.

Chuckling at the memory, Rooney added, "I thought then we were dead. At kickoff, I knew it. There must have been about 125 fans in the stands."

The memory didn't keep Rooney from standing up for New Orleans as NFL owners debated where to hold Super Bowl VI. New Orleans wanted the game, but it was eliminated on the first ballot. The front-runners, Miami and Dallas, were hopelessly deadlocked. Neither could muster the necessary 20 votes. The owners bickered and balloted without success.

"Nobody really cared where the next Super Bowl game would be played except those from Dallas and Miami," Rooney recalled. "Finally, I told (Minnesota president) Max Winter and (Chicago owner) George Halas that I thought the damn thing ought to be settled.

"So I proposed that we go to New Orleans. My motion got 19 votes and one abstention. So Pete Rozelle called another vote and New Orleans won it."

During Super Bowl VI week, city fathers, who by then knew more about the NFL than Mayor Maestri, threw a plush party for league moguls at the Cabildo. Rooney hadn't planned to attend, but he ran into friends as he left Mass at St. Louis Cathedral.

They urged him to show his face. So he entered the Cabildo. Rooney, one of the most recognizable faces in the NFL, reached the door, explaining that he had left his invitation at the hotel. The guard told Rooney, "No soap."

"He wouldn't let us in," Rooney recalled with a laugh. "I kiddingly told the guy, 'Look, I'm supposed to be in there.' He just said, 'Not without a ticket you're not.'

"Finally, I started to walk away and I told him, 'If it wasn't for me, you wouldn't be having a party in there.' He looked at me and must have thought I was some kind of nut."

Instead of getting someone to identify him, Rooney retreated to his hotel. He hadn't wanted to party anyhow.

That tells you all you need to know about Art Rooney. The Chief, as they called him, was one of the most colorful and kind persons I ever knew. His word was his bond, good as gold. They don't make many like him anymore.

He was a master storyteller and was far from one-dimensional. He loved his Steelers and the Pirates. Horses? He could talk endlessly about 'em.

He enjoyed politics and politicians. And dogs, too. The kind you bet, not pet. He liked newspapermen, especially those who enjoyed facing up to a mutuel window at the track.

Once Art and some sportswriters were Irishing it up at a West Palm Beach track operated by his sons. As a first-time starter in dog-wagering, I wondered how anyone could possibly handicap an animal that didn't have a rider. I couldn't have cared less about racing dogs, but it was a chance to be with him, so I accepted his invitation. He talked about Johnny Blood and Davey O'Brien and I loved it.

"New to this, huh?" Rooney said. "Let's see your program." Rooney circled a number in each race and returned it.

Guess what? All but one of Art's picks won. I was impressed. "Can we come again tomorrow night?" I asked.

Rooney, flashing a big Irish grin, replied, "That won't happen again, ever."

Roesler thought of another special time with Rooney in a pretty special place. "I used to see him at the owners' meetings and they were always held in the poshest resorts," said Roesler. "One of the nicest moments I ever had with him was on the porch of the Royal Hawaiian Hotel in Honolulu. He'd go out there to smoke his cigars. We'd talk about the old days. We'd talk about the Steelers in the late '30s, that exhibition game in New Orleans, stuff like that.

I asked him it if was true that he'd won all that money in two days at the horse tracks. He said it wasn't true. "If it wasn't true," I asked him, "why has that story stayed around so long?" He said, "Well, it's a great story, isn't it? It's hard to kill a good story."

You have to understand how we regarded this man. Those of us who lived in the new frontier of the NFL looked upon him like he was Daniel Boone, or the Lewis & Clark of pro football. You think of him and George Halas, and not necessarily in that order, and you think about the beginnings of the league. Yet Art Rooney was one of us, the common people. I got to know him (in 1965) the year before New Orleans came into the NFL. He was Mr. NFL.

He went to Mass at St. Anthony's Church in New Orleans. I'm a new Catholic, a convert. I knew the priest there, a Dominican named Father Lever. He said they were always delighted when Mr. Rooney came to town. The priest said the handle went up when he came to church. He said when the Steelers came to town the collection plate got heavier. He was very generous. Even today, when I pass St. Anthony's, I think of Mr. Rooney.

"The life, the escape from routine.
That's what was great about playing pro football.
If you didn't like neckties, it was hard to beat."
— Johnny Blood, legendary player
and coach in the '30s

Bob Roesler, at right, hopes to see Dave Anderson of *New York Times* at Super Bowl XXXVI in New Orleans.

Pro Football Hall of Fame

Former Steelers star Byron "Whizzer" White, left, was appointed to Supreme Court by President John F. Kennedy. At 45, Justice White was the youngest so honored.

> *"He was the essence and embodiment of our city. There are very few men and women whose names are synonymous with their particular city, but Art Rooney will always mean Pittsburgh to all of us."*
> — Mayor Sophie Masloff

Pro Football Hall of Fame
The gang's all there

"It's always been a big deal in Canton."

Any sports fan from Pittsburgh or western Pennsylvania will point with hometown pride to many of the exhibits to be found at the Pro Football Hall of Fame in Canton, Ohio.

It's a turnpike auto trip of about 110 miles from downtown Pittsburgh into another era, a less-sophisticated time, when the football was a little rounder, and football heroes all seemed to have nicknames and wore mud-caked uniforms, and the uniforms weren't quite as fancy as those found today in the National Football League.

There's something for everyone, though, not just older fans. The present-day NFL stars are well-acclaimed, for instance. The Steelers of the '70s still hold forth in a strong manner in this fascinating museum.

The Super Bowl accomplishments of Chuck Noll's troops are well-documented in Canton by film, photographs, displays, their four Super Bowl rings, and Bill Cowher comes in for his due as well.

Lynn Swann became the 17th individual mainly associated with the Steelers to be inducted into the Pro Football Hall of Fame at ceremonies on August 4, 2001. He was preceded by Bert Bell and Johnny "Blood" McNally in 1963, Art Rooney in 1964, and then Bill Dudley and Walt Kiesling (1966), Bobby Layne (1967), Ernie Stautner (1969), Joe Greene and John Henry Johnson (1987), Jack Ham (1988), Mel Blount and Terry Bradshaw (1989), Franco Harris and Jack Lambert (1990), Chuck Noll (1993), Mike Webster (1997) and Dan Rooney (2000).

The 1979 Hall of Fame class was of interest to a Pittsburgh sports fan because native son, Johnny Unitas, the great quarterback of the Baltimore Colts, was inducted, and Pat Livingston, the sports editor of *The Pittsburgh Press*, received the Dick McCann Award for long and meritorious service to pro football through his writing. Livingston also served on the selection committee for the Hall of Fame for many years. Myron Cope later served as Pittsburgh's representative.

From the start, once you pass through the turnstiles and by the 7-foot bronze statue of Jim Thorpe, there are exhibits of special interest to the fan from the Pittsburgh area.

For openers, before one finds the exhibitions of the Canton Bulldogs and the Pottsville Maroons, there's a glass-encased display paying tribute to some of the pioneers of the pro sport. There's a faded and cracked copy of an agreement by which Ivy League hero, William "Pudge" Heffelfinger of Yale, was paid $500 to play for the Allegheny Athletic Association of Pittsburgh, one of the early barnstorming teams, in 1892. He's now heralded as the first pro football player.

For a time, it was thought that the first pro football player was Dr. John K. Brallier, a quarterback who was paid $10 and "cakes" for leading the Latrobe YMCA team to a 6-0 win over Jeannette on September 3, 1895, three years later than Heffelfinger's pro debut.

In either situation, a case could be made for having the Pro Football Hall of Fame headquartered in Pittsburgh or Latrobe. It's unlikely, though, that either would have done as good a job as the community of Canton has in hosting the history and tradition of the game. The Hall of Fame has always been a big deal in Canton.

The NFL was founded in 1920 in a meeting in Canton, so the Ohio community has a legitimate claim to being the site of the sport's shrine. Pittsburgh and western Pennsylvania are well-represented by inductees like Unitas, from Mt. Washington and Brookline; Joe Schmidt, from Mt. Oliver; Mike Ditka and Tony Dorsett, both from Aliquippa; George Blanda, from Youngwood; Joe Montana, from Monongahela.

Bobby Layne is another NFL legendary figure who played for the Steelers late in his career. Layne led the Detroit Lions when they dominated the NFL in the 1950s with four division titles and three league championships. Under head coach Buddy Parker, the team won back-to-back league titles in 1952 and 1953. The Lions' battles with the Cleveland Browns in those days were classic confrontations between two giants of the blossoming NFL. Parker and Layne worked the same magic when they were later reunited in Pittsburgh. They provided some thrills and were always competitive but they couldn't grab the brass ring.

Layne's running buddy when he was in Pittsburgh was Steelers' favorite Ernie Stautner, one of the NFL's all-time toughest defensive linemen. Stautner played 14 seasons with the Steelers, a longevity record when he retired after the 1963 season to get into coaching. He later became a long-time assistant on Tom Landry's staff with the Dallas Cowboys. He was born in Bavaria and came to the Steelers from Syracuse University.

Another favorite is "Bullet Bill" Dudley. He came out of Bluefield, Va. to star at the University of Virginia and was the Steelers' No. 1 draft choice in 1942. He starred for the Steelers that season and — following a two-year stint in the Air Force — in 1945 and 1946. He won a rare triple crown in 1946 when he led the league in rushing, interceptions and punt returns.

Dudley didn't care for Coach Jock Sutherland and forced a trade. He played for the Detroit Lions and Washington Redskins in later years.

Kiesling coached the Steelers on three different occasions, including their days as a Philadelphia-Pittsburgh combine. Kiesling was not considered much of a coach by long-time followers of the Steelers. He's the team's answer to the Pirates' popular manager Billy Meyers whose No. 1 jersey is retired, mysteriously, even though his 1952 team lost a record 112 games. Kiesling's Steelers were usually a sorry sight, but he did guide the team to its first winning season in 1942. He was quite the ballplayer, apparently, a tackle with distinguished service for the Duluth Eskimos, Pottsville Maroons, Chicago Cardinals and Chicago Bears. He was in pro football for 34 years.

Johnny "Blood" McNally, known as the "Vagabond Halfback," did not qualify for the Hall of Fame for his stay with the Steelers, as a player at the end of his career, and certainly not as a coach. A tale is told of how he once went to scout a Chicago Bears/Green Bay Packers contest because he thought his Steelers weren't scheduled to play that weekend. The Steelers met the Philadelphia Eagles that day without a head coach on the sideline.

An elusive runner and gifted pass receiver in his heyday, Blood played for the Green Bay Packers, and played a major role in their drive to their first three championships in 1929, 1930 and 1931, and also played for the Milwaukee Badgers, Duluth Eskimos, Pottsville Maroons and the Steelers.

Among the leading rushers in NFL history is John Henry Johnson, who put in several seasons with the Steelers in a storied pro football career that began in Canada. Johnson is pictured in a 1960 game against the Cleveland Browns in which he gained 114 yards. In his best game against the Browns, however, Johnson gained 200 yards in an upset victory.

There's plenty more, and the Hall of Fame continues to update its displays and entertainment technology to compete with other tourist attractions in the area. Anyone who cares a hoot about football and its history and traditions would enjoy a visit, and many of us return each year to check it out.

Detroit Lions' president Bill Ford presents Pittsburgh's Joe Schmidt for Hall of Fame induction in Canton, Ohio.

The Greatest Football Reunion
Dan Rooney joins father in Canton

"That is really something special."

D an Rooney's timing was perfect. The Steelers owner and president could not have picked a better year or a better day to enter the Pro Football Hall of Fame than the Class of 2000.

There has never been a gathering of great football players to top this one that assembled on the last Saturday of July. National Football League Commissioner Paul Tagliabue thought it would be a good way to start off a new century by inviting every living member of the Hall of Fame to the sport's shrine in Canton, Ohio.

It was billed by the NFL spinmeisters as "Pro Football's Greatest Football Reunion."

Canton is located just 110 miles west of Pittsburgh, but it was a trip back in time, to when many of those football heroes were hale and hardy, when they were bubble gum cards stored in a drawer in a boyhood bedroom. It was a great way to celebrate the NFL's 80th anniversary.

An early morning rain made Hall of Fame officials nervous, but the gray gave way to a sunny and warm afternoon.

Everyone who was there should have felt honored by the occasion. There were 110 of the 136 living members of the league's elite who came to Canton on July 29, 2000. Sid Gillman, who taught Chuck Noll so much about football, came in a wheelchair. A half dozen walked with the aid of a cane. Many more moved with great difficulty — up and down the steps of the building with a football-shaped facade.

"All the important men of the game are here," offered the 68-year-old Rooney, the fifth and final inductee to be introduced during the ceremonies in front of the Pro Football Hall of Fame.

Earlier, he had said, "When I think of my father being in there, that is really something special. I am very, very pleased and humbled to be with such great people."

Rooney remembered being at the Hall of Fame for his father's induction back in 1964, the second class to be so honored. Dan was 31 at the time. Dan had witnessed many other Steelers being similarly honored, and he had been there to present defensive back Mel Blount in 1989 and coach Chuck Noll in 1993. Blount and Noll had been key contributors to the Steelers' four Super Bowl triumphs when they were named "the team of the decade" in the '70s.

And now he was being recognized for the outstanding way in which he had run the Steelers and contributed to the success of the league at large with his behind-the-scenes involvement. Rooney preferred to believe that he was representing the Steelers and the city of

Joe Greene (top photo) presented Steelers president Dan Rooney for induction at the Pro Football Hall of Fame in Canton, Ohio. Jack Lambert (center) leads cheering on steps of Hall of Fame. Class of 2000 includes, left to right, Joe Montana, Howie Long, Dan Rooney, Ronnie Lott and Dave Wilcox.

Pittsburgh and the Steelers' fans at the Canton ceremonies. It was a team thing.

"I look at it as a Steelers' event," he said at Canton. "This is about the fans, too — the greatest fans in the world." Rooney seemed reluctant to think he was being honored as an individual.

"The best part of it was being a member of the Class of 2000," remarked Rooney a week later, when he was walking through the press box at Three Rivers Stadium as the Steelers were starting their final season there with a pre-season contest with the Miami Dolphins. "It was really great to be with those guys, to get to know them better. The camaraderie was great. It was really a special group."

Tagliabue paid tribute to Rooney, saying, "It is a well-deserved honor for one of the game's great people. Dan has been one of the most respected leaders in the NFL for many years. He helped build and manage one of the premier franchises in sports and he has been a tremendous contributor to the overall success in the league."

Rooney also faced the task in early August of moving the Steelers' offices from Three Rivers Stadium to the UPMC practice facility they share with Pitt on the city's South Side. It had to be difficult to watch the movers taking photos down off the wall of his father's former office, which had been turned into a library. It had to be difficult to move out of a stadium where the Steelers had enjoyed so much success since it opened in 1970 — the stadium made the Steelers a first-class outfit for the first time in the team's history — and move to new digs, no matter how desirable and state-of-the-art they might be. Moving ranks high on the stress scale, right up there with death and divorce in the family.

Even with the honors being bestowed on him at the Hall of Fame, it had been a difficult and demanding year for Rooney. He and his oldest son, Art II, his heir apparent in the Steelers' front-office, had to make some difficult decisions to help the team turn things around after a disappointing 6-10 record, the worst in Bill Cowher's six years as head coach.

When it became obvious that Cowher and operations director Tom Donahoe could not co-exist in the Steelers' complex, they made the hard call to dismiss Donahoe, who had been a good friend of the family and a loyal lieutenant in the organization for most of his adult life. Donahoe took a year off before taking the top job with the Buffalo Bills.

Rooney remains optimistic that the best is yet to come. Rooney routinely piloted his own airplane in passes over the North Side site where a new stadium was under construction for the Steelers, as well as the University of Pittsburgh Panthers, and PNC Park where the Pirates would be playing.

"Three Rivers Stadium was just a tremendous thing for our team," related Rooney. "We played our first game there against the Giants. Terry Bradshaw was in his first year. After we beat the Giants (21-6), he wrote 'WINNERS' on a blackboard in the clubhouse. We

226

went from being a team to being a great team at Three Rivers. You take the '70s. No city could equal what we did, and I'm talking about Pitt and the Pirates, too. It was great for Pittsburgh. We were the City of Champions. I look forward to a new time in a new stadium. Our team in the '70s was the best team ever, I think, but I'm biased. We were the best defensive team; that's for sure.

"It's not easy to sustain that sort of greatness with the new rules regarding player contracts, free agency, and player movement today. You can't hold on to all your players anymore; it's tough to get a team anymore. We're going to have to find a way for teams to keep their best players."

"Those are pretty good people."

When I spoke to Rooney in the press box at Three Rivers Stadium the week after the Hall of Fame ceremonies, I asked him if he saw the spot where his bronze bust and brief bio would be displayed in the Hall of Fame. He had not seen it. "It's the same situation you were in at the induction ceremonies," I told Rooney. "You're next to a Raider and a 49er. You're to the right of Leo Nomellini of the 49ers and Jim Otto of the Raiders."

Rooney smiled. "Those are pretty good people," he said.

The Steelers were originally called the Pirates because Art Rooney was such a fan of the baseball team. When the Steelers' founder was growing up on the North Side, or Old Allegheny as it was then called, the Pirates played there at Exposition Park.

The Rooneys became only the second father-son tandem in the Hall of Fame, preceded by their lifetime friends, Tim and Wellington Mara of the New York Football Giants.

Dan Rooney had been a part of the Pittsburgh Steelers for more than 45 years, working his way up the organization. His first job was as a ballboy, before moving into personnel, public relations and management. He graduated from Duquesne University in 1955, and that's when he really went to work for his father.

He was a pretty fair quarterback at North Catholic High School and was miffed when he was named second-team on the Catholic League all-star team. A fellow named John Unitas of St. Justin's was the first-team pick. "I thought at the time, 'How can this guy beat me out?'" recalled Rooney. "Of course, that proved to be a pretty good choice after all."

The Steelers drafted Unitas in 1955 and the young Rooney used to catch passes with Unitas on the sideline at summer training camp. He and his brothers kept telling their father that Unitas was a good passer. But Walt Kiesling cut Unitas, keeping Jim Finks, Ted Marchibroda and Vic Eaton as quarterbacks. Unitas ended up playing sandlot football for the Bloomfield Rams for $7 a game, before he got a call from the Baltimore Colts when they were desperate for a quarterback. The rest is history.

Rooney was asked if he ever thought, when he was the quarterback at North Catholic, that he would someday be going into the Hall of Fame. Rooney smiled at that question. "I don't think I'm here as a quarterback," he came back.

That exchange came at a press conference inside the Hall of Fame that preceded the induction ceremonies for the Class of 2000. Each of the five inductees was limited to 15 minutes, and they were on the clock. A Hall of Fame official made sure they stuck to it, something they should have done during the actual ceremonies when speakers are supposed to limit their remarks to eight minutes, but run as long as 20 to 25 minutes at times. Only Dan Rooney restricted himself to eight minutes. He has always been one to follow the rules. It took three hours to honor five Hall of Famers.

Dan Rooney was asked about his father beforehand and he said, "I'm trying not to think of those things right now." He felt he would get too emotional if he dwelled on his dad, Arthur J. Rooney, who founded the Steelers in 1933, and his mother, Kathleen Rooney, and his daughter, Kathleen, who had died. He and his wife, Pat, had nine children altogether, but it was the one who was missing that was on his mind. "Guys, I don't want to get into that," he said to fend off such questions at the press conference. "If I do, I won't be able to handle this!"

Later, Dan did talk about his father's influence on him. "My dad gave me the understanding of what this league meant," Rooney said. "He gave me the commitment to do everything possible to keep it strong and viable. He was one of the men who forged this league. My father was one of the early men who did everything to make the NFL successful. To join him here today is special."

In an earlier interview in Pittsburgh, Dan stressed the difference between him and his father.

"All this you see around you, this whole organization, my father really made all this possible for us," said Rooney "But I realize I'm going a different route from him. I really never felt I was the same as him. Maybe I never had the same desires or approach. I wanted to make my contribution differently.

"My father was a 'people' man. He was a politician. His first reaction was 'What will people think?' My philosophy was that you have to do what is right and logical, even if it's unpopular. Like raising season ticket prices. I think a person has to do his job, hold up his own end. My father worried about everyone's feelings constantly. Sometimes it infuriated me, but that's just the type of person he was. He really worried about people. We had our differences, but I listened to what my father had to say."

> ## *"My father really was a man of the people."*
> — Dan Rooney

"The players should be friends."

Dan Rooney visited the Steelers' training camp at St. Vincent College in Latrobe a week before he made the trip to Canton. While there, he was asked by the writers who cover the team on a daily basis to talk about his upcoming honor. It was July 19, one day before his 68th birthday, and he was in a reflective mood.

True to form, Rooney was reluctant to talk about himself, but he talked about the good old days, which related to why he felt so good about what was happening in his life. It had been a long time since he was a wide-eyed five-year-old ballboy, of sorts, at similar Steelers training camps.

He remembered the influence his father, Arthur J. Rooney, Sr., had on his life.

"It's a special feeling and honor to join him," said Dan, saying something he would say often in the next week or so. "But to go in there with so many of the people I was fortunate enough to meet — George Halas, who started the National Football League, the commissioners (Bert) Bell, Pete Rozelle was a friend of mine, (George Preston) Marshall, the Maras (Tim and Wellington), (Charles W.) Bidwell — I had the opportunity to see them all and talk to them and hear what they had to say. I had humorous times, tough times, things like that.

"On the other side, just being with the Steelers and seeing some of the players that we had from the beginning until now. You young guys think the team started in 1970. There were some great players in the early days, and some great people.

"I really say that I got here through the fans, the players, the coaches and my father. That really makes it special. I really feel that I, hopefully, represent them in this whole thing."

He was asked to talk about today's brand of NFL football.

"The game is faster, the players are bigger," he said. "They work harder, and they really prepare, so from that standpoint, I think it's better.

"I think there are some things that I might say should be changed. No. 1, I think the coaches spend too much time telling players what to do. I think the players might be better off if there was, let's say — what's the word? — if they could be more spontaneous. I'm not trying to change the game completely. I'm just saying I think spontaneity would be good. It would help the game.

"The other thing that I really feel should happen is there should be more camaraderie. I've talked to (NFL Players Association Executive Director) Gene Upshaw about this. Once the game ends, the players should be friends with each other. They have respect for each other; I'm not trying to say they don't. But I'm saying there should be something special. I think the players that are getting to the Pro Bowl have this to an extent, but I also feel that it should be general."

"This means so much to my dad."
— Art Rooney II

A week later, as he stood front and center on the steps of the Pro Football Fall of Fame, Rooney wanted to share the spotlight. Dan asked his family members to stand and take a bow during his induction speech. He praised Pat Rooney, in particular, to whom he had been married for 48 years. "I've been fortunate to have a lot of support," he said. He thanked his four brothers, Art, Jr., Tim, Pat and John. "I thank God for so many things he has given me and my family," declared Dan.

Rooney's family, friends and front office personnel made the two-hour trip from Pittsburgh on three chartered buses.

Among the eight Rooney children in the crowd, Art II, the oldest, has been the closest to the Steelers' scene and has been designated to succeed his dad someday as the head of the organization.

"It's an emotional day for me because I'm so close to my dad, and I was so close to my grandfather," said the oldest of Dan and Pat Rooney's sons. "So this is really special. And I can tell this means so much to my dad. He's honored that people look upon him as someone who's important in the NFL."

His dad wrote his speech, and showed it to Art II for his approval. He suggested a few changes. His dad went with a few of them.

"We are not here to celebrate statistics," said Rooney in his speech. "We are here to celebrate excellence."

He praised league officials, and demonstrated that he had picked up some political skills from his father in the way he cited so many people for helping him get to Canton. He expressed some concerns about what was going on in the NFL and with its players. He said the game had to be protected, that the game was the most important aspect of what they were involved in. "We have to be watchful and make sure the game remains the same," he said. "The game is the whole works. We have to protect the game. We should spend more time on the game. It's America's No. 1 sport. You have my commitment that I'll do whatever it takes to protect the game. The National Football League, the game, is your legacy. Protect it. Don't let anyone tarnish it."

Rooney was much smaller than everyone else on the dais, and certainly the palest, but the fires were still burning in his belly.

During an interview on Saturday, Rooney said, "I'd like to win one more Super Bowl."

Former Steelers who were present at Canton included "Bullet Bill" Dudley (1966), Ernie Stautner (1969), Joe Greene (1987), John Henry Johnson (1987), Blount (1989), Franco Harris (1990), Lambert (1990) and Noll (1993). Jack Ham (1988), Terry Bradshaw (1989) and Mike Webster (1997) were not in attendance.

Those who showed up were, as former 49ers owner Eddie DeBartolo, Jr. put it when he introduced the most popular of all the inductees, Joe Montana, surrounded "by the very best of the best."

"Joe Greene is always a champion."
— Dan Rooney

The Class of 2000 was heralded as one of the best classes of inductees as well. It was a class that made anyone from Pittsburgh or Western Pennsylvania feel especially proud. The class was headed by Montana, a hometown hero from Monongahela, and Rooney.

They were the last to be inducted in the ceremonies. They saved the best for last. They were preceded by Dave Wilcox and Ronnie Lott, two of the hardest hitters in pro football history, representing two different eras of excellence for the 49ers. Lott had been a teammate, close friend and admirer of Montana during the great run when the 49ers won four Super Bowls in the '80s.

Howie Long of the Oakland Raiders, who wore No. 75 because of his admiration for the Steelers' Joe Greene, was the other member of the high-profile class. Greene was there, too, as a former inductee and as the man chosen by Dan Rooney to present him in the induction ceremonies.

He had chosen Greene because he believed he was the foundation of the Steelers of the '70s. "Joe symbolizes what the Steelers were all about," he explained.

When he first revealed that he had asked Greene to present him at the Hall of Fame, Rooney related, "First, Joe Greene is a very good friend and did so much for the Steelers during his playing and coaching days with the team. This induction is a celebration of the Pittsburgh Steelers and the great fans. I felt he (his presenter) should be a Steeler, and Joe was always on my mind. Joe really represents the Steelers players and is indicative of what we represent.

"Joe Greene is always a champion. He is a man of intense desire to win and a person of integrity who I admire as a friend. I am very privileged to have him present me."

Greene was only too glad to oblige his old boss. "Probably the last time I felt this good was when we won the Super Bowl," said Greene. "If I hadn't been sitting down when he asked, I would've fallen over. I'm truly honored. Truly honored."

At the Canton ceremonies, Greene paid tribute to his former boss on several fronts, talking about what a firm leader he has been, while showing compassion and personal interest in the players and their families. He spoke of his strong spiritual side, his Catholic upbringing, the backbone for his simple lifestyle.

"I'm a coach today because of Mr. Rooney," said Greene. He was pleased that he had been permitted to be part of the interview process when the Steelers were seeking a coach to succeed Noll in January of 1992. He was disappointed Rooney did not choose him, opting instead for Bill Cowher. "I trusted his judgment," said Greene, "and the record shows he picked the right man.

"The Steelers players have always been a part of Dan's family. You can read a lot about him, but you can't read about the great friendship Dan has shown me, or the kindness he has shown my family.

"Through 31 years of trust and respect, my relationship with Dan Rooney has transcended football. Dan loves the Steelers organization and he loves the people of Pittsburgh. Dan has always led with humility. When things go as planned, he's in the background. When things don't go as planned, he's in the forefront."

I've seen and heard Greene give better talks, more from the heart, but he was reading from a script and it stole something from his usually more spirited delivery.

When Greene was on Noll's coaching staff, he once complained at St. Vincent College that he was not able to attend Hall of Fame induction ceremonies when former teammates were being honored. Greene thought the Steelers would have benefited more from going to Canton and seeing one of the team's former players be honored than to stay at St. Vincent for one more day of training camp activity. I agreed, for what it's worth.

Greene is one of those guys who gushes about being in the company of the game's greats. Greene gets inspired by the company a visitor keeps in Canton. Seeing them and the rest of their fellow Hall of Famers stirred different memories for those in a record crowd of 18,000. In his recent fan's memoir, *Home and Away*, Chicago-bred writer Scott Simon wrote, "Sports stories can be memories and daydreams by which we measure our growth, like a parent's strokes inching up the unseen insides of a doorway."

"The Irish were not meant to be out in the sun."
— New York Giants owner Wellington Mara

I go to Canton every summer to enjoy these gatherings. It has become a rite of summer. I love this stuff. I go there with two good friends, Bill Priatko and Rudy Celigoi, who played the game in college. Priatko spent enough time over a two-year period with the Browns, Packers and Steelers to serve him in good stead the rest of his life.

When the formal ceremonies were concluded, I was ready to go home. I'd been out in the sun too long and knew I would be punished for it. As Wellington Mara of New York Giants once told me through winced blue eyes, "The Irish were not meant to be out in the sun."

Priatko never gets enough of this scene. He wanted to look for Mike Ditka. I didn't think there was a chance we could find Ditka in the crowd. Priatko persisted and Rudy and I followed him, reluctantly.

We showed our credentials to get through three different lines of security guards and, before we knew it, we were at a party for Hall of Famers and their families. We spent a half-hour with the likes of Mike Ditka, George Blanda, Joe Greene, John Henry Johnson, Tony Dorsett and Al Davis. Oh, if only Joe Namath and Montana and Dan Rooney and his late father, Art Rooney, had been there.

Jan Stenerud, the great place-kicker of the Kansas City Chiefs, and Don Maynard, one of Namath's main passing targets when the Jets won the Super Bowl after the 1969 season, were both talking nearby.

I had two ice-cold beers that helped take the burn out of my forehead. Mixing with so many personal favorites, catching up with their current activities, seeing Dorsett mimic the way John Henry Johnson once punished would-be tacklers with a fierce forearm was a priceless experience. Any fan would have loved to be in their company.

Jim O'Brien

Banners saluting Joe Montana of Monongahela and Dan Rooney of Pittsburgh hang from Fawcett Stadium alongside Pro Football Hall of Fame in Canton, Ohio.

Joe Montana
Pride of Monongahela

"I was always a Steelers fan."

Joe Montana was the main man in the Class of 2000 at the Pro Football Hall of Fame. He drew the loudest and longest ovation from a record crowd estimated at 18,000 that sat in the rain and then searing heat to hear what he and four other inductees had to say as they were enshrined in their sport's mecca.

Montana merely smiled when he heard the roar. Then he smiled some more. Then he waved and thanked everybody. And the roar erupted again. For one of the few times in his fabulous public life, Joe Montana wasn't sure what to do next. This was different.

No matter how good you've been, you get humbled by the company you are keeping at the Hall of Fame. That was especially true on July 29, 2000 when 110 Hall of Famers from the past were present in Canton at what NFL Commissioner Paul Tagliabue billed as "Pro Football's Greatest Reunion."

The Class of 2000 included Montana and teammate Ronnie Lott of the San Francisco 49ers, linebacker Dave Wilcox from earlier 49er teams, defensive end Howie Long of the Oakland Raiders and Steelers owner and president Dan Rooney.

Montana had been introduced by his former boss with the San Francisco 49ers, Eddie DeBartolo, Jr. of Youngstown. "We took a chance on a skinny kid from Notre Dame, and he changed our lives," said DeBartolo, whose late father owned the Pittsburgh Penguins when they won the Stanley Cups and who bankrolled him in his venture into the National Football League.

DeBartolo was a Notre Dame grad himself, so he was always biased about Montana. His early enthusiasm paid off. "I loved watching Joe turn losses into wins," said DeBartolo. Montana paid tribute to DeBartolo, as well, in a press conference prior to the induction ceremonies, and then when it was his turn to be honored on the steps of the Hall of Fame.

This was the kind of Saturday afternoon Montana relished when he was quarterbacking the Fighting Irish. He had also been a star at Ringgold High School near his home in Monongahela and his birthplace in New Eagle.

He had a storybook career with the San Francisco 49ers and the Kansas City Chiefs. He paid tribute to family and friends and former coaches — like Chuck Abramski, Paul Zolak and Jeff Petrucci at Ringgold — who had helped him find his way to Canton. Montana was the first native of Washington County ever to be inducted into the Pro Football Hall of Fame.

"Joe is the greatest ambassador we had," said Zolak, now the athletic director at Bethel Park High School, whose son Scott had just completed an eighth year career as a backup quarterback in the NFL. "Ringgold and Joe are synonymous."

Ringgold was a new school, only about four years old, when Montana put it on the map. There had been some growing pains when previous heated rivals like Donora High and Monongahela High, among others, were merged into a single school district.

The small towns of Donora and Monongahela sit along the west bank of the Monongahela River, about 25 miles downstream from Pittsburgh. Donora is famous for St. Louis Cardinals Hall of Famer Stan Musial, former Cincinnati Reds' outfielder Ken Griffey, Sr., NFL standout "Deacon" Dan Towler, and college athletic standouts Arnold "Pope" Galiffa and Lou "Bimbo" Cecconi. Monongahela was best known for turning out former University of Pittsburgh, Vikings and Browns placekicker Fred Cox, before Montana emerged, that is.

Taken by the 49ers in the third round of the 1979 National Football League draft, Montana became the master of the late-game comebacks. He directed his teams to 31 fourth quarter come-from-behind victories during his illustrious 16-year pro career.

Everyone remembers the 92-yard drive in the closing seconds of Super Bowl XXIII. He produced the winning touchdown against the Cincinnati Bengals at the Pontiac Silverdome. He did this time after time and it was known as "Montana Magic."

I covered that contest for *The Pittsburgh Press*, and I recall the pride everybody from western Pennsylvania felt when Montana won the MVP award. There wasn't a tougher, hard-nosed football player in the league, at any position, than Montana. The way he walked, his shoulders slouched, the profile, the nose, reminded one of Joe Namath, another Hall of Fame quarterback from back home.

"That drive was something I had done many times in my back-yard," said Montana when he first learned in January, 2000 that he had been elected to the Pro Football Hall of Fame during Super Bowl Week in Atlanta. "You accomplish a lot of things in your backyard. I won a bunch of Super Bowls by the time I was nine. But I never got into the Hall of Fame before. The one thing I did not dream about, or was unfathomable, was the Hall of Fame."

He won the NFL's passing title in both 1987 and 1989. He led the NFC in passing five times. He passed for more than 300 yards in a game on 39 occasions. In seven of those games, he passed for more than 400 yards. His six 300-yard passing performances in the post-season are an NFL record.

He led his team to the playoffs 11 times. Along the way, he captured nine divisional championships and victories in Super Bowls XVI, XIX, XXIII and XXIV. He was the only quarterback this side of the Steelers' Terry Bradshaw who could say he directed his team to four Super Bowl titles in as many tries. He topped Terry by being named the MVP in three of those championship contests.

He never threw an interception in 122 passes over four Super Bowls, which is unbelievable. Steelers fans could only wish that were true of Neil O'Donnell in one Super Bowl.

He spoke of great catches made by Dwight Clark — remember how high he went in the end zone to make that game-winning catch? — and Jerry Rice, John Taylor, Roger Craig and Mt. Lebanon's John Frank. Montana was named All-NFL three times, and he was voted to the Pro Bowl eight times, which was a league record for a quarterback at the time.

Montana missed 31 consecutive games because of an injury to his throwing arm, but made a dramatic comeback in 1992. In the second half of the regular season finale, a Monday Night Football Game vs. the Detroit Lions, he completed 15 of 21 passes and two touchdowns as the 49ers defeated the Lions, 24-6. The bigger the spotlight the more Montana rose to the occasion.

At the time of his retirement, he ranked among the leaders in every passing category. He finished his career as just the fourth quarterback in history to pass for more than 40,000 yards.

"I feel like my teammates are the biggest part of what got me here," said Montana. "When you look at football, it's really the only team sport where it takes a whole team to get something accomplished. One guy can go in and score 70 points in a basketball game. A guy can come up and hit two or three home runs. But to get the ball into the end zone, it takes a team effort."

Montana's middle school, high school and college career coincided with the Steelers great run when they were the "team of the decade" and Pittsburgh was hailed as "The City of Champions." Like Dan Marino, who came up behind him, Montana was a big fan of Terry Bradshaw.

Montana liked Bradshaw because he never gave up despite some early challenges in his career. "When he was with the Steelers in those early years, he was getting hammered," said Montana. "It was nice to see him turn it around."

Sitting next to Rooney and in front of Steelers' Hall of Fame great Joe Greene on the steps of the Hall of Fame reinforced old feelings.

Now Montana was joining Bradshaw, Greene, and other western Pennsylvania quarterbacks like Namath, George Blanda and John Unitas in the Hall of Fame. When he went to Notre Dame, he followed in the tradition of other quarterbacks who went to South Bend from western Pennsylvania like Johnny Lujack of Connellsville,Terry Hanratty of Butler and Tommy Clements of McKees Rocks. He cited Clements at the Hall of Fame induction, saying that when he was at Notre Dame he just wanted to be like Tommy Clements. Now Clements was the quarterback coach of the Steelers.

Montana's roots shaped him, for sure, even though he has been criticized for his reluctance to return home to be honored by his early followers, or to lend his presence to any fund-raising programs in western Pennsylvania.

"I've always been a Steeler fan, all my life," said Montana, nodding in the direction of Dan Rooney. "Yeah, I loved them back then…I still do. It's somewhat scary, though, when I see Joe Greene sitting behind me. I keep thinking he's going to break through the line and get me.

"Growing up in this area was one of the luckiest things that happened to me. It was an area that was very, very sports-oriented. People loved sports there. I grew up loving baseball, basketball and football, and the people were always behind it. As a kid, it was so easy to walk out your door and play basketball. You would find five or six teams waiting to play. You didn't want to lose on the basketball court because you had to sit out so long to play again."

Montana had mixed feelings in some other ways. He felt strange when he first learned he was being considered for the Hall of Fame. "I thought, 'Hey, I'm only 44, and I feel like I'm in my coffin, still alive, and they're throwing dirt on me. I really got the true meaning of what this is all about when I arrived here, and met so many of those who have been honored before.

"This is for the rest of our lives. This is a beginning, not an end. We're only going to another team. From my Pop Warner days, I'd heard about some of these guys. Now I was going to join them on the Hall of Fame team. I'm going to be a part of a great team again. In the middle of the night, I woke up and told my wife, Jennifer, I got the meaning.

"I'd compare it to the week of the Super Bowl. All the preparation leading up to this. Getting together with a lot of the older guys, hearing some pretty good stories, it was pretty amazing. You have a natural bond with guys in the NFL, no matter when they played.

"Somebody asked me if I thought I could be the starting quarterback of this team, and I said, 'I better be.'"

That points up the positive manner in which Montana always approached the game. When he neared the microphone at the pre-induction press conference, a writer posed an ice-breaking question, "Are you nervous, Joe?"

Montana didn't mull on that one too long. "Me … nervous … never," he said, succinctly summing up what he's always been about, and the real secret behind his success.

Even at the Hall of Fame, though, he still needed coaching. "My wife told me to stand up straight, and to quit slouching," he said. "I guess I was slumping in my seat at the table during dinner last night."

> *"My dad was dying, and on his deathbed he was still critical of me for not drafting Danny Marino. He never forgave me for that. I have to share some of the blame, but the final choice wasn't mine. In hindsight, we should have taken him."*
> — Art Rooney Jr.

"My parents wanted me to be the best."

Joe Montana wasn't always comfortable in front of a microphone, whether at a press conference, or during the one season he served as an analyst on NFL football telecasts, but being honored by the Hall of Fame brought out the best in him. He was boisterous, engaging, serious and funny and, best of all, he spoke from the heart. He wasn't a slave to his script.

He spoke about the support he received, right from the beginning, at his home in Monongahela, from his parents, Joe and Theresa Montana. "I learned that winning is what is expected of you," he said. "They taught me not to quit. My parents wanted me to be the best. They made sacrifices to make sure I accomplished all that I wanted to do."

He credited his family, and his wife, Jennifer, for their help along the way. Jennifer is his second wife. Some of his critics back home in Monongahela haven't forgiven Montana for divorcing his first wife, who had been his high school sweetheart.

While he always appeared cool on the surface, Montana confessed that his wife and family knew better. "Inside, we're a mess," he said. "They have to deal with a lot that people don't see."

He spoke about how difficult it was under Dan Devine at Notre Dame, when he saw his name listed seventh on the depth chart at the quarterback position. "I got off to a slow start at Notre Dame," Montana admitted. "But I learned what big-time football was all about, and how to deal with the media like I'm doing today. Notre Dame was a great experience."

He credited Bill Walsh, his coach with the 49ers, for making him strive for perfection.

He credited Ronnie Lott, his friend and former teammate on the 49ers, for pushing the team to greatness. He said that Lott and Eddie DeBartolo, Jr. kept the team inspired. "Mr. D. drove us," said Montana. "If the team needed a kick in the rear end, if it wasn't Ronnie, it was Mr. D. He made it possible for us to compete."

He said it was a difficult decision to choose someone to introduce him at the Hall of Fame. "I thought about Eddie, and then I'd go back and forth between him and Bill Walsh and my dad. Eddie meant so much to me," said Montana. "He's the whole reason the 49ers had such a great organization from top to bottom. He was a great leader on and off the field.

"I feel like a little kid up here. I'm still trying to grow up. I'm trying to fight off growing old. My wife says she has to deal with five kids, not four.

"What it's all about is the loving and sometimes dying and striving together. To make things happen on the football field truly takes 53 players and coaches working together."

He said going into the Hall of Fame with Lott, the godfather for one of his children, "makes it a little bit sweeter." He had a lot of respect for Ronnie, one of the hardest-hitting cornerbacks in NFL history.

"Here was a guy who not only talked about it," said Montana, "but he went out and did it. He talked the talk and walked the walk."

Lott complimented Montana on his leadership role. "Joe taught us how to compete in practice," allowed Lott. "If we didn't come to play, we got our butts kicked. When you compete against people you love and respect, you want to beat them. It's like when you're competing in anything with your brothers. That's the kind of respect and admiration I had for Joe." Howie Long praised Montana during the pre-induction press conference. "Joe was like El Cid," allowed Long. "You could prop him up dead on a horse and the other side would retreat. Whatever it is, he has it."

Jim O'Brien

Monongahela's Joe Montana meets the press prior to his induction at Pro Football Hall of Fame in Canton, Ohio as member of the Class of 2000.

Tony Dorsett, Hall of Fame, 1994
At Pro Football's Greatest Reunion
Canton, Ohio July 28-29, 2000

"I love being at the Pro Football Hall of Fame and seeing all these guys I looked up to all my life. Seeing John Henry Johnson...I heard a lot about him when I was growing up in Hopewell, and how he was such a tough, hard-hitting fullback for the Steelers. When I got older, I used to see video of John Henry, and how he hit would-be tacklers with the fiercest forearm you ever saw. Bam! And they'd be gone. He had the greatest stiff-arm in the game to knock away tacklers. He hurt people. I see all these Steelers here. I was a big Steelers fan when I grew up, and when I was with the Cowboys we had some great games against each other. They cost us a few Super Bowls. I feel at home here. To see all these guys I admired, like Gale Sayers. I talked to Joe Namath. I tell him, 'Joe, I was a big fan of yours. Joe, you're my hero.' He was from Beaver Falls, not far from my home, and I identified with him. My brothers knew him. When he was in high school, he threw passes and he'd walk to the sideline before the receiver scored. He knew it was six points."

John Henry Johnson, left, shows Tony Dorsett how to use forearm as a weapon to ward off would-be tacklers as two Pittsburgh favorites meet at "Pro Football's Greatest Reunion" at Canton, Ohio the last weekend in July, 2000.

Will McDonough
The Last Hurrah

*"If I weren't an owner I'd want
to be a sportswriter."*

Will McDonough, 65, of The Boston Globe *is one of the most respected
writers and commentators on the National Football League beat. He
has been to all the Super Bowls and he votes for the Pro Football Hall
of Fame and believes he had a special relationship with Art Rooney.*

We don't have many characters left in the sports writing
business. The Super Bowl is like an annual convention for
sportswriters. The old guys are storytellers. The young guys
are all opinion guys. I call these guys Mexican hat dancers. It's all
I-I-I-I. Guys like Blackie Sherrod would spin stories all night. Jim
Murray could do that. John Steadman was such a sweet man, and he
loved to tell stories. I could sit up all night listening to those guys.
They wrote stories about other people, about other characters. You
had guys like Ring Lardner. Jimmy Cannon. Those guys got along
with the people they were writing about. They spent a lot of time with
them. They ignored a lot of things, but in the long run they had more
entrée to the top guys. They got the good stories and they knew what
was going on. Today it's all very sterile. Sound bites. Press
conferences. I still have pretty good relationships with a lot of people
in the business. I can get information. People trust me. Guys who
can't get stories bitch about the guys who can get the stories. I've been
with *The Boston Globe* for 41 years, and I've been in the building for
44 years since my student days at Northeastern University.

I was around the New England Patriots from the start, and I was
with the AFC all the way from 1960 to 1970. I was there in 1970 the
first time we played the Steelers. That was Terry Bradshaw's rookie
year. We played a pre-season game against them in Shreveport, La.
That's where Bradshaw had gone to school at Louisiana Tech. He was
the league's No. 1 draft choice and they thought he'd attract a good
crowd. We had a fullback named Eddie Ray, who wasn't very good,
and he fumbled the ball on an end run. He gets hit and the ball flies
out. L.C. Greenwood comes by and picks up the ball and runs with it.
Eddie Ray runs like crazy after L.C. Everyone is standing around,
holding their helmets, hollering at them both to stop. L.C. was running the wrong way. Eddie Ray catches him and tackles him. They
both jumped up like they'd done something really good. They beat us
(31-3). After the game, I'm talking to Len St. Jean, one of our offensive
linemen. We had played the Lions in Montreal the week before, and
he had lined up against Alex Karras. St. Jean tells me, 'I didn't think
he (Karras) was that good, but I just played this young guy tonight

and he killed me. He's the greatest I've ever faced." That guy was Joe Greene, who was beginning his second year in the league.

I remember when I first saw the Steelers. They'd be playing the Giants on TV and they'd always lose.

Art Rooney, in my opinion after 40 years of sports, of all the guys I met, was the guy I loved the most. I still think of him a lot. In fact, just last month I came across this photo showing Dan Rooney sitting at the base of his father's statue. I had never asked anybody for an autograph in my life, but I called Dan to ask if he could please send me that photo and autograph it. I left a message. Dan called me after he got my call. He sent me a small photo of it. It's this big (wallet-size). He managed to write "to the greatest Irish-American sports writer in America." I called him back and asked him why he put "Irish-American" in there.

They were having an owners' meeting in Maui once, and I was not there. Art Rooney called me in Boston. He said, "'This is Chief. I called you to find out what's going on down here.'" That was a great compliment.

I knew he had been quite the amateur fighter. He had won some titles in Boston. He always had a special affinity for Boston. He had a friend there, a former boxer named Tansey Norton. They met each other in the 1920s. Tansey lived 35 miles south of Boston. Chief would have him come down as his guest for games in Pittsburgh. I used to bump into Tansey at the airport and we'd fly to Pittsburgh together for games, and come back to Boston on the same planes. I'm sure Chief picked up the total tab for Tansey. He was like that with old friends.

Art invited me to a party once. He said, "Will, I'm going to have a little get-together of Irish guys tonight. You're welcome to come." My Ryan was eight or nine years old at the time. He remembers that. Everyone was seated at a long table. He went to my son Ryan and said, "Son, you're going to sit next to me." He died two months later.

The Chief used to say that the day the television money stops coming in the league is over. He said, "We spend beyond our means." He also said there weren't many owners left who had the NFL in their blood.

The guy I admired the most in sports was Pete Rozelle. He was the most influential person in sports for the century. He never talked about himself. He had the same quality as Art Rooney in that respect. Art Rooney was a sports fan, first and foremost. He's the guy in sports I loved the most.

I loved going to Pittsburgh and I loved going into Art Rooney's office. It was like going into your own living room. I saw all the play-off games. You know Lenny Pasquarelli, the sportswriter in Atlanta? He's from Pittsburgh, as you know. Well, Lenny Pasquarelli's father let me in at the press gate. Stuff like that. He'd say, "Will, how ya doin'?" It made you feel comfortable all the way. Art Rooney would say the same thing when I'd see him.

We'd go back in the kitchen in the Steelers' offices. Tansey Norton would be there. Myron Cope would come in and sit down. He'd go over the lineups. Art would talk to us. He never talked about the Steelers. It was always about other stuff

When I'd leave the press box early to get to the locker room I'd run into Mr. Rooney. He'd say, "I'm going down to the locker room. You take care of yourself." I was there the day of "The Immaculate Reception." He had no idea what happened. He didn't know his guys had scored. He was going down because he wanted to console the players after what he thought was a tough loss.

He was sharp as a tack until the day he died. The league meetings aren't the same without him. When he was in his 80s, he fell down at one of the league meetings and hurt himself. I felt his pain.

Jim O'Brien

Boston Globe columnist Will McDonough, one of the most respected pro football commentators, compares notes with Sean Rooney, son of John Rooney and an executive with Aramark, a national food service company, during Super Bowl XXXV activities in Tampa, Florida.

"I love Pittsburgh . . . The people, the traditions, the ethnicity of the place, the feeling of neighborhood. Lord knows it's not the weather. But this is where my family made their money, and I want to stay and help the area."
— Richard Mellon Scaife
Publisher
Pittsburgh Tribune-Review

Joe Greene
The first building block

"We upped our standards
after we got Joe Greene."
— Chuck Noll

Joe Greene goes back to the beginning, those dark days of 1969 when he was the Steelers' No. 1 draft choice and Chuck Noll was the No. 1 hope of a franchise that had floundered for nearly 40 years.

"I remember the first meeting," said Greene. "Coach Noll said our goal is to win the Super Bowl. And I was thinking of that team and the present and, frankly, it wasn't that pretty. Coach Noll was looking down the road."

And what a road it was. Nine straight playoff appearances, four Super Bowl championships and the recognition as the best pro football team of the '70s.

Greene gained a reputation as the fiercest, often nastiest No. 75 in the league, looking to kill quarterbacks with a single blow and leap over opposing linemen in a bound, hell-bent on terrorizing everybody and everything in his path. On this day, February 9, 1982, Greene could only grin at such an Attila the Hun image.

He was known as Mean Joe Greene, and he came by his nickname honestly, though he was never comfortable with the tag.

"I've enjoyed the whole journey," said Not-So-Mean Joe. "But it has come to an end." Thinking better about that, he added, "It's the beginning."

In a sense it was both. It's been said that athletes die twice, when their athletic careers come to an end and, like the rest of us, when their heart stops beating.

At age 35, and after 13 mostly glorious seasons with the Steelers in the National Football League, Greene was giving up the ghost. He was retiring as a player, one of the proudest ever to play the game.

This was in the Pirates Room, of all places, part of the Allegheny Club complex, and Greene was in good company. Sharing the dais were Art and Dan Rooney, Chuck Noll and Joe's wife, Agnes. There were framed photographs on the walls of earlier Pittsburgh athletic greats such as Honus Wagner, Ralph Kiner, Roberto Clemente and Dick Groat, who like Greene, grabbed the hearts of sports fans in Pittsburgh and continue to tug on them even today.

He wasn't alone. Jon Kolb would soon announce his retirement, too, joining the likes of Sam Davis, Rocky Bleier, Mike Wagner, Steve Furness, L.C. Greenwood and Dwight White among the missing from the Steelers' star-studded cast of the '70s.

Mike
Webster

I could remember the first time I ever saw Joe Greene in the flesh, or in uniform, anyhow.

It was in the summer of 1979, and it was Photo Day at the team's training camp at St. Vincent College in Latrobe. I'd been watching rookies and free agents and a few veterans going through two-a-day workouts for nearly a week when the bulk of the Steelers' All-Pro cast came to camp.

I couldn't get over Greene. Sure, I'd watched the Steelers from a distance, following their fortunes on TV and in the newspapers during my ten years away from my hometown, but this was different. Greene came out of the dressing room and down the hillside and he seemed larger than life.

He was so big and so beautiful — there was no other way to express it honestly — and he just dominated the scene. There were other familiar faces like Franco Harris and Terry Bradshaw and Jack Lambert and Jack Ham, Mel Blount and Mike Webster, Lynn Swann and John Stallworth, Rocky Bleier and Larry Brown, Sam Davis and Jon Kolb, Donnie Shell and Mike Wagner, but none of them loomed as great as Greene. None of them glowed like Greene.

Frankly, I was surprised by my own gee-whiz attitude upon gazing at Greene and these other guys in black shirts. I thought I had been around longer than that. But I was impressed. There was something special about Greene. There was a grace about Greene that few men his size possess, indeed, a presence. He spoke carefully, with well-thought-out reflections, and he continued as long as anyone stood in front of him with a pad and pen or tape recorder. Joe Greene seemed too good to be true.

Later that night, I was walking through a dark hallway in the dormitory where the Steelers were staying, and I saw two large figures coming through a doorway. I couldn't make them out, at first. It turned out that the duo was Joe Greene and Mel Blount. Both smiled and said hello. I was grateful that they were such pleasant fellows off the field.

Greene set a standard for the other Steelers. "We upped our standards after we got Joe Greene," said Chuck Noll during an all-too-brief commentary on Greene's retirement.

Greene was asked that first day of camp in the summer of 1979 about the Steelers' chances of repeating as Super Bowl champions, winning the NFL title for a fourth time, and he responded, "You better believe we can. The Pittsburgh Steelers, if they put their minds to it, can do anything they want to do. They don't always do it, but, man, they always try."

The Steelers put their mind to it and they did win the Super Bowl that year.

Then Joe Greene got into a marketing gimmick and called for "One For The Thumb in '81 — a fifth Super Bowl ring — to fill out his hand. But it eluded Greene's grasp. He chased it for two more years.

He had planned on playing his final game in the Silverdome in Pontiac, the site of Super Bowl XVI a month earlier. "When I was watching Cincinnati and San Francisco, I was a little bit jealous," he said at his retirement announcement.

So he didn't go out on top, the way he once envisioned he would.

Once, after Greene had chased after Johnny Unitas during his final and futile season with the San Diego Chargers in October of 1973, Greene felt badly. "He's being tarnished and I hate to see it," Greene said of Unitas. "He was too good a player to be going out this way. It would be better if he went out the way my man, Jimmy Brown, did."

Few ever got to leave like his man, Jimmy Brown. He played nine strong seasons, then said goodbye, prematurely surely from a physical standpoint, to go into the movie business.

Greene may not have believed Chuck Noll at that first meeting when the new coach spoke about Super Bowl ambitions, but Greene was confident he could do it with the right supporting cast. Noll and club president Dan Rooney and the Steelers scouting staff made sure Greene got what he needed. But Joe was certainly the first block in building a dynasty for the next decade.

Greene came to his first camp late, after holding out for more money than the Rooneys offered him at first. Greene knew he was good.

Following practice at the South Park Fairgrounds that first year, Greene was asked how he regarded the veterans. "They're here, I'm here," he responded. "What they can do, I can do."

From the start, he knew his role. "I'm hoping I'll start right off the bat," he said. "I've never taken a back seat in football. I'm ready to play with the so-called big boys. I've spent the last ten years learning how to play this game. Football is my life, my career. I've got to make myself succeed."

No one succeeded any better.

"They allowed a country boy to come up from Texas and be himself."

He's seldom mentioned in the same breath as Roberto Clemente and Mario Lemieux, but Joe Greene was as important to the Steelers' success as either of those all-timers were to their respective teams in baseball and hockey.

Greene looked down the dais and said, "I'd like to thank the Pittsburgh Steelers, but I don't think that's possible. Words don't quite get there. Mr. Rooney and Dan and Chuck and the staff...they allowed a country boy to come up from Texas and be himself, and say what he wanted to say, good or bad. I'm grateful for being able to be myself.

"I could have been labeled as a radical or misfit. I bumped on all the boundaries. I pushed on them, not for any particular purpose. That was me, and they allowed me to be myself."

He was thrown out of a game early in his rookie season for a late hit on Fran Tarkenton, the quarterback of the New York Giants. Tarkenton, a scrambling type, had frustrated him all afternoon and he was out to level him.

Greene talked about that ejection experience the following day at a Curbstone Coaches luncheon at the Allegheny Club. "It's the way I play football," said Greene. "I really get angry at an opponent for being on the same field with me."

He said that back in high school in Temple, Texas, it had been the same way. "I got thrown out of my first game my freshman year for fighting," he said.

Talking about the Giants in general, Greene allowed, "I don't remember any of their linemen giving me any particular trouble."

Greene was never a shy guy. People listened when he talked.

Greene hollered at quarterbacks. "I'm going to get you!" he'd holler.

When Greene was banished for playing overly-aggressive football, Noll noted, "It's a first for the Steelers."

Greene's rule of thumb on going after quarterbacks: "My theory is that when you kill the head, the body dies."

He was thrown out of another game later that season, at Minnesota, when he belted Viking lineman Jim Vellone with a forearm across the face. "I don't relish getting thrown out of a game," said Greene. "The true mark of a champion, I know, is to shake off adversity and keep playing football. I hope to be like that from now on."

He kept his word. Which is why it was easy for Dan Rooney to remark at the retirement luncheon that "Joe Greene has been exciting and brought exciting times since the first day he came here. I was talking to Chuck and he said this is quite a transition. The day after we drafted him, the *Post-Gazette* had a headline that said, 'Steelers Draft Joe Who?' Joe never liked that, and he said so. He said many things and did many things in the 13 years he's been here, and they were all positive."

At least it seemed so over lunch that day. There were times when not everyone concurred with Rooney's remarks.

There was the time Greene blasted the game officials and vowed, "If I get half a chance, I'll punch one of them out and it'd give me a whole lot of satisfaction." He drew a fine from NFL Commissioner Pete Rozelle for that remark.

There was the time when he spit into the face of a Pittsburgh sportswriter, Pat Livingston. Greene later apologized and they became good friends.

During the 1975 season, Paul Howard of Denver and Bob McKay of Cleveland both claimed that Greene kicked them. Greene's response was to smile and say, "I think I've been too nice lately."

Two years later, he was fined $5,000 for punching Howard in the stomach in the midst of the madding war in the trenches.

When the Steelers were warring with the Oakland Raiders, both on and off the field, when George Atkinson and Jack Tatum were trash-talking all the time and leveling Lynn Swann every time he ran across the middle, Greene issued an at-large warning. "We have the kind of guys who can play it dirty. We can play it any way they want to play it. I won't shy away from the dirty stuff. In fact, you might say I'm capable of leading the way."

When Swann was leveled by a hard shot while going over the middle for a pass against those Raiders, it was Greene who picked up Swann's limp body and carried him off the field. It's a picture that stays in the mind. Noll, on the other hand, was unhappy with what he was reading in the newspapers back then, what he thought was negative writing on the Steelers. "It could have an effect," said Noll. "People put it in there that we're dirty. We're clean. We hit hard. If you don't hit hard, it's basketball."

But when Noll went to court after Atkinson sued him for statements he made about his aggressive style, Noll listed Greene, Mel Blount and Ernie Holmes, as well as several Oakland players, as belonging to a "criminal element" in the league. Noll later insisted his attorney made up the list to prove a point. Blount sued Noll, but Greene chose to turn his cheek this time. He didn't see how any good could be accomplished by getting into an argument with his coach.

He had good timing, too, and a sense of what was good for the Steelers. He could be a good guy, as depicted in that award-winning Coca-Cola commercial.

During a players' strike in the summer of 1974, Greene stayed home. "I didn't want to carry a picket sign against the Rooneys," he explained then. "They're the nicest people I know. If the other owners were like the Rooneys, there wouldn't be a strike."

At his retirement luncheon, Greene said he would miss the Steelers' scene, his teammates most of all, the strategy meetings, the weekly challenges, all but the pain and hurt and questions about his and the Steelers' decline and fall.

He had such good memories of the Steelers' best days.

"The Super Bowl experiences were above my wildest dreams," said Greene. "I walked on clouds, all four times. It was just a wonderful, wonderful feeling. I'm going to miss the fans, too, and seeing them filling the stadium and waving their 'Terrible Towels' and screaming and shouting and understanding when I didn't sign or did sign an autograph, or frowned or smiled at them. Joe Greene wasn't always at his best. But he tried."

Greene was having a hard time saying goodbye, even to the persistent sportswriters who surrounded him. "I'll come back next year and conduct a press conference after every game," he said to cheer them. "We respected one another...the sharing of ideas."

He had a glad and firm hand for everyone, a goodbye that would be remembered by each. That wonderful wink. "It's time," he said. "Right now I think I'm ready to go out in the real world and live.

"The other day my mother showed me an old scrapbook and there was a picture of me when I signed my first contract with the Steelers. I looked at it and said, 'Wow, that looks like my son.' So I'm sure it's time."

Steelers owner Art Rooney is flanked by two Hall of Famers at Dapper Dan Sports Dinner at Hilton in the '70s, with Willie Mays of the Giants and Joe Greene of the Steelers at his side.

Joe Greene and wife, Agnes, join Art Rooney Jr. and Bill Nunn Jr., proud members of the Steelers' personnel and scouting department during glory days of the '70s.

Terry Bradshaw
Better than Sammy Baugh?

"He's got a special talent."
— Chuck Noll

Ted Thompson

Art Rooney always regarded Slingin' Sammy Baugh as the best quarterback in pro football history until Terry Bradshaw became the Steelers' savior.

"He can do everything Baugh did, and then some," the Steelers' 80-year-old owner told me during an interview in his office at Three Rivers Stadium a few days before Thanksgiving in 1981. "Bradshaw has more ability than Baugh. He's the best I ever saw."

The previous Sunday in Atlanta, Bradshaw had fired five touchdown passes to steer the Steelers to a 34-20 victory over the Falcons. The five touchdown passes were a Steelers' record and one more than Bradshaw ever threw in a game before.

(Mark Malone, by the way, would tie this record four years later when he threw five touchdown passes against the Indianapolis Colts. Bradshaw, Bubby Brister and Jim Finks all had three games in which they threw four touchdown passes. Malone, Dick Shiner and Ed Brown each had four touchdown passes in a game.)

Bradshaw's five touchdown passes at Atlanta gave him a career total of 189, moving him by Baugh's 186 for 14th place on the all-time list. Bradshaw finished after the 1983 season with 212 career TD passes. Bradshaw was 33 years old during the 1981 season, but Chuck Noll thought he still had some record-breaking days ahead of him. "He's never done this before," Noll noted of Bradshaw's five TD pass outing, "so who knows what he might do next?

"I don't think Terry has peaked out as a quarterback. He's had lots of accomplishments, but he's a very talented individual. He's very accurate and he's got more changeups than anybody I've ever seen. There are a lot of things he can do that other people can't. I just think he's got a special talent."

Rooney agreed with Noll. "I think he can do anything better than anybody," said Rooney. "I don't think he's done it all, either, even though he's the only quarterback ever to win four Super Bowls (this was before Joe Montana matched it).

"Look, Baugh was as good as any quarterback. Who knows who's the best? He could've been the best because he did the most. He passed, he ran, he kicked the ball.

"Baugh was a single-wing tailback for most of his career. Bradshaw would have been a great tailback in the single-wing system. He's a stronger passer than Baugh, a stronger runner, and if he wanted to — and he doesn't — he could punt as well as anybody. I've watched him punt in practice ever since he came here and he could be a great punter."

Bradshaw was moving up the career ladder in several statistical categories, bypassing the likes of Baugh, Bobby Layne, Bart Starr, Babe Parilli, Otto Graham, Norm Van Brocklin and Charlie Conerly and he was closing in on the likes of Joe Namath, Len Dawson, George Blanda and Sonny Jurgensen. "That's something you think about when it's over," said Bradshaw. "I know about it because (Steelers publicist) Joe Gordon tells me about it after the game. But I never think about records or yardage, or stuff like that.

"Maybe when the game is over, or the season or your career is over, you look back on that stuff. Then, it's important. Right now, the most important thing is winning. Everything else falls into place."

Bradshaw had some bumps along the road in recent years, and had gotten involved in movies and TV and singing, and some thought he might be thinking about retiring.

"I'm a full-time football player now," he insisted. "I'm where I ought to be. Hey, I'm just beginning. I'll play five more years and I'll ride out on a horse."

The week before, following a disappointing setback at Seattle, Bradshaw was approached by someone with a tape-recorder who wanted Bradshaw's life story in ten minutes.

"How are you different from the Terry Bradshaw of, say, five years ago?" the inquisition began.

"Well, for one thing, I'm five years older," began Bradshaw in one of his vintage good-fun deliveries. "I was 28 then; I'm 33 now. I lost a little more hair in the meantime, but I'm a little faster now."

"What was the biggest day of your career?"

"Today could have been a big day. I'll wait for it. I'm never satisfied," Bradshaw said.

"What's the most important thing in your life?"

"That's sort of serious to get into now," said Bradshaw, "but the most important thing to me is happiness."

Terry Bradshaw wields baseball bat between two outstanding participants in the 1971 World Series, Willie Stargell of the Pirates and Jim Palmer of the Baltimore Orioles, during a light moment at Three Rivers Stadium.

Ted Thompson

Terry Bradshaw and
Cliff Stoudt

**Cliff Stoudt, former Steelers
quarterback (1977-1983)
At Tony Dorsett McGuire Memorial Celebrity
Golf Classic, Father's Day, June 17, 2001:**

*"When I left the Steelers after being a backup
quarterback behind Terry Bradshaw for seven
seasons to sign with the Birmingham Stallions
of the United States Football League it really
upset the football fans in Pittsburgh. It was
unreal. I received death threats before we came
to Pittsburgh to play the Maulers.*

*"Security was increased at Three Rivers
Stadium. They even had special security for my
parents who were in a booth near the press
box. They took me off the airplane before it
arrived at the gate. It was spooky. And, of
course, the fans threw stuff at me when I came
onto the field at Three Rivers Stadium. It was
a bad scene.*

*"But Art Rooney arranged for a catered
dinner for me and my parents after the game
in the clubhouse. He sent me letters and cards
in Birmingham. He said he was sorry I didn't
stay with the Steelers. He wished me good luck
and success. He said I would always be a part
of the Steelers family, and that I would always
be welcome in the Steelers' offices.*

*"I wrote a letter to Chuck Noll a few years
ago and expressed my thanks to him for trying
to teach me more than football when I was
here. It took me awhile to realize that. I came
back for a reunion of the team two years ago
and it was great to see everyone. His wife,
Marianne, told me I had no idea what that
meant to Chuck. She said he didn't get many
letters like that."*

Johnny Unitas
The great one that got away

"Johnny Unitas was a miracle."
— Dan Rooney

Johnny Unitas has often been acknowledged as the greatest quarterback in the history of pro football. Some will hold out for Joe Montana, John Elway, Danny Marino, Terry Bradshaw, Otto Graham or Slingin' Sammy Baugh, but Unitas is still No. 1 in most books. It's safe to say Johnny U. was one of the all-time greatest performers at his position. They said he was peerless as a passer with poise and accuracy under fire and, indeed, he once owned a restaurant in Baltimore named The Golden Arm, which was his nickname.

Unitas was the focal figure in what was called "the greatest game ever played." That was the 1958 National Football League championship, when a cool Unitas, just 25-years-old, led the Baltimore Colts to a 23-17 victory over the New York Giants in "sudden death" overtime. If that was not really the greatest pro football game ever played it was certainly the most important.

It was the first overtime game in regular or post-season history in the NFL. As America watched in fascination on NBC, network executives began to realize the potential for the NFL on television. The impact of that game is still felt today. It completely changed the picture of pro football. It was the dawning of a new era for the sport. Fifteen participants in that game, including three coaches — Weeb Ewbank, Vince Lombardi and Tom Landry — are honored in the Pro Football Hall of Fame.

"I think that particular game accelerated football into what it's become now," said Unitas, who was present at Super Bowl XXXV in Tampa to root for the Ravens, Baltimore's current pro football club and the NFL's championship team for the 2000 season.

Unitas was upset when the Colts left Baltimore for Indianapolis in the dark of the night, and never wanted to be associated with the team. The Ravens have worked hard to get him on their side, and seem to have succeeded. He is often seen standing on their sideline during games.

Unitas hails from Pittsburgh and any die-hard Steelers fan worth their salt knows the story of how the Steelers cut him from their squad during the summer of 1955. He had been their No. 9 draft choice out of the University of Louisville, but they let him go in favor of a rookie quarterback from Missouri named Vic Eaton, who could double as a defensive back. Eaton, their No. 11 draft pick, was retained as the No. 3 quarterback behind Jim Finks and Ted Marchibroda.

"There were only 33 players on a team then," pointed out Steelers' president Dan Rooney, "so it made sense to keep a more versatile player. There were only 12 teams then. A lot of guys got cut."

Unitas ended up playing sandlot football for $6 or $7 a game for the Bloomfield Rams that season. The following season, the Colts were short on quarterbacks — backup Gary Kerkorian quit to go to law school — and were desperate for a signal-caller so they contacted Unitas and invited him to join their team. The rest, as they say, is history.

I spoke over the telephone with Unitas, at age 67, in late November of 2000 and asked for his version of a story I had heard from several sources through the years. I wanted to hear it from Unitas.

"I'd come home to Pittsburgh from Cincinnati, where we had beaten the Steelers in an exhibition game," said Unitas. "I wanted to pick up my wife and our baby who were with my brother at his place on Mt. Washington.

"I was driving down West Liberty Avenue in Brookline near the intersection of Brookline Boulevard. I was stopped there at a traffic light. Who pulls up alongside me but Art Rooney. One of his sons (John) is driving the car. His dad is next to him in the front seat, with the cigar in his mouth. Walt Kiesling, the coach of the Steelers at the time, is in the back seat. He's the coach that cut me.

"I said to my wife, 'Do you know who that is? That's Mr. Rooney.' So I hollered out, 'Hi, Mr. Rooney.' He always called me U-nide-EES.' We stopped alongside each other at the next light. Mr. Rooney leans out the car and says, "Hey, John, I hope you go on to become the greatest quarterback in the game."

According to Art, Jr., his dad immediately wanted to take back his words because he didn't want it to sound like a criticism of Kiesling.

It's a true story, though, Unitas says, confirming one of Art, Jr.'s favorite tales about his father. Rooney and his contingent, by the way, were in the neighborhood to attend a funeral.

Unitas remembers seeing Mr. Rooney again before one of the Super Bowls. "He was sitting down to dinner and he spotted me," recalled Unitas, "and he offered me congratulations on my career."

What a career Unitas had. He played pro football for 18 years, with the Baltimore Colts from 1956 through 1972 and finished up, somewhat sadly, at San Diego with the Chargers in 1973. He was recognized as possibly the finest clutch quarterback in the game. The round-shouldered 6-1, 195-pound passer was All-NFL five times and he played in ten Pro Bowls, four NFL championship games, two AFC title contests, Super Bowls III and VI.

His career figures are staggering — 2,830 pass completions in 5,186 attempts good for 40,239 yards and 290 touchdowns. When he retired, no other passer even remotely approached those totals. Most of them have since been surpassed and then some by Marino, another

Three quarterbacks competing for jobs in Steelers' 1955 training camp at St. Bonaventure University in Olean, New York are, left to right, Jimmy Finks, John Unitas and Vic Eaton. Ted Marchibroda was also in the competition. Unitas was cut in favor of that trio.

John in grade school days

John's mother, Helen Unitas, was his real hero.

Unitas visits Terry Bradshaw in Steelers clubhouse at Three Rivers Stadium.

quarterback out of Pittsburgh, Fran Tarkenton, Elway, Warren Moon and Montana, among others.

"I never look back."

Johnny Unitas still appears in the NFL record books, and remains in the Top Ten in several statistical categories. His most unbeatable mark is his string of 47 straight games in which he threw at least one touchdown pass, starting in 1956 and ending in 1960. Some people compare that to Joe DiMaggio's 56-game hitting streak.

Relate any of those numbers to Unitas and it doesn't stir his juices. "I never look back," he said. Unitas still has the cool exterior. He can be proud of his accomplishments, though, especially considering how he nearly did not get a chance to display his talents.

"I have to believe," Dan Rooney remarked, "that there must have been other guys who got cut who could've been great players if given the opportunity to play. It's scary. Johnny Unitas was a miracle."

Rooney made this remark in July of 1979, just before Unitas was inducted into the Pro Football Hall of Fame in Canton, Ohio. I had just reported for duty at *The Pittsburgh Press* a few months earlier, and had been assigned the pro football beat, covering the Steelers and the NFL. So I was dispatched to Canton to cover the Hall of Fame induction ceremonies. It meant a lot to me.

Dan Rooney, by the way, had played quarterback at North Catholic High School at the same time Unitas starred at St. Justin. Rooney bristled when he was named second-team all-league behind Unitas. "It turned out they had it right," remarked Rooney before Rooney joined his father, Art Rooney, Sr., and Unitas in the Pro Football Hall of Fame in July, 2000.

"Bullet Bill" Dudley, then the president of the National Football League Alumni Association, introduced Unitas and the Class of 1979, which included Dick Butkus, Yale Lary and Ron Mix, and read of their numerous achievements during the induction ceremonies in Canton.

The Hall of Fame should be a high for the honorees. "It is not every day," wrote William N. Wallace in *The New York Times*, "that a person is paraded in an open automobile before 100,000 people; hears himself extolled as one of the greatest athletes of his time, and witnesses the unveiling of a bronze bust and a portrait that are remarkable likenesses."

Unitas was introduced in Canton, surprisingly enough, by Frank Gitschier, a retired FBI agent who was the backfield coach at Louisville in the early 1950s. He taught Unitas the rudiments of the T-formation quarterback position. In gratitude, Unitas asked him to introduce him at the Hall of Fame.

Unitas had been my boyhood hero. I usually played center or linebacker on the midget football league teams of my youth. One year

I got to play halfback for St. Stephen's Grade School and quarterback for the Hazelwood Steelers. I played in the Pittsburgh Catholic League on Saturday mornings and in the Greater Pittsburgh Midget Football League on weekday evenings. Playing under the lights was a special thrill. Playing on an oil-coated Arsenal Field in Lawrenceville where Unitas had played was a thrill, too, though my mother couldn't appreciate it when she had to get the oil stains out of a white football jersey in the wash that week. I've visited Dean Field, under the Bloomfield Bridge, where the Rams played some of their games. Dan Rooney was coaching St. Peter's in the Pittsburgh Catholic League in 1956, the same year I was an eighth grader in the same league.

That year I played quarterback I wanted to be like Johnny Unitas. I wore No. 19 on my jersey. I wore black high-top shoes. My hair was shorn in a crew-cut style. I mimicked Unitas' close-by-the-ear throwing motion, with a downward thrust on the follow through. If I had been more athletic, more mobile, taller and not near-sighted I could have been the next Unitas. But I loved to write and wanted to be a sportswriter. So I settled for being a sportswriter.

I wrote two long letters to Unitas during the 2000 football season seeking an interview with him. I told him he had been my boyhood sports hero. He was wary of sportswriters, I was warned, believing he had been burned a few times. In my second letter, I mentioned having a conversation with his good friends, John Steadman, the legendary sports columnist in Baltimore, and Tom Matte, the former Colt running back and emergency quarterback who was an analyst on Colts' radio broadcasts. I mentioned some mutual friends we had from his days at St. Justin's High School and on the sandlot playing fields of Mt. Washington and Brookline, such as Ralph Jelic, Dan Kanell, Tom Bigley, Pat and Jon Botula. The second letter worked.

"I used to play baseball with Tom Bigley at Olympia Park." said Unitas. "Is he still married to Joanie Weaver?" I told Unitas that the Bigleys were still a couple, happy in each other's company, and that I frequently bumped into them at Pittsburgh sports events. They go to high school football games most Friday nights. Jelic likes to tell a story about how he, a fullback, passed for more yardage in a game than Unitas when he was playing for Dayton against Louisville. "Of course, Unitas got hit and knocked out of the game in the third quarter. I threw a wobbly pass that went for a touchdown in that game," said Jelic.

"I never doubted my ability. "

One day I came home and one of the messages on my telephone went like this: "Jim O'Brien, this is John Unitas in Baltimore. You called and said you wanted to speak to me." It sounded like a voice from heaven. I told my wife, Kathie, to keep it on the message system the remainder of the month. I wanted to hear it again from time to time.

Unitas sounded like he was calling out signals in that game against the Giants in 1958. It reminded me of a line offered by one of his Colts teammates who, when asked what it was like to be in a huddle with Unitas, said, "It's like being in the huddle with God."

That was some week. I also heard from Marino and Mike Ditka during an eight-day stretch. These were three of the finest football players ever to come out of western Pennsylvania. They were all big fans of Art Rooney and Pittsburgh.

I had just picked up a photo the same morning Unitas left his message from John Nicolella that I was excited to get. It showed Nicolella's friend Joe Schmidt, an All-American at Pitt in the mid-'50s and later a Pro Bowl middle linebacker and coach with the Detroit Lions, with his former Lions' teammate Bobby Layne. That made my day. Then to get a phone call from Unitas was a real bonus. I got back to him immediately to interview him. I learned, coincidentally enough, that Schmidt was the opposing player Unitas admired the most during his days in the NFL.

Unitas recalled how he used to play pitch-and-catch at the Steelers' training camp at St. Bonaventure University in Olean, New York with Art Rooney's twin sons, Pat and John, and sometimes Tim and Dan. It was Tim who drafted a 22-page letter to his dad back in Pittsburgh, extolling the virtues of Unitas when he thought Kiesling wasn't giving him a fair chance to compete for a spot on the squad.

"I never doubted my ability," Unitas told me over the telephone during our interview. "I knew I could play the game. I just didn't get an opportunity with the Steelers. I scrimmaged all the time with them at the training camp. I always did fairly well. They made a judgement about quarterback, and I lost out. Those things happen."

The Steelers gave Unitas $10 for travel back to Pittsburgh from Olean. He was broke, so he pocketed the $10 and hitchhiked back to Pittsburgh with another player who had been released by the Steelers.

"I remember some of the Steelers I was with at that camp," said Unitas. "They had Dale Dodril, Elbie Nickel, Bill McPeak, Fran Rogel, Lynn Chandnois, Ray Mathews, Ernie Stautner, Jack Butler, Jim Finks and Ted Marchibroda at the time. They had some good backs and ends. They had Lou Ferry, Willie McClung, Goose McClairen and Richie McCabe, too.

"I'd never seen a professional football game until I was in high school. The first game I ever saw was between the Cleveland Browns and Philadelphia Eagles. I liked the Eagles for some reason. They had Tommy Thompson and Pete Pihos and Steve Van Buren. I liked Van Buren the best. That was in 1950 or 1951.

"My high school coach, Max Carey, took some of us to the game in Cleveland. He worked at the Veterans Administration and he also coached a sandlot team."

The Unitas tale is a true rags-to-riches story. There are few examples of a more dramatic climb from the depths to the dizzying heights that Unitas reached.

"The Rooneys are Pittsburgh."
— Jack Mascaro

He was born May 7, 1933, into a Lithuanian family in Pittsburgh. Unitas knew hardship early in his life. Unitas' father, Francis, was a West Virginia coal miner who died in Pittsburgh when Unitas was five years old. His mother, Helen Unitas, at one time scrubbed floors in office buildings in downtown Pittsburgh to support the family. Even today, Johnny will insist that his mother was responsible for instilling into him the traits of courage and determination that served him so well in football.

At St. Justin's High School, he played halfback for two years and might have become an end had not the regular quarterback been hurt in John's junior year. Because he had a strong arm, Unitas was moved to quarterback where he was a two-year sensation, winning All-Pittsburgh Catholic honors each season.

When it came to college, both Notre Dame and Indiana turned him down because of his 145-pound size and he flunked an entrance examination to the University of Pittsburgh. So he took the only opportunity remaining, the University of Louisville, where he was a regular for almost four full years.

He played on weak teams at Louisville, but he managed to account for more than 3,000 yards passing as a college quarterback against some stiff competition. With the Steelers, he was cut before he could throw a single pass in a pre-season game.

So he spent the 1955 season playing for the Bloomfield Rams, about three miles from Forbes Field. Following that season, a fan wrote a letter on his behalf, extolling his talents, to Colts' coach Weeb Ewbank. Don Kellett, the Colts' general manager, made the call to Unitas. Since the Colts needed a backup to starter George Shaw, they decided to check out Unitas. Both John's coach at Louisville and an assistant at Pittsburgh gave Ewbank positive reports. More importantly perhaps, he received a strong recommendation by none other than Art Rooney. So Unitas was signed to a $7,000 contract on a make-it basis. There was no guarantee, no bonus for signing.

In the fourth game of the 1956 season, Shaw was severely injured and Unitas had to take over. His very first pass was intercepted and returned for a touchdown by the Chicago Bears. From thereon in, it was all uphill for Unitas.

Unitas marvels at the fates. "You know," he said, "after Pittsburgh released me, I originally intended to go to Cleveland. I had heard through a scout that Paul Brown was interested in me, and I later sent a telegram to Paul asking for a tryout. But just then, Brown talked Otto Graham out of retirement. That was 1955. Then, in 1956, when I was still looking around, Otto retired again. But I knew the Browns still had George Ratterman, Babe Parilli and Tommy O'Connell at quarterback. So I weighed both situations and decided Baltimore was a better place for me."

If Unitas had gone to the Browns he might have been played in the same backfield as Jim Brown. That's mind-boggling. "I think things turned out just fine for me," he said.

As John Steadman observed at the time Unitas retired before the 1974 season, "Superstars are constantly making the scene, but Johnny Unitas was maybe the last of the real sports heroes. He was the kind of athlete little kids could admire and copy and whose stories were the kind you could read with your breakfast cereal. We won't see anyone quite like him again."

"Pittsburgh is still home."

Unitas takes pride in his Pittsburgh roots. "I have a sister and aunts and uncles and other relatives there," said Unitas. "Pittsburgh is still home. I get there once in while for family functions or to visit. I've been in Baltimore for 44 years. My first two children, who are now in their mid-40s, were both born in Pittsburgh. That's Janice and John, Jr. My next three were born in Baltimore. They're in their 30s. There's Robert Francis, Christopher and Kenneth. I have three children to my present wife, Sandra. There's Francis Joseph, 26, Chad, 21,and Paige, 18. We have a 19-acre spread, called Passing Fancy, just northeast of Baltimore. We raise some cattle; Chad had a horse. The kids took horse-riding lessons. I went to Art Rooney's horse farm in Maryland a few times. It's called Shamrock Farms.

"I still have my Pittsburgh connections. Joe Schmidt is a very good friend of mine. I played with him in a lot of Pro Bowls. He's a great guy. Joe's done very well in the auto parts rep business in Michigan. He was a very smart player. You had to work real hard to beat him."

When I told him about the photo I had picked up that same morning of Schmidt and Layne, Unitas said, "I knew Bobby a long time. He was a wild man. I played against him a few times, too. He was known for his antics. He was known for drinking pretty heavy after the games, and having a good time with his pals.

"Everybody had their own way of doing things. Bobby liked to holler and scream at his guys in the huddle. I had my own way of doing things. I never liked people who had to holler and scream. I did it by being calm and operating the way I did.

"Nobody else talked in the huddle with our team. I always got my information from the players on the way back to the huddle. They'd tell me if they thought they could get open, or if the other team was open to doing something. I think pro football has lost something by having coaches call the plays from the press box or the sideline.

"I think it's slipped. Nobody is in a better position to call the players than the quarterback. Nobody should have a better feel for what's going on out on the field. He should be able to see and exploit weaknesses. That's one of my major complaints about the game today. I think they've taken the game away from the quarterback.

"The attitude today among the coaches is that I'm not going to turn my football team over to a 22-year-old kid. I get the calls I want to call. But I don't buy that. You have a game plan and you go over it all week and think about it. By game time, the quarterback should know the game plan. But he's not allowed to put his own thinking into the game. I don't think the kids learn the game as well because of it. How many times do you see quarterbacks call timeouts when they don't have to?

"We never called timeouts. We saved them for the last two minutes of each half."

Unitas recalled certain pass patterns — down-and-out to Raymond Berry, a slant-in to Lenny Moore — he liked to call to get the ball into the hands of Berry, Moore and Jimmy Orr. He thinks today's quarterbacks throw too many short or dump passes to their running backs.

"The last guy I want to throw to is a halfback coming out of the backfield," continued Unitas. "My whole idea was to get the ball 15 or 18 yards down the field. I wanted first downs.

"I would talk to my receivers and I'd talk to my linemen. I'd ask the linemen, 'Is he playing you inside? Can you hold him? Can you drive block him? Do you need help?' You always want to know when and how you can run."

I had asked John Steadman, who covered every one of the 213 games Unitas played for Baltimore, to explain the secret to Unitas' success. He said, "He was beyond intimidation." I passed this observation along to Unitas.

"I never let that stuff bother me," said Unitas. "Just growing up the way I did in the street, or working at home. If you had a problem you looked it in the eye and resolved it. We had a big garden in our backyard when I was a kid. My mother planted tomatoes and cabbages that she put up for the winter. We did what we had to in order to get along. We didn't panic. My mother had real challenges raising us without a husband and father. Playing football couldn't compare. We lived in several houses in Mt. Washington and Brookline. I remember a house we had on Williams Street near the end of Grandview Park on Mt. Washington. It had a very nice view of the city. We lived there from the time I was nine till I was a junior in college. I remember coming home from college once during the holiday season. I went to the door of our home, and couldn't get in. Our door was never locked. A woman came to the door and asked me, 'Who are you?' I told her who I was. She told me that she had bought the house from my mother three months earlier.

"I found out my mother had moved to Berkshire Avenue in Brookline. When I saw her, I asked her if she was trying to tell me something by not letting me know she had moved. I'm not sure why my mother thought it was okay to leave our door unlocked. We had three murderers and two bank robbers living on our street, so it wasn't necessarily safe.

261

"My mother cleaned offices at night. She worked at a bakery in the daytime. She continued her education in between and she eventually landed a job with the city as a bookkeeper. She kept that for 22 years. My mother was something else.

"I learned more from her than any football coach, not about the game but about life, about being tough, about hanging in there. She was a tough, tough lady. She died about seven or eight years ago. She had been in a nursing home in McMurray. My sister, Shirley Green, lives in Bethel Park. I see her once a year. I have a brother, Leonard, who lives in Jacksonville. My other sister is Millicent, who lives in Gettysburg. I have a cousin, Joe Unitas, who played semi-pro football in Pittsburgh (Valley Ironmen). He has a photo studio in McMurray. I have a cousin Bill Unitas, who lives in Gibsonia."

Shirley speaks of her mother with reverent tones, too. "We all got our work ethic from her," said Shirley. "They don't make them like her any more. She had a thing where she'd say 'Is it a need, or a want? We don't have any money, but we'll discuss it if it's a need, but not a want.' She was a tough cookie, but fair.

"John was just so very focused from the time he was young. That's all he ever wanted to do. He was not a talker. He just did it. There were no obstacles that anyone could put in front of him, like his size — he was always so slight — and other things, that he wouldn't climb over. He was very tough. He never complained when he was hurt, and you couldn't keep him out of the lineup. He always went to work; I think we got that from our mother.

"The Steelers made a real boo-boo. Who ever heard of Vic Eaton again?"

I mentioned to Unitas that so many great quarterbacks had come out of western Pennsylvania, such as Blanda, Namath, Marino and Montana, and wondered if he had any explanation for this phenomenon. "It must be the water," said Unitas. Montana had once said, "It must be the Iron City beer."

"They're all good people," added Unitas. "And they were all exceptionally talented."

Unitas said he had been working for the past 13 years for Matco Electronics. "We build high technology electronic circuit boards for military and commercial customers," said Unitas. "It's a $500 million dollar company out of Birmingham. I run an office for them near Baltimore. I am on call to different reps. We're in sales and solving any problems. I do a few card shows and appearances a year. I have my own company, John Unitas Management, which my son, John, Jr., runs. It's to control the use of my name. We sell signed items and memorabilia. It's to protect how my name is used to promote things. You have to be careful about that these days because there's a lot of abuse. There's a lot of people out there you can't trust. This is the only way you can handle it.

262

"Yes, I am careful about what interviews I do," he continued when I asked him about this touchy subject. "I'm careful. You don't want to do interviews where you might get hurt. You can't trust some guys."

Johnny Unitas was on the cover of the May 7, 2001 issue of *Sports Illustrated* for a feature story called "Play Now, Pay Later." It revealed that Unitas, 68 by then, could no longer use the right hand that once flung a football like no other. Like so many former NFL players, "he is doomed to a life of pain and disability."

Unitas told writer Bill Nack, "I have no strength in the fingers. I can't use a hammer or saw around the house. I can't button buttons. I can't use zippers. It's very difficult to tie shoes. I can't brush my teeth with it, because I can't hold a brush. I can't hold a fork with the right hand. I can't pick this phone up. You give me a full cup of coffee and I can't hold it. I can't comb my hair."

Johnny Unitas was the first winner of the NFL Man of the Year award back in 1970. It has since been renamed in honor of the late Walter Payton, who won the award in 1977. Others with Pittsburgh ties who won the award for their accomplishments on and off the field included Len Dawson (1973), George Blanda (1974), Franco Harris (1976) Joe Greene (1979), Lynn Swann (1981), Dan Marino (1998) and Jim Flanigan (2000). Flanigan's father, also Jim Flanigan, played on a WPIAL championship team at West Mifflin North High School, at the University of Pittsburgh and with the Green Bay Packers.

Dick Schaap
Remembers special walks

"He looked like Pittsburgh."

Long-time journalist and TV observer, Dick Schaap of ESPN Radio had his memoirs published in 2000 under the title, "Flashing Before My Eyes." He appears on the cover between boxing great Muhammad Ali and comedian Billy Crystal. When he appeared in Tampa, Florida during Super Bowl XXXV week to trumpet his new book, he looked quite dapper. He wore a blue dress shirt with a white collar and white cuffs with cuff links, and a navy blue sport coat.

When I'd go to Pittsburgh, I would make a point to walk around with Mr. Rooney. He knew everybody's name. He was — if you had to capture him in one word — real. There was no façade. It was a delight to be in his company, to walk through the stadium with him. He must have said hello to everyone and he stopped to say hello to them. If you walked through Yankee Stadium with George Steinbrenner, the team's owner, people would cower and hide. Art Rooney was the way sports used to be. My friend and mentor Jimmy Breslin really liked him. He has good stories about Art Rooney.

He didn't act like he was a big guy in sports or anything else. We all have egos, but he didn't flaunt it. He always seemed to be having fun. Today, the owners and players don't seem to be having any fun. He was the perfect guy for Pittsburgh. Art Rooney looked like Pittsburgh. I don't think of him in a tie and a jacket, even when he was wearing a tie and a jacket.

Photos by Jim O'Brien

ESPN's Dick Schaap does a telephone interview regarding his recently-published memoirs, "Flashing Before My Eyes," in lobby of Marriott Waterside Inn in Tampa during Super Bowl XXXV.

John Steadman
"Mr. Quarterback"

"My mother thought Art Rooney was royalty."

Ialways knew that John Steadman was an admirer of Art Rooney, the owner of the Pittsburgh Steelers. I didn't realize to what degree until I was sitting with Steadman in the media dining area behind the press box at Three Rivers Stadium prior to the next-to-the-last home game of the 1999 National Football League schedule.

"Art Rooney was the best person I ever met in sports," said Steadman, the sports columnist for *The Baltimore Sun.* "No one else even came close."

Steadman, who chronicled Baltimore's pro football teams for a half century, was a close friend and confidante of Johnny Unitas, who quarterbacked the Colts to NFL championships and was thought to be the greatest player at his position in the history of the league.

Unitas, who grew up in Pittsburgh, was my boyhood hero. I asked Steadman what set Unitas apart from the pack. "I can sum it up in two words," said Steadman, who had obviously been asked this question before. "Beyond intimidation. John knew what he wanted to do, and didn't care about the circumstances or the challenge. He knew he'd get it done. He had so much confidence in his ability to do what was necessary to win a game. He couldn't be intimidated. John always reduced things to simplicity and basics."

John Steadman was one of the grand old men of the sports writing world.

He was loved and respected by everyone in the business. He looked like a writer, and he dressed like a writer, or the way writers used to dress when they didn't want to be mistaken for a fieldhand. He always wore a sport coat, a dress shirt and tie, and a smile. He often wore a pocket handkerchief, too. He also covered the Orioles, showing disdain for the lax press box dress code by maintaining his own sartorial splendor.

He was a proud and stubborn Irishman who was a lot like Art Rooney in many respects. He would stop and talk to sports fans for hours, making sure he learned all their names. Frank Cashen, the former Orioles' general manager, said of Steadman, "Not many of us can say we did what we loved — and won at it."

He had bright eyes and bushy eyebrows and those eyebrows danced over those dark eyes, and accented his commentary. His presence was such that he demanded your attention when he was telling stories. "He was the best of the best as company, original and opinionated, a listener and a peerless storyteller," said a fellow traveler, John Eisenberg of *The Sun* in Baltimore.

Art Rooney loved to talk to sportswriters like John Steadman. The Steelers' owner often said that if he wasn't an owner and promoter he would want to be a sportswriter. I recall him saying, "I love to spend time with old sportswriters and old politicians." I also recall Rooney remarking, "If I were a sportswriter I would go to the losing locker room first. That's where the action's going to be."

Steadman maintained contact with Art Rooney and later with his second son, Art Rooney, Jr. When I was working on this chapter, I learned that when Steadman felt poorly while attending the Ravens-Steelers game in 1999 that Art, Jr. left the stadium midway through the game and drove Steadman to the Pittsburgh International Airport for his return trip to Baltimore.

"He sends me cards from time to time," said Steadman. "Artie is more like his dad that way than Dan. We've become good friends."

When I related to Art, Jr. that Steadman had told me of his kindness, Rooney said, "I thought I was doing the right thing. I'm glad I could be of help. I know how much my father thought of John. He was always a class act."

Steadman was one of the few sportswriters to attend every Super Bowl. I went to seven Super Bowls in my sportswriting career, the last two with the Steelers under Bill Cowher in 1995, and then Super Bowl XXXV in January, 2001 on my own. Among the highlights of attending the weeklong festival at the Super Bowl site were the gabfests in the pressroom. I always sought out the company of the great writers such as Steadman to hear what they had to say.

I wanted to be with the likes of Furman Bisher of the *Atlanta Journal-Constitution*, Edwin Pope of *The Miami Herald*, Arthur Daley, Red Smith and Dave Anderson of *The New York Times*, Jim Murray of *The Los Angeles Times*, Melvin Durslag of the *Los Angeles Herald-Examiner*, Jerry Izenberg of the *Newark Star-Ledger*, Blackie Sherrod of the *Dallas Times-Herald*, Woody Paige of the *Denver Post*, Hubert Mizell of the *St.Petersburg Times*, Larry Felser of the *Buffalo News*. Joe Falls of the *Detroit News*, Joe Gilmartin of the *Phoenix Gazette*, Stan Hochman of the *Philadelphia Daily News*, Larry Merchant of ESPN and former columnist of the *Philadelphia Daily News* and the *New York Post*, Will McDonough and Bob Ryan of the *Boston Globe*. I liked talking to them, always eager to know what they thought about the sportswriting business.

What prompted me to go to the last Super Bowl was the death of John Steadman on Monday, January 1, 2001. He died of cancer at age 73 while I was working on this book. I decided I better go and spend time with the giants of the sportswriting game before it was too late. When I went there, I learned that six of them were planning to retire soon. The Super Bowl was going to be the closing act for some of them. So my timing was perfect.

Some of those sportswriting greats and some of those newspapers are gone now, but I will always cherish the time I spent in their company. They were bigger to me than any of the pro football players

Jim O'Brien

Baltimore sports columnist John Steadman, at left, speaks with an old friend, Blesto scouting service director Jack Butler, one of the best defensive backs in Steelers history, in media room behind press box at Three Rivers Stadium.

From Joe Rooney collection

Steelers owner Art Rooney is flanked by two Hall of Fame football coaches, Chuck Noll of the Steelers and Don Shula of the Miami Dolphins. Noll was a defensive assistant coach for Shula on his staff with the Baltimore Colts when he was hired in 1969 by Steelers president Dan Rooney.

who participated in those Super Bowls. I read stories some of them wrote in *Sport* magazine when I was a teenager. Beano Cook and I started and operated a newspaper called *Pittsburgh Weekly Sports* for 5½ years (1963-68) and we reprinted their writing efforts in our irreverent and provocative tabloid publication. They wrote for some of the best newspapers in the country and yet they still liked talking about our sports weekly. It was a publication that was ahead of its time.

Beano Cook, more famous now as an ESPN college football analyst, introduced me to the best sportswriters and, in turn, the best sports writing in the country at an early age and I will always be grateful for that. Steadman, for instance, carried himself with a certain dignity, dressed in a certain signature style, not as flamboyant as Bob Prince, mind you, but different than those around him. I can picture him clearly and can't help smiling at the image of this grand old man who brightened every press box he ever entered.

He had seen a lot of sports in his day, and delighted in talking about it. He could hold an audience. He could poke fun at himself. He once produced a book with a collection of his columns called "The Best and Worst of John Steadman."

Steadman's 1997 book, "From Colts to Ravens," underlined his love of pro football, and especially pro football from a Baltimore slant. Hall of Fame quarterback Johnny Unitas offered this endorsement on the back cover of Steadman's book. "I've known John Steadman since the day I joined the Baltimore Colts in 1956, and no writer is better equipped to tell their story."

Steadman was inducted into the National Sportscasters and Sportswriters Hall of Fame in April 1999.

"John Steadman is the sports reporter I grew up reading," bestselling author Tom Clancy once said. "I think he's about the most knowledgeable sports journalist in America, and certainly the single best authority on Baltimore's rich football history."

He once wrote a column for 12 years about pro football for *The Sporting News* called "Mr. Quarterback."

Jon Eisenberg eulogized him in *The Sun* by writing, "As fierce and emotional as he was, even as he grew older and became ill, he was always the gentleman, always ready with a smile, an ear, a generous hand. John Steadman made you proud to be in the newspaper business. If only the rest of us could handle the job so deftly."

Another writer for *The Sun*, Michael Olesker, offered, "He was the great rememberer. He thought a clean conscience counted for more than anything. He saw sports as a great common denominator and helped create a whole era of good feeling around here. He believed in underdogs, and he wrote about them with passion. He saw the world with a twinkle in his eye."

The Sun devoted several pages to praising Steadman upon his death. It was a great tribute to a great man.

He had a Pittsburgh sports background, too. In his early years, Steadman aspired to become a major league baseball player, but he languished as a catcher in the Pittsburgh Pirates' farm system before turning to journalism. His first newspaper job was with the old *Baltimore News-Post*.

He was the beat writer for the newspaper when the old Baltimore Colts of the All-American Conference went out of business after one year in the National Football League in 1951, and he resumed writing about the team when it returned as an NFL entry in 1953. He was the publicity director for the Colts from 1955 to 1957, but longed to return to newspaper work. At age 30, he became sports editor of the *News-Post* in 1958.

After the paper folded in 1986, Steadman became a columnist with the *Baltimore Evening-Sun* until that paper closed in 1995. He then took the same job with *The Sun*, a morning daily.

He was a wonderful human being, loved by all his compatriots. He was president of the Pro Football Writers Association of America, and represented his hometown of Baltimore on the Pro Football Hall of Fame selection committee.

"I wish every town had an Art Rooney."

I spoke to John Steadman the last time on the telephone for about an hour at midday on September 11, 2000. We had spoken during his visits the previous two seasons at Three Rivers Stadium, and this was a follow-up call. The Steelers had opened the season against the Ravens on September 3. He was generous with his time, and with his stories. From all that I had been told by his fellow travelers with the Ravens' party, I had a feeling it would be our last conversation.

"The first time I ever met Art Rooney was at the Bellevue-Stratford Hotel in the winter of 1950," said John Steadman, sitting at a table in the pressroom at Three Rivers Stadium in its last season. "It was right after the NFL and the old All-America Conference got together. There were a number of players whose contract rights were disputed. Bert Bell, the commissioner, said the clubs could work it out by a flip of a coin. I went up to Rooney's room at the hotel. It was no suite; it was a tiny room. He was sitting there in his underwear, long-johns, smoking a cigar. What a picture that was.

"I was a reporter with the *Baltimore News*, a Hearst newspaper. He was happy to see me. They didn't keep you out, or behind ropes back then. They were glad to have you around. Not like today. He said, 'I better get out there and flip the coin.' He wanted to get Jim Owen, an All-American end at Oklahoma who was later a successful coach at the University of Washington. He'd already been out to the racetrack that day in New Jersey, maybe Monmouth Park, and had bet on eight races without a winner. So Ed Kiely, the Steelers' representative, flipped the coin and the Steelers lost to Baltimore for the rights to Owen. Rooney said, 'That's my ninth loser of the day.' Owen ended up starting for us that year.

"Baltimore had a dreadful season. We later played the Steelers at Forbes Field in Pittsburgh. It was a fiercely competitive game. Owen got hurt, a kidney injury, I think. He had to be hospitalized in Pittsburgh. The club was so poor they didn't leave anybody behind with him. We never saw him again. He went home. He was a nice kid, too, respectful. I looked him up when the University of Washington was having all those great seasons.

"Baltimore had a team in the merged league for one year. There were 13 teams, and we were the weak sister. Baltimore was called the 'swing team' and we played every one of the other 12 teams once that season. The NFL was very happy to push us over a cliff. It took us a while to get back in the league when a team from Texas moved to Baltimore a few years later.

"I liked Art Rooney right from the start, and I think he liked me, too. I guess he liked my enthusiasm. Rooney was so friendly and down to earth. He wasn't as reserved, say, as Wellington Mara of the Giants, who had a preppy education and was a country club guy. Rooney used to send me postcards from all over the world. He was always coming from a racetrack or a religious shrine, which was sort of an interesting parlay.

"I went to this NFL meeting in Philadelphia. I was about to leave to go back to Baltimore and he asked me how I was getting home. I said I was taking the train. He said he wanted to go to his horse farm in Maryland and wanted to know if he could go with me on the train ride. I was pleased to have his company. What writer wouldn't want to be with a guy like him?

"It snowed all the way from Philadelphia to Baltimore. When we got there the town was shut down. There were no buses or streetcars running. No taxis. I told Art he could stay at my mother's house. She had a three-bedroom house. Her maiden name was Mary Loretta Dolan, a real Irish gal. When I called her from the train station to tell her I was bringing Art Rooney home she thought I was bringing royalty. Before I left that night, I told her to make sure he had a real good home-cooked breakfast in the morning.

"She got up and cooked a big breakfast for him. Then she called up to him in his room. She got no answer. He was gone. Here's what he had done. He carried his shoes through the house so he wouldn't wake anyone up, and he sat out on the porch and put on his shoes. You could tell by the way the snow looked on the porch. He went to Mass that Sunday morning at Blessed Sacrament a few blocks from our home. He had breakfast when he came back. That tells you a lot about the guy.

"Years later, we'd talk about John Unitas, and how the Steelers let him slip out of their hands. I remember Unitas was with us only a couple of games in 1956 when George Shaw from Oregon, who had been the Rookie of the Year in 1955, got hurt. His knee was torn up. John went in and his first pass was picked off by J.C. Caroline of the Bears and returned for a touchdown. Some start.

"I only wish every town had an Art Rooney. I used to love it when he was telling stories about George Halas trading him broken-down players for the best he had. He said one came in on a cane and the other on crutches.

"Once the Steelers were interested in a guy from Baltimore named Bob Williams. He was a quarterback. He was 24 years old and he had several children. He had been the No. 1 choice of the Chicago Bears in 1951, and was a backup for them. Kyle Rote of SMU was the bonus choice of the New York Giants that year. Bob was called into the Navy. When he came back, he was a big story in Baltimore. He had been a star at Loyola of Baltimore. As a 19-year-old, he had quarterbacked Notre Dame to a national championship

"When he came out after two years in the Navy he said he didn't want to play pro football anymore. He said he had to make a life for his family; remember pro football players weren't making big money then. The Bears agreed to trade him, and Art Rooney got permission from Halas to talk to him.

"Art came down from his farm on a beautiful spring day in May. He called me. He said, 'Do you know where Williams lives?' I said, 'Yes, I can take you right to where he lives.' So I took him there.

"When we get there, he tells me to come inside with him. I said, 'No, you're going to be talking dollars, stuff I don't need to know.' So I gave him an hour before I returned to pick him up. I asked him how it went. He said, 'The boy convinced me he doesn't want to play.' Then Art said, 'He's such a fine boy. I'm so glad I met him.' That's Art Rooney for you. The majority of owners would have said, 'What a wasted trip.' This was an unusual man. He had ethics. He was a notch above the rest of them. Bob Williams today, by the way, is a president of a bank in Baltimore Harbor.

"I remember Art Rooney's funeral so well. The family was receiving callers at St. Peter's Church on the North Side, his church. I got there real early. The church had just opened. The ushers were standing outside by the street light poles at the corner. Nearby there were about 20 guys, rugged-looking guys. Some of them were wearing red T-shirts. I asked the ushers if those guys were from the fire department. 'That's the ground crew from Three Rivers Stadium,' I was told. Art always gave them a hot meal when they were making the changeover from baseball to football or vice versa. I found out he started taking two of them on road trips. One time, he had to get two of them out of jail in Houston. The usher said it was sad. He said, 'You have no idea the regard they had for him. Art was good to them.'

"It's funny what you remember. Art knew his boxing, and he always said Charley Burley was the best boxer in Pittsburgh. Burley was black, and Art said he had a hard time getting fights against the contenders. He said that even though Billy Conn was a frequent companion, and he knew Fritzie Zivic, too. He had a funny way of pronouncing Conn's name. He also referred to ballplayers as "ath-a-letes."

"It's tough on a guy like Dan and the rest of them to have had such a popular father. He's a tough act to follow. I think Dan inherited his mother's traits. She was a good woman, too. I hear she hated the farm. It was really a working farm. It had linoleum on the floor. They were quite a pair.

"I remember how distraught he was when Dan fired his brother Art as the personnel guy. The Chief went to his horse farm to brood about that. But he didn't want to interfere with Dan directing the franchise. I don't know how he got away with that. The other three brothers are all big boosters of Artie. It's like a monarchy. Dan is the oldest son and now he will automatically be succeeded by his oldest son (Art II). I don't know how that works. Maybe one of the other brothers has a real sharp kid. Don't they all own the same percentage of the club? I've always been fascinated by that.

"Art Rooney is definitely No. 1 on my list of people I've met and known in sports. Without question. There will never be another man like him. I liked him because he never put anyone down. He liked to keep company with some of his players, like Elbie Nickel, or their broadcaster, Joe Tucker, and the guy (Richie Easton) who drove the newspaper truck. There was no pretension to this man."

"That's one of the best stories."

There is a certain chilling and sobering aspect to this business of books and biographies. More often than not the people I interview or plan to interview are up in their years and often ailing. Sometimes they are not on the same schedule as I am. I can only interview so many people in a certain period. I have certain subjects and books in mind, and it's best to stay focused on the next one. How often have you heard coaches and managers talking about the importance of taking them one game at a time?

You see someone and you want their stories and you wonder — especially if you know they are challenged by health problems — if you better do it now before it's too late.

I wanted, for instance, to interview Joe Gasparella for this book. He grew up in Vandergrift and played quarterback at Notre Dame in the late '40s when the Fighting Irish ruled the college football world. He played quarterback for the hometown Pittsburgh Steelers in 1948 and in 1950 and 1951, one of the backups to Jim Finks. He coached the Carnegie Tech football team for 13 years from 1963 through 1975, while teaching architecture at the Oakland institution. He was an architect, a rare calling for a football guy. He was brighter than the average bear, and I thought he might have some interesting insights into those Steelers of the early '50s. I saw him at a party of a friend who was a home decorator who was celebrating the opening of new offices. I was told he was ill and not faring well. I made a note to see him soon, but never followed up on it. There were other demands on my schedule, other things to do. Joe Gasparella died in December of 2000, before I had a chance to sit own with him and discuss his days at Notre Dame, as a teammate of Johnny Lujack of Connellsville and Leon Hart of Turtle Creek, who both won the Heisman Trophy and were stars on national championship teams, and his days with Art Rooney and the Steelers. I knew that John Steadman was sick. I interviewed him three times over a two-year period, twice in the press room at Three Rivers Stadium when the Baltimore Ravens came to Pittsburgh to play the Steelers, and once afterward over the telephone at his home in Baltimore.

The first interview took place before the ballgame on December 12, 1999. The second interview took place on September 3, 2000, the Steelers home opener that season. It was the day before Labor Day. I had to take my mother, Mary O'Brien, then 93, to St. Clair Hospital that holiday for a check-up. She was having some internal problems. Later that same Monday, my wife and I visited her parents, Harvey and Barbara Churchman, at their home in White Oak on the outskirts of McKeesport. They were in their 80s. Her father had all sorts of health concerns, some real and some imagined. Her mother had recently learned that she had breast cancer and would require chemotherapy and radiation treatments. It's hell to get old and to see your parents get old. Old age isn't for sissies, says a bumper sticker. (My mother-in-law died on Friday the 13th in July, little more than a month before her 84th birthday.)

People in the press box whispered that Steadman had cancer and was not expected to live long when he came to Pittsburgh in 1999. I thought it might be the last time I would see him. He was visiting with old friends like Art Rooney, Jr. and Jack Butler and Ed Kiely, all veterans of the Steelers scene. I did get to see him one more time.

Steadman, on his next visit in 2000, had been driven from his home in Baltimore by his wife, Mary Lee, to be at the game. He couldn't travel with the team any more. He looked like he had lost weight, but he was doing fine. Or so it seemed. He urged me to tell one of my stories he had enjoyed on an earlier visit to his buddies from Baltimore. He knew the lines, but he laughed at every one of them. He made me feel like Steve Martin or Billy Crystal. "That's one of the best stories I've ever heard," he said more than once.

He went to one of the Ravens' home games in Baltimore in a wheelchair, with Mary Lee pushing him, just so he could keep his streak alive of attending every pro football game played in Baltimore.

"He has been the heart and soul of Baltimore professional football," said Ernie Accorsi, the Colts' public relations director from 1970 to 1974 who became general manager of the New York Giants, when he learned of Steadman's death. "I just loved the man."

He died the same week that Jack Fleming, the former "Voice of the Steelers" and "Voice of the Mountaineers" died at age 77, and there was no mention of their passing on the popular "Inside The

NFL" show on HBO that week. Marty Glickman, a New York sports-caster who came up with the idea for the show and hired Len Dawson and Nick Buoniconti to be on it, was properly eulogized, but no mention of Steadman or Fleming, two fixtures on the pro football scene for so many years. That was sadder than the news of their deaths. There was no reflection on their deaths on ESPN radio sports talk shows, either. Their deaths were noted on the news segments, but no discussion about them. Will McDonough was a guest on ESPN radio two days after Steadman's death, and Steadman's name never came up for discussion. The subject was coaching changes in the NFL. And no one loved John Steadman any more than fellow Irishman Will McDonough. Steadman simply wasn't that day's story, except in Baltimore. Fleming had been the radio voice of the Steelers for over 30 years and West Virginia University football and basketball for 42 years.

I visited Harvey Haddix, the great Pirates pitcher, at his home in Springfield, Ohio on April 12, 1993, and he was suffering from emphysema. He was having difficulty breathing. He died several months later. It was the last in-depth interview he would ever do, his wife would later tell me.

I was not planning on interviewing Sam Narron, the bullpen catcher for the Pirates when they won the World Series in 1960. Heck, you can't interview everyone associated with a ball club. I was in Raleigh, North Carolina on a Thanksgiving break, however, and I was antsy to talk to someone, and he was not that far away when I checked my roster of Pirates alumni to see if anyone lived anywhere nearby in North Carolina. Sam and his wife, Sue, turned out to be two of the dearest people you would ever want to meet, and together they shared some wonderful stories. I didn't know Narron had played for "the Gashouse Gang" of the St. Louis Cardinals in the early '40s, or that he had been a coach or backup catcher with the "Boys of Summer" edition of the Brooklyn Dodgers in the early '50s. Narron had shared the same locker room as Jackie Robinson, Roy Campanella, Duke Snider, Pee Wee Reese, Gil Hodges, Carl Furillo and Carl Erskine. He was a wonderful storyteller and host.

I stopped to see them a few times afterward at their home in Middlesex, North Carolina. I came once, unannounced, and learned that he was in a nursing home. He would die soon after.

When traveling through North Carolina, I visited Mace Brown four times over a three-year period. His wife, Sue, to whom he had been married for 69 years, died during that span. I knew what a great loss that was for him and his family. You get close to some of these people after you've been to their homes and it hurts when they suffer such setbacks or when they die.

Ray Mansfield, known as "The Ranger," was easily the best storyteller of the Steelers of the '70s, and he was also the first to die. He was only 55 when he died of an apparent heart attack while hiking through the Grand Canyon with his son, Jim, in early November of 1996. His coach, Chuck Noll, sat directly behind me at Westminster Church during a memorial service for Mansfield. Noll had often scolded me for urging him and his Steelers to reflect and reminisce about their heydays, insisting it was too soon to look back. I was glad and grateful I had talked to Mansfield on more than one occasion at his home in Upper St. Clair and chronicled his stories. His early years with his family, migrant farmers in the fields of Washington, California and Arizona, were fascinating. I'm glad I didn't wait. John Steinbeck wrote about such families in his classic, "The Grapes of Wrath."

I would have liked to talk to Joe Gilliam, the beleaguered quarterback of the Steelers of the early '70s, a starter and then a backup on the team's first Super Bowl championship team. Gilliam looked good when he participated in the parade of Steelers of the past at the team's final game at Three Rivers Stadium on December 16, 2000. He said his drug problems were behind him for good. He died 11 days later, just short of his 50th birthday, of a heroin overdose.

One time, while doing one of my books about the Pittsburgh Pirates, I planned on interviewing Diz Bellows during the coming summer. Bellows had been the bartender in the media room at Forbes Field and Three Rivers Stadium for over 30 years and knew all the news people well, especially Bob Prince. I told Bellows of my plans. I bumped into him in the auxiliary press box at a Steelers' game in the winter, by accident, and asked him if we could do the interview. He obliged me. He had some great stories. He died that spring.

A copy of my book with the story about him was put in the casket during his viewing at a funeral home in Oakland. The same thing happened when Jackie Powell died. My book on the Penguins, with a full-length chapter about Powell, was placed in his casket. It was strange to see that. Powell had been a minor official, a goal judge, for the Pittsburgh Hornets at Duquesne Gardens and the Civic Arena, and for the Pittsburgh Penguins at the Arena, now known as Mellon Arena. Powell had seen more pro hockey games up close than anyone else in Pittsburgh, and had been around Pittsburgh sports, pro football and college basketball, most of his life.

After the holiday season of 2000, I started the New Year trying to pick up the pieces of the craziness of my Christmas schedule that has me signing books at some shopping mall every day for more than a month. I wanted to get things organized before I began to get back to writing this book in earnest. I came across a long yellow legal pad with all my notes from my last interview with John Steadman. It said STEADMAN in all capital letters at the top of the first page of the ledger. I held it in my hands, happy to have come across it.

The very next day I was driving into the city and listening to a nationally-syndicated ESPN show. I learned that John Steadman, the venerable Baltimore sports columnist, had died. It hurt. He had died the day before, on Monday, the same day I had discovered my notes from my last interview with him. That was sort of eerie. I said a prayer for him, though I didn't think he needed any to join Art Rooney and his NFL buddies somewhere in the great beyond. Or was the prayer for me?

Tom Matte
Son of a Pittsburgh Hornet

"I'm a Pittsburgh guy, too."

I was sitting with John Steadman, a sports columnist for *The Baltimore Sun*, in the media room behind the press box at Three Rivers Stadium on Sunday, December 12, 1999. The Steelers were playing the Baltimore Ravens in the final game of the home schedule. Steadman was telling stories about Art Rooney and Johnny Unitas.

A fellow I recognized came toward our table and sought Steadman's attention. Steadman introduced Tom Matte to me. Matte was a former halfback for the Baltimore Colts who was the color man on radio broadcasts (WJFK and WQSR—CBS outlets) of the Baltimore Ravens games.

"I was interviewing John about Johnny Unitas, a Pittsburgh guy," I said to Matte as we shook hands.

"Hey, I'm a Pittsburgh guy, too," Matte said, much to my surprise.

"How's that?" I inquired.

"My father, his name was Roland Joseph Matte, played for the Pittsburgh Hornets hockey team here in the mid-'30s, maybe 1936 to 1940 or thereabouts," said Matte. "He was a French-speaking Canadian from Vant Leek Hill, just north of Ottawa. The sportswriters preferred to call him Joe. The last name is really pronounced Ma-TAY; that's the French pronunciation. It's been Americanized to MATTY.

"He broke in with the Detroit Red Wings at 18, and later played for the Chicago Black Hawks. Then he played for the old St. Louis Flyers and in Kansas City. I think he got traded to Pittsburgh. Later, he was traded to Cleveland. He played with Freddie Glover for the Barons for years.

"He met my mother when he was playing in Pittsburgh. She was Dorothy Stevens from Brookline. She lived near a Chrysler-Dodge dealership on West Liberty Avenue. Her father was a salesman there. They later moved to an apartment in Dormont. My dad lived at her grandparents' place in Brookline; they were renting out some rooms. That's how he met my mother. He only spoke French when he first came here.

"I was born in Pittsburgh in (June 14) 1939. I lived in Brookline for a brief period. Then my Dad got traded to the Cleveland Barons. He played a total of 17 years of professional hockey. He shattered his knee and he had to stop playing. He played about seven years in the National Hockey League, with the Red Wings and Black Hawks, and the rest, for the most part, in the American Hockey League. So I grew up in Cleveland."

This was the first time I had ever heard that Tom Matte was a native-born Pittsburgher. One of the pleasures of writing books is what you learn along the way that you never knew before. Matte enjoyed a special place in National Football League folklore, and it was great to learn that he was, indeed, "a Pittsburgh guy," and a big fan of Steelers' owner Art Rooney. He had lived, even if briefly, in Brookline, where Unitas lived before he became a legend in the NFL. That was another coincidence. The hair stands up on the back of my neck when I make discoveries like that.

Tom Matte was a fine football player and hockey player at Shaw High School in East Cleveland and he went to Ohio State University to play quarterback for Woody Hayes. Ohio State was famous, of course, for its "three yards and a cloud of dust" offense. They ran the ball most of the time, and seldom passed the ball.

"Bo Schembechler was the offensive line coach then," said Matte. "I had to report to him. We're still good friends. He went from Ohio State to Miami of Ohio. My brother Bruce went there and was his quarterback. Bruce was drafted by the Washington Redskins and the Toronto Argonauts in football and by the New York Mets in baseball. I come from an athletic family. My grandfather on my dad's side was a decathlon champion while at McGill University. He was a lawyer. I had an Uncle Henri who played professional hockey. I had another uncle, Jacque, who was a Dominion tennis champion. So was his sister. Uncle Jacque got into curling and became the captain of a team that represented Canada in international competition."

Playing quarterback at Ohio State was the worst possible preparation for the pros, so Matte was moved to halfback when he was drafted on the first round by the Baltimore Colts in 1961. At 6 feet, 215 pounds, he was a fine running back on some of the Colts' greatest teams. It was when he was forced to play quarterback again, however, that he grabbed the attention of the nation's football fans.

It was at the end of the 1965 season. The Colts were playing the Green Bay Packers in the next-to-the-last game of the regular schedule with the Western Conference title on the line. The week before, Johnny Unitas, the Colts' No. 1 quarterback, had been knocked out of action for the season. In this contest against the Colts, Gary Cuozzo, the No. 2 quarterback, was hurt.

The Colts had no No. 3 quarterback. Coach Don Shula turned to Tom Matte. He remembered that Matte, a 26-year-old fifth-year pro, had played quarterback in college.

He sent him into the fray. Matte trotted onto the field. "Listen, fellas," he said as he entered the huddle. "I need all the help I can get." He looked at Lenny Moore, the great running back from Penn State. "Lenny, you'll have to run harder than you ever have."

Matte asked his teammates to suggest plays and he kept things moving until Cuozzo could return late in the game. He had the pain in

"*Three Rivers Stadium could be a tough place to play when the wind was blowing in off the lake.*"
— Bubby Brister

his shoulder deadened by a drug. Cuozzo wasn't too effective and the Colts lost the game. Cuozzo couldn't play the following week. Matte had to take a cram course in quarterbacking before the Colts played the final game against the Los Angeles Rams.

Shula had given Matte a tryout at quarterback during training camp, just in case he needed a third quarterback, but quickly abandoned the project because Matte had such a squeaky voice. "Stop," Shula had shouted at one point, laughing at the same time, "and talk like a man!"

Now Shula couldn't be concerned about Matte's high-pitched voice. He had no other choice. Shula simplified the offense as best he could. Matte's wife, Judy, even helped him review the playbook that week. The Colts needed a win over the Rams to win the conference title. Matte was getting more attention from the media than he had ever experienced before. He was a handsome, clean-cut kid with a charming manner about him and the press was pulling for him to succeed. That also put a lot of pressure on him. His teammates were trying to calm him down.

Worse yet, Matte had nearly died a year and a half earlier from bleeding ulcers. He had lost four and a half pints in one episode. "The system only holds eight pints, you know," he told sportswriters who asked about that incident.

The day before the big game, a Saturday contest, Matte made his famous "crib sheet." It was a brown plastic wrist-band with a clear plastic window under which was a piece of paper with formations and plays printed on it.

His arm was sore and he felt numb when he woke up that Saturday morning. Matte managed to lead the Colts to a 20-17 victory. Matte didn't complete one pass in the entire game, but he led both teams in rushing with 99 yards. That shouldn't have been a big surprise. After all, Matte had led the Colts in rushing in 1963 when Moore was hurt.

Now the Colts would be playing the Packers once again. Everyone who wasn't a Packers' fan was cheering for Matte, a man facing a challenge no one else would want to have, to win the championship. He still had his "crib sheet" or "cheat sheet," and everyone who ever used one to help them on a test in school could identify with Tom Matte. The Colts led, 10-0, at halftime. The Packers tied the score and beat the Colts, 13-10 on a Don Chandler field goal in the 14th minute of sudden-death overtime. It was a heart-breaking defeat for the Colts, but Shula said he was proud of his team and particularly of the way Matte had come through under difficult circumstances. Everyone praised his courage.

"Matte had every reason to be proud," said Shula. "He gave everything he had."

When he discarded his wrist-band "crib sheet" in the clubhouse after the Green Bay game, Steadman, who was covering the game, picked it up and took it back home to Baltimore. He later handed it over to the Hall of Fame in Canton, Ohio. It's still on display at the Hall of Fame. "That's how I cheated my way into the Hall of Fame," says Matte with his signature smile.

Steadman said that Pete Elliott, the former director of the Pro Football Hall of Fame, told him it was one of the most popular exhibits at the Canton complex.

They had a Playoff Bowl back in those days, so the Colts had one more game, a consolation contest of sorts with the Dallas Cowboys in Miami, Florida. The Colts won that one easily, 35-3, and Matte passed for two touchdowns and two of his other passes put the Colts in scoring position. He wasn't supposed to be much of a passer, but he threw long and he threw short and he ran when he had to in leading the Colts to victory.

When the Colts came into the dressing room after the game they were bragging that Matte could have shot down the Eastern Division champion Cleveland Browns.

"Shula let me throw in that so-called Playoff Bowl, since it didn't really mean anything," recalled Matte. "We called it the Toilet Bowl. He had a meeting with the defensive team in the locker room, I learned later, and told them they might be in a for a long day because he was going to let me throw the ball. I turned out to be the MVP."

Matte played 12 years with the Colts in his distinguished pro career, but it was what he did when he was pressed into playing quarterback during those four games at the end of the 1965 season that made him a football hero forever. He averaged nearly four yards a try on 1200 attempts in his Colts' career, and completed 12 of 42 passes for 246 yards during regular season competition.

He was traded to San Diego, but he didn't go. Unitas would have been wise to have done the same thing. "My ulcers were so bad they had to cut my stomach out," said Matte. "I decided I had enough of pro ball. I had to get into something less physically demanding."

I spoke with Matte before the Steelers-Ravens game on December 12, 1999 and again before the Steelers-Ravens season-opening contest on September 3, 2000 at Three Rivers Stadium. I was interested in learning more about his former teammate, Johnny Unitas.

"He kept me in the league," said Matte. "He said he always knew where I was going to be. I was his safety net if no one got open downfield. He was such a great reader of defenses. He'd check the coverage and he'd come back to the weak side. I was always the outlet, and he'd find me.

"I remember when Weeb Ewbank, our coach, would send me into the game and call me over to talk with him on the sideline before I'd go in. Weeb would say, 'Tell John the call is...tell John the call is...tell John the call...hell, just tell John to get the first down.'

"I'd come into the huddle and John says, 'What you got for me? The usual?' And I'd say, 'Yeah.' And John would call his own play. It would work; we'd get a first down or a touchdown, and the next day the story on the game would say that Weeb Ewbank sent in this play or that play for the game-winner. We'd just smile when we saw that. Weeb was no good on game day. He was a basket case. But he really prepared us well for every game.

"John was always the smartest quarterback. He knew how to make the adjustments. He had everything under control. He had an air of confidence about him. You'd walk into a huddle — behind by two touchdowns — and John would say, 'We have everything under control.' He'd call the offense. There was no one better. John knew what was going on all the time. Ewbank didn't have to tell him anything.

"He'd talk to Jimmy Orr and Raymond Berry as they were coming back to the huddle, and he'd ask them, 'What you got?' They'd tell him what they thought would work. He might wait a play or two, but he'd come back to them. There's no communication like that in today's game. Everything comes in from upstairs as far as play-calling is concerned. I think they're missing something.

"The chemistry of that team was outstanding. It was more like a close-knit fraternity. We'd have a weigh-in on Friday and then we'd retreat to Andy's Bar & Grill, a little place in Baltimore. There'd be 30 or 35 guys from the team there. I wanted to leave early this one time, and Gino Marchetti wanted to know where I was going. I said, 'I've got to do some Christmas shopping.' Marchetti said, 'Kid, this is a team meeting. You stay right here!' My wife, to this day, still believes that we had team meetings on Friday nights."

"Kid, this is a team meeting."

Tom Matte remembers what that scene was like. "We'd sit there and eat hamburgers and drink some beers, and talk about the game coming up. We had a guy named Bill Pellington. He'd be 236 at the weigh-in, and he'd be 260 by game time.

"We did some charity stuff when I was playing for the Colts. I had played club hockey at Ohio State in my fifth year, when I went back to get the six credits I needed for my degree — hockey was my first love — and I agreed to play in a charity hockey game with the Baltimore Clippers. I got some of the guys from the Colts to agree to play. When the Colts' general manager, Don Kellett, found out about this he had a fit. He refused to permit us to play. He said there was no way we were going out on the ice. I liked hockey because you could play both ways.

"To this day, we're still a close group. The former Colts get together at golf tournaments and things like that now. I'm involved with a program called 'Baltimore Reads,' a literary program to get the city kids reading more. We've raised over $550,000 in nine years for that with our golf tournament. Cal Ripken of the Baltimore Orioles has another similar program. I probably see John (Unitas) about three or four times a month. I was involved in that documentary ESPN did on him. They did a great job.

"I work for ATC Logistics, Inc., which is headquartered in Jacksonville, Florida. I have a ten percent interest in the company. We're a port processing company. We import and export automobiles. Right now we have ports in Mexico and Baltimore, but we're looking for another location

"I have a company of my own called Tom Matte's Celebrity Events. I represent about 500 or 600 athletes on a non-exclusive basis. If I can line them up with something they might be interested in then we're in business. I line up celebrities and sports figures for different commercial endorsements, appearances, stuff like that. I line up something for John (Unitas) now and then. His son, John, Jr. runs a company that handles the majority of John's memorabilia and signing appearances.

"I'm more identified today because of that brief spell I played quarterback than anything else. It was most unbelievable. Everybody has a dream and I always wanted to play quarterback, like I'd done at Ohio State. This was my ultimate dream. When my turn came, I wasn't so sure about it. Everybody seemed to be behind me, though. I got telegrams from all over the world acknowledging what I did. Everybody likes an underdog. Everyone has their own adversity and they could relate to the challenge. I think it brought the team closer together. Everybody remembers me for that. I led the league in scoring touchdowns one year (in 1969) with 11, and nobody remembers that. I led the league once in total offense — running, passing and kick returns. I am only remembered for being the instant quarterback.

"I think I still hold one record in the Super Bowl: most yards per carry (10.5 yards on 116 yards on 11 carries). I had the longest run from scrimmage in the Super Bowl for about 20 years. I had a 58 yard run from scimmage; if I had any speed I'd have gone 80 yards. Marcus Allen broke it.

"I used to like to visit with Art Rooney when I came to Pittsburgh. I had family living here. Whenever I played in Pittsburgh or came here as an announcer, I always made a point to pay a visit to Art Rooney. Sometimes I would see him in the press box and stop by to say hello. Always. He was a legend to me and my grandparents.

"My wife's sister, Marilyn German, lived on the North Side near the Rooneys so she kept us posted on their activity. They used to see him at St. Peter's Chuch on the North Side. That was his church.

"The Rooney are all caring people. Last year I was talking to Art Rooney, Jr. and I told him John Steadman was not well, and that he was struggling while the game was going on. I asked him if he could get someone to take him to the airport. Without hesitating, Art said, 'I'll take him to the airport.' And he did. Now John is here again. How he's doing this is beyond me. I don't know how he's still alive.

"I only wish every town had an Art Rooney."
— John Steadman

"I don't know how you wouldn't like Art Rooney. He's like an Art Modell or what Carroll Rosenbloom was for us when we were the Colts. He was a great owner for the players. He was such a special guy to Pittsburgh. All the years they had so many teams here that struggled, yet he stayed with them and hung in there. He was always a special guy to the NFL. People have got to remember people like him. People have got to remember the Baltimore Colts.

"Chuck Noll turned things around here. He was great with the players. They were lucky to get him. I knew him from his days in Baltimore. He was a great defensive coach with us. He brought team unity. He was a former player who could speak the language of the players. It's different today, but Modell is doing his best to get good players in Baltimore, and to keep them there. No one will ever be able to keep a championship team together like they did here in Pittsburgh."

Jim O'Brien

Former Baltimore Colts star Tom Matte, left, enjoys time with Steelers president Dan Rooney in press box during last season at Three Rivers Stadium.

> *"Cigars and stories. That's what I think of first when I think of Mr. Rooney. He was always telling stories."*
> — Lynn Swann
> Hall of Fame receiver

The Final Game at Three Rivers
Mayor Murphy comes through

"It was just a building. It was
the people who made it special."
— Joe Greene

The Steelers closed down Three Rivers Stadium in grand style. It's a shame Art Rooney wasn't there. He always enjoyed a good Irish wake.

The day, Saturday, December 16, 2000, came up perfect for a funeral. It began with dark gray skies, rain and then more rain, downright dreary. It was 42 degrees at kickoff, but it felt colder. It was a typical December day in Pittsburgh or in Ireland, for that matter. There's something about the Steelers and their fans, however, that seem to gain spirit and strength from such foreboding conditions. Or so they'd like to think. The bad weather would somehow give the Steelers the edge over the visiting Washington Redskins. Thunder and lightning were greeted with cheering. It would have been even better if it had been snowing, some suggested, as it often did during all those storied playoff games in the '70s when the Steelers won four Super Bowl titles and Pittsburgh was heralded as "The City of Champions."

Those were the days, my friend, we thought they'd never end, to borrow a phase from a popular song from that same period.

Art Rooney would have relished the scene, though surely it would have been a bittersweet experience for him as well. No one knew better than the team's owner and founder how much Three Rivers Stadium meant to the Steelers. It was a place where he loved to loaf — an expression the late NFL Commissioner Pete Rozelle always associated with Pittsburgh and Art Rooney — and entertain his cronies.

"We were never looked upon as a big league team until we got here," Art Rooney often said. His father, Dan Rooney, once operated a saloon on the site where the stadium stood.

"We lived on the second floor of my father's saloon — Dan Rooney's Saloon," Art once related. "He owned it for years and years. It was a rough neighborhood, in a way, but in those days kids were on the playgrounds from the time the sun came up to the time it went down. We played baseball and football and boxed. We were too busy to get into trouble."

Exposition Park where the Pirates first played had been there once upon a time. Rooney loved to play baseball and he loved the Pirates. In fact, when he first got into the National Football League his team was called the Pirates. He later changed that to the Steelers to avoid confusion. The North Side, or Old Allegheny or the First

Ward — he referred to it both ways when he told stories — was always hallowed ground to Rooney. He remained in a home in what deteriorated into a ghetto neighborhood because he liked his neighbors and he was comfortable there.

"We were rich and my dad had us living in a ghetto," Art, Jr. once said.

It was an 11-room, high-ceilinged Victorian-style home that was 133 years old. There were white columns in the front. His son, Dan, had it remodeled — the renovations took a year to complete — and moved into it in 1995. Dan's daughter and her family had lived there for awhile, right after Art Rooney had died. No one would have dared suggest the property be sold. The Rooneys regarded the two-story red brick home as if it were Tara.

The Rooneys obviously didn't feel the same way about Three Rivers Stadium, just 31 years old. Dan Rooney, initially, wanted civic officials to help him fund a significant improvement of Three Rivers Stadium into a football-only edifice. When he saw the plans for PNC Park where the Pirates would play nearby, and when he saw the new stadiums in Baltimore and Cleveland and Charlotte, and knew what was coming in Cincinnati, he decided the Steelers shouldn't settle for anything less than a new state-of-the-art stadium.

So everyone who truly cared about the Steelers came to say goodbye, to pay their last respects. They told stories, laughed and cried, as people usually do at funerals. It was one of the hottest tickets in town. Brokers and scalpers were asking for $300 to $500 for tickets with a face value of $40 or $45.

Art Rooney's five sons were all there. Dan, Art, Jr., Tim and the twins, Pat and John, were all in the building, along with their wives. There were lots of grandchildren and great-grandchildren, even an Art, IV. Chuck Noll, the coach who made the Steelers and Pittsburgh respectable and deserves most of the credit for the club's turnaround in its fortunes, was there, and many of his players were also present. Some of them had played for the Steelers' greatest teams, and some for less-than-stellar teams. On this day, they were all greats from the past.

Joe Gilliam was there, for instance, and he looked good. He told everyone who would listen that he had cleaned up his act, and that he was clean of drugs. He was lying, as addicts will do. A week later, Gilliam, the once so-gifted passer, was dead from an overdose of cocaine. Jack Fleming, the former Steelers' radio play-by-play announcer, famous for his "Immaculate Reception" call, was there, too. He died a few weeks later. The times they were a changin'.

The Rooneys knew what moving to a new stadium would mean for the Steelers. "Three Rivers was a big deal for us," recalled Art Rooney, Jr. "and in 1970 it was a classy joint."

Dan remembered those days at Forbes Field how "the Pirates treated us like poor second cousins." Hopefully, he would do better by Pitt at the new football stadium.

photos by Mike Fabus/Pittsburgh Steelers

Surrealistic scene at Steelers' final game at Three Rivers Stadium on Saturday night, December 16, 2000. Steelers' president Dan Rooney is flanked at on-the-field activity by coaches Bill Cowher, left, and Chuck Noll who braved the rain to make appearances for fans in fabulous goodbye and victory over Washington Redskins. Cowher is signed to coach the Steelers another five years.

There would be a parade — Steelers of the past strutting across the turf one more time — and fireworks, and nothing draws a crowd in Pittsburgh better than parades and fireworks. Building implosions appear to be moving up on the charts as crowd magnets as well.

There would be a recreation of the "Immaculate Reception," the touchdown run by Franco Harris after he picked off a rebound of a Terry Bradshaw pass that was aimed at Frenchy Fuqua. When Fuqua collided with Oakland Raiders' defensive back Jack Tatum the ball came back at Bradshaw and Franco found it at his feet, and picked it off his shoetops for a TD scamper.

The recreation started with Bradshaw tossing a pass on a live telecast from Fox Sports that was shown on the jumbo screen at Three Rivers Stadium, with Fuqua and Harris reenacting their roles on the playing field. It's a play that couldn't really be recreated. No one's sure today what really happened. But it was all in good fun, and it brought back some great memories. The "Immaculate Reception" and the 1972 season began a change in the Steelers fortunes that would lead to four Super Bowl titles. "It was like Moses crossing the desert," said Art Rooney, Jr. "After 40 years, you're *somebody*."

Dan Rooney related some of his personal memories to Jerry DiPaola of the *Tribune-Review* prior to the final game.

His fondest memory was the "Immaculate Reception" touchdown by Franco Harris in the 1972 AFC playoffs. "That actually put us on the level to start to play with the big boys," he said. "Our team started to believe in itself.

"The stadium gave our team, the players a sense of belonging. A sense that this was it. It was a special place. It was very professional. They could come in and sit at their lockers. It was their home.

"There were other things, of course, that contributed to it. There was Chuck Noll coming on the scene, our drafting, my brother Art was handling that, you know. And the success we had built on it and just kept building. When you think of Three Rivers Stadium…it was the success that both the Pirates and the Steelers had and the fans thinking that they had a part in it."

Some of the former Steelers players on hand offered their favorite memories as well:

"I remember working out there one off-season," former Pro Bowl linebacker Andy Russell related, "and there was going to be a big concert there that night. The stage was already built. I was running wind sprints in the outfield and on the stage was Stevie Wonder, playing his music. We were the only two in the stadium."

Rocky Bleier, former running back of the Steelers, said, "We played Kansas City in our last regular season game in 1980, and it didn't mean anything because we weren't going to the playoffs. I scored the game-winning touchdown, and I heard the fans chanting, 'Rocky, Rocky, Rocky.' I could have died right there."

Two of Steelers' all-time greatest linebackers, Levon Kirkland (99) and Jack Lambert (58), team up during on-the-field ceremonies at Steelers' final game at Three Rivers Stadium.

Neither rain, nor sleet nor snow can stop Bill Hillgrove and Myron Cope from talking about Steelers' exploits as they braved the elements for final showing at Three Rivers Stadium on December 16, 2000.

John Banaszak, a former defensive lineman, said, "The two games against Houston in 1978 and 1979 are memorable. Three Rivers Stadium was a sea of Terrible Towels. That is pretty intimidating for a visiting team to come and see. The fans were part of what we were trying to do."

Mike Wagner, former safety, said, "Members of Franco's Italian Army, there would be 10,000-15,000 of them at the stadium for pre-game warmups chanting, 'Here we go, Steelers, here we go.' The visiting team would be wondering what they were cheering for because the game hadn't even started."

And L.C. Greenwood, the great defensive end of those celebrated teams of the '70s, had this to say: "The most important thing to me are the players I played with and the fans who came out to support us. Every time we walked on the field, we felt and heard their presence. Many of them would be waving signs or Terrible Towels."

"I'll see you at the Stadium."
— Mayor Tom Murphy

I was bummed out in the days leading up to the to Steelers' final game. I had to request a press box credential on a game-to-game basis in 2000 for the first time in my 21 years of reporting on the team. The Steelers had tightened requirements for all the media across the board. Because of "overwhelming demand" for press box accommodations, the Steelers "regrettably" would not be able to take care of me for the last game. As a free-lance writer and publisher, I didn't fit the NFL profile to merit such seating. I knew that. I was hurt just the same.

It turned out to be a blessing in disguise. I went to a Christmas party the night before the Steelers' final game that was held at a most unlikely site. It was hosted by Jack Mascaro of Mascaro Construction Company at the city jail.

Mascaro was on top of the world because his Mascaro Construction Company was building the new $250 million football stadium in collaboration with Hubert Hunt & Nichols of Indianapolis, as well as building the UPMC Sports Complex on the South Side. He had invited his friends, city officials and business associates to his annual holiday celebration. Both the stadium on the North Side and practice facilities on the South Side would be shared by the Steelers and by Mascaro's alma mater, the University of Pittsburgh, and its football Panthers. Mascaro was also responsible for refurbishing the downtown jail. It is a strangely beautiful building that the famed Frank Lloyd Wright once declared was the only building in Pittsburgh architecturally worth preserving. Wright would not have thought much of Three Rivers Stadium. Not too many Pittsburghers did, either, until it was time to level it.

Two of the Steelers' all-time finest running backs, Franco Harris (32) and Jerome Bettis (36) meet at midfield for final game at Three Rivers Stadium on December 16, 2000.

Two of the Steelers' all-time most popular performers, Franco Harris and Jack Lambert, showed up to mix with fans during final game ceremonies.

Tom Murphy, the mayor of Pittsburgh, was among the celebrity guests at Mascaro's Christmas party at the jail. After Mayor Murphy made his way through the crowd, shaking hands with everybody along the way, he approached me to say hello and offer his holiday season greetings. I introduced him to my wife, Kathie, and he said to her, "How do you live with a guy who has such a passion for Pittsburgh and its history?"

Kathie smiled at Mayor Murphy and replied, "I'm used to it. I've learned to live with it."

Then, to me, Mayor Murphy said, "Well, I guess I'll see you at the stadium tomorrow. Another big day in Pittsburgh sports history. You can get another book out of it, I'm sure. You know, I think there's a national book in how these stadiums were financed and brought to reality."

That's when I told the mayor my tale of woe, that I didn't have a press pass to attend the Steelers' final game at Three Rivers Stadium.

"I may have an extra pass," Mayor Murphy told me. "Meet me at Gate A at 12:15, and I'll get you a ticket."

"Stop by and have a glass of wine."
— Jack McGinley

I had an early appointment in downtown Pittsburgh on Saturday, December 16. I was scheduled to appear on KDKA-TV news to reflect on the final game just across the Allegheny River from KDKA's studios in Gateway One. I was interviewed by Brenda Waters during the 10 a.m. news segment. Following that, I grabbed a telephone and did a sports talk radio show segment with Tom Dinga from Ford City on the same subject. I had stored my car in a parking lot at Gateway Center. I walked through Point State Park and across a span leading to Three Rivers Stadium.

No sooner did I reach the other side, around 11 a.m., when it began raining hard. I ran to get under cover in the inner circle of the stadium. This rain, I thought, was going to put a real damper on all the tailgating activity around the stadium. The parking lots and roads surrounding the stadium were all torn up, to begin with, and tailgating had become a challenging enterprise. The rain wouldn't help. It would be a real mess before long.

I got to Gate A about an hour early. I was out of the rain. I had never stood at Gate A, or any other gate for that matter, and waited an hour before a ballgame. It was an interesting scene. I saw a lot of well-known individuals walking by on their way to the press gate and where most of the box-holders passed through.

I could check out the activity at the new football stadium just 65 feet away. I was surprised to see that they had put in a lot of large

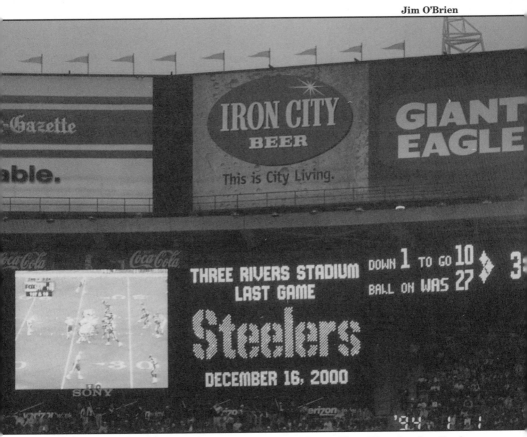

Author Jim O'Brien was guest of Pittsburgh Mayor Tom Murphy for final game at Three Rivers Stadium. Mayor Murphy takes great pride in pushing financing for PNC Park for Pirates and Heinz Field for Steelers and University of Pittsburgh.

Dave Malone

windows on the side closest to Three Rivers Stadium. To me, it seemed a foolhardy exercise. Wouldn't those windows be in danger of breaking when they dropped Three Rivers Stadium in early February?

I could hear Bill Hillgrove, Tunch Ilkin and Myron Cope doing a pre-game radio broadcast that was being aired over the public address system. Cope was doing his best to be up to the occasion — like he wanted to utter some Lincolnesque line to capture the moment — and he was shouting even louder than usual, or so it sounded, from where I was standing. Cope was screeching so much so that I thought the stone pillars supporting Three Rivers Stadium might come tumbling down prematurely.

This would be a day when the fans would use their Terrible Towels to dry off their seats before they started waving them to stir up the Steelers.

I saw Jack McGinley and his family dropped off in a van at the curb nearest to the press gate. His grandson, Joe, was driving. McGinley is a minority partner in the Steelers. He and his sister, Rita McGinley, have a one-fifth share of the team and its profits (the Rooneys owned 80 per cent of the team). Rita dropped her ticket as she exited the van in haste.

"Are you going to stop by our box?" Mr. McGinley asked as he shook my hand in greeting. "Stop by and have a glass of wine. Get something to eat. So we'll see you upstairs."

Then I saw John Rooney, one of the twins and the youngest of Art Rooney's five sons. He was wearing a camel-haired topcoat. He had a cigar in his mouth. A wisp of white hair was dangling over his forehead. I was struck by how much John, at age 61, resembled his late father at that same age. I had seen enough old photos of his father to make the comparison. John looked more like his father than any of the five brothers.

Then came his twin brother, Pat, wearing a dark blue topcoat. He and John have a strong resemblance. Then came Tim, wearing a dark topcoat. He was wearing a dark suit with a gray sweater vest. John and Pat had come to Pittsburgh from Palm Beach, where they operated a greyhound racing track, and Tim had come from Yonkers, New York, where he operated a harness racing track. Those three show up on occasion, usually when something special is going on, for a Steelers' home game.

Art Jr., who looks after the family's real estate interests from an office building in Upper St. Clair, just down Washington Road from his home in Mt. Lebanon, attends all home games. He is usually in the company of two old scouts, Jack Butler of Blesto and long-time Steelers birddog Bill Nunn, Jr. Dan usually is seen strolling the stadium with his oldest son, Art II, a Pittsburgh attorney who is the designated heir apparent to the president's seat in the Steelers' organization.

"My main thought was that I was hoping we'd win the game," confessed Tim Rooney. "It was sad to see the stadium go. We had so

292

many great teams, so many great players, so many great memories. I was happy that we'd be moving into a new stadium. From the ramp behind the press box, you felt like you could just reach out and touch the new stadium. It was so close."

I saw Mark Nordenberg, the chancellor of the University of Pittsburgh, driving by in a Buick. I thought about how his predecessors, Wesley Posvar and J. Dennis O'Connor, both had chauffeurs. Nordenberg and the school's athletic director, Steve Pederson, had become strongly allied with the Rooneys while negotiating to become tenants in the new stadium, and for the final season at Three Rivers Stadium after they leveled Pitt Stadium.

Within a year, two buildings where I worked — I actually occupied new offices in Pitt Stadium for three of my five years at Pitt — were being leveled. I'm a sentimental guy, and it was tough on me emotionally to handle this. They were landmarks that were reminders of many wonderful times and even more wonderful people.

I saw two of the city's top banking officials, Sy Holzer of PNC Bank and Harrison Vail of Three Rivers Bank, go through Gate A. John Paul, the executive vice president of UPMC, arrived in a dark Cadillac. I saw Danny Rains, the former linebacker for Mike Ditka's Super Bowl champion Chicago Bears, and Gordon Oliver, a former lineman for Pitt's 1955 Gator Bowl team. Rains was now with McCarl's Plumbing in Beaver Falls and Oliver with Metaltech in Coraopolis. Both were good buddies of Redskins' assistant coach, Foge Fazio, from Coraopolis, and Fazio had gotten them sideline passes so they could watch the game from the visitors' bench. It was fitting that Fazio would be home to see the last pro game there.

No one cared more about football in western Pennsylvania than Fazio, Rains and Oliver, so I knew this Three Rivers Stadium finale would be working on them as well. They wouldn't forget the scene and the enthusiastic crowd for this last game.

Joe Greene, the great building block of the Steelers of the '70s, may have expressed it best when he offered in a video-taped interview, "It was just a building. It's the people who made it special. It's where I went to work. It served its purpose. The bottom line was that it was the people who made it special."

Greene had said in an earlier interview that he was always emotionally moved by a banner that was hung in the end zone at Three Rivers Stadium. It read: YOU'RE IN STEELER COUNTRY.

"The fans really made it special today, without question," said Donnie Shell, the greatest strong safety in Steelers' history, and one of about 50 former Steelers who showed up for the goodbye event. "The fans made football in Pittsburgh."

Mike Fabus/Pittsburgh Steelers

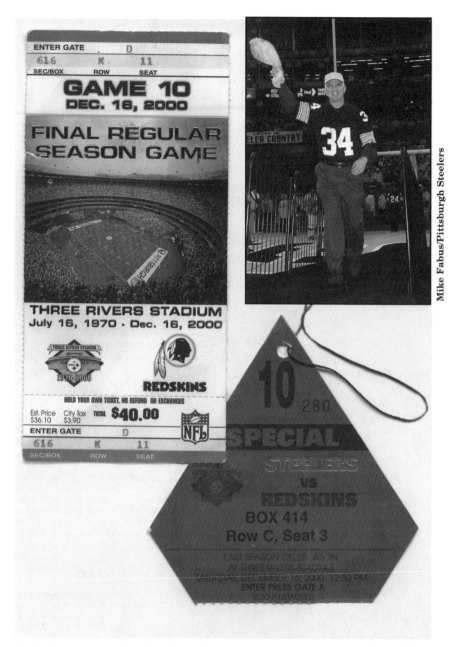

Andy Russell, one of the Steelers' all-time linebackers, returns to Three Rivers Stadium for one last introduction. Author's tickets for final game are a keepsake. Mayor Tom Murphy provided one at lower right.

As I stood at Gate A, I was approached by Ed Boyle, a 47-year-old maintenance mechanic at the Federal Building in downtown Pittsburgh. He and his wife Linda, 45, of Castle Shannon, were going to Super Bowl XXXV in Tampa the next month on an all-expenses paid trip for Ed's winning entry in a contest sponsored by the Steelers. He had submitted the winning entry in a contest to name the top ten plays of the Steelers at Three Rivers Stadium.

"I'm just glad we were there. It really was special."
— Mike Hagan

When the mayor showed up, he handed me a triangular red ticket that was on a string. It was for Box 414, Row C, Seat 3. "You'll be with some City Council members and I'll be right next door," said Mayor Murphy. "You can move back and forth."

I swelled with pride. The mayor had come through. He had been good for his word. I had grown up in Hazelwood, at the eastern end of the city, and I thought there was something special about getting a ticket from the mayor of the city for the final Steelers' game at Three Rivers Stadium. It beat getting a press pass any day of the week.

I have purchased four season tickets of my own from the Steelers for 21 years, or since I covered the club for *The Pittsburgh Press*, starting in 1979. I covered them when they won their fourth Super Bowl at the end of that 1979 season.

During the first half of the final game, I sat in one of my seats — Sec. 616, Row K, Seat 11 — with a good friend and patron, Mike Hagan, the president of Iron & Glass Bank on the South Side. Mike worked in the comptroller's office when I first worked at Pitt, later as the vice-president of NorthSide Bank, and for three years — 1993 through 1995 — as comptroller for the Steelers, with an office at Three Rivers Stadium. Those were good years when Bill Cowher's club went to the playoffs three years and twice played in AFC championship contests on its home turf, and went to Super Bowl XXX in the third. Mike was sitting with his daughter, Jennifer, and his son, Michael. Jennifer was a third-year student at the University of Pittsburgh School of Medicine, and Michael was a freshman at the University of Notre Dame. Mike and Jennifer were ND alumni. Jennifer knew my older daughter, Sarah, who had preceded her by two years at Pitt's Med School. Mike and I shared stories about their school and hospital-related experiences when we'd meet for lunch on the South Side.

"I'm just glad we were there," said Hagan a week later. "It really was special."

I'd forgotten what great seats I'd had at Three Rivers Stadium all those years because I always had customers and business associates sitting in those seats while I was in the press box. There was a tremendously strong and vibrant spirit in Three Rivers Stadium for the Steelers' finale. The team had to get a lift from the boisterous crowd. The Steelers had selected four of their Hall of Fame players as honorary captains for the final contest. They were Jack Lambert, Jack Ham, Franco Harris and Mel Blount. Lambert wore a black beret, tipped just so on his blond head. I had to smile. Leave it to Lambert to stand out in the crowd, I thought. I wondered what he was thinking that morning when he checked out his black beret in the mirror. Lambert was always combat ready. This day was no different. He was pumped and those near him fed off his spirit.

"Pittsburgh fans were always the best fans," said Harris. "I've always appreciated them. They're special people."

The Steelers had won the week before at Three Rivers Stadium in a 21-20 thriller over the Oakland Raiders. This time they whipped the Washington Redskins, 24-3. "They gave the fans everything they were looking for," said Lynn Swann, the former wide receiver who was just over a month away from learning he had been voted into the Professional Football Hall of Fame.

Some of the old banners from earlier days were hung out in the rain, like The Steel Curtain and Dobre Shunka (Polish for Good Ham). There were some new ones, too, to capture the spirit of the occasion, such as Farewell Old Friend to We're Moving Out, See Yinz Next Door. "It was really something here in the '70s," said Myron Cope, who was part of the magic mix as much as anyone. "Even the backups had fan clubs. There were banners all over for everybody. Then you had the stadium filled with Terrible Towels waving. You had no other stadium that could match it. But time marches on."

The Steelers were becoming successful at the same time the steel mills were closing, and they kept people's spirits up. "You can't put a price tag on how valuable it was to the human spirit here," Cope continued. "Wherever people gathered, the Steelers were the dominant topic. It gave people something pleasant to talk about, for a change, instead of, 'Where the hell am I going to get work?'"

Jim O'Brien

Heinz Field rises next to Three Rivers Stadium rubble.

"People are going to think a ghost came back."
— Mayor Tom Murphy

John and Pat Rooney were standing outside the Rooney's box — No. 341. They were joined by Mayor Tom Murphy and Bob O'Connor, the president of Pittsburgh City Council. Murphy and O'Connor were preparing for Democratic primary campaigns for the mayor's office. Mayor Murphy told John, "You look so much like your dad that people are going to think a ghost came back. You look more like your father than any of the boys."

John just shrugged in acknowledgment. He had obviously heard it many times before. I had told him the same thing a few minutes earlier. I asked him how he felt when people offered that observation.

"It's sorta embarrassing," he said. "I'm not him, surely. He always used to say to me that I should comb my hair straight back. I had long hair in college, and he never liked that. Now I'm told I look like him. I guess I'm getting old."

Chuck Noll and his wife, Marianne, were sitting in the Steelers' owners luxury box, which was twice as wide as most of the other boxes and was situated right on the 50-yard line. Box 341 had some of the best seats in the house. I asked Noll how it felt to see the Steelers playing their last game at Three Rivers Stadium.

Noll has never been overly sentimental, and he wasn't about to change. Life has to be easier the way Noll approaches it, if he was being totally honest.

"The thing that pops up right away," said Noll, "it's today and tomorrow. It isn't yesterday. Time marches on.

"New stadiums can help a program. It certainly helped us. I was an assistant in Baltimore before I came here. We were playing in an old stadium. The facility wasn't very good. When I saw what was on the drawing board here, I saw it as an opportunity. That's one of the things I liked about this situation. A new stadium was being built. To me, that was an attraction. Our players took pride in playing in Three Rivers Stadium. We practiced at the Fair Grounds at South Park my first year here, and that was the humblest of facilities.

"I went for my interview with the Steelers about the head coaching job, and *I interviewed them*. I didn't want to take just any head coaching job. I wanted to know what the management was like. I had heard that the Steelers didn't want to spend any money and that's why they never had a winner.

"But Dan Rooney was willing to give me whatever I needed and he never went back on that. There were a lot of negatives here, though. The offices were in a rundown hotel. They were just horrible. The practice facilities were bad. You can't win a championship from a rundown office. Not these days, anyway. You've got to have a first-class operation in every respect. When you treat players first-class they'll start to believe they are first class. In the era of free agency, you have to sell players on choosing your team over others.

297

"I remember the first game we played here. It was a pre-season game against the New York Giants. The Giants were one of the NFL's old guard teams. I remember seeing the players in the locker room before the game. Their eyes were sparkling. They had a look about them like they were better than they were before. They had a great feeling calling this home. We beat the Giants that night. I am convinced our new stadium was a part of our turnaround here."

It was a great day for Steelers fans, though.

The Steelers had won to keep their playoff hopes alive. Jerome Bettis had rushed for more than 100 yards. There was good news on the local sports front. Dan Rooney always thought that the Pittsburgh teams fed off each other's successes in the '70s. On the hockey front, Mario Lemieux had announced that he was coming out of retirement after a 3½-year layoff from the Penguins, Pitt was going to a football bowl game, and Pittsburgh was abuzz about its sports teams for the first time in five years heading into the final week of Christmas shopping.

Reflecting on Lemieux's comeback and the implosion of Three Rivers Stadium, Tom Rooney, a Penguins executive and a cousin of the Steeler Rooneys, offered, "How about that — a resurrection and a burial, all in one week."

I had book signings scheduled every day until Christmas Eve and I knew that these events were going to be good for business. I'd spent the day in the company of Mike Hagan and his kids, the Steelers' faithful, Mayor Murphy, the McGinley and Rooney families, Chuck Noll and Jim Lally, who all understood the significance of the day, and I felt good all over.

Lally looked on, deeply moved by the occasion. "I've been looking after this place, for the most part, since it was built. I'm feeling a lot of emotion today," he confessed, a trace of a tear visible in the corner of his eye. It had stopped raining, briefly, as I was exiting Three Rivers Stadium. There were puddles everywhere. I wanted to dance right through them, waving my umbrella, just like Pittsburgh's Gene Kelly in that wonderful 1952 movie, "Singin' In The Rain."

Jim O'Brien

PNC Park is near completion next to Three Rivers Stadium.

Snapshot:

Chuck Noll, Hall of Fame coach of the Pittsburgh Steelers (1969-1991) At Mario Lemieux Celebrity Invitational at The Club at Nevillewood:

"One of the things that stands out in my mind is that I would try to go to lunch on occasion with Art Rooney. You couldn't walk through a restaurant with him. I'd have a time frame where I had to get back to work, but it never phased him. He'd talk to everybody. He knew everybody. He knew their father. He knew their hometown. He was such a people person. It was quite a gift. What I appreciate most about Art and Dan Rooney is that they gave you a job to do and they let you do it."

Marianne and Chuck Noll sat in the club owners' box on 50-yard line for Steelers' final game at Three Rivers Stadium.

Dick Stockton
Steelers boosted him to CBS

"You were the best."
— Art Rooney

Dick Stockton is best known as an NBA play-by-play man on network telecasts for over 30 years, but he also does NFL telecasts for Fox Sports. He has been their No. 2 man after Pat Summeral and gets many key games. Stockton is smooth, knowledgeable and versatile, well-versed in most sports. Stockton got his start as a big-time sportscaster on KDKA-TV in Pittsburgh and credits the Steelers for boosting his network career. By coincidence, Stockton worked the first Steelers telecast at Three Rivers Stadium and he worked the last game. He did so with former Penn State star Matt Millen as analyst. They would work together on a radio broadcast of the Super Bowl as well before Millen moved to Detroit where he had accepted a position as general manager of the Lions.

It's an amazing coincidence. None of this was planned. The only one who would really know that I broadcasted the first game in Three Rivers and the last one was me. They don't keep it on the stat sheet. It was a thrill for me to be there. The Rooneys were always at my back.

The thing I remember best, after I left Pittsburgh, is that at some point when I would be doing the NBA finals on CBS-TV each year I'd get a letter from Art Rooney. He'd remember my days when I was working in Pittsburgh, at KDKA-TV, of course, and he'd write "Dear Dick, We were in New England and I saw you on TV...," and "you were the best" or "you were the class," or something like that. It always made me feel great. I have eight of those letters framed and on display on the wall in my home in Boca Raton, Florida.

Bill Burns, who was the main guy on KDKA News, was a close friend of Art Rooney. And I mean a close friend. He was with him a lot. I was 24-years-old when I began my first major television job in Pittsburgh in 1967. I was a native New Yorker, and I was going on at 6 and 11 as the new sports guy in town. I had that New York brashness about me, and I'm sure it didn't go down well with everyone there. Burns was the star of the show and he wanted to make sure I knew that. I got into an elevator one day at Gateway Center and Burns was with some of his buddies. He kept right on talking when I got on. He was telling them what players the Steelers were going to leave unprotected in an expansion draft to stock the New Orleans Saints. None of the sports guys in town knew who was on that list, not yet anyhow, but Burns wanted me to know that he knew. He was telling these guys for my sake. He was telling me, "You may be a hot-shot coming in here, but I still know more than you. I'm still more connected than you'll ever be."

They were playing a pre-season game with the Bengals at Forbes Field. I told Art Rooney my dad was coming to the game with some other family members. He said, "Tell your father they can sit with me." So my dad had a chance to meet the great Art Rooney.

The Rooneys were responsible for me getting into network TV. They recommended me to the powers-that-be at CBS. They talked to Bill McPhail and Bill Pitts on my behalf. I'd only been at KDKA a short time when they did that. They had me do a post-game show on the Steelers. They helped me get my foot in the door at CBS.

Dan Rooney was directly responsible for me getting a network connection. Bill Pitts, the executive producer of NFL football, was looking for someone to do a few post-game shows. Dan recommended me to him. Pitts saw a tape I did, and liked it. I got to do six games that first year, all Steelers games from Pitt Stadium, and that was the start of my network assignments with CBS.

When I did my strong opinionated commentaries at KDKA, I don't know whether you noticed it or not, but I never came down too hard on the Steelers. I always seemed to miss the Steelers. That's because of Art Rooney. He's the No. 1 owner I've ever known. I knew people that I respected and admired like Red Auerbach, Wellington Mara and Tom Yawkey, but no family in sports was ever kinder, friendlier, warmer and as sincere as the Rooney family.

Now I appreciate my four years in Pittsburgh. I really became a broadcaster. It was a period in which I really gained polish on the air. From then on, I was ready for any assignment. I went from a guy who didn't know what he was doing to being a guy who knew his stuff.

If I started out in any other city, I don't know if I'd be where I am today. Pittsburgh was the ideal city to get my act together. But I was always wondering where I was going. I wanted to get back to New York, and work in my hometown.

Jim O'Brien

Heinz Field as it looked in May after bluegrass sod was laid.

Jack McGinley
The silent partner

"God be with you now."

Jack McGinley Jr. and his dad visit Steelers' offices at Three Rivers Stadium.

His name was always listed second in the Steelers' administrative directory, right after Daniel M. Rooney, president. His name is John R. McGinley, vice president. His friends, and they are many and devoted, call him Jack, or Jack Sr. The R. is for Regis. Most Steelers fans are unaware of him. He likes it that way. He is the ultimate silent partner.

Arthur J. Rooney II, vice president and general counsel and the oldest son of Dan Rooney, leapfrogged over McGinley into the second spot for the 1999 Media Guide. It's just another sign that someday, sooner than later, Art II will replace his father on the Steelers' throne. The Steelers' succession system, it seems, works like the British monarchy.

The Steelers have never had photos of their officials in their annual media guide, so few people even know what Jack McGinley looks like. That's OK, too. This is a man comfortable in himself and with his coterie of family, friends and the good fathers from the clergy ranks.

"I'm not that interested in getting my picture in the newspapers," he said. "When I was involved with boxing, I got a lot of that because I was a matchmaker. But it never bothered me one way or another."

He and his sister, Rita McGinley, a former guidance counselor in Braddock and later the Woodland Hills School District, each owns ten percent of the Steelers. Their father, Barney McGinley, was a good friend and partner of Art Rooney in several sports ventures, including the Steelers. They shared a love for sports and, in tandem, promoted boxing shows in the Pittsburgh area.

They formed Rooney-McGinley Sports Enterprises, a boxing promotion operation, in 1938. Barney McGinley bought his share of the Steelers in 1946 when Bert Bell, who had been an equal partner with Art Rooney, left to become the commissioner of the NFL. Bell had to sell his interest in the Steelers to do that. Rooney bought some of his shares so he would have a majority interest in the club, and McGinley got the rest.

The Rooneys now own 80 percent of the team, so each of the five Rooney brothers owns 16% per cent of the team. "Originally, Art owned 58 percent of the club, and my dad owned 42 percent," said Jack. "When my brother Bill died, the Rooneys bought his share."

They divvy up the profits accordingly on an annual basis. A handsome check goes out to each of the owners.

Jack McGinley gave Mel Blount the Steelers 1983 NFL/Miller Man of the Year award.

Jim O'Brien

Jack McGinley and Art Rooney join Joe Bach for coffee after Bach signed a two-year contract on Dec. 26, 1952 to succeed John Michelosen as coach of the Steelers. Bach coached the year before at St. Bonaventure University.

One last time: The McGinleys gather in their private box at Three Rivers Stadium. Jack McGinley, at right, hosts his sister, Rita McGinley and his wife, Marie, sitting in front row. Standing, left to right, daughter Mary, and sons Barney, Jack Jr. and Mike.

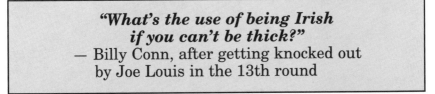

"What's the use of being Irish if you can't be thick?"
— Billy Conn, after getting knocked out by Joe Louis in the 13th round

Jack is married to Art's kid sister, Marie Rooney, and they have a home on Beechwood Boulevard in Squirrel Hill. So Jack is the uncle of the five Rooney boys, and Marie is their aunt. Jack and Marie were close friends of the late KDKA news anchorman Bill Burns and are the godparents of Patti Burns who followed in her father's footsteps.

Marie and her sister, Margaret Laughlin, who still lives on Marshall Avenue on the North Side, were the only survivors of Art Rooney's eight siblings as this book went to press in the summer of 2001. Margaret was married to the late Johnny Laughlin, who owned Johnny Laughlin's Shamrock Room, a landmark restaurant on the North Side, not far from the new football stadium.

It is fascinating to trace some of the connections within the Rooney empire. Art Rooney had some other partners at various times in the early days of the franchise, like Milt Jaffe and then Bert Bell, but they were bought out at different junctures. The McGinleys may have sold some of their shares to the Rooneys through the years, but no one wants to discuss that in any detail.

Jack joined the Steelers' operation in 1941, working in ticket sales and publicity after he graduated from the University of Pittsburgh. Then he did a three-and-a-half year stint as an officer in the U.S. Navy. Jack McGinley has always enjoyed talking to sports writers and broadcasters. The media, in turn, have enjoyed Jack McGinley. You have to press Jack to tell stories whereas Art offered them up without prodding. There are subjects — such as early gambling room and horse room activity downtown involving the Rooneys — that Jack wouldn't touch with a 10-foot shillelagh. You know not to go any further. The silence is deafening.

He prefers to look at the world with a more positive outlook. "I've had many happy moments with the team and some great relationships over the years," he said. "I enjoy being around the guys. I enjoy the business and I understand the business because I've been around it a long time. I'm very comfortable with the way things are."

"Jack swims every day, religiously."
— Jim Lally

Jack McGinley had a private box — No. 309 — at Three Rivers Stadium, right next door to the Pirates box for Steelers games. The McGinley box was always filled to the brim with family and friends. Jack McGinley often stood in the aisleway, leaning against a wall, welcoming those who stopped in to say hello. The McGinleys weren't sure what their arrangement would be in the new football stadium, but they knew security would be tighter, and it wouldn't be as easy for friends to simply stop by for a beer or a glass of wine, or a bite to eat. They were always generously offered to visitors. The McGinleys would miss the casualness of that arrangement. The McGinleys have never stood on ceremony or on formality. Printed invitations were never required to join them.

McGinley usually wore a sport coat and tie, sometimes a button-down navy blue wool sweater. On this particular day he was wearing that sweater under a gray glen plaid sport coat, dark slacks, a white dress shirt with a blue and red tie. He favored a beige trenchcoat and hat, and always seemed dressed for bad weather. There's something very Irish about that. On the other hand, he might have taken his dress cue from Columbo, the TV sleuth.

Jack McGinley is a nice man. He is a pleasant, warm fellow. He always has a well-scrubbed look, with full rosy cheeks, and a welcoming grin or smile. Anyone who missed out on meeting or spending any time with Art Rooney, the late owner of the Pittsburgh Steelers, ought to say hello to his old friend and partner, Jack McGinley. You'd get a good idea of what you missed, and maybe then some.

He won't forget your name. He's more apt to address you by your baptismal or formal name. He often calls me James or Shamus, as in, "James, be well." Or, "James, you take care now." Or, "Shamus, God be with you now."

He has pet phrases the way Art Rooney and his sons have pet phrases. "He has a soft way of saying hello and goodbye, and they have become part of the lexicon of his children as well," said Jack McGinley, Jr., an attorney and partner of the law firm of Grogran Graffam McGinley & Lucchino, with offices at 3 Gateway Center. At the end of our telephone conversation one day, sure enough, Jack Jr. said, "James, be well."

I have probably known Mr. McGinley almost as long as I knew Mr. Rooney, but it wasn't until I interviewed him on several occasions for this book that I came to fully appreciate him. One day, as we were having lunch at his club, the Pittsburgh Athletic Association, or the P.A.A., it struck me like a bolt of lightning.

My God, Jack McGinley was just like Art Rooney. He was Art Rooney. They were so much alike; McGinley could be a ringer for Rooney. Their look, those too-snug button-down sweaters, their modest manner, some of their favorite phrases, their concern, their genuine interest in everyone, their religious devotion, keeping company with priests, their feelings about family, their goodness, the list goes on, are so similar. Their style, or lack of it, was much the same. They were real Pittsburgh guys, to the core. They were proud Irish Catholics — they wore it on their sometimes-frayed sleeves — who walk the talk. McGinley's got a soul of his own and attributes that might have been missing from the Rooney repertoire. He's his own man, mind you, and he's a good man. He has many virtues.

Dan Rooney recognizes that more than most observers. He knows he's got a great uncle in Jack McGinley. "Sure, we're family, but I still say it's an unusual situation," Rooney related several years ago. "There are a number of examples of people who have had problems in family ownership situations in our league. It's no secret that the Maras had problems in New York and the Bidwells had problems in Chicago and St. Louis and the Rams had a situation with Dan Reeves.

"Our relationship with the McGinleys has been super from the beginning. I'm not saying there's never been a difference of opinion, and I can't speak for the old days, but there aren't any problems."

McGinley called me one day in early March 2001 from his winter retreat in Palm Beach, Florida because I had left word at his office that I needed to check out something with him. When I asked him when he expected to be back in Pittsburgh, he said, "Holy Week." It caught me off guard, and I had to think a few seconds to know what week he was talking about. Is that a venial sin?

How many people do you know who'd say that? Holy Week!

This is a man who goes to Mass every morning and goes to the P.A.A. each day, sometimes for lunch, but every day of the week to swim 40 laps in the club swimming pool. That's how he stays in shape. That's why he always looks so darn clean-cut, so well scrubbed as I said earlier. Sometimes he swims at the same time as Fred Rogers — yes, TV's Mr. Rogers — another famous fellow who favors snug button-down sweaters. For years, McGinley did his swimming at the Downtown YMCA.

One of McGinley's dearest friends, Jim Lally, who looked after Three Rivers Stadium and the labor front for the previous 30 some years, often joins him at the P.A.A. "I can vouch for the fact that Jack swims every day, religiously," allowed Lally.

McGinley does so many things religiously. He is a man of routine. He keeps to a schedule. Every Wednesday, for instance, he has lunch with Monsignor Owen Rice, a feisty old Irish-Catholic priest with a presence in Pittsburgh. Anytime you try to book a date with McGinley, he begins by saying, "Wednesday is not good for me." No one is going to bounce Monsigner Rice from McGinley's luncheon schedule.

Monsignor Rice was an outspoken critic and columnist for *The Pittsburgh Catholic* weekly newspaper for many years. Monsignor Rice got on the wrong side of a few bishops in his time. He was pro-labor to the nth degree. He fought ardently for the little people, sometimes annoyingly so. He could be a maverick, but he was never dull. Barry Fitzgerald would play him in a movie. "You got him right on that," said McGinley when I shared that observation.

I shared a glass of dark red wine with Monsignor Rice in the company of the McGinleys after a few Steelers' games at Three Rivers Stadium. The McGinleys, including children and grandchildren, always gathered there for a family dinner after the home games. I was often invited to join them for a glass of wine. I've never quite understood why the McGinleys and the Rooneys always seem to be in the company of priests. Do they bless the food and wine? Are they good luck charms, like shamrocks? Or are they insurance policies?

Jim Lally looks over Three Rivers Stadium scene one last time.

Jack McGinley inherited his father Barney's share of Steelers and has served as club's vice president.

Pittsburgh Post-Gazette sportswriter Ed Bouchette talks about Steelers latest developments with colleague Gerry Dulac as Jack McGinley Jr. and his dad listen in at Steelers' offices at Three Rivers Stadium.

I confess, I've always enjoyed talking to priests, ministers and rabbis, just to cover all bases, or in case I need references on Judgment Day. I've always found the clergy interesting and engaging company.

"We go to St. Joseph's in Bloomfield," said McGinley. "We used to go to St. Augustine's, just around the corner from here, but they changed their Mass schedule. We go to the 11:30 a.m. Mass and try to be a daily communicant."

When McGinley got back from his winter's stay in Florida, we made a date to get together again. We met this time, Tuesday, April 24, 2001, at Del's Restaurant in Bloomfield. We were joined by Jim Lally and Father Francio Fagini from St. Augustine's in nearby Lawrenceville.

Lally told stories about his boyhood in Oakland, where he still lived on Bellefield Avenue, when he met and befriended Babe Ruth and Lou Gehrig and Dizzy Dean and the like while hanging around Forbes Field and the nearby Schenley Hotel, and how he and his friends found ways to get to New York for both of Billy Conn's fights with champion Joe Louis. Lally mentioned how Fritzie Zivic lent him $20 to carry him over during one of those New York stays. All those magic names...

"If you weren't living in that era," pointed out McGinley, "it's hard to envision how big a man Billy Conn was in this city. He was like Michael Jordan."

Lally and I had visited McGinley's office before going to lunch. We both found ourselves once again looking at all the wonderful framed photos he has on the walls there.

McGinley visits his office most days at Wilson-McGinley Beer Distributors on 36th Street in lower Lawrenceville. His original partner was Fritz Wilson, who previously had been in the clothing business. Fritz had gone to Notre Dame and been a classmate of Fred Miller. Fred was from the same Miller family that founded the Miller Brewing Company. That's how Wilson got the franchise for Miller Beer in western Pennsylvania. Another case of having the right connections. Wilson brought McGinley into the business. Wilson's brother, Father Jerome Wilson, became a vice-president at Notre Dame. He served many years as an aide to Father Hesburgh at South Bend. There is a second generation and third generation of McGinleys and Wilsons working at the Lawrenceville warehouse.

Wilson-McGinley is one of the major beer distributors in western Pennsylvania. They're on the same level as Frank Fuhrer Wholesale Distributing on the South Side. Wilson-McGinley has a warehouse on the other side of the railroad tracks in Lawrenceville where the row houses say hello to the warehouses, hard by the Allegheny River. It's about five miles upstream from the new stadium and new ballpark on the city's North Side.

It's a familiar neighborhood for me. My mother, Mary O'Brien, herself a feisty Irish-Catholic, lived nearby on 36th Street, just up the hill at the St. Augustine Plaza, an apartment residence for senior citizens. She lived there for 22 years, from 1977 to 1998. She moved in the same week our younger daughter, Rebecca, was born, that's how I remember the date so well. Then she moved to Mt. Lebanon's Asbury Heights, an assisted-care residence four miles from my home. Jack McGinley often asked me how she was doing, the way Art Rooney always asked me how she was doing.

McGinley's office was a treat to visit, for much the same reason as Art Rooney's office was always so inviting and interesting. There are framed photographs from the past. Jack McGinley is a young man in many of them. He and Marie and the boys are in several. Art and Dan Rooney are in others.

There were photos, for instance, showing McGinley presenting the Miller Lite Man of the Year awards to Rocky Bleier, Mel Blount, Lynn Swann, Mike Webster and Jack Lambert.

There are lots of fight photos. Jack's dad, Barney McGinley, co-promoted the famous Ezzard Charles vs. Joe Walcott heavyweight championship fight at Forbes Field on July 18, 1951. Buck McTiernan, a Pittsburgh boxer in his day, was the referee for that fight, and is shown in several of the photos. A crowd of 28,272 watched Walcott upset the 5-to-1 favorite Charles. It was on CBS television.

The trunks that Ezzard Charles wore that night are draped over a chair in a corner of the office. Several hats worn by Billy Conn rest atop the chair. There's boxing memorabilia from Fritzie Zivic, one of the Zivic fighters who grew up in the same Lawrenceville locale. They were all champions. "Billy and Fritzie were good friends of mine," said McGinley, and he was not boasting.

"There was nobody like Billy Conn. It's hard now to realize what it was like. He was terrific. After the first Louis fight, he didn't fight during the War, except exhibitions. They were charades. I thought promoter Mike Jacobs didn't help the situation. He didn't want either of them to fight. He was trying to protect a big gate for a rematch. So they didn't have any real fights in between their title fights. If Billy had two or three tune-ups before their second fight, I think he would have had a better showing. Who knows?"

During one of my visits, I brought along a buddy of mine, Jack Curley, a spirited Irishman who grew up on Mt. Washington, did a little amateur boxing in his youth and drove a truck all over the East until he retired at age 68. I knew that Curley, at age 71 and still playing competitive basketball with men half his age twice a week, would enjoy Jack McGinley and his gallery of boxing memorabilia. There were letters from Angelo Dundee, who trained Muhammad Ali among many other championship fighters, and was an old friend from my days of covering boxing in Miami and New York.

When I went to Miami in 1969 to be a sports writer with *The Miami News*, I was welcomed and accepted by Angelo and Chris Dundee, who promoted boxing shows on Miami Beach. The Dundees, originally from Philadelphia, had been involved in some boxing promotions in Pittsburgh back when the Rooneys and McGinleys were fixtures in the fight game. If I knew the Rooneys and McGinleys I was all right with the Dundees. It was a door-opener.

When McGinley was wintering in Palm Beach, in a condominium where Kathleen and Art Rooney, Jr., also stay, he told me he had spoken to Angelo Dundee, who lived in Weston, Florida, not far from the home of Dan Marino, Sr. "Ange is doing fine," reported McGinley.

In his office that day, McGinley encouraged Jack Curley to pick up the black trunks with white trim once worn by Ezzard Charles and hold them against his own slacks. Curley was reluctant, at first, to touch these treasures, lest they come apart in his hands. He smiled like a lighthouse when he held the trunks to his midsection, and when he doffed one of Conn's ballcaps. Charles came from Cincinnati, but he was managed by Jake Mintz, a Pittsburgh boxing icon who resided in Squirrel Hill.

There were Irish blessings on the wall and in the wall cupboard and boxing items here, there and everywhere in Jack McGinley's office, dinner programs piled high, you name it, and Curley was in a sports fan's heaven. "Ah, this is great!" he said more than once. McGinley got a kick out of Curley and invited him to join us for lunch later at the P.A.A. "I want to do this while your friend can make it, too," said McGinley. That's the kind of guy he is.

I was checking out some of the memorabilia in the office closet and when I looked back, I caught Curley throwing some imaginary jabs at Jack McGinley to put some punch in one of his boxing stories. McGinley countered with a wide grin. I knew they were getting along well.

There was a team photo of one of Jock Sutherland's football teams at Pitt back in the late '20s, when Art Rooney's brother, Jim, was a running back on the squad. "They were on their way to play Stanford in the (1928) Rose Bowl," said McGinley.

There was a photo of Jack and Marie McGinley having dinner with Walt Kiesling and TV newsman Bill Burns and their wives.

"We used to see them a lot. Bill Burns was maybe my best friend. We loafed together. Our wives were good friends. We had dinner every week. His wife was from Houtzdale, just six miles from my dad's hometown of Osceola. I was friendly with Bob Prince, too. He was just starting at WJAS.

"We were promoting this one fight at Hickey Park. Bill Burns did the blow-by-blow description and Pie Traynor from the Pirates did the color. That was some combination."

"Game Plan for Success"
"Above all, we look for motivation. When I look at the most successful people I've worked with, I always see the same attributes: common sense, passion and dedication. Give me managers with those qualities, and I'll give you an unbeatable team."
— William R. Johnson
President and CEO
H.J. Heinz Co.

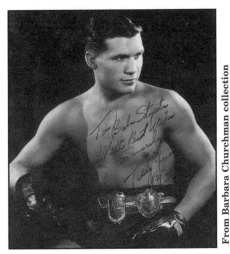

From Barbara Churchman collection

Teddy Yarosz of Monaca

Pittsburgh Steelers Archives

Art Rooney in boxing days

Carnegie Library of Pittsburgh

Harry Greb of Garfield

Jim O'Brien

Boxing figures Freddie Manns, Tim Conn, Jack McGinley and Art Swiden meet at ceremonies to name street in Oakland after legendary fighter Billy Conn.

Boxing training camp at Eagles Nest in Shaler in summer of 1939 has impressive lineup, left to right: Billy Marquart, Rich Gregory, Emil Josephs, Glenn Lee, Barney McGinley, Billy Conn, Art Rooney, Sammy Angott, Fred Apostoli and Jimmy Leto.

From Billy Adams collection

"It's a heartache to go through there."

Jack McGinley grew up in Braddock, where his father owned a neighborhood bar right after World War II. "It was a terrific town," recalled McGinley. "There was really a lot of activity; it was one of he busiest main streets in the area. There was lots of action.

"All those mill towns — Braddock, McKeesport and Homestead — were so alive round the clock. The mills were going 24 hours a day, three eight-hour work shifts. Braddock is a shell of itself now. It's a heartache to go through there.

"I went to Braddock High School. Our church was St. Brendan's, an Irish-Catholic church. Sacred Heart was the Polish church in town. St. Joseph's was the German church for Catholics.

"There were two department stores, and you often had to walk in the streets because the sidewalks were so crowded. People would come from the surrounding towns to shop. I remember three movie theaters, the Times, the Capitol and Paramount. My dad's name was Barney McGinley, and he had a bar called Barney's Place right on Braddock Avenue. He managed the Moose Club before that. There must have 50 bars on that avenue. Art Rooney's dad owned the General Braddock Brewing Co. right after prohibition ended, from maybe 1933 to 1939. Then he had Dan's Saloon on the North Side.

"There were four children in our family. My brother Bill has been gone 25 years now, and my sister Mary Ann has been gone for 12 years. So there's just Rita and I now.

"My dad was originally from a small town in Clearfield County called Osceola Mills. Then he moved to South Fork, where he ran a hotel, before he came to Braddock. That was in 1920. You know Carl Hughes, the old sports writer who ran Kennywood Park for years? Well, his father was a banker in South Fork.

"Carl Hughes covered boxing and football for *The Pittsburgh Press*, and he took care of everybody. About three or four times a year, I get together for lunch and conversation with Carl and his good friend, Roy McHugh. Now there's a great boxing writer. We get together at Carl's house up on Mt. Washington. Sometimes Bill Henniger, the CEO from Kennywood, joins us.

"I think my father met Art Rooney at a restaurant in downtown Pittsburgh owned by Owney McManus. He was a little guy, about 5-2, but a tough little guy. He was a boxer in his day. He hung out with Patsy Scanlon, who was about 5-5, and had been a good fighter. He fought pro."

Pittsburgh sports writer Pat Livingston provided a story about Owney McManus. "He owned a very popular restaurant in downtown Pittsburgh," recalled Livingston. "He used to run train trips to Steelers' games on the road, and to big fights or other sports events. They were called ham & cabbage specials. He and his buddy were both little guys. They made nearly every road trip with the Steelers in those days. We were playing the Redskins at Washington, and I was talking to their team's owner, George Preston Marshall, before the game. Marshall said, 'Where's the Prez?' That's what he called Art Rooney. I told him that he'd be along soon, that he had probably stopped to speak to someone. Then Rooney shows up on the field with McManus and his buddy at his side. Marshall looked at them and said, 'Here comes Art and his Mick Midgets.' It was funny."

"We didn't know what hit us."

I saw some photos on the wall of McGinley's office from his days in the U.S. Navy and asked to talk about those days. "I was in the Navy for three and a half years, mostly over in North Africa," said McGinley. "I was aboard an LST (landing ship, tanks). We made the landing at Tunisia, Sicily and Salerno and Normandy. We took a load in for the D-Day invasion and went back across the English Channel. We got sunk on June 6 when we were returning to England to get another load.

"We got hit around 4 o'clock in the morning. We got hit by Nazi torpedos (referred to as "tin fish" in one newspaper report). We didn't know what hit us; we couldn't see anything. But it was an E-boat, we realized. We were about 20 miles off the coast of Cherbourg. Many of us were just floating around in the water, for about two and a half hours. We were wearing life-jackets and we had rafts. We got picked up at dawn by a British destroyer. We lost half our guys, about 60 guys, when we got hit. I was in getting a cup of coffee when we got hit. We lost a lot of guys, James. I was an engineering officer. I had 24 men reporting to me. We lost 16 of them. The torpedoes hit in the back of the crew's quarters. Lots of them were sleeping...

"I was in the battle area for 15 months. I went in at age 19. I was there from May 1942 to November 1945. See these photos here on the wall...we lost these two doctors. We lost this boy. This fellow here was an old gunner's mate. I spoke to him the night before the invasion....

"I wound up a lieutenant. I got to come home for awhile in August, and I finally got a chance to see our son, Jack Jr., who was eight months old at the time. He was the first of our six children. We were living on Perrysville Avenue on the North Side at the time."

During his stay overseas, he ran into his wife's brother, Father Silas (Dan) Rooney, in England. He was serving as a chaplain with the American Forces. In Palermo, he ran into another brother-in-law, John Rooney, who was with the American Invasion Forces in Italy.

"My dad didn't get involved with the Steelers until 1943. Art and Bert Bell had the team then. Art had sold his team to a New York guy named Alexis Thompson. Thompson wanted to run a team from New York, so Bell arranged for him to get the Eagles team. Bert brought the Eagles to Pittsburgh and sold them to Art. He and Art had been 50 percent partners before that with the Steelers. The Steelers have operated ever since with franchise papers that were originally awarded to the Eagles.

"My dad was like Art, an extremely bright guy. He worked in the mines as a kid. He led the donkeys out of the mine. When he became a businessman, though, an entrepreneur, he dressed like he was the president of Mellon Bank. He wore a sharp Stetson all the time.

"Art Rooney was a good man. He was a generous man. He was a very religious man. He just did his best and that was pretty good.

"I was doing publicity for the club in 1941 and Bell was the coach when we were in training camp at Hershey, Pennsylvania. Bert was a super guy. We lost the first four games and the team was turned over to Buff Donelli. He was the football coach at Duquesne University at the time. He was very successful at Duquesne. We trained at Moore Field in Brookline. Buff would coach us in the morning and coach Duquesne in the afternoon. It didn't work. He lost the next four games. Then Duquesne had a game with St. Mary's Gallopin' Gaels, and Duquesne was going out there by train. Donelli was expected to be with the Duquesne team. So Art turned the Steelers over to Walt Kiesling. We had three different head coaches that year, and we finished with a 1-9-1 record.

"I remember how we found out Donelli was missing. One of the trainers called and said Buff Donelli hadn't shown up for practice. I called Doc Skender, who was the athletic director at Duquesne. I said, 'Hey, Doc, Buff didn't show up this morning.' He said, 'Jack, he's on the train with our team and they're heading for San Francisco.' So Kiesling finished out the season as coach. We went to Philadelphia and tied the Eagles, 7-7. We won the next game at home against Brooklyn for our only victory of the year.

"We went through several coaches the next four seasons, Kiesling, Greasy Neale, Phil Handler and Jim Leonard, and then Sutherland stepped in.

"We had two rooms at the Fort Pitt Hotel, rooms 241 and 243. That was it. We expanded our offices in 1946 when Sutherland became the coach. There was only Joe Carr, the ticket manager, and me in the office. I'm a young guy, 32, and I have a lot of responsibility. We didn't have any secretaries. All of Sutherland's assistants were part-time coaches. Jock was getting paid $27,500 as the head man. I'd been in the Navy and Jock had been in the Navy. He called me Jock.

"I never knew how much difference a coach could make. Jock Sutherland...what a coach he was. He was a strong disciplinarian. He was extremely bright. He was terrific. He'd have been great for the Steelers if he hadn't gotten sick and died. You know, he lived here at the P.A.A. and he walked to the office downtown each day from here.

"His contract called for him to get 25 percent of the profits in addition to his salary. Fran Fogarty, the business manager, went over the books at the end of the year and figured out what we owed Sutherland. Fran and I were sitting in the office when Sutherland showed up to get his final check for the season. Fran had all the books out for Sutherland to see. Sutherland never took his hat off. He said, 'Did you and Art go over the books? Well, whatever you came up with is fine with me. I don't need to go over the books.' He never questioned anything. 'Just send me the check,' he said. That story goes against his reputation for being a parsimonious guy.

"I was in the office one day, on a Saturday, when we got a telephone call. Art answered the phone. A doctor was calling from Kentucky to tell him that Sutherland had been found in a farm field down there.

"He said, 'We have a fellow here who works for you people. We found his car along the side of a road. He's not well. His name is Sutherland. We don't have the hospital facilities here to help him.'

"So Art called John Michelosen and he got hold of a fellow named Dave Thompson, who lived in Mt. Lebanon and owned an airplane. Michelosen and Thompson went down and brought Sutherland back here. They took him to the hospital here in Oakland. He had a brain tumor. He died at age 58."

I asked McGinley about his own personal philosophy. "That's pretty hard, Jimmy," he said. "My grammar is rather limited. You're pretty limited in what you can do. You do the best you can each day, and you try not to hurt anybody."

From Jack McGinley collection

Good friends, left to right, Jack McGinley, long-time KDKA news anchor Bill Burns and Steelers publicist Ed Kiely attend shindig in downtown hotel in '60s.

Len Pasquarelli
The Bloomfield connection

"I still get goosebumps."

Pittsburgh-born and bred Len Pasquarelli has reported on the National Football League for 22 years, most while based in Atlanta. He was a beat writer for the Atlanta Journal-Constitution *for 10 years (1989-1999) and then joined CBS SportsLine in 1999. He is a friend of Dan Marino and his father, and they enjoy reminiscing about their days in Pittsburgh. Let Len tell you his story:*

My father's name was Joe Pasquarelli and he grew up in Oakland, not far from Forbes Field. He was born in 1927, the year the Yankees swept the Pirates in four games in the World Series. The Yankees had the famed "Murderers' Row," led by Babe Ruth and Lou Gehrig. He and his brother Al both worked at Forbes Field from the time they were teens. Al was older and he was an usher at Forbes Field during the 1927 World Series. My Uncle Al is in his late 80s.

So my father never saw the Pirates play in the World Series until 1960. It was one of his great memories. He was a ticket taker at the gate at Forbes Field that year. He worked two jobs. He was home from his first job at 4 o'clock. The table would be set and we'd all eat dinner. Then he'd be off to Forbes Field. Sometimes he'd take me and my brother, Danny, and one of his friends on the ushering staff would seat us somewhere. My father was 33 when the Pirates played in the 1960 Series. I was 10 at the time. I never saw my father cry until the Pirates won that World Series. He was not supposed to cry, but he wept openly. He never thought he'd ever live long enough to see the Pirates play in the World Series.

He had entrée to the locker room, and he could get some souvenirs for us. He crawled on the second tier and grabbed some red, white and blue bunting and brought it home. We still have the bunting. He went to the locker room and got a bat Roberto Clemente had used in the Series. Years later, he asked me what I thought that bat was worth. I took my dad out to a sports collectors' show at Robert Morris College and the traders there took a lot at the bat and appraised it being worth $3,400. It was signed Momens Clemente; it was the last year he signed his bats that way.

My dad worked at Three Rivers Stadium and he always got a kick out of seeing Art Rooney coming and going. My dad worked the press gate for years and he was proud when I passed through the bar with my buddies in the business. I was interested in sports all through school and I became the editor of a weekly newspaper devoted to the Steelers. The Chief didn't know me from a bag of beans, but he embraced me right from the start and made me feel so comfortable to be around the Steelers. He walked me into his office. He was interested in what I was doing. I really didn't hear half of what he said. I was just soaking up being there. He slipped me a cigar. It's still in my home. I never opened it. There was a picture of Chief, Dan and Art with three Super Bowl trophies, and I got them all to sign it. I still have it. That sits on my desk with the cigar right under it.

There are some old-time owners in this (2001) Super Bowl, like Art Modell and Wellington Mara, but they don't mean nearly as much to me as Art Rooney. But that's because I'm from Pittsburgh and it will always be my home. There's a great bond between Pittsburghers. I'm 50 years old now and I have lived much of my adult and professional career in Atlanta, but I wear Pittsburgh like a badge of courage. I'm worse than some Southerners with the Civil War stuff.

I bumped into Dan Marino at Super Bowl XXXV and did an interview with him. He called his dad, Dan Sr., in his room and told him to come down and see me. "You haven't seen Lenny in a long time, Dad, c'mon down," said Dan. I cherish that kind of relationship from somebody I knew way back when.

My dad moved to Bloomfield when he got married and that's where I grew up. We traveled back and forth across the Bloomfield Bridge to Oakland. I coached a Catholic grade school team where I'd gone to school, St. Joseph's. One of the teams we played was Immaculate Conception on Polish Hill. Their coach was "Bear" Rodgers. He had coached Johnny Unitas when Johnny was playing sandlot football for the Bloomfield Rams after he was cut by the Steelers. When I'd go up against him, I'd think about how "this guy coached Johnny Unitas!" They had played and practiced at Dean Field, just under the Bloomfield Bridge.

I made sure I was at the Steelers' last game at Three Rivers Stadium. When I walked in there and the fans were waving those Terrible Towels it got to me. I still get goose bumps just thinking about it. I had Art Rooney's name as a reference on my resume for years. When he died, I mentioned that to Dan, and Dan told me I could put his name on it for future reference. The Rooney family has always been beyond gracious with me.

> *"I think the thing I'll remember most is that during the darkest hours for me when I was managing the Pirates, Mr. Rooney would show up in my office. I don't know how he figured it out, but he would always show up at those times. He knew what I was going through, and he was there to cheer me up and tell me to hang in there. I'll never forget that. In a short period of time, I think we became close friends, and I had a tremendous amount of respect for him."*
> — Jim Leyland, former manager
> Pittsburgh Pirates

Tex Schramm
A classy Cowboy who respected Pittsburgh's Team

"Art was a good guy and he believed
everybody was like him."

Tex Schramm was one of the most influential figures in the National Football League during the period of its greatest growth. He was part of the founding of the Dallas Cowboys. He had the name, Texas E. Schramm — yes, that's his real name — and the plan to put the Cowboys in an elite category. Under his direction, and the ownership of Clint Murchison, they became "America's team," and no NFL team was more image-conscious. They had the classiest organization in the league, from top to bottom and were the darlings of network TV. Football fans in Pittsburgh and other places resented their status and often hated the Cowboys. Schramm was the club's first general manager and later its president. He hired Tom Landry as the team's first coach. He brought in Gil Brandt, the recruiting guru, and gave him the computerized support system and a generous expense account and those were thought to give the Cowboys an edge in evaluating talent. Early in his career, as general manager of the Los Angeles Rams, Schramm recruited Pete Rozelle into the league as the Rams' public relations man. In 1966, Schramm helped negotiate a merger agreement with the American Football League that resulted in the Super Bowl, and he chaired the NFL Competition Committee from 1966-1988. At age 80, Schramm was 12 years removed from the Cowboys' scene, but still a respected figure among NFL leaders. I visited him for an hour in his room on the 21st floor of the Marriott Waterside Inn in Tampa the day after Super Bowl XXXV. I noticed his right hand shaking as he spoke on the telephone for a few minutes during my visit. Otherwise, he looked fine. Here's what he had to say:

I thought Art Rooney was a wonderful person. He was one of the great men of the game. He was one of the builders of our sport. He went through the tough times that too few of those today who are enjoying the success of our league had to go through. He was just a great individual, a great person and a man I loved very dearly. I knew him from 1947 or 1948 when I was running the Rams. My first real association with Art came in the late '40s and early '50s when I was general manager. I was there from 1947 to 1957, before I went to CBS and then to the Cowboys. I dealt directly with him. We had one full-time scout at the time, a fellow named Eddie Kotal. The reason I bring that up is that I always had a lot of fun with Art trying to work out a trade. You didn't have all the tiers of management you have now. It was much simpler then.

At the time, we had a lot of football personnel, and we were looking to unload some guys. We played for the championship in 1950. We were defeated in a difficult game by the Cleveland Browns in the first sudden death game in the league. We got beat by a field goal by Lou Groza in the extra period. The next year we beat them. We traded some of our guys to the Giants, and we gave them too much in Andy Robustelli and Harland Svare. I'm not proud of that.

I wanted to make a trade with Art Rooney. I'll tell you how close we were. We trained at Redlands, California then, and I told him to send a man out to take a look at our players. I didn't want him thinking I was pulling anything over his eyes. I told him, "You don't have to believe me about these guys." He sent someone out and he spent a few days watching us practice. Then I made a trade with him for five players. One of the players we traded to him played in a game for us the night before they were to leave for Pittsburgh. His name was Spud Murphy, a lineman. He broke a bone in his hand or wrist. Art got on me. He said, "You sent me a player and he's in a cast." I told him he was a good player. But I don't think he ever ended up playing for the Steelers.

We had a lot of fun. He was an honest person. We just always got along. He was just a loveable gentleman. George Halas of the Bears was always picking on him, and they got into some great debates. Art was a good guy and he believed everybody was like him. He helped other people. I know Halas helped the cross-town Cardinals when they ran into a money problem. He helped Bill Bidwell. They were among the originals. It wasn't easy to make money then and they were having trouble staying afloat. In those days, nobody had any money.

I remember how much Art loved the track and racing. He had grown up with it. He had all these fabulous stories. He had a big hit one day, at Saratoga Springs, I think, and that's supposed to be where he got the money to buy his NFL franchise. At least that was the story making the rounds in those days. And the Rooneys were always close to the Maras, from Tim and Jack through Wellington. I respect these people. That's why I liked this Super Bowl because it had Wellington in there against Art Modell. I knew Wellington and Art very closely. Wellington always had a presence about him. He wasn't a real social person. I don't remember ever going out and having a drink with him. Wellington was always very reserved, except when he'd get away at an owners' meeting. He was kind of the elder statesman of the league.

I'm close to Dan Rooney, too. As he's grown up, he's taken over most of his dad's responsibilities along the way. I did a lot with him. Dan was definitely different from his father. He thinks well. Now he's been there for years. He was just becoming an influence when I was still on the committees. You'd want him on a committee because he worked toward resolutions. He put personal gains aside for the good of the league. Dan was an honest person and a logical person and you knew you could count on him.

I knew Art Jr., too. He was a personnel man for them. Art Rooney, Jr. reminds you more of Art Sr. than Danny does.

Things are still fresh in my mind from those early years. So many of the people around now weren't even born then. The Rooneys represent the league, to me. When I came into the league, you had people like the Rooneys in Pittsburgh, Curly Lambeau in Green Bay, George Halas in Chicago, George Preston Marshall in Washington, Tim Mara in New York, though I didn't know him that well, and Dan Reeves in Los Angeles.

Art Rooney was not an aggressive person, but everyone knew he was there. Wellington Mara was that way, too. In later years, when he got into his 70s and 80s, Wellington took on a new stature. When Art was gone, Wellington became the patriarch of the league. Art seldom stood up to speak at league meetings, but when he did people listened. He was so forthright and so honest. There were people you didn't trust very far, but he had the history and background, and you knew he had seen it all from the beginning.

I knew he loved the football team, but he was the kind of guy who'd rather be out at the racetrack or a baseball game. George Preston Marshall was a driven man, for instance, a very aggressive person. George Halas was a very aggressive person. Lambeau was one of the originals, and he had everyone's ear.

I know the Maras were into racing, too. Tim was a bookmaker at the track before he bought his NFL team. That was something that always hung over the Maras, even though bookmaking wasn't illegal in those days. Art Rooney was a big racetrack gambler; everyone was aware of that. It was a different era. Those were the kind of guys who made the league successful. In the early days you had to fight to promote pro football. They did things like special tours with Red Grange, and they'd sell out the Polo Grounds, stuff like that.

I always had a close relationship with Art and I have a close relationship with Danny. That reminds me of a funny story. It involves Art's wife, Danny's mother, Kathleen. We're playing Pittsburgh in a Super Bowl in Miami. And I'm in a box right next to a box where Kathleen is sitting. Art wasn't with her. I'm one who sometimes used expletives with five- and four-letter words when something bad happened. I said something not so nice and, all of a sudden, I look over at her and I say, "Oh, my God, she can hear me!" Shortly after that, I saw her and I'm still embarrassed. And I told her, "I want to apologize for some of the stuff I said." She said, "With the five boys I have, I didn't hear one thing I hadn't heard before."

I had a lot of respect for Chuck Noll. I was one of the people who liked him. A lot of people didn't think he was very friendly. I'll always have a certain respect for him. He ruined a couple of days for us. I'm told he's got a boat that's one of the slowest boats you can buy. I'm told he's really taking it easy. That's good that he can do that. Socially, we were friends. He's a victim of the same thing that Tom Landry was a victim of. They seemed so stern, so cold. But, up close, both of them

320

were wonderful people. We went to the Super Bowl five times in the '70s, so we weren't about to criticize Landry for not being as social as Don Shula, for instance. Noll comes up with a funny line every now and then. He tries. Shula and Paul Brown and I were on the competition committee and we got Noll as a fourth for awhile, and we got along very well.

We had some guys on our team and in our organization who had Pittsburgh backgrounds, like Mike Ditka and Ernie Stautner, and they don't come any tougher than those two guys. And we had Tony Dorsett, and he put us over the top. He made a big difference in our team. Those people all knew Art Rooney and they had a great deal of respect for the Steelers and Art Rooney.

I've been at all 35 Super Bowls and I've been around a lot of great people. I know all the sportswriters, guy like Blackie Sherrod, Edwin Pope, Furman Bisher, John Steadman, Jim Murray, Dave Anderson, Jerry Izenberg, Bob Oates, Larry Felser; they're all good guys. They're all geezers now. I spent a lot of time with those guys. I got along great with the writers. They were great people. I got along with the younger guys, too, like Randy Galloway. I got along with the newspaper people in Dallas. I told them if they'd work with me — instead of trying to beat me — I'll work with you. I was honest with them and kept them abreast of what we were doing. I never led them astray. There were times I couldn't tell them some things, not right then, but I leveled with them, and had the kind of relationship that worked best for all of us. I miss seeing those guys like I used to. We had our fights and disagreements, but overall I'm proud of the way we got along. They might not love me the way they loved Art Rooney, but I think I had their respect. That's good enough.

Jim O'Brien

Former Cowboys boss Tex Scramm and wife Marty pose in their room at Marriott Waterside Inn, the NFL headquarters for Super Bowl XXXV in Tampa, Florida.

Jim "Popcorn" Brandt
He signed the little red book

"Mr. Rooney always called me Pops."

W hen I was checking my files for information and materials for this project, I came across a little red autograph book from 1953. It was in great shape. I was 11 years old and in fifth grade at St. Stephen's Grade School at the time. Sister Mary Lucy was my teacher. My favorites, according to a list in the front of the little red autograph book, were popular music, history, football and baseball.

I took this autograph book to a sports banquet in the school hall one evening and got all the celebrity guests to sign it. Now this was a parochial school in Hazelwood and I know that none of the guests got a dime for coming to the dinner. The lineup was impressive and you couldn't match it today at anything less than the annual Dapper Dan Sports Banquet at the Hilton in downtown Pittsburgh.

One of the names in that book belonged to Jim "Popcorn" Brandt, a reserve running back with the Pittsburgh Steelers from 1952 to 1954. I always loved his name. It ranked right up there, as magical names go, with Byron "Whizzer" White, Johnny "Blood" McNally, John "Zero" Clement, "Bullet Bill" Dudley, Val Jansante, Jim "Cannonball" Butler, John Henry Johnson and John "Frenchy" Fuqua among Steelers stars.

Brandt was back in Pittsburgh to help celebrate his mother-in-law's 90th birthday when he called me on the telephone. I had told his relatives in West Mifflin, the Nagy family, that I wanted to talk to him. Brandt and I had brunch on Tuesday, March 13, 2001 at Eat'n Park Restaurant near South Hills Village, about a mile from my home.

I brought my little red autograph book with me. Brandt checked out his signature, which was right above teammate Jack Butler, a great defensive back from that era. "That's my hand-writing all right," declared Brandt. I had him sign another page in the back of the book just to be sure I had his authentic autograph.

Brandt smiled as he checked out the other signatures in the book. They brought back some memories for him, too.

Those who signed it included Danny O'Connell, an infielder for the Pirates, and Frankie Gustine, a former infielder for the Pirates and one of the post popular sports figures in the city. Gustine was the owner of a restaurant near Forbes Field in Oakland. I would become a close friend of Gustine as an adult. I was an honorary pallbearer at his funeral, a great honor. "He talked about you like you were one of us," said one of his sons, Bobby Gustine, a Pittsburgh attorney.

Pete Dimperio, the legendary coach of all those City League championship football teams at Westinghouse High School, returned to his hometown for this fete.

So did Julius "Moose" Solters, the only major league baseball player to come out of Hazelwood. I didn't realize how good Solters was until I met his son, Steve Solters, an executive with USFilter, and spent some time with him at Super Bowl XXXV in Tampa, Florida where he works. "Moose" Solters, who went blind after his ballplaying career, played nine years in the big leagues and had a .289 career batting average. In a three-year stretch, from 1935 to 1937, he had 112, 134 and 109 RBIs. He scored over 90 runs each of those three seasons as well. He got those numbers in 154-game seasons. He batted over .300 three times.

"Moose" Solters showed up for every Little League and Pony League awards banquet I attended in Hazelwood. Now that I know how good he was I feel even better about that. He had been struck in the side of his head by a thrown baseball and that contributed to a physical problem which left him blind in his early 30s.

Solters' signature appeared on a page right below the signature of David L. Lawrence, the mayor of Pittsburgh and later the governor of Pennsylvania. He was a close friend of Steelers' owner Art Rooney. Yes, Mayor Lawrence was at the dinner as well.

Father Conroy, an assistant priest at St. Stephen's, signed that page, too. On the next page was the signature of Rev. Paul M. Lackner, Jack Butler (I got him twice), Rev. A. R. Spisak, another parish priest, and Lee McHugh, the local alderman. Bill Mackrides, a rookie quarterback for the Steelers from Nevada, was there, too. He was with the Steelers for that one season.

"We never got paid for going to those sports banquets," said Brandt. "So they usually sent the rookies or young players to those community affairs. It was a free dinner and you might make some good contacts."

"It was the smartest play in Steelers' history."
— Joe Tucker

It points up how times have changed. Those ballplayers were making less than $10,000 a year back then. Now that they're making millions they can't be bothered to go to sports banquets. Brandt said $7,000 was his top salary. Today, some ballplayers make that much for gracing the dais at some of the major sports banquets, or for an appearance at a sporting goods store.

"We paid our own way to come to training camp," recalled Brandt. "You bought your own shoes. You didn't get paid during the exhibition season. If you got cut you got a ticket home and that was it.

Sometimes Art Rooney would slip some money to such a player. He was like that. George Halas was supposed to be good about that sort of thing. The Bears were the best-paid team in the league back then."

Brandt, 72-years-old, wore a new blue and brown NFL Alumni ballcap to our meeting. He had round shoulders. He wore a blue jacket over a brown jersey, buttoned to the neck. He said he was a borderline diabetic and had to watch his diet. He said he was feeling pretty good. He had a bright look in his blue/gray eyes and was a delightful conversationalist. He was never a star with the Steelers, but he shared some good stories. Brandt had insights about his boss, Art Rooney. He spoke about what it was like in those simpler days of the early '50s.

He was on the Steelers' team that I first followed, with Jim Finks at quarterback, Fran Rogel at fullback, and Lynn Chandnois and Ray Mathews as halfbacks in a T-formation lineup. Mathews was one of the team's top pass-catchers. He often gave way in the backfield to Brandt on third-and-two and third-and-one situations. "I was our short-yardage guy," recalled Brandt. "It was Rogie and me. He could really hit in there. We blocked for each other. "

The Steelers had just switched from playing the single-wing after the 1951 season when John Michelosen gave way to Joe Bach as the coach. "You heard about the play where we beat the Eagles in 1954 by throwing a pass to Elbie Nickel from around the 50-yard-line, didn't you?" asked Brandt. "Finks faked a handoff into the middle to me, and flipped the ball to Elbie over the middle and he ran it in for a touchdown. We had lost six straight games to the Eagles and we finally beat them (17-7) that day. We felt pretty good about that."

I was not familiar with that play, so I checked with my former boss at *The Pittsburgh Press*, sportswriter Pat Livingston, and Elbie Nickel for more details.

"That might have been the best known play in Steelers history until Franco Harris and 'The Immaculate Reception' play came along," allowed Livingston. "That completely surprised the Eagles. They had a big crowd, a night game at Forbes Field, and they sold standing room only tickets. They put in temporary bleachers. The playing field was surrounded by fans.

"Two weeks before that, the Steelers got cheated in a big game in Philadelphia (losing by 24-22). The Steelers were fighting with the Eagles for first place in the East Division. Pittsburghers were still upset about that first game."

A check of a game report revealed that it was third down and one yard to go on the Steelers' 48 at 6:25 of the third quarter. The Steelers were leading 3-0 thanks to a 24-yard field goal by Ed Kissell in the first quarter. The Steelers had moved there from their own 20 on passes to Mathews and Nickel. Brandt came off the bench and replaced Mathews in the backfield. The Eagles were sure it was a running play. They had nine players on the defensive line and the other two backs were pressing right behind. It was Nickel who called

Jim "Popcorn" Brandt

JIM "POPCORN" BRANDT
Steelers Fullback (1952-1954)

Pittsburgh Steelers Archives

the play. He called time out and he and Finks huddled with Kiesling on the sideline and Nickel suggested they run a fake 32 and flip it to him. He thought he'd be wide open.

The Steelers huddled briefly on the ballfield so as not to tip off their strategy. How long would it take to call a simple dive play? Finks took the ball and turned as if he were to hand off the ball. Rogel rushed into the guard slot ahead of Brandt, as if he were blocking for a bull rush. Finks fired a pass to Nickel who ran under the ball at the Eagles' 35-yard-line and ran in untouched for a 52-yard-scoring play.

Joe "The Screamer" Tucker, who was calling the game on the radio, termed it "the smartest play in Steelers' history."

Nickel recalled it in a telephone conversation from his home in Chillicothe, Ohio. "It was a simple play, really," he said. "They had all their backs up crowded at the line, and I simply slipped downfield. I went right by their halfback. He was coming up to make the tackle. It was a short pass, but I was wide open."

"How's the corn look out your way?"
— Art Rooney

Jim Brandt provided some background about how he became a Steeler. "I was drafted out of St. Thomas in St. Paul in 1951, but I had to go into the military service that year," said Brandt. "So I didn't report to the Steelers until 1952. I also won a Golden Gloves boxing title that year as a heavyweight boxer in the Twin Cities. So I could handle myself pretty good. Art Rooney liked the fact that I was a boxer.

"Johnny Blood was coaching at St. John's in Collegeville, Minnesota and we played against them. That was Blood's alma mater. He recommended me to the Steelers. He had been a player-coach with the Steelers (in the late '30s) and had remained a close friend of Art Rooney. Another guy (Olie Haugsrood) who had been an owner with the old Duluth Eskimos talked me up, too. I was drafted on the 12th round in 1951. Then, too, Walt Kiesling, the Steelers' coach, had gone to St. Thomas. Joe Bach was born in Minnesota.

"I was from Olivia, in the western end of the state, about a hundred miles west of the Twin Cities. I was from out in the country. Art Rooney was always asking me how the corn and wheat and oats were growing out there. He always played the commodities market out in Chicago. He'd say, 'I just bought some corn. How's the corn look out your way? What are the crops like?' I think he played the commodities market as much as he played the horses. I'm told he made a lot of money in that, too. But when I played ball, he wasn't a rich man. When we'd go to Chicago, Mr. Rooney would meet a friend and be off to the commodities market.

"The Steelers offices in those days were at the Union Trust Building on Grant Street. They had some rooms on the floor level for the front-office people, and the coaches were on the fifth floor. I remember Rooney's business man was Fran Fogarty. His father had been the head of the ground-keeping crew at Forbes Field.

"I had a room in a home in Oakland, about eight blocks from Forbes Field where we practiced and played our home games. Each player would get four complimentary tickets for the home games. The tickets cost about $7 or $8 in those days. Those were good seats. You could get in for a buck, too. I remember we used to eat breakfast at Scotty's Diner on Forbes Avenue — Scotty was a real character — and we'd have a few beers after practice at The Clock, or at the Home Plate Café or at Coyne's near the ballpark. Sometimes we'd go over to Homestead to Chiodo's, which was at the end of the (High-Level) bridge. A wonderful little guy named (Joe) Chiodo owned the place. He was a big Steelers' fan.

"We had a good backfield and ends, but our line wasn't so hot. Chandnois was a good runner. He was 6-2, 210. He was left-handed, you know. I was 6 feet tall, 200 and I could run the 100 in 10 seconds and change. Finks had a good head for football. He was a defensive back in the beginning when they were playing single-wing ball. I played both ways myself.

"Finks left the Steelers early to be an assistant coach on Terry Brennan's staff at Notre Dame. Finks went on to have a great career as an administrator in the NFL, with the Minnesota Vikings, Chicago Bears and New Orleans Saints. I'd get to see him from time to time. I spent some time with Ted Marchibroda when he brought his Buffalo team into Minneapolis. Marchibroda came to the Steelers as a backup to Finks in 1953.

"I played with Fran Rogel from North Braddock, and Bill McPeak from New Castle and Rudy Andabaker from Donora. We got our first black player on that team the same year I came here. His name was Jack Spinks. He was a fullback from Alcorn A&M. He had huge hands. He'd hold a beer can in his hand and crush it by squeezing it."

Spinks averaged 4.3 yards a carry on 22 rushes as a rookie and was cut by Walt Kiesling the following year. "I think Kiesling was afraid he'd push Rogel for the starting fullback job," said Brandt. "That's the way he operated.

"We played some exhibition games in the South and they still had segregated housing," said Brandt. "Rooney tried to keep the team in the same place as much as possible. He didn't like having anybody separated from the team. The Rams had more blacks on their ballclub than anybody else. They were known around the league as the Harlem Rams.

"The Browns had Marion Motley, and he was such a powerful man. He came to the Steelers in 1955 for his final year in pro ball. I gave way to Leo Elter as the top reserve running back that year. The

Browns used to have the best team and Paul Brown didn't pay those guys much. They were the opposite of the Bears in that regard.

"Rooney was looking after us one way or another. He was always giving us horses to bet on at places like Waterford and Wheeling Downs. He'd come to practice and he was always chewing tobacco, or the end of his cigar. The players would have a tin of Mail Pouch tucked in the back of their pants, and he'd come by and borrow some. We'd say, 'You got any good horses for us?'

"He had a horse farm in Maryland, and I think he had about 20 or 22 horses down there. He'd say, 'They tell me I've got some winners, but I haven't seen any checks yet. All I get are bills for oats.' He talked so low, so funny. He always called me 'Pops.' I'll bet you can't find too many people, can you, who talk against him? He was a very caring person.

"He was the kind of person who didn't want people to know he did anything. I'll bet he helped more people than you know about. I heard he used to drive the people at Three Rivers Stadium crazy the way he'd bring little kids through the gate with him. There'd be kids waiting for him at the gate and they'd go in with him. They didn't have tickets. But who was going to turn them away? They were with 'The Chief.'

"He epitomized Pittsburgh. He liked this town; that's for sure. You know I'm married to a Pittsburgh girl. She's from West Mifflin. Her name was Aurella Heidel. We got married in 1958. My mother-in-law, Dolores Nagy, is celebrating her 90th birthday this week. That's why I'm in town."

"I appreciated the opportunity to play."

I asked "Popcorn" Brandt how he came by his nickname. "I sold popcorn at the ballpark as an 8-year-old," he said. "You did stuff like that to get in the ballgames. That was in the early '40s, and somebody just started calling me 'Popcorn.' It stuck. People remember me for that as much as anything.

"I didn't think much of Joe Bach or Walt Kiesling as coaches. Kiesling had played at my old school, St. Thomas, and he'd been quite a ballplayer for the Green Bay Packers. Gus Dorais from Notre Dame was an assistant coach my rookie season. He and Knute Rockne were a passing combination at Notre Dame. Dorais had coached with the Detroit Lions and was at the end of his career. He was always complaining about the heat at practice. He was always telling me I should stand under a tree and stay out of the sun as much as possible. I think he wanted company.

"They fired Bach during the exhibition season in 1953. We came back to Oleans, New York, where we trained at St. Bonaventure, and some of the coaches didn't come back with us. We had a meeting at 7 o'clock and they told was Kiesling was going to be the coach. Walt was one of Art's old friends; that's why he was always there.

"Art's brother, Father Silas — we called him Father Dan — was the athletic director at St. Bonaventure. He bet on the horses, too. Those priests weren't supposed to have any money, but, as he told us, 'We've got to have a little fun, too.' Art's brother, Jim, was there, too.

"Olean was about 22 miles from Bradford, Pennsylvania. Sometimes we flew out of Buffalo for games and sometimes we flew out of Bradford. We had some real trips, I'll tell you. I remember one time we played an exhibition game with the New York Giants in Des Moines, Iowa. We'd take a bus at 7 a.m. from Olean to Buffalo. We took a train from Buffalo to Chicago. We took a sleeper out of Chicago to Des Moines. Those trains were called 'milk runs' because they stopped at every town to drop off milk and mail. We got to Des Moines at 6 a.m. the day of the game. We'd go to a hotel and they'd have extra beds in each room, like three or four beds to a room. We'd just lie around all day. We played the Giants at Drake Stadium. We'd take a sleeper out of Des Moines after the game and we'd get to Buffalo around midnight. We'd take a bus to Oleans and we'd get back to the dorms around 3 a.m. How'd you like a road trip like that?"

(Pat Livingston added: "I used to make all those trips. One of the buses would always break down. The guys would be trying to figure out in advance what buses were the best bets to break down.")

"We made some trips by airplane to the West Coast," continued Brandt. "It took you all day to get to L.A. or San Francisco back then. You'd fly by DC-4s or DC-6s.

"I remember in my rookie year that we played an exhibition game against the Green Bay Packers at Parade Stadium in Minneapolis. Bach started me because it was my home area. On the first play I had the ball I ran 75 yards for a touchdown. That was on the third play of the game. It was for the benefit of some Father Meagher Catholic program in Minneapolis. It was a Catholic Welfare benefit; they looked after thousands of kids.

"And you didn't get any money for playing in those games, either. They get good money now just for being in camp. We carried only 33 players on the team then and it was tough to make the team. You had to be versatile if you weren't a star. I had another good game against Green Bay, a regular season contest in 1953. I got my first start of the season, in place of Ray Mathews, and scored two touchdowns on short bursts. Rogel gained 168 yards in that game. I played three years with the Steelers and then one year with the Montreal Alouettes in the Canadian Football League. Then I decided I better go to work.

"I got into sales. I went into the distributing business with my brother back in Minnesota in 1962. Later, I went to work with the Peerless Chain Company in Winona, Minnesota and was with them for 30 years before I retired in 1994.

"I've got some team pictures from those days with the Steelers. There were pictures in the game programs and I had everybody sign some of them. I still have my playbook with all the directives and offensive plays in it.

"Art Rooney wasn't the only special man I met when I was in Pittsburgh. I was a pretty good baseball player, too, and Branch Rickey, who was the general manager of the Pirates, wanted to talk to me. That was in 1953. The Pirates were pretty bad the year before (they lost 112 games that season) and they needed help. Branch Rickey was one of the greatest men I ever met. I talked to him several times. The first time we were together for two-and-a-half hours. We talked about a lot of things, and I learned a lot from him. I was an outfielder and a catcher, and I could hit the long ball.

"He asked me if I wanted to go to spring training. I was playing semi-pro baseball during the off-season and making pretty good money for it. I was 27 or 28 at the time, and I didn't want to go play Class D baseball somewhere for $200 a month. Rickey was a special man, though. So was Rooney. Rooney rates near the top. He always had time for somebody. He had a lot of deep feeling for a lot of people. Money wasn't the main reason we were in football back then. You loved the game and you wanted to play. There were only 12 teams and you felt honored to be playing. My ambition as a little kid was to play pro ball. I appreciated the opportunity to play pro ball.

"I enjoyed it. I met a lot of nice people. Money isn't everything. It's something they can't take away from you. I'm doing something worthwhile with my time now. I'm doing volunteer work at Gary Elementary School near my home. I have first graders read to me one day a week, and I have third graders with slow learning ability work with me another day. They're mostly minority kids. I've been doing it since I retired in 1994. My neighbor is a teacher there, and one day she said, 'I have a job for you.'

"The rest of the time I like to play golf — about three times a week — and we've got some great trout fishing out our way. I do some hunting. I go to Montana each year for some hunting. An old customer of mine has a place out there. It's beautiful in Montana."

I told him I thought Art Rooney would be proud of him. He smiled. "That's good enough for me," he said.

Jim O'Brien

Art Rooney statue outside Three Rivers Stadium

Sid Hartman
Tribune star

"Everybody liked the Rooneys."

Sid Hartman is one of the veteran sportswriters on the NFL scene, as the sports editor and columnist for the Minneapolis Tribune. *He had covered sports for 54 years and was a member of the Hall of Fame selection committee.*

The greatest thing about Art Rooney that I can remember goes back to 1953, when he brought his Steelers to Minneapolis for a pre-season exhibition game. We had a Catholic Welfare Fund and Father Meagher was the head of it. It took care of a lot of needy kids, including orphans, and boys and girls homes in Minneapolis. This game was played for the benefit of that fund. Art Rooney received a $15,000 check as his share of the gate, and he gave it back to the promoters, saying it should go to the Catholic Welfare Fund. And he didn't have a lot of money back then. I go back a long way with the Rooneys. Dan and I are good friends, too. He and Max Winter, who owned the Vikings, were very close friends. Everybody in the business liked the Rooneys.

Ed Morgan/Sun-Telegraph in PG Archives

Arthur J. Rooney, president of the Steelers, watches a workout from temporary bleachers installed at Forbes Field in anticipation of soldout game with Philadelphia Eagles in December of 1954.

Father Reardon
Game day companion

Jim O'Brien

"I learned what loyalty meant from Art Rooney."

The Rev. Robert J. Reardon was nearing his 68th birthday when he reflected on his friend Arthur J. Rooney. Father Reardon was serving as the pastor of St. John Capistran Roman Catholic Church in Upper St. Clair, a suburb nine miles south of Pittsburgh. He was having some problems with his hips, which hindered his movement. He required a cane. It wasn't easy for him to get in and out of cars, but it was easy for him to stoop to pet his dog, Cappy, a Welsh corgi, or to reminisce about his days with The Chief. We met March 29, 2001 for lunch at Atria's Restaurant & Tavern in nearby Mt. Lebanon.

I first got to know Art Rooney in 1960, the same year the Pirates beat the Yankees to win the World Series on Bill Mazeroski's famous home run. I was a good friend — a golfing friend — of his son, Tim, and a friend of Tim's wife, June, when they were living in Brighton Heights on the North Side. I was serving at the time at St. Francis Xavier on California Avenue near where they lived. We have been friends ever since.

I was down to Palm Beach the week before and just after the Super Bowl in Tampa, and I stayed with Tim and June. I said Mass for them each morning in their home. They have a beautiful home down there and I was at the place they had in Scarsdale, New York, before they moved to Greenwich, Connecticut. Tim's twin brothers, John and Pat, live in the Palm Beach area year-round and Art Jr. was there, too. Art, Jr. was staying in the same condominium as Jack McGinley and his wife, Marie, who is Art, Sr.'s sister. I used to go down there with The Chief after they bought the track.

I used to sit with Tim and Art Jr. at the Steelers football games. Then a few of The Chief's priest friends died. Father Flanigan and Father Campbell passed away in the early '70s. He needed a new priest. So the Rev. Bob Friday and I joined him and his friends, like Richie Easton, in his box at Three Rivers Stadium. I was there during the best days of the Steelers. Richie Easton lived in Brookline. He drove a delivery truck for *The Pittsburgh Press*, and he drove The Chief back and forth from his home to the stadium, and other places. Richie is deceased now, too, but his son, Richard, is a professor at Washington & Jefferson College. Father Friday is the vice-president of Catholic University in Washington D.C.

Art would always spend some time with his good friend, Tom Foerster. I think Art was his mentor and sponsor as Tom came up the political ranks. They were always close. Tom had coached kids' football teams on the North Side, the Perry Atoms, and they had a lot in common.

Senator John Heinz would stop in the box, too.

I think I was thought to be OK for Art's box because I was a serious football fan and I didn't talk a lot. I spoke at appropriate times. Art never liked to talk too much during the game.

Art Rooney was very comfortable with priests. He had a lot of trust with priests. His brother was a priest, a Franciscan. I didn't know until you told me that Art had spent some time in a seminary himself. I never knew that. That's interesting. He was a daily communicant at Mass. He was a very special person and a most religious man. His family and religion were of paramount importance to him. He was a man who could be at great peace with himself.

When I was sitting with him at Steelers' games, around the third quarter or so, he'd take out his rosary and pray the rosary. It had nothing to do with the outcome of the contest. His religion had a great impact on his sons. The five sons go to Mass every day, or most days anyhow. They're very faithful to that.

"He was at peace with God."

I remember a game where Kenny Anderson, the quarterback of the Cincinnati Bengals, got KOd by the Steelers and had to be helped off the field. I know Art wrote him a letter, and said he hoped he'd be OK and that it wouldn't shorten his career. Art was like that. Our booth was right next to the visiting team's radio booth. Years later, Anderson was the analyst on the Bengals' broadcasts, and he'd always come over and say hello to Art. The year (1988) Art died, Anderson came over and spoke to me. He said he had swallowed hard when he entered the stadium that day, knowing that Art Rooney wouldn't be there.

Everyone misses him. What was the essence of Art Rooney? I think he was at peace with God, and because of that he was at peace with everybody else. No matter what religion or color, he was comfortable with everyone. He was such a religious man, we used to call him "Bishop." And I remember how Myron Cope always called Chuck Noll "the Emperor Chaz" and "Pope."

I remember going to the racetrack — I believe it was Bowie in Maryland — and he'd send different people to place his bets. There were bettors who'd wait to see who was going to place the bet for Art and they'd follow them to the window. They wanted to see what horse Art Rooney was getting down on. They knew he was knowledgeable about horses. He was very talented at handicapping horses. I went to his horse farm in Maryland with him a few times, too. That was always a great getaway.

I don't see any conflict with him being so religious and liking to gamble. He wasn't hurting anyone. It wasn't like his habit was hurting his family, as is the case with a lot of people who like to gamble.

He was just doing something he liked. There was nothing deceptive about it. I don't think there was any conflict with his religious side.

He had a great sense of humor, too. I remember once, after he and his wife, Kathleen, had gone to Ireland, someone asked him, "How did you like Ireland." And he said, "It was beautiful, but I'm glad my grandparents didn't miss the boat." Do you know this year would be his 100th birthday? He was born on (January 27, 1901) the very same day, same year, as my mother, Catherine Scheuble Reardon. That was Mozart's birthday, too.

I conducted the wedding of Kathleen Rooney, the daughter of Tim and June, to Chris Mara, the son of Wellington Mara, the owner of the Giants. That was at Immaculate Heart of Mary Church in Scarsdale about 20 years ago. There was a clip about it on the end of NBC News that night, and I heard a lot about that. They made a lot about a wedding between the Steelers family and the Giants family, the AFC and the NFC. I got to know Wellington Mara from that. I've had three other weddings involving Rooneys. In two of the four weddings I was the main celebrant, and two of them I was a co-celebrant.

Art Jr. has become a dear friend. He's a lot like his dad. I don't think a week goes by that he doesn't send me a card. He and Kay came over and we watched the Super Bowl game with them. Tim had gone to Tampa to see some of his friends with the Giants.

It was something that two of Art's dearest friends in the league, Wellington Mara and Art Modell, were the owners of the competing teams, the Giants and Baltimore Ravens, in the Super Bowl. I know Modell, and I like him. He was at the Mara-Rooney wedding, too. He gave a great toast at the rehearsal dinner. He was very sincere.

Early on, when the Steelers got good, the Cincinnati Bengals were playing the Pittsburgh Steelers in an exhibition game (in 1969). I was the spotter for the Cincinnati radio station. Terry Hanratty started to warm up to come in during the second half and the fans got excited. The play-by-play man from Cincinnati asked me, "What's that?" I said, "That's Hanratty." And the announcer said, "My spotter is Father Reardon, the Diocesan Director of the Confraternity of Christian Doctrine (religious education). He's all excited because Notre Dame's Terry Hanratty is warming up." That was funny.

Chuck Noll was in my parish, you know, when he lived in Upper St. Clair during his twenty-some years as the Steelers coach. He and his wife, Marianne, attended Mass regularly at St. John Capistran.

"He wasn't a show-off."

Any time famous people would come to Pittsburgh they always wanted to meet Art Rooney. So famous people were always stopping by the box before the game to shake hands with Art and wish him well. I remember this time, during the mid-'70s, when the cast of "Hill

Street Blues" came by to say hello. Three members of their party were graduates of Carnegie Mellon University and they were in town for some event at CMU. They had the hottest show on TV at the time. It was No. 1 in the ratings. After they left, Art asked, "What show are they in?"

He was told it was called "Hill Street Blues." And he said, "What time's that on?" He was told it was on at 10 o'clock. He said, "Oh, I'm in bed by then."

Art and Dan came to my 25th anniversary of my ordination as a priest. You hardly knew they were there. They knew it was my day. Art's whole thing was to fall into the cracks. He didn't want any fanfare. He saw me beforehand and expressed his good wishes, not when everyone else was there. He wasn't a show-off. He impressed people who knew him as a very good person. Loyalty was a big thing with him. I learned what loyalty meant from Art Rooney.

It was a blessing to get to know him and spend so much time with him. The priests loved him. That was evident at his funeral Mass. St. Peter's was packed, and many of the people present were priests and nuns. Bishop Leonard presided at the Mass, and Bishop Wuerl assisted him. I remember when he called for the peace offering that Al Davis of the Oakland Raiders and Pete Rozelle, the NFL Commissioner, shook hands. And they had been in a feud. Everyone talked about that.

It was exhilarating to be with him at the games. The TV people always showed him during the game and, since I was sitting next to him, I got on sometimes, too. One time I was chomping down on a hot dog when the camera came on us. Friends of mine on the West Coast called and asked, "Hey, was that hot dog good?"

Toward the end of his life, the great part for me was not going to the Steelers games, but being with Art. I was just happy to be with Art. He was sincere as anything when he'd pull out his rosary in the late going. It gave him a certain peace.

Arthur J. Rooney and Father Robert J. Reardon were constant companions in box at Three Rivers Stadium in '70s and '80s.

It wasn't easy
Kissing Three Rivers Stadium goodbye

"I got tears in my eyes."
— Mrs. Bob Prince

A little bit of all of us went down with Three Rivers Stadium. That was certainly true for Betty Prince who watched the extensive television coverage of the implosion of the stadium that unforgettable Sunday morning, February 11, 2001.

Mrs. Prince was comfortable in her bathrobe, sitting on a well-stuffed couch in her townhouse in Mt. Lebanon, just south of Pittsburgh and about eight miles from the home of the Pirates and the Steelers. She thought of the great times she and her husband, Bob Prince, enjoyed during the early years of the stadium, especially 1971 when the Pirates won the World Series.

Bob Prince was a Pittsburgh institution. For 28 years, from 1948 to 1975, he was "the voice of the Pirates," broadcasting their games on radio and TV. In his early years, he also was a broadcaster for Steelers and Penn State football. KDKA sportscaster John Steigerwald said one of his best memories of Three Rivers Stadium was when Prince returned to the broadcast booth for a few Pirates games in early May, 1985. Prince died from cancer on June 10 that year.

KDKA's Saturday night special on the implosion of Three Rivers Stadium was called "Kissing It Goodbye," borrowing its title from one of Bob Prince's signature home run calls.

Prince was one of the people I thought about as I watched the implosion coverage in my family room, happy to be warm, with a cup of hot coffee at hand. I thought there was no better way to watch the whole thing than by surfing the three local TV channels that were carrying stories about the most-covered event since the Vietnam War, or at least the comeback of Mario Lemieux.

I thought of Art Rooney and Danny Murtaugh, Chuck Noll and Chuck Tanner, Jack Fleming and Myron Cope, Lanny Frattare and Steve Blass, Roberto Clemente and Willie Stargell, Terry Bradshaw and Franco Harris, Jack Lambert and Joe Greene. I thought of so many wonderful people associated with the Steelers and Pirates and my colleagues in the sports media. I thought about special times with my family there.

Mrs. Prince and I agreed that Greene, the great defensive lineman of the Steelers, summed up the leveling of Three Rivers Stadium best by saying, "It was a building. It's where I went to work. The people in the building made it special. It served its purpose well. The bottom line is that it was the people."

That landmark reminded us of those people, and that's why we'll miss it the most, not because of the games played there, great as many of them were. "I got tears in my eyes and a lump in my throat when it went down," said Mrs. Prince over the telephone, "and I said something to Bob."

Did Bob say anything back?

"I'm still waiting to hear from him," said Mrs. Prince, laughing at her own remark. "I'm still on hold."

She and Bob also shared a great sense of humor during their 44 years of marriage. Mrs. Prince, 84, said she felt fine except for a piercing pain — "like a hot sword" — in her right shoulder.

"I was amazed to see it all happen," Mrs. Prince continued. "It was such an absolutely phenomenal event. They took it all down without damaging the new football stadium 65 feet away. That was impressive. I was just sitting here and I thought, 'There goes our lounge box 334.' We called it 'The Jesters' Box.' That's where we'd take the granddaughters. I remember our friends being critical of us for having the grandkids in those seats that were priceless during the World Series. Bob would tell them, 'They're my grandkids.' That was enough for him."

Mrs. Prince planned to discuss the stadium implosion with her daughter, Nancy Prince Thomas, of Bethel Park, and her son, Bob, Jr., who lives in Michigan. The grandchildren, Kim Bacchiochi, 35, and Casey Gold, 33, who both reside in Venetia, were saddened by the event. "Kim wanted none of this business," said Mrs. Prince. "She said, 'They are destroying all of my youth.' She remembered how much fun we had there."

All of us do. I wasn't feeling so hot to begin with over the same weekend, fighting a lingering head cold. This didn't help. We were supposed to be excited about what was to come, the openings of a new football stadium that would be called Heinz Field, and PNC Park, but Three Rivers Stadium will be missed on the North Side skyline. It hurt to see it go.

Bob Prince waves to crowd at Three Rivers Stadium during his brief comeback at KDKA microphone for Pirates-Dodgers series in early May of 1985. Looking on are Lanny Frattare, at left, and Bob's daughter, Nancy, at far right.

The Implosion
Going . . . Going . . . Gone!

Three Rivers Stadium is leveled

On February 11, 2001, the demolition crew used more than 4,800 pounds of dynamite to topple this massive structure. Opened on July 16, 1970, the stadium was home field for Pittsburgh's professional baseball and football teams for over 30 years.

Three Rivers Stadium
Still has a wedding ring to it

I was telling my wife Kathie about some of my fondest memories of Three Rivers Stadium. Then she told me some of hers. I liked hers better. Hers weren't about games. They were about special times and special people in our lives. That's what stadiums and ballparks are really all about.

It was the home field for a whole generation who never saw the Pirates play at Forbes Field or never saw the Steelers at the ballpark by Schenley Park or at Pitt Stadium.

During its 31 years of existence, Three Rivers Stadium was a great home field for the Pirates and the Steelers, especially during the decade of the '70s when Pittsburgh was called "The City of Champions."

I missed most of that period. I was away for ten years, one year in Miami and nine years in New York, and returned home in time to cover the Steelers for *The Pittsburgh Press* during the 1979 season. I remember standing in the end zone at Three Rivers Stadium as the Steelers were completing an AFC championship victory over the Houston Oilers. Rocky Bleier ran behind Ted Petersen on an inside smash play for the final TD in a 27-13 win over Bum Phillips' ballclub on January 6, 1980. The Steelers would be going to the Super Bowl, I thought, and I'd be going with them. I was so excited. I had picked a good time to come home.

Others may hold out for the "Immaculate Reception" by Franco Harris in the Steelers' AFC playoff victory over the Oakland Raiders in 1972, or those years when the Pirates were winning the World Series in 1971 and 1979, or the National League East titles in the early '90s. I remember being there to salute the Penguins in a parade at the Stadium in the early '90s after they had won their second straight Stanley Cup.

Kathie has different kinds of memories. She remembers us going to a concert featuring Elton John and Billy Joel about six or seven years earlier — it might have been the best doubleheader ever played there — when she nearly lost her wedding ring at a Steelers-Browns game in the early '80s, and a Pitt-Penn State game on Thanksgiving Weekend in 1976. She didn't remember the significance of that Pitt-Penn State game. She just remembers that we were with college classmates of mine, friends from our New York days, and that she was pregnant with our second daughter, Rebecca. That puts it all in its proper perspective.

I reminded her that Pitt beat Penn State, 24-7, to complete its regular season and went on to beat Georgia, 27-3, in the Sugar Bowl. They finished with a 12-0 record, a national championship and star Tony Dorsett won the Heisman Trophy as the nation's outstanding football player. It is an oft overlooked sports highlight in the history of Three Rivers Stadium.

That Pitt-Penn State game was played under the lights at Three Rivers Stadium on Friday night, Nov. 26. It was originally scheduled for Pitt Stadium the next day, but was moved so it could be shown in prime time on national television. Those were the days when Pitt and Penn State played each other in the traditional final game of the season.

Kathie went to one Steelers game a year when I was covering the club. She has always been very selective about her sports viewing. During the summer of 2000, she stayed up to 11:30 every night to watch the Olympic Games, one of her favorites along with Wimbledon and the U.S. Open Tennis Championships.

At one of those Steelers games, when she was with her brother and sister-in law, Harvey and Diane Churchman, she was standing on a walkway at the top of the stadium before the game, watching the crowd coming in below.

Her wedding ring slipped off and fell to the ground at the base of the stadium. A gentleman picked up the wedding ring, then looked up to Kathie, and waved for her to come down and retrieve it. She did. She thanked the man profusely for his kind act.

She drove by Three Rivers Stadium every day on the way to work as a social worker in the oncology unit at Allegheny General Hospital for ten years. Seeing the stadium reminded her of some good times in our lives.

One of the author's most cherished memories of Three Rivers Stadium was taking his daughters to a Steelers practice where they met team owner Art Rooney and some of the players. Sarah O'Brien, at 7, and her sister, Rebecca at 3$\frac{1}{2}$, sat on rolled up tarp on sideline during the 1980 season.

Barry Foley
Foreman at Three Rivers Stadium

"He treated us like we were one of his sons."

Barry Foley, a former foreman of the ground crew at Three Rivers Stadium, enjoys playing with his grandchildren at his home in Beechview. He was pleased to be asked about Art Rooney and his relationship with the ground crew.

I was on the ground crew at Three Rivers Stadium from the start in 1970. I got my start as a part-time member of the ground crew at Forbes Field in 1960. Pretty good timing, huh? I grew up in Oakland and my uncle was Eddie Dunn, who was in charge of the ground crew. He gave me the job. So I was there when Mazeroski hit the home run, and I knew all those guys: Clemente, Hoak, Haddix, Friend, Law, Burgess, Groat, all of them.

I went to all four of the Super Bowls the Steelers won. There were 16 men on the full-time ground crew and we all got to go. No wives, just the guys. Some of the wives went on their own and met up with us. The Steelers started taking two guys from the ground crew on each charter flight starting in the early '70s. We picked the games out of a hat. It was a free ride all the way, airplane, hotel and meals.

Art Rooney was great with us. He treated us like we were one of his sons. Danny was just as well with us. He has many of the qualities of his father, even if he does have a different personality.

I became the foreman of the ground crew in 1992 when Steve "Dirt" DeNardo stepped down and retired. He was a legend on his own. When the Steelers went to Phoenix for their last Super Bowl, Dan Rooney took me and my wife on the charter, and he took two other guys. I think there are so many in the Rooney family now that there wasn't room for the entire ground crew this time.

He was something else. He treated us all the same, and that was with great dignity. He was one of us. That's why he was named an honorary member of the ground crew. I think they gave him that award at the Dapper Dan Sports Dinner.

"When my dad died, our family held a draft to divvy up his possessions. I took his prayer book with my No. 1 choice. It's filled with funeral cards."
— Art Rooney Jr.

Rocky Bleier
A bar story

"That story was our bond."

Robert "Rocky" Bleier of Appleton, Wisconsin was a popular running back for the Steelers for 12 years (1968, 1970-1980), and one of the team's all-time Top Ten groundgainers. He turned 55 on March 5, 2001. Bleier was a valued member of the Steelers' four Super Bowl teams of the '70s. He was a 16th round draft choice of the Steelers in 1968 after a fine career at Notre Dame. He suffered wounds in battle in Vietnam that prompted some doctors to question whether Bleier would walk again, but he battled back and proved he could play with the best. Art Rooney talked his son, Dan, and Chuck Noll into giving Bleier some extra time to rehabilitate before making a final decision on him. Noll had cut him from the squad on two different occasions. There was a book and TV movie about his career called "Fighting Back." He won the George Halas Award in 1974 as the NFL's Most Courageous Player, and the NFL Man of the Year Award in 1980. He appeared at the Mario Lemieux Celebrity Invitational Golf Tournament at The Club at Nevillewood on June 8, 2000 and talked about Art Rooney. I saw him again with his wife, Jan, at Atria's Restaurant & Tavern on April 22, 2001, not far from their home in the Virginia Manor section of Mt. Lebanon. They have two daughters, Ellen, 3, and Rose, 2, (named for their grandmothers) whom they adopted from the Ukraine.

Mr. Rooney always had a story about each person. That was their bond. He'd tell you stories and you'd tell him stories. Somewhere in there was a story that he always associated with you, and would bring up from time to time. He had a favorite story for so many people. One of our bonds was that we both grew up living over our dad's saloon.

The Steelers were playing the Green Bay Packers in an exhibition game in Green Bay in 1969. When they got to Green Bay, Mr. Rooney asked Ed Kiely, "Doesn't Bleier's parents have a restaurant around here? That's where we should have dinner tonight."

Now Appleton was about 25 miles from Green Bay, so they weren't just walking around the block. My parents, Bob and Ellen, operated a popular neighborhood bar-restaurant. They usually packed the place on weekends. When Mr. Rooney arrived, he asked a waitress if she could get Mrs. Bleier for him. "I'm Mrs. Bleier," she said. And Mr. Rooney said, "Oh, you couldn't be. You're too young to be Rocky's mother." He said, "I'm Art Rooney with the Pittsburgh Steelers," and my mother said, "Oh, Mr. Rooney, it's so nice to meet you and to have you here." He said they needed a table for four for dinner. "That's wonderful," she said. "Hold this. It's your number on the wait list."

Mr. Rooney loved that. He always mentioned what my mother did when they went to our family's restaurant. My mother denied the story, so I don't know. I think we had some other bonds between us, too. My religious faith was important to me. When I was in sixth grade, I came down with Oshgood Slaughter disease. It's when you grow faster than your joints. It's quite painful. I couldn't play sports that summer. I wasn't supposed to go out for sports in seventh grade at St. Joseph's Grade School, but I sneaked out, but someone told my dad what I was doing, and I had to quit.

I was on very successful high school basketball and football teams. We almost never lost. Everybody came to my dad's place and talked about sports. I wanted to please people and I wanted to be liked. Being a small town, everybody knew my father. My father always said the only thing you really had was your reputation. I never forgot that. From my mother, I learned to have a sense of yourself and to be an individual. At what point did I turn into my father?

I set different goals as I went along. At first, it was great just to be on the high school team. I was lucky to have a terrific coach in Torchy Clark. Then I thought it would be great if I could make all-conference. That would be the greatest thing. I did that as a sophomore. I made all-conference on offense and defense. I figured if I could score two touchdowns a game I could make all-state and I did that as a junior. Then I made the *Parade* All-America team as a senior. In high school, I didn't think about being a professional. Not even college. I was worried about the next game. I was worried about my next date for the high school dance. Then I go to Notre Dame and I was on a national championship team in 1966. I was the captain of the team my senior year. Then I defy the odds and make the Steelers and come back from being injured in Vietnam to stick with the Steelers, and play on all those Super Bowl teams. I have been so fortunate all the way.

When I look back, I think about that experience in sixth grade when I got Oshgood Slaughter disease. I had a Sister Hilaire, and she gave me a novena. It was a nine-week novena, not the usual nine-day novena. It lasted for 63 days. I had to say the rosary every night and pray for healing. I prayed for good health. That sparked a good appreciation for my faith.

I got healthy. I believe that novena led to all those good things down the road, being at the right place at the right time. I never told this to anyone, but I think that novena really defined my soul. It was something that was so powerful in my life. Art Rooney was a man who certainly believed in the power of prayer and no one had a greater respect for saying the rosary than he did. We didn't talk about that, but it was a bond, I'm sure.

> *"Being a pro football player is a great life.*
> *It gave me a status different from my peers,*
> *and I liked the attention. So I was going to try*
> *everything to make it."*
> — Rocky Bleier

Jan and Rocky Bleier enjoy a wine-tasting party at Station Square.

Photos by Jim O'Brien

Mellon Mario Lemieux Celebrity Invitational at The Club at Nevillewood always attracts a star-studded lineup including, from left to right, Rocky Bleier, John Paul, executive vice president of sponsor UPMC, and Mel Blount.

Lynn Swann
A Hall of Famer, at last

"I just started crying."

A rt Rooney always said that any football team, even a bad football team, could have a good highlight film. As long as the Steelers had Lynn Swann on their team they were always assured of having a good highlight film. Swann always made these dives and grabs and aerial acrobatics to snare the ball out of the high-flying defender's grasp, especially in the big games, and starred in so many of those annual promotional reflections on the previous season.

Consider Swann's performance in Super Bowl X. He made three sensational catches of Terry Bradshaw passes that still rank among the greatest catches in championship game history. He had four catches altogether for a Super Bowl record 161 yards. One was a 64-yard touchdown pass with 2:02 left in the final quarter at the Orange Bowl that would prove the game-winner in a 21-17 victory over the favored Dallas Cowboys. Swann was voted the game's MVP.

Swann only stayed nine seasons with the Steelers, however, and that shorter-than-usual career became an albatross around his neck when it came time for Hall of Fame consideration.

He had good reasons to step down when he did. The injuries started to pile up toward the end, and kept him sidelined for longer stretches and, besides, he had always known he wanted to get into the TV broadcasting business. He majored in public relations and took graduate courses in radio-TV production at the University of Southern California. He had other opportunities.

Even so, it was those nine seasons that proved a stumbling block when it came time for the voting for the Pro Football Hall of Fame when Swann became eligible five years after he retired following the 1982 season. He had some spectacular catches and game-winning heroics to his credit and three Pro Bowl appearances but his overall numbers paled by comparison to some receivers who had stuck around longer. No one questioned Jim Brown's qualifications for the Hall of Fame when he quit after nine seasons to devote full time to movies, but no one had numbers like Jim Brown managed in that sensational stretch.

So Swann had a hard time getting into the Pro Football Hall of Fame. And it hurt. He thought he deserved such honors. Swann was only 5-11, 180 pounds, but he was never short or light on self-confidence. He believed he belonged up there, enshrined in Canton, Ohio. Yes, he truly believed he belonged with the best.

He could beat the biggest baddest defenders to the ball when Terry Bradshaw tossed those bombs his way, and he wanted proper credit for it.

He is a handsome fellow with a smooth cocoa-colored complexion and a smooth style. He could talk the talk and walk the walk. It's a shame that Lance Alworth of the San Diego Chargers had already claimed the nickname of "Bambi" because it would have suited Swann even better.

Swann had been on the ballot for 14 years and came close a couple of times, but no cigar. He knew there were other deserving Steelers in the team's history who had disappeared from consideration after awhile, like L.C. Greenwood, one of his teammates on those great Steelers' teams of the '70s, and Andy Russell and Jack Butler and John Henry Johnson. Johnson got in later, by vote of a special panel that considers exceptional players who might have been passed over in the initial balloting process.

Dan Rooney, the president of the Steelers, was voted into the Pro Football Hall of Fame with the Class of 2000, and he was sensitive to the suggestion that he might have delayed Swann's induction another year. So Rooney went to bat for Swann and called all the members of the media who vote for the Hall of Fame and put in a strong recommendation for Swann. Chuck Noll, who was voted into the Hall of Fame in 1993, two years after he retired as coach of the Steelers — coaches come up for election earlier than players — also lobbied for Swann.

"Lynn Swann was one of the greatest receivers ever to play the game," said Rooney. "He not only played super in the Super Bowls, but he did so much in the regular season and the playoffs to get us in the Super Bowls. He played at a time when the ball was not being thrown on every down, but he was a very important part of the success of the Pittsburgh Steelers running game. When the NFL changed the rules to emphasize the passing game, he proved to be one of the great receivers in the league."

Noll, who coached the Steelers from 1961 to 1991, knew how much Swann meant to the Steelers' success after they drafted him in the first round out of USC in 1972. That was the first season the Steelers made the playoffs. That was the year of "the Immaculate Reception." Here's what Noll had to say:

"Lynn Swann was like an acrobat, the way he would come across the middle and catch the ball high in the air, knowing that he might get hit. Nobody played better in big games, and that's the mark of a great player. The reason he doesn't have as many receptions as some players is because we ran the ball so much. That was my choice. If we threw the ball a lot more, he could easily have as many catches as other players who are in the Hall of Fame."

Steelers' analyst Myron Cope offered some kind words as well. Cope always had a soft spot for Swann because he appreciated how Swann helped popularize "the Terrible Towel" by waving it on the sidelines to stir up the crowds at Three Rivers Stadium.

"Lynn Swann changed the game of football," declared Cope. "He raised the level of expectations for players and coaches all over the country. The only player that came close to his style was Paul Warfield, and he's in the Hall of Fame. When people made a spectacular catch, they called it a 'Lynn Swann catch.'"

Said Swann: "I always felt I had an impact on the game, but this is the culmination, and I stand here representing what I feel was the greatest single collection of talent ever on the same football team at the same time."

Swann joined Joe Greene, Jack Ham, Jack Lambert, Mel Blount, Franco Harris, Terry Bradshaw, Mike Webster and Noll in the Hall of Fame, along with club owners Art Rooney, Sr. and Dan Rooney, from those Steelers of the '70s.

"It will make me appreciate it more."

I spotted Lynn Swann in the lobby of the Regency Hyatt in Tampa, Florida on Friday night, January 26, 2001, on the eve of the annual meeting of 38 media members on the Hall of Fame selection committee. They always meet the day before the Super Bowl.

I had lobbied for Swann with one of the voters, Furman Bisher of the *Atlanta Constitution*. I had breakfast with him the day before and put in a pitch for Swann as a deserving candidate. Bisher said he thought John Stallworth was more deserving. Stallworth stayed 14 seasons with the Steelers and, of course, had better numbers.

I told Bisher they were both deserving, but that when they were in the same lineup that Bradshaw looked first to Swann when he was checking out his receivers. Swann was the go-to guy in those glory days. Stallworth would bristle about that, but to himself. He did address the subject on occasion with Bradshaw, but in the privacy of the locker room.

Swann and Stallworth were both proud men. They both believed in their own abilities, that they were second to none. Unlike Troy Edwards and Plaxico Burress, two wide receivers who were the Steelers' No. 1 draft choices in 1999 and 2000, respectively, they never jawed about it on the field, in the locker room and certainly not to the media.

Swann and Stallworth spoiled us. They were so skilled, so smooth, so discreet, so classy — on and off the field. Both were well spoken, though Swann was more apt to get on the grandstand. Stallworth was more a silent weapon.

Both were born in the South and had a Southern charm about them. Swann was born in Alcoa, Tennessee — where Pittsburgh-based Alcoa had an aluminum plant — but grew up in California. Stallworth was born in Tuscaloosa, Alabama, the college town where Bear Bryant held sway, but had to go to a small black school, Alabama A&M, to play ball. He has always gone home to Alabama, whereas Swann has, somewhat surprisingly, chosen to call Pittsburgh home.

Joe Greene carries teammate Lynn Swann off the field after a fierce hit by Oakland Raiders defensive backs leveled the Steelers' star receiver.

Celebrity lineup at fund-raiser at Hilton Hotel includes, left to right, Foge Fazio, Franco Harris, President George Bush, Marcus Allen, Dinah Shore, Danny Marino and Lynn Swann. There were four future Hall of Famers in the picture.

When I saw Swann in the hotel lobby in Tampa, I approached him and greeted him. He was wearing a black sport coat over a black jersey. He was looking good, as always. He was nearing his 49th birthday (March 7, 1952 birthdate), but he appeared younger.

I wished him good luck in the next day's voting, and told him I hoped he would be elected. Swann has very expressive dark eyes. He likes to make faces. He rolled his eyes and made a face when I suggested he had a good chance to be elected to the Pro Football Hall of Fame. He shrugged his shoulders. "We'll see," he said, almost resignedly. "We'll see." Swann always played games with sportswriters and wasn't sure what to make of them.

I went to the Tampa Convention Center around noon the next day to attend a press conference to announce the Class of 2001 for the Pro Football Hall of Fame.

Swann was at his hotel, staying in his room. He called his wife and told her he was going to be all right. He didn't think he'd been selected. He told her he wasn't too dejected and wanted to make sure she'd be fine, too. He hadn't gotten a call to tell him he had been elected. He had waited for that call so many times, yes, 13 times and now he thought that he was going to be passed by once again.

He felt sorry, he said, for his two young children who had wished him good luck and told him they would say some prayers for him.

As Dodgers' fans in Brooklyn used to say, "Wait till next year."

Then he got the call. He made it. Yes, he was in. The Hall had called the Class of 2001. There were seven of them. They would be billed in the headlines of the next day's issue of *The Tampa Tribune* as "The Magnificent 7."

The subhead read: "Lynn Swann and six others get word saying they'll be inducted into the Pro Football Hall of Fame."

Swann seemed to get star billing in most of the reports from Tampa, including the international wire service stories. He was at the head of the class. He was at the far left in the picture of the five honored players who were present at the press conference at the Tampa Convention Center. The others, left to right, were Marv Levy, Jackie Slater, Jack Youngblood and Nick Buoniconti. I was happy for all of them, especially Buoniconti. I had broken into the pro football writing ranks as a member of *The Miami News* in 1969 when Buoniconti was the Dolphins' defensive captain. I'd had a reunion with him the previous June at the Mellon Mario Lemieux Celebrity Invitational at The Club at Nevillewood.

Dan Rooney was among the first to congratulate Swann when he entered the room. This was some stage. There were 22 TV cameras at the back of the hall, and pro football's most distinguished writers and broadcasters were assembled in the room.

Asked what happened when he heard the good news, Swann smiled that million-dollar smile and said, "I tried to take a deep breath and I just started crying.

"You just don't know what an honor it is to be here after 14 years," Swann told the assemblage. "I've seen guys at the podium (in Canton); I introduced Franco. I've seen guys cry and I said, 'No, that won't be me.' I cried all the way over here."

He said he didn't know what would happen when he stood on the steps of the Hall of Fame come August 4. He hoped he would be all right.

He met with writers from Pittsburgh backstage a half-hour after the ceremony and had regained his composure by then.

"I appreciate the fact," said Swann, "that while it may have taken me 14 years and while that may have been difficult, maybe it will make me appreciate it more to be in the Hall of Fame."

He personally thanked Ed Bouchette, the beat writer for the *Post-Gazette* and Pittsburgh's representative on the selection committee, for making a strong pitch on his behalf at the voting session.

Swann said he didn't know who he would get to introduce him at the Hall of Fame. During the next month, he selected Stallworth, which was fitting. He hoped it would help Stallworth's chances for election to share the spotlight in Canton.

Dan Rooney said he was more emotional about Swann's selection than he was about his own the year before. "I couldn't be more pleased," remarked Rooney. "Now, it's all great that he's in. I really was concerned. I didn't want to be here in place of him. Now, it's complete." Well, almost. Stallworth comes next.

Swann made the Hall along with offensive linemen Jackie Slater, Mike Munchak and Ron Yary, defensive stalwarts Nick Buoniconti and Jack Youngblood and Coach Marv Levy. No more than seven can be elected and all received at least 80 percent of the votes. Munchak and Yary were not present at the press conference.

Bisher came by and told me he voted for Stallworth early on, but gave in and went with Swann as the voting continued.

On March 6, a long-waited announcement came forth that the veterans committee had selected Pirates second baseman Bill Mazeroski to the Baseball Hall of Fame. The committee had met in Tampa by coincidence. So two of Pittsburgh's most popular athletes were voted into the Hall of Fame in the same Florida city. Maz, who was at the Pirates training camp in Bradenton when the word came, rushed to Tampa for a press conference. Maz would be inducted in ceremonies at Cooperstown, New York on August 5.

I go to the Pro Football Hall of Fame ceremonies every summer, usually in late July or early August. It is a rite of summer. I have gone there for at least ten years in the company of my pals, Bill Priatko and Rudy Celigoi. We immediately made plans to attend both Hall of Fame inductions.

Two of Pittsburgh's finest clutch performers, two big game guys, were going to be properly recognized. In both cases the wait had been too long. At last, they were getting their due. It would be a great doubleheader for anybody who cared about sports in Pittsburgh or its tri-state area. It would be an idyllic weekend. I couldn't wait.

"We are the best receivers on one team."

Seeing Lynn Swann and John Stallworth together again, this time on the steps of the Pro Football Hall of Fame in Canton, would bring back some great memories for all the Steelers' people, from Dan Rooney, the team president, up to the team's fans filling the bleachers and hillsides by Fawcett Stadium. Steelers' fans always make their presence known in Canton, with their black and gold uniforms, their "Terrible Towels" and their often raucous behavior. They turn it into a tailgate party.

Swann and Stallworth both made terrific touchdown catches in the Steelers' last Super Bowl victory, the 31-19 triumph over the Los Angeles Rams in Super Bowl XIV in Pasadena, California. My wife Kathleen and I were there to witness that, less than a year after we had returned to Pittsburgh after ten years away, one in Miami and nine in New York. It was a game we'll never forget.

Afterward, I asked Swann about the Swann-Stallworth combination. "I believe that John and I are the best pass receivers on one team," said Swann without a flinch. "If I didn't think we were the best, then we wouldn't be. We've proven over the years that we are. We have never been intimidated. I think John and I will catch the ball anywhere, under any circumstances, under any conditions — wind, rain or snow. There is no foundation for any other opinion, except that we are the best 1-2 pass-catching combination in pro football. John Stallworth and Lynn Swann are the complete receivers."

Stallworth was so spectacular with two difficult over-the-shoulder receptions that many felt that he, and not Bradshaw, should have been the game's most valuable player.

Swann was already working part-time in broadcasting when he offered that striking commentary in assessing his and Stallworth's abilities. He began his broadcasting career in 1976. Upon retirement from playing football in January, 1983, he went to work full-time with ABC Sports, which continues through today.

Bradshaw was the biggest fan of Swann and Stallworth in those glory years. "It's a nice situation," he said, "to be able to take your pick of those guys when you're going deep with a pass. They make me look pretty good."

Other teammates of Swann offered tributes to him in a lobbying effort to get him into the Hall of Fame.

"In the big game, Lynn Swann made it happen for us," said Joe Greene. "He made so many spectacular catches, and he did it so gracefully that he made it look routine. But they were more than routine; they were the type of catches that win games."

Mel Blount went one better. "Without him, we would not have won four Super Bowl rings," said Blount. "If he played under today's rules, there's no telling what he would do."

Jon Kolb came to his support as well. "People forget that Lynn Swann led the league in punt return yardage as a rookie because of his great running ability," commented Kolb. "Our quarterback took a seven-step drop and we ran deeper routes than anyone in the league. Terry Bradshaw liked to throw deep, and Lynn's ability to go get the ball helped Terry a great deal. It wasn't the high-percentage passing game that many teams run today. But no receiver came up with more big plays. His ability as a receiver helped open up the running game."

Bradshaw could throw into double coverage, a no-no to so many of the TV analysts, because he believed that Swann and Stallworth would go up and get the ball. Swann was small in stature, but he had that track and field and dancing background to give him the leaping ability and timing to soar over others to get the ball. He was an outstanding long jumper, high jumper, pole vaulter, hurdler, you name it in his schoolboy days.

"My football playing was a fluke," he once told me. "I only played football because my older brother played. Gene Kelly should have been a football player and I should have been a dancer."

Swann said at the Mellon Mario Lemieux Celebrity Invitational that his boyhood heroes were not sports people. He admired Sammy Davis, Fred Astaire and Pittsburgh-born Gene Kelly, all dancers and entertainers. "If you thought I was fast on a football field," he said, "you should have seen me running home from dancing school so the kids in the neighborhood wouldn't see where I'd been."

His mother made him go to dancing school, but he came to like it.

"I never wanted to play football," said Swann, in a surprising revelation. "I played at USC because I had a scholarship and I couldn't afford college without it. I played professional ball because I was a first round draft choice. I promised myself I would not play more than five years. Then six came, then seven, then eight, then nine."

Swann stays active in the community, serving on several boards of directors and as a spokesperson for several national organizations. Since 1980, Swann has been the national spokesman for Big Brothers Big Sisters of America. He has won NFL Man of the Year honors for his community service.

"I knew that young people looked up to me when I was playing. I think that really good ballplayers see themselves as heroes, making great catches and great runs," said Swann. "Then whenever it happens, you say, 'Hey, I knew I could do it.' I'd been wanting to do something super for a long time.

"I take with me most of all the character of the people I played with. It was a great opportunity to grow and mature in Pittsburgh. The Steelers insisted we do something in the community, to give back something to the city and our fans. Some people are surprised I stayed here since I grew up near San Francisco and played college ball in Los Angeles and do a lot of work out of New York City. But I like the people here — we were always the city's team — and I feel comfortable here.

> **"I consider myself a Pittsburgher.**
> **This is my town."**
> — Mario Lemieux

"I just want to be remembered as one of several people who played on one of the greatest teams ever assembled in American sports history, and as someone who gives to his community and his friends above and beyond his athletic abilities.

"I take personal pride as a person who played his best games under pressure. When the game meant the most and we had our backs up against the wall, my teammates could count on me to come through. Maybe it was fear of failure that made me play better in such circumstances."

He said he was grateful for the support he felt he received from Day One from Dan Rooney, the team president, and his father, Art Rooney.

"Mr. Rooney had this reputation as a nice, old grandfather type," said Swann. "But he was tough, especially when it came to contract time with the players, and he passed that on to Dan. Mr. Rooney was in the background, but he was still giving advice to Dan, and he didn't want him to give away the bank.

"Cigars and stories, that's what I'll remember the most about Mr. Rooney. He always had those cigars and he was always telling stories."

Jim O'Brien

Five of the seven members of the Class of 2001 for the Pro Football Hall of Fame were present in the Tampa Convention Center at Super Bowl XXXV, including, left to right, Lynn Swann, Marv Levy, Jackie Slater, Jack Youngblood and Nick Buoniconti.

Paul Zimmerman
Dr. Z loved Art Rooney

"He was the perfect owner."

One of the most respected observers of the pro football scene, Paul Zimmerman is known to his faithful followers as Dr. Z. He has been with Sports Illustrated *over 20 years, and prior to that he covered the New York Jets for the* New York Post *when I was working at that same afternoon tabloid newspaper in the '70s. It's known that Zimmerman didn't vote for Dan Rooney for induction in the Pro Football Hall of Fame because Dan had fired his brother, Art, Jr., someone Zimmerman long admired in the organization. "I know I should be more objective about such things," he said, "but I couldn't' shake that. I'm not proud of that."*

Art Rooney was the nicest person I ever met connected with football, flat out, slam dunk. It's not even close. Bill Veeck, the baseball owner, was the most impressive person I ever met in sports. Art Rooney was the nicest. His son, Artie, is not far behind. I hear from Artie a lot to this day. He keeps me posted on Pittsburgh and sends me postcards with drawings of his dad on them.

My son, Michael, is the most avid Steelers' fan in the state of New Jersey. I remember this Steelers' game in 1980, which marked the end of the dynasty. Jim Plunkett and Oakland beat them (45-34) in Pittsburgh. Mikey was about 8 at the time, and he just adopted the Steelers for some reason, probably because they had been so good. The game was on Monday Night Football. Mikey could only watch till half time and he had to go to bed. Terry Bradshaw got hurt, and Jack Lambert got hurt. Mikey was sitting there in his pajamas. Tears were running down his cheeks.

The next time I was in Pittsburgh I told Art Rooney that story. Three days later, an autographed football came to our home from the Steelers. Mikey went tearing out of the house like a madman to show his friends his football. Two years later, I took him to Pittsburgh to see the Steelers against San Diego in an AFC playoff game. I took him to see Mr. Rooney. He rushed over to Mr. Rooney and hugged him. I didn't think nine-year olds did things like that. With Mr. Rooney, I just think he felt comfortable to do that. He was the perfect owner.

I always enjoyed seeing his son, Artie, too, because he loved to discuss the nuts and bolts of football. We'd test each other. When I go to Pittsburgh, I always make sure I see him. He has the stories of his father. He's a very, very nice person. He says good things. He's very pungent. When my son was there in 1982, you know how open their offices were at that time. Artie was watching film in his office. One of the college teams he was looking at had dark numbers on dark jerseys and it was hard to make out the numbers. He asked Mikey who was sitting closer to the screen, "Is that 88 or 89?" And Mikey said, "It's No. 89, Mr. Rooney." And Artie said, "Thanks, son." Later on, Mikey said to me, "Daddy, do you realize the Steelers might have drafted the wrong guy if I hadn't helped Mr. Rooney with those numbers?"

I told my son he was never to ask for autographs when he occasionally accompanied me on the pro football scene. We were in Pittsburgh and I told him to stay in the hallway outside the Steelers' locker room while I was interviewing players inside. "I'll be out in awhile," I told Mikey. The next thing I know he's in the locker room, standing off in a corner. I went over to ask him what he was doing there. I found out that Art, Jr. found him in the hallway and brought him in the locker room.

He recently sent me a postcard showing his father and his uncle in their baseball uniforms when they were playing with a team called the Wheeling Stogies. I had it framed. Artie has done me a lot of favors through the years. He's a Pittsburgh guy. If I'm ever in Pittsburgh, he's the first guy to call.

I've always been friendly with Chuck Noll and Dan Rooney. I just always got flat comments from them. They just never told me anything of value. It was all platitudes stuff. I always liked Noll. When I did a two-part series on him for *SI*, his first response was that he didn't want me to do it. He gave me a couple of weeks to talk to him. He showed me a picture of his team from a Catholic grade school he went to in Cleveland. Half of the ball team was black. In the 1940s, that was a bit unusual. He was trying to show me that he had always played with and gotten along just fine with blacks all his life. It's no secret why he had such a good rapport with black players.

I remember talking to Art Rooney back in 1974, right after the Steelers had beaten the Oakland Raiders (24-13) to win the AFC title, the first title Rooney had earned in 42 years. They were going to the Super Bowl in New Orleans. "I'm going to enjoy the plane trip back to Pittsburgh," Rooney told me. "If we'd have lost…well, that plane trip would have been like bringing back the body of a close relative."

They gave the game ball that day to Rocky Bleier — who gained 98 yards on 18 carries — and that had to make Rooney feel good. After all, it was Rooney who had recommended that the Steelers keep Bleier on the payroll during the years he was recuperating from the shapnel wounds he suffered in Vietnam. The coaching staff had suggested that Bleier gracefully retire.

Rooney told me something else that day. "This ream reminds me of some of the great teams we've had. You know, we've had some great players here, some great quarterbacks…John Unitas, Lenny Dawson, Bill Nelsen, Jack Kemp, Earl Morrall.

"Of course, we gave 'em all away. I was once speaking at a banquet, and I told them, 'If you want to ask me any questions, ask me about quarterbacks. We're experts there." He thought Bradshaw had the stuff to be a great quarterback. Who knew then that Bradshaw would quarterback the Steelers to four Super Bowl titles?

356

JACK KEMP

Lenny Dawson, the Steelers' No. 1 draft choice from Purdue in 1956, is flanked by Fran Fogarty, team business manager, and owner Art Rooney at Variety Club luncheon.

BILL NELSEN

EARL MORRALL and JOHNNY UNITAS

> *"My dad went to 50 Kentucky Derby races and he went to a Catholic shrine in Canada for St. Anne for 50 years. Mom and Dad went to countless novenas and holy hours. They always had something to pray for. Dad was big at lighting candles in churches."*
> — From a tribute to his parents by Art Rooney Jr.
> Rooney Reunion at Idlewild Park
> July 13-15, 2001

Art Modell
An old friend from Brooklyn

*"Art Rooney was the first to embrace me
when I came into the National Football League."*

Art Modell, at age 75, was on top of the mountain, at long last. After 40 years in the National Football League, the Brooklyn-born Modell had made it to the league's championship game, and his Baltimore Ravens had knocked off the New York Giants by 34-7 in Super Bowl XXXV. Over the years, he survived eight operations, a heart attack and a close encounter with blood poisoning that damned near killed him. So he wanted to enjoy this ultimate triumph. He pressed the Vince Lombardi Trophy to his heart. "It only took me forever to get here," he said, proudly.

Modell had appeared at a press conference on Thursday afternoon prior to the big game, sitting on a raised platform in a huge white tent outside the Hyatt Regency Westshore where his team was staying in Tampa. He was under harsh lights and, too often, harsh questioning. Too many of the questions were about how Modell was hated in Cleveland for taking its team away from them five years earlier, or about his star defensive player, Ray Lewis, who had been involved in a double-murder at an incident following the Super Bowl the year before in Atlanta. Modell grimaced more than once. They were spoiling his day in the sun.

I caught up with Modell as he was walking through the parking lot after his press conference stint. I asked him about his relationship with Art Rooney. Modell wrapped his left arm around my shoulders as he reflected on Rooney. When he finished, he gave me a playful cuff on the chin and a wink of the eye. A friend in the business, who'd witnessed this, said, "I didn't realize you knew Modell so well." I smiled. "I don't," I said, "but do you think he'd rather talk about how much they hate him in Cleveland, about the Ray Lewis mess, or about Art Rooney?" Here's what Modell had to say that day:

Would I like to have Art Rooney's reputation? Everybody would like to have Art Rooney's reputation. Art Rooney was the first man to embrace me when I first came into the National Football League in 1961. Most of the owners weren't happy about how much money I had to spend to get into the NFL. They thought I had raised the stakes. They didn't realize that it was increasing the value of all their franchises as well. They would benefit in the long run. I was not a football guy, as such, even though I had been a big fan of the New York Giants all my life. I was coming in from television and advertising and was something of an outsider. But Art Rooney, on a personal level, couldn't have been nicer. The first year I didn't even answer roll call at the owners' meeting. I've since made up for lost time. Art Rooney was my dearest friend in the league from the beginning. Now I'd say that Wellington Mara is my dearest friend. That's why it's so great that we both have our teams in the Super Bowl.

Art Rooney was a man of high morals, integrity and honor and love for his fellowman. And...he was a great competitor.

We were part of an important move that helped make the NFL the successful league it is today. When we merged with the American Football League in 1970 we had to move some NFL teams so we'd have a balanced number of teams in each conference. The Baltimore Colts were willing to switch to the American Football Conference, and I was willing to go, but I wouldn't go unless the Steelers came with us. I wouldn't have done it without Art Rooney going with me. We were their meal ticket when they came to Cleveland and when we went to Pitt Stadium. Art Rooney was my friend. Our teams and our cities had a rivalry. They were having financial trouble. I wanted to keep the rivalry alive for both our sakes. There was that...but I never would have gone without approval from Wellington Mara, either. We had a rivalry, too. Mara and Rooney were my best allies in the league. They were the National Football League, as far as I was concerned. I still buy my 67 season tickets every year for the Giants. I told the commissioner, Pete Rozelle, 'I'll go, but only with the Steelers.' They were stunned. While we were at these meetings, I got terribly sick, and was rushed to the hospital in New York. I had internal bleeding and was in bad shape. Mara and Art Rooney and Dan Rooney came to my room at the hospital. They were by my bedside. We started talking about moving our teams to the AFC. 'I don't like it,' Dan said. 'There's no way the Steelers are moving to the AFC.' The Chief was silent for awhile, standing there chomping on his cigar. Finally, he says, 'Dan, you stay in the National Conference. I'm going with Art Modell!' And that was it.

Everyone asks me how I could leave Cleveland (after the 1995 season), when we did so well there. Economics forced my hand. I had to leave to survive. Was it worth it? I don't think I would subject my family to the ordeal of the last five years...leaving the place we loved. Still do. Thirty-five years in that city. We were part of the social, civic and charitable fabric of that town. No family did more for that city, including the Rockefellers 200 years ago, than the Modells did. I served the last nine years before I left as president of the Cleveland Clinic. (Son) David was president of the Diabetes Foundation. (Wife) Pat helped raise the money and we built the largest free-standing hospice installation in the country. We loved it. We had to leave precipitously.

But I've got to say this: What makes it somewhat gratifying, in a subtle way, is that the new stadium in Baltimore, with the revenue streams, gave me the economic wherewithal to compete and do business. I could not in Cleveland. Oddly enough, they ended up building a new stadium for somebody else, and I left my colors there, my name, my legacy, my heritage for the people of Cleveland. I did not take that with me. But the pure, pure unadulterated fact is, you've got to have money to compete in the free agency market, in coaching, in scouting, what have you. This gave me the economic well-being to build this team from scratch. As I said when we announced we were moving to Baltimore (Nov. 6, 1995), I had no choice. It hurt that I could not attend the funeral of my dear friend Lou Groza when he died this year. I was very tempted to go back. But I decided I would be a distraction. I didn't want to take anything away from the solemnity of the occasion. I didn't want to do anything to hurt Jackie (Groza) and the kids. I got a beautiful note from Jackie the other day. I cried when I got it. But part of my heart is still in Cleveland.

Time will tell. I would love to go back and say hello to a lot of people and the public. I really love Cleveland. I love the people there. I really do. The people there gave me enormous support for 35 years. Enormous. But I'm welcome in Baltimore. People tell me I own the town. I don't own it. Who would I sell it to? I want to deliver a product. They treated me well. They gave me a stadium. They treated me with open arms and warmly, and they're deserving of all the rewards we can muster on the playing field. All the wins we can give them. The fans come first.

Earlier in the week, Art Modell was just sitting in the stands on Media Day at Raymond James Stadium, the site of Super Bowl XXXV, discussing his relationship with Art Rooney and the Pittsburgh Steelers. This was a story about an incident in 1964, October 10 to be exact, a Saturday night in Cleveland. Rooney's downtrodden Steelers were about to play Modell's Browns, who would go on to win the NFL championship that season. The Steelers would finish with a 5-9 record. Modell said his old friend begged for mercy when they met that night.

I moved the game from Sunday afternoon to Saturday night. We had Pete Rozelle and the networks approve it so we could duck the World Series on Sunday. Art came in walking with Pennsylvania Governor David Lawrence and six priests, collars and all. I said, 'What's this, Art? Where do I get a rabbi at this hour? It's ridiculous; you win, hands down.'

Art Rooney says to me, 'I want you to do me a favor. You guys go easy. We have one healthy linebacker, Myron Pottios. All the others are hurt. I hope you go easy on us.' I was fully confident we could handle the Steelers. I said, 'Don't worry, Art; don't worry, Chief.'

The Steelers then went out and pulled one of their biggest upsets in team history, beating us, 23-7. John Henry Johnson set a Steelers' record with 200 yards rushing that night. I was appalled. Buddy Parker was their coach. They put up a defense that might have been a forerunner of the 46 defense in Chicago. I was beside myself. He told me to go easy and they're piling it on.

So I leave the stands and I stomp back to the office in the stadium, and I hear, 'Hey, Art! Art!' I thought it was some disgruntled bettor, so I didn't turn around. 'Art! Art!' I recognized the voice. It was

The Chief. I turned around; he was 20 yards away. Then he really surprised me. He put his hand up to his face, his thumb to his nose, and he wiggled his fingers. I couldn't believe it. He didn't do it in a mean manner, though. He did it in fun. I can smile about it now.

Jim O'Brien

Baltimore Ravens' owner Art Modell addresses media assembly at Super Bowl XXXV press conference in Tampa.

"There are few people you meet in your life that you respect any more than Mr. Rooney and his family. He was my kind of guy. Loyal. Never took himself seriously. Always concerned about everybody but himself. He didn't make money just to make money. He was the easiest touch, I suppose, in the whole city for the right kind of people. He's the kind of guy you just hope you have a little of in yourself."
— Joe Paterno, Head Coach
Penn State University

Larry Felser
A big fan from Buffalo

*"I felt like I was talking
to my grandfather."*

*Larry Felser, 67, planned to retire three weeks after Super Bowl XXXV
in Tampa. Or at least slow down, writing once a week and doing some
radio reports. He had been covering pro football for the* Buffalo News
*for 38 years. He said he had been a newspaper reporter since 1953. He
hadn't missed a single Super Bowl and planned on going with his wife,
Beverly, to the next one in New Orleans merely as a spectator. He said
he just wanted to enjoy the big bash without any deadlines. He said he
might go to the one after that, too, in San Diego.*

I remember a game between the Bills and Steelers in 1972. That
was a breakout year for O.J. Simpson. He really came on strong
and he won the NFL's rushing title that year. The Steelers came to
Buffalo Memorial Stadium early in the season. They were 4-2 coming
in. They beat the Bills in a tough, pretty even game that day (38-21).

I remember the play that turned the game around that day.
Terry Bradshaw threw a pass down the middle and Franco Harris
made a finger-tip catch at the back of the end zone for a touchdown.
Harris was a rookie that year and he really impressed people that day.
He had taken a backseat to Lydell Mitchell at Penn State. Some were
saying Harris might be a better pro than he was a college player
where he had a reputation for not always putting out.

I remember telling people after that game that the Steelers were
going to be pretty good. And I was right. Harris made "The
Immaculate Reception" in the AFC playoffs to beat Oakland that year,
and then they lost to Miami in the next playoff game. That was the
first time the Steelers ever won a playoff game.

We played the Steelers in the second game of the season in
Pittsburgh in 1975. By then, O.J. is the Michael Jordan of the NFL.
The Steelers had one of the strongest defensive teams in the league.
They had gone 14 straight games without allowing a team to gain 100
yards. O.J. went 88 yards the first time he touched the ball. It was one
of the biggest runs I'd ever seen. He shook Jack Ham off his feet, and
beat the Steelers secondary down the sideline. O.J. had almost a pho-
tographic memory of his long runs, and he said he shifted from running like a football player to a track stride for the final 50 yards. He
gained 227 yards that day and the Bills beat the Steelers (30-21). The
Steelers went on to win the Super Bowl that year, their second
straight championship.

I remember talking to Joe Greene after the game, and he said,
"At least, I can tell my grandchildren some day that I played against

362

O.J. Simpson." How can you not love a team like that? They were just as easy to talk to after they won the Super Bowls.

I met Art Rooney for the first time at the first Super Bowl in Los Angeles back in 1967. I felt like I was talking to my grandfather. I had heard about Art Rooney for years and he was as good as advertised. I had heard about him from Sy Kritzer, who was a sports columnist for the *Buffalo Evening News*, and from Pat McGroder, a beer distributor and local businessman who helped get Ralph Wilson to buy the American Football League franchise for Buffalo.

Kritzer and McGroder were big fans of Art Rooney. His brother, Father Silas Rooney, was the athletic director at St. Bonaventure University, not far from Buffalo. Jack Butler and Ted Marchibroda had both played at St. Bonaventure. The Steelers had trained there. So Art Rooney was revered in those parts. I found him to be twice as good as I expected. The Steelers were the best opposing team I ever covered in sports.

Jim O'Brien

Two Hall of Famers from Penn State and the Steelers, Franco Harris and Jack Ham, meet in press box at Three Rivers Stadium during final season there.

363

Wellington Mara
A Giant in the business

"Art Rooney had that ability great gamblers have to have."

Mara and Rooney at 1938 meeting

Wellington T. Mara, age 84, has been associated with the New York Football Giants since he was 9 years old when the Giants played their first home game on October 18, 1925 against the Frankford Yellow Jackets. He is one of the leaders of the National Football League. His Giants have won 17 NFL divisional championships, six NFL championships, including Super Bowl XXI and Super Bowl XXV. He was elected to the Pro Football Hall of Fame in 1997. Mara, and his father Tim, who was the founder of the Giants and a charter member of the Hall of Fame, were the first father and son to be so honored, until Dan Rooney joined his father Art Rooney in the Canton shrine in the summer of 2000. We caught up with Mara at Super Bowl XXXV in Tampa, where his Giants lost to the Baltimore Ravens, and we spoke again over the telephone on May 2, 2001.

Art Rooney was more my father's contemporary than mine. He was someone you looked on with a great deal of almost reverence. My father used to say he was the original rolling stone. If he was at a league meeting and it went a day longer than expected, he'd simply send Fran Fogarty, his business manager, out to buy him a new white shirt, or a razor and shaving cream at the drug store, and he'd never complain. He always rolled with the punches.

I remember seeing him in 1938 down at the old Lincoln Hotel on Miami Beach. Art had taken a house right around the corner from the hotel where my folks were staying. Artie was a little blond kid about two years old at the time. Art would take a walk with Artie past our hotel each night. Artie would grab onto the railing and chin himself on the front porch of the hotel. I don't remember where Dan was; I don't remember seeing him. Art was accompanied by his brother, Jimmy, the great boxer Billy Conn, who was a light-heavyweight contender at the time, and one of the Steelers' linemen, a tackle named Ed Karpowich, from Catholic University back when Catholic University had its own football team. Milt Jaffe, one of Art's partners at the time, was with them, too. Walt Kiesling, the Steelers' coach, might have been along for the ride.

Those guys went deep sea fishing someplace down in the Florida Keys. Art was quite the fisherman, I'm told. He fished in the fresh waters of Canada and he fished in the Atlantic off the coast of New Jersey. There were local natives, known as Conch, who lived in the

WELLINGTON MARA
New York Giants owner and Art Rooney admirer

Florida Keys. These guys worked as guides and went out on the fishing boats. When Art and his guys came back on one of those rental boats they had caught a lot of fish. These natives said the fish belonged to them, and they tried to claim the catch. A debate ensued. There were about eight to ten of these Conchs, and they were soon joined by others who were on shore.

When it ended a lot of Key West natives were swimming for their lives. Those six guys had knocked them all into the water. The next day Art came by our place, and he was telling us all about what happened. His arms were all bruised when he had fended off some boards or poles these guys had swung at him. Those Conchs couldn't have picked four tougher guys ever than that Pittsburgh Six. But those natives stabbed Jimmy Rooney in the ribs and hurt him pretty good, and they hit Karpowich with a grappling hook in the head and hurt him, too. It got pretty bloody, I'm told. The local police authorities told the Pittsburgh guys never to come back again. They also told them they were lucky to get out of that mess alive.

I always thought of Art as an easy-going, happy go lucky grandfather type, but he was brought up in Allegheny and learned how to fight and how to take care of himself with a tough crowd. He was quite the competitor. My father marveled that he could do something like that, fight off those guys in Florida.

He was always on the side of administration in the league, whether it was Bert Bell or Elmer Layden or Pete Rozelle. Art Rooney was one of the reasons Pete Rozelle became the commissioner of the National Football League. We had a long, drawn-out owners' meeting at the Kenilworth Hotel on Miami Beach back in 1960.

Art was regarded as an open-minded minority at those meetings. Bert Bell had died the year before, and we needed to name a new commissioner, someone who could take us forward and help steer the league in the right direction, help us promote our game. I was part of the majority who were trying to get Marshall Leahy from the West Coast as the commissioner. We couldn't get enough votes, however, to swing that. We even talked about Vince Lombardi as a possible commissioner. Art had said he would go along with Joe Donahue of the Eagles and do what they would do. Carroll Rosenbloom of the Colts and George Halas of the Bears were with that minority group. Art didn't have an agenda. He wasn't pushing anyone. He wanted to do what would be best for the league.

Dan Reeves of the Los Angeles Rams thought his publicity man, Pete Rozelle, was a young guy with great vision. Reeves didn't want to lose Rozelle for the Rams, but he thought he'd do a good job as commissioner. I had a lot of respect for Art Rooney and I went to him and talked to him about what we might be doing. I was asked to represent our group to Rooney and try to sell him on a compromise choice.

Carroll Rosenbloom cried out, "Who the hell is Pete Rozelle?"

And Art said, "I don't know him, either, but 'Well' tells me he's OK, and that's good enough for me."

So we voted and Pete Rozelle was a unanimous choice.

My father, Tim Mara, said that Art Rooney personified the integrity he found in his experience at the racetrack, where a guy's word was better than a written contract.

You've heard the stories about how Art Rooney made a big killing at Saratoga, winning money in six figures. I was there at Saratoga with my father when that happened in 1936. I was 20 at the time and my father would let me bet $1 a race. Art was getting a lot of his tips from Steve Owen, who was working for us at the track, and was one of our football coaches. Art was betting big money and winning big money.

He was betting a lot of that money with my father, but my father was laying off some of the bets with other runners at the track, as they would do, to spread out the risk. There wasn't parimutuel betting back then; the bets were placed with bookmakers at the track. It was all legitimate.

After he won big that day he came to our family's summer place on Lake Luzerne, about 16 miles north of Saratoga. Art spent the night up there. He was eating ice cream on the veranda that night to celebrate his good fortune. His wife, Kathleen, meantime had gone into the hospital sooner than expected to deliver a son, their third boy. Art told my dad, "I'll never let you forget this day. I'm going to name my son Tim after you." That's how Tim Rooney got his name.

I was always at ease with his company. He went back to the track the next day. His horse won the first race. I don't know if he bet $10,000 or that $10,000 was the money he would have won. They disqualified his horse. He didn't cry about it. He said, "My luck has changed. I'm going home and see that baby of mine."

Art Rooney had that ability great gamblers have to have. He didn't push his luck. When it came to betting on the horses he could be very cold-blooded. He was anything but cold-blooded with everything else. He went home to see the baby.

His son Tim had a daughter named Kathleen. She married one of my sons, Chris, about 20 years ago. They're a great couple. So it all came full cycle with the Rooneys and the Maras. My son's father-in-law is named after his grandfather.

> *"You can talk about Man o' War and Arcaro all you want. The Chief for my money is the biggest figure in horse racing history."*
> —Roy Blount, Jr., Author
> *About Three Bricks Shy Of A Load*

George Young
The good scout

*"When things were bad he didn't cry;
when things were good he didn't gloat."*

George Young is a former general manager of the New York Giants and super scout with the Giants and Baltimore Colts, and was a close friend of fellow personnel chief Art Rooney, Jr. of the Steelers during the team's glory years. Young spoke about the Rooneys at Super Bowl XXXV in Tampa:

I read this book about Al Capone, the Chicago gangster, and I gave my copy to Art, Jr. and recommended it to him. He read it and gave it to his dad. His dad gave it back to him and said, "It's a nice book. It was interesting because I knew most of the people in the book." His dad told me a story how George Halas asked him and Bert Bell, Jr. to do him a favor. A fellow named Ed McCaskey, a student at the University of Pennsylvania, had taken a shine to Halas' daughter, Virginia, who was a student at nearby Drexel University. McCaskey was also moonlighting as a singer in a smoky bar in Philadelphia. Virginia was talking marriage and her father wasn't so sure he liked the idea of his daughter tying the knot with a saloon singer, only if the kid did such gigs to get spending money while he was in college.

So Art Rooney and Bert Bell both wore double-breasted suits and dark hats and camelhair overcoats when they went to scout McCaskey's act. Rooney said they looked like they were right out of a Chicago mob. They must have been a real sight. Halas gave them pictures of his daughter and McCaskey. They tailed them around Philadelphia for a few days, and checked them out with their friends. Art was enjoying telling this story. He said, "If you'd seen the way the two of us looked... Ed almost keeled over when he saw us. He figured these two hoods were coming to get him. Bert Bell went up to him and said, "You McCaskey? I'm Bert Bell and this is Art Rooney. Halas sent us here to investigate you." McCaskey said the two men left and caught up with him later that night at the saloon where he was singing. They had been to see Bill Lennox, the ticket manager at Penn. Bell told him, "Bill Lennox said you're OK and if you're OK with Bill Lennox, you're OK with me." Then Art Rooney took his cigar out of his face and said, "If you're OK with Bert, you're OK with me. And whoever said Halas was an angel?" Art, Jr. said his Dad told him, '"We really liked the kid, so we went back to George and told him we liked the kid. I'm not sure that's what he wanted to hear. They ended up getting married and they've been a great family. Ed ended up as an executive with the Bears and, eventually, succeeded George in running the organization. McCaskey could sing Irish songs, and loved to do so at parties. So we liked him more than ever."

I first met Art, Jr. at UCLA in the spring of 1968. Tommy Prothro was the coach at UCLA then. He was smoking cigarettes and drinking Coca-Cola when we talked to him. We were interested in some lineman at UCLA; I forget his name now. You got to know the people on the road in those days. Spring practices were more formalized, and you got a chance to see more of the players. So you saw more of the other scouts.

I don't know why Artie and I hit if off right away. What we had in common, other than the game, was that we both had a lot of other interests we liked to talk about. Plus, he had a familiarity with Baltimore. His dad had a horse farm in Maryland, and visited the tracks in Baltimore back in those days.

I remember we were standing on the sideline on a warm day in southern California, and we're both wearing coats and ties, with the ties knotted at the neck. Artie said I must've grown up with a father like his where you were expected to have a suit and tie on when you appeared in public. I told him he was right about that.

I was scouting for the Colts at the time in my hometown of Baltimore. Don Shula hired me. Johnny Unitas was still there. I coached the offensive line in 1970, so I had to work with Unitas on the running game. I knew Unitas when he was a rookie. I was a high school teacher — history and political science — and a coach at a school just three blocks from Memorial Stadium and I used to go to their practices. Weeb Ewbank came in as the coach in 1954 and I got along well with him. I became friends of Shula and Gino Marchetti, who were players on the team. I was at a pre-season scrimmage in 1956 when he threw three TD passes. That's when people were still calling him U-nah-taz. John was not the sort of athlete who looked good to you right away. When I saw baseball players like Yogi Berra, the Yankees' catcher, or Ron Cey, the Dodgers' third baseman they called "The Penguin," I always wondered who the scout was that said "We should take this guy." It took some guts. There are some guys who just don't look like athletes. John Unitas was kind of a stiff athlete, bent at the shoulders. We tend to spend too much time talking about negatives when we're assessing prospects. They did the same thing to Kurt Warner, the St. Louis quarterback, and look at what he's done. There are a lot of players like that. I've said from the day I came into the league that the greatest decisions were often made by Divine Providence.

On the day of the game, Weeb was a wipeout. John called all the plays. Weeb was a tremendous teacher and a great judge of talent. Shula was good like that. He brought Chuck Noll in as an assistant coach in 1966. I knew him well. He replaced Charley Winner when he went to St. Louis as the head coach. I like Chuck. He was never the Coach of the Year, but he was the Coach of the Decade ('70s). He never changed. He was the same person he was when he was an assistant coach. Some guys change, but he didn't. He had a lot of interests besides football; he had the same interests toward life. He kept the same values. I remember telling Artie when they got down on Noll early in his career (when he was 1-13 in 1969) that they should be patient. I told them, "When Chuck Noll is your coach the Rooneys will still be the owners." A lot of coaches come in and they become big shots. He's not that way. He won't steal the team's attention away from the owners. He stayed away from doing commercials and he never sought the spotlight. It doesn't always happen that way. Often times, the guy on the field becomes the dominant figure in the franchise, and not the guys who took the chances a long time ago.

I always liked the Rooneys. They loved football the same way I did. I started going to NFL games in 1942. I remember seeing the Steagles (in 1943) when they merged the Steelers with the Eagles during the War and played some of their home games in Philadelphia. I remember the Card-Pitt team when they joined forces the following year with the Chicago Cardinals. I used to go to Washington to see them play the Redskins. In 1947, I was an usher at Memorial Stadium and saw every game. The first game I saw was against the Brooklyn Dodgers. I saw the New York Yankees play the Colts, too.

I thought Artie had a great run as the head of the Steelers' personnel department during the '70s. He helped them get a lot of great players. I know how disappointed he was when Danny took the job away from him. I told Artie, "You've had a wonderful life. People knew who you were when you were the top dog." I respected him a great deal as a talent scout, but I never tried to hire him to work for us. I couldn't put him against Danny. Danny was more interested in the business side of the Steelers. He did things Artie didn't like to do.

Everyone liked Art Rooney, the father, the first time they met him. What's not to like? You talked to him like you knew him ten or 20 years. He felt particularly comfortable with Irish types. He was a delightful man. He loved to hear my stories about Baltimore. I knew Carroll Rosenbloom, the owner of the Colts, and Art loved to hear my stories about Rosenbloom. Every time I was with him, I had to entertain him with a story about Rosenbloom. I loved to be with Art Rooney. He's an icon in this business. I admired him because when things were tough he didn't cry; when things were good he didn't gloat.

I remember one time he was at an owners' meeting at the Biltmore in Phoenix. Some heart doctor in Phoenix gave all the owners a free heart exam. I remember seeing him walking around the lobby after his exam. I said, 'How did you do?' He said, 'I flunked.' He had a hardening of the arteries. They had a lot of guys watching him after that, but his health declined soon after that.

I enjoyed his company. I remember having dinner with him at the family's dog track in West Palm Beach, and at their harness racing track at Yonkers. I was not interested in racing, but I loved being with Art Rooney.

I saw him in his last year and he still wanted to hear some stories about Carroll Rosenbloom. I'd tell some stories and he'd laugh.

They told me it was the first time he got out of his slump in a long time. Rosenbloom had graduated from the high school where I taught for 13 years, and I taught with teachers who had known him. They told me good stories about him; he was a real character. I remember that Art Rooney told me after Carroll Rosenbloom died, "You know that guy still owes me 500 Super Bowl tickets."

When I left the Colts, I went to work for Wellington Mara, who was a great friend and admirer of Art Rooney. They share some common background, but Wellington is very much a Jesuit-educated person. Art is a guy in the neighborhood; Wellington is more of a guy at the country club. They're different.

The Rooneys have made a great contribution to the National Football League. Art was most respected, but Danny has made such an important contribution on his own. The players' union has always had a lot of respect for him and Wellington.

They take football seriously. It was a major part of their life. They recognized that owning an NFL franchise was a partnership. They knew it was important to share the wealth. They knew the history of the league. They knew it got to be a successful venture because of people cooperating.

I remember the scene in the church (see photo on next page) when Art Rooney was laid to rest. I never saw so many priests in one place in my life. I told Art, Jr., "I would hate to be a Catholic dying in this city today. There aren't going to be any priests available to give the last rites. They're all at Art Rooney's funeral."

Jim O'Brien

George Young, former Giants general manager, is long-time friend of Art Rooney Jr., going back to their traveling days as college football scouts.

"I would hate to be a Catholic dying in this city today. There aren't going to be any priests available to give the last rites. They're all at Art Rooney's funeral."
— George Young

Susie Post/Pittsburgh Post-Gazette Archives

Jim O'Brien

Art Rooney, Jr.
The good scout

"My dad was really a sportsman."

Art Rooney, Jr. was in charge of the scouting and player personnel department during the Steelers' great successful run in the '70s, and was given much credit for the club's four Super Bowl victories. He ran afoul of Chuck Noll somehow in the early '80s and was removed from his position by his brother, Dan, who wasn't happy with the way things were going, either. The other brothers were opposed to the idea, but Dan threatened to leave the organization if he didn't get his way. It's too bad. Art, Sr. was 86 at the time, and went to his horse farm to grieve over this decision. But he didn't step in to stop it since Dan was in charge of the team. Art, Jr. had differences of opinion with Noll from the beginning. Noll didn't like scouting combines such as BLESTO, which the Steelers had helped to organize. Then, too, Artie argued in favor of taking Franco Harris as the team's No. 1 draft choice in 1972 rather than Robert Newhouse who ended up with the Dallas Cowboys. Noll thought Newhouse was the better prospect. His brothers believe Artie should be in the Hall of Fame, too. They think he had as much to do with the Steelers' success in the '70s as anybody in the organization. The brothers were pleased to hear that Artie was nominated for consideration for the Hall of Fame at the outset of 2000.

I just heard that Lowell Perry died the other day. I sent a card and a letter to his family. He was a great player, or he could have been if he hadn't been hurt. He showed a lot at our training camp (in 1956) and in the early part of the season. He got hit by two great players from the New York Giants, Emlen Tunnell and Rosey Grier. He got hit from both sides. They wrecked his hip. The doctors said it was broken the way it usually happens only in an automobile accident. It was really bad. I believe Bill Nunn recommended Lowell Perry to Buddy Parker. Nunn was the sports editor for the *Pittsburgh Courier*, the black newspaper, but did some scouting for us, too.

Perry was smart and had done well in school at Michigan. My dad sent him to Duquesne Law School. He worked as an assistant coach with us while he was going to law school. He was the first black football coach in the National Football League.

We had only a few black players on the team back then. We had Jack "Goose" McClairen and Willie McClung on the team at the time. We went down South for an exhibition game and the black players were not allowed to stay in the same hotel as the rest of the team. Lowell wasn't used to being treated that way. "Goose" told him they wouldn't have a curfew, that they'd get good food at the house where they stayed, and that they'd have the best time of their lives. Later,

373

"Goose" reminded him, "I told you that you'd have the time of your life." And Perry told him, "I did have a great time, but you just don't get what it's all about. You can't accept that; it's not right."

That game was in Jacksonville. My father wasn't with the team when it arrived in Jacksonville. He came the next day. When he found out what happened, that the players couldn't all stay in the same hotel, he met with the black players and apologized to them. He said, "This will never happen again, I promise you."

The next year, when he couldn't get a guarantee that the players could all stay in the same hotel, he quietly cancelled an exhibition game in Atlanta. They were trying to get an NFL franchise in Atlanta at the time. We were getting a good guarantee for going there. My dad cancelled the game way in advance so other plans could be made. But he was sensitive to stuff like that. He cared about his players, all his players.

He stuck to his word. He was way ahead of his time.

He was one of the first owners to have a black on his team. Ray Kemp from Duquesne, who was from Cecil, out in Washington County, was on our first team in 1933. That was 14 years before baseball broke the color line with Jackie Robinson.

Things like that come back to me now. I guess I'm at the age where you should be more reflective. Maybe it's time for us to do a book about the early days of the Steelers. I don't know how you'd handle the early years of my father, the gambling and two-fisted stuff. That's the good stuff. Many of the old people who knew him have passed away and the ones who are left won't talk about it. Jack McGinley, Jr. is a guy who knows a lot, for instance, but he won't even talk to me about some of that stuff.

Times were different back then. My dad was really a sportsman. Maybe you could do it in fiction. I think you need someone like Mark Twain to do it, someone with a sense of humor who wouldn't come down on him too hard about some things. That way you could work in some of the stories about what went on. Different things were accepted then. The North Side was like the Wild West. They could have Wild Bill Hickcock walking around, and maybe they did. And Wild Bill Hickcock was Art Rooney.

If you made a movie — and my dad loved some of those old movies — you'd want Spencer Tracey or James Cagney to play the part of my father.

Were the Maras like that? Yes, in a way. Tim Mara got his start as a bookmaker at the track. That reminds me of a good story, like I'm talking about.

We were at Forbes Field and we were playing the New York Giants. My dad is in the locker room before the game and he's checking out the game program. He sees a story about Tim Mara in the program. He finds a reference to Tim Mara getting his start as a bookmaker. The story was written probably by Jack Sell or Jack Henry, one of the Pittsburgh guys who wrote about the Steelers. My dad was furious. He didn't want Tim Mara to see that and take it the wrong way. He didn't want to hurt Tim Mara's feelings. He didn't want to upset anybody. Being a bookmaker was legitimate back then, but it didn't look good. It might be misinterpreted. My dad gets Dan and the rest of us boys and he instructs us to tear out this one page in every program before they go on sale for the game. We had about 10,000 to 15,000 game programs. There was a full-page ad on the back of that page, and Dan had to make good on it with the advertiser. What a lesson! I think I was about 13-years-old at the time. I'm glad I was able to do that for my dad.

My dad believed you did things the right way. Tim Mara was his friend and he didn't want to hurt him. So when you get a chance to do the right thing you ought to do it. That was the lesson.

You know I have spent a lot of time in recent years writing down my father's stories. And I still don't know him. I still don't know who the real Art Rooney is.

"Treat people the way you want to be treated."

My father could be so tough. He always taught us, "Treat people the way you want to be treated." But then he'd add, "But never allow them to mistake your kindness for a weakness."

In his first few years in the league, he got into an argument with George Halas about an agreement they had regarding compensation for an exhibition game between the Bears and Steelers in Rockford, Illinois. My dad demanded that Halas make good on the agreement and pay him what he thought he was due. Halas was a big tough guy — about 6-2, 205 when he was playing end in the pros — much bigger than my dad, and Halas said, "I'll fight you for it." My dad told him he didn't want to fight. Finally, Halas came around and gave my dad what he wanted. As my dad was leaving the room, he turned around and hollored back, "Hey, George, by the way, fighting me wasn't any sure bet on your part, either."

The Chief loved to tell that story, and it was fun to hear him tell it.

I have to smile when I think of how he's remembered as he was at the end as a kind, old, wise gentleman. He was all that and more, but he was also a swashbuckler in his day. He was Clark Gable and Spencer Tracy in 'Boom Town' and 'San Francisco.' He lived a full life in a lot of different ways.

I saw a movie on TV recently called "The Cotton Club," and it was about a club in Harlem where they had a stage show and dancing to a band up front and gambling in the back room. My dad knew guys who owned places like that, and I'm sure he enjoyed places like that.

I know it's crazy. I'm 65 and I still worry about what my father would think about everything I do. There isn't a day goes by that I don't think about him. "What would he say? What would he think? Would he approve of what I'm doing?" I don't think about my mother like that, and she was prettier and wittier than he was. But that's the influence he has on us.

He never wanted us driving Cadillacs, for instance. When we dedicated the statue to him, my wife Kay said he should get a limousine to take us there because we had some friends in from out of town, and we had too many for one car. I agreed, reluctantly, knowing how my dad felt about such things. As we neared the statue, I jumped out of the car and walked the rest of the way. It's funny now, but I guess I didn't want my dad — even the statue of my dad! — to see me getting out of a limousine.

My dad was a tough cuss in the early days. He got into fights with two of his first three coaches, real fights. Luby DeMelio, who'd been a lineman at Pitt, coached our club in 1934. He and my dad got into an argument in the office. They sent over to Joe Goetz at his sporting goods store and had him send over some boxing gloves. They pushed the furniture back to the walls in my dad's office, and put on the gloves and they went at it. It must have been something. My dad beat up Luby DeMelio really bad. He really beat the stuffing out of him. My dad always said there was a big difference between fighting and boxing. DeMelio was bigger than my dad, but my dad was a good boxer. They say DeMelio couldn't gain the respect of the players after he'd been beaten up by the owner. He never had a chance.

Then my dad got into a fight with Joe Bach, who was one of his buddies, on a train ride back from a game in his first year (1935) as a coach. My mother told me this story. Bach was upset that my dad had farmed a home game out to New Orleans when the Steelers were in contention and needed a victory badly. The Steelers lost and Bach was blaming my dad for moving the game. They got into it in the dining car. They got into a helluva fight. Bach had been one of the "Seven Mules" at Army, and he'd wrestled there. So Bach gave my dad a better fight than DeMelio. But, just imagine, the owner of the team has real fights with two of his first three coaches. Those were rough and tumble times. My dad must have been a terror in those days. He and Bach were the best of friends, and my dad even brought him back as a coach, as he did with Walt Kiesling. My dad got into his face a few times, too.

He didn't care how big they were.

Words of Wisdom
"I have been quoted as saying 'Winning is the only thing.' That's a little out of context. What I said is that winning is not everything — but making the effort to win is. Not everyone can be a winner all the time, but everyone can make that effort, that commitment to excellence. And I say that the quality of any man's life has got to be a full measure of that man's personal commitment to excellence and to victory, regardless of what field he may be in."

— Vince Lombardi

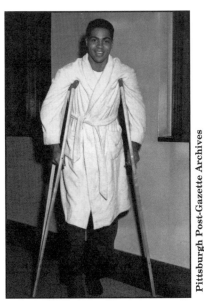

Some Christmas present. Lowell Perry, a rookie receiver from Michigan, suffered career-ending hip injury the week before Christmas in 1957.

Receiver Frank Lewis, the Steelers' No. 1 draft choice in 1971 from Grambling, gets checked out by Art Rooney, team's player personnel director.

Art Rooney Jr. oversees scouting department during glory years of the '70s

"We wanted world championships."

I got my start as a scout for the Steelers when Buddy Parker was our coach. Parker was a great coach with a lot of expertise (who was with the Steelers for eight seasons, 1957 to 1964). But he had a philosophy that the way to win was with veterans who didn't make mistakes. So he kept trading away our draft choices for veteran players. We didn't have a No. 1 draft choice in 1958 or 1959. In 1959, we didn't have a choice in the first seven rounds. Mike Ditka got New Orleans in a fix like that a few years ago when he traded all those draft choices to get Ricky Williams from Texas.

Our drafts in those days were frustrating. We'd look up at the board on draft day and see all these beautiful names and there was nothing we could do about them. I finally started going on scouting trips in 1964, Buddy's last year as a coach. The guy who had the most influence on me was Jack Butler, a former Steelers player who had done some scouting for us.

We would take trips around the country and we'd sit in the car and figure out what the good teams were doing and what we could do. He finally came up with the BLESTO idea, the idea that we couldn't get the coverage of college players unless we joined together with other teams and pooled our information.

The irony of the BLESTO thing was that Buddy Parker was the guy who pushed the idea. He convinced my father. Buddy was so anti-draft, but he was the guy who got BLESTO off the ground. He told my dad, "You should be able to afford this because you'll get the coverage that will allow you to compete with the good drafting teams like Los Angeles and Dallas."

We did not want instant credibility. We wanted world championships. We had traded away too many draft choices and too many quarterbacks over the years only to see them come back and haunt us. We were convinced that the draft was the best way to go. The number one pick is so important. You look for different types of players in the draft. That first pick you're looking for a guy who can be a starter and so on, a guy who can contribute to your team, a guy who can make your team, and not a guy who's just a prospect.

Our method of scouting players was not unique. I'm sure the other clubs had the same ideas we did. I'd love to tell you that we were all geniuses here, but I don't believe that. When you look for players, you're looking for critical factors: quickness, control, strength potential, athletic skills, and the normal height-speed ratio. Then what you have to do is figure out their toughness and football intelligence.

This was especially true when you were looking for free agents, and I'm talking about the kids who weren't selected in the draft, not veteran players from other teams. We really relied on the computer for free agents. After you'd gone over all the written reports you went to the computer.

"You're brand new."

I recall some of those trips to our horse farm in Maryland. We all did some driving. Dad was a tough passenger when his sons were doing the driving. He'd be shouting constant instructions and complaints about what we were doing. "Turn here...ya already passed the turn...I wanna get to the track for the first race, you know...let's get there for the kickoff...you're gonna get us killed...slow down...you're gonna get us pinched...you're brand new when it comes to driving... I was the best driver I ever saw. Barney Olfield wanted me to join his driving team."

Jim, we never believed a lot of dad's boasts about things, like the Olfield boast. But years later, we always seemed to find out that they were true. My father had an image in Pittsburgh once upon a time as being a gambler, a bumbler, and cheap as far as running his football team. But my father was the best in the business at handicapping horses. There was no one who could compare with him in the country. I always admired the fact that he never spoke up in his own defense and said, "Hey, I'm the best at this."

If you ever made a real bone-headed move, The Chief would say, "You're brand new." My brother John said he remembers dad calling him "brand new" on several occasions. If it were worse, he'd say, "You're right off the shelf." Still worse, he'd say, "You're unwrapped," or "You're right off the farm." Those Rooneys had a music to their speech. And great body language, too.

Dad would call us "saps" a lot because we did, in fact, do a lot of dumb things. He would make a fuss with his sons about little things, but he would be very understanding about bigger failings.

John brought up something else that I had forgotten about. When Dad was giving a non-family member hell, Dad would use a very strong voice and body language, but he would never swear. I had seen this a few times, and was very amazed about it. Dad would say, "You bum you. You dirty bum, you big bum." He'd go on vehemently, but he would never swear.

He could never tell a joke the right away. Mom said he always got the punch line messed up, or altered the joke to take out a cuss word and ruined it. Or just plain forgot something. At the same time, he was great at sharing stories. I say share because he wanted to give people something humorous or exciting or ironic. Irony was never one of his words, but he loved irony. Bert Bell was the same way. It was so wonderful to be with Bert or my dad. When Bert Bell died of a heart attack — ironically, while attending a football game between two teams he had once owned, the Steelers and the Eagles in Philadelphia — my father was mobbed by the Bell family at the funeral. He was like an uncle or grandfather to that family. They really leaned on him. My mother says he was shaken and drained when he came back to Pittsburgh following that funeral. For me, as a kid, it was unbelievable to be with both of them together. They shared their stories with big shots to waiters, shoeshine guys and elevator operators. St. Peter must have been a little bit like that, talking about The Lord.

Dad surrounded himself with enough good people to fend off what the bad people were promoting. A lot of his brothers and some of the earlier Rooneys got sidetracked by booze. He kept good company. All those priests you wondered about and people like that, Rich Easton, Iggy Borkowski, Ed Kiely. My mom, the best driver of them all. People like Father Reardon, Father Flanigan, Father Lackner, Father Campbell, Father Bosen Pierre, the Franciscans, Bishop Leonard, spirituality. Those were his saviors. Jim, just how do you think Dad made it out of the North Side and that tough environment without ever becoming like so many of the questionable people he was with? His spirituality, I think. He was never phony about it either. He always said the family rosary. Dan and Tim knew Dad best; I just listened to him.

He even told us late in his life that it would be OK if we ever decided to sell the team. He reminded us we weren't big-money people. This isn't well known, but toward the end of his life, one of his great desires was to own a minor league baseball team. He thought it would be neat to be involved with young, hungry kids on their way up.

No one was in his league when it came to going to funeral homes. After he died, the family had a draft to divide his belongings. I picked his prayer book with my No. 1 pick. He kept his funeral cards in there. There were hundreds and hundreds. The rest were in the books in his library. He used them for book marks.

He loved the ground crew. He used to yell at me for not taking the free little bottles of whiskey when I flew first class. He made me bring them back for (head groundskeeper) Dirt DiNardo to give to his men.

My dad helped the Homestead Grays stay afloat, I've been told by relatives of Cum Posey, the Grays' owner. I've been told the Chief helped keep the team going financially. I had heard bits and pieces about that over the years, but to hear it in such detail was amazing.

"My dad ended up paying the whole bill."

I remember a few years back there was a story on TV and in the newspapers about a local magistrate named Cross who was in a lot of trouble because he had been fixing traffic tickets for years. He was on trial for that.

The media carried a story that Cross told about how Art Rooney, Sr. called him once and asked him to help former light-heavyweight boxing champion Billy Conn to get back his driver's license. The magistrate looked into the case and found out that Conn had not paid his fine for a traffic offense and that's why he lost his license.

Art Rooney Jr. found final season at Three Rivers Stadium a nostalgic trip. Rooney compares notes with fellow North Catholic alumnus and director of football operations Kevin Colbert.

Photos by Jim O'Brien

Well, Billy Conn was known as "America's Guest" because he never paid for anything. He was always eating and drinking and being entertained on somebody else's tab. Cross told my dad the fine was $125 and another $25 for additional expenses. Some time went by and Conn still didn't have his license and was complaining to my dad. My dad called Cross. He found out that Conn's check had bounced. My dad ended up paying the whole bill. Well this story by Cross got big play by the local media, especially on TV.

That reminded me of another story my dad told many times. It was after World War II, about 1946 to 1949. My dad was driving to Florida and was pinched somewhere in the state of Georgia. There were no interstate highways in those days and anyone with a Northern license plate was a top candidate to be stopped and arrested for traffic violations, some real and some imagined.

After The Chief was arrested, he was taken to a local police head-quarters. He said the place was no more than a house with more than usual parking areas around it. There were four other people there who had been picked up for traffic violations. All were Yankees. One was a young sailor. The serviceman was in a bit of a shock. He asked the policeman how long he had to wait around. The trooper said he would have to wait until the judge came along. The kid said he had a three-day pass. His ship was in Norfolk, Virginia and he was driving to Jacksonville, Florida to see his wife. He said it would take a day to get down there, then a day with his wife, and then a day to drive back to Norfolk. The cop said, "Well, the judge should be here in three days." The young sailor protested, "I told you I only had three days." And the cop said, "You can plead guilty, pay the fine of $50 and leave." The kid said, "I only have $50." Then the cop said, "Well, you will have to wait for the judge." My dad stepped up, pulled $100 from his pocket and said, "I'm guilty, the sailor is guilty, and here's a hundred bucks to pay our fines. Now let's get out of here, kid!"

"Stay at home if you can't stand the night work."
— Bobby Layne

My brother, John, was golfing in Palm Beach, Florida recently when a short, portly fellow approached him. The man asked him, "Are you Art Rooney's son?" John replied, "Yep, I am." The man said, "I met your dad back in the late 1950s. I was a good friend of Tom Tracy." John replied, "Oh, yes, Tom 'The Bomb' Tracy, I knew him...he was a good running back...played for Buddy Parker."

"Yeah, that was Tom," the man came back. "That's how I met your dad. I told Tracy that I had a good idea for a bar business in Michigan, near the college, lots of action. I told 'The Bomb' that if he came up with $2,500, he could be my partner. Well, Tom tells me that he did not have $2,500, but he might be able to get it by borrowing against his next season's contract with the Steelers. He would have to call Art Rooney to see if he could swing it.

Well, Tom Tracy was a real good little running back, but he tended to be inconsistent. He was only about 5-9 to 5-10, and weighed 205 pounds. If he gained any weight, he would lose a lot of quickness. Tracy didn't watch his diet, either. Our trainer, Doc Sweeney, said he'd sit around all night watching TV, drinking beer and eating salty nuts and buttered popcorn. Once, he went out the night before a game with Bobby Layne and Ernie Stautner and they had a rip-roaring, hell of a good time. Tracy was playing poorly the next day, and feeling poorly. Layne asked him what was wrong. Tracy told him he had a hangover. "Hell," Layne snapped at him, "stay at home if you can't stand the night work."

Anyway, back to the story. My dad talked to Tom and his friend by phone and was not overly thrilled about giving Tom Tracy an advance. Tom never struck us as being that sharp, and he was sure to blow that money. And on a bar. That might be a disaster for a guy like Tom.

Now this fellow told my brother that our dad was very nice to them on the phone, but said he would have to meet with them before he could make up his mind about the advance. So Tracy and his friend caught the next train to Pittsburgh and met with my dad at his Roosevelt Hotel office the following afternoon.

The short, fat guy said he was introduced to our dad and, to be truthful, he said he was pretty frightened about trying to sell this big shot on a college town bar. He told John that he opened the conversation by telling our dad that he was not a big shot or financial wizard. He had a good spot and he knew the bar business. He repeated that he was not a big shot.

He said his grandfather and father were both bartenders and that his mother was a waitress in a bar. That's all my dad had to hear. The guy said he was shocked when my dad turned to his business manager and instructed him to write out a check for $2,500. He said they did well with the little bar in the college town and years later sold it for $70,000. He said, "Your dad was quite a guy. He made you feel comfortable."

My brother John said he had to laugh to himself. He told the guy that when Dad heard his parents were in the business that sold him on the idea. After all, his dad had been a bar owner and a bartender. In Dad's mind the guy had a good chance of making it in that business even if he wasn't a business wizard.

> *"When I spoke at the Rooney Reunion this year (July 13-15, 2001), I told the family that my father belonged to St. Peter's Church on the North Side for 80 years. He really believed in the power of prayer. His mother was quite ill when he was 13 and he went to St. Peter's and prayed for 12 straight hours. She got better the next day. Mom and Dad and Mom's sister, Aunt Alice McNulty, prayed so much their prayer books had holes in them."*
> — Art Rooney Jr.

"Her doggie was named Art Rooney."

My daughter, Sue, was finishing up the school year as a kindergarten teacher at Baker School in Upper St. Clair. The kids were told to bring their teddy bears to school for the last day for a teddy party.

One of the kids stood up to introduce her teddy as all the other kids had done. Sue asked the student, "What is your teddy named?" The little kid said, "I call my teddy Arthur Rooney." My Sue said, "That's my dad's and grandfather's name. How did you get that name?" The kid said, "I got the name from my grandma. Her doggie was named Arthur Rooney."

So much for famous names.

"He would fly underneath some of the bridges."

Dad had a friend who had been a pitcher for the Pirates Baseball Club. This fellow was an airplane-flying enthusiast. Dad said airplanes always impressed him. The friend gave flying lessons and told The Chief that he could get him into his class. Now there were two parts to the piloting class. The first was the practical which was held at the old Bettis Field (Allegheny County Airport) and another one out near Fox Chapel. The other part of the class was all academic and was given at Carnegie Tech. Dad said he did rather well at the airfields, but told his friend that the classes at Carnegie Tech might as well have been taught in Greek as far as he was concerned.

Dad's teacher friend asked Dad who he thought was the best student in the class at Carnegie Tech. The Chief said the name of the top student in his estimation. Dad's friend said, "That's right. But, do you know something? We are going to wash him out. He has no idea of how to fly a plane. He will be killed. We will let him fly around a little bit, but he is out of here." Then he looked at my Dad, and said, "You, on the other hand, are the best or nearly the best flyer we have. Just show up for all the classes and keep your mouth shut."

Dad said, "I'll never pass the written test." His teacher said, "Put your name on the test paper, be patient and wait until most of the other students turn in their test, and then hand yours in."

Dad did just that...and passed.

On the other hand, the smart student turned in his test paper first and got an "A" for it. On his solo flight, however, he wrecked the plane and almost was killed. Dad's teacher told Dad, "I knew that we should not have let that guy try to solo."

When asked how he did on his solo flight, Dad said, "It was perfect until I landed. It was up in that little field near Fox Chapel. The wind changed and I ended up going over some trees into the Field Club golf course. The airplane was OK, but we had to get a truck to move it out of there."

Art Rooney Jr. shares box at Three Rivers Stadium with longtime friend and scout Bill Nunn Jr., and talks football with two current NFL scouts, Ken Herock of the Green Bay Packers, and Mike Butler of the Indianapolis Colts. Butler, the son of Jack Butler, and Herock both hail from Munhall.

Jim O'Brien

Dad had a reputation as a flyer of those by-wing airplanes as a bit of a daredevil. Mom said he would fly underneath some of the bridges in Pittsburgh.

My brother, John, said that he heard that Dad got into a little trouble when he buzzed the City-County Building. I think that Dad and Mom were married in 1930. She flew with Dad at least once. Mom told us that she made Dad promise never to fly again when she became pregnant with Dan. To the best of my knowledge, he was true to his word and never did fly again. It's interesting that my brother Dan took up flying and flies his own plane.

"Don't be a sap about that streaker guy."

When Dad was in his 80s, I saw him get upset with a non-family member only once and that was Myron Cope.

We were playing at Three Rivers Stadium when a man jumped out of the stands and ran past the field guards onto the playing field. This was not totally unusual except that the guy was naked. He streaked right down the middle of the field. Everybody, including the players, got a big kick out of this. Everybody but Dad, that is. Dad always had a prudish side to him. The streaker really upset him.

Well, Myron Cope, the Steelers' radio color man knew a good story when he saw it. He somehow got in touch with the streaker. This naked runner was a bit touched in the head, as it was later discovered. He craved attention. Cope seemed, at least to The Chief, to be giving the fellow publicity.

The runner showed up in a couple of the places around town. Myron seemed to be ready to call attention to these capers. The Chief got more and more irritated at Myron. Usually, he would have called Myron into his office or just bumped into Myron somewhere at Three Rivers Stadium, accidentally on purpose. Dad would then kid Myron about the streaker. Dad called it, "Kidding on the square." It meant Dad was telling someone off or giving advice in a funny way. It was "the old spoonful of sugar makes the medicine go down," though I'm sure Dad wouldn't know who Mary Poppins was.

Well, Dad had his fill of Myron Cope and his streaker. There would be no "kidding on the square" this time. Each morning, the media, coaches, and front office staff all congregated in the kitchen area of the Steelers' offices at Three Rivers for coffee and a sweet roll. It was informal and off the record. My Dad went after Cope like he was one of his sons.

Dad shouted, "Myron, don't be a sap about that streaker guy. He's a nut, but smart enough to be playing a tune on you. A screwball like that could cause some kind of riot!" Now Myron was trying to get a word in edgewise, "but Mr. Rooney..."

My Dad came back, "Myron, he'll give the other nuts the idea, and they will all come out of the woodwork. That's the way they are, you know." With that, The Chief spun on his heels and left the kitchen area very briskly, especially for a man in his eighties.

It was quiet, very quiet. I said, "Well, Myron, now you have been treated just like one of Dad's sons. I don't think anyone actually heard me...especially Myron Cope."

"Give him what he wants."

Rocky Bleier told me this story while having breakfast at Sea Island, Georgia a couple of years ago. Bleier said he was trying to get some extra money from his first Steelers' contract with Fran Fogarty. Fogarty was a great guy who pretty much ran all of dad's day-to-day business. He knew the value of a buck and, in particular, where every dollar and cent in the organization was going.

To an outsider, Fran could seem outspoken and cynical. In fact, he was, indeed, a tough ex-hockey player and a combat veteran of World War II. Fogarty was captured by the Germans, escaped from a moving railroad train and spent time with the French underground before making his way back to the American lines.

This was before Rocky became a war hero in his own right. He was just a kid from Wisconsin and Notre Dame trying out for the Steelers. In those days, the Steelers offices were in the Roosevelt Hotel. Dad and Fogarty shared a cramped office on the ground floor on that hotel.

Rocky Bleier said dad had been out of that office while he was talking to Mr. Fogarty. Rocky was trying to get a $1500 bonus he hadn't technically earned his rookie year. He wanted Fogarty to take some other things into consideration. ("Hey, I needed the money," related Rocky.) The meeting was going nowhere. Neither Rocky nor Fran would budge an inch. Rocky had been a late draft pick so Fran was not going to become too excited about re-signing the kid even if he had been the captain of the Notre Dame team. Rocky said that all of a sudden he heard a low, but forceful voice from another office call out, "Who is that?"

Bleier cringed because he recognized the voice belonging to The Chief.

"It's Rocky," replied Fogarty.

"Give him what he wants," Rooney hollered.

"OK," said Fogarty.

"Art Rooney is the voice of the man in the street."
— Cardinal John J. Wright

Tim Rooney
Remembers long car rides

"He specialized in static."

It was February 28, 2001 and the box on the calendar said it was also Ash Wednesday, a Holy Day of Obligation in the Catholic faith. Tim Rooney and his brother, Art, Jr., who was visiting from Pittsburgh, both went to St. Edward's Catholic Church in Palm Beach, Florida that morning and came away with a dark smudge on their foreheads. They had received their ashes, the parish priest applying them with his index finger and thumb. Their father would have been pleased. Tim, who was born August 8, 1937, was 63 years old at the time we spoke. Tim was thought to be a lot like his dad. The other brothers always accused him of living the good life. He always lived in the best places. He had homes in Palm Beach, Greenwich, Connecticut and in Ireland. He took pride in having nearly every book that was ever written about the Kennedy Family.

We went to the same church where my father used to go when he was here. I saw one or two guys really get dusted. They came away looking like they'd been working in the coal mine. I think the priest did that on purpose. Art and I just had breakfast here. It's great to have him and (his wife) Kathleen here in the winter. Pat and John live around here and we enjoy getting together and sharing stories. When we talk we just bounce one story after another off each other. We really get going and have a lot of laughs. It's more difficult to tell you, or anyone else, the stories. They don't come as easy. You forget some good stories. The best ones about my dad are about his early days.

We've been down here ever since we bought the Palm Beach Kennel Club in 1970. I worked here in the beginning, but we bought Yonkers Raceway the following year and I've been there ever since, serving as the president. We winter here every year. So it's more than 30 years now. We're trying to sell Yonkers Raceway now and hope to get that completed soon.

It's never been easy. It's always been a struggle. Sonny Werblin opened the Meadowlands in New Jersey in 1976. You had off-track betting legalized in New York and in Connecticut . You had jai-alai come into Connecticut. Then Atlantic City got all those gambling casinos. We're on the Connecticut border and just across the Hudson River from New Jersey, and you've got action across the border in Canadian cities. So we've always had so much competition. When things were going good in the early '70s, we were making a lot more money from Yonkers Raceway than we were with the Steelers. There was no comparison.

But we're at the end of the rope now. The business has gone down so much and property values have gone up. Yonkers Raceway is open 356 days a year, but it's not as profitable anymore. We can do better by selling it. We can sell it for a lot of money. We paid $48 million for it and it's all paid off. Once we sell it there won't be a track there anymore. It will be developed commercially. It's 90 prime acres.

"I've never known anybody as religious as my father."

All of my memories of my early days in Pittsburgh are fond memories. My family was the source of most of my fond memories. The kids we grew up with. We just had a lot of good friends.

My mom was the centerpiece of our home, like with most families. The biggest thing about her was that she was very, very shy, at least with outsiders. Anyone outside the family would have thought she didn't have much to say. But she was so witty. She knew all these Irish sayings, and she could make you laugh.

I remember riding with my dad in his car. Maybe we'd be making the trip from Pittsburgh to Winfield, Maryland, the site of Shamrock Farms, our family's thoroughbred stable. One of his friends, or someone else in the family would be doing the driving. He'd have the windows wide open, even in the middle of winter. He was chewing tobacco and spitting out the window. He'd be playing with the radio, trying to get a baseball game from somewhere. He specialized in static.

We'd drive somewhere for four or five hours. The whole time he was trying to pick up a baseball game. If there was the slightest hint of a baseball game he'd stay with it for awhile. It would be just rattling, and you could hardly make it out. It was so annoying, but he never complained. If he had a piece of a station that was good enough. In daylight, he'd read his missal or say the rosary while he was riding along. He could say the rosary in the dark.

I've been associated with a lot of religious people. I've kept the company of a lot of priests. But I never met anybody, whether they were cardinals or bishops, who were more religious than my dad.

When I was in Pittsburgh, we went to a lot of funerals. You'd go to see some primary diseased person, but while you were in the funeral home you'd stop in and pay your respects to everyone else who was there, too. You always knew somebody there.

When he had his offices at the old Roosevelt Hotel in downtown Pittsburgh it was really something to see. If you looked outside his office there were always 12 or 15 guys lined up to see my dad. It was like they were waiting for the mayor of Pittsburgh to get jobs or something. People needed things. He did a lot of things to help out people.

He may have been helping some of the old guys with their rent at the Roosevelt, but he was not unbelievably foolish with his money, I can assure you of that. My father was frugal in some ways, generous in other ways.

I remember this guy called him from Chicago and told him that unless he mailed him some money he was going to jump to his death from the church belfry. My father tried to talk him out of that, but I also know he didn't send him any money to make sure he wouldn't jump.

I tried to convince my dad that Johnny Unitas was a good quarterback and that we should keep him. My brothers and I all played catch with Unitas at our training camp, and we all thought he was good. He was the best passer. We had Jim Finks, Ted Marchibroda and Vic Eaton. We were training at St. Bonaventure University that summer (1955), but we had a pre-season game at Green Bay and we stayed for awhile at some college campus in De Pere, Wisconsin. We left there and went to Miami for a game. While we were in Wisconsin, I wrote a 22-page letter to my dad about Unitas. We didn't think the coach, Walt Kiesling, was giving him much of a chance. I'm told that Artie was with my dad when he got my letter at his office in Pittsburgh. I'm told that he rolled the letter up in a ball and pitched it in his waste can. He told my brother, 'That fresh punk thinks he's some kind of football expert.' He thought all of us were fresh punks. But Unitas turned out to have some ability, didn't he?

So we could have had Unitas and there's another story about how we could have had Kelso, one of the greatest race horses in history. There was a guy name Cal Hanford, who was a trainer for us and some other stables. His brother had ridden for us. We were at Garden State when Hanford was offered a job to train horses for the Du Pont family. He had to give up his other commitments if he did so. He was training a three-year-old gelding for the Du Ponts that had a lot of problems. Mrs. Du Pont's advisors told her she should sell the horse. Hanford was an honest guy, and he kept telling her he thought the horse was a good one and that she ought to keep it. She said she'd let it run one more time and if it didn't do well she was going to sell it. So Hanford called my father and told him that if the horse didn't win he ought to buy it. I think it was for sale for $10,000 or $20,000, at the most. My father said he would buy the horse. The horse won that next race. So Mrs. Du Pont kept the horse. It went on to win Horse of the Year honors, and did so for the next few years. And that horse, of course, was Kelso. That was in the '60s. And Kelso is still considered one of the greatest horses in history.

Note to Art Rooney:
   "You are the best influence in Pittsburgh."
               — Father Robert J. Reardon
                  Priest, St. John Capistran
                  Upper St. Clair, Pa.

"We went to football camps in the summer."

I had a lot of favorites among the Steelers in my early years. I liked Johnny "Zero" Clement, Val Jansante — I remember he used to sell shoes at Horne's just around the corner from our offices at the Roosevelt Hotel — and Elbie Nickel was a fabulous receiver. I liked Jim Finks, Bill Walsh and Jack Butler. They were all great guys. My dad liked those guys, too.

I remember we practiced one summer at Alliance College in Cambridge Springs up near Erie. We had an exhibition game in Erie. That was in 1947. This guy named Paul Stenn, a tackle from Villanova, saw me sleeping in the dorm, and he tossed a newspaper over me that hid me. The team left without me and, when they realized they had left me behind, they sent one of the buses back to pick me up.

I never got into too many fights in our neighborhood when I was growing up. Most of my fights were with my brothers. Artie tells a story about getting upset with me when I hit a kid over the head with a piece of sidewalk. Artie told my dad what I had done because he didn't think it was right. My dad didn't get on me about that. He said, "When you fight, you fight with whatever you need."

I remember one time we had an Ireland Fund dinner at Yonkers. One of our employees got punched by a guy in the investment business at the get-together. I called up my father and told him what happened. He said, "You know I always wondered whether that Ireland Fund was really for the Irish. Now that they had a fight I guess they are."

I know we have picked up many of our father's habits. We keep in close touch with one another. We talk to each other just about every day. Yes, we go to church frequently and we all count priests among our close friends and confidantes. We should have picked up more of his habits. One thing we learned from him is that we never thought we were better than anybody else.

My father was a disciplinarian. He expected us to do certain things. We better do this and not do other things. He had strong opinions on how you should behave. There should be more fathers like him today. He was tough on us.

We'd go to religious shrines in Canada every year, and there were so many priests around. They'd have a Mass every half hour. We'd start out going to Mass at 8 a.m., and we'd get there about ten minutes early and there'd be a Mass going on. And he'd say, "You know if we got here a little earlier we'd have been in time for the 7:30 a.m. Mass." And we'd go to the 7:30 a.m. Mass and we'd get there ten or fifteen minutes early, and he'd say, "You know if we got here a little earlier we could have been here in time for the 7 a.m. Mass." By the time our stay was coming to a close, we were going to Mass at 6:30 a.m.

He understood life. The way he grew up and the things he experienced, he understood the world. He understood people. He went through some tough times, and he was as tough as the times.

My wife's name is June Marracini; she's from Clairton. We've been married 42 years, I think. I always get into trouble when I tell people that. I'm usually off by a few years. We have five children. There's Kathleen, 41; Margaret, 39; Bridget, 38; Timmy, 35; and Cara, 28. Kathleen is married to Chris Mara. His first name is really Timothy, the same as his father who's known as T. Wellington Mara. He was named for his father and grandfather, who was the founder of the New York Giants football team. I'm Timothy Rooney, and I was named after Tim Mara who was a close friend of my father. So it's a real coincidence that my oldest daughter is married to one of the Maras.

One time we had a chance to buy Bowie Race Track. It was offered to my father for $1 million. Somebody asked my dad if he was going to do it, and he replied, "Where am I going to get $1 million in cash?" The thought never crossed his mind to borrow any money. His sons borrow money. We're different from him in that respect. We had to borrow about $60 million to buy the tracks that we bought. We had to borrow, relatively speaking, a lot of money.

It's been a wonderful ride. I've lived a life that would be as good as any kid's dream. We didn't go to fancy summer camps like some other kids. We went to football camps.

Being around the team was spectacular. My father and the respect he had from so many people made us all proud. We were always running into people who knew him, no matter where we traveled in North America. When we'd go to Gulfstream or Hialeah, someone in the parking lot would say hello to my father by name. When we went to New York or New Jersey, people knew him.

I remember once he stopped at a bar before he went over a bridge to the Canadian border to get some directions. The bartender recognized him. We went to the World's Fair in Montreal and we were going into the Czechoslovakian pavilion. We were in a line about 30 yards long. The captain came out and called out, 'Mr. Rooney, come on up here. Bring your family along.' And we went to the head of the line. It wasn't that way when we traveled in Europe, but it was that way everywhere else. I don't think the people in Pittsburgh knew that my dad was a celebrity everywhere we went.

I always enjoyed going to Ireland. I'm involved with a group that owns a farm in Ireland. But Ireland has changed. It's not the Ireland I once knew. The religious fervor is gone. The more money that has come into the country has made it different from the way I knew and loved it. The richer it's gotten the poorer of spirit it's gotten.

It's been great to see the Steelers prosper. Danny has done a great job in that respect. He hardly ever leaves Pittsburgh unless it's to go to the NFL owners' meeting or to go to Ireland. Otherwise, you can't get him out of Pittsburgh.

I think that if each one of us boys was given a decision about what we really wanted to do all five of us would have wanted to run the team. No doubt about that. And you look at those teams of the '70s and you'd have to say Artie had quite an impact on those teams when he was running the draft for the Steelers. That was completely Artie's doing. He was picking the right players for the team. He got all the great ones. We sure had a great run. It would be nice to make a similar run one more time. It might not be possible these days.

Tim Rooney and his father check out one of their racing horses.

Art Rooney's five sons in the '70s, from left to right, Dan, John, Art Jr., Pat and Tim.

John Rooney
One of the twins

*"The Chief wasn't a businessman;
he was more of a sportsman."*

*John Rooney, age 62, is the fifth-born son of Art Rooney's five sons. He
and Pat are twins. When we talked to John, on January 12, 2001, we
were struck by how much he sounded like his father on the telephone.
He and Pat and Art, Jr. are most alike in that respect. When John told
a funny story, for instance, he would chortle — that's the only word
that captures what he does — at his own story. His father did the same
thing. He was at his home in West Palm Beach as we talked. I pulled
him away from post-holiday season chores.*

I'm trying to get things cleared away from Christmas. My wife likes
to put a tree and all the decorations up, and now she wants me to
put it away. It kills my back. I hate this part of it. So I'm happy to
take a break to talk about sports. You want to know about my background?

I was always, just about always, I was with the guy who made
all the deals. His name was John T. McCartney. He was a
Philadelphia lawyer and loan arranger. I worked with him when we
were acquiring things. I used to go with him to check out deals we
might make. He was a genius. I watched him making all these deals,
and I was signing all the checks. He became the secretary-treasurer of
our Yonkers corporation. We had the William Penn and Continental
Racing Associations at Liberty Bell Park in Philadelphia. The Chief
was involved, but not that much. The Chief wasn't a businessman; he
was not a wheeler and dealer. He was more of a sportsman. He liked
the action. He liked taking a chance.

We came here to Palm Beach back in 1970, after I had turned 30.
I went to Philadelphia in 1964. So I have spent almost 37 of my 61
years working away from Pittsburgh. Plus, I was away at school for
four other years. So I lived most of my life away from Pittsburgh.
There was a fellow named John Boggiano. Don't ask me to spell that.
He owned the Palm Beach Kennel Club. He was an acquaintance of
my father from Monmouth (N.J.) Park. He owned a restaurant in New
York. He bought the Kennel Club in Palm Beach. He wanted to sell
the place and he called The Chief to see if he might be interested, or
know anyone who might be interested. There's a funny story about
that. My father said he was interested, but said he wanted to have
someone check out the place.

Boggiano asked my father, "Will you be coming down?" My father
says, "No, I'll be sending my boys down." Boggiano got upset by that
remark. Boggiano says, "Hey, we don't do business that way

anymore." He thought my dad was going to send down some kind of tough guys or something. My dad said, "No, I'm talking about my sons. I'm sending my sons down to check it out."

I was the president of the place in the beginning. Then my brother Tim came down. Tim had been working as a stockbroker at a firm in Pittsburgh. He wanted to get out of that.

We bought this place and then we bought Yonkers soon after. I was president there, at first. Pat was supposed to run that. He was running a thoroughbred track in Philadelphia, the Keystone Racing Assn. The track was called something else; I can't remember right now. Timmy was working down here. I was around McCartney. I could sign papers that way and see that everything was being done. We decided to send Timmy to Yonkers.

I became the president here. I was handling this place when we bought Green Mountain in Vermont, near Bennington. It was near Williams, Massachusetts, right on the border.

So, at one time, we had five different tracks, Liberty Bell, Keystone, West Palm Beach Kennel Club, Green Mountain and Yonkers. We had owned part of a track before that, Randall Park in Ohio when I was in college. My dad was in that with a guy from Pittsburgh named Dan Parrish. He owned a construction company. Some people think my dad made sure that all his sons had some piece of the pie, but that's not the way it happened. We bought all these tracks on our own. His name helped because he was well known in the racing business, but we made these acquisitions on our own.

My twin brother Pat and I went to Mount St. Mary's College of Maryland, near Frederick and Gettysburg. It was the oldest independent seminary in the country in addition to being a college. I went to St. Peter's Catholic Grade School on the North Side and then North Catholic High School. All the Rooney boys did that.

I taught school for three years at Plum Boro. I taught English, history and coached the track & field team. You'd take any job that came your way back then. I got an English degree somehow at Mount St. Mary's. There was a Dr. Dillon who was the head of the English department at Mount St. Mary's. His dad was a big detective in Pittsburgh and he knew my dad. I took a lot of courses from him because he looked after me. Next thing I knew I had a major in English and a minor in education. A fellow named Jim Hamer, an old referee, an old Welshman, took me to see a guy named "Mush" at North Park, and he knew about an opening at Plum. A guy named Jack Cummings was out there and he gave me the job. I think I got the job myself, but my brother Dan might have helped me. I'm not sure.

Teaching was the most rewarding job I ever had. I never had another job where you got a rush every day about what you were doing to compare with that. You looked into the faces of the students and you saw that something was coming through. Some learning was taking place. You didn't get that same sort of rush in business.

I was paid $3,800. It was hard to sustain six kids on that sort of money. I had some kids right away and knew we'd be having more. Plum Boro was really pretty rural at the time. My wife's name is JoAnn. She is from the Spring Hill section of the North Side. She went to St. Benedict's Academy, a Catholic girls' school. I met her when I was at North Catholic High School. Our schools did a lot of social things together. Her school was just off Rt. 19, near West View. There was a car barn there. St. Benedict's is now a retreat house.

"Now I cry about everything."

I have five kids now and 15 grandkids. That's pretty good with only three of the five getting married. I lost one of my boys. That was Jimmy. He'd be 35 now. He was killed in an automobile accident when he was 17. That was so difficult for all of us.

When we were talking about me teaching, you asked me if I saw that Robin Williams movie, "Good Will Hunting," about a special teacher at a prep school. Didn't that have a sad ending? I think one of the kids committed suicide. With my situation, I have a hard time watching that stuff. My son didn't commit suicide — I lost him in an auto accident — but I can't deal with kids dying like that. It brings back too many bad memories. I'm emotional. I never used to cry and now I cry about everything. I cry all the time.

My oldest son, Sean, is with Aramark. He runs restaurants at stadiums and arenas around the country. He does very well. Mary Jo, is 38, a good wife and mother, with four kids. Alice is 36. She's like Mary Jo; they're old-fashioned women. They take care of their kids. Jimmy came next. Then we had Peter. There was some time between our first group and second group of kids; which was good. Peter is 28. He is a professor at a school in Dublin, Ireland. Peter teaches English and American Literature. He loves it. I have a son named Matt — he's 26 — who wants to be in your business. He's a writer who just finished graduate school at Columbia. He lives in New York. He's struggling.

I got to Philly when I was 24 years old, so I know what it's like trying to find oneself. I had apprehensions about it when I left Pittsburgh and went away to work. I didn't know if I had done the right thing by giving up teaching. I had a couple of kids right away, and knew we'd have more. It was a tough life then.

When I first went to Philadelphia, I'd come home during the summer and work with the Steelers. In Philly, our track was open a total of 50 racing days, 25 days in the spring and 25 days in the fall, and I'd come home in between.

Did I want to be a part of the Steelers' operation? Sure, I wanted to stay. We all did. That was pretty evident. But the door wasn't really open to anyone but Dan. The rest of us knew — it was made pretty clear to us — that we had to find something different to do. There was no job for me with the Steelers.

396

John Rooney, rear left, and Johnny Laughlin and Dan Rooney, rear right, shared coaching duties for St. Peter's Grade School squad in the Catholic Grade School Football League in 1956. Jim Parks (No. 20 in front of Dan Rooney) provided this photo.

Jim O'Brien

Taking in final game at Three Rivers Stadium are three wives of the Rooneys, left to right, Kathleen (Art Jr.), JoAnn (John) and Sandy (Pat).

Jim O'Brien

John Rooney at final game at Three Rivers Stadium.

Sam Quincy/Palm Beach Kennel Club

Art Rooney with previous Palm Beach Kennel Club owner John Boggiano.

We did things according to age in our family. Even eating. I was the youngest. So I know how that works better than anybody in the family.

Personally, I don't think it works. But age determines everything. It sets up the succession link. Danny worked with the Steelers because he was the oldest. It's that simple. I don't say that begrudgingly. It's the way it was. As far as young Artie goes, we didn't know if he'd be the heir apparent. But Dan has declared him as such, so that's the way it is. If something happened to Dan, hey, we're not that far behind Dan in age. Dan is the most capable because he was trained in the field. He's been in the football business all his life.

Danny was older than the rest of us and he started in the football business. Art got into scouting. Art was very very capable. I think he should be in the Hall of Fame. He's every bit as deserving as Dan. He had as much to do with our team's success. Art wasn't groomed to be in the business end of things. Artie studied to be an actor. It was difficult for the rest of us when Dan decided that Art didn't fit into the football picture anymore. That was difficult for my father to accept.

We never had any problems in our family aside from that.

I ran a racetrack that made a lot of money. Our jobs were bigger jobs. Danny wouldn't want to admit this, but we were making more money in the '60s and '70s. It was great to run a racetrack. But the football business has grown, and things exploded for the National Football League, and the value of the franchise has soared. We split the profits pretty evenly each year and we have all benefited by the boon in pro football.

We weren't involved in the Steelers' business one bit. That's been Dan's baby, and he's been grooming his oldest son, Artie, or Art II, to succeed him.

Yep, my father didn't care about what we thought until we were adults. He wasn't trying to be your friend. He wasn't trying to be our buddy. He was our father. From the time you were ten till you were 21, he was your father. I don't know if it would work today. We raised our kids a little differently; we were more involved with them.

Times were different. My father was always out working; he was away a lot. My mother would say when your dad gets back he's going to straighten you out. My dad was involved with us. He played with us when we were little kids. He wasn't going to take you on a fishing trip. The older I get the more I appreciate him being that way.

What was his secret? I don't know if you've ever experienced this. Have you ever gone into a roomful of people, and someone came in who was special? That person is not always a good guy. I remember a time when I met Mr. (Ernest) Gallo at the Super Bowl. He was the wine maker. I knew who he was, but he grabbed the attention of every one in the room when he entered. Jack Kent Cooke...he wasn't our cup of tea, but you knew he was special. I've met a few guys like that. The Chief was like that. He goes into a full room and it belongs to him. He was one of those guys who had an air about them. The special thing about The Chief...he made everybody feel like he was their best friend.

So many of the Steelers thought they were his favorite ballplayer.

"All you have to do is go to Ireland and you'll know you're not Irish."

Sometimes you'd get him going at the dinner table. He'd tell stories about when he was a boy. He could keep you in a spell. I don't remember the specific stories; Art knows them. At Thanksgiving or Christmas, he'd talk more than he would otherwise. You could sit around and be mesmerized. Unlike young people today, we respected our elders. I hate to be critical of young people; they're doing OK. But we sat down to dinner every night, and our dad was the center of our attention.

My Aunt Alice lived with us. My mother and aunt never sat down. They fed us. Aunt Alice was my wife's sister. That was like the Irish; there's always one who doesn't get married. She lived there with us. She was a McNulty. She and my mother were cousins of Father McAnulty, the president of Duquesne University. My dad had a great relationship with Father McAnulty. They spelled their name differently because someone dropped a letter when they came through Ellis Island, or something like that. Once upon a time they all had the same name.

Being Irish was important in our house. Where we came from on the North Side, everybody was Irish. We'd always do something special on St. Patrick's Day. I don't think the Irish thing got to be a big thing until we got involved with the Ancient Order of Hibernians. Our dad didn't talk about being Irish. Other people talked about us being Irish. I think my dad always talked about himself as being an American. My mother used to say, "Be proud of being Irish, but not too proud."

Art and I are not as crazy about being Irish. I think of myself being of Irish heritage. I'm not Irish, really. All you have to do is go to Ireland and you know you're not Irish. As soon as you talk, they know you're a Yank. Danny loves it over there. Tim has a place over there. Pat rents a place over there. Pat likes Ireland because of golf.

The Irish people are wonderful. They know how to laugh.

I remember some special times with my father. Being in a car with him going to the racetrack. Being with my mom and my wife. He'd be relaxed. He loved it. People in Pittsburgh didn't realize it. They didn't know how much of a race guy he was. He enjoyed it as much as football. He liked the action. The football team wasn't as big a deal then as it is now.

> ### A Man For All Seasons
> *"I would have to look to my background and what my dad taught me. That is: You are just as good as anyone, but you're no better than anyone. Never forget it.*
> — John Wooden

He was a big shot at the racetrack. Not with the big shots, but with the bettors, with the guys in the parking lot, with the maître d' in the dining room, by the regular people. They all knew my dad. He was a big shot in the racing business. Not like the Galbreaths, who owned the Pirates. The Galbreaths were big shots with the horse owners. They had a big horseracing farm in Columbus. The Chief didn't own a big time horse. He had some horses that ran at smaller tracks. He was mostly into the gambling end of it.

He was always telling us not to buy Cadillacs or Lincolns, or luxury cars. He thought Buicks were big enough and good enough. I owned a Lincoln when I had Liberty Bell. It was a Lincoln Continental Mark IV with the fake tire thing in the back. I didn't think he knew what it was. He said, "What kind of car is that?' I said, 'It's a Ford.' Figuring it was a Ford-Lincoln car, I didn't think I was really lying to him. He said, "Don't take me for some kind of rube. I know it's a Lincoln. How are you going to negotiate a contract with the mutuel union? Get yourself a Buick; they're not so showy and they're good cars."

The Buicks he bought were always loaded. They were as classy inside as any Cadillacs. My mother's father, you see, owned North Side Buick. It was the first Buick agency in Pittsburgh. He owned the dealership. Dad was loyal to that sort of thing.

My dad called us all every day and now we're pretty good about staying in touch with each other. I know I sound like my dad on the phone. I'm getting old and fat, and I'm looking more like he did.

My brother Pat plays more golf than Jack Nicklaus. He played on his wife's birthday and on Christmas. I don't play much anymore because my back is bad. Everybody is down here except Dan during the winter. Tim comes down every year. Tim is staying in Swellsville. He's over in Palm Beach with the rich dudes. Art is on his way here right now. He and his wife, Kathleen, are on their way here. Kay, as we call her, is really a nice lady. She's fun.

Since I can't play golf much anymore, I go fishing. I always did fish. My dad fished. Not many people knew, but my dad went up to Canada now and then. He said he was going fishing. Maybe there was a place to gamble up there. Who knows? I just know I never went fishing with him.

He'd get upset at you for some small thing and he'd holler at you and give you a rough time. He didn't really swear, but he substituted other words that were nasty in the way he said them. But when there was a real problem he'd be there for you. It was like when my boy died. He was there for me. He was calling me up every day; he was sympathetic all through that difficult time.

He called me up every day of his life, every day. I guess that's why I do it; after growing up like that. I talk to Pat every day. I see Pat every day. I don't talk to Tim every day; he's always going somewhere. Dan isn't available every day.

My dad was great. He was always your dad. He sent us postcards from everywhere in the world. He wrote funny remarks on the cards.

I can remember when I was in Pittsburgh. He'd call me and tell me to come down to the office. He said we had to go to a funeral. I'd ask, "Who are we going to see?" He'd say, "I don't know, but we'll know when we get there." We'd stop at four five places and he'd stop to see everyone who was there.

My brothers and I used to have to be pallbearers for these homeless people who were buried through St. Vincent de Paul Society. My dad thought he was Digger O'Dell. Some guy with no family would die and he'd volunteer us for pallbearers at the funeral. One day I'm there alongside the casket of some guy we're burying. His daughter and son showed up at the last moment. "Can you open the box so we can see him?" they asked. The funeral director protested vehemently. "We can't do that; it's against the law," he said. "Once it's sealed, we're not allowed to open it."

"Can't you do this one last thing for us so we can see him before he's buried," they asked. The priest said, "Open it." So the funeral director opens the casket and the guy was in the casket stark naked. The funeral director had stolen the guy's clothes that the St. Vincent de Paul Society people had given him for his funeral.

We'd be going to a ballgame together and he'd see some guys he knew outside the ballpark. He always had you give your tickets to somebody. He'd say, "You don't need it. You just walk into the ballpark with me. Nobody is going to stop you." He was great at giving things away — of yours!

Rooney boys check out UPMC Sports Complex on South Side a few days before final Steelers game at Three Rivers Stadium. From left to right, they are Tim, Art Jr., Pat, Dan and John.

Pat Rooney
One of the Philly Whiz Kids

"No one knows me in the Steelers offices anymore."

Pat Rooney is one of the twins. He and John are the two youngest of Art Rooney's five sons. They turned 62 on March 7, 2001. Pat was in his office at the Palm Beach Kennel Club in Florida when we spoke. Two of his other brothers, Art, Jr. and Tim, were wintering nearby. So four of the five Rooney boys spent a lot of time together at the outset of 2001. Dan, the oldest, was back in Pittsburgh looking after the Steelers and the completion of their new stadium and North Side development plans. "I'm glad you talked to my brothers Tim, John and Pat for your project," wrote Art, Jr. in a postcard he sent to me in early March from Palm Beach. "They've always felt left out and they have much to offer."

I remember when we were just starting out at Liberty Bell Racetrack in Philly. John and I were there, and Jerry Lawrence, who was the son of David L. Lawrence, the former mayor of Pittsburgh and governor of Pennsylvania, were in charge. Jack Kiser, who covered harness racing, wrote a wonderful article about us in the *Philadelphia Daily News*. John probably still has the clipping. They called us "The Whiz Kids." That was in the summer of 1964. Of course, the Philadelphia Phillies once had a terrific baseball team they called "The Whiz Kids" back around 1950. Kiser was crazy, but he was smart and respected in the business. I don't think anyone will be calling us "Whiz Kids" any more.

Betting on harness racing had just been legalized in the state and we were in on it at the beginning. We've been away from Pittsburgh since then so we never really were that involved with the operation of the Steelers. We spent so little time in Pittsburgh.

We were all there for the Steelers' final game at Three Rivers Stadium and that was something to experience. There were a lot of good memories there, but we're excited about the new stadium, too. It should be something special. We had our picture taken — the five of us Rooneys — at the new training complex on the South Side. I have it here on my desk.

The last connection I had with the Steelers' front office, aside from my brother Dan, was Mary Regan, who had been my dad's secretary all those years. When they left Three Rivers Stadium for the new set-up on the South Side, Mary Regan retired. When I went in there before Mary Regan was the only one who knew me. I don't know who to see now. That's the way it is.

We bought this place (Palm Beach Kennel Club) in 1970. I moved here in 1984 and I've been in Florida ever since. We have a new home here in Jupiter. We also have a small farm in Hellertown, Pennsylvania. I spent a lot of time here in the beginning. I have seven kids. I have Pat, Jr., Joe, Theresa — we call her Terry — and Christopher, Thomas. Brian and Monica — we call her Molly. My oldest son was born in Pittsburgh, when we lived in Green Tree.

My son, Pat, the lawyer, loves to play golf even more than I do and he's quite good. Joe has a master's and doctorate degrees and is a professor at Lynn University. He pooled some money from his brothers and sisters and is the manager of Rooney's Public Houses. There are now three of them in the South Florida area. They are Irish pubs, like the kind my grandfather had on the North Side, only nicer. Chris, who's getting his master's degree at Pitt, is working in the new family business as manager of one of the Rooney Public Houses. The kids have done well in school and are all doing well.

My twin brother John and I went to Philadelphia to open Liberty Bell, so the rest of my kids weren't born in Pittsburgh. My wife is Sandy. You knew her as Sandy Sully in Hazelwood. Didn't you go to school with her younger sister, Susan? Yeah, their dad was a guard at Western Penitentiary.

John and I had both gone to school together, too, when we went to Mt. St. Mary's in Maryland. We went there with Johnny Laughlin, our cousin, who was the son of the owner of Johnny Laughlin's Shamrock Restaurant, which was a big hangout of my father and his friends on the North Side. It's still there.

I was a tennis player when I was growing up on the North Side. I learned how to play on the courts at Monument Hill, not far from our home. My brother Timmy had his own baseball team. He was the worst baseball player you ever saw. Timmy couldn't play, so he started his own team. Richie McCabe, who played football at North Catholic, Pitt and with the Steelers, was one of our friends. Richie and his brothers all hung out with us at Monument Hill.

You could play basketball and baseball up there. Sometimes you had to wait your turn to play. They had real good tennis courts at West Park, too. They were well taken care of. Sometimes we'd go over there. You know Gus Karalis, the fellow who sells ice balls, peanuts and popcorn there? We'll, we knew his parents when they had that stand. They've always been out there. They used to be on the other side of the railroad bridge there, closer to St. Peter's Church and School. Then they moved down by the tennis courts.

It was fun growing up on the North Side. We were just talking about it. It was a great place. It changed dramatically during the time I was away at college. When I went away it was okay. Contrary to what people might think today, the North Side was a vibrant place. St. Peter's was a big church. It was a friendly place. It was a tough place, too, like Hazelwood when you were young, but it wasn't so dangerous. A lot of the people on the North Side didn't have much money, but they behaved better back then. When you went to St. Peter's it was packed with people.

We'd hang out at the local YMCA. It was a great place. In the old days they had a great cafeteria and people lived there. It was a real action place. Up around Allegheny General Hospital, all the German people lived there, in Deutschtown. That was a great area up there, up around Western Avenue and Madison Avenue. Above that was Troy Hill, another great neighborhood.

There was a farmer's market up at East Ohio Street. The old Boggs & Buhl Department Store was there. Sears & Roebuck had a store. There was a Carnegie Library, a Heights Drug Store and, as I said, the Market House. It was a disgrace that they ever tore that down. I thought they killed the North Side with redevelopment. The same thing happened with East Liberty. They took the heart out of it. Manchester was a very, very great area. A lot of people lived there. There were some magnificent homes there. Some of them, I'm told, have been restored, but they've never been able to get the whole neighborhood back to the way it was, which was the plan.

You had St. Andrew's and St. Joe's. There were a lot of activities there. Getting into North Catholic (High School) was a real honor back then.

I was reading in the paper prior to the Super Bowl about Wellington Mara, the owner of the New York Giants. He was talking about things his father told him. He was eight years old when the Giants got into the NFL. He said his father said the NFL would never be a big thing, but it would be fun.

That's so true. Some fans today don't understand that pro football wasn't the way it is today back in the late '40s or '50s. People can't understand that today. It was totally different. It wasn't the big deal it is today. I can remember when we were quite young that all the boys would be out at the steel mills passing out season ticket flyers to the workers when they'd be coming to work or going home from work. You could get a season ticket for $25 or $30 back in those days.

The guys who owned the teams then were sportsmen and guys who enjoyed being around sports activity. My dad had been a ballplayer — semi-pro football and minor league baseball — and a top-notch amateur boxer. A lot of the owners, like George Halas, were guys of that ilk. Up until 1920 or 1925, football wasn't much of a sport. Baseball was clearly the No. 1 sport, and lived up to its name as the national pastime. Boxing was bigger, so was horseracing, even golf back then. When football became important it was college football and not pro football.

My dad used to talk to us a lot. He talked to every one of us every day. Forever. I talk to John every day. I talk to Tim about three or four times a week. I talk to Art several times a week. I talk to Dan now and then. John talks to Dan almost every day, and he tells me what Dan said. I talk to Art II. Yeah, I talk to young Art about different things that we're involved with. I talk to them about the American Ireland Fund in Washington D.C., stuff like that. I'm not as involved as Dan, but I've been involved in it from Day One. Dan and Tony O'Reilly of the H.J. Heinz Co. really started it. It's involved in peace efforts, culture and charity work.

I've been involved in several projects in Ireland. Some peace projects, trying to have safe houses, trying to bring both sides together to discuss issues, not on the political side, but on a personal level. We've set up charitable gifts. I had a house in County Clare for ten years. I sold it last year. I rent a place now. I spend about two months a year over there. I must go over three times a year. We have an American Ireland Fund meeting in June. Dan goes over there, too. We have a Rooney prize for literature over there.

(Author's note: When I told Pat I was reading a book called How The Irish Saved Civilization, he said he knew about it. "The Scottish and Welsh have books like that, too," he said with a laugh.)

My interest in Ireland started with my parents' interest in Ireland, of course. And I was educated at St. Peter's. The Mercy nuns taught there and their order originated in Ireland. The first time I went over I went with Tim and our good friend Baldy Regan. Baldy and his wife both had family in Ireland. We met them all. I've enjoyed going over there. I travel around the country and play golf. Playing at a place like the Black Bush. I've enjoyed going to my grandfather's place in Newry. My mother's people were from Derry in Northern Ireland. I love the Irish people and always feel good when I'm there.

Jim O'Brien

John and Pat Rooney take in Steelers' final game at Three Rivers Stadium from club owners' box.

Fans of Art Rooney
They remember him fondly

"You do go back a way."

John Henry
Johnson

Jim Kriek has been writing sports for the Uniontown
Herald-Standard *since 1979. Before that, he wrote
sports for the* Connellsville Courier *from 1961 to 1979. He was officially retired in 1991, after he had reported on the Pittsburgh Steelers
for eight years, but he continues to contribute stories on scholastic
sports happenings in Fayette County. Kriek, who turned 73 in May,
2001, treasures those years with the Steelers, but enjoys the high school
kids just as much.*

"Art Rooney came into the media room one day at Three Rivers
Stadium. He sat down and started to talk to us. He said, 'There are
two kinds of people I like to talk to — old politicians and old
sportswriters.' Our buddy Norm Vargo, from the *McKeesport Daily
News*, was there and he piped up. 'Well, you should talk to him,' he
said, pointing his finger in my direction. 'He's the oldest sportswriter
here.'

"Mr. Rooney said, 'Is that so? How old are you?'

"Vargo came back, 'Heck, he interviewed Curly Lambeau. That'll
give you some idea of how old he is.'

"Mr. Rooney said, 'Is that true?'

"And I said, 'No, but I did interview George Halas.'

"Mr. Rooney smiled and said, 'Well, you do go back a way, don't
you?'"

"That man was one of God's good people."

Leona Johnson is the wife of John Henry Johnson, who played
fullback for the Steelers from 1960 and 1965, and had some great
seasons. Leona was with her husband at the Pro Football Hall of
Fame in Canton, Ohio in late July, 2001

"When John was traded to the Steelers we initially stayed at the
Roosevelt Hotel in downtown Pittsburgh where the team had its
offices. The first Sunday we were there we went to eat dinner in the
dining room. John Henry told me they had the best prime rib in the
world. When we went into the dining room, the whole Rooney family
was there. They saw us. Mr. Rooney was so gracious. He came over
and visited with us. He said, 'Is this your sweetheart?'

"His family was taking up about four or five tables. There were
so many of them. He introduced us to every one of them.

"Toward the end of his stay with the Steelers, John Henry asked Dan Rooney for a raise. He said he couldn't give John a raise. John lost his temper. He told Dan that his dad would have given him the raise, that he was fair and always appreciated what he did for the team. When they had the 50 Seasons celebration, Mr. Rooney asked John and me to sit next to him. He said he was heart-broken that John was upset with the Steelers. He said, 'If John had waited for me, I'd have given him the raise.' When John was inducted into the Pro Football Hall of Fame, he wanted Mr. Rooney to be his presenter. He said Mr. Rooney was always good to him and was a big reason for his success in Pittsburgh. He liked playing for Mr. Rooney. He respected him. That man was one of God's good people."

Andy Russell, Pro Bowl caliber linebacker for 12 seasons (1963, 1966-76), and a successful businessman in Pittsburgh:

"In the final game of my rookie season, we were playing the Giants in New York to determine who'd finish first in our division. We had beaten New York easily (31-0) early in the season. I thought we were going to the championship game. I was starting at linebacker and was so proud of what we'd done. We blew it and we lost (33-17) and we shouldn't have. We finished with a 7-4-3 record. To this day, the classiest act I ever saw Art Rooney do came after that game. We came that close to winning a championship for him, and we let it get away. It was not a pretty game. The coaches coached it badly and we played it badly. Yet he went around the locker room in Yankee Stadim and shook hands with each player, and wished us all a good off-season. To this day, that's the single-most classy thing he ever did."

Beano Cook, ESPN sports analyst, former sports information director at the University of Pittsburgh:

"I kidded Art Rooney once about letting all the priests in free to the games. He got upset with me. He said, 'I let the ministers and rabbis in for free, too.' I could tell he'd taken the heat. But he smiled and he knew I was just kidding him. He was the best."

Sophie Masloff, former mayor of the City of Pittsburgh:

"We all knew and loved The Chief. He stopped to talk to every-one. To Art Rooney, everyone he met was someone special. He made you feel important."

Pro Bowl and Hall of Fame linebacker Jack Lambert:

"My fondest memory of playing for the Pittsburgh Steelers was the twinkle in Arthur J. Rooney's eyes. When we pass the statue, we will be forever reminded of that twinkle. We meet so few truly great men in our lifetime. As members of the older generation, it is our duty to tell the stories of Art Rooney, to tell his acts of generosity. Most of all, tell them how he cared not whether his players were black or white, Catholic, Protestant or Jew. We were all his boys. And, in this day and age, what a beautiful legend to leave behind."

Hall of Fame running back Franco Harris:

"This remarkable and grand man has made a lot of special times for all of us. He was always there to help and to give. And this feeling filtered down to the players. I think the Steelers players give more to their community than any other team in professional sports."

John C. Veasey, editor of *Fairmont Times West Virginian*:

"I have always been a very strong Pirates fan, but I've only seen the Steelers in action once in my life, and that was the playoff game with the Miami Dolphins the week after Franco Harris' 'Immaculate Reception' in 1972.

"I vividly remember attending that game with *Morgantown Dominion-Post* sports editor Mickey Furfari on Dec. 31 on a 70-degree New Year's Eve just because of all the excitement sparked by that great victory over Oakland one week earlier.

"I can recall casual chats with Art Rooney at Pittsburgh Pirates games over the years. Even though I'm sure he had no idea who I was, he was always the perfect gentleman and it was always a pleasure running into him on the old elevator, in the press box or wherever, and exchanging a few words. Even today, years later, I can recall no one ever being any nicer to an out-of-state sportswriter than he was, even though I was only a fan of his team through the magic of television."

Jerry Green, sportswriter for *The Detroit News*:

"Art Rooney was much more available than most owners I knew. He was more of a people person, for instance, than William Ford, the owner of the Lions. Ford was from a famous family, the grandson of Henry Ford, and he was from a different background than Rooney. Ford was born into money. I remember how people thought about the Steelers when they started going to Super Bowls. They were a franchise that came from the pits. They were favorites with a lot of people. Art was fortunate to pick Chuck Noll to coach the team. He was probably the dullest coach we ever listened to at a Super Bowl — he put us down a lot — so the writers were happy the team had a friendly, quotable owner with good stories to tell."

"It is our duty to tell the stories of Art Rooney."
— Jack Lambert

Jerry Magee, sportswriter for the *San Diego Union-Tribune*, started covering pro football when the Chargers moved from Los Angeles to San Diego in 1961, the second year of the AFL. Magee has covered every Super Bowl:

"After he became aware of my fondness for cigars, Art Rooney used to send me a box of cigars each Christmas with a little note. They were of a quality better than I normally smoked or could afford. Among the highlights of my years on this beat was observing Pittsburgh's four Super Bowl championship teams. Having an association with the late Art Rooney was another. When I last saw him he was sitting around with a cop and a truck driver. Rooney did not have to walk with the mighty. After Rooney's death, I was in Pittsburgh for a game and I asked Ed Kiely if he would take me out to the cemetery where Rooney was buried. I went there with Kiely to pay my respects. I'd like to think Art Rooney was aware of my presence. Anyone who knows anything about fast horses and good cigars has not lived in vain."

Andy Rooney, social critic and curmudgeon for CBS "60 Minutes," and long-time season-ticket holder of the New York Giants:

"I went to an NFL owners' meeting once in Palm Springs. I went to pick up a rental car at the airport and they gave me Art Rooney's car by mistake."

Leonard Shapiro, a sportswriter for 32 years with *The Washington Post* and a member of the selection committee for the Pro Football Hall of Fame:

"To me, Dan Rooney is the most cooperative owner in the National Football League. He's totally unlike anybody I've been around in the league. Art Modell is like that, too. There's no pretentiousness. Dan walks around, looking as if he's still the ballboy. The first time I ever saw Dan Rooney he treated me like he had known me for 20 years. He ought to be the role model for every owner in the league, especially a young owner like Daniel Snyder of the Washington Redskins. With Dan Rooney, everything is about the team, the city and not Dan Rooney. One of the great pleasures in life was voting him into the Hall of Fame. I was one of those who spoke on his behalf. With him, there's no flash; it's all substance. At league meetings, he's always there for us. Most of those guys dash to the airport. He stops. Not to get publicity; he knows we need to find out what's going on. He doesn't have a television face. It's the same face all the time. He helped Lynn Swann's candidacy for the Hall of Fame. I think he called every voter on behalf of Swann. He didn't have to do that. I expect he'll do the same for Stallworth. He knew they weren't going in as a package deal."

409

Cathy Pawlowski of Castle Shannon works for Cold-Comp Typography and has set the type for all the books in the "Pittsburgh Proud" series. Her beloved mother, Bernie Bonnar, died as we were completing this book but Cathy continued her work during a difficult time which was appreciated by everyone associated with the project:

"My brother, Father Dave Bonnar, celebrates Mass for some of the Steelers players before the home games over the past four years. He usually goes to one or two away games with the team. Dan Rooney attends sometimes. Dave is one of the biggest Steelers fans I know. When he was studying in Rome, he created a 'Pittsburgh Room' at the North American College. A little story about Dave's first Mass for the Steelers ... He asked the players if there was anyone they wanted to pray for. Various players prayed for some serious things and then Jim Sweeney said that ever since he was a kid growing up in Beechview his parents always taught him to pray for his opponent. So he said he would like to pray for their opponent. The next day the Cowboys beat the Steelers. The following week when Dave was celebrating Mass he once again asked if anyone wanted to pray for something in particular. Mike Tomczak spoke up right away and said, 'Let's not pray for our opponent!' The Steelers won the next day.

"Celebrating Mass for the Steelers is a dream come true for my brother. Last season he was in the owners' box with Art II and Dan for the Titans game. The Steelers lost that game in the last few seconds. As they were leaving, when the elevator doors opened, Bud Adams, the Titans' owner, was standing there. The first thing Dan Rooney did was shake his hand and congratulate him on a great game. It was a class act all the way. Dave feels Dan is a reflection of his father. When my mother died, Dave received a card from Art Rooney, Jr. He wrote that the Irish believe the mothers of priests go straight to heaven."

Dave Wannstedt, the head football coach of the Miami Dolphins, played football at the University of Pittsburgh and Baldwin High School:

"When I was at Pitt, I always admired Mr. Rooney. The first thing that comes to my mind is seeing him on TV, surrounded by children, in that United Way ad. The Steelers were lucky to have a man like him at the top. His attitude seemed to be that we'll find a way to get through this. I used to go to their camp every year, and I had a good rapport with George Perles and Woody Widenhofer, their defensive coaches. I've always been a big Steelers' fan. They say I finished second to Bill Cowher when they picked the coach to succeed Chuck Noll, so they must have liked me, too. It worked out well for them and it's worked out fine for me."

> *"One thing I've really enjoyed is the fact that the team has always been a strong part of the city. We are Pittsburgh's Steelers, not just some team with the name of a city."*
> — Lynn Swann

Marcy Canterna, a school teacher at Franklin Regional whose father, Oland "Dodo" Canterna, was the athletic director at St. Vincent College when the Steelers conducted their summer training camp at the Latrobe campus in the 1970s:

"I was introduced to Art Rooney in the parking lot at St.Vincent College in August of 1978. He was pleasant and we spoke for a few minutes. It was the first time I'd ever met him and the last time I saw him until the Super Bowl. I went to Miami with some friends for the Super Bowl. I walked out of the front door of the hotel as he was stepping out of the door of an automobile. I said hello, figuring he wouldn't know me from Adam. I was wrong. After five months, and after having met me once in his life, he spoke to me and called me by name. He asked me how I was and if I was having a good time. I wished him well and expressed my hope for a Steelers' victory. I am still astounded that after a lifetime of meeting people — many important sports figures, businessmen, celebrities and media personalities — and that he remembered my name from one meeting five months earlier. That's the kind of person he was. He always made you feel important."

Bob Oates, veteran sportswriter for *The Los Angeles Times*, and a charter member of the selection committee for Pro Football Hall of Fame:

"I saw an item in our paper that reminded me on an event I attended. Art Rooney was out here in Los Angeles for the funeral of Carroll Rosenbloom, the owner of the Rams. Rooney was here with Ed Kiely, the Steelers' public relations guy. Dan Reeves, the original owner of the Rams, used to call Rooney 'Mr. Lucky' because of his success at the horseracing tracks. A man attending the funeral came up to Art Rooney and congratulated him on his success with the Steelers and at the racetracks. When the man left, Rooney turned to Kiely and said, 'He was a nice fellow. What does he do?' Kiely replied, 'Art, that was the movie actor Cary Grant.'"

Jack Wagner, Pennsylvania State Senator, Vietnam veteran and former member of Pittsburgh City Council:

"I remember how I first met Mr. Rooney. I was walking near his home on the North Side campaigning for City Council. I was about 30 years old. I spotted him walking on the sidewalk and went up to him. 'Mr. Rooney, I just want to say hello,' I said. 'I've been an admirer of yours for a long time.' He extended his hand in greeting. 'I'm Jack Wagner,' I said. He looked at me and took the cigar out of his mouth. 'Wagner, huh? Wagner. Are you the guy who has those signs all over town?' He invited me into his home, had someone get me a cold soda, and sat down and talked to me for about 20 minutes. It's a precious memory."

Bill Hillgrove grew up in Garfield and graduated from Central Catholic High School and Duquesne University, and has been "the voice" of both the Pittsburgh Panthers in football and basketball, and the Steelers:

"He knew I was Irish, but he said he could never find the name Hillgrove on any maps of Ireland. My ancestors came in from England to County Cork. I told him they were in the hotel business, and he liked that because his dad had been in the hotel and tavern business. He said, 'You're golden people, real lace curtain, not shanty Irish like the Rooneys.' He always had fun with me. He was one of the most honest sports figures I ever met."

Bill Priatko, 69. who played at Pitt and briefly with the Steelers with his good friend, Richie McCabe, remembers a story McCabe told him. McCabe played at St. Peter's Catholic Grade School and North Catholic and was close to the Rooneys. He was a water boy at the Steelers' summer camps along with the Rooney boys and played for the Steelers in 1955, 1957 and 1958:

"I remember Richie telling me when he found out just how rich Art Rooney was. He used to go to horse racing tracks with him and place bets for him. Richie said they were at Thistledown in Cleveland and Mr. Rooney gave him $2,000 to bet to win. Richie went to the wrong window and by the time he got to the 'Win' window it was closed. He blew it. He went back and apologized to Mr. Rooney for not getting his bet down. The horse was a 20-to-1 shot and it won. Mr. Rooney told him, 'Don't worry, Rich, we'll get the next one.' Richie said he also realized the peace of mind that Mr. Rooney enjoyed. He said that one time Mr. Rooney held up both of his hands to Richie and said, 'See those five fingers on each hand. In your lifetime if you're fortunate to have two good friends (he kept two fingers up to make his point) you're lucky. I have a lot of people who say they're my friends, but they're not really my friends. They're acquaintances or people I've met.'"

Philip Monti, 87 years old as of May, 2001, lives in retirement in Mt. Lebanon. He worked all his life in service positions in hotels and restaurants in Downtown Pittsburgh. He was a bartender, a host, you name it. He is always well dressed, though he confesses his clothes are all 40 years old. He remembers Art Rooney from his early days in the business:

"He had a horseracing room on Liberty Avenue in downtown Pittsburgh. I was working at The Pittsburgher Hotel at Diamond and Grant streets and later the Villa Madrid Restaurant on Liberty Avenue. I remember Rooney coming around, always dressed well, coat and tie, paying off bets. Everybody knew him. He had his paper money wrapped in a rubber band. I never heard him swear. People would tell

412

you how he was taking care of nuns on the North Side and in Millvale. He did so much charity work, and he did it quietly. He had such a great reputation. He was in the gambling business, but he had a high moral character. There's nothing wrong with gambling. Now the state is in the business. So how can it be bad? Rooney was a good man. Everyone trusted him. His word was gospel. That wasn't true of everybody in that business. Guys like that are gone. Those guys were great sports."

PHILIP MONTI
Hotel service

DAVE WANNSTEDT
Dolphins Coach

ANDY RUSSELL
Steelers linebacker

Andy Russell

RICHIE McCABE
Steelers defensive back

> *"I'm a Pittsburgh guy and that'll never change."*
> — Mike Ditka
> Hall of Famer

Val Jansante
He went back to Bentleyville

"He's still my hero."
— Zeb Jansante

Val Jansante is sitting across from me at a table in Ruby
Tuesdays at The Galleria in Mt. Lebanon, about two miles from
my home in Upper St. Clair. His son, Zeb Jansante, is sitting
next to him. Zeb lives in nearby Bethel Park. He drove down that
morning to Bentleyville, about 25 miles south, to pick up his dad to
deliver him to me for a luncheon interview. This is Wednesday, April
18, 2001.

Zeb, dressed in black shirt and slacks that went well with his
dark hair and eyes, is the principal of a middle school in the Quaker
Valley School District of Sewickley. The school is on spring break. Zeb
is pushing photographs of his father toward me. Most of them are
cracked, dog-eared, faded, but intriguing just the same. A few are in
good shape. Zeb is telling me about his father's feats, when he led the
Steelers in receiving five straight years (1946-1950).

The father just smiles as his son extolls his virtues and accomplishments. He is wearing a plaid flannel shirt that looks warm and
comfortable, like his smile.

Val Jansante played two seasons for the Steelers under Jock
Sutherland, and four more under Sutherland's disciple, John
Michelosen. In his sixth season with the Steelers, he was traded at
mid-year to the Green Bay Packers. He didn't like being that far from
home and retired at the end of the 1951 season. He was only 29 at the
time. Zeb thought his father could have posted some impressive pass-
catching numbers had he stayed in the game longer. Zeb keeps
prompting his father to tell me about this or that aspect of his life.

Val wasn't one to boast about such things.

Both Jansantes had a gleam in their dark eyes. "As you can see,"
said Zeb, "he's still my hero. He's the only Steeler ever to lead the
team in receiving five straight years. I never knew how good he was
— he never talked about it — until I started doing some research on
my own. He was really a terrific player."

My mind is wandering, like it did sometimes when I was sitting
at my desk as a freshman at Central Catholic High School in Oakland.
Val Jansante was the head football coach of the Vikings at the time.
I remember seeing him in the hallways at school where he was also a
teacher, seeing him in the gym, and on the sidelines at practice and
the team's games.

I was always impressed with Val Jansante. For one thing, I loved
that name. I still enjoy saying it aloud. For another, I had his bubble
gum card when I was in grade school, at St. Stephen's in Hazelwood,

414

a community at the southeastern tip of inner-city Pittsburgh. I had his card when it was black and white, and also when the cards went to color.

I was sitting in Ruby Tuesday's, but I was back at that red-brick castle on Fifth Avenue that they call Central District Catholic High School.

I went out for the football team that first year at Central, back in the fall of 1956. I was foolhardy to do so. I was one of the smallest kids in my class, 1F. I was a real shrimp. I had started at halfback as an eighth grader for St. Stephen's and that prompted me to think I could continue to play for the school team. I ran some laps in gym shorts around the field behind the school after classes at the opening day of tryouts. I was not invited to return. Thus my high school football career at Central began and ended on the same day.

I never held a grudge or resentment against Jansante or his assistants, Fran Collins and Ed Fay. There were several players from my hometown on the Vikings' football team, like Johnny Kirsh, Paul Rowser, Joe Burns, Buddy Hanka and Marty Moran, and I went to their games and rooted for them. I still remember the school cheers. You had to learn them or you couldn't go home from school until you did.

I went out for the school newspaper, *The Viking*, and the yearbook, *Towers*, and wrote sports for both publications. I would do the same when I went to Pitt. In between, I went to Taylor Allderdice for two-and-a-half years, where I did neither. I continued as the sports editor of *The Hazelwood Envoy*.

"There wasn't any better than Jansante."
— Art Rooney

It was good to see Val Jansante again. He was now 80 years old, but appeared in good shape. He recently had an ankle replacement operation, but he was moving easily. Zeb had picked Ruby Tuesday's for our meeting, I learned upon arrival, because his dad was one of several Steelers from the '40s and '50s who were pictured in a framed montage on the wall just inside the doorway of the restaurant. "I thought this would be appropriate," said Zeb when he pointed out the photographs.

Jansante, the son of Italian immigrants, was married to Germaine Sloan of Richeyville in 1946, his rookie season with the Steelers. Now she was 78, yet still went to work every day as a secretary in the Bentworth School District. Her husband was still a member of the Bentworth Board of Education. Val Jansante had been a teacher and coach at Bentworth in his hometown of Bentleyville until retiring in 1982. Jansante was born on September 27, 1920 in nearby LaBelle.

He was, indeed, a hometown hero. He and Germaine had 12 children altogether, but three had died as infants. The survivors included Christopher, Val, Tim, Cindy, Kevin, Zeb, Jill, Dion and Maureen.

Jansante made $5,000 his rookie season with the Steelers. "I had a meeting with Art Rooney at the end of the year and he gave me a $500 raise," recalled Jansante. "That was the only raise I got during my stay with the Steelers. I made $5,500 from thereon in. That was it. I thought he was fair; I thought he paid me what he could afford to pay me. We figured he needed the money to feed his horses. I respect him more than anyone I had contact with in football."

In 1982 when the Steelers celebrated their 50th year in the National Football League, Jansante was on the ballot for the All-Time Greatest Steelers team. Art Rooney remarked at the time, "There wasn't any better than Jansante. He was listed as one of the All-Time Greatest Steelers in the 1998 book, "Total Steelers: The Official Encyclopedia of the Pittsburgh Steelers." In 1999, he had the distinction of being listed as one of only six receivers to be considered for the Steelers All-Century Team.

"Art Rooney said a lot of good things about me," Jansante said. "I often wonder how I would have done if I played with a T-formation team. I was called 'Glue Fingers.' We had some good players when I was there. In practice, I went up against Bill Dudley. He was a good defensive back. He was like a safety. He was always in the right place. He wasn't real big, but he was quick, and he knew where to go."

Jansante has been honored by being elected to the Duquesne University Sports Hall of Fame, the Washington County Chapter of the Pennsylvania Sports Hall of Fame, the Pittsburgh Sports Hall of Fame. In 2000, he was inducted into the Mid-Mon Valley Sports Hall of Fame in a class that included Monongahela's great quarterback, Joe Montana, and Lee Sala, an outstanding boxer in the '40s and '50s from Donora. I have since nominated him for the Italian-American Sports Hall of Fame.

After retiring from football, Jansante was a teacher and head football coach at Central Catholic High School, Mon Valley Catholic High School in Monongahela and Bentworth High School in Bentleyville. He was also athletic director at Mon Valley Catholic High School. He coached both boys' and girls' sports teams in the WPIAL for more than 25 years.

"I was ready to leave."

With 154 receptions in six seasons, Jansante held the club's reception record for awhile. That was quite an accomplishment, considering that the Steelers seldom passed while utilizing the single-wing offense during that span, plus the Steelers had another talented receiver, Elbie Nickel, during five of those seasons. Nickel is now regarded as the better end, but that wasn't always the case when they both lined up at opposite ends of the offensive line.

416

Card from Topps series

Jim O'Brien

Val Jansante points to his picture on wall display of Steelers of the past at the Ruby Tuesday Restaurant at the Galleria in Mt. Lebanon.

Jansante was 6-1, 190 pounds and was an All-Pro first or second team selection several times. This was before there was a Pro Bowl contest. The Pro Bowl began in 1951, and Nickel was named to it on three occasions.

Jansante set a club record with 35 catches for 599 yards and five touchdowns in 1947, the first year the Steelers went to the playoffs. It was their only playoff competition until 1972. Jansante caught ten passes in a game for the Steelers on two occasions, against the Eagles and against the Rams. The Steelers' record book credits him only for the game against the Eagles, but Zeb said he found the other 10-catch game in his personal research of game stories. During his heyday, Val Jansante drew comparisons to the great Don Hutson of Green Bay.

Jansante got his start under Alex Ufema at Bentleyville High School. Then he played for Buff Donelli at Duquesne University. He played for the Dukes during their 26-game winning streak. Duquesne was undefeated in 1941, playing Division I football in those days. He went into the Navy in 1942.

During part of his time in the service, Jansante, who was an ROTC member, was a student at Harvard and then Villanova. While at Villanova, he starred in a scrimmage against the Steagles, a wartime combination of Steelers and Eagles. In this scrimmage in Philadelphia, Jansante reportedly sacked the quarterback 11 times and had seven receptions. Bert Bell, from the Steagles' front office, put Jansante on the NFL draft prospect list.

Jansante was a 10th round pick of the Steelers in 1944, but did not join the team until 1946 because of a World War II commitment. During his time in the military service, Jansante played for the Naval Base Fleet City team near Oakland, California. His first six catches were good for touchdowns, according to his resume, and the Fleet City team, led by scatback Buddy Young, won the league championship.

"I went to my first training camp with the Steelers at Cambridge Springs, and nobody gave me much attention," Jansante said. "I was ready to leave. I was at the train station ready to go home. Chuck Mehelich, another end, who was a friend of mine, talked me out of it. I had played with Mehelich at Duquesne and at Fleet City.

"Jock Sutherland was tough. You couldn't mess with him. You weren't allowed to drink water no matter how hot it was. He put oatmeal in the water in the bucket so you wouldn't drink it. I would take ice and suck on it. We played in 97 degree temperatures once in St. Louis and I lost 17 pounds. I only weighed 180 at the time to begin with. You couldn't drink water that day, either.

"He had that single-wing and we never threw that many passes. I led the team in catches my rookie season with ten catches. Johnny Blood led the Steelers with that many catches several years earlier (1937). That was the lowest total for the team's top pass-catcher in club history.

"One time in 1947, we practiced a whole week without getting paid for it for a playoff game with the Philadelphia Eagles. I was our top player and the guys on the team asked me to represent them. They said, 'Why don't you see if you can get us any money for this?' When Sutherland came by, they all ducked out on me and left me alone with him. I mentioned about the money. He stared at me fiercely for a moment. Then he shouted, 'Get out of here!' He was really angry about it. He was kinda mad at me; he was mad at the whole team. Yet, when he died, I was one of his pallbearers.

"When Sutherland died suddenly, of a brain tumor while he was on vacation in the South, John Michelosen succeeded him. Michelosen had played for Sutherland at Pitt, and was one of his assistants with the Steelers. Michelosen tried to emulate Sutherland. He would have done better if he'd been his own man.

"Jim Finks was our best passer, but Michelosen used Joe Geri (1949-1951) at tailback. Then he used a rookie named Chuck Ortmann. We'd tell Michelosen that Finks was our best passer. Geri had small hands; he was always bouncing the ball off my knees or ankles, or throwing it behind me. We had another good passer in Johnny 'Zero' Clement. I heard that Michelosen was told by Art Rooney that he had to abandon the single-wing formation if he wanted to keep his job. He refused and he was let go.

"Then Michelosen goes to Pitt, and what does he do? He plays the T-formation. Try to figure that out. He could have kept his job with the Steelers if he would have changed the offensive scheme. I guess he was too stubborn. That was a Sutherland trait, too."

I asked Jansante what he learned from his experience with Sutherland and Michelosen that helped him when he became a high school football coach. "I learned not to use the single-wing," he said with a smile.

"When I played end for Sutherland, he never told me what to do. I was on my own. He never talked much to the players. I moved out away from the tackle, so I could get free easier to go out for passes. He told me to get back where I belonged, back inside. Little by little, I moved out. In a way, I think I became the first split-end.

"I never saw that much of Art Rooney. He never made himself too visible. We always figured he was away at a racetrack or with his horses. That was his main interest in those days. The only time I'd see him was after the year was over. We'd all go down to his office when the season was completed to talk about a contract for the next year.

"He'd review what you'd done. If you were satisfactory, he'd give you a small raise. Otherwise, you'd stay the same. You had to try out every year. There were no long-term contracts; it was a year-to-year deal. He had a guy named John Houlihan who was a scout and recruiter and handled some of the business. You dealt with him more than Mr. Rooney.

"Mr. Rooney didn't have any notes or statistics in front of him. He went by his memory, what he saw. He believed you. If you told him, 'I'm a good end,' he'd believe you and give you a raise. He gave me a $500 raise after my first year and that was it. I went to Green

Bay during my last season in 1951 and I got another $500 raise. Tobin Rote was the quarterback there at the time, and he was a good one. But that was too far away. So I hung it up after that season. I could make as much teaching and I wouldn't get beat up. I didn't realize how important it was to be a pro football player at the time.

"I was always happy for Rooney when they finally put together a championship team. He always talked good about me; he never criticized me. I was glad for him. He went through some tough times.

"In my first year with the team, I learned that Dan Rooney wanted to go to Duquesne, my old school. Dan was taking care of the equipment in those days at training camp. He asked me if I could help him get into Duquesne. I spoke on his behalf, so maybe I helped him. I hope so.

"When I was finished with pro football, I got into coaching. I went to Central Catholic, then Mon Valley Catholic and, finally, I went back home to Bentleyville. Then Bentleyville merged with Ellsworth, and 84 and Scenery Hill, some other Washington County schools, and it became Bentworth. Bentleyville was where I grew up. My father was a coal-miner there. He worked in different mines in that area, in Vista No. 4 in Belleville, then in Ellsworth and then Gibson. His name was Germanio and my mother was Pauline. They both came over from Italy. They never spoke any English at home.

I had a brother named Jimmy and five sisters, Lilly, Eva, Evelyn, Virginia and Cecelia.

"I worked as a life-guard at Piney Fork Swimming Pool in Library, Pa. when I was in school, and I spent time in London during World War II, otherwise I always stayed pretty close to home. I've always been comfortable there."

From Jansante family album

Val Jansante (No. 54) watches as hands-on Coach Jock Sutherland shows a defensive lineman how he wants it done during practice at South Park Fairgrounds.

Bill Lyon
Liked simplicity of Steelers

"He was never artificial."

Bill Lyon is a columnist for the Philadelphia Inquirer, *where he has worked since 1972, and has been a sportswriter since 1956.*

I can't remember an owner revered as Art Rooney was. More often than not, they are villified. He didn't meddle; he didn't interfere. That's the sort of thing you think about with owners today. They figure they spend so much money that it gives them the right to run all aspects of their team. Art Rooney was loved as a person. I don't think I ever heard an unkind word about Art Rooney. I'd love to have that for an epitaph on my tomb. I visited him in his office a few times. He was never artificial or pretentious. I always thought the Steelers did as tasteful a job of displaying the Super Bowl trophies as anyone. They were just there in a clear plastic case in the front of the lobby in their offices at the stadium. It was like wow! There wasn't just one, either. There were four of them. The simplicity of it was like Art Rooney himself. I don't know he was so identified with the town. What a reputation. He didn't seem to have any ego at all. He was a common man, and that's a compliment. I think the true measure of the man is that he was wealthy and powerful and yet he didn't act like it. He was a breed apart. Today's owners have more money than he ever had, but not as much class.

Photos by Jim O'Brien

421

Mike Wagner
Wondered where the cigars came from

"I'll tell you when to quit."
— Art Rooney

Mike Wagner was a starting safety for the Steelers for ten seasons (1971-1980), and a member of four Super Bowl championship teams. He was an immediate starter after being an 11th round draft choice out of Western Illinois. He was selected to the 1975 and 1976 Pro Bowl games. He has an MBA from the Joseph Katz School of Business at the University of Pittsburgh. He spent over 15 years in investment banking in Pittsburgh and is a health benefit consultant for the UPMC Health Plan. He was honored at age 52 as a "legend" by the Italian-American Sports Hall of Fame at an awards dinner at the Hilton on April 29, 2001. I had won the same award two years earlier. We sat next to each other on the dais and discussed his days with the Steelers:

I read something about the Steelers being cheap and not paying the players that well, and I found myself bristling. I believe the Rooneys paid top dollar to us. They paid for a championship team. The money we made pales by comparison to the salaries today, but we were well rewarded for what we did in those days. There were two incidents in my career where the Rooneys were very generous to me. One year it was announced that I had been picked for the Pro Bowl, and then I was removed. The league office said an error had been made in the vote count. Dan Rooney was very upset by it.

He called me into his office, and he told me that he considered my season to be a Pro Bowl caliber season, and that he was going to pay me the Pro Bowl bonus that was in my contract. He didn't have to do it, but he did. Then, after the 1980 season, I went to Chuck Noll and told him I was retiring. He was Chuck. He just accepted it. He always said that if you are thinking of retiring then you ought to retire. Then I went to Dan and told him I was retiring. I told him I couldn't stay healthy anymore — I had come back from some serious injuries in my last few years — and that it was time to try something else. I had some other opportunities I felt I should look into. Dan did not try to talk me out of it.

A few days later, I got a call from The Chief. He wanted me to keep on playing. He said, "I'll tell you when to quit. I'll know when you're finished. And you're not there yet." It's nice to know, after all those years with the team, that someone still wanted me to stay. But I knew it was time. I told him I was just getting beat up, and it was time to give up the ghost.

Two days later, I got a call from Jim Boston at the office, and he tells me to come in. Boston negotiated the contracts in those days. He says he has something for me to sign. I told him I was serious about retiring, and that I wasn't just using this as a negotiating ploy. He said he understood, but told me to come in anyhow.

They had a two-year or three-year contract for me to sign, and it had a signing bonus. "Just sign it," Dan Rooney instructed me. "This is our going-away gift." I wanted to share this story because the Rooneys always did things quietly, and didn't get credit for it. The public doesn't realize what went on behind closed doors. Dan is not one to beat his own drum.

It's not important that they gave me the money. It was the gesture and the gratitude that meant the most.

My grandfather used to come here to see me. I would take him on a tour of the Steelers' complex, and into the clubhouse to meet the players. The Chief would come upon us, and he'd stop and say hello. My grandfather's name was Frank. The Chief would offer him a cigar. My grandfather talked about it the rest of his life. We were walking around the next year and The Chief came upon us again. He remembered my grandfather's name. My grandfather was stunned. So The Chief had some special things. Everybody has a little special spot for The Chief.

Some people would be cynical when they'd hear about The Chief. They couldn't believe he could be that good. The legacy remains with his sons. I have letters and notes and cards from all five of the sons. They take the time to try and touch people.

I remember how we used to get on the airplane after a road game and we'd get two cans of cold beer to take back to our seats. The Chief was always passing out these long cigars to the guys who liked them. I always got one. By the time we took off, about 20 guys would have The Chief's cigars. I always wondered where he kept all those cigars.

As I reflect on what we did, it's mind-boggling to me that eight of my teammates, my coach, and two of our owners are all in the Hall of Fame. Lynn Swann will be the eighth player when he goes in this summer. We must have been pretty good. I think The Chief would be proud of us.

Mike Wagner
23

Jim O'Brien

Chuck Noll and Mike Wagner wax nostalgic at the Mellon Mario Lemieux Celebrity Invitational at The Club at Nevillewood.

Edwin Pope
An admirer in Miami

"Everyone always calls him Mr. Rooney."

Edwin Pope has been the sports editor and lead columnist for The Miami News *before the Dolphins came into being, and votes for the Pro Football Hall of Fame.*

I was always impressed by how different the Steelers and Pittsburgh of Chuck Noll and Art Rooney were in regard to their football team and the Dolphins of Don Shula and Joe Robbie were at the same time. It was something that money can't buy and you can't pack in a suitcase.

It was the way the Steelers loved Pittsburgh and Mr. Rooney, the team owner. Mean Joe Greene said a lot of what the Steelers were all about was about Mr. Rooney. Everyone associated with the Steelers, for one thing, always referred to the boss as Mr. Rooney. There's something old-fashioned and right about that.

I mean his players went to his home and serenaded him with carols at Christmas time. Ask yourself how many pro sports owners have been serenaded lately by players.

There was a lot of Mr. Rooney in the Steelers locker room. Steeler dressing quarters were as brightly opposite from the Dolphins' grim, stay-the-hell-outta-here locker room as Miami's weather is from Pittsburgh's.

The Steelers were good because they were big and strong and fast and were playing football like no one did over such a period. They were tough turkeys. Just like Mr. Rooney.

Once he walked away from a racetrack with $300,000 in won cash stuck in every pocket. Back around Woodrow Wilson's presidency, he was a good enough amateur fighter to be named to our Olympic team, but didn't fight "because it wasn't such a big thing then." He still had the fighter's face. Ridged eyebrows ran above an off-center nose. His thick lips bespoke some battering. Thus his words poured out like nectar from a bent tin can.

And he still said, "Goodness."

He was always available for an interview. He said he enjoyed being interviewed. He said he appreciated being interviewed. Imagine that.

Yet he was the most humble man you'd ever meet. Humility was the old man's natural gig. He refused to flaunt success. You had to read to the 22nd paragraph of the team's history in the press guide to find a Super Bowl mentioned.

The city painted its buses black and gold, Steelers colors and Pirates colors and Penguins colors. It called itself the City of Champions. The rest of Pittsburgh took its championships and the hell with nice guys, except for Mr. Rooney.

Putting Pittsburgh and Mr. Rooney together is a tough combination, like a one-two punch in boxing.

Ray Mathews
Farmer from McKeesport

"Art Rooney was always fair with me."

Ray Mathews made an appearance at the Thompson Club in West Mifflin on April 19, 2001 to receive the "Man of Yesteryear" award. It is presented to an athlete who was outstanding in his sport over 20 years ago. Mathews certainly qualified in that respect. It's been a lot longer than that since he last starred for the Pittsburgh Steelers.

Mathews came out of Port Vue, McKeesport High School and Clemson University to star as a running back and receiver for the Steelers from 1951 to 1959. He finished his pro career with one year of reserve duty with the Dallas Cowboys in their first season of 1960.

At age 72, Mathews was still a handsome fellow. He had the look of an old Hollywood movie star, like Paul Newman, and everyone who greeted him told him he was looking good. They used to call him "Maverick" because he looked like James Garner.

Nellie King, the former Pirates pitcher and sidekick to Bob Prince on the Pirates' broadcasting team, and Pete Dimperio, the former head football coach at Westinghouse High School, used to delight audiences at the Thompson Club's annual Sports Night with their comic banter. They both told an adage about how there are three stages in our lives: when you're young, when you're middle aged and when you're looking good.

Mention Mathews to anyone who has followed the Steelers for a long time, like Joe Chiodo, the legendary Homestead restaurateur who has had a front row table for all 43 years of the Thompson Club's annual craziness, or Myron Cope, the voice (yoi!) of the Steelers for over 30 years, and they agree that Mathews was a helluva football player in his day. He was an all-around threat.

Cope, who made the award presentation, came prepared with plenty of statistics to show just how good Mathews was during his nine-year stay with the Steelers. Mathews played in the Pro Bowl three times. He led the Steelers in pass catching three straight seasons (1954-1956), succeeding Elbie Nickel as the team's top receiver.

Cope was most impressed with the fact that Mathews averaged 17.03 yards per catch on 230 catches. His total receptions places him 8th on the team's all-time pass receiving list. Lynn Swann, who went into the Pro Football Hall of Fame in August, averaged 16.24 yards on 336 catches, and John Stallworth, who should be entering the Hall of Fame in the near future, averaged 16.24 yards per catch. Cope didn't mention that Roy Jefferson (18.4) and Buddy Dial (20.6) both bettered the Swann-Stallworth combo in regard to yards per catch.

Mathews has the third best punt return average in a season (1951) in team history with 15.4 yards per return, just ahead of Swann's 14.1 yards. Mathews returned three punts for touchdowns. Louis Lipps (1984-1991) tied that for the club's career record.

Mathews ranks sixth in career receiving yards with 3,919 and in touchdown catches with 34. Only Jefferson caught more touchdown passes in a game (four) than Mathews' three against the Cleveland Browns.

There is also a consensus that Mathews might have posted even more impressive numbers if he hadn't joined the Steelers when they were still using the conservative run-oriented single-wing offense for one year under John Michelosen, and if he had played with a better and deeper squad.

Mathews lives in Harrisville, Pennsylvania, up near New Wilmington and Grove City and the Prime Outlets of Grove City. They are both "dry" towns, so the college students ("if they're 21") from Westminster and Grove City, as well as the old guys in the area, frequent a bar-restaurant owned by Mathews called "Your Brother's Place." Mathews also works a small farm there.

"I'm still a farmer," Mathews told Norm Vargo, the sports editor of *The Daily News* in McKeesport, who attended the Thompson Club dinner. "I was born in Dayton (near Kittaning) and I came to Port Vue to live. But I spent my summers on my uncle's farm. I love farming."

He's always liked riding horses.

Growing up in Munhall and working most of his life in McKeesport, Vargo has always been a big fan of Mathews, a likable character with an easy laugh. Mathews not only plays golf with former Steelers, but he often shows up at Pirates Alumni affairs. He frequently plays golf with Bill Mazeroski, the former Pirates second baseman who was inducted into the Baseball Hall of Fame in the summer of 2001. They are often joined by Paul Blanda, the former Pitt linebacker and brother of George Blanda, from Youngwood. Mathews appears at a lot of fund-raising golf tournaments in the tri-state area.

Mathews was a standout basketball player under the legendary Clarence "Neenie" Campbell at McKeesport High School. His football coach with the Tigers was another legendary scholastic figure, namely Harold "Duke" Weigle. Mathews also played baseball and soccer in his senior year. He was good enough to play a few years in the minor league system of the St. Louis Cardinals.

"When I was at McKeesport, you had to play three sports just to keep a girl friend," said Mathews. "That's why I went out for the soccer team as a junior. But that's all changed now. The coaches try to get the kids today to concentrate on one sport. I don't think that's such a good thing."

When Mathews came out of Clemson, he was a seventh round draft choice in 1961. "They're making too much money these days, these kids coming out of college," he said. "So much money; there's no way they can keep their minds on playing the game.

427

"And that's not good. You gotta love football to play it well. I loved football. That's why I played. Hell, it wasn't for the money in those days."

He said he made about $6,500 a year when he starred for the Steelers. "And in those days, that was big money," he said. "They say the Steelers are cheap, but I'll argue that. Mike McCormick was a first-round draft pick with the Browns, and I was making more money than he was.

"Art Rooney was a hard guy to deal with, but he was fair. He loved football. He played the game. He paid you what he thought you were worth."

Mathews said he felt Michael Vick, the Virginia Tech quarterback who ended up being the first pick by the Atlanta Falcons in the NFL draft in 2001, was making a mistake giving up college eligibility to come to the pros early.

"Like I said, it's the money," Mathews said. "These kids today are not using their heads. They're going to make so much money, they'll never go back and finish college. They'll say they don't have to. But that's a mistake. You just never know when a degree will come in handy down the road.

"When I came out of McKeesport, I had a shot at going to Tulane and Maryland. But I picked Clemson because I wanted to go to a school that taught about agriculture. Tulane and Maryland were city schools. Clemson was out in the country. And that's what sold me."

When Mathews completed his pro playing career, he stayed on with the NFL as an assistant coach, along with Moe Scarry of Duquesne, on Otto Graham's staff with the Washington Redskins, then later as a scout with the New York Jets.

When he was taken in the expansion draft by the Dallas Cowboys, Mathews may have made a mistake by telling Dallas sportswriters about how he could always beat Tom Landry when Landry was a defensive back for the New York Giants. Landry was in his first year as the head coach of the Cowboys.

Mathews may have mentioned how the Steelers upset the Giants, 63-7, back in 1952 at Forbes Field. That might explain why Mathews didn't get to play much in his last NFL season. He just smiles at the suggestion. It's a Hollywood smile accented by squinted eyes.

Mathews had his biggest day as a Steeler against another vaunted opponent on October 17, 1954 when he scored four touchdowns in a 55-27 victory over the Cleveland Browns before a sellout crowd of 33,260 fans at Forbes Field.

The Browns had beaten the Steelers in their previous eight meetings and they would go on to win nine of their next ten games, including the NFL championship. They beat Buddy Parker's Detroit Lions, 56-10, in the title game.

In that big win over the Browns there were several Steelers who stood out. Quarterback Jim Finks had a tremendous afternoon. He completed 11 of 15 passes for 239 yards and four touchdowns. Pittsburgh's defensive backs intercepted five passes. Jack Butler returned one of those 41 yards for a touchdown in the second quarter and Russ Craft returned one 81 yards for a touchdown in the fourth quarter.

Mathews, a versatile 185-pound halfback, scored the first of his four touchdowns on a twisting, leaping catch in the end zone. He made the score 34 to 20 with a 78-yard run after taking another Finks toss in the clear behind Don Paul. Mathews' two other touchdowns came in the second half. He made a three-yard dash around end and caught a 45-yard TD pass from Finks down the middle, showing good speed as he darted away from Cleveland defenders.

It was something he could point to at season's end when he sat down to discuss his next year's contract with The Chief.

"I used to ask Art Rooney for a raise each season," said Mathews with a smile. "One time he took the last cigar out of a tin container and gave me the container. He said, 'Here, take this with you, and maybe you can pass this around and collect some more money with it. You don't need a raise.' I always managed to get something. I got eight raises in a row. Not big. But raises. He'd always tell me some stories, too. He was a good story-teller. He was a rich man that way, and I guess getting to know him and spending time with him was one of the perks of the job."

Jim O'Brien

Two of Pittsburgh's all-time favorite professional ballplayers, ElRoy Face and Ray Mathews, enjoy a good time at Thompson Club's annual Sports Night dinner on April 19, 2001. Mathews received the "Man of Yesteryear" award that Face received at the previous banquet.

John Mamajek
He almost made it with the Steelers

"Sports were a vital part of the community."

I remember how proud the people in our community were when John Mamajek was playing for the Pittsburgh Steelers. That was back in 1953 when I was 11 years old. The Steelers were only 20 years old. I was an ardent sports fan and devoured the daily newspaper sports sections. My brother Dan, then 16, told me all about John Mamajek. Dan was a classmate of John's kid brother, Jim.

John Mamajek, who had been a star running back and track and field performer at Central Catholic High School and at The Citadel, was trying out for the Steelers as a place-kicker. He was getting plenty of action during the team's exhibition season, back when they played six games before the start of the real stuff in the NFL.

Mamajek did OK, it seemed, but he was one of the last cuts. Mamajek joined a long line of top-notch athletes from our area who almost made it to the major leagues. Lots of local guys got scholarships, but returned home before they finished their first year at college. Others went to the minor leagues in baseball briefly, and then came home, usually to work in the mills. That's where Mamajek went to work before he became a teacher and coach.

Our hometown was Hazelwood. Sometimes I thought it should have been called Almost. Or What Might Have Been. Or Hazelwooda.

I played sandlot football with a fellow named Dave Fleming. He had a tryout as a running back with the Steelers in 1963. He almost made it, too. He did play ten years as a defensive back with the Hamilton Tiger-Cats of the Canadian Football League (CFL). John Sklopan, who played in the same backfield with the Hazelwood Steelers, played two years with the CFL Edmonton Eskimos. Another local product, Eddie Vereb, a star running back at Central Catholic and an All-America on Maryland's national championship team of 1953, played for the Washington Redskins.

This all came running back to me on Tuesday, April 17, 2001 when I received a half-dozen telephone calls informing me that John Mamajek had died at age 70 from complications of diabetes in Jefferson Hospital, Jefferson Hills.

One of those who called me was Carmine Bellini, the brother-in-law of John Mamajek. Bellini is one of the owners of Bellini Brothers Lawn & Garden Center in Mt. Lebanon. His sister, Lena, was married to Mamajek for 45 years.

I got a telephone call the previous summer inviting me to a get-together at Eddie Howard's home in Greenfield to spend some time with his older brother, John, and John Mamajek. Both were having serious health problems. John Howard had been the coach of the J.J.

Doyle's football team in Hazelwood that Mamajek played for after he was cut by the Steelers. Eddie now resides in Scott Twp.

The J.J. Doyle's were one of the best sandlot football teams in the area, right up there with the Sto-Rox Cadets, the Rox Rangers and Butler Cubs. Mamajek looked much like Willie Stargell did when I saw the Pirates Hall of Famer in September of 2000. He looked like a man on borrowed time.

Mamajek didn't make it with the Steelers, but he made a successful career out of his athletic abilities. He began a teaching and coaching career at Central Catholic in 1958 and then moved in 1962 to Serra Catholic High School in White Oak, where he and Lena have lived ever since. He coached football and several other sports and was a social studies teacher there for 32 years.

Jerry Vondas, who grew up helping out at his father's restaurant in Hazelwood, wrote a wonderful story in the *Tribune-Review* about Mamajek when he died. It began: "In Hazelwood, where sports were as vital a part of the community as the coke ovens and blast furnaces of J&L Steel, John Mamajek was long remembered as a standout athlete."

His family found some solace in the outpouring of praise. His son, John Mamajek, who oversees the men's grill at the St. Clair Country Club, recalled what it was like having his father as a teacher and a coach at Serra. "My dad was a good teacher and a good coach, so it was fine," he said. "He had the ability to size up a young athlete and place him where he thought he could do his best."

Young John also recalled how his dad used to rib his mom. She had attended Taylor Allderdice High School. "Dad never let her forget that in a football game between Central Catholic and Taylor Allderdice, he had scored 28 of the 31 points, the most in his high school career," said John.

Those were the glory days, of course. There were hundreds of photos from his football days and family events on placards throughout the Jaycox-Jaworski Funeral Home in White Oak. His brother, Jim, who still lives in Hazelwood, was there, too, telling stories about his brother, like those days when he played for the Pittsburgh Steelers.

"John was a good football player."

John Mamajek was born in Braddock, the grandson of Polish immigrants. He was one of three sons of John V. and Rosella Mecynski Mamajek. His father, better known as "Ace" Mamajek, was a machinist for the Mesta Machine Company in West Homestead. He worked in the same machine shop as my father, Dan O'Brien.

"Ace" Mamajek played football for the semi-pro McKeesport Crimsons. I remember him having protruding bushy eyebrows, like

John L. Lewis, the famous union leader. His boys all had those same bushy eyebrows.

I had lunch at Twin Oaks Restaurant in White Oak prior to attending the funeral of John Mamajek with a buddy of mine, Bill Priatko of North Huntingdon, and his friend, Don McMahon of Irwin.

When Priatko learned that I was going to pay my respects to John Mamajek, he said he would join me. Priatko played football for Pitt and had briefs stints with the Green Bay Packers, Cleveland Browns and Pittsburgh Steelers. He remembered playing against John Mamajek when Bill was at North Braddock Scott High School in the late '40s. "John was a good football player," Priatko said, and that sufficed.

Priatko brought along some pages from one of his old scrapbooks. There were newspaper clippings pasted in it about a game where North Braddock Scott beat Central Catholic, 40-20. Scott led by 40-0 at halftime. Mamajek scored the only touchdown for Central Catholic before 6,000 fans that Friday night at the stadium in North Braddock.

Priatko didn't know that Mamajek had been born in Braddock. That made that victory even sweeter. There was such a rivalry beween Braddock and North Braddock back then. It also made the death of Mamajek that much more poignant.

There was also a clipping on that same page about how Bill's life-long friend, Rudy Celigoi, blocked two punts in a shutout victory over Duquesne. Celigoi went on to become superintendent at Swissvale High School and later an administrator at Woodland Hills High School.

"John Mamajek was quite a football player," said Priatko, now retired after finishing his career as the athletic director at Yough High School. "He was a good man in our profession. He touched and helped a lot of young people. That's his real contribution."

After I left the funeral home, I drove about five miles through White Oak to Coultersville, Art Rooney's birthplace. The sun was out, temperatures were in the high 60s, almost balmy. Coultersville, now called Coulter by some, is a little community in South Versailles Township. It abuts Boston and North Huntingdon and White Oak; it's about 25 miles east of Pittsburgh

It's a community of mostly modest homes, even mobile homes. It was a coal-mining town once upon a time and the railroad tracks still run through it. It seemed that half the homes had American flags flying from poles or porches.

Dan Rooney, the father of Art Rooney, operated a small business as an innkeeper there. When the family of six sons and two daughters moved to Pittsburgh, Dan Rooney's saloon on the North Side near Exposition Park became the sports center for discussion and information. Sports stars and celebrities enjoyed the adulation, conversation and debates at Dan's Place. Nickel beers and free lunches drew standing-room-only patronage.

The Rooney clan were miners and steel puddlers. Art's relatives fought for union recognition long before the terrible Homestead Steel Strike occurred. Art's relatives were involved in that tragic confrontation. That's why he was always sympathetic to the formation and development of the National Football League Players Association.

He was always adamant that the black players on the team have the same treatment as the white players, that the team be housed as a unit in one hotel. I came upon a man working under his car, later a woman mowing her lawn — she said she'd lived there for 50 years — and they both knew that Art Rooney had been born there. "That's what I heard when I got here," the woman said. They told me to go up the hill from Railroad Street and that I would find Rooney Street. Sure enough, I did. Rooney Street is only about 40 yards long, at best. Art Rooney lived in a house there at the beginning, though no one could point out a particular structure.

I stopped at a war memorial and at a cemetery, but couldn't find any Rooneys on any of the plaques or grave markers.

I felt Art Rooney's presence, though, and I could see him smiling. He had a hand, I'm sure, in making sure I got to the funeral home that day to pay my respects to John Mamajek, who'd been a Steeler. I don't go into a funeral home these days that I don't think of Art Rooney. He's always there, paying his respects, touching people, offering his condolences. He would have told Lena Mamajek that things will get tough at times, that there will be some bad days.

She would be comforted by his presence and his soft-spoken words. It would also have confirmed the fact that her husband had been a Steeler.

Recalling memorable days with the J.J. Doyles sandlot football team in Hazelwood were John Mamajek, Coach John Howard and Billy "Ace" Adams during reunion picnic in 2000. Former teammates came to see Mamajek and Howard, who were having health challenges.

433

Rick Gosselin
An admirer in Dallas

"It's still all about football."

Rick Gosselin writes about the National Football League at large for the Dallas Morning News.

I am a lot more familiar with Dan Rooney than I was Art Rooney. I like him. He's up front. No bull crap. He tells you what he's thinking. He respects your questions. You don't have to agree with him to be his friend. He's a man of the utmost integrity. I'm told he's like his dad. I've always enjoyed being around the Steelers. They never made me feel like an outsider, or uncomfortable.

So many of the Steelers have been very classy guys. Mel Blount and Donnie Shell come to mind. Their facilities were never the finest, but there was something appealing about the simplicity of the operation. Their practice field, for instance, was a 60-yard field near Three Rivers Stadium. Who else in the NFL had a field like that in the 90s? There was something spartan about them. It spawned a no excuses philosophy.

Their logo was so simple, appearing on just one side of their helmets. I feel badly that you're losing all that. I'm going to miss Three Rivers Stadium. That whole scene. Mr. Rooney was one of those owners, like Mara, Hunt, Modell and Wilson, who made pro football important in this country.

We all liked dynasties. The Steelers of the '70s were special. Pittsburgh fans were so proud of their team. And that all happened at Three Rivers Stadium. I miss Cleveland Municipal Stadium. When I went in there I thought of Jim Brown. When I went into Three Rivers Stadium I thought of the Rooneys. So I'll miss it.

The Rooneys are a reminder to us that it's still all about football. People are making millions on the game, but the Rooneys are reminders that it's still about football. They're the owners of a football team. I'm glad they won. I'm a historian. I like the way the game was with the Steelers and Three Rivers and Joe Greene. That was football. That was the game I came to love.

Dan was approachable to talk about the game. Here's a guy who owns a multi-million operation and he acts like a guy who lives next door. He treats you like he's at your level. It's still about people. He's the last of the breed that understands that.

> ### *"I don't think he'd be too thrilled about what's going on today. I can remember him telling me, 'You'll rue the day you take all that money from the networks. It won't be our game as much anymore. It'll be their game.'"*
> ### — Dan Rooney

Palm Beach
A royal getaway in South Florida

"It's not bad."
— Marie McGinley

Palm Beach is a tropical paradise. It is located on the East Coast of Florida, 65 miles north of Miami. It is known around the world as the most wealthy, glamorous, opulent, decadent, self-indulgent spot on earth, according to "The Season," subtitled "Inside Palm Beach and America's Richest Society," by Ronald Kessler, a *New York Times* reporter and best-selling author. "With their beautiful 3.75 square-mile island constantly in the media glare," writes Kessler, "Palm Beachers protect their impossibly rich society from outside scrutiny with vigilant police, ubiquitous personal security staffs, and screens of tall hedges encircling every mansion."

Palm Beach has been a Rooney retreat for over 70 years, especially the last 35 years, and several of the sons of Steelers' patriarch Art Rooney and their children and grandchildren now call that area home. They live in Palm Beach or West Palm Beach, the two communities separated by the narrow Intracoastal Waterway. The Rooneys live well there, on a higher plane than in Pittsburgh. They are pale-faced Irishmen, however, and I have never seen any of them sporting a tan. They get sunburned on occasion, but never tanned.

The family believes that Art Rooney started staying in Palm Beach during the racing season — when it lasted only a few months in the winter — back in the late '20s or early '30s. He frequented the Palm Beach Kennel Club which features greyhound racing long before he bought the facility in January of 1970.

I visited Palm Beach for five days, May 9-14, 2001. I had an opportunity to talk once more with Pat and John Rooney, the twins and youngest sons of Art Rooney. I went to the Palm Beach Kennel Club and the Rooney Public House in West Palm Beach and the one at the airport, touring all three places on two separate occasions over the weekend. I met Art and Dan Laughlin, sons of Margaret Rooney Laughlin, one of Art Rooney's two surviving sisters. Art and Dan Laughlin are the general manager and operations manager, respectively, of the Palm Beach Kennel Club. I met Joe and Chris Rooney, sons of Pat Rooney and grandchildren of Art Rooney, who manage the Rooney Public House chain. A third pub was to open in mid-June in nearby Jupiter, where Pat lived. It is near Roger Dean Stadium where the Montreal Expos and St. Louis Cardinals conduct their spring training. There were plans to expand the restaurant chain to Pittsburgh, Philadelphia and other places the Rooneys have called home. They hoped to have a presence in Heinz Field, the new football stadium on the North Side.

My wife Kathleen and I went to Palm Beach primarily to spend some time with our younger daughter, Rebecca O'Brien. Like Joe Rooney, she has a degree in food service management. Rebecca, who turned 24 earlier in May, graduated in 1999 from Ohio University. She was in Palm Beach for an 11-week management training session with California Pizza Kitchen. She would be departing Palm Beach on May 26 to work as a manager of a new restaurant opening at the Easton Shopping Mall in suburban Columbus, Ohio, where she had been living the past year. It's a trendy restaurant chain that features gourmet pizza, fancy sandwiches and salads and is often located in upscale shopping malls and resort communities across the country, mostly on the West Coast and Southwest, but moving toward the East Coast. Pat's wife, Sandy Rooney, said she had dined at California Pizza Kitchen at the Gardens Mall in Palm Beach Gardens and loved it. "Their décor is black and gold — Steelers colors," noted Sandy. I had made the same observation. Rebecca had her choice of places to go for her training, and she picked Palm Beach. I seconded the motion since I wanted to visit the Rooneys there anyhow.

"It's the first time in my life," Rebecca remarked midway through her Palm Beach stay, "where I felt like the poor little girl in town. But this is a great place. I'd like to stay here."

Rebecca drove us around Palm Beach to see the beachfront mansions and the fabulous Breakers Hotel at 1 South County Road, which was originally built by Henry M. Flagler (1830-1913), who made a fortune in oil and railroads, and developed Palm Beach and Miami. We toured Worth Avenue, Palm Beach's answer to Rodeo Drive in Beverly Hills, where all the fancy shops and stores are located. No signs along Interstate Route 95 point to Palm Beach. The residents prefer privacy to tourists.

On our ride we saw a sign for the LeMont Restaurant on the 20th Floor of the Northbridge Centre. It was opened in March by Anna and Ed Dunlap of Upper St. Clair, who bought and completely renovated the restaurant of the same name on Mt. Washington. It's been a Pittsburgh landmark since Jim Blandi first opened it.

Among those who spend time at Palm Beach in the winter are celebrities such as Celine Dion, Aretha Franklin, Tom Cruise, Ivana Trump, Roxanne Pulitzer, Christie Brinkley, Whitney Houston, Marla Maples, Pamela Anderson Lee, Rod Stewart and Harrison Ford. The families of American business such as Hutton, Hilton, Pillsbury, Firestone, duPont, Scripps and Ford (Henry, not Harrison) have lived there. When John F. Kennedy was President and had a home in Palm Beach it was called the Winter White House.

Four of the Rooney Boys wintered in Palm Beach, and Jack McGinley, the minority owner of the Steelers, was staying there during the same period, known in South Florida as "the season." I learned a lot during my stay there. I wish I could have stayed longer. I came to appreciate Art Rooney and his family even more. It filled in some blank spaces in the Rooney story.

Just before I went to Palm Beach, all five Rooney boys and McGinley were in Pittsburgh for a meeting of the owners of the Steelers, something they do on a regular basis. Pat and John went to Philadelphia after that, then back to Palm Beach, then to Ireland. Pat departed for Ireland on Mother's Day and John was to join him a week later. They were going to be playing in some fund-raising golf tournament in Ireland, among other things. Pat is on the board of trustees of the American College in Dublin and had to attend a meeting in that respect.

Dan Rooney and Tony O'Reilly of the H.J. Heinz Co. are among the leaders in The American Ireland Fund and are active in fund-raising for peacekeeping activities in O'Reilly's native land. The Rooneys realized a dream by having the Steelers play the Chicago Bears in an exhibition contest at Croke Park in Dublin before the 1997 season. Dan Rooney doesn't share his father or brothers' passion for Florida. If he is not in Pittsburgh, he would rather be in Ireland. He went there in June, 2001, as did his brother, Tim, joining the twins there.

Like their father, the Rooneys are on the go quite a bit. They can't stand still for too long. The Rooneys are like rolling stones; they gather no moss on their shoes or backsides. I never realized that Art Rooney spent so much time in South Florida before I started doing the research for this book. I don't remember in my youth reading about his off-season sojourns in the columns of Al Abrams and Chester L. Smith, or the stories by Jack Sell and Pat Livingston in the Pittsburgh newspapers. I think Art Rooney wanted it that way.

There are about 9,800 Palm Beach residents and 87 percent of them are millionaires. Art Rooney, Sr. often lectured his five sons not to be showoffs. He said they shouldn't make a display of their wealth, and that they should never think or act as if they were better than anybody else. They weren't to buy Cadillacs, for example. Buicks would do just fine. He often admonished them, saying "We're not rich people..." In truth, however, the Rooneys are rich people. They can't deny that. Hey, they needn't apologize for it.

They are going to get richer as their coffers continue to swell. They will be fattened by lucrative NFL TV contracts, league expansion, increased ticket sales, seat license fees, naming rights fees and a sweetheart financial arrangement on the new stadium on the North Side and practice facilities at the UPMC Sports Medicine complex on the South Side. They have gained the rights to developing the area around the stadium.

The Rooneys continue to unload some of their gaming properties. They have sold off tracks like Liberty Bell in Philadelphia and Green Mountain in Vermont, and a jai-alai fronton in West Palm Beach. They were trying to sell Yonkers Raceway in the summer of 2001. Some day they will probably sell the Palm Beach Kennel Club. Some day, and no one wants to consider the possibility, they will probably sell the Steelers. It will make sense when they do it.

There are estate tax problems with family-owned businesses — the Maras have gone through this in New York with the Giants and their other interests — and it's a complex matter the Rooneys and their financial advisors and attorneys will have to continue to address. The O'Malleys had to sell the Dodgers because of such considerations, the Wrigleys unloaded the Cubs for the same reason. Clint Murchison sold the Cowboys and Joe Robbie ran into estate problems with his ownership of the Dolphins because of imminent tax claims on the family fortune. They were all proud pro sports owners.

The Rooneys may not have as much money as many of the new NFL owners, or their neighbors in Palm Beach, but they won't have to hold any raffles to fund their retiring years. They have been industrious, prudent and resourceful with their finances. They can't be called cheap. The Steelers had the highest payroll in the AFC for the 2000 season.

Nonetheless, they are keeping well-heeled company in Palm Beach. The infamous Donald Trump, for instance, has a place and owns several properties in Palm Beach. Palm Beach is also home to many members of the Kennedy clan of Massachusetts. The Rooneys always had a high regard for JFK and RFK and Teddy. In a sense, the Rooneys are Pittsburgh's answer to the Kennedys.

The Rooneys remain down to earth in their behavior. It's not an act. By maintaining a modest residence in a neighborhood on the North Side that knew better days they maintained an image that suited them like dark blue suits in the summer.

They have appealed to Pittsburghers because they didn't act like big deals. Pittsburghers prefer their sports heroes to be humble, which helps explain why Bill Mazeroski was a hometown hero long before he got the call from the Baseball Hall of Fame.

Three of Art Rooney's sons maintain principal residences in Palm Beach County. Tim, the president of Yonkers Raceway, has homes in Greenwich, Connecticut and in Ireland — he raises thoroughbred horses on a farm there — but his principal residence is in Palm Beach. He has to spend at least six months a year there. One of the benefits is that there is no personal income tax in Florida. He used to own a beautiful 11-room home in Scarsdale, New York before going to Greenwich. I remember attending a party he threw in New York City over 25 years ago, and it was a classy affair.

John Rooney, who ran Liberty Bell in Philadelphia, is the vice-president of the Palm Beach Kennel Club. He has also done well in the oil and gas business. He lives in a home on the Ibis Country Club in West Palm Beach. He loves golf and fly-fishing. He used to live in a home on the Bear Lakes Country Club. I walked by the Bear Lakes Country Club every morning during my stay in West Palm Beach and it looked like a country club ought to look like in that part of South Florida. It was from another era. There was a "Members Only" plaque prominently displayed at the entryway, and "No Tresspassing" signs at junctures along a pale pink stone and black wrought iron fence that surrounded the facility. There was a restaurant nearby named

Gatsby's of Palm Beach that had two spacious billiards rooms. One could easily picture Jay Gatsby and Daisy Buchanan, or author F. Scott Fitzgerald and his wife, Zelda, walking up the front steps of the Bear Lakes Country Club.

Pat Rooney, the president of the Palm Beach Kennel Club, had built a new home a year earlier in nearby Jupiter, just north of West Palm Beach. He also had a place in Ireland, and was part of an investment consortium that converted castles in Ireland to bed & breakfast establishments. He also had a small farm in Hellertown, Pennsylvania, near Bethlehem.

Pat loves to go to Ireland. "He goes to Ireland," said his uncle, Jack McGinley, Sr., "like he's going from Palm Beach to West Palm Beach."

Sean Casey, the outstanding hitter for the Cincinnati Reds who grew up in Upper St. Clair, had purchased a new home in Jupiter that same year. During my stay in West Palm Beach, I was saddened to learn that Perry Como, the beloved crooner from Canonsburg, had died at age 87 in Jupiter Inlet Beach Colony. Como, who started out as a barber in Canonsburg, often returned to the Washington County community, and never forgot where he came from. That appeals to Pittsburghers as well.

Art Rooney, Jr. and his wife, Kathleen, and Jack McGinley, Sr. and his wife, Marie, spent "the season" at Palm Beach in the winter of 2001. They were there from mid-January to mid-April. They stayed at Ocean Towers, where Art, Sr., the Steelers' founder, once owned a condominium. "Some of the old-timers there remembered my father and mother," reported Art, Jr. "They share stories of those days. My brother, Tim, has a beautiful old, old house on the beach nearby. We went to Mass every morning together. I'd see Jack and my Aunt Marie, too. They are wonderful people."

When I asked Marie McGinley about Palm Beach, she said, "It's not bad."

Asked about her brother, she said, "Arthur was always good to me. We stayed with him every year. His place was lovely and big — they had three bedrooms — and Jack and I would go there in February and stay a couple of weeks. Our daughter, Mary, was close to him. My brother Dan liked to go there, too.

"Arthur and Jack would go to Miami every day to the racetracks. Then they'd come home and take a shower and go to the dog track for the evening. It was all so wonderful. We had wonderful times together. We'd get on a ship, a fancy ship, and go on all kinds of cruises.

"I remember once reading about a ship having a bad fire and it was a ship we were booked on a month or so later. I told Arthur about it, but he told me to keep that under my hat. He said he cut the item out of the newspaper because he didn't want his Kathleen to see it. They put us on a different ship, a Greek ship, and it was awful. It was not a fancy liner. Arthur's room had a leak. It could have been disastrous. But we still had a wonderful time. Arthur always enjoyed himself. It didn't take much to make him smile.

439

"We went to the Super Bowls together, too. As we got older, after Kathleen died, I'd stay with Arthur back at the hotel and watch the game on TV. There were many good times. Arthur was wonderful. We never had any cross words between us.

"I enjoyed the family reunion we had ten years ago and I'm looking forward to the one this summer. Dan really did a wonderful talk there. Sandy and Pat did a great job, too. Dan had a nice luncheon for us at the cafeteria at St. Vincent's College after we went to Mass there.

"Yes, I think my Jack is a lot like Arthur. That's why they got along so well. I was the eighth in our family of nine and much younger than Arthur. I remember when I was in a Catholic high school we had to help raise money by selling chances. And Arthur would buy my whole book of chances.

"One year, we were in Miami, and Arthur took me to a racetrack. They stopped me and said I had to be 18 to get in. Arthur said, 'She's my wife.' And they let me in. I have so many great memories of Arthur. He was a great brother."

"It's like you're in a Technicolor movie."
— Susie Rooney

Art Rooney, Jr. lives in a mansion in Mt. Lebanon, has a condominium in Palm Beach, and a weekend getaway in Deep Creek, Maryland. "Deep Creek doesn't look as good after you've been to Palm Beach," said Art, Jr. He also has an office in Upper St. Clair where he looks after the family's real estate interests. Yet he doesn't realize that he's a rich man. There is a naivete about him that is appealing. He has a magic name, but doesn't use it as a door opener. He has never realized his own potential in that regard. He's boisterous and entertaining as a storyteller, but backward and bashful in regard to his own role in the Rooney clan. He is self-deprecating, part of his charm.

"Hey, I'm smart enough to know I never would have had the job I had with the Steelers if my name wasn't Rooney, and my dad didn't own the team," he said. "At the same time, I think I can be proud of the job I did. I worked at it, and thought I made a major contribution to the success of the Steelers."

He studied to be an actor, and loves making movie analogies, but lacks the self-confidence to go on the main stage. He is a sweet man. He has an engaging grin, and a great sense of humor. He knows a good story when he hears one. He is like his dad in that regard. Some of his brothers favor the father more appearance-wise, but none are closer in character than Art, Jr. He works at that, too.

"I'd rather look like my mother," said Art, Jr. "My dad was a tough-looking guy. My mother was a beautiful woman. Did you see that photo of her in an evening gown?"

He does much to preserve and promote the legacy of his father and the family. He has commissioned artist Merv Corning to do a series of ink sketches of his father, for instance, and the walls of Rooney's office complex are a Wall of Fame for his father and the Steelers. He has reprinted those Corning sketches on post cards and notepaper, and a color rendering of a bubble-gum card showing his dad and his dad's brother, Dan, when they were with the Wheeling Stogies in minor league baseball. "I wanted to show your father doing something he really enjoyed," is the way Corning explained his choice. Corning was happy to hear that an enlarged version of his baseball card on the Rooneys was displayed on the wall at the Rooney Public House at the airport in Palm Beach. Art, Jr. has also made copies of an ink drawing of his father by internationally known New York artist Leroy Nieman.

Art, Jr. does a lot of things that his father did in his later years, such as writing letters and writing cards to family, friends and sportswriters around the country. But he lacks the role — the stage and spotlight — that his father enjoyed when he was in his office at the Steelers' complex at Three Rivers Stadium when the team ruled the National Football League. Art, Jr. does his act in exile, so to speak, at his well-appointed office in the suburbs. There's a secretary and receptionist, Dee Harrod, and a property manager and bookkeeper in Maureen Butler Maier, the daughter of his good friend, Jack Butler, sharing the same office suite. That's it. There's little media attention. He was fired as the Steelers' player personnel director by his brother Dan in a shocking move on January 6, 1987, yet for years he has continued to provide scouting reports on college prospects, almost out of habit. He has never been sure whether or not the Steelers bothered to read his reports.

Art, Jr. is trying to ward off advancing age with swimming, walking and weight training. He loves to do e-mail, though he says his fat fingers and spelling shortcomings often make for interesting hieroglyphics. I can vouch for that.

I spoke to Art, Jr. in mid-May, 2001, after I returned from a 5-day stay in Palm Beach. He had returned from a three-month stay there only a few weeks earlier. I was telling him how much my wife, Kathleen, and I enjoyed Palm Beach and West Palm Beach. "My wife Kay wants to go back now," said Art. "She's enjoying decorating our condo. She loves it there.

"Our son, Art, is moving his dental practice to Naples, Florida. There are a lot of Pittsburghers in that state. You run into a lot of Pittsburgh people at the Palm Beach Kennel Club and at the Rooney Pub. Kay and I had lunch at the Rooney Pub at the airport there. I asked the waitress if her grandfather's photo was on the wall. She said 'no' and looked at me as if I was some kind of nut. I said, 'Well, that's my grandfather right there.' She seemed to think that was funny. Of course, Kay, told me to stop being a bore."

Palm Beach provides quite a contrast to the Rooney roots in Pittsburgh. Art's daughter, Susie, said, "When you get on the plane in Pittsburgh in the winter it's like you're in a black-and-white movie, and when you get off the plane in Palm Beach it's like you're in a Technicolor movie."

I had a similar observation. When we were in Palm Beach, I felt as if my vision had improved. "I feel like I did when I got my first pair of glasses," I told my wife as we were driving to downtown West Palm Beach. "I came out of the optometrist's office and went directly across the street to a movie theater and saw Howard Keel, playing the part of a Canadian mountie, in a musical called 'Rosemarie.' The color was sharper — the reds were redder — everything had such definition. Trees had leaves. It was as if I was seeing for the first time."

In South Florida, all the automobiles looked new because they didn't have any rock salt stains or grime on them. They are better cars, too. You see more BMWs, Mercedes-Benz, Lexus, Jaguars, Porsches, Rolls-Royce, Ferraris, Lincolns and, yes, even some Cadillacs and Buicks.

The colors of the city are different. There are so many homes and buildings in pastels: pale pink, pale yellow, pale orange, pale green, peach, plum and apricot. "It's a nice place, no doubt about it," said Art. Then there is that blue, blue sky and constant sunshine. It was warmer, by 20 degrees most days, than it was in Pittsburgh. Then there are those stately palm trees that line every major thoroughfare. When you see those palm trees outlined against the blue, blue sky you know you're not in Kansas (or Pennsylvania) anymore.

"My father always loved South Florida," said Art, Jr. "He didn't start staying in Palm Beach until he bought the Palm Beach Kennel Club in 1970. Before that, he used to go farther down in South Florida, like Miami and the Florida Keys, during the off-season.

"He loved Miami. They had Gulfstream, Hialeah and Tropical Park for thoroughbred horse racing. There was Pompano Downs for harness racing. John McCartney, who was our lawyer and original partner when we had tracks in Philadelphia, remembers driving with my dad from Palm Beach to Miami and back one day.

"He said they drove down to Hialeah for the horse racing program, and on the way back they caught four races at the harness track in Pompano Beach, and then they got to Palm Beach for the last four races at the Kennel Club. McCartney said he went from watching horses with riders, to horses pulling carts and drivers, to dogs — all in one day! My Dad did things like that all the time. He was a man of enormous energy.

"Back in the 1930s, he drove down with some friends from Pittsburgh to Hialeah, without stopping. He had a horse running in the first race. He bet on his horse to win and parlayed that with another horse in the second race for a daily double bet. His horse was beat in the first race. He didn't stick around for the second race. They returned to Pittsburgh right after the first race.

"He would go down there to gambling houses in Daytona Beach — it was wide open — and to Palm Beach.

"He went to a cockfight (a contest of gamecocks usually armed with metal spurs) somewhere in South Florida. Gangsters came into the room with machine guns pointed at the crowd. They were there to rob them. Jock Whitney, the millionaire from New York, was in the crowd. The Whitneys and Vanderbilts had mansions in that area. Jock Whitney wanted to fight these guys. My dad hollered out, 'Give them the money! It's just money!' Whitney was smart enough to listen to my dad. My dad came back the next day for more cockfighting. What a time. He was the man. That's why it bothered me when someone would criticize my father for something to do with the Steelers. Like he was some kind of bozo. They just knew him from the Steelers. They didn't know what he was doing all over the country, how he was regarded in the horse racing and gaming industry. My dad was pretty smart, all right.

"I'll tell you another driving story. There are so many of them. My uncle, John McNulty, who was my mother's brother, shared the driving with my dad en route to South Florida. He worked at North Side Buick, which his father owned. He said my dad's car broke down in Washington, D.C. They went to a garage and the mechanic said it would take a few days to make the repairs. My dad said he didn't have a few days. So he bought a new car right on the spot. This was in the '30s. No one had any money. But my dad had money. He had money when everyone else was broke. And they continued on their way to South Florida.

"Geez, it was an experience to drive with him. The cigar and tobacco juice; his fedora hat, worn like John Wayne wore his in the movies ("The Quiet Man"), the speed, the radio tuned to a ballgame, or I should say nearly tuned to a ballgame. If not the ballgame, then saying the rosary at 70 miles per hour. Mom had a lot of confidence in him as a driver, but she gave him that old line that even St. Christopher gets out of the car when you're going 80 miles per hour.

"Who needed Kennywood Park with The Chief at the wheel? It was a thrill a minute. He was a great driver. I don't remember ever hearing of him being in any accidents.

"I never heard any stories of him going to Havana, but he went to Las Vegas lots of times. Jack Butler and I went with my dad to Las Vegas once after a game on the West Coast. As we walked through the crowded casino, you could hear a buzz in the place. Someone said, 'Art Rooney is here.' Some casino officials took us backstage, so to speak, where all the guys who ran the place were located. They showed us a sign on the wall in which they listed about five gamblers who could give the house difficulty because of their expertise. My father's name was on the list. Some people back in Pittsburgh thought he was some bumbler who could not run a football team or a Chinese fire drill. Dad had the discipline to let them think what they wanted to think without protesting. He knew what he could do.

443

"With The Chief's legacy, it's like he's still alive. Everybody has his own spin on each story. I have 15 journals on his legendary stories that I started to write down when I turned 60. I hope I don't get kicked out of the family for doing this, or for sharing some of these stories."

As far as all the brothers getting along, Art, Jr. said, "Everybody grouses, but there's no real viciousness."

"He enjoyed being on stage."
— Pat Rooney, Jr.

There are legendary stories about the time when Art Rooney, at age 19, played craps at the same table as Pancho Villa in a gambling house somewhere in Mexico. His boys talk about how he wore ties with his golf shirts — he had his own ideas about being dressed properly — and how he boxed and wrestled with his coaches. He received cigars from Frank Sinatra. He was quite the minor league baseball player (once leading the league in hitting), a national AAU boxing champion and a co-promoter of a heavyweight championship bout in Pittsburgh between Jersey Joe Walcott and Ezzard Charles at Forbes Field.

When he was in training to be an airplane pilot, Art Rooney reportedly buzzed the City-County Building and swooshed under some bridges in downtown Pittsburgh. He must have been a daredevil in his younger days.

This is a man memorialized by a statue outside the new football stadium on the North Side, and by having buildings named after him at St. Vincent College and Indiana University of Pennsylvania.

Pat, Sr. said, "He was a man who enjoyed being on stage."

Reflecting on some of the stories I checked out with him, Pat, Sr. said, "Some of the stories are tremendously embellished, I'm sure. But they're good stories. My dad used to say that all ex-baseball players ended up being .300 hitters.

"My dad was great with his team when you had to meet the payroll. Dan is great in a time when the financial aspect is so much bigger. It took both of them to get it where it is today."

Asked how he feels about living in South Florida, Pat said, "From October to July first, I don't think you can beat it. I don't like July and August much. September's not so bad. Anybody's who's 50 or over who doesn't come down here in the winter is nuts."

> *"I am of Ireland,*
> *And the Holy Land of Ireland,*
> *And time runs on,' cried she.*
> *'Come out of charity,*
> *Come dance with me in Ireland.'"*
> *— W. B. Yeats*

Bobby Layne with Art Rooney

With Ernie Stautner at Hall of Fame induction

With grandson Art II

With Bob Prince at Dapper Dan Dinner

With Frank Sinatra at Steelers' practice at Palm Springs, California

West Palm Beach
At Rooney's Pub
and the Kennel Club

"We try to celebrate our heritage."
— Joe Rooney

CityPlace

West Palm Beach is divided from Palm Beach by the Intracoastal Waterway. Once upon a time it was connected to the mainland, but that natural bridge was cut away to make it an island unto itself. West Palm Beach has been called the island's poor cousin. There are three bridges connecting West Palm Beach with Palm Beach. There are about 70,000 residents in West Palm Beach, about seven times as many as can be found in Palm Beach.

My wife Kathie and I came to West Palm Beach in early May of 2001 to visit our younger daughter, Rebecca, and it gave me further opportunity to talk to the Rooneys and their relatives, the Laughlins, who worked and resided in the area. My daughter Rebecca was close to completing an 11-week training period with California Pizza Kitchen, Inc. Her training site was located at The Gardens Mall in Palm Beach Gardens. Rebecca was training to be a manager at a brand new restaurant at the Easton Mall in suburban Columbus, Ohio. She was delighted by the environment in which she found herself. She was telling me stories about seeing tennis greats Andre Agassi, Steffi Graff and Jennifer Capriatti eating at California Pizza Kitchen. There are rich people — or "swells" as they are known — living in West Palm Beach, but not to the same extent as in Palm Beach. Some of the people who provide services for the rich people live in West Palm Beach. In short, it's not nearly as exclusive. It's more of a mixed bag. I wouldn't mind having a winter home there. I could fit in. If I did, I'd hang out at the Rooney Public House.

The Rooney Public House is at 213 Clematis Street in the Clematis section of the business district, just a short block from the Intracoastal Waterway where all the beautiful boats are docked. It's near Pizza Girls, which is reported to have the best pizza in that part of town, Starbucks Coffee and Pig City. In Ireland, they have a word for having a good time — *craic* — which is pronounced crack. You can have a good time on Clematis Street. It reminded me of Walnut Street in Shadyside or Forbes Avenue in Squirrel Hill. Only with the sun shining and a body of water nearby.

There are photos of Art Rooney and his family to be found on every wall in the Rooney Public House, or the Rooney Pub as the regulars refer to it. There are Steelers pictured everywhere, personally signed photos of Johnny Unitas and Jack Kemp alongside a head-shot of Byron "Whizzer" White, the Steelers' star running back in 1938 who became a Supreme Court Justice. Even the great ones who got away remain a significant part of the Steelers' story. Art Rooney would approve of their pictures being in the pub. There's a drawing of him above that grouping in which he appears to be looking on approvingly at the scene below.

"When we first opened," recalled Joe Rooney, "someone from Pittsburgh came walking in and said, 'I don't know if Art Rooney would approve of you stealing his name this way.' We think he would. That's why we did it. Anyway, it's our name, too."

There are photos and signed helmets and jerseys of Pittsburgh-area pro stars such as Danny Marino, Joe Namath and Joe Montana on display in the same case as some Waterford crystal. There is an eclectic mix of memorabilia from the sports and Irish literary world to be found in this popular pub that attracts a lot of former Pittsburghers or tourists from Pittsburgh. There are 50 or 60 who show up regularly during the football season when the Steelers' games are telecast via a satellite dish.

There's a "Notre Dame corner" on the left, just inside the doorway, featuring photographs of Jerome Bettis, Johnny Lattner, Frank Varrichione, Terry Hanratty, Rocky Bleier and Oliver Gibson. How about Red Mack and Myron Pottios and Bill Walsh and Joe Gasparella? Where have you gone, Joe Gasparella?

There's a photo of Rooney's original Hope-Harvey football team on a wall near the first bar in the house.

The photos aren't all of sports figures. Irish writers are celebrated in this dark, cavernous restaurant-bar that is furnished with authentic benches, tables and white stone Celtic high crosses. There is fresh corned beef. There is much that could be found in an Irish pub across the Atlantic Ocean. It would be a good place to celebrate or brood. The Irish love to do both, which is why they love wakes. There is a despairing, melancholy quality to much of Irish literature.

By the fireplace and in some of the booths there are photos, drawings and illustrations of James Joyce, George Bernard Shaw, Brendan Behan, Samuel Beckett, Oscar Wilde, William Butler Yeats, J.M. Synge, Kathleen Raine, Liam O'Flaherty, Frank O'Connor and Sean O'Casey. There are even a few books about the Steelers by Jim O'Brien, yes, yours truly, to be found among the books on shelves by these same booths. What an honor. Imagine how I felt to find my books keeping that kind of company. I found the same book titles displayed in a wall unit in the office shared by John Rooney and Art Laughlin at the Palm Beach Kennel Club.

The Rooneys are really into Irish literature and have presented a prize for 30 years to an outstanding writer in Ireland. "This race did ever love great personages," someone once wrote of the Irish.

The whiskey choices at the Rooney Pub include Bushmills, John Powers, Jameson and Kilbeggan. The beer offerings include dark Guinness, of course, Killians Irish Red, New Castle from England,

Harp from Ireland, Rolling Rock from Latrobe and, at times, Iron City and I.C. Light imported from Pittsburgh. While you are eating or drinking, you can read *The Irish Times* delivered daily at the doorstep, or the latest copy of *Steelers Digest*. There's plenty of Irish fare, but we were happy with the hamburgers we ordered. Especially when they were topped with Stilton cheese from the British Isles.

Joe Rooney, the 36-year-old son of Pat Rooney, sat on a tall stool at the corner of one of the bars at the Rooney Public House. As he talked, I had to smile. He had a lot of Rooney in his full-cheeked face. He resembled both of his grandfathers, Art, the son of a saloonkeeper in Western Pennsylvania, and Joe Sully, a guard at the Western Penitentiary in Woods Run, just down the Ohio River from the North Side. Joe Rooney appreciated hearing that. He combed his dark brown hair straight back, the way his grandfathers, dad and uncles did.

"The family heritage is important to all of us," said Joe, who is schooled to manage restaurants and bars, and teaches others how to do it at Lynn University in Boca Raton, just south of West Palm Beach. "We're trying to stay as loyal to that family heritage as we can. Even with our beer labels and our company name. In our corporate filings, we're the General Braddock Brewing Co., for instance, which was the name of my great-grandfather's brewery in Braddock. We've had a beer of our own called Rooney's Old Irish Ale and we had one of the original bottles and labels and we copied both. Now we're introducing another beer with a great odd name. It's Veterans & Civilians Safety Brew. That's a lighter lager, whereas our other brand is a dark ale. And we try to get Iron City and I.C. Light here, when we can, to keep our Pittsburgh roots intact.

"My goal, drawing on our heritage, was doing things the way our family had always done them. I made a few trips to Pittsburgh to visit museums, archives and such to do research and find out as much as I could about our family's business. We draw on our history in New York, Philadelphia and Vermont. Our Green Mountain Track was originally a thoroughbred track and then it became a dog track.

"My great-grandfather, Dan Rooney, owned the Colonial Hotel in Monaca around 1900, then the General Braddock Brewing Company in Braddock, then his saloon on Robinson Street on the North Side. Somewhere in there, between Braddock and the North Side, I think, he may have owned a bar in McKees Rocks, too. We're not certain about that."

Like the Kennedys, the Rooneys have been linked with bootlegging during Prohibition (1920-1933). There was a 13-year period when the manufacturing, transportation and sale of alcoholic beverages were banned by the U.S. Government. It was outlawed by the 18th Amendment and the Volstead Act. Rumors persist that the Rooneys continued to brew and peddle beer during that time when it was illegal to do so.

Joe Rooney smiled and shook his head when I asked him if he came across anything relating to that in his personal research. "I don't know anything about that," he said.

Pat Rooney Jr., an attorney, offers legal advice to his brother Joe, who oversees the family's Rooney Public House chain of Irish pubs. They are seen in the one in West Palm Beach.

Kathie and Jim O'Brien enjoy a visit with Joe Rooney at Rooney's Public House on Clematis Street in West Palm Beach in May of 2001.

When I returned to Pittsburgh after my visit to Palm Beach and West Palm Beach, I asked Art Rooney, Jr. about the stories relating the Rooneys to bootlegging activity, and I also asked him about another story I heard upon my return.

A fellow who lives in the same Mt. Lebanon community as Art Rooney, Jr., approached me at a booksigning at Waldenbooks at South Hills Village in late May. He introduced himself as Jude C. Pohl. He produced dinner theater shows at the Radisson Hotel in Green Tree and he had published books (including "The Blooper Man — The Rip Sewell Story"). When he heard about my plans for a book about Art Rooney, he stopped me cold by declaring, "I have no use for Art Rooney."

When I asked him why, Pohl told me that his late father had been run over by a car Art Rooney was driving. His father — Charles Pohl — was attempting to walk across a street on the North Side back in the early 1930s when he was struck by a speeding automobile. Remember, Rooney was known for driving automobiles with a heavy foot on the gas pedal.

"Both of my dad's legs were broken," said Pohl. "He had just stepped off the curb when this car came careening around the bend. My dad tried to sue Art Rooney for his hospital expenses and lost wages and had to take him before a magistrate on the North Side. If you couldn't work in those days you didn't get paid. There was no disability insurance or workmen's compensation at the time. I wasn't around then. My dad had just gotten married. My dad said that Art Rooney came into the magistrate's hearing room and walked up to the magistrate — he seemed to know him — and spoke to him quietly for awhile before the proceedings got underway. The magistrate dismissed the case for lack of evidence. My dad never got a chance to plead his case."

Art Rooney, Jr. told me he had never heard any stories about his father being involved in any automobile accidents.

I asked him if he knew of any bootlegging background in the Rooney family history. Some people who knew the Rooneys from the North Side had told me they'd heard stories about that.

"Pop Rooney had the General Braddock Brewery that made Rooney's Beer," answered Art, Jr. by e-mail. "But there could not have been too much action during Prohibition (1920-1933). Or was there? Jack and Marie McGinley are the people to ask about that, but Jack never tells me anything about those days. Pop hurt his leg or hip and might have been relegated to a political job about then. Was my grandfather a bootlegger? I don't know, but that was looked on by many as a noble Irish profession. You got me on that one, Jim."

Prohibition was deemed a big failure. Alcoholic consumption actually went up during that 13-year period, so did crime and corruption. Speakeasies sprung up in every neighborhood. Bootleggers often bought protection from political officials, the local police and judges for the illegal traffic and sale of alcoholic beverages. Organized crime was involved in bootlegging, drugs, prostitution and the "protection" racket. Homicide rates soared as well.

I remember going to "speakeasies" in our neighborhood with my father in the late 1950s when saloons weren't allowed to be open on Sunday. Social clubs like the American Legion, VFW and Hungarian Club were more popular in Hazelwood then as well because they were places one could go and get alcoholic beverages — a shot and a beer — on the Sabbath.

If the Rooneys were involved in such shenanigans in the '20s and early '30s, there is no record of it in the Rooney Public House in West Palm Beach.

"Ireland is important to our family."

Dan Rooney was born in Ireland and came to this country when he was 12 years old. That's something Joe Rooney, his great-grandson, knows for sure. That Dan Rooney was the father of Art Rooney and eight other siblings.

"Ireland is important to our family," said Joe. "I was the dean of students at American College in Dublin for three years. My Dad (Pat Rooney) is on the board of the college and goes over there for meetings from time to time.

"We're Irish-Americans, and that's not something that they think about or promote in Ireland. They don't seem to know how much Americans like to retain their ethnic roots and ethnicity. We go to Ireland often. We have tried to replicate pieces of Ireland that have a strong appeal to us in our pubs here. There's an archway in the middle of our restaurant, for instance, that is a reproduction of an arch at the college where I taught in Ireland. My family's been there and we try to bring those links out in our pubs. It legitimizes us as not only barkeepers but as Irish barkeepers.

"It's important that we draw on our legacy of being saloon-keepers and bar owners, but also Irish saloonkeepers and Irish bar owners. We try to celebrate that heritage.

"My father and my brothers and my wife have all spent time in Ireland. We enjoyed it so much that when we established ourselves here we decided we wanted a piece of Ireland here, and hence we have the Irish pub. The look and environment of our place is pretty true to that you'd find in most pubs in Ireland.

"We all travel so much. My father doesn't seem to be able to stay in one place longer than two weeks before he wants to be on the move. My wife calls it 'the Rooney ants in the pants trait.' That's why we'd like to expand our pubs to places in Pennsylvania, like Pittsburgh and Philadelphia, maybe New York and Vermont.

The Rooney Public House reflects the love of and loyalty to the family heritage. There are news telecasts from Ireland available on

TV if anyone is interested. You can almost hear the whine of bagpipes or strains from a fiddle or two as you walk about the pub. There is an Irish band on certain nights. There are signs from front to back. There's a bumper sticker in the front window for Jim Rooney for State Senate back in Pittsburgh. There's a wooden sign on the wall that reads "Thirst is a shameless disease, so here's to a shameless cure." And "May You Be Across Heaven's Threshold Before The Old Boy Knows You're Dead."

Joe Rooney said the family all has a stake in this enterprise. "All my brothers and sisters and my dad are involved in this financially," he said. "My brother, Chris, works here full time. The others are just investors....

Dan said his wife, Renee, was from Quakertown, Pennsylvania and that they had taken over a little bed and breakfast in Bucks County.

Joe Rooney did his undergraduate work at Indiana University of Pennsylvania. His degree was in food service management. When he looked at schools, he checked out only three schools, IUP, St. Francis of Loretto and St. Bonaventure University, all schools with a Rooney history. A woman who was aware of his IUP heritage, brought him a copy of the 1920 yearbook from Indiana (Pa.) Normal because his grandfather, Art Rooney, was pictured in its pages. What was wild, though, was that when Joe opened it he found an inscription on the first page. This is what was written in dark ink: Arthur J. Rooney, 528 N. Robinson St., N.S. Pittsburg Penna Indiana State Normal School, 1920. "That was the address of the Rooney saloon on the North Side," said Joe Rooney. "I realized that this was my grandfather's yearbook." What are the odds on that? I mentioned to him that Pittsburgh was often spelled without the "h" at the end of it in those days, and that the abbreviation for Pennsylvania was "Penna." and not Pa. or PA. The N.S. was for North Side, which was thought by its citizens to be a different world than Pittsburgh.

"I was at IUP from 1983 to 1987," said Joe Rooney. "It meant a lot to me that my grandfather had gone to school there, too. That also put me closer to Pittsburgh, and I had a chance to see my grandfather more often. He died in 1988. So I got to spend a lot of time with him in his last years. I got to know him a little bit. Before that, I only got a holiday glimpse of him at Thanksgiving. I got a sense of him by the regard that was held for him in Pittsburgh. I sort of got a sense of him as a legend."

Joe Rooney just might be the most scholarly saloonkeeper in the Southeast. He has a master's degree and doctorate degree in hotel management from Florida International University in Miami and doctorate in business administration from Nova Southeastern in Fort Lauderdale. He also taught at Lynn University.

His wife Renee (Gibson) has a mater's degree in women's studies from Trinity College in Dublin. She is restoring their historic home in West Palm Beach. I also met his brother, Chris, age 32, during a second visit to the Rooney Public House on Clematis Street.

"I went to college at Lehigh, then Washington & Jefferson and then Lynn" commented Chris, who expressed an interest in being a writer. "I am working right how on a master's degree in journalism at Point Park College in Pittsburgh."

Chris, a handsome strawberry blond, was married in Kilfanora, a community in County Clare near Lahinch. He, too, loved to go to Ireland.

He looked the part. He exuded a carefree spirit. He wanted to be a writer, but he was in no hurry, it appeared.

Chris recalled how he and his brothers and cousins kept teasing Al Davis of the Raiders when he showed up at the luncheon at the Allegheny Club following the burial of their grandfather, Art Rooney. "We kept reminding him that the Steelers beat the Raiders in some big games," said Chris. "He didn't back down. He thought it was good fun."

"CityPlace is someplace special."

One of the highlights of the visit to West Palm Beach was touring CityPlace on two occasions. This is an impressive $550 million entertainment-retail complex in a downtown area that was a ghetto best avoided a few years earlier. It is a development that opened in 2000 and completely transformed the area. CityPlace includes national retailers, local and regional speciality shops, restaurants, private town homes, live/work lofts, rental apartments, a restored 1920s church that's been adapted to serve as a multi-purpose cultural center, a 20-screen Muvico cinema complex fashioned after the Paris Opera House and a $3.5 million show fountain in the center of the main plaza.

It would fit beautifully between the Steelers' new football stadium and PNC Park on Pittsburgh's North Side. At first glance, it seems like the most obvious answer to what is needed in Pittsburgh. Just do the same thing in Pittsburgh. On second thought, though, it might be a little too pricey for Pittsburgh. There's more money in South Florida, more tourists, and more sunshine. They all add up to make CityPlace so popular. The 586 residences are the key to the 24-hour success of the site. To have a vibrant downtown you must have greater number of people living downtown. A scaled-down version might succeed on the North Side.

I had a chocolate ice cream soda at the Ghiardelli's, and enjoyed it in a European-plaza like setting. I had a terrific dinner at a Legal Seafood restaurant, which I had first visited in Boston.

Best of all, and here's a novel idea. There's free on-site parking in a garage. One sees a stunning lineup of automobiles in that garage. There are a lot of Jaguars, Porches, Ferraris, Lexus, Mercedes-Benz, BMWs, on occasion a Rolls Royce, Cadillacs, a few Buicks. There are not too many junkers.

453

A signed Mario Lemieux jersey was on sale at a collectibles store for $ 899. There is similar stuff on sale with the signatures of Dan Marino, Joe Montana, Joe DiMaggio, Michael Jordan and Jaromir Jagr at sports memorabilia stores throughout the South Florida area. Marino, understandably, is especially popular in those parts.

"It's the Wrigley Field of dog racing."
— Art Laughlin

The visit to the Palm Beach Kennel Club reminded me of my year in Miami, back in 1969, when I worked as a sportswriter for *The Miami News*. In those days, we could go to any of the horse racing tracks — Hialeah, Gulfstream or Tropical Park — and the greyhound tracks and jai-alai frontons — and have dinner on the house. I hardly ever wrote any stories about those subjects because my beat was pro football. You always met a lot of interesting characters at those betting venues.

There's a Leroy Nieman ink drawing of Art Rooney in the lobby behind two ebony greyhound statues. I got to know Nieman during my New York days (1970-1979), especially when I was on the boxing beat. Nieman was a colorful character and always had an interesting entourage.

You felt like you were living the good life when you were treated to a grand evening at those places. It reminded me of something Dick Young once told me, in explaining why he liked being a sportswriter: "I don't want to be a millionaire," said Young. "I just want to live like a millionaire."

Palm Beach Kennel Club looked to have the same kind of cast. There are two levels of the grandstand. Admission is $1 for the upper level and 50 cents for the lower level. Most of the regulars at the track have season passes, compliments of the house. "They don't like to pay because they don't like coming in feeling like they're already in the red," explained Art Laughlin, the track's general manager.

The upper level looks like a casting call for "Guys and Dolls" with the men wearing bright attire, red sport coats, electric blue sport coats, canary yellow, with lots of white and tan shoes. The women are usually just as flashy in their costumes.

The lower level reminded me of a bus station in Cincinnati where we stopped en route home from Fort Knox, Kentucky, outside Louisville, on the way to Pittsburgh during the Christmas season back in the mid-60s.

The theme song from the old TV series "Miami Vice" came on every so often in the dining area. I was enjoying a dinner of stuffed shrimp in the highly-acclaimed Paddock Restaurant. It wasn't as crowded as it had been during "the season," which has just concluded, according to Art Laughlin. The "snowbirds," as they call those who winter in the area, had gone back north.

I went through the program for that night's races and bet $5 on each of the first six races. So I bet $30 altogether. I won $18.50, cashing tickets for a win and one for a place. So I lost $11.50. Nobody will be talking about my "big day" at the track 60 or 70 years from now.

The track boasts of paying out $80 million to bettors last year for "live" greyhound racing. There are 500 TV screens carrying racing elsewhere in the nation. There's a classy poker room on the second level. Art Laughlin took my wife, Kathie, and I on a tour of it and the rest of the facility on my second visit.

On the screens at the Palm Beach Kennel Club were races at Churchhill Downs, Delaware Park, Belmont Park, Pimlico, Hawthorne Park, Lone Star, Mountaineer, Charleston, Penn National, Wheeling Downs. There was a TV monitor at each table and you could flip it to whatever track suited your fancy.

"If it was like this when my Uncle Art was alive," said Art Laughlin, "he'd have never left the place. He could sit here and bet on action all around the country. He'd have loved this setup."

Art Laughlin, age 52, sat with me during five races at Palm Beach Racing Track and his brother, Dan, age 60, sat in on half of that session. Art lives in West Palm Beach with his wife, Debbie. Dan was previously the manager of a jai-alai fronton in West Palm Beach, but the Rooneys sold that, so now he was working as the operations manager at the Kennel Club. Dan's wife, Janet, was there that evening with Sandy Rooney, the wife of Pat Rooney, the president of the Kennel Club. Pat's brother, John, is the vice-president of the track. Janet graduated from St. Benedict's Academy in the North Hills.

Dan went to North Catholic and coached football at Central Catholic from 1962 to 1965. When I commented on how the Rooneys and their relatives all seem to have the same names, Dan smiled and said, "We figured out once that there were 9 Dans and 7 Arts in the family, but that may have changed," said Dan Laughlin. Dan and Art went to St. Peter's and then Annunciation before they went to North Catholic.

Another Laughlin brother, Jim, 58, comes down in the winter and believes he's quite the handicapper. In the summer, he manages the concessions at Settler's Cabin Wavepool near Pittsburgh. He lives with their mother, Margaret Rooney Laughlin, on Marshall Avenue on the North Side. He used to drive "The Chief" around quite a bit, too.

Joe Rooney and his wife, Renee, and their children showed up at the track while I was there. Joe and Renee have two sons, JoJo and Lawrence. JoJo is Joseph Arthur Rooney. He is in third grade at Rosarian Academy. He plays baseball, soccer and flag football. Lawrence is in first grade. He enjoys all water activity, soccer and surfing. He loves football and is a big fan of the Steelers.

At one point, my attention was drawn to another table when I heard JoJo announce to his dad, "We're winning on a power play goal by Straka!" He was watching a Penguins' playoff game on one of the monitors. He was definitely a Pittsburgh sports fan.

Art said he started working for the Steelers, initially, when he graduated from North Catholic High School. When he graduated from the University of Pittsburgh in 1970. Art said be began working for the Steelers part-time, in the ticket office at the new Three Rivers Stadium under the supervision of Gerry Glenn.

"I was supposed to come down here in 1973," recalled Art. "But the Steelers got real good, and I couldn't come down. We were selling more tickets. So I didn't come down here to Florida until 1974. I worked the first two Super Bowls, and then I went back up there to help after that. In those days, the track was open from January to the end of May. So I'd come down for the winter meeting and then I'd go back to Pittsburgh and work in the Steelers offices. In 1978-1979, the track here expanded its meeting from October to June and in 1988 they went year-round with racing.

"Pat is the president of the track. He's here a lot during the season, but he tries to stay out of Florida in the summer time. Pat has a place near Bethlehem, Pennsylvania, and he likes to go there. He travels a lot.

"John is here from the middle of October to middle of April. He lives in Jupiter. He goes to Philadelphia quite a bit. He goes to Tallahassee to lobby for tax relief, racing dates, legislation relating to dog racing and pari-mutuel betting.

"We have more kinds of competition for the betting dollar than we used to.

Nowadays, we have more betting here on horses than on dogs, but we don't get as good a cut on the betting activity at other tracks. We're taking bets on racing all over the country. We have action for tracks in New York, Philadelphia and Kentucky. They'd stay here all night if we kept the machines on for racing from West Coast. This place used to be packed at night.

"The Rooneys have had this place since 1970, the same year that Three Rivers Stadium opened." Art Laughlin went on. "It's right next to the airport. It's easy to get here. It's 59 acres of prime property. It's valuable land. The bulding was built in 1962. It's just the right size. It's like the Wrigley Field or Fenway Park of dog racing. Some of the ones they built since then were too big. It's the perfect size for the business we do. There are about 250 people employed by the track.

"Business is better in January, February and March. We do half of our business in three and a half months." I told him the same was true of the book business.

In Art's corner of the office, he has framed photos of Steelers' four Super Bowl squad photos, and another photo in which he is pictured with Jack Nicklaus. Art is an avid golfer, something he and John and Pat have in common. He had three of my Steelers books, plus one by Ed Bouchette of the *Post-Gazette* "Dawn of A New Steel Age," on display in a bookcase on a wall facing his desk.

There were sets of Super Bowl tickets preserved under glass. They all prompted good memories.

"When I first went to work for the Steelers, I used to drive The Chief a lot," said Art Laughlin. "I was supposed to get a job with the County Parks & Recreation through Doc McClelland. One time Doc McClelland came through the Steelers' offices and he asked me when I would be reporting, and The Chief heard him. After he was gone, The Chief said. 'What are you doing? I want you work for me. I want you with the Steelers.' I was 18 at the time. I had just graduated from North Catholic. I was supposed to start at Pitt in the fall. I wanted to go to summer training camp with the Steelers, but they kept me at the Roosevelt Hotel. We'd go to Charleston or Shenandoah. We'd go to Pimlico in Baltimore or to Liberty Bell Park in Philadelphia. We'd leave Saturday morning and be gone all day.

"I was hoping to learn something about handicapping. All he did was preach to me, 'Don't bet.' He wouldn't teach me about the horses. He'd say, 'You can't make any money doing this.' My dad had a bar, and he was preached against drinking. Between the two of them, I was told no gambling, no drinking.

"He treated me so well, though. That's the way he was with just about everybody. He made everyone he met feel like someone special. I traveled a lot with him. My brother Jimmy drove him a lot before I did, and then he drew the job again later on. I took The Chief to Montreal. We'd go to all those churches. Tim and June and The Chief and I would go to church. Sometimes The Chief would fall asleep in the car during a long ride.

"I remember another time when I was bringing him to the farm in Maryland and we got off the turnpike in Breezewood. They stopped us at the toll booth there. They'd been on the lookout for Mr. Rooney. They told him he had to call home. His mother, Margaret Rooney, had died. He said, "We're going back to Pittsburgh. Your grandmother died.'

"John and Pat told me a story about how when they graduated from college, their father came up to them afterward and said, 'Hurry up and get out of those caps and gowns. We're going to the track. You have to remember that he took his wife to Belmont on their honeymoon."

"I've had a wonderful life."
— Margaret Rooney Laughlin

When I returned to Pittsburgh from West Palm Beach, I called Margaret Laughlin, the mother of the Laughlin boys and the older of the two surviving sisters of Art Rooney. She was at her home on Marshall Avenue with her son, Jimmy.

457

"Arthur was a real good brother," said Margaret. "You could depend on him. I don't think he was the favorite son or anything. We were all treated equally. But he was always a leader. He stood out."

When I asked her how old she was, she hesitated a few seconds and then said, "I'm 87. My Jimmy is laughing because I don't usually tell anyone my age. But what's the difference now? At my age, you're lucky to be around. I haven't been feeling so well lately, but I've had a wonderful life.

"My boys, Artie and Danny and Jimmy, all drove for my brother at one time or another. They've got lots of stories. My Artie went to work for them right out of high school. Danny coached football for awhile and then went up to their track in Vermont. Jimmy worked at Yonkers for awhile, but he's been home sow since 1981. He drove for Arthur a lot in his last years.

"Arthur was a wonderful brother. We lived next door to each other when we lived over our restaurant on Western Avenue. We could holler out the window to each other. Then they moved to Lincoln Avenue and that's where they stayed. We moved to Marshall Avenue in 1951. We also lived next door to each other when we had cottages up in Ligonier. I went there first, and he came the year after. I have fond memories of those days."

"I wish I could take credit for Bill."
— Art Rooney, Jr.

Bill Nunn, Jr. is a frequent visitor to the Palm Beach Kennel Club. He has a place nearby where he winters. Sometimes his friend, and one of my boyhood heroes, Herb Douglas, is in his company. Douglas, a retired businessman who won a bronze medal in the long jump in the 1948 Olympic Games, has a place in the same complex as Nunn. They also get together in Pittsburgh.

Nunn was one of Art Rooney, Jr.'s top scouts during the glory days of the Steelers, and was the director of the team's annual summer training camp at St. Vincent College. He was a sportswriter and editor for the *Pittsburgh Courier*. His father had preceded him in the same roles. "My dad said his dad was a real nice guy and a terrific writer," said Art, Jr. (Bill, Jr.'s son), also Bill Nunn, is an actor who has performed in movies with Harrison Ford, Whoopie Goldberg, Samuel Jackson and Morgan Freeman, and is often seen on TV shows.

"Ric Roberts of the *Pittsburgh Courier* talked Dad into hiring Bill," said Art, Jr. "Dad was a friend of his father. It worked out so well that I wish I could take credit for Bill. He and Jack Butler and Dick Haley, and some of our regional scouts like Joe Krupa, were a big part of our success in getting good players.

"When he was at the *Courier*, Bill put together the black All-America football team. He had tremendous contacts at black schools, and really helped us in that regard. He improved our relationship tremendously with those schools. The people associated with those schools had a great deal of respect for Nunn. Nunn scouted and/or signed Frank Lewis, Sam Davis, John Stallworth, Fats Holmes, Donnie Shell, L.C. Greenwood, Mel Blount and Glen Edwards. That's eight starters in the Super Bowls. There are five Pro Bowl players there. Blount is in the Hall of Fame. Stallworth should be in there soon.

"Nunn and Butler knew their stuff, and they kept me from making more mistakes. I remember how Butler begged me to take Howie Long from Villanova. I thought of that last summer when Howie Long was inducted with my brother Dan into the Pro Football Hall of Fame. Ugh, he was such a great defensive lineman for the Raiders. I wasn't always that smart.

"When Bill Nunn ran our training camp, he roomed the rookies by alphabetical order. So blacks and whites were often roomed together as rookies. A few stayed roommates after their rookie year. He later paired the veteran John Brown with a young Joe Greene. He thought Brown would be a good influence on Greene, and he was. Brown became a bank executive with PNC Bank and he gave Greene a lot of sound guidance.

"Bill is supposed to be retired, but he still does some scouting and special assignments for the Steelers. He lives close to where my brother John used to live and where the Laughlins still live. He visits the dog track and he comes to John's home to watch Steelers games. He is in demand for those games with his insights and anecdotes. He has meant a lot to the Rooney family and the Steelers."

Jim O'Brien

Art Laughlin looks after Palm Beach Kennel Club, a greyhound racing operation the Rooneys have owned since 1970, the same year they moved into new Three Rivers Stadium. That's an ink sketch of Art Rooney by famed New York artist Leroy Nieman in the background.

Bob Oates
Hall of Fame voter

"Most owners are anxious to get away."

Bob Oates admits to being in his mid-80s. He is retired, so to speak, from the Los Angeles Times, *but continues to write a weekly column on pro football for the newspaper's website. He is the only charter member of the selection committee for the Pro Football Hall of Fame, dating back to its inception in 1962. He has voted for all 38 classes. The committee consists of 38 members, one media member from each NFL city and several at-large voters. He and Marnie, his wife of 60 years, were in Tampa, Florida for Super Bowl XXXV. He has attended every Super Bowl ever played. We spoke in Tampa and again on a telephone call to Los Angeles.*

I've been on the Hall of Fame selection committee from the start, and Art Rooney was the first (in 1964) who ever wrote me a letter and thanked me for voting for him. He's still one of the few who has ever done that. And, hey, someone has to vote for you to get into the Hall of Fame. I was pretty impressed with Art Rooney.

This is my 63rd year of writing football. I was the first national college and professional writer; that is I was assigned to cover both the college and pro game on an at-large basis. I went to the best games on both levels. So I have seen some of the best football possible. I once wrote for the *Los Angeles Herald-Examiner* and I've been with the *Los Angeles Times* for 33 years. I started out with the *Yankton Press & Dakotan* in Yankton, South Dakota while I was still in college. I replaced Jimmy Jordan who married the prettiest girl in town and moved to Pittsburgh where he was a sportswriter the rest of his life.

There were more great players on the Steelers team in the '70s than any other team, even the Green Bay Packers of the Vince Lombardi era. That's why it's hard for a Lynn Swann or John Stallworth to get voted in, or for L.C. Greenwood to get in. They're competing against each other for space in Canton. Now that Swann is in, I think Stallworth will get in the next time, or the year after that.

My son, Bob Oates, Jr., wrote a book about those Steelers. Art Rooney used to talk to me about that book. He seemed pleased with the way it came out. My son knows more about pro football than anyone I know. I'm glad Rooney liked it.

I loved running into Art Rooney at the owners' meetings. He'd sit and talk to you as long as you wanted to stay. He'd be pleasantly talking with anybody who struck up a conversation with him. He would stay there and talk to you at great length. Most owners are anxious to get away. They figure if they stay long enough you'll ask about something tough that they don't want to talk about.

The only other person who was like that in pro football was none other than O.J. Simpson. He would talk to you indefinitely. He was that way at USC. He'd stand in the locker room and talk as long as anyone wanted to talk to him. There were 21 daily newspapers in Los Angeles County, and I think he gave one-on-one interviews to all of them sometimes. He'd wrap a towel around his middle and just stay there forever.

Art Rooney would do that, and I always appreciated that quality in him. He was one of those guys who remembered back when they couldn't get anyone to talk to them. I talked to George Halas about those early days. In the beginning, Halas had to write every advance story and game-day story for every newspaper in the Chicago area. That was in addition, of course, to running and coaching the Bears.

I remember covering a game in Pittsburgh and I left the press box with about five or six minutes to go so I could get to the dressing room right after the game. I ran into Art Rooney in the hallway. He was leaving. Pittsburgh was up by two touchdowns, but I was surprised to see him ducking out. I hollered out, "Art, where are you going?" And he replied, "I've got to get home and see the second game." I think he's the only owner who would leave a game to see another game. He loved his football; he loved all sports I'm told. He was just so for real.

Jim O'Brien

Dan Rooney and Chuck Noll are reunited in lobby of Steelers' office complex at Three Rivers Stadium.

Sam Davis
"The Gentle Giant"

"Everybody liked Sam."
— Craig Wolfley

Jim O'Brien

Sam Davis speaks with difficulty these days. Once upon a time he was the Steeler who was the easiest to speak to; he was such an intelligent, charming individual. That was before he had the bad fall. Now he is among the more challenged in that regard. It's a shame, a Steelers' tragedy.

He is not alone. Two of their team's most fearsome fullbacks, Fran Rogel and John Henry Johnson, suffer from dementia — a condition of deteriorating mentality — and have difficulty with their recall. Their gait is often unsteady. They grasp the arm of an escort when they walk anywhere. They may have taken too many hits to the head in their heyday. They took pride in punishing would-be tacklers.

Ray Mansfield, a former Steelers' center who lined up alongside Davis in the early '70s, was once told by a chiropractor that he had the neck bones of a 90-year-old man. Mansfield was 52 at the time. Mansfield died of an apparent heart attack in 1996, at age 55, while hiking with his son, Jimmy, through the Grand Canyon. He was the first to die of the Steelers of those glory days.

His successor, Mike Webster, went on to have a Hall of Fame career. But Webster's world started falling apart just prior to his induction in Canton, and he's had a series of personal behavioral problems. He has separated himself from his family and some of his best friends among the Steelers, the ones who were trying to help him. It's not a pretty picture. Now we are learning that these were not Men of Steel. They always asked us to see their human side, and now we were.

Many of them have gone on to successful business careers, and everyone likes to point with pride about how well they've done. Some have fallen on hard times. There are stories about players selling their Super Bowl rings because they needed the money. Sam Davis was doing just fine until he had that bad fall. Now he's one of the Steelers' sadder stories.

Davis was a starting guard for the Steelers on four Super Bowl championship teams, and was one of their most durable performers in his 13 seasons, from 1967 to 1979. He was the offensive captain since 1970. There was a line in his biographical sketch in the Steelers' press guide in 1979 that went like this: "Is very popular with teammates and frequently assumes role as a club spokesman."

He was pictured on the same page in the 1979 guidebook with Tony Dungy, a defensive back, and also a starter on the Steelers' all-time nice guy team. Dungy was traded to the San Francisco 49ers that same summer, a personal loss for many of the Steelers. Dungy got into coaching and became the head coach of the Tampa Bay Buccaneers.

There's quite a disparity in the direction in which Davis and Dungy have gone since their playing days came to an end. Sam Davis was also a special man, much respected and loved by his teammates. He was humble and had a quick smile and a good word for everyone. He was a sweet man. He was one of the great success stories in Steelers' history and one of Art Rooney's all-time favorites.

His was an inspirational story. He came out of Allen College, a small NAIA school of 900 students in Columbia, South Carolina, and made the Steelers as a free agent in the summer of 1967. He was discovered by Steelers' scout Bill Nunn, Jr. Davis ran the 440 and threw the shot put for the Allen track & field team. He was quite an athlete. Davis and players like Donnie Shell, John Banaszak and Randy Grossman gave hope to other undrafted prospects who came to Pittsburgh with a dream to play for the Steelers. He was an outstanding role model in so many ways. His nickname was "Tight Man" because he kept the team tight.

"I had a 50-50 scholarship," Davis once disclosed to me, reflecting on his college experience at Allen. "I worked for half of it, and played for half of it. I've stayed with that program the rest of my life, it seems. I've always been involved with some type of work outside of sports."

Davis, who was No. 57 for the Black and Gold, was a natural to go to work for the H.J. Heinz Company not far from Three Rivers Stadium on the North Side and help peddle some of its 57 or so varieties. He worked with Heinz for eight years on a part-time basis while playing for the Steelers before taking a full-time position upon retiring as a player in 1981. He had tried to stick with the Steelers in 1980 and 1981, but bad knees prevented that. Life might have worked out better for Davis if he had remained at Heinz. He was a natural salesman and had been quite effective for them in sales and marketing. He would have advanced in their front-office ranks.

"Everybody liked Sam Davis," said Craig Wolfley, who came along in 1980 and succeeded Davis as one of the Steelers' offensive guards. "I learned so much from him. He was a super guy."

Davis had quick feet, mobility and he was one of the keys to the Steelers' penchant for trap-blocking their opponents. He was admired for his agility. The Steelers' offensive line was smaller than most, its members bared their biceps before it became routine to do so, and outworked and out-witted bigger defensive linemen. Chuck Noll nearly snickers these days when he discusses how his line outwitted so many bigger foes. That was his strength when he played for the Browns.

Davis wanted to call his own shots career-wise, however, and be an entrepreneur. He tried different business ventures, including a gift shop called Only Happiness at South Hills Village in suburban Pittsburgh. He sold "Smurfs" when they were the rage, and other small gift items. The shop didn't last much longer than the "Smurfs" craze. He ended up in the cement business that required steep financing.

Davis was injured, according to him and his family, in a bad fall at his farm house on a 55-acre spread in Zelienople on September 9, 1991. He stumbled and fell down a stairway into his basement, says Sam and his wife, Tamara Davis, who now lives on Mt. Washington.

"He suffered serious brain damage," said his wife. "Sam is still a nice man, and he'll do anything for anybody. So he's vulnerable. I get calls from people telling me Sam promised them tickets to the Super Bowl, or that he'd take them up to the Steelers' training camp at St. Vincent. So we try to protect him."

I took a fall down the steps into the basement of my home on November 1, 1997. I broke my right wrist in two places and was knocked unconscious when my head struck a door and knocked it two inches off its hinges. Seeing Sam Davis made me realize how lucky I was.

I spotted Sam Davis while I was driving through McKeesport, about 15 miles east of Pittsburgh, in late May, 2001. I had not seen him in at least seven or eight years, since he appeared and signed autographs at a Steelers' open house promotion for fans at Three Rivers Stadium. He seemed so quiet and reserved that day at the stadium. I had last talked to him at length when I interviewed him in Room 503 at the Allegheny Neuropsychiatric Institute in Oakdale shortly after he was injured.

In recent years, Sam Davis had virtually disappeared from the Steelers scene. I saw Davis taking a walk down the street where he lives in a rather modest personal care home. It was a large home, a duplex, that had been converted into a personal care facility. There are several on the same stretch of road, the way some communities have a cluster of antique shops. I was coming from McKeesport Hospital and was on my way to the home of my in-laws, Harvey and Barbara Churchman, in White Oak. I couldn't stop when I first saw him strolling down the street because I had some time pressures.

Barbara was a patient at McKeesport Hospital and Harvey was a patient at nearby Riverside Nursing Center, by the Youghiogheny River. Within a few days, both would be joining my mother, Mary O'Brien, at Asbury Heights, a personal care residence in Mt. Lebanon, about four miles from my home in Upper St. Clair. It was a difficult time for our family. I was too familiar with the anxieties and challenges of having family health problems and loved ones in need of professional care on a full-time basis. So I felt I was sensitive to what Sam Davis and Tamara Davis and their children were going through.

My wife and older daughter still didn't think it was a good idea to interview Sam Davis. My wife, Kathie, was in her 10th year as a medical social worker in the oncology department of Allegheny General Hospital, where Davis had initially spent time after his fall. Our daughter, Dr. Sarah O'Brien-Zirwas, was in her first year as a resident pediatrics physician at Children's Hospital in Pittsburgh. Sarah had spent a summer during her student days at the University of Virginia as an intern at the Allegheny Neuropsychiatric Institute (ANI), where Davis had been sent early in his rehabilitation effort.

464

I can't pretend that Sam Davis doesn't exist anymore. He has problems that can't be fixed. He'll never be right again. This should not be an embarrassment to his children. Davis isn't to blame for his dilemma. His story can't be ignored. It's a compelling tale that has to be told. This is a man who walked and worked with giants, and was a public figure on one of the greatest sports teams ever assembled.

Those children have been robbed of living with and interacting with the Sam Davis I knew and admired so much during his days with the Steelers. Those children should know that Sam Davis was a cut above the crowd. He may have been one of the ablest and most personable of all the players on those championship teams. He was a wise old owl. He was the oldest player, on the team, at age 35, when I returned to Pittsburgh in the summer of 1979 to report on the Steelers for *The Pittsburgh Press*. He and Rocky Bleier were the only two ballplayers left from the regime of the previous coach, Bill Austin.

I had covered the Steelers in 1967 and 1968, Austin's last two seasons, for *Pittsburgh Weekly Sports*, a tabloid newspaper that Beano Cook and I published on a shoestring for nearly six years.

Davis and Bleier were both building blocks, and both inspirational stories, men of special courage, in the championship teams put together by Chuck Noll when he arrived in 1969. I depended on Davis so much that first year I covered the Steelers. He explained the personalities and paranoia of his teammates. He shared insights that helped me find my way in the locker room and to establish trust with the Steelers' players and coaches. Sam was a go-between and a bit of an ambassador for me in several cases. He had helped me. So it hurt to see him diminished in so many ways.

"He's nice to everyone."

I drove back to the block where I had seen Davis later that same day. I talked with a school crossing guard who talked to him all the time, and to clerks at a nearby store where he often stopped for Copenhagen snuff and Snickers candy bars. I learned that Sam Davis did that same stroll down the street about three or four times each day.

People in the neighborhood knew he had once played for the Steelers. "Some of the school kids found out he was a Steeler, and they looked up stuff about him on the Internet," said Mae Etta Grimball, a gray-haired woman he later told me was "my adopted mother." Mrs. Grimball gave Davis treats from time to time. "I know he likes sweets," she said. Davis signed autographs for a few of the students, she said, adding that he was good with the kids.

"My son knew all about him," she added. "My son, George Grimball, played football for the McKeesport Little Tigers when Bill Lickert coached the team and he's a big football fan. He's 50 and he's out in California now." She pointed out the store where Sam liked to go during his walks.

"He hangs out here a lot," said Sheila Guzewicz, who was in charge behind the counter at a neighborhood delicatessen. "He's nice to everyone. We call him the 'Gentle Giant' because he's such a good-natured fellow and such a big man, compared to the kids and us. But he helps us keep the kids in order just by his presence. We've never been robbed or anything like that."

Another employee, a 19-year-old woman, said she had been an aide at a personal care home in the same area a year earlier when Sam Davis was in residence there. He had been at that home for two years, I later learned, and his present one the previous year. The first place had 84 residents and this one had 18 residents. He preferred the latter arrangement.

Davis played for the Steelers at 6-1, 255 pounds. He's got more of a paunch now than he did when he was playing for the Steelers, but so do some sportswriters who were on the beat back then. I felt a tap on my shoulder when I was speaking to Sheila Guzewicz. I turned around and Sam Davis was standing directly behind me. I was startled to find him there. "I hear you're looking for me," he said.

I treated him to a can of Copenhagen snuff, a Snickers candy bar and M&M peanuts and asked him if we could talk for awhile. He begged off, saying he had to be back at the personal care home for a meal at 3 p.m., but that he could see me afterward.

I said I'd come back at 3:45 p.m. When I did, I saw Sam Davis coming down the hill, as he promised he would.

"Maybe they couldn't find me."

Even with his problems, Sam Davis proved to be a better interview than many of the current Steelers. His thoughts still ran deeper than most professional athletes. The problem was, though, that he had to dig so hard to find them, to find the right words to express himself.

I was used to that because my mother, who was 94 when I completed this book, found it difficult to collect her thoughts and express herself the way she once did. "I know what I want to say, but I can't say it," she often said, frustrated by her difficulty. "You know how sharp I used to be."

When I told Sam Davis about the book I was writing, and why I wanted to talk to him, he smiled and said, "I think about Art Rooney a lot. He was good to me."

He went on to speak of his admiration for Art Rooney and Chuck Noll and Bill Nunn, Jr. "He scouted me," he said of Nunn. "He's the one who brought me here." He said his wife thought he needed special care, someone to make sure he was OK, somebody to make sure he took his medications, someone to keep him safe from harm. "She wanted me to relax, and take it easy," he said.

When I asked him if he watched the Steelers' games on TV anymore, tears filled his eyes and crept out onto his cheeks. I asked him why that question made him sad. He said, "Because I can't play football no more."

For years, earlier in the ten-year span since he suffered head injuries, Davis thought he was still playing for the Steelers. He wanted to be ready for the next game.

I hadn't seen Sam Davis during the ceremonies at the last home game of the 2000 schedule, a victory over the Washington Redskins, when they closed down Three Rivers Stadium. There were over 50 former Steelers who paraded across the field that day in a moving procession.

"Nobody asked me," said Davis, explaining his absence that afternoon. "I didn't know about it until later. Some people asked me why I wasn't there. That's how I found out about it. Maybe they couldn't find me."

I asked him if he had any visitors from the Steelers. "I haven't seen anybody for about two years," he said. "They used to come and see me when I was at the other place."

I later bumped into John Brown, Craig Wolfley and Tunch Ilkin within a few days and told them about what Davis said. They all confessed that they had not been by to see him in that long. "Tunch and I took him out to lunch about two years ago," said Wolfley. "We just haven't gotten back to him. We'll have to do that. Did he wander when he was talking to you?"

Sometimes, I said, but overall he was pretty good. Hey, I wander when I'm talking, and have become increasingly forgetful. I'd been advised that John Henry Johnson would be tough to interview and I never had any difficulty talking to him. Friends had told me about other people who were suffering from Alzheimer's Disease and my experience was that they were never as bad as I had been forewarned.

John Brown, a former offensive lineman with the Steelers (1967-1972), had been a close friend of Sam and Tammy Davis. He knew there were money problems. Brown had been an executive with PNC Bank for nearly 30 years and had spoken to and advised the Steelers on financial matters when he was still playing and after retiring as a player. He thought that Tamara Davis was doing the best by Sam that the family could afford. He felt she had been loyal to him.

Sam said she and the children came to visit him regularly, sometimes twice a week. That's not always easy to do, I know from personal experience.

"As players, we should be paying more attention to Sam," said Brown. "He was a good friend. It's been two years since I went to lunch with him. I don't think the Steelers are responsible for us for the rest of our lives, however. We played for them. They paid us. The responsibility is ours to make it the rest of the way. They can't bail us out of our business and health problems. The NFL has a special fund to help needy players, but you can tap that only so many times."

Sam Davis said he roomed with Jon Kolb during his career with the Steelers. He didn't know that Kolb was now coaching football at Grove City College. "Jon Kolb and I were like brothers," said Davis.

As Davis talked to me, his hands were shaking. My mother's hands shook like that on occasion. That same thing happened when I was talking to Tex Schramm, the retired general manager of the Dallas Cowboys. When Davis did it I was reminded of Muhammad Ali, the champion boxer who suffers from Parkinson's Syndrome. Davis reminds one of an old boxer.

"Art Rooney knew what you had to do to survive," said Davis, as he stood in the sunlight in front of a neighborhood church that afternoon in McKeesport.

"He didn't look at anything too lightly, though he had a great sense of humor. But he was real serious about some things. He'd joke a lot, but you knew when he was serious, too.

"It was funny how he missed the 'Immaculate Reception.' He thought we had lost and he was coming down to show us he felt bad for us. He didn't see Franco pick that ball out of the air after Bradshaw threw it to Frenchy. He missed that. I didn't see it, either. I was blocking. I don't remember who the pass receiver was supposed to be, but it wasn't Frenchy when we were in the huddle. It was a roll-out to the right. I was blocking either a tackle or defensive end. I'm not sure.

"But Art Rooney was on his way down to the locker room when it happened. He was always coming into the locker room to talk to us. He was always asking me about my wife and kids. We talked to players on other teams and some of them never saw the owners during the week.

"I never really went into his office and sat down and talked about football or anything. I'd usually talk to him about my salary.

"Maybe I'd already talked to his son, Dan, about my salary and I wasn't happy with that or something. Sometimes I didn't think Dan was fair with me about money. He was tough. Everybody you talk to thought he was tough when it came to money. Otherwise, he was OK. I think I got a $1500 bonus when I signed and maybe $15,000 my first year. The best salary I ever made was $50,000."

I told him they should have paid him at least $57,000 a year, owing to his Heinz association. He smiled and said, "They should have paid me $157,000.

"I loved playing for Art Rooney and I loved playing for Chuck Noll," added Davis. "He was the most important one. If it weren't for Chuck Noll we wouldn't have had the players we had. They did the job. Chuck Noll...he was such a genius when it came down to picking players and coaching them."

Read that paragraph over again. Does it sound like it came from a man who was mentally-challenged? Sam Davis has difficulties with his speech at times and, yes, he can laugh or cry in a burst when he's talking to you, and there's something child-like about his demeanor at times, but he still makes sense. He still has something to say that is worth listening to and repeating.

"Chuck Noll deserves more credit for what he did for the Steelers," added Davis.

"I knew I could play for them. I wasn't drafted, but I knew I could play in the NFL. I just had confidence in myself. Bill Austin was the coach when I first came here. I came from a small school — Allen College — and everyone said I didn't have a chance. I said, 'I've got a good chance. The players who don't have a chance are the players who think they have it made.'"

When he talked about how much he missed playing the game, I told him how I had hurt my knee a month earlier playing basketball and that it continued to bother me. I said I might have to quit playing and I hated the thought.

When you play a game, no matter how old you might be, even at age 58 or so, you feel young again. "Don't quit playing," said Davis, giving me a little pep talk. "Put a sleeve on your knee. You don't want to quit playing."

He smiled when he said that. "I want to play football," he said. "I was a little bit *excited* about playing football. I saw it as a way of proving some things. For one thing, the Steelers didn't draft me. And for another thing, the players they had starting weren't players that could keep the position.

"They had Larry Gagner and Bruce Van Dyke when I got here, and I thought I could beat them out sooner or later. I started out playing on special teams and I proved I could contribute there. They played all three of us at guard for awhile. I thought Austin had a lot of determination. He'd been an offensive guard himself when he played for the New York Giants. I think he might have been successful if he hadn't tried to be like Vince Lombardi. He wanted to be like Vince Lombardi.

"Nobody bought that. Roy Jefferson didn't like him, and Roy Jefferson had a lot of talent. He might have been our best ballplayer at the time. But he forced a trade to the Redskins. He was the biggest loss the Steelers ever had.

"I'm glad I stayed with the Steelers. It was good for me. I liked Pittsburgh. I should have stayed at Heinz. I went to work for them in 1975 and stayed even after I retired from the Steelers. Yeah, I should have stayed. I wanted to get into business for myself. I had a gift shop called Only Happiness. I had a hard time getting product; that's where I had the problem. I didn't have enough to sell. The store did pretty good. Everybody was surprised. They didn't think the store could be successful.

"I don't think about the Steelers anymore. The Steelers is a history, like a history book. I don't think what we had will ever be back. I liked Chuck Noll a lot. He was a coach who could be considered just like Vince Lombardi as far as success is concerned. They should pay more honor to Chuck Noll.

We loved playing for Chuck Noll. We loved playing for Art Rooney. There will never be another Chuck Noll. There will never be another Art Rooney."

And there may never be another Sam Davis.

Sam Davis shares Steelers stories with McKeesport High School athletes, from left to right, William Chaffin, DeVon Jeter and Jamie Chaffin in spring of 2001.

Sam Davis (No. 57) discusses upcoming Super Bowl XIV at Newport Beach, California site in January, 1980 with *Pittsburgh Press* sportswriters, Jim O'Brien and John Clayton.

Joe Chiodo
An Italian leprechaun

"Art Rooney cared about me."

With Chuck Noll

It was a shame that Joe Chiodo couldn't be there when he was inducted into the Italian-American Sports Hall of Fame on April 29, 2001. Chiodo, a Homestead icon whose family restaurant has drawn national media attention through the years, was ill at the time.

He had been battling the gout since, interestingly enough, St. Patrick's Day. He may have contracted it from eating corned beef and cabbage at some Irish gathering and the Gaelic fare didn't agree with his Latin lining.

The gout is a metabolic disease marked by painful inflammation of the joints. It's tough to move about on sore feet. It is caused by uric acid in the blood and can be debilitating. So Chiodo's loyal customers had not seen much of him at his landmark restaurant on Eighth Avenue at the Hi-Level Bridge.

He would have been thrilled to be honored at the Italian-American Sports Hall of Fame's 15th annual dinner at the downtown Hilton. He was one of three men inducted. Former pro golfer Jim Masserio, Jr. and bowling standout Rocco Coniglio were the other two men similarly enshrined. Chiodo has great pride in his Italian heritage, so this was significant.

Then, too, some of the top achievers in about a dozen categories were honored at the same dinner. An old friend of Chiodo's, Charles "Corky" Cost, former Pitt three-sport standout and construction magnate from Wilkinsburg, was honored as "Man of the Year." He followed Armand Dellovade, a construction magnate from Avella and one of Pitt's most loyal boosters, who had been similarly honored the previous year.

It was apparent that Chiodo wasn't doing well when he failed to appear at his front row table for the 43rd annual Thompson Run Athletic Association's Sports Night at the West Mifflin club a week earlier. Chiodo had perfect attendance at the first 42 award dinners and was always among those to be acknowledged in the audience. Chiodo stands only 5-feet 4-inches tall, but he's a big man in the Steel Valley.

I was honored to be asked to accept the award for Chiodo by Tony Ferraro, a national director of the Italian-American Sports Hall of Fame. Ferraro has serviced Chiodo's Restaurant for years as a sales executive for the Pittsburgh Brewing Company. Ferraro's wife, Kathy, and my wife, Kathie, are friends on the medical staff at Allegheny General Hospital.

I had been honored as a so-called "legend" at the same dinner two years earlier. Not many Irishmen are honored at these affairs, so it was real special. Maybe they found out that I grew up surrounded by Italian families on Sunnyside Street in Hazelwood.

Chiodo's award and medals are now on display, along with the magnificent sports memorabilia adorning the walls and ceiling of Chiodo's Tavern. Everyone was rooting for the grand old gentleman, 83 at the time of the dinner, to rally and get back to his bar so he could share the good news with friends and customers.

Chiodo is a little guy with a big heart, something of an Italian leprechaun — a tricky little old man in Irish folklore who, if caught, may reveal the hiding place of treasure — and a tough cookie in his heyday.

He had been a Steelers' fan from the start, and has been running bus trips to away games in Cleveland, Cincinnati, Philadelphia, Detroit, Chicago and other NFL outposts since he formed a football club when the bar opened back in 1947. At last count, he held 36 season tickets to Steelers' home games.

Chiodo once nixed the sale of his saloon when the prospective buyer insisted that the 36 Steelers tickets be part of the deal. "I couldn't do that to my loyal customers," Chiodo said.

During the Steelers' run in the '70s when they won four Super Bowls and were honored as the NFL's Team of the Decade, Chiodo's Tavern received a great deal of attention from network and local TV, magazines, newspapers, you name it, as a retreat for loyal Steelers' fans. Pictures of favorite players, banners, newspaper clippings, helmets, trophies, even colorful bras, can be found at Chiodo's. God only knows what all is up in the rafters, maybe even some of those infamous "Mystery" sandwiches they create at Chiodo's.

Chiodo's Tavern was a magnet for travelers from all areas of Pittsburgh, and from the Oakland campuses, long before The Waterfront was on the planning boards. It was Joe Chiodo who made it someplace special. The college kids loved to talk to him. He had so many stories to share, and he appreciated those who frequented his place.

For the record, Joe Chiodo was born in the little town of St. Tommaso Soveria Mannelli in the Province of Catanzaro, Italy in 1917. In 1927, at the age of 10, he came to America with his mother to join his father, who was already here.

As a young boy, he learned the shoemaker trade and worked in a shop in Homestead. It was there that the Chiodo family decided to live.

At the age of 18, Chiodo attained Eagle Scout ranking. In 1941, he served in the U.S. Army, where he progressed from corporal to sergeant. He served five years and, during the Battle of Normandy, was given a field commission to lieutenant.

In 1947, he and his father opened the Chiodo's Tavern on 8th Avenue in Homestead. It was to become well known as a sports hangout, and was popular with the workers at nearby U.S. Steel and Mesta Machine Company, when those mills were going full blast.

472

One of Joe's biggest thrills came when he was pictured on a Steeler ticket in 1992, the team's 60th anniversary season. He was so honored because he had been a lifetime Steelers' fan.

He has sponsored teams in golf, bowling, baseball and softball. So he was honored as a contributor in the sports world.

Joe and his wife, Florence, celebrated 50 years of marriage the previous year and they lived up on the hill in West Homestead.

"The Irish are good people."

I was coming from Clairton to Pittsburgh on a dreary night, Tuesday, June 5, 2001. I was driving along Rt. 837, called the River Road — by the Monongahela River — from Clairton to Duquesne and past West Mifflin and Munhall before I hit Homestead. They were once all great steel towns and football towns. I had attended the funeral of my Aunt Mildred K. Clark, my mother's kid sister, that evening. Aunt Millie was 87 when she died. My mother, Mary O'Brien, was 94 and struggling toward 95. It hurt that I couldn't tell my mother that her sister had died. It wouldn't have registered.

When I spotted Chiodo's Tavern, I thought I better stop to see if by any chance Joe might be there tending bar. I had heard he wasn't coming in much lately, since his battle with the gout, but I also thought there might not be too many opportunities to catch Chiodo in action. So I pulled into the parking lot next to his place.

There were only a few customers at the bar when I walked through the door to check it out. Business picked up later. Out of the corner of my left eye, I caught Chiodo coming down the hall, greeting me enthusiastically, the only way he ever greeted anyone who came through that door. "Jimmy, it's so good to see you!" Chiodo cried out. "I saw you through the window and it made me feel so good."

He extended his left hand to shake mine, saying his right hand still hurt too much to have anyone squeezing it.

He ushered me into the dining room where he had been sitting with two good friends, Tom Lacey, a retired instructor from the art department at the University of Pittsburgh, and his wife, Eileen. Lacey, who grew up in Munhall, was a sculptor, working at Pitt with the renowned Virgil Cantini. One of Lacey's steel renderings paying testimony to Chiodo's beginnings as a shoemaker was on display in the bar next door. Lacey once taught art and coached the wrestling team, an usual combination, at West Mifflin High School and also later served on the school board.

Chiodo called for a bottle of I.C. Light with a frosted glass for me and, after I had turned him down several times, succeeded in talking me into having a cheeseburger. It was just right, and hit the spot, as did the I.C. Light. Chiodo kept his elbows on the red and white checkered oilcloth table covering as he spoke.

There was a GUINNESS mirror directly behind Chiodo and that got him talking about a trip he made to Ireland. Then he brought out some Ireland guidebooks to show me his picture in both of them. He's pictured in a bar in Ireland drinking a glass of Guinness.

"I got better treatment in Ireland than I did in my homeland of Italy," said Chiodo. "The Irish are good people. I was disappointed the way my wife and I were treated in Italy. I'm not eager to go back."

Chiodo told me he had gone down to the UPMC Sports Complex the Steelers share with the University of Pittsburgh football program on the city's South Side. Chiodo was not happy with his seat location in the new football stadium, Heinz Field, and was bitter about the treatment he was getting from the Steelers.

"I asked them to put me on the Steelers' side of the stadium," he explained. "I thought I might get some special consideration after all these years, with all those tickets I've had, with all those bus trips I lined up to take my customers to away games. I wanted to be on the shady side of the stadium. Hey, at 83, I can't handle staring into the sun anymore. It's hard enough to see."

Chiodo recalled the days when he'd go down to the Fort Pitt Hotel, or the Roosevelt Hotel, or Three Rivers Stadium and see the owner of the team and talk to him about his needs. Chiodo recalled how he used to bring a box of chocolate candy for each of the secretaries at the Steelers' offices.

"I don't know anyone there any more," Chiodo complained. "I couldn't get to see the people I wanted to talk to. The receptionist kept telling me this one or that one was busy, or at a meeting and couldn't be disturbed. It's not the same anymore. I went over to the Pitt side of the building, and was able to see Coach Walt Harris. He was great. He took me on a little tour of the place. He signed a miniature Pitt helmet for me. Come, let me show it to you."

Chiodo escorted me into the bar area, and proudly pointed toward the ceiling, where a shiny new blue and gold helmet hung from the rafters, right up there with the bras and the shoulder pads and you name it. What a sports museum!

He showed me his own little Hall of Fame. He had affixed the name plates of some of his departed friends in the sports business to a counter top along the window facing 8th Avenue. The names included Art Rooney, Bob Prince and Steve Petro, who'd all been to his place.

"When my mother died — back on June 1, 1973 — some of my own neighbors did not come to the funeral," he said. "Art Rooney was at a cottage in Ligonier when he learned of my mother's death. He and Joe Carr and Jim Boston came to my mother's funeral. I was just a lowly customer of his, but he came all that way to pay his respects. That's the kind of man he was.

"When I first started buying all those tickets, Joe Carr, their ticket manager, gave me three books of season tickets for free. I got three books when they played at Forbes Field, two books for free at

Pitt Stadium, and nothing for free when they moved to Three Rivers Stadium. Shouldn't I have gotten at least one at Three Rivers? Now I can't get anyone's attention about my ticket location. It's not as good as it was at Three Rivers. I had 72 people going to games on the road with me at one point. Doesn't that count for anything anymore? We'd charter a bus from the DeBolt people in Homestead and we had a great time."

My late brother Dan used to go on those trips, along with his good friends, Bob "Blue" Martin and Bob Vavro. Chiodo told me Vavro, a retired barber and barbers' union official from Hazelwood, was still handling the business books for Chiodo's football club.

He said Joe Gordon, the former public relations director for the Steelers, was always good to him, and sent sportswriters and broadcasters out to see him and his bar during the glory days of the Steelers. "The attention was good for business," claimed Chiodo. "I appreciated that."

His friend had a big book on the table that I recognized. It was a book about John Adams, our second President, by David McCullough, a Pittsburgh-born writer who was educated at Pitt and Yale. McCullough won the Pulitizer Price with his biography "Truman" a few years earlier.

That prompted another story by Chiodo. "When someone dies, I like to buy memorial books for the Carnegie Library in Homestead," he said. "When Mrs. Rooney died, I didn't buy flowers. I sent money to St. Peter's, the Rooney's church on the North Side, for them to buy some books in her memory for the grade school there. I did the same thing when Mr. Rooney died. Flowers last a few days. Books are forever."

Joe Chiodo, in black jersey at far right in rear, oversees bus trip to Steelers' road game from his famous Homestead bar and restaurant site at end of High-Level Bridge.

Gordon Forbes
A fan from Philadelphia

*"He gave me the longest
cigar I'd ever seen."*

Gordon Forbes has been the NFL columnist for USA Today *since 1982. "I started out in the midst of a player strike," he recalled. Before that, he covered the Eagles and the league at-large for the* Philadelphia Inquirer.

I remember the Eagles were playing the Steelers at Pitt Stadium. If you looked out behind the press box you could see a cemetery on the hill nearby. I was in my second year with the *Philadelphia Inquirer*. I met Art Rooney before the game. He found out I liked cigars. He gave me the longest cigar I'd ever seen. It must have been a $50 cigar. I lit it midway through the second quarter. It was still going strong at the end of the third quarter. It was a great cigar. It spoiled me for the kind of cigars I usually picked up.

What I liked about Art Rooney was that he was so unassuming. He could talk to kings of countries and busboys with the same feeling. I remember having dinner with him at the old Liberty Bell Park racetrack in Philadelphia. I was at the track and he invited me to join him.

I had a couple of winners. He said, "Gordon, you're a pretty good handicapper." I had to smile. It was quite a compliment, coming from him. I miss him. He was great.

The new guys can't compare with Art Rooney. He was from a different era. There weren't as many problems associated with teams. Art could give you more time. They can't, or they won't. He never failed to return a phone call. He was never down on his team. He was always upbeat all the time. He must've had some bad Sundays, but he never let it show. If he walked into a room, you knew it would be a different day. He was one of a kind.

I remember the first Super Bowl they played in. There was a feeling then that a team that came to the Super Bowl for the first time wouldn't win. The Steelers, perhaps reflecting Art Rooney, behaved like it was their fifth Super Bowl. They were loose and having fun. They were so free-spirited when they came to New Orleans.

I loved the team. I loved to go to Pittsburgh to cover the team. I loved everything but the parking situation. That was never good. The Rooneys made it special.

Joe Gordon was a terrific, accommodating public relations guy. I was doing a story once about the "Steel Curtain," and Joe lined up all four of the front four to call me in Philadelphia. Within a two-hour period, I talked to Joe Greene, L.C. Greenwood, Dwight White and

Fats Holmes. That was quite a trifecta, plus one. Ed Kiely was good, too, when he had the job before Gordon did.

Dan Rooney is a wonderful man, too. The Rooney family made it different from all the other franchises.

Steel Curtain defense began with front four, from left to right, of Dwight White (78), Ernie Holmes (63), Joe Greene (75) and L.C. Greenwood (68).

Back in 1967 or 1968, Art Rooney brought New York writer Jimmy Breslin into the Steelers' locker room one day. Bill Austin, the coach, was visibly upset and chased Breslin out, shouting at him in front of the players. Rooney approached Austin the next day at the South Park practice site and told him he wanted a few words with him. "I follow the rules around here," Rooney told Austin, "but I don't want you to forget that I own this team. If you're delivering a Knute Rockne speech at halftime, I can bring Alexander and his Ragtime Band into the locker room if I want to. Don't you ever forget that."

Joe Santoni
He named the Steelers

"I got to meet Art Rooney and Billy Conn."

I was trying to finish writing this book, but I kept bumping into people, former players, coaches or fans that I felt compelled to include in just one more chapter.

I was running from one hospital to another hospital, from one funeral home to another funeral home — there was lots of bad stuff happening to family and friends and it made it difficult to focus on my writing when I was in the home stretch — but good things were happening, too.

Whenever I have worked on books about the Steelers, I always felt that Art Rooney was right there with me, helping me at the task. I sat at his former desk, in his chair, to do research on "Doing It Right" and "Whatever It Takes" at the Steelers' offices at Three Rivers Stadium. He was with me even more on this book. I thought he was up there in heaven, doing what he always did best, even back in his early days as a ward politician, and that's pulling strings. I became his puppet. People were popping up in front of me who had a story to tell about the Steelers.

I do strange things when I am working on a particular project. I pick coffee cups in the morning to suit my mood or need for the day. It may be a coffee cup with shamrocks if I want to feel Irish or one with a dog or teddy bears on it if the day comes up cold, or one with the slogan "Whatever It Takes," something Chuck Noll used to say, if I'm struggling.

At lunchtime, I may pick a glass with the likeness of Jack Lambert on it, or one with Art Rooney or Bob Prince or Roberto Clemente visible on the side. I have quite a collection. I want them with me. It's a team thing. When there was a Three Rivers Stadium, I might touch the nearby statue of Art Rooney as I passed it for strength and inspiration, as if I'm visiting a church. Or say something under my breath to Mr. Rooney as I am passing St. Peter's Church on the North Side. My pal Pat Hanlon tells me to keep this stuff to myself for fear someone will think I'm a bit *teched*, but it works for me.

On this particular day, Thursday, June 7, 2001, I went to the Mario Lemieux Celebrity Invitational at The Club at Nevillewood in Presto, Pennsylvania, just south of Pittsburgh and Bridgeville. I knew I'd see a lot of stars there, and I wasn't disappointed. I bumped into Lynn Swann, the former Steelers' wide receiver who had recently been voted into the Pro Football Hall of Fame, and he was standing at the clubhouse door, leaning on crutches. He said he had undergone hip surgery, but promised to be ready for the induction in Canton on August 4.

478

Later, I spoke to former Steelers' quarterback Mark Malone and Coach Chuck Noll. They filled in some blank spaces. Then I spoke to Emil Boures, one of Noll's favorites as a versatile lineman who could take a turn at every offensive line spot in the '80s, former Pitt performer Emil Boures. He was caddying for his good friend, Dan Marino. I had a chance to say hello to him, too. The former Dolphins star always attracts one of the biggest followings at this celebrity golf tournament where he, Lemieux and Michael Jordan are the marquee stars. I went to a party afterward at the palatial home of Armand Dellovade in Lawrence in Washington County. Dellovade has a spread like the Ewings in "Dallas". He came out of Avella and worked hard to build a successful national steel sheet siding and roofing company in Canonsburg, and became one of Pitt's biggest boosters and supporters through the Golden Panthers and — though he hates the name and rejects it — Team Pittsburgh.

Dellovade throws the best parties this side of Pearl Mesta in western Pennsylvania history. His Christmas and July 4th parties are part of local legend and his Italian Day get-together isn't far behind. He's always treating good friends at Tambellini's Restaurant in Bridgeville. This was Italian Day, which looks like a casting call for "The Sopranos," but you wouldn't find a gathering of more good-hearted, warm guys anywhere in the world.

The two newest members of Bill Cowher's Steeler coaching staff were present. Russ Grim, the line coach and former Washington Redskin standout from Mt. Pleasant, and Tommy Clements, who came out of McKees Rocks to star at Notre Dame — Joe Montana said he wanted to be like Tommy Clements when he went there — and in the Canadian Football League, had been busy that same day at a team mini-camp at the team's South Side training complex. Clements was coaching the Steelers' quarterbacks.

Boures was there, too, as was Jimbo Covert of Conway, who was a Pro Bowler with the Chicago Bears, along with his former Bears teammate under Mike Ditka, Danny Rains of Hopewell. Joe Moore, who had coached so many future pro linemen at Pitt, Temple and Notre Dame, was giving them all a hard time, which is part of his charm. Jerry Olsavsky, a former Steelers' and Pitt linebacker from Youngstown, came late. They were hugging a half dozen more former Panthers like Bill Cherpak of Steel Valley, Dave Jancisin of West Mifflin and Tony Recchia of Vandergrift who were invited to the affair. Bill Fralic, Dan Marino and John Congemi have been to these all-star affairs in the past, but were not present. I was dining under the Dellovade tent with friends Joe Natoli, Joe Chiodo, Tony Ferraro, Don DeBlasio, Jon Botula, Gordon Oliver, John Nicolella, Lou "Bimbo" Cecconi and Reno Virgili — you get the idea — when I spotted an old friend from Monongahela. Aldo Bartolotta is in the super market business and claims "I never had a bad day."

He was with friends from the Mon Valley at another table. When I sat down to talk to him, he introduced me to one of them, Joe

Santoni, a retired restaurateur from Charleroi. After a few pleasant exchanges, when I told Bartolotta about the book I was working on, Santoni spoke up and said, "I named the Steelers." That got my attention. Bartolotta and his buddies vouched for Santoni's story.

There was Art Rooney at work again, an Irishman working his magic at an Italian get-together. Don't ask me, by the way, how I get invited to this shindig. Hey, I'm happy to be an honorary Italian for a day. They just move the "O" to the back of my name for an evening of pasta, hot sausages and the sweetest music this side of Perry Como and Dean Martin.

"In 1940, when I was 20 years old," said Santoni, "I submitted the name 'Steelers' when the *Post-Gazette* was running a contest to re-name the team. They had been the Pirates since 1933, but they kept getting confused with the baseball team so they decided to change it. I had my photo taken with Art Rooney. No, I don't have it. I misplaced it somewhere along the way. I just thought Art Rooney was great.

"I won a pair of season tickets at Forbes Field. I sat next to Billy Conn and that beautiful blonde from Pittsburgh that he married (Mary Louise Smith). She was something. We were in great box seats on the sideline, close to the field. There were about eight in the box. I was a big fight fan, and sitting with Conn meant more to me than the Steelers winning. Later on, I bought season tickets for the Steelers. I used to go with guys to road games in Buffalo and Cleveland and Philadelphia, places like that. I went to California when they won their last Super Bowl in Pasadena. I went down to Dallas and Houston to see them play. I'm still a Steelers' fan, though I think something is amiss these days.

"I had a restaurant — Santoni's — in Charleroi for 48 years. It was on Main Street. I sold it about two years ago and the new owners kept the name. I'm 80 now and it's time to take it easy. Dan Rooney was in our restaurant when I still had it. He came up a few years ago to promote voting for the referendum to build a new stadium for the Steelers. It was good to have him in our place. I told him my story about naming the Steelers. He liked that."

Joe Natoli of Morningside, Joe Santoni of Charleroi, Aldo Bartolotta of Monongahela and Joe Chiodo of Homestead spend a day at Armand Dellovade's Italian Day picnic at his palatial home in Lawrence.

John Brown
A cut above

"I've already paid my dues."

I found John Brown sharing space under a large umbrella with our good friend Gus Kalaris at his ice ball stand in West Park on the city's North Side. It was Friday evening, June 3, 2001, and Brown and I were both killing time before going to an event in the neighborhood. I was planning on attending a Pirates' game with the Atlanta Braves at PNC Park, a little more than a mile away, and had a date to interview Bill Virdon, a popular Pirates' coach who would be turning 70 in a week. John Brown was planning on attending a dinner under a tent in the parking lot at the Carnegie Science Center, about two miles from West Park, and across the street from Heinz Field, the new football stadium. The dinner was being held by the Allegheny Club as part of a reorganization effort. It had been raining, but lightly. Now it was raining harder. Prospects for outdoor activities didn't appear good. Gus got his yellow raincoat out of his van and put it on. "I'm not going home," he said. "I did that last week and then it cleared up and I missed about five hours when I could have been selling stuff. I'm not out here in the winter, so this is when I have to make hay."

John Brown shared a similar work ethic with Kalaris, who often puts in a 12- to 14-hour day during the summer. That was part of their bond. Brown had first come to know Kalaris when Brown came to the Steelers from the Cleveland Browns back in 1967 and stayed in an apartment at the Allegheny Center nearby. Gus was the godfather for one of Brown's sons, Jay, when he was baptized at St. Peter's Church, just past the Aviary.

Brown was in his 15th year on the board of directors of the Allegheny Club, which lost its home when Three Rivers Stadium came tumbling down. The club had not been offered space in the new football stadium by the Steelers or in PNC Park by the Pirates. The Allegheny Club had been a vital part of the original financing package of Three Rivers Stadium, but now the club was out in the cold. Its officers and administrative staff were going to try to make a go of it in space provided at the Carnegie Science Center. They felt betrayed by the city's ballteams and the Sports and Exhibition Authority. "Where's the loyalty?" asked one of the long-time bartenders.

It had been a difficult year for the Allegheny Club. The service staff had gone on strike a year earlier and club officials were challenged during the previous baseball and football seasons to provide the usual first-rate offerings.

At the Allegheny Club at Three Rivers Stadium, a club member could watch the Steelers and Pirates play while having dinner on the terrace, or from the bar above. To me, that was the main appeal of the place. During the week, the view of the stadium playing field or the

481

three rivers was worth the price of lunch or dinner. How was the club going to survive not having those amenities?

"I've already paid my dues," said Brown. "One of the magnets is that they have 300 parking spaces for members at the Science Center, within easy walking distance of the new stadiums."

Brown had performed with honor at offensive tackle for 11 seasons in the National Football League, the first five (1962-66) with the Cleveland Browns, and then six seasons (1967-72) with the Steelers. He was the offensive captain of the Steelers. He expressed admiration for Art Rooney and Art Modell, his bosses during his pro football career, and shared stories and reflections about both club owners.

Brown could talk with equal ease about Ernie Davis and Ernie Stautner, Paul Brown and Chuck Noll, Jim Brown and Muhammad Ali, Moon Mullins and Sam Davis. It was Davis who succeeded him as captain. Brown had special insights. I remember Dwight White telling me when I interviewed him for an earlier book, "I'm smarter than the average bear." The same could be said of John Brown.

"I'm not *that* smart," said Brown when I praised him in that regard. "When I played with the Browns we had a quarterback named Frank Ryan, who had a doctorate degree in math. Now he was smart. One time in the huddle, after Paul Brown had sent in a play from the sideline, Ryan said, 'I'll have to *cogitate* on that.' No one else in the huddle knew what that word meant. Finally, one of the guys in the huddle said, 'Frank, you're not going to do that on national television, are you?' We all broke up."

Cogitate, for the record, means to meditate upon, think over, ponder, plan. Brown said he didn't know at the time what the word meant, either, but he does now and he is certainly good at cogitating.

"Paul Brown believed you had to have a certain intelligence to be a good professional football player," said John Brown. "He used to give an intelligence test for new players on opening day at training camp. It took eight hours to take that exam. It was like the College Boards. Later on, he'd give us a test about our playbook."

I told Brown I'd heard that Chuck Noll aced those tests when he was a guard and linebacker for the Browns. "I'm not surprised," Brown came back.

Brown sat on a tall bar stool under the stationery umbrella that protected Gus Kalaris' bright orange cart from the elements, overhead trees and ubiquitous pigeons. The umbrella was striped and had as many colors as did the bottles of sweet flavors that flanked a large block of ice in the middle of that cart. A cloth was draped over the ice when Gus wasn't running a steel scraper over it to make another ice ball. There were glass-covered cases at each end of the cart, one containing hot popcorn and the other bags of roasted peanuts.

Brown sat on the stool, or on one of the nearby park benches, to rest his knees, as Kalaris kept serving his customers. When it started to thunder and lightning, Brown jumped off the stool. "I've got steel rods in both of my legs," he said, "and I'm a virtual lightning rod. I better take cover."

So he got behind the wheel of his wife's 1999 black Jeep Grand Cherokee parked along the curb nearby. I got in next to him. The rain started to come harder and flowed fast down the windows. I hadn't planned on this, but there I was with my notebook in my lap, listening to John Brown talking about his playing days with the Browns and the Steelers, and his schooldays at Syracuse University. I felt like I was interviewing him in an aquarium.

I remembered how Chuck Noll, who played for the Browns in his hometown of Cleveland, and coached the Steelers in Pittsburgh, once observed that football takes on a life of its own, that you can't plan everything that happens. So does a book. John Brown belonged in this book. After all, he was one of Art Rooney's favorites, and he always had something insightful to offer.

It said PA BROWN over his heart on the gray sweatshirt he was wearing on this blustery day. The blue and gold ballcap was from Pitt's jazz program, courtesy of its director, Dr. Nathan Davis. Brown had the heart of a grandfather and the soul of a musician.

John Brown had come out of a broken home in Camden, New Jersey, where he had knee surgery for the first time at age 14 as the result of a football injury, and starred at Syracuse under Ben Schwartzwalder in the early '60s, where he underwent several more surgeries on both knees. He hurt his knees as a freshman and sophomore flying downfield on kickoffs in scrimmages, and getting cut down by blocks.

I had seen him play against Pitt at the old Archbold Stadium when Ernie Davis was an All-American running back for the Orangemen, and I was the sports editor of the campus newspaper at Pitt. "I still have a photo at home I took of Davis in the dressing room after that game," I told Brown. "I got good pictures that day because it was cloudy overhead, it rained, and it was damp. The colors came out richer."

Brown smiled at my observation. "It was always cold and damp at Archbold Stadium," he said. Or so it seemed, anyhow, to a young man with balky knees.

"I had two or three operations at Syracuse," he said. "The pros probably wouldn't have drafted me today. There's too much money involved and they wouldn't want to take the risk. They don't know what you have in your innards."

He persevered, however, and missed only four games in his first ten seasons in the National Football League. Like many football players, he paid the price. He had both knees replaced in 1991, and the rehabilitation period was quite demanding and, at times, frustrating.

People who've met and associated with John Brown always knew he was something special, both on and off the field, as a ballplayer and team leader, as the father of a fine family and as an executive at PNC, going back to its days as Pittsburgh National Bank and PNB.

Three days after I interviewed Brown a second time, I spoke with Chuck Noll at the Mario Lemieux Celebrity Invitational at the Club at Nevillewood. "John Brown was unusual," noted Noll. "John was very bright and very reliable. He had a great work ethic, and he had the thing that separates people — attitude. You can have all kinds of talent and screw it up. He had a great attitude and he was a great competitor and leader."

Ed Kiely, who was the team's publicist when Brown became a Steeler, said Brown was "always a class act." Brown credits Kiely for promoting him to the powers-that-be at Pittsburgh National Bank, and for getting him named to the Allegheny Club's board of directors. "He was one of the best, in so many ways," said Kiely.

Brown, at age 62, had recently retired after nearly 30 years at PNC. He was a vice-president and regional director at the end. Now he had more free time on his hands, he was taking piano lessons, resuming an activity he enjoyed as a child. He was taking computer lessons at Community College of Allegheny County. He was serving on 15 boards. In addition to the Allegheny Club, he was on four different boards for Allegheny County including cultural and development programs; Vintage, a senior citizen group in East Liberty; Mount Ararat Community Center and the Art Rooney Scholarship Fund. He was loafing, as Art Rooney might say, with Gus Kalaris at the ice ball stand.

Brown always takes the high road, no matter what he's driving. We were talking about his days at Syracuse, and he started to explain how in his days there the school recruited black ballplayers in pairs, so they could room together. He said the blacks had to be above average students, preferably superior students, and that they had to toe the line. The demands on them were a cut above the rest of the school's athletes.

"That's just the way it was then," recalled Brown. "I can't look back and be bitter. I got through Syracuse for free. I'm not going to complain about that. It was that way at a lot of places."

When I said it was that way at Pitt when I was a student there during a comparable period. Brown came back, "After Bobby Grier, who I got to know, I don't think Pitt had any black ballplayers on their football team for awhile. I can't remember seeing any blacks on the Pitt team during the four years I played at Syracuse. I also knew Henry Ford, who played at Pitt before Grier."

I told Brown he didn't see any blacks on the Pitt football team in his days at Syracuse because there weren't any. Pitt went five years without a black until the coaches brought in Eric Crabtree, a running back from Monessen, and Jim Jones, a big lineman from Easton, in 1962.

I asked Lou "Bimbo" Cecconi, who was an assistant coach on the staff of John Michelosen, to recall that period. "I don't think they roomed together," he said. "It wasn't a big deal, like 'Hey, we got a black player.' It was never an issue. I recruited Crabtree, and I got some help from Frank Bolden from *The Pittsburgh Courier*. Eric was a good one." Frank Lauterbur recruited Jim Jones.

Brown didn't think the stricter guidelines hurt him any. "I just don't dwell on what used to be," said Brown. "I'm too busy trying to make things better." Brown refused to be bitter about anything. His oldest son, Ernie, age 30, named after football great Ernie Davis, had been released by the Steelers just three weeks earlier. Ernie, a 6-4, 285-pound defensive tackle and end, had been on the Steelers' practice squad the previous two seasons. He had played for a championship team in NFL Europe during that time. Prior to playing with the Steelers, he had put in four years in the Canadian Football League. "I thought he was good enough to make the team," said his father. "I know how that works. They have big bonuses invested in other players. I'm disappointed, but not bitter."

He's glad he came to Pittsburgh. He listed his two biggest thrills during his stay with the Steelers as Franco's "Immaculate Reception" and "meeting Mr. Rooney." He was on the sideline when Franco found a deflected football coming his way and picked it off and ran for a game-winning touchdown in an AFC playoff contest with the Oakland Raiders in 1972, Brown's last season with the Steelers.

Brown is a big booster of the Steelers' organization. "They taught me how to play the game," he said, "and I mean the game of life.

"I came here from Cleveland. I left Cleveland under questionable circumstances. I had arguments there about salary. When I got here, Dan (Rooney) came to my room, and said, 'Here's what we'll pay you. Here's what we expect of you. You're starting clean with us.' I'm sort of a second-hand Steeler because I didn't start out here. But his dad, Mr. Rooney, developed a relationship with me. It was always, 'How's your family?' We went to church at St. Peter's on the North Side, so that made it easy to see him. He'd say, 'John, I saw your son at Mass. Have him come over to see me when he's there.' I'd say, 'He doesn't want to do that.' Things like that. When they had the 50 Seasons Celebration, Art and Dan Rooney asked me to participate. Heck, I had never been a big star. When they had the statue fund to build the memorial to Mr. Rooney, they again asked me to participate. That means a great deal to me.

"They respected me; I respected them. I tell guys if you're going to play for a team then you should live in that city. You should get involved and you should keep yourself clean. You can't cause them any embarrassment." Brown nodded in the direction of the stadiums and said, "People think the only thing you learn out there is football. But you learn how to live."

"I'm too busy trying to make things better."
— John Brown

"You're in that fake world."
— John Brown

I ended up not going to PNC Park that night. It was still raining when I was scheduled to meet Virdon during batting practice. I learned later that the Pirates took batting practice in the cages under the stands. I rescheduled my interview with Virdon for noon on Monday at PNC Park. I called John Brown and asked him if we could meet at Gus's ice ball stand at 2 o'clock. I wanted to do a full-blown interview with Brown. I had a quick lunch beforehand at the Shamrock Inn on Western Avenue. That restaurant used to be owned by Johnny Laughlin, who was married to Margaret Rooney, one of Art Rooney's sisters. I had corned beef on rye, just to stay with an Irish (or is it Jewish?) theme. Call me strange, but I believe you have to stay focused in every way, as Noll might say, and do whatever it takes to help the cause.

This neighborhood was so familiar to the Rooneys. The Rooney Manse was two blocks away on North Lincoln Avenue, in the direction of the Point. The Regans used to live in a modest rowhouse on North Taylor Avenue. The Regan girls shared beds in cramped rooms in those days. Pat went on to marry Dan Rooney, the oldest of Art Rooney's five sons. Mary went on to become the Steelers' secretary and receptionist and, for many years, Art Rooney's personal secretary. She had retired when the Steelers left Three Rivers Stadium. Mary began working for the Steelers in 1952. I can remember calling the Steelers in the '60s when I was in college, and Mary Regan answering the phone by saying, "Steeeeelers! Hold on!" Another sister, Geraldine, who became Gerry Glenn when she got married, became the director of ticket sales. Joan became a secretary for local political leader Tom Foerster, one of Art Rooney's proteges. In recent years, I would come upon Mary and Joan and their mother, also Mary, who lived together in Mt. Lebanon, on a frequent basis on Friday evenings at Eat'n Park Restaurant at South Hills Village. They went there most Fridays for a fish dinner. They had another sister, Irene, and two brothers, Marty and John, but I never met them.

When I got together with Brown a second time, I learned that he didn't keep his Friday night date, either. "I talked to some people who went and they said it went well," he said. He was supposed to meet his wife, Gloria, at Gus's stand and she arrived after he had already returned to their home in Ross Township. She had been held up with school activities. She had been teaching for 25 years at Northview Heights Elementary School on the North Side.

"I didn't want to go without her," said Brown. They had been married for 36 years and that got us off on another subject. We both knew several players whose wives had walked out on them after their playing days were over, for one reason or another.

"You have to marry someone who has their own identity," said Brown. "When you're a professional athlete, you're in that fake world, an unreal world. If your spouse doesn't have some worth it will be difficult for her. When I retired as a player, she went to work, first as a substitute, as a teacher. She's still at it.

"I called the National Football League to ask some questions about my NFL pension. The woman I spoke to said I was an anomaly in the way I wanted the money divided between my wife and me, and that I had been married to the same woman for 36 years.

"It can't be easy for a woman to be married to a professional athlete. A lot of athletes have gotten accolades all their lives. They get so much personal attention, and favors, in grade school, in high school, in college and again in the pros. Everybody is always doing something for you, looking after, cleaning up your mess. You really think you're something. So many things are done for you. You live in a truly unreal world.

"No matter how much money you make, you better prepare to do something when you're finished playing ball. I remember how I felt when I was finished playing pro ball. I was scared. You live at least 72 years, according to the actuarial charts, so you've got around 40 years after you're done as a ballplayer. What are you going to do?

"Some guys are in bad shape by then. I went to Marion Motley's funeral in Ohio a year ago. Some of the old ballplayers there were in bad shape. Some looked great for their age. Joe Perry, who was 75, spoke at the funeral service, and he was outstanding. So he's OK. I owed a lot to Marion Motley, who'd been a great fullback for the Browns. He helped me play pro ball. At Syracuse, our whole offense was run-oriented. We always had the great running backs at Syracuse. I had a difficult time with the Browns in the beginning when I tried to set up to block in pass protection. Marion was playing for the Browns' basketball team when I got there, even though he had to limp up and down the floor. At every opportunity, he would take me aside and show me how to pass block.

"It's funny, but I learned how to pass protect from a fullback. But Marion, as someone pointed out to me, was one of the league's best blocking backs."

Motley, I mentioned to Brown, played his last NFL season (1955) with the Steelers. He was one of the players (Alan Page and Dan Dierdorf were the others) who grew up in Canton and were enshrined in the Pro Football Hall of Fame.

I asked Brown to talk about another Hall of Famer, Steelers' founder Art Rooney. He told me something I had never heard before.

"I first heard about Mr. Rooney when I was still playing for the Browns in Cleveland," said Brown, "and I could see what an influential man he was in Pittsburgh. Jim Brown was tight with Muhammad Ali, and he had the rights to promote his fights with Top Rank, Inc. in certain cities. Jim wanted to get some of his friends on the Browns involved, and he lined up me, Ernie Green, John Wooten, Paul Warfield and Sidney Williams as part of a boxing promotion team. We got a few cities we could work with, and one of them was Pittsburgh.

When we inquired about rental rates at the Civic Arena in Pittsburgh we were told that we would have to go through Art Rooney. He had the rights to promote boxing shows there. He had to be a part of the promotional team.

"What I liked about Mr. Rooney was I could always stop in his office and talk to him, even after I retired," continued Brown. "I always felt welcome, never an intruder. He'd always ask me about my wife and kids. One time Gale Sayers wrote a letter to protest against the lack of black coaches and administrators in pro football and I wouldn't go along with that. I felt the Steelers had always been fair in that respect. I didn't add my name to that protest.

"From Day One, I always felt so comfortable with Mr. Rooney. I thought this might not be such a bad place to play. I remember when I was at Syracuse and we came here in 1958 to play Pitt. It was gray and dark and sooty here that day. I remember talking to Ernie Davis at our hotel about how I would never want to play, stay or live in a place like Pittsburgh. Here I am in Pittsburgh 34 years after I first reported to the Steelers, and I couldn't be happier or more content.

"I'm from the 'Armpit of America,' which is what they called Camden in a national magazine. Sixty-five percent of the people there are on the public dole, some form of government assistance. Crime is high. So I'm happy to be in Pittsburgh. I'm glad I came to Pittsburgh.

"I know that Art Modell loved Art Rooney to death. I got to know Art Modell because he did so much to try and help my roommate Ernie Davis when he learned he had leukemia. Davis had won the Heisman Trophy as a senior at Syracuse and he was the Browns' No. 1 draft choice. They were looking at him to be the next Jim Brown. Davis came to Syracuse from Elmira, New York, but he was originally from Uniontown and was 12 years old when he moved from Uniontown to Elmira. That impressed me about Art Modell. He really cared about his players." He took a keen interest in trying to help Ernie beat leukemia."

In an interview in 1991, Brown discussed Davis at greater length. "We became great friends," said Brown back then. "If Ernie Davis had lived he would have been greater than Jim Brown because he was such a greater person than Jim Brown. Jim Brown was a great player, don't get me wrong, but Jim was always such a hardass.

"Athletes have super egos, but Ernie was just like another person. Even with his superstar status, he was easy to be with, and to talk to. He cared about you. When I was at Syracuse, he made me become a better student. I followed his lead. I had a brother, but I had a fragmented family because of certain circumstances, and he was truly like a brother to me.

"It was about the time of the All-Star Game in Chicago that we learned that Ernie had leukemia. When he was ill during my first year in Cleveland, Art Modell wanted him to play, but Paul Brown did not want him to play. I was having difficulty adjusting to playing offensive line in the pros. It was so different from what I'd done in college. It was a big adjustment. I was feeling sorry for myself. But I took heart from Ernie. His exact words were, 'I may not make it, but I don't have to give up trying.'

"He'd shave and he'd end up bleeding profusely. He had to have transfusions all the time. He had sores around his mouth. He'd sneak away for treatments. He didn't want anyone feeling sorry for him."

After a 16-month battle, Ernie Davis died on May 18, 1963.

Ernie's mother, Mrs. Marie Fleming, is the godmother for John Brown's son, Ernie. During our most recent interview, Brown told me he had accompanied Mrs. Fleming on a trip to Dallas two weeks earlier when Ernie Davis was posthumously inducted into the Cotton Bowl Hall of Fame. She had asked Brown what she ought to do with all the memorabilia she had from her son's playing days. Brown told her she should send it to Syracuse University where they had a special display honoring the memory of Ernie Davis. "My son, Ernie, said he would like to have something, too," added Brown.

"My mother was a strong woman."

John Brown said he had a history with Chuck Noll. "Chuck Noll recruited me for the San Diego Chargers when the AFL was competing with the NFL for college players," said Brown. "Sid Gillman, the great offensive coach, was the head coach of the Chargers. I had played in my last regular season game at Syracuse, but we still had a bowl game to play. The pros weren't supposed to sign us until the bowl games were over. They didn't care. They signed guys while they were still in school. I went out to San Diego and met with Noll. He said, 'John, you don't want to go to Cleveland. I've been to Cleveland, and San Diego is a nicer place to work.' Gillman gave me a beautiful watch. He said, 'I know you'll be here.' I sent it back to him when I didn't sign with them. Chuck remembered that when he came to the Steelers and I was on the team. He said I was the only one who ever sent back the watch to Gillman. Maybe I was too naïve, but that's the way I was raised. My mother was a strong woman and that's the way I was brought up. She taught me what was right. When she was 68 years old, she had a boyfriend. We told her it was OK if she wanted to live with him rather than get married again. We said we were adults and we could handle that. We told her if she got married she'd lose out on her Social Security payments. She said, 'I'm a church lady. I can't do that.' My mother died three weeks ago. She was 89. She didn't like my wife, at first, because nobody was good enough for her Johnny. But they became very close through the years.

"I started out in Chester, Pennsylvania, but when my parents broke up, I ended up in Camden. I took piano lessons from the time I was eight years old until I was 13. I gave it up when I got deeply involved in sports. I've been taking lessons for a year now — at the African-American Music Institute in Homewood — and I'm playing some pretty good stuff. They tell me I have an aptitude for it. Maybe in 14 years I'll be as good as Walt Harper."

With that remark, Brown got off the bench and went over to his car and retrieved some sheet music to show me what he was doing. He showed me how his teacher had made some special notes on a song called "It's All Right With Me." He had some Duke Ellington and Ludwig van Beethoven music, some minuets, some pop music. "Some of this is pretty challenging," he said, "but I'm coming along."

I asked him if he knew much about Pittsburgh's rich jazz heritage, how the city had turned out the likes of Erroll Garner, Lena Horne, Billy Eckstein, Earl "Fatha" Hines, Dakota Staton, Mary Lou Williams, Maxine Sullivan, Stanley Turrentine, George Benson and Walt Harper. He said he did, thanks to Nathan Davis at Pitt's Jazz program. He had seen the Jazz Hall of Fame in the lobby of Pitt's William Pitt Union.

I told him I once came upon Erroll Garner as he was coming out of the Royal York Hotel in Toronto, when I was there with the Penguins for a National Hockey League meeting back in 1968 or 1969. I asked Garner how he explained why so many great jazz musicians came out of Pittsburgh. Garner tugged at his signature goatee a moment and said, "I guess because we were all born there." It wasn't deep, but Garner may have gotten to the heart of it.

Brown recalled bumping into "Big Daddy" Lipscomb, the legendary defensive tackle of the Los Angeles Rams, Baltimore Colts and Steelers, when he was at a jazz club in the Hill District during their playing days.

"In my first year with the Browns, I was on all the special teams, and I had to deal with 'Big Daddy' on one of them," said Brown. "Someone hollered to me from the sideline during an extra point attempt. 'John, pick up Big Daddy if he comes.' Big Daddy heard that and he hollored at me with this squeaky voice he had, 'You're damn right, Big Daddy is coming!' He's laughing and pointing at me. I did all right."

Brown also recalled that in his first starting assignment for the Browns, he had to go up against Ernie Stautner of the Steelers. "He had his arms all taped up, with cardboard wrapped under the tape. His arms were weapons. You could slap a lineman upside his helmet in those days, and they did it every play. Mike McCormack and Monte Clark couldn't play, so I started. I was black and blue the next day, but Ernie didn't get to the quarterback. By that time, though, he was about 40 years old. But he was still one of the toughest guys in the league."

Talking about tough tackles brought the Browns' Lou Groza to mind. "He was not only one of the great place-kickers of all time," said Brown, "but he made the Pro Bowl as an offensive tackle, too."

The Browns had an end named Horace Gillom who was also their punter. Marion Motley could play fullback and linebacker and kick, if needed. Noll went both ways. That's why Noll was never crazy about kicking and punting specialists. He thought they should contribute some other way, like real football players.

Brown remembers he signed with the Browns for a $5,000 bonus and a first-year salary of $11,500. He said Groza, who signed with the Browns in 1942 for something less, was still kicking for the Browns in 1962. "I think he filled in at offensive tackle for a game that year when we had some injuries in the line," said Brown. "He'd tell me, and not in a malicious way, that I was getting too much money. I told him he came to the Browns in 1942 and I came in in 1962 and the money situation had improved.

"I was with the Steelers in 1969 when Joe Greene joined the team. He signed for about three or four times as much money as I did. I knew how Groza felt. But things change with the times. Joe and I became roommates during his first year. My first couple of roommates all got cut. I think Bill Nunn paired us, but Dan Rooney might have told him to do it. Greene was beating up everybody when we had one-on-one drills. I'm saying, 'I'm going to stop this kid.' Everyone was taking a step back to set up and block him. He was quick as hell and he went right through them or around them. Instead of going back, I fired into him, and got up under his chin. He went down. He respected that. We became fast friends.

"I think we were good for each other. I may have passed along some wisdom I had picked up along the way, about things on and off the field, mostly off the field. But he was good for me, too. Here was a young guy coming in, and I'm getting older. My knees were falling apart. He had such an intense desire. I can't tell you how much drive he had. You couldn't be rooming with a guy like that and not be playing well. I had to play harder to stay with him. He was a good influence on me that way.

"Joe was so far ahead of everybody. He was not a strong weight person. He didn't get into lifting weights like they do today. If he had started out earlier, I think he could have lasted longer. L.C. Greenwood was not a weight person, either. He was just so quick, and got off the ball so fast that he beat people to the punch.

"In my last season of 1972, I broke my thumb in training camp. I didn't tape my hands that day, for whatever reason, and my thumb got caught in some equipment during a contact session, and my thumb was completely reversed. My thumb was broken, my knees were shot, and I just hung in there for one more year on smarts and heart. I did a lot of holding that year. I had to go up against Buck Buchanan and clutched his jersey all day. I did all right, but I couldn't get out of bed the next day. My wife reminds me of that when I tell someone I miss playing football. She doesn't miss it."

Brown said he was lifting three times a week while in retirement to stay as toned as possible.

Looking back at how Noll molded a championship team in the '70s, Brown said, "He moved people into the right positions. Jon Kolb came here as a 218-pound center and he made him a tackle. Moon Mullins and Larry Brown both came in as tight ends and he made them into interior linemen. Moon had quick feet; that was his best asset. Sam Davis had quick feet, too. Sam was such a good person. It's a shame what happened to him. He made some mistakes in business, and he's paid dearly. There wasn't a nicer guy on the team."

Brown has always been a big booster of Chuck Noll.

"Chuck Noll did not remind me of Paul Brown in his mannerisms or what he said as much as in his overall approach to the game. Chuck was truly a dedicated coach, in the same sense that Paul Brown was. Paul was a teacher and so was Chuck a teacher, and despite what some people might say who played for them, I liked them both. They both made you better.

"Chuck and Paul demanded respect. If you played for them, you had to give them respect. That was their way of controlling the team. They felt if they couldn't control the team they couldn't win consistently. Paul didn't yell at people. Chuck didn't yell at people. I don't recall them ever yelling at their players.

"Hey, we had a helluva guy there. Chuck Noll is not going to be easily replaced in Pittsburgh. He did so much for this city."

Jim O'Brien

Gus Kalaris keeps company with his buddy John Brown at ice ball stand in West Park on city's North Side. Kalaris is the godfather for Brown's son, Jay.

Class of 1980
They missed the glory years

"Are you the janitor?"
— Nate Johnson

he Steelers' Class of 1980 in the college draft had great expectations. They joined the Steelers at their summer training camp at
St. Vincent College six months after the team had won its fourth
Super Bowl in six seasons and everyone thought the giddy success
would continue. The Steelers failed to make the playoffs that year,
however, and no one in the Class of 1980 came away with a Super
Bowl ring. The glory days were over.

Mark Malone, Tunch Ilkin, Craig Wolfley and Bill Hurley were
good football players and even better people. It was quite a quartet.
They bonded that summer and they have remained good friends
through the years.

I spotted Malone, Ilkin and Hurley at the practice tee at the 2001
Mellon Mario Lemieux Celebrity Invitational on June 8. I bumped
into Wolfley, who lives in my neighborhood, one morning before I went
to The Club at Nevillewood, about four miles away, to catch the action
in the four-day event that draws a big crowd and big bucks for local
charities.

Malone, now an ESPN studio host and football analyst, lives in
Bridgeville, even closer to Nevillewood, and has a townhouse in
Stamford, Connecticut where he stays during the football season.
Malone was a quarterback with the Steelers for eight seasons (1980-
1987), and finished up with the San Diego Chargers in his hometown.
Chuck Noll used him at wide receiver in a few games, and Malone set
a Steelers' record for longest touchdown reception with a 90-yard
scamper on a pass from Terry Bradshaw at Seattle on November 8,
1981. When Joe Theismann, the former Redskins' quarterback,
walked by Malone at the practice tee, I pointed them out to former
Steelers' coach Chuck Noll, who was also participating in the celebrity golf event. Malone was much more physically impressive than
Theismann, but never accomplished as much in the NFL as
Theismann.

"Mark would've made a terrific receiver," noted Noll. "But he
wanted to be a quarterback."

Ilkin was an "American Dream" story. He came to America as a
child from Turkey. He was a Muslim, but he became a devout
Christian during his stay with the Steelers. Ilkin's parents both converted to the Christian faith as well.

Ilkin was cut during his first training camp, but kept in shape
while working as a janitor in a health club in Chicago and was called
back by Noll when injuries created an opening. Ilkin played 13
seasons as an offensive tackle with the Steelers (1980-1992) and then

493

finished up for one additional season with the Green Bay Packers. Ilkin played in two (1989 and 1990) Pro Bowls.

He followed in Malone's footsteps, working with Sam Nover at WPXI-TV in Pittsburgh, and was doing local TV as well as joining Bill Hillgrove and Myron Cope in the WDVE broadcast booth as an analyst for Steelers' coverage. He was covering the Lemieux event for Fox Sports. He lived in Upper St. Clair and often teamed up with Wolfley to deliver Christian-oriented talks at local churches and schools.

Wolfley was a guard and tackle for ten seasons with the Steelers (1980-1989), and wound up his NFL career with two years with the Minnesota Vikings. He was operating the Martial Arts and Sports complex in Bridgeville and doing free-lance radio (97 the Burgh and ESPN) and television (WPXI-TV) assignments in Pittsburgh. He was quite good.

Bill Hurley accompanied Ilkin to the Lemieux Invitational. Hurley played only one season (1980) as a defensive back with the Steelers before being traded to the New Orleans Saints. He operates a prep scouting and counseling service and was living in Bridgeville.

They all had good memories of their boss, Art Rooney.

Mark Malone: "He was a super caring person. I have so many good memories of him. I used to remain in the locker room after most of the guys had left following practice sessions. The Chief would always come into the locker room and wander around, saying something to everybody.

"I'll cherish those times when I'd be sitting on a stool in the center of the locker room, smoking a cigar and playing gin with The Chief. Just us, one-on-one. He was one of the most famous sportsmen of the century and I was playing gin with him.

"There was another time when I saw what resiliency he had. We were practicing in the cold at Three Rivers Stadium. The Chief came out and walked around the practice field. He was by himself. Somebody threw an out route pass — I don't think it was me — and the receiver caught the ball and kept running. He ran right over Mr. Rooney and knocked him flat.

"Everybody on the field panicked. He was eighty-some years old at the time. Oh, man, did we kill The Chief? The trainers went over to him and checked him out. Mr. Rooney got up, dusted himself off, smiled, and just resumed his walk. That was about a year or so before his death."

Tunch Ilkin: "Art Rooney was a beautiful man. Every time he walked by me, he'd say, 'Tunch, my boy, how are things in Turkey? Are they still killing each other? It's just like Ireland.'

"I remember when I first reported for a physical after I was drafted out of Indiana State in 1980. I was sitting in the lobby of the Steelers' complex at Three Rivers Stadium waiting to see the team doctor. There were two other rookies with me: Ted Walton and Nate Johnson.

494

"The Chief came out to the lobby. He was wearing a light blue cardigan sweater over a golf shirt. It was snug. I'm not sure if the buttons were buttoned right or not. He came over to where we were sitting, and he was dumping the ashtrays as he walked toward us. He was cleaning up.

"He said, 'How are you fellas? What's your names?' We all identified ourselves. Then Nate Johnson says, 'Who are you? Are you the janitor or something?' The Chief chuckled. He got a kick out of that comment. 'I do a little bit of everything around here,' he said, still smiling. That showed you the sense of humor he had. He was unreal."

Bill Hurley: "When I went to New Orleans, he sent me a card or letter every two weeks, I swear. He liked me because I was an Irish-Catholic. There'd be four or five lines. He'd tell me to come and see him when I was back in town. He signed them simply 'Art.' I wish now I had saved them. During the off-season, I came back to Pittsburgh and I'd go down there to work out with some of the guys I knew. He saw me in the hallway one day and he told me, 'Let me know if anyone gives you a hard time. You're welcome to work out here any time.' He was a great guy. I was there for only a year, and I was a peon. But he treated me like a king."

Craig Wolfley: "I remember his kindness most of all, and him sitting down at my dressing stall and talking to me in the off-season. He was like a politician the way he worked the locker room. He connected with everybody. When he heard my brother (Ron) went to West Virginia University, he told me stories about his days of barnstorming through West Virginia playing baseball and football. He'd tell me stories about my hometown of Buffalo, and playing the ponies in upstate New York. He'd say, 'Let me tell you about your Buffalo...' He told me about a blizzard in Buffalo he'd been in where they had to string ropes from one building to another so you could find your way. That's how bad it was. Ted Petersen had a buddy who had played football and minor league baseball. His name was Jeff Gossett, and he sneaked into a practice one day at Three Rivers Stadium to see Ted practice. Mr. Rooney came upon him, and Jeff figured he was going to get the boot. Mr. Rooney ended up taking him to lunch at the Allegheny Club and feeding him, and telling him some stories. Just like you'd expect."

Jim O'Brien

Tunch Ilkin, Bill Hurley and Mark Malone meet at Mellon Mario Lemieux Celebrity Invitational in June of 2001.

Author's Page

Jim O'Brien and Dick Schaap enjoyed a reunion at Super Bowl XXXV in Tampa, Florida in January, 2001. O'Brien was a contributing writer for SPORT when Schaap served as editor of that national monthly publication. Schaap, now with ESPN and ABC News, was promoting his newest book, a memoir called "Flashing Before My Eyes." Schaap is the author or editor of 33 books at last count.

"Jim O'Brien is the poet laureate of Pittsburgh sports. He knows the streets and the stars and he is passionate about both. I have great respect for him and cherish our long friendship. Have a few laughs."

— Dick Schaap
ESPN, ABC News
June 5, 2001

PITTSBURGH PIRATES PROFI

FRONT ROW--LANTZ-CLARK-JANACEK-KATTIER-DE
MIDDLE ROW--ARTHUR J. ROONEY, (PRESIDENT)
SWARTZ-SORTET-SHAFFER-COOPER-CRITICHFIEL
BACK ROW--HOLM-TANQUAY-OEHLER-MOSS-TESSEF
MOORE-BROVELLI-DOUDS (COACH)